Wesley's Notes on the Bible
The Old Testament: First Samuel - Psalms
by John Wesley
Edited by Anthony Uyl

Woodstock, Ontario, 2017

Wesley's Notes on the Bible - The Old Testament: First Samuel - Psalms
by John Wesley (1703-1791)
Edited by Anthony Uyl

The text of Wesley's Notes on the Bible - The Old Testament: First Samuel - Psalms is all in the Public Domain. This edition is published by Devoted Publishing a division of 2165467 Ontario Inc.

**What kind of philosophies do you have?
Let us know!**

Contact us at: devotedpub@hotmail.com
Visit our shop on Facebook: @DevotedPublishing

Published in Woodstock, Ontario, Canada 2017

For bulk educational rates, please contact us at the above email address.

ISBN: 978-1-77356-068-7

Table of Contents

NOTES ON THE FIRST BOOK OF SAMUEL 4
NOTES ON THE SECOND BOOK OF SAMUEL 36
NOTES ON THE FIRST BOOK OF KINGS 59
NOTES ON THE SECOND BOOK OF KINGS 93
NOTES ON THE FIRST BOOK OF CHRONICLES 116
NOTES ON THE SECOND BOOK OF CHRONICLES 133
NOTES ON THE BOOK OF EZRA 151
NOTES ON THE BOOK OF NEHEMIAH 157
NOTES ON THE BOOK OF ESTHER 167
NOTES ON THE BOOK OF JOB 173
NOTES ON THE BOOK OF PSALMS 217

NOTES ON THE FIRST BOOK OF SAMUEL

This book and the following bear the name of Samuel, (tho' he wrote only part of the former, and some other of the prophets, perhaps Nathan, the rest) because they contain first a large account of Samuel, and then the history of the reigns of Saul and David, who were both anointed by him.

I

The affliction of Hannah, ver. 1-8. Her prayer to God, with Eli's blessing, ver. 9-18. The birth and nursing of Samuel, ver. 19-23. The presenting of him to God, ver. 24-28.

1. Ramathaim-zophim - Called Ramah, ver. 19. Eparathite - That is, one of Bethlehem-judah, by his birth and habitation, though by his original a Levite.

2. Two wives - As many had in those ages, tho' it was a transgression of the original institution of marriage. And it is probable that he took his second wife, namely, Peninnah, because Hannah was barren.

3. Yearly - At the three solemn feasts, when he, together with all other males were obliged to go to worship God in the place appointed; and at other times, when he as a Levite, was to go thither in his course. To sacrifice - Not in his own person, which the Levites could not do, but by the priests. Were there - Or, were the priests of the Lord there, under their father Eli, who is generally conceived to have been the high-priest, but being very old and infirm, his sons ministered in his stead. This is the first time in scripture, that God is called the Lord of hosts or Armies. Probably Samuel was the first who used this title of God, for the comfort of Israel, at the time when their armies were few and feeble, and those of their enemies many and mighty.

4. Portions - Out of the sacrifice of his peace-offerings, the greatest part whereof fell to the offerer, and was eaten by him, and his friends or guests, before the Lord. And out of this he gave them all portions, as the master of the feast used to do to the guests.

5. Shut up her womb - Yet Elkanah did not withdraw his love from her. To abate out just love to any relation, for the sake of any infirmity which they cannot help, is to add affliction to the afflicted.

6. Her adversary - Peninnah: so her envy or jealousy made her though so nearly related.

7. When she went-This circumstance is noted as the occasion of the contention, because at such times they were forced to more society with one another, by the way, and in their lodgings; whereas at home they had distinct apartments, where they might be asunder; and then her husband's extraordinary love and kindness was shewed to Hannah, whereby Peninnah was the more exasperated; then also Hannah prayed earnestly for a child, which hitherto she had done in vain; and this possibly she reproached her with. Did not eat - Being overwhelmed with grief, and therefore unfit to eat of the sacred food. Which they were not to eat in their mourning.

8. Ten sons - Oughtest thou not to value my hearty love to thee, more than the having of as many sons as Peninnah hath? She would willingly change conditions with thee.

9. A seat - Or, throne; for it is manifest it was raised higher than ordinary, chap. iv, 18. Here he might sit, either as the judge; or rather as high-priest, to hear and answer such as came to him for advice, and to inspect and direct the worship of God. Temple - That is, of the tabernacle, which is frequently so called.

10. Bitterness - That is, oppressed with grief. Prayed unto the Lord - They had newly offered their peace-offerings, to obtain the favour of God, and in token of their communion with him, they had feasted upon the sacrifice: and now it was proper to put up her prayer, in virtue of the sacrifice. For the peace-offerings typified Christ's mediation, as well as the sin-offerings: since by this not only atonement is made for sin, but an answer to our prayers obtained.

11. Give him - That is, consecrate him to God's service in his temple. No razor - That is, he shall be a perpetual Nazarite.

12. Continued - Hebrew. multiplied to pray. By which it appears that she said much more than is here expressed. And the like you are to judge of the prayers and sermons of other holy persons recorded in scripture, which gives us only the sum and substance of them. This consideration may help us much to understand some passages of the bible.

13. Drunken - Because of the multitude of her words, and those motions of her face and body, which the vehemency of her passion, and the fervency in prayer occasioned.

16. Count not, &c. - Thus when we are unjustly censured, we should endeavour not only to clear ourselves, but to satisfy our brethren, by giving them a just and true account of that which they misapprehended.

18. Find grace - That favourable opinion and gracious prayer which thou hast expressed on my behalf, be pleased to continue towards me. Sad - Her heart being cheared by the priest's comfortable words, and especially by God's spirit setting them home upon her, and assuring her that both his and her prayers should be heard, it quickly appeared in her countenance.

19. Remembered - Manifested his remembrance of her by the effect.

20. Samuel - That is, Asked of God.

21. His house - Hannah only and her child excepted. His vow - By which it appears, though it was not expressed before, that he heard and consented to her vow, and that he added a vow of his own, if God answered his prayers.

22. Weaned - Not only from the breast, but also from the mother's knee and care, and from childish food; 'till the child be something grown up, and fit to do some service in the tabernacle: for it seems that as soon as he was brought up he worshipped God, ver. 28, and presently after ministered to Eli, chap. ii, 11.

23. His word - His matter or thing; the business concerning the child, what thou hast vowed concerning him, that be may grow up, and be accepted and employed by God in his Service.

24. Three bullocks - One for a burnt-offering, the second for a sin- offering, and the third for a peace offering; all these sorts being expedient for this work and time. Flour - For the meal-offerings belonging to the principal sacrifices, which to each bullock were three tenth-deals, or three tenth parts of an ephah, and so nine parts of the ephah were spent, and the tenth part was given to the priest. Wine - For drink-offerings.

25. A bullock - The three bullocks mentioned ver. 24, the singular number being put for the plural, which is frequent.

26. Soul liveth - As surely as thou livest. Which asseveration seems necessary, because this was some years after it.

28. Lent him - But not with a purpose to require him again. Whatever we give to God, may upon this account be said to be lent to him, that tho' we may not recall it, yet he will certainly repay it, to our unspeakable advantage. He worshipped - Not Eli, but young Samuel, who is spoken of in this and the foregoing verse, and who was capable of worshipping God in some sort, at least with external adoration.

II

Hannah's song of thanksgiving, ver. 1-10. Elkanah leaves Samuel to minister before the Lord, ver. 11. The wickedness of Eli's sons, ver. 12-17. A farther account of Samuel and his parents, ver. 18-21. Eli's too mild reproof of his sons, ver. 22-25. Samuel's growth, ver. 26. God's dreadful message to Eli, ver. 27- 36.

1. Prayed - That is, praised God; which is a part of prayer. Rejoiceth - Or, leapeth for joy: for the words note not only inward joy, but also the outward demonstrations of it. In the Lord - As the author of my joy, that he hath heard my prayer, and accepted my son for his service. Horn - My strength and glory (which are often signified by an horn,) are advanced and manifested to my vindication, and the confusion of mine enemies. Mouth enlarged - That is, opened wide to pour forth abundant praises to God, and to give a full answer to all the reproaches of mine adversaries. Enemies - So she manifests her prudence and modesty, in not naming Peninnah, but only her enemies in the general. Salvation - Because the matter of my joy is no trivial thing, but that strange and glorious salvation or deliverance which thou hast given me from my oppressing care and grief, and from the insolencies and reproaches of mine enemies.

2. None holy - None so perfectly, unchangeably and constantly holy. None beside - Not only none is so holy as thou art, but in truth there is none holy besides thee; namely, entirely, or independently, but only by participation from thee. Any rock - Thou only art a sure defense and refuge to all that flee to thee.

3. Talk no more - Thou Peninnah, boast no more of thy numerous off-spring, and speak no more insolently and scornfully of me. She speaks of her in the plural number, because she would not expose her name to censure. Of knowledge - He knoweth thy heart, and all that pride, and envy, and contempt of me, which thy own conscience knows; and all thy perverse carriage towards me. Actions - That is, he trieth all mens thoughts and actions, (for the Hebrew word signifies both) as a just judge, to give to every one according to their works.

4. Bows - The strength of which they boasted. Stumbled - Or, were weak, or feeble, in body and

spirit.

5. Hired themselves out for bread - It is the same thing which is expressed both in divers metaphors in the foregoing, and following verses. Ceased - That is, ceased to be hungry. Seven - That is, many, as seven is often used. She speaks in the prophetick style, the past time, for the future; for though she had actually born but one, yet she had a confident persuasion that she should have more, which was grounded either upon some particular assurance from God; or rather upon the prayer or prediction of Eli. She - That is, Peninnah. Feeble - Either because she was now past child-bearing: or, because divers of her children, which were her strength and her glory, were dead, as the Hebrew doctors relate.

6. Killeth - The same person whom he first killeth, or bringeth nigh unto death, he afterwards raiseth to life. Me, who was almost consumed with grief, he hath revived. The name of death both in sacred scripture, and profane writers, is often given to great Calamities.

8. From the dunghill - From the most sordid place, and mean estate. Inherit - Not only possess it themselves, but transmit it to their posterity. Throne - That is, a glorious throne or kingdom. Pillars - The foundations of the earth, which God created, and upholds, and wherewith he sustains the earth, and all its inhabitants, as a house is supported with pillars; and therefore it is not strange if he disposeth of persons and things therein as he pleaseth.

9. Feet - That is, the steps or paths, their counsels and actions; he will keep; that is, both uphold, that they may not fall into ruin; and direct and preserve from wandering, and from those fatal errors that wicked men daily run into. Silent - Shall be put to silence: they who used to open their mouths wide against heaven, and against the saints, shall be so confounded with the unexpected disappointment of all their hopes, and with God's glorious appearance and operations for his people, that they shall have their mouths quite stopped. Darkness - Both inward, in their own minds, not knowing what to say or do; and outward, in a stat e of deep distress. Prevail - Namely, against God, or against his saints, as the wicked were confident they should do, because of their great power, and wealth, and numbers.

10. Exalt - Increase, or advance the strength. Of his anointed - Of his king. This may respect Christ, the singular anointed one of God, and the special king of his people. In this sense also, the Lord shall judge the ends of the earth: David's victories and dominions reached far. But God will give to the Son of David, the uttermost parts of the earth for his possession. And he will give strength unto his king, for the accomplishing his great undertaking, and exalt the horn, of the power and honour of his anointed, till he hath put all his enemies under his feet.

11. Minster - In some way agreeable to his tender years, as in singing, or playing upon instruments of musick, or lighting the lamps. Before Eli the priest - That is, under the inspection, and by the direction of Eli.

12. Knew not - They did not honour, love, or serve God.

13. Boiling - As the Lord's part of the peace-offerings was burnt upon the altar, so the priest's and offerer's parts were to be boiled.

14. Took - Not contented with the breast and shoulder which were allotted them by God, they took also part of the offerer's share; besides which they snatched their part before it was heaved and waved; contrary to Levit vii, 34.

15. The fat - And the other parts to be burnt with it. So this was all additional injury; for they took such parts as they best liked whilst it was raw.

17. Abhorred - But we know the validity and efficacy of the sacraments does not depend on the goodness of those that administer them. It was therefore folly and sin in the people, to think the worse of God's institutions. But it was the much greater sin of the priests, that gave them occasion so to do.

18. Ministered - That is, performed his ministration carefully and faithfully. Before the Lord - In God's tabernacle. Ephod - A garment used in God's service, and allowed not only to the inferior priests and Levites but also to eminent persons of the people, and therefore to Samuel, who, though no Levite, was a Nazarite, from his birth.

21. Grew - Not only in age and stature; but especially in wisdom and goodness. Before the Lord - Not only before men, who might he deceived, but in the presence and judgment of the all-seeing God.

22. Very old - And therefore unfit either to manage his office himself, or to make a diligent inspection into the carriage of his sons, which gave them opportunity for their wickedness. To Israel - Whom they injured in their offerings, and alienated from the service of God. The door - The place where all the people both men and women waited when they came up to the service of God, because the altar on which their sacrifices was offered, was by the door.

23. He said, &c. - Eli's sin was not only that he reproved them too gently, but that he contented himself with a verbal rebuke, and did not restrain them, and inflict those punishments upon them which such high crimes deserved by God's law, and which he as judge and high-priest ought to have done, without respect of persons.

25. The judge - If only man be wronged, man can right it, and reconcile the persons. Against the Lord - As you have done wilfully and presumptuously. Who shall, &c. - The offense is of so high a

nature, that few or none will dare to intercede for him, but will leave him to the just judgment of God. The words may be rendered, Who shall judge for him? Who shall interpose as umpire, between God and him? Who shall compound that difference? None can or dare do it, and therefore he must be left to the dreadful, but righteous judgment of God. They had now sinned away their day of grace. They had long hardened their hearts. And God at length gave them up to a reprobate mind, and determined to destroy them, 2 Chron. xxv, 16.

27. Man of God - That is, a prophet sent from God.

29. Kick ye - Using them irreverently, and profanely; both by abusing them to your own luxury, and by causing the people to abhor them. He chargeth Eli with his sons faults. honourest thy sons - Permitting them to dishonour and injure me, by taking my part to themselves; chusing rather to offend me by thy connivance at their sin, than to displease them by severe rebukes, and just punishments. Fat - To pamper yourselves. This you did not out of necessity, but out of mere luxury. Chiefest - Not contented with those parts which I had allotted you, you invaded those choice parts which I reserved for myself.

30. I said - Where, or when did God say this? To Eli himself, or to his father, when the priesthood was translated from Eleazar's to Ithamar's family. Walk - That is, minister unto me as high-priest. Walking is often put for discharging ones office; before me; may signify that he was the high-priest, whose sole prerogative it was to minister before God, or before the ark, in the most holy place. For ever - As long as the Mosaical law and worship lasts. Far from me - To fulfil my promise, which I hereby retract.

31. Arm - That is, I will take away thy strength, or all that in which thou placest thy confidence, either,

1. the ark, which is called God's strength, Psalm lxxviii, 61, and was Eli's strength, who therefore was not able to bear the very tidings of the loss of it. Or,

2. his priestly dignity or employment, whence he had all his honour and substance. Or rather,

3. his children, to whom the words following here, and in the succeeding verses, seem to confine it. Father's house - That is, thy children's children, and all thy family which was in great measure accomplished, chap. xxii, 16, &c.

32. Shalt see,&c. - The words may be rendered; thou shalt see, in thy own person, the affliction, or calamity of my habitation; that is, either of the land of Israel, wherein I dwell; or of the sanctuary, called the habitation by way of eminency, whose greatest glory the ark was, chap. iv, 21, 22, and consequently, whose greatest calamity the loss of the ark was; for, or instead of all that good wherewith God would have blessed Israel, having raised up a young prophet Samuel, and thereby given good grounds of hope that he intended to bless Israel, if thou and thy sons had not hindered it by your sins. So this clause of the threatning concerns Eli's person, as the following concerns his posterity. And this best agrees with the most proper signification of that phrase, Thou shalt see.

33. Of thine - That is, of thy posterity. Shalt grieve - Shall be so forlorn and miserable, that if thou wast alive to see it, it would grieve thee at the heart, and thou wouldst consume thine eyes with weeping for their calamities. Increase - That is, thy children. Flower - About the thirtieth year of their age, when they were to be admitted to the full administration of their office.

35. Raise a priest - Of another line, as it necessarily implied by the total removal of that office from Eli's line. The person designed is Zadok, one eminent for his faithfulness to God, and to the king, who, when Abiather, the last of Eli's line, was deposed by Solomon, was made high-priest in his stead. Build,&c. - That is, give him a numerous posterity, and confirm that sure covenant of an everlasting priesthood made to Phinehas, of Eleazar's line, Num. xxv, 13, and interrupted for a little while by Eli, of the line of Ithamar, unto him and his children forever. Anointed - Before Jesus Christ, who is the main scope and design, not only of the New, but of the Old Testament, which in all its types and ceremonies represented him; and particularly, the high-priest was an eminent type of Christ, and represented his person, and acted in his name and stead, and did mediately, what John Baptist did immediately, go before the face of the Lord Christ; and when Christ came, that office and officer was to cease. The high-priest is seldom or never said to walk or minister before the kings of Israel or Judah, but constantly before the Lord, and consequently, before Christ, who, as he was God blessed forever, Rom. ix, 5, was present with, and the builder and governor of the ancient church of Israel, and therefore the high-priest is most properly said to walk before him.

III

God's first manifestation of himself to Samuel, ver. 1-10. God's message to Eli, ver. 11-14. His faithful delivery of that message, and Eli's submission to God, ver. 15-18. The establishment of Samuel to be a prophet, ver. 19-21

1. Before Eli - That is, under his inspection and direction. Word - The word of prophecy, or the

Revelation of God's will to and by the prophets. Precious - Rare or scarce, such things being most precious in mens' esteem, whereas common things are generally despised. Open vision - God did not impart his Mind by way of vision or Revelation openly, or to any public person, to whom others might resort for satisfaction, though he might privately reveal himself to some pious persons for their particular direction. This is premised, as a reason why Samuel understood not, when God called him once or twice.

2. His place - In the court of the tabernacle.

3. Went out - Before the lights of the golden candlestick were put out in the morning.

7. Did not know - He was not acquainted with God in that extraordinary or prophetical way. And this ignorance of Samuel's served God's design, that his simplicity might give Eli the better assurance of the truth of God's call, and message to Samuel.

10. Came and stood - Before, he spake to him at a distance, even from the holy oracle between the cherubim: but now, to prevent all farther mistake, the voice came near to him, as if the person speaking had been standing near him.

12. In that day - In that time which I have appointed for this work, which was about twenty or thirty years after this threatning. So long space of repentance God allows to this wicked generation. When I begin, &c. - Tho' this vengeance shall be delayed for a season, to manifest my patience, and incite them to repentance; yet when once I begin to inflict, I shall not desist 'till I have made a full end.

13. Restrained them not - He contented himself with a cold reproof, and did not punish, and effectually restrain them. They who can, and do not restrain others from sin, make themselves partakers of the guilt. Those in authority will have a great deal to answer for, if the sword they bear be not a terror to evil-doers.

14. Have sworn - Or, I do swear: the past tense being commonly put for the present in the Hebrew tongue. Unto - Or, concerning it. Purged - That is, the punishment threatened against Eli and his family, shall not be prevented by all their sacrifices, but shall infallibly be executed.

15. Doors - Altho' the tabernacle, whilst it was to be removed from place to place in the wilderness, had no doors, but consisted only of curtains, and had hangings before the entrance, instead of doors; yet when it was settled in one place, as now it was in Shiloh, it was enclosed within some solid building, which had doors and posts, and other parts belonging to it. Feared - The matter of the vision or Revelation, partly from the reverence he bore to his person, to whom he was loth to be a messenger of such sad tidings; partly, lest if he had been hasty to utter it, Eli might think him guilty of arrogancy or secret complacency in his calamity.

17. God do so, &c. - God inflict the same evils upon thee, which I suspect he hath pronounced against me, and greater evils too.

18. It is the Lord - This severe sentence is from the sovereign Lord of the world, who hath an absolute right to dispose of me and all his creatures; who is in a special manner the ruler of the people of Israel, to whom it properly belongs to punish all mine offenses; whose chastisement I therefore accept.

19. Fail, &c. - That is, want its effect: God made good all his predictions. A metaphor from precious liquors, which when they are spilt upon the ground, are altogether useless.

20. From Daniel, &c. - Thro' the whole Land, from the northern bound Daniel, to the southern, Beersheba; which was the whole length of the Land.

IV

Israel smitten by the Philistines, ver. 1, 2. They bring the ark into the camp, which affrights the Philistines, ver. 3-9. Israel beaten and the ark taken, ver. 10, 11. The news brought to Shiloh and the death of Eli, ver. 12-18. The travail and death of his daughter-in-law, 19-22.

1. The word - That is, the word of the Lord revealed to Samuel, and by him to the people. A word of command, that all Israel should go forth to fight with the Philistines, as the following words explain it, that they might he first humbled and punished for their sins, and so prepared for deliverance. Went out - To meet the Philistines, who having by this time recruited themselves after their loss by Samson, and perceiving an eminent prophet arising among them, by whom they were likely to be united, and assisted, thought fit to suppress them in the beginning of their hopes.

3. Wherefore, &c. - This was strange blindness, that when there was so great a corruption in their worship and manners, they could not see sufficient reason why God should suffer them to fall by their enemies. The ark - That great pledge of God's presence and help, by whose conduct our ancestors obtained success. Instead of humbling themselves for, and purging themselves from their sins, for which God was displeased with them, they take an easier and cheaper course, and put their trust in their ceremonial observances, not doubting but the very presence of the ark would give them the victory.

4. Bring the ark - This they should not have done without asking counsel of God.

5. Shouted - From their great joy and confidence of success. So formal Christians triumph in

external privileges and performances: as if the ark in the camp would bring them to heaven, tho' the world and the flesh reign in the heart.

7. Heretofore - Not in our times; for the fore-mentioned removals of the ark were before it came to Shiloh.

8. Wo, &c. - They secretly confess the Lord to be greater than their gods, and yet presume to oppose him. Wilderness - They mention the wilderness, not as if all the plagues of the Egyptians came upon them in the wilderness, but because the last and sorest of all, which is therefore put for all, the destruction of Pharaoh and all his host, happened in the wilderness, namely, in the Red-sea, which having the wilderness on both sides of it, may well be said to be in the wilderness. Altho' it is not strange if these Heathens did mistake some circumstance in relation of the Israelitish affairs, especially some hundreds of years after they were done.

10. Tent - To his habitation, called by the ancient name of his tent. There fell - Before, they lost but four thousand, now in the presence of the ark, thirty thousand, to teach them that the ark and ordinances of God, were never designed as a refuge to impenitent sinners, but only for the comfort of those that repent.

11. The ark - Which God justly and wisely permitted, to punish the Israelites for their profanation of it; that by taking away the pretenses of their foolish confidence, he might more deeply humble them, and bring them to true-repentance: and that the Philistines might by this means he more effectually convinced of God's almighty power, and of their own, and the impotency of their gods, and so a stop put to their triumphs and rage against the poor Israelites. Thus as God was no loser by this event, so the Philistines were no gainers by it; and Israel, all things considered, received more good than hurt by it. If Eli had done his duty, and put them from the priesthood, they might have lived, tho' in disgrace. But now God takes the work into his own hands, and chases them out of the world by the sword of the Philistines.

13. The ark - Whereby he discovered a public and generous spirit, and a fervent zeal for God, and for his honour, which he preferred before all his natural affections, not regarding his own children in comparison of the ark, tho' otherwise he was a most indulgent father. And well they might, for beside that this was a calamity to all Israel, it was a particular loss to Shiloh; for the ark never returned thither. Their candlestick was removed out of its place, and the city sunk and came to nothing.

18. He fell - Being so oppressed with grief and astonishment, that he had no strength left to support him. The gate - The gate of the city, which was most convenient for the speedy understanding of all occurrences. Old - Old, and therefore weak and apt to fall; heavy, and therefore his fall more dangerous. So fell the high-priest and judge of Israel! So fell his heavy head, when he had lived within two of an hundred years! So fell the crown from his head, when he had judged Israel forty years: thus did his sun set under a cloud. Thus was the wickedness of those sons of his, whom he had indulged, his ruin. Thus does God sometimes set marks of his displeasure on good men, that others may hear and fear. Yet we must observe, it was the loss of the ark that was his death, and not the slaughter of his sons. He says in effect, Let me fall with the ark! Who can live, when the ordinances of God are removed? Farewell all in this world, even Life itself, if the ark be gone!

20. Fear not - Indeed the sorrows of her travail would have been forgotten, for joy that a child was born into the world. But what is that joy to one that feels herself dying? None but spiritual joy will stand us in stead then. Death admits not the relish of any earthly joy: it is then all flat and tasteless. What is it to one that is lamenting the loss of the ark? What can give us pleasure, if we want God's word and ordinances? Especially if we want the comfort of his gracious presence, and the light of his countenance?

21. I-chabod - Where is the glory? The glory - That is, the glorious type and assurance of God's presence, the ark, which is often called God's glory, and which wast the great safeguard and ornament of Israel, which they could glory in above all other nations.

22. The ark - This is repeated to shew, her piety, and that the public loss lay heavier upon her spirit, than her personal or domestic calamity.

V

The Philistines carry the ark into the temple of Dagon, ver. 1, 2. Dagon is overthrown, ver. 3-5. The men of Ashdod and Gath plagued, ver. 6-9. The Philistines determine to send it back, ver. 10-12.

2. By Dagon - By way of reproach, as a spoil and trophy set there to the honour of Dagon, to whom doubtless they ascribed this victory.

3. They - The priests of Dagon. Set him - Supposing his fall was casual.

4. Cut off - The head is the seat of wisdom; the hands the instruments of action: both are cut off to shew that he had neither wisdom nor strength to defend himself or his worshippers. Thus the priests by concealing Dagon's shame before, make it more evident and infamous. The stump - Hebrew. only

dagon, that is, that part of it from which it was called Dagon, namely the fishy part, for Dag in Hebrew signifies a fish. It - Upon the threshold; there the trunk abode in the place where it fell, but the head and hands were slung to distant places.

5. This day - When this history was written, which if written by Samuel towards the end of his life, was a sufficient ground for this expression.

6. Emerods - The piles.

8. To Gath - Supposing that this plague was confined to Ashdod for some particular reasons, or that it came upon them by chance, or for putting it into Dagon's temple, which they resolved they would not do.

9. Hidden parts - In the inwards of their hinder parts: which is the worst kind of emerods, as all physicians acknowledge, both because its pains are far more sharp than the other; and because the malady is more out of the reach of remedies.

11. The city - In every city, where the ark of God came.

VI

The Philistines send the ark back, ver. 1-12. The Israelites receive it, ver. 13-18. The people of Beth-shemesh, smitten for looking into the ark, desire those of Kirjath-jearim to fetch it, ver. 19-21.

1. Seven months - So long they kept it, as loath to lose so great a prize, and willing to try all ways to keep it.

3. It shall be known - You shall understand, what is hitherto doubtful, whether he was the author of these calamities, and why they continued so long upon you.

4. Emerods - Figures representing the disease. These they offered not in contempt of God, for they fought to gain his favour hereby; but in testimony of their humiliation, that by leaving this monument of their own shame and misery, they might obtain pity from God. Mice - Which marred their land by destroying the fruits thereof; as the other plague afflicted their Bodies.

5. Give glory - The glory of his power in conquering you, who seemed to have conquered him; of his justice in punishing you, and of his goodness if he relieve you.

6. Wherefore, &c. - They express themselves thus, either because some opposed the sending home the ark, though most had consented to it; or because they thought they would hardly send it away in the manner prescribed, by giving glory to God, and taking shame to themselves.

7. Milch kine, &c. - In respect to the ark; and for the better discovery, because such untamed heifers are apt to wander, and keep no certain and constant paths, as oxen accustomed to the yoke do, and therefore were most unlikely to keep the direct road to Israel's land. From them - Which would stir up natural affection in their dams, and cause them rather to return home, than to go to a strange country.

9. His own coast - Or Border, that is, the way that leadeth to his coast, or border, namely, the country to which it belongs. Then he, &c. - Which they might well conclude, if such heifers should against their common use, and natural instinct, go into a strange path, and regularly and constantly proceed in it, without any man's conduct.

12. Beth-shemesh - A city of the priests, who were by office to take care of it. Loving - Testifying at once both their natural and vehement inclination to their calves, and the supernatural power which over-ruled them to a contrary course. The lords went - To prevent all imposture, and to get assurance of the truth of the event. All which circumstances tended to the greater illustration of God's glory.

14. They - Not the lords of the Philistines, but the Beth-shemites, the priest that dwelt there. Offered the kine - There may seem to be a double error in this act. First, that they offered females for a burnt-offering, contrary to Levit i, 3. Secondly, that they did it in a forbidden place, Deut. xii, 5, 6. But this case being extraordinary, may in some sort excuse it, if they did not proceed by ordinary rules.

18. Villages - This is added for explication of that foregoing phrase, all the cities; either to shew, that under the name of the five cities were comprehended all the villages and territories belonging to them, in whose name, and at whose charge these presents were made; or to express the difference between this and the former present, the emerods being only five, according to the five cities mentioned, ver. 17, because it may seem, the cities only, or principally, were pestered with that disease; and the mice being many more according to the number of all the cities, as is here expressed: the word city being taken generally so, as to include not only fenced cities, but also the country villages, and the fields belonging to them. Abel - This is mentioned as the utmost border of the Philistines territory, to which the plague of mice extended. And this place is here called Abel, by anticipation from the great mourning mentioned in the following verse. It is desirable, to see the ark in its habitation, in all the circumstances of solemnity. But it is better to have it on a great stone, and in the fields of the wood, than to be without it. The intrinsic grandeur of divine ordinances ought not to be diminished in our eyes, by the meanness and poverty of the place, where they are administered.

19. Had looked - Having now an opportunity which they never yet had, it is not strange they had a

vehement curiosity to see the contents of the ark. Of the people - In and near Beth-shemesh and coming from all parts on this occasion.

20. Who is able, &c. - That is, to minister before the ark where the Lord is present. Since God is so severe to mark what is amiss in his servants, who is sufficient to serve him? It seems to be a complaint, or expostulation with God, concerning this great instance of his severity. And to whom, &c. - Who will dare to receive the ark with so much hazard to themselves. Thus when the word of God works with terror on men's consciences, instead of taking the blame to themselves, they frequently quarrel with the word, and endeavour to put it from them.

21. Kirjath-jearim - Whither they sent, either because the place was not far off from them, and so it might soon be removed: or because it was a place of eminency and strength, and somewhat farther distant from the Philistines, where therefore it was likely to be better preserved from any new attempts of the Philistines, and to be better attended by the Israelites, who would more freely and frequently come to it at such a place, than in Beth-shemesh, which was upon the border of their enemies land.

VII

The ark remains at Kirjath-jearim twenty years, ver. 1, 2. Samuel reforms Israel from idolatry, and Judg. Israel, ver. 3-6. The Philistines come up against Israel, are overthrown, and restore the cities they had taken, ver. 7-14. Samuel administers justice thro' all the land, ver. 15-17.

1. Fetch up - That is, by the priests appointed to that work. Hill - This place they chose, both because it was a strong place, where it would be the most safe; and an high place, and therefore visible at some distance, which was convenient for them, who were at that time to direct their prayers and faces towards the ark. And for the same reason David afterwards placed it in the hill of Zion. Sanctified Eleazar - Not that they made him either Levite or Priest; for in Israel persons were not made but born such; but they devoted, or set him apart wholly to attend upon this work. His son - Him they chose rather than his father, because he was younger and stronger, and probably freed from domestic cares, which might divert him from, or disturb him in this work. To keep the ark - To keep the place where it was, clean, and to guard it that none might touch it, but such as God allowed to do so.

2. Kirjath-jearim - Where it continued, and was not carried to Shiloh its former place, either because that place was destroyed by the Philistines when the ark was taken, or because God would hereby punish the wickedness of the people of Israel, by keeping it in a private place near the Philistines, whether the generality of the people durst not come. Twenty years - He saith not, that this twenty years was all the time of the ark's abode there, for it continued there from Eli's time 'till David's reign, 2 Sam. vi, 2, which was forty years: but that it was so long there before the Israelites were sensible of their sin and misery. Lamented - That is, they followed after God with Lamentations for his departure, and prayers for his return.

3. Spake - To all the rulers and people too, as he had occasion in his circuit, described below, mixing exhortation to repentance, with his judicial administrations. If - If you do indeed what you profess, if you are resolved to go on in that which you seem to have begun. With all your heart - Sincerely and in good earnest. Put - Out of your houses, where some of you keep them; and out of your hearts, where they still have an interest in many of you. Ashtaroth - And especially, Ashtaroth, whom they, together with the neighbouring nations, did more eminently worship. Prepare your hearts - By purging them from all sin, and particularly from all inclinations to other gods.

6. Poured it out - As an external sign, whereby they testified, both their own filthiness and need of washing by the grace and Spirit of God, and blood of the covenant, and their sincere desire to pour out their hearts before the Lord, in true repentance, and to cleanse themselves from all filthiness of flesh and spirit. Before the Lord - That is, in the public assembly, where God is in a special manner present. Judged - That is, governed them, reformed all abuses against God or man, took care that the laws of God should be observed, and wilful transgressions punished.

7. Went up - With an army, suspecting the effects of their general convention, and intending to nip them in the bud. Afraid - Being a company of unarmed persons, and unfit for battle. When sinners begin to repent and reform, they must expect Satan will muster all his forces against them, and set his instruments at work to the uttermost, to oppose and discourage them.

8. Cease not, &c. - We are afraid to look God in the face, because of our great wickedness: do thou therefore intercede for us, as Moses did for his generation. They had reason to expect this, because he had promised to pray for them, had promised them deliverance from the Philistines, and they had been observant of him, in all that he had spoken to them from the Lord. Thus they who receive Christ as their lawgiver and judge, need not doubt of their interest in his intercession. O what a comfort is it to all believers, that he never ceaseth, but always appears in the presence of God for us.

9. Cried - And he cried unto the Lord. He made intercession with the sacrifice. So Christ intercedes in virtue of his satisfaction. And in all our prayers we must have an eye to his great oblation,

depending on him for audience and acceptance.

12. A stone - A rude unpolished stone, which was not prohibited by that law, Lev. xxvi, 1, there being no danger of worshipping such a stone, and this being set up only as a monument of the victory. Eben-ezer - That is, the stone of help. And this victory was gained in the very same place where the Israelites received their former fatal loss. Helped us - He hath begun to help us, though not compleatly to deliver us. By which wary expression, he exciteth both their thankfulness for their mercy received, and their holy fear and care to please and serve the Lord, that he might help and deliver them effectually.

13. Came no more - That is, with a great host, but only with straggling parties, or garrisons. All the days, &c. - All the days of Samuel that is, while Samuel was their sole judge, or ruler; for in Saul's time they did come.

14. Peace - An agreement for the cessation of all acts of hostility. Amorites - That is, the Canaanites, often called Amorites, because these were formerly the most valiant of all those nations, and the first Enemies which the Israelites met with, when they went to take possession of their land. They made this peace with the Canaanites, that they might he more at leisure to oppose the Philistines, now their most potent enemies.

15. Samuel judged - For though Saul was king in Samuel's last days, yet Samuel did not cease to be a judge, being so made by God's extraordinary call, which Saul could not destroy; and therefore Samuel did sometimes, upon great occasions, tho' not ordinarily, exercise the office of judge after the beginning of Saul's reign; and the years of the rule of Saul and Samuel are joined together, Acts xiii, 20, 21.

16. In all places - He went to those several places, in compliance with the people, whose convenience he was willing to purchase with his own trouble, as an itinerant judge and preacher; and by his presence in several parts, he could the better observe, and rectify all sorts of miscarriages.

17. Built an altar - That by joining sacrifices with his prayers, he might the better obtain direction and assistance from God upon all emergencies. And this was done by prophetical inspiration, as appears by God's acceptance of the sacrifices offered upon it. Indeed Shiloh being now laid waste, and no other place yet appointed for them to bring their offerings to, the law which obliged them to one place, was for the present suspended. Therefore, as the patriarchs did, he built an altar where he lived: and that not only for the use of his own family, but for the good of the country who resorted to it.

VIII

Samuel's decay and the degeneracy of his sons, ver. 1-3. The people petition him for a king, who refers it to God, ver. 4-6. God directs him what answer to give, ver. 7-18. They insist upon their petition, ver. 19, 20. Which he promises, shall be granted, ver. 21, 22.

1. Old - And so unfit for his former travels and labours. He is not supposed to have been now above sixty years of age. But he had spent his strength and spirits in the fatigue of public business: and now if he thinks to shake himself as at other times, he finds he is mistaken: age has cut his hair. They that are in the prime of their years, ought to be busy in doing the work of life: for as they go into years, they will find themselves less disposed to it, and less capable of it. Judges - Not supreme Judges, for such there was to be but one, and that of God's chusing; and Samuel still kept that office in his own hands, chap. vii, 15, but his deputies, to go about and determine matters, but with reservation of a right of appeals to himself. He had doubtless instructed them in a singular manner, and fitted them for the highest employments; and he hoped that the example he had sent them, and the authority he still had over them, would oblige them to diligence and faithfulness in their trust.

2. Beer-sheba - In the southern border of the land of Canaan, which were very remote from his house at Ramah; where, and in the neighbouring places Samuel himself still executing the office of judge.

3. Took bribes - Opportunity and temptation discovered that corruption in them which 'till now was hid from their father. It has often been the grief of holy men, that their children did not tread in their steps. So far from it, that the sons of eminently good men, have been often eminently wicked.

5. A king - Their desires exceed their reasons, which extended no farther than to the removal of Samuel's sons from their places, and the procuring some other just: and prudent assistance to Samuel's age. Nor was the grant of their desire a remedy for their disease, but rather an aggravation of it. For the sons of their king were likely to be as corrupt as Samuel's sons and, if they were, would not be so easily removed. Like other nations - That is, as most of the nations about us have. But there was not the like reason; because God had separated them from all other nations, and cautioned them against the imitation of their examples, and had taken them into his own immediate care and government; which privilege other nations had not.

6. Displeased - Because God was hereby dishonoured by that distrust of him, and that ambition,

and itch after changes, which were the manifest causes of this desire; and because of that great misery, which he foresaw the people would hereby bring upon themselves. Prayed - For the pardon of their sin, and direction and help from God in this great affair.

7. Hearken - God grants their desire in anger, and for their punishment. Rejected me - This injury and contumely, reflects chiefly upon me and my government. Should not reign - By my immediate government, which was the great honour, safety, and happiness of this people, if they had had hearts to prize it.

8. So do they - Thou farest no worse than myself. This he speaks for Samuel's comfort and vindication.

9. Ye protest - That, if it be possible, thou mayst yet prevent their sin and misery. The manner - That is, of the kings which they desire like the kings of other nations.

11. Will take - Injuriously and by violence.

12. Will appoint - Hebrew. To, or for himself; for his own fancy, or glory, and not only when the necessities of the kingdom require it. And though this might seem to be no incumbrance, but an honour to the persons so advanced, yet even in them that honour was accompanied with great dangers, and pernicious snares of many kinds, which those faint shadows of glory could not recompense; and as to the public, their pomp and power proved very burdensome to the people, whose lands and fruits were taken from them, and bestowed upon these, for the support of their state. Will set them - At his own pleasure, when possibly their own fields required all their time and pains. He will press them for all sorts of his work, and that upon his own terms.

13. Daughters - Which would be more grievous to their parents, and more dangerous to themselves, because of the tenderness of that sex, and their liableness to many injuries.

14. Your fields - By fraud or force, as Ahab did from Naboth. His servants - He will not only take the fruits of your lands for his own use, but will take away your possessions to give to his servants.

15. The tenth - Besides the several tenths which God hath reserved for his service, he will, when he pleaseth, impose another tenth upon you. Officers - Hebrew. To his eunuchs, which may imply a farther injury, that he should against the command of God, make some of his people eunuchs; and take those into his court and favour, which God would have cast out of the congregation.

16. Will take - By constraint, and without sufficient recompense.

17. His servants - That is, he will use you like slaves, and deprive you of that liberty which now you enjoy.

18. Cry out - Ye shall bitterly mourn for the sad effects of this inordinate desire of a king. Will not hear - Because you will not hear, nor obey his counsel in this day.

20. Be like - What stupidity! It was their happiness that they were unlike all other nations, Num. xxiii, 9 Deut. xxxiii, 28, as in other glorious privileges, so especially in this, that the Lord was their immediate king and lawgiver. But they will have a king to go out before them, and to fight their battles. Could they desire a battle better fought for them than the last was, by Samuel's prayers and God's thunders? Were they fond to try the chance of war, at the same uncertainty that others did? And what was the issue? Their first king was slain in battle: and so was Joshua, one of the last and best.

21. Rehearsed - He repeated them privately between God and himself; for his own vindication and comfort: and as a foundation for his prayers to God, for direction and assistance.

22. Go - Betake yourselves to your several occasions, till you hear more from me in this matter.

IX

A short account of Saul, ver. 1, 2. Seeking his father's asses, he is advised to consult Samuel, ver. 3-10. He is directed to him, ver. 11-14. Samuel being informed of God concerning him, treats him with respect, and prepares him for the news, that he must be king, ver. 15-27.

2. Goodly - Comely and personable. Higher - A tall stature was much valued in a king in ancient times, and in the eastern countries.

3. The asses - Which were there of great price, because of the scarcity of horses, and therefore not held unworthy of Saul's seeking, at least in those ancient times, when simplicity, humility, and industry were in fashion among persons of quality.

6. honourable men - One of great reputation for his skill and faithfulness. Acquaintance with God and serviceableness to the kingdom of God, makes men truly honourable. The way - The course we should take to find the asses. He saith, peradventure, because he doubted whether so great a prophet would seek, or God would grant him a Revelation concerning such mean matters: although sometimes God was pleased herein to condescend to his people, to cut off all pretense or occasion of seeking to heathenish divination.

7. A present - Presents were then made to the prophets, either as a testimony of respect: or, as a grateful acknowledgement: or, for the support of the Prophets themselves: or, of the sons of the

prophets: or, of other persons in want, known to them.

9. Seer - Because he discerned and could discover things secret and unknown to others. And these are the words, either of some later sacred writer, who after Samuel's death, inserted this verse. Or, of Samuel, who, being probably fifty or sixty years old at the writing of this book, and speaking of the state of things in his first days, might well call it before time.

12. Came today to the city - He had been travelling abroad, and was now returned to his own house in Ramah. High place - Upon the hill mentioned ver. 11, and near the altar which Samuel built for this use.

13. Find him - At home and at leisure. To eat - The relicks of the sacrifices. Doth bless - The blessing of this sacrifice seems to have consisted both of thanksgiving, this being a thank-offering, and of prayer to God for its acceptance.

15. His ear - That is, secretly, perhaps by a still small voice.

16. Philistines - For though they were now most pressed with the Ammonites, yet they looked upon these as a land-flood, soon up, and soon down again: but the Philistines, their constant and nearest enemies, they most dreaded. And from these did Saul in some measure save them, and would have saved them much more, if his and the people's sins had not hindered.

20. On whom - Who is he that shall be that, which all Israel desire to have, namely, a king. Father's house - That honour is designed for thee, and, after thy death, for thy family or posterity, is by thy sin thou dost not cut off the entail.

21. The smallest - For so indeed this was, having been all cut off except six hundred, Judg. xx, 46-48, which blow they never recovered, and therefore they were scarce reckoned as an entire tribe, but only as a remnant of a tribe; and being ingrafted into Judah, in the division between the ten tribes and the two, they in some sort lost their name, and together with Judah were accounted but one tribe.

22. Chief place - Thereby to raise their expectation, and to prepare them for giving that honour to Saul, which his approaching dignity required.

24. I said - When I first spake that I had invited the people to join with me in my sacrifice, and then to partake with me of the feast, I then bade the cook reserve this part for thy use.

25. Communed - Concerning the kingdom designed for him by God.

27. Pass on - That thou and I may speak privately of the matter or the kingdom. Which Samuel hitherto endeavoured to conceal, lest he should be thought now to impose a king upon them, as before he denied one to them; and that it might appear by the lot mentioned in the next chapter, that the kingdom was given to Saul by God's destination, and not by Samuel's contrivance. Word of God - That is, a message delivered to me from God, which now I shall impart to thee.

X

The anointing of Saul, ver. 1. Samuel gives him signs and instruction, ver. 2-8. The signs accomplished, ver. 9-13. His return to his father's house, ver. 14-16. He is elected, solemnly inaugurated, and returns to his own city, ver. 17-27.

1. Poured it - Which Is was the usual rite in the designation, as of priests and prophets, so also of kings, whereby was signified the pouring forth of the gifts of God's spirit upon him, to fit him for the administration of his office. These sacred unctions then used, pointed at the great Messiah, or anointed One, the King of the church, and High-priest of our profession, who was anointed with the oil of the spirit without measure, above all the priests and princes of the Jewish church. Kissed - As a testimony of his sincere friendship and affection to him. His inheritance - That is, over his own peculiar people. Whereby he admonisheth Saul, that this people were not so much his, as God's; and that he was not to rule them according his own will, but according to the will of God.

2. Rachel's sepulchre - In the way to Bethlehem, which city was in Judah; her sepulchre might be either in Judah, or in Benjamin; for the possessions of those two tribes were bordering one upon another. The first place he directs him to was a sepulchre, the sepulchre of one of his ancestors. There he must read a lecture of his own mortality, and now he had a crown in his eye, must think of his grave, in which all his honour would be laid in the dust.

3. Plain - Not that at the foot of mount Tabor, which was far from these parts; but another belonging to some other place. Bethel - Properly so called, which was in Ephraim, where there was a noted high-place, famous for Jacob's vision there, Gen. xxviii, 19, where it is probable they offered sacrifices, in this confused state of things, when the ark was in one place, and the tabernacle in another.

5. Prophets - By prophets he understands persons that wholly devoted themselves to religious studies and exercises. For the term of prophesying is not only given to the most eminent act of it, foretelling things to come; but also to preaching, and to the making or singing of psalms, or songs of praise to God. And they that wholly attended upon these things, are called sons of the prophets, who were commonly combined into companies or colleges, that they might more conveniently assist one

another in God's work. This institution God was pleased so far to honour and bless, that sometimes he communicated unto those persons the knowledge of future things. Psaltery - Such instruments of musick being then used by prophets and other persons, for the excitation of their spirits in God's service. Prophesy - Either sing God's praises, or speak of the things of God, by a peculiar impulse of his spirit.

6. Will come - Hebrew. will leap, or rush upon thee. Another man - That is, thou shalt be suddenly endowed with another spirit, filled with skill of divine things, with courage, and wisdom, and magnanimity; and other qualifications befitting thy dignity.

7. Thou do - Hebrew. do what they hand findeth to do; that is, as thou shalt have a call and opportunity. He doth not intend that he should take the kingly government upon him, before his call to it was owned by the people, but that he should dispose his mind to a readiness of undertaking any public service when he should be called to his office.

8. Till I come - This, though now mentioned and commanded, was not immediately to be performed; as is evident, partly from the whole course of the story, (which shews, that Saul and Samuel, and the people, first met at Mizpeh, ver. 17, &c. where Saul was chosen by God, and accepted by the people as king; and afterwards went to Gilgal once before the time here spoken of, chap. xi, 14, 15,) and partly, by comparing this place with chap. xiii, 8, &c. where we find Saul charged with the violation of this command, two years after the giving of it. It seems this is given as a standing rule for Saul to observe while Samuel and he lived; that in case of any great future difficulties, as the invasion of enemies, Saul should resort to Gilgal, and call the people thither, and tarry there seven days, which was but a necessary time for gathering the people, and for the coming of Samuel thither. And Gilgal was chosen for this purpose, because that place was famous for the solemn renewing of the covenant between God and Israel, Josh. iv, 19-24, and for other eminent instances of God's favour to them, the remembrance whereof was a confirmation of their faith; and because it was a very convenient place for he tribes within and without Jordan to assemble, and consult, and unite their forces together upon such occasions.

10. Prophesied - The accomplishment of the two former signs is supposed, and this only is expressed, because this was more eminent than the former; the other were only transient acts, which passed in private between two or three persons meeting together; but this was a more permanent and notorious sign, done in a more solemn manner, and before many witnesses.

11. Is Saul - A man never instructed, nor exercised in, nor inclined to these matters.

12. Who is, &c. - Who is the father of all these prophets, among whom Saul now is one? Who is it that instructs and inspires them but God? They have it not from their parents, nor from their education, but by inspiration from God, who, when he pleaseth, can inspire Saul, or any other man with the same skill. And therefore wonder not at this matter, but give God the glory of it. A proverb - Used when any strange, or unexpected thing happened.

13. High place - Returning thither with the prophets, to praise God for these wonderful favours, and to beg counsel and help from God in this high business.

16. Told not - In obedience to Samuel, who obliged him to secrecy: and from an humble modesty.

19. Now therefore, &c. - He puts them upon chusing their king by lot, that all might know God had chosen Saul (for the disposal of the lot is of the Lord) and to prevent all dispute and exception.

20. Benjamin - Which tribe was now preferred before Judah, because the kingdom was freely promised by God to Judah, and was to be given to him in love; but now the kingdom was in a manner forced from God, and given them in anger and therefore conferred upon an obscure tribe.

22. Inquired - Either by Urim or Thummim, which was the usual way of enquiry. Or, by Samuel, who by his prayer procured an answer. Stuff - Among the carriages or baggage of the people there assembled. This he probably did, from a sense of his own unworthiness.

24. None like him - As to the height of his bodily stature, which was in itself, commendable in a king, and some kind of indication of great endowments of mind. God save the king - Hebrew. let the king live; that is, long and prosperously. Hereby they accept him for their king, and promise subjection to him. None will be losers in the end by their humility and modesty. honour, like the shadows, follows them that flee from it, but flees from them that pursue it.

25. Manner of the kingdom - The laws and rules by which the kingly government was to be managed; agreeable to those mentioned Deut. xvii, 16, &c. Before the Lord - Before the ark, where it was kept safe from depravation.

26. Went home - Not being actually inaugurated into his kingdom, he thought fit to retire to his former habitation, and to live privately 'till he had an occasion to shew himself in a more illustrious manner. Then went - To give him safe and honourable conduct to his house, though not to abide with him there, which did not suit his present circumstance.

27. No presents - As subjects in those times used to do to their kings. This was an evidence both of his humility, and the mercifulness of his disposition. So Christ held his peace, in the day of his patience. But there is a day of recompense coming.

XI

The distress of Jabesh-gilead, ver. 1-3. Saul's readiness to relieve them, and success, ver. 4-11. His tenderness to them that opposed him, ver. 12-13. He is confirmed in his kingdom, ver. 14- 15.

1. Then - That is, about that time; for that this happened before, and was the occasion of their desire of a king, may seem from chap. xii, 12, although it is possible, that Nahash's preparation, might cause that desire, and that he did not actually come 'till their king was chosen. Will serve - The occasion of this offer was, that they saw no likelihood of relief from their brethren in Canaan.

2. Thrust out, &c. - Partly for a reproach, as it here follows; and partly, to disable them. He leaves them one eye, that they might be fit to serve in any mean and base office.

5. After the herd - For being only anointed king, and not publickly inaugurated, nor having yet had opportunity of doing any thing worthy of his place, he thought fit to forbear all royal state, and to retire to his former private life, which, howsoever despised in this latter ages, was anciently in great esteem. Good magistrates are in pain, if their subjects are in tears.

7. Sent them - Wisely considering, that the sight of mens eyes does much more affect their hearts, than what they only hear with their ears. Samuel - Whom he joins with himself, both because he was present with him; and that hereby he might gain the more authority. Fear - A fear sent upon them by God, that they should not dare to deny their help. The fear of God will make men good subjects, good soldiers, and good friends to their country. They that fear God will make conscience of their duty to all men, particularly to their rulers.

8. Men of Judah - Who are numbered apart to their honour, to shew how readily they, to whom the kingdom was promised, Gen. xlix, 10, submitted to their king, though of another tribe; and how willing they were to hazard themselves for their brethren although they might have excused themselves from the necessity of defending their own country from their dangerous neighbours the Philistines.

14. Then - While the people were together by Jabesh-gilead, wherein Samuel's great prudence and fidelity to Saul is evident. He suspended the confirmation of Saul at first, whilst the generality of the people were disaffected, and now when he had given such eminent proof of his princely virtues, and when the peoples hearts were eagerly set upon him, he takes this as the fittest season for that work. Renew - That is, confirm our former choice.

15. Made - They owned and accepted him for their king.

XII

Samuel clears himself from all imputation of abusing the power which he now resigns to Saul, ver. 1-5. He reminds them of the great things God had done, ver. 6-13. He sets before them the blessing and the curse, ver. 14, 15. He calls upon God for thunder, ver. 16-19. He encourages and exhorts them, ver. 20-25.

1. Said - While they were assembled together in Gilgal. And this is another instance of Samuel's great wisdom and integrity. He would not reprove the people for their sin, in desiring a king, whilst Saul was unsettled in his kingdom; lest through their accustomed levity, they should as hastily cast off their king, as they had passionately desired him, and therefore he chuseth this season for it; because Saul's kingdom was now confirmed by an eminent victory; and because the people rejoiced greatly, applauded themselves for their desires of a king; and interpreted the success which God had given them, as a divine approbation of those desires. Samuel therefore thinks fit to temper their joys, and to excite them to that repentance which he saw wanting in them, and which he knew to be necessary, to prevent the curse of God upon their new king, and the whole kingdom.

2. Walketh - Ruleth over you. To him I have fully resigned my power, and own myself one of his subjects. Old - And therefore unable to bear the burden of government. My sons - Or, among you, in the same states private persons, as you are; if they have injured any of you, the law is now open against them; any of you may accuse them, your king can punish them, I do not intercede for them. Walked before you - That is, been your guide and governor; partly, as a prophet; and partly, as a judge.

3. Behold - I here present myself before the Lord, and before your king, ready to give an account of all my administrations. And this protestation Samuel makes of his integrity, not out of ostentation; but for his own just vindication, that the people might not hereafter for the defense of their own irregularities, reproach his government, and that being publickly acquitted from all faults in his government, he might more freely reprove the sins of the people, and, particularly, that sin of theirs in desiring a king, when they had so little reason for it.

7. Righteous acts - Hebrew. the righteousnesses; that is, mercies or benefits the chief subject of the following discourse; some of their calamities being but briefly named, and that for the illustration of God's mercy in their deliverances.

John Wesley

8. **This place** - In this land: in which Moses and Aaron are said to settle them; because they brought them into, and seated them in part of it, that without Jordan; because they were, under God, the principal authors of their entering into the land of Canaan; inasmuch as they brought them out of Egypt, conducted them through the wilderness; and thereby their prayers to God, and counsel to them, preserved them from ruin, and gave command from God for the distribution of the land among them, and encouraged them to enter into it. And lastly, Moses substituted Josh. in his stead, and commanded him to seat them there, which he did.

9. **Forgat** - That is, they revolted from him, and carried themselves, as if they had wholly forgotten his innumerable favours. This he saith to answer an objection, that the reason why they desired a king, was, because in the time of the Judges they were at great uncertainties, and often exercised with sharp afflictions: to which he answereth by concession that they were so; but adds, by way of retortion, that they themselves were the cause of it, by their forgetting God: so that it was not the fault of that kind of government, but their transgressing the rules of it. **Fought** - With success, and subdued them.

11. **Bedan** - This was either Samson, as most interpreters believe, who is called Bedan; that is, in Daniel, or of Daniel, one of that tribe, to signify that they had no reason to distrust that God, who could raise so eminent a saviour out of so obscure a tribe: or, Jair the Gileadite, which may seem best to agree, first, with the time and order of the Judges; for Jair was before Jephthah, but Samson was after him. Secondly, with other scriptures: for among the sons of a more ancient Jair, we meet with one called Bedan, 1 Chron. vii. 17, which name seems here given to Jair the judge, to distinguish him from that first Jair. **Safe** - So that it was no necessity, but mere wantonness, that made you desire a change.

12. **Your king** - That is, when God was your immediate king and governor, who was both able and willing to deliver you, if you had cried to him, whereof you and your ancestors have had plentiful experience; so that you did not at all need any other king; and your desire of another, was a manifest reproach against God.

13. **Ye have chosen** - Though God chose him by lot, yet the people are said to chuse him; either generally, because they chose that form of government; or particularly, because they approved of God's choice, and confirmed it. **The Lord** - He hath yielded to your inordinate desire.

14. **Then, &c.** - Hebrew. then shall-ye-be, (that is, walk, or go) after the Lord; that is, God shall still go before you, as he hath hitherto done, as your leader or governor, to direct, protect, and deliver you; and he will not forsake you, as you have given him just cause to do. Sometimes this phrase of going after the Lord, signifies a man's obedience to God; but here it is otherwise to be understood, and it notes not a duty to be performed, but a privilege to be received upon the performance of their duty; because it is opposed to a threatening denounced in case of disobedience, in the next verse.

15. **Your fathers** - Who lived under the Judges; and you shall have no advantage by the change of government, nor shall your kings be able to protect you against God's displeasure. The mistake, if we think we can evade God's justice, by shaking off his dominion. If we will not let God rule us, yet he will judge us.

17. **Wheat-harvest** - At which time it was a rare thing in those parts to have thunder or rain; the weather being more constant in its seasons there, than it is with us. **Rain** - That you may understand that God is displeased with you; and also how foolishly and wickedly you have done in rejecting the government of that God, at whose command are all things both in heaven and in earth.

18. **Samuel** - Who had such power and favour with God. By this thunder and rain, God shewed them their folly in desiring a king to save them, rather than God or Samuel, expecting more from an arm of flesh than from the arm of God, or from the power of prayer. Could their king thunder with a voice like God? Could their prince command such forces as the prophet could by his prayers? Likewise he intimates, that how serene soever their condition was now, (like the weather in wheat harvest) yet if God pleased, he could soon change the face of their heavens, and persecute them with his storms.

19. **Thy God** - Whom thou hast so great an interest in, while we are ashamed and afraid to call him our God.

20. **Fear not** - With a desponding fear, as if there were no hope left for you.

21. **Turn aside-**After idols; as they had often done before; and, notwithstanding this warning, did afterwards. **Vain things** - So idols are called, Deut. xxxii, 21 Jer. ii, 5, and so they are, being mere nothings, having no power in them; no influence upon us, nor use or benefit to us.

22. **His name's sake** - That is, for his own honour, which would suffer much among men, if he should not preserve and deliver his people in eminent dangers. And this reason God alledgeth to take them off from all conceit of their own merit; and to assure them, that if they did truly repent of all their sins, and serve God with all their heart; yet even in that case their salvation would not be due to their merits; but the effect of God's free mercy. **To make** - Out of his own free grace, without any desert of yours, and therefore he will not forsake you, except you thrust him away.

24. **Only, &c.** - Otherwise neither my prayer nor counsels will stand you in any stead.

XIII

Saul and Jonathan's life-guard, ver. 1, 2. Jonathan smites a garrison, and the people are called together, ver. 3, 4. The Philistines come up, and the Israelites are terrified, ver. 5-7. Saul sacrifices, ver. 8-10. Is reproved by Samuel, ver. 11-14. The people diminished, plundered, and disarmed, ver. 15-23.

3. Blew - That is, he sent messengers to tell them all what Jonathan had done, and how the Philistines were enraged at it, and therefore what necessity there was of gathering themselves together for their own defense.

4. Saul - Perhaps contrary to some treaty.

5. Thirty thousand chariots, &c. - Most of them, we may suppose, carriages for their baggage, not chariots of war, tho' all their allies were joined with them.

6. Strait - Notwithstanding their former presumption that if they had a king, they should be free from all such straits. And hereby God intended to teach them the vanity of confidence in men; and that they did not one jot less need the help of God now, than they did when they had no king. And probably they were the more discouraged, because they did not find Samuel with Saul. Sooner or later men will be made to see, that God and his prophets are their best friends.

7. All the people - That is, all that were left.

8. Seven days - Not seven compleat days; for the last day was not finished.

11. Camest not - That is, when the seventh day was come, and a good part of it past, whence I concluded thou wouldst not come that day.

12. Supplication - Thence it appears, that sacrifices were accompanied with solemn prayers. Forced myself - I did it against my own mind and inclination.

13. For ever - The phrase, forever, in scripture often signifies only a long time. So this had been abundantly verified, if the kingdom had been enjoyed by Saul, and by his son, and by his son's son; after whom the kingdom might have come to Judah.

14. A man - That is, such a man as will fulfil all the desires of his heart, and not oppose them, as thou dost. Commanded - That is, hath appointed, as the word command is sometimes used: but though God threatened but Saul with the loss of his kingdom for his sin; yet it is not improbable, there was a tacit condition implied, to wit, if he did not repent of this; and of all his sins; for the full, and final, and peremptory sentence of Saul's rejection, is plainly ascribed to another cause, chap. xv, 11, 23, 26, 28, 29, and 'till that second offense, neither the spirit of the Lord departed from him, nor was David anointed in his stead. "But was it not hard, to punish so little a sin so severely?" It was not little: disobedience to an express command, tho' in a small matter, is a great provocation. And indeed, there is no little sin, because there is no little God to sin against. In general, what to men seems a small offense, to him who knows the heart may appear a heinous crime. We are taught hereby, how necessary it is, that we wait on our God continually. For Saul is sentenced to lose his kingdom for want of two or three hours patience.

20. Philistines - Not to the land of the Philistines, but to the stations and garrisons which the Philistines retained in several parts of Israel's land, though Samuel's authority had so far over-awed them, that they durst not give the Israelites much disturbance. In these, therefore, the Philistines kept all the smiths; and here they allowed them the exercise of their art for the uses following.

22. Sword - It seems restrained to the six hundred that were with Saul and Jonathan; for there were no doubt a considerable number of swords and spears among the Israelites, but they generally hid them, as now they did their persons, from the Philistines. And the Philistines had not yet attained to so great a power over them, as wholly to disarm them, but thought it sufficient to prevent the making of new arms; knowing that the old ones would shortly be decayed, and useless. There were likewise other arms more common in those times and places, than swords and spears; to wit, bows and arrows, and slings and stones.

XIV

Jonathan proposes to his armour-bearer the attacking of the Philistine's army, ver. 1-10. They make the attack; the Philistines are terrified, ver. 11-15. They slay one another, and are pursued by the Israelites, ver. 16-23. Saul adjures the people to eat nothing 'till night; Jonathan eats honey, ver. 24-30. The people smite the Philistines, and eat the spoil with the blood, ver. 31, 32. Saul remedies this, ver. 33-35. Dooms Jonathan to death, who is rescued by the people, ver. 36-46. A general account of Saul's exploits and family, ver. 47-52.

2. Tarried - In the outworks of the city where he had entrenched himself to observe the motion of the Philistines. In - Or, towards Migron, which was near Gibeah.

3. Ahiah - The same who is called Abimelech, chap. xxii, 9, 11, 20, the high-priest, who was here

John Wesley

to attend upon the ark which was brought thither, ver. 18. Ephod - The high-priest's ephod, wherein the Urim and Thummim was.

4. Passages - Two passages, both which Jonathan must cross, to go to the Philistines, between which the following rocks lay, but the words may be rendered, in the middle of the passage, the plural number being put for the singular. Rock - Which is not to be understood, as if in this passage one rock was on the right hand, and the other on the left; for so he might have gone between both: and there was no need of climbing up to them. But the meaning is, that the tooth (or prominency) of one rock, (as it is in the Hebrew) was on the side; that is northward, looking towards Michmash (the garrison of the Philistines) and the tooth of the other rock was on the other side; that is, southward, looking towards Gibeah, (where Saul's camp lay): and Jonathan was forced to climb over these two rocks, because the common ways from one town to the other were obstructed.

6. Uncircumcised - So he calls them, to strengthen his faith by this consideration, that his enemies were enemies to God; whereas he was circumcised, and therefore in covenant with God, who was both able, and engaged to assist his people. It way be - He speaks doubtfully: for tho' he felt himself stirred up by God to this exploit, and was assured that God would deliver his people; yet he was not certain that he would do it at this time, and in this way. Work - Great and wonderful things.

10. A sign - Jonathan not being assured of the success of this exploit, desires a sign; and by the instinct of God's Spirit, pitches upon this. Divers such motions and extraordinary impulses there were among great and good men in ancient times. Observe; God has the governing of the hearts and tongues of all men, even of those that know him not, and serves his own purposes by them, tho' they mean not so, neither does their hearts think so.

12. Come up, &c. - A speech of contempt and derision. The Lord - He piously and modestly ascribes the success which he now foresees, to God only. And he does not say, into our hand, but into the hand of Israel; for he fought not his own glory, but the public good. His faith being thus strengthened, nothing can stand against him: he climbs the rock upon all four, though he had nothing to cover him, none to second him, but his servant, nor any probability of any thing but death before him.

13. They fell - For being endowed with extraordinary strength and courage, and having with incredible boldness killed the first they met with, it is not strange if the Philistines were both astonished and intimidated; God also struck them with a panic; and withal, infatuated their minds, and possibly, put an evil spirit among them, which in this universal confusion made them conceive that there was treachery among themselves, and therefore caused them to sheathe their swords in one anothers bowels.

15. Field - That is, in the whole host which was in the field. All - That is, among all the rest of their forces, as well as those in the garrison at Michmash, as the spoilers, mentioned chap. xiii, 17, the report of this prodigy, and with it the terror of God speedily passing from one to another. Trembling - The Hebrew is, a trembling of God, signifying not only a very great trembling, but such as was supernatural, and came immediately from the hand of God. He that made the heart knows how to make it tremble. To complete their confusion, even the earth quaked; it shook under them, and made them fear it was just going to swallow them up. Those who will not fear the eternal God, he can make afraid of a shadow.

19. Withdraw - Trouble not thyself to inquire; for I now plainly discern the matter.

21. Which went - Either by constraint, as servants; or in policy, to gain their favour and protection.

23. The battle - That is, the warriors who were engaged in the battle, and were pursuing the Philistines. Yet it is said, the Lord saved Israel that day: he did it by them: for without him they could do nothing. Salvation is of the Lord.

24. Distressed - With hunger, and weakness, and faintness, and all by reason of the following oath. Avenged - As Saul's intention was good, so the matter of the obligation was not simply unlawful, if it had not been so rigorous in excluding all food, and in obliging the people to it under pain of an accursed death, which was a punishment far exceeding the fault.

26. Honey - Bees often make their hives in the trunks of trees, or clefts of rocks, or holes of the earth; and this in divers countries, but eminently in Canaan.

27. Enlightened - He was refreshed, and recovered his lost spirits. This cleared his sight, which was grown dim by hunger and faintness.

28. People - They that came with Saul, whose forces were now united with Jonathan's.

32. Slew - At evening, when the time prefixed by Saul was expired. With blood - Not having patience to tarry 'till the blood was perfectly gone out of them, as they should have done. So they who made conscience of the king's commandment for fear of the curse, make no scruple of transgressing God's command.

33. Transgressed - He sees their fault, but not his own, in giving the occasion of it.

36. Draw near - To the ark, in order to inquire of God.

39. Answered - None of those who saw Jonathan eating, informed against him; because they were satisfied that his ignorance excused him; and from their great love to Jonathan, whom they would not expose to death for so small an offense.

41. Perfect lot - Or, declare the perfect, or guiltless person. That is, O Lord, so guide the lot, that it may discover who is guilty in his matter, and who innocent. Escaped - They were pronounced guiltless.

42. Jonathan - God so ordered the lot; not that he approved Saul's execration, ver. 24, or his oath that the transgressor should die, ver. 39, nor that he would expose Jonathan to death; but that Saul's folly might be chastised, when he saw what danger it had brought upon his eldest and excellent son; and that Jonathan's innocency might be cleared.

44. For thou,&c. - We have no proof, that Saul did not act in this whole affair from a real fear of God.

45. With God - In concurrence with God, he hath wrought this salvation. God is so far from being offended with Jonathan, that he hath graciously owned him in the great service of this day.

47. Took the kingdom - That is, resumed the administration of it, after he had in a manner lost it by the Philistines, who had almost turned him out of it.

49. Ishui - Called also Abinadab. chap. xxxi, 2. Ishbosheth, Saul's other son is here omitted, because he intended to mention only those of his sons who went with him into the battles here mentioned, and who were afterwards slain with him.

XV

God commands Saul utterly to destroy the Amalekites, ver. 1- 3. He destroys them, but not utterly, ver. 4-9. Samuel pronounces sentence upon him for his disobedience, yet consents to honour him before the people, ver. 10-31. Slays Agag, ver. 32, 33. Takes his leave of Saul, yet mourns for him, ver. 34, 35.

1. Hearken - Thou hast committed error already, now regain God's favour by thy exact obedience to what he commands.

2. I remember - Now I will revenge those old injuries of the Amalekites on their children: who continue in their parents practices. Came from Egypt - When he was newly come out of cruel and long bondage, and was now weak, and weary, and faint, and hungry, Deut. xxv, 18, and therefore it was barbarous instead of that pity which even Nature prompted them to afford, to add affliction to the afflicted; it was also horrid impiety to fight against God himself and to lift up their hand in a manner against the Lord's throne, whilst they struck at that people which God had brought forth in so stupendous a way.

3. Destroy - Both persons and goods, kill all that live, and consume all things without life, for I will have no name nor remnant of that people left, whom long since I have devoted to utter destruction. Spare not - Shew no compassion or favour to any of them. The same thing repeated to prevent mistake, and oblige Saul to the exact performance hereof. Slay, &c. - Which was not unjust, because God is the supreme Lord of life, and can require his own when he pleaseth; infants likewise are born in sin, and therefore liable to God's wrath. Their death also was rather a mercy than a curse, as being the occasion of preventing their sin and punishment. Ox, &c. - Which being all made for man's benefit, it is not strange if they suffer with him, for the instruction of mankind.

6. Kenites - A people descending from, or nearly related to Jethro, who anciently dwelt in rocks near the Amalekites, Num. xxiv, 21, and afterwards some of them dwelt in Judah, Judg. i, 16, whence it is probable they removed, (which, dwelling in tents, they could easily do) and retired to their old habitation, because of the wars and troubles wherewith Judah was annoyed. Shewed kindness - Some of your progenitors did so, and for their sakes all of you shall fare the better. You were not guilty of that sin for which Amalek is now to be destroyed. When destroying judgments are abroad God takes care to separate the precious from the vile. It is then especially dangerous to be found in the company of God's enemies. The Jews have a saying, Woe to a wicked man, and to his neighbour.

7. To Shur - That is, from one end of their country to the other; he smote all that he met with: but a great number of them fled away upon the noise of his coming, and secured themselves in other places, 'till the storm was over. 8. All - Whom he found. Now they paid dear for the sin of their ancestors. They were themselves guilty of idolatry and numberless sins, for which they deserved to be cut off. Yet when God would reckon with them, he fixes upon this as the ground of his quarrel.

9. Vile - Thus they obeyed God only so far as they could without inconvenience to themselves.

11. Repenteth - Repentance implies grief of heart, and change of counsels, and therefore cannot be in God: but it is ascribed to God when God alters his method of dealing, and treats a person as if be did indeed repent of the kindness he had shewed him. All night - To implore his pardoning mercy for Saul, and for the people. Is turned back - Therefore he did once follow God. Otherwise it would have been impossible, he should turn back from following him.

12. A place - That is, a monument or trophy of his victory.

13. They - That is, the people. Thus, he lays the blame upon the people; whereas they could not do it without his consent; and he should have used his power to over-rule them.

18. A journey - So easy was the service, and so certain the success, that it was rather to be called a

journey than a war.

20. The king - To be dealt with as God pleaseth.

21. But the people, &c. - Here the conscience of Saul begins to awake, tho' but a little: for he still lays the blame on the people.

22. Sacrifice - Because obedience to God is a moral duty, constantly and indispensably necessary; but sacrifice is but a ceremonial institution, sometimes unnecessary, as it was in the wilderness: and sometimes sinful, when it is offered by a polluted hand, or in an irregular manner. Therefore thy gross disobedience to God's express command, is not to be compensated with sacrifice. Hearken - That is, to obey. Fat - Then the choicest part of all the sacrifice.

23. Rebellion - Disobedience to God's command. Stubbornness - Contumacy in sin, justifying it, and pleading for it. Iniquity - Or, the iniquity of idolatry. Rejected - Hath pronounced the sentence of rejection: for that he was not actually deposed by God before, plainly appears, because not only the people, but even David, after this, owned him as king. Those are unworthy to rule over men, who are not willing that God should rule over them.

24. I have sinned - It does by no means appear, that Saul acts the hypocrite herein, in assigning a false cause of his disobedience. Rather, he nakedly declares the thing as it was.

25. Pardon my sin - Neither can it be proved that there was any hypocrisy in this. Rather charity requires us to believe, that he sincerely desired pardon, both from God and man, as he now knew, he had sinned against both.

26. I will not - This was no lie, though he afterwards returned, because he spoke what he meant; his words and his intentions agreed together, though afterwards he saw reason to change his intentions. Compare Gen. xix, 2, 3. This may relieve many perplexed consciences, who think themselves obliged to do what they have said they would do, though they see just cause to change their minds. Hath rejected thee, &c. - But he does not say, he "hath rejected thee from salvation." And who besides hath authority to say so?

29. Strength of Israel - So he calls God here, to shew the reason why God neither will nor can lie; because lying proceeds from the sense of a man's weakness, who cannot many times accomplish his design without lying and dissimulation; therefore many princes have used it for this very reason. But God needs no such artifices; he can do whatsoever he pleaseth by his absolute power. Repent - That is, nor change his counsel; which also is an effect of weakness and imperfection, either of wisdom or power. So that this word is not here used in the sense it commonly is when applied to God, as in Jer. xi, 1-23, and elsewhere.

31. Turned - First, that the people might not upon pretense of this sentence of rejection, withdraw their obedience to their sovereign; whereby they would both have sinned against God, and have been as sheep without a shepherd. Secondly, that he might rectify Saul's error, and execute God's judgment upon Agag.

33. As, &c. - Whereby it appears, that he was a tyrant, and guilty of many bloody actions. And this seems to be added for the fuller vindication of God's justice, and to shew, that although God did at this time revenge a crime committed by this man's ancestors 400 years ago, yet he did not punish an innocent son for his father's crimes, but one that persisted in the same evil courses. Hewed - This he did by divine instinct, and in pursuance of God's express command, which being sinfully neglected by Saul, is now executed by Samuel. But these are no precedents for private persons to take the sword of justice into their hands. For we must live by the laws of God, and not by extraordinary examples.

35. To see Saul - That is, to visit him, in token of respect or friendship: or, to seek counsel from God for him. Otherwise he did see him chap. xix, 24. Though indeed it was not Samuel that came thither with design to see Saul, but Saul went thither to see Samuel, and that accidentally.

XVI

Samuel is appointed to anoint one of the sons of Jesse king, ver. 1-5. The elder sons are passed by, and David anointed, ver. 6- 13. Saul growing melancholy is eased by David's music, ver. 14- 23.

1. Mourn - And pray for his restitution, which the following words imply he did. Oil - Which was used in the inauguration of kings. But here it is used in the designation of a king; for David was not actually made king by it, but still remained a subject. And the reason of this anticipation was the comfort of Samuel, and other good men, against their fears in case of Saul's death, and the assurance of David's title, which otherwise would have been doubtful. I have provided - This phrase is very emphatical, and implies the difference between this and the former king. Saul was a king of the people's providing, he was the product of their sinful desires: but this is a king of my own providing, to fulfil all my will, and to serve my glory.

4. Trembled - Because it was strange and unexpected to them, this being but an obscure town, and remote from Samuel, and therefore they justly thought there was some extraordinary reason for it.

Peaceable - The Hebrew phrase, comest thou in peace, is as much as to say (in our phrase) is all well?

5. He sanctified - It seems evident that there was something peculiar in Jesse's invitation. For first, both he and his sons were invited, whereas the others were only invited for their own persons. Secondly, the different phrase here used, that he sanctified these, when he only bade the other sanctify themselves; argues a singular care of Samuel in their sanctification. Which makes it probable, that the rest were only to join with them in the act of sacrificing; but these, and only these, were invited to feast upon the remainders of the sacrifices.

6. Before him - That is, in this place where God is now present. For it is observable, that not only the sacrifice is said to be offered, but even the feast upon the remainders of it is said, to be eaten before the Lord, Deut. xii, 7, that is, before or near his altar, where God was present in a special manner. This I take to be the person I am sent to anoint: wherein yet be was mistaken, as other prophets sometimes were, when they hastily spake their own thoughts, before they had consulted God.

10. Seven - There are but seven named, 1 Chron. ii, 13-15, because one of them was either born of a concubine: or, died immediately after this time.

11. Keepeth sheep - And consequently is the most unfit of all my sons for that high employment. Either therefore he did not understand David's wisdom and valour, or he judged him unfit, by reason of his mean education. And God so ordered it by his providence, that David's choice might plainly appear to be God's work, and not Samuel's, or Jesse's. David signifies beloved: a fit name for so eminent a type of the Beloved Son. It is supposed, David was now about twenty years old. If so, his troubles by Saul lasted near ten years: for he was thirty years old when Saul died. Samuel having done this went to Ramah. He retired to die in peace, since his eyes had seen the salvation, even the scepter brought into the tribe of Judah.

13. Anointed him - David's brethren saw David's unction, yet did not understand, that he was anointed to the kingdom; but were only told by Samuel, that he was anointed to some great service, which hereafter they should know. Thus Jesse only, and David, understood the whole business, and his brethren were able to attest to that act of Samuel's anointing him, which, with other collateral evidences, was abundantly sufficient to prove David's right to the kingdom, if need should be. The spirit,&c., - That is, he was immediately endowed with extraordinary gifts of God's Spirit, as strength, and courage, and wisdom, and other excellent qualities which fitted him for, and put him upon noble attempts.

14. Departed - God took away that prudence, and courage, and alacrity, and other gifts wherewith be had qualified him for his public employment. From the Lord - That is, by God's permission, who delivered him up to be buffeted of Satan. Troubled - Stirred up in him unruly and tormenting passions; as envy, rage, fear, or despair. He grew fretful, and peevish, and discontented, timorous and suspicious, frequently starting and trembling.

16. Be well - And the success confirms their opinion. For although music cannot directly have an influence upon an evil spirit to drive him away; yet, because the devil, as it seems, had not possession of him, but only made use of the passions of his mind, and humours of his body to molest him: and because it is manifest, that music hath a mighty power to qualify and sweeten these, and to make a man sedate and chearful; it is not strange, if the devil had not that power over him when his mind was more composed, which he had when it was disordered; as the devil had less power over lunaticks in the decrease, than in the increase of the moon: Matt. xvii, 15, 18. And seeing music prepared the Lord's prophets for the entertainment of the good Spirit, as 2 Kings iii, 15. Why might it not dispose Saul to the resistance of the evil spirit? And why might not the chearing of his heart, in some measure strengthen him against those temptations of the devil, which were fed by his melancholy humour? And by this means, David without any contrivance of him or his friends, is brought to court, soon after he was anointed to the kingdom. Those whom God designs for any service, his providence will concur with his grace, to prepare and qualify them for it.

18. Prudent - Wonder not, that David was so suddenly advanced, from a poor shepherd, to so great a reputation; for these were the effects of that Spirit of the Lord which he received when he was anointed. The Lord, &c. - That is, directs and prospers all his undertakings.

20. Sent him - This present, though in our times it would seem contemptible, yet was very agreeable to the usage of those times, and to the condition of Jesse, which was but mean in the world. And it seems to have been the custom of those times, (as it is yet in the eastern countries) when they made their appearance before princes, or great persons, to bring a present.

21. Stood before him - That is, waited upon him. And he loved him greatly - So there was something good in Saul still: he had not lost all, tho' he had lost the kingdom. armour-bearer - He had that place conferred upon him, though we do not read that he ever exercised it; for it seems he was gone back to his father upon some occasion not related; and had abode with him some considerable time before the war described, chap. xvii, 1-53, happened.

23. Departed - Namely, for a season. And the reason of this success, may be, partly natural, and partly supernatural, respecting David; whom God designed by this means to bring into favour with the king, and so to smooth the way for his advancement.

XVII

Goliath challenges the armies of Israel, ver. 1-11. David coming into the camp, hears his challenge, ver. 12-27. Eliab chides David, whose words are related to Saul, ver. 28-31. David undertakes to fight Goliath, ver. 32-37. He rejects Saul's armour, and goes with his sling, ver. 38-40. He attacks and slays Goliath, ver. 41-51. The Israelites pursue the Philistines, ver. 52-53. David returns: the notice taken of him by Saul, ver. 54-58.

1. Gathered, &c. - Probably they had heard, that Samuel had forsaken Saul, and that Saul himself was unfit for business. The enemies of the church are watchful to take all advantages, and they never have greater advantage, than when her protectors have provoked God's Spirit and prophets to leave them.

4. Six cubits - At least, nine feet, nine inches high. And this is not strange; for besides the giants mentioned in Scripture, Herodotus, Diodourus Siculus, and Pliny, make mention of persons seven cubits high.

5. Coat of mail - Made of brass plates laid over one another, like the scales of a fish. The weight, &c. - The common shekel contained a fourth part of an ounce; and so five thousand shekels made one thousand two hundred and fifty ounces, or seventy- eight pounds: which weight is not unsuitable to a man of such vast strength as his height speaks him to be.

6. Greaves - Boots.

7. Beam - On which the weavers fasten their web. It was like this for thickness. And though the whole weight of Goliath's armour may seem prodigious; yet it is not so much by far as one Athanatus did manage: of whom Pliny relates, That he saw him come into the theatre with arms weighing twelve thousand ounces. A shield - Probably for state: for he that was clad in brass, little needed a shield.

8. Come down - That the battle may be decided by us two alone.

11. Afraid - This may seem strange, considering the glorious promises, and their late experience of divine assistance. And where was Jonathan, who in the last war had so bravely engaged an whole army of the Philistines? Doubtless he did not feel himself so stirred up of God as he did at that time. As the best, so the bravest of men, are no more than what God makes them. Jonathan must sit still now, because this honour is reserved for David.

12. Old man - Therefore he went not himself to the camp.

15. Went - From Saul's court: where having relieved Saul, he was permitted to go to his father's house, to be sent for again upon occasion.

18. Pledge - That is, bring me some token of their welfare.

19. Fighting - That is, in a posture and readiness to fight with them; as it is explained, ver. 20, 21.

20. Went, &c. - Jesse little thought of sending his son to the camp, just at that critical juncture. But the wise God orders the time and all the circumstances of affairs, so as to serve the designs of his own glory.

24. Fled - One Philistine could never have thus put ten thousand Israelites to flight, unless their rock, being forsaken by them, had justly sold them and shut them up.

25. Free - Free from all those tributes and charges which either the court or the camp required.

28. Naughtiness - Thy false-confidence, and vain gloried curiosity. See the folly and wickedness of envy! How groundless its jealousies are, how unjust its censures, how unfair it representations? God preserve us from such a spirit!

29. A cause - Of my thus speaking? Is this giant invincible? Is our God unable to oppose him, and subdue him? However David is not deterred from his undertaking, by the hard words of Eliab. They that undertake public services must not think it strange, if they be opposed by those from whom they had reason to expect assistance, but must humbly go on with their work, in the face, not only of their enemies threats, but of their friends slights, suspicions, and censures.

30. He tarried - For being secretly moved by God's spirit to undertake the combat. He speaks with divers persons about it, that it might come to the king's ear.

32. Let no man's heart, &c. - It would have reflected upon his prince to say, Let not thy heart fail: therefore he speaks in general terms, Let no man's heart fail. A little shepherd, come but this morning from keeping sheep, has more courage than all the mighty men of Israel! Thus doth God often do great things for his people by the weak things of the world.

33. A youth - Not above 20 years old; and a novice, a raw and unexperienced soldier.

37. The Lord, &c. - The lion and the bear were only enemies to me and my sheep, and it was in defense of them I attacked them. But this Philistine is an enemy to my God and his people, and it is for their honour that I attack him.

38. armour - With armour taken out of his armoury. He seems to speak of some military vestments which were then used in war, and were contrived for defense; such as buff-coats are now.

39. Proved them - I have no skill or experience in the managements of this kind of arms.

40. Staff - His shepherd's staff. These arms in themselves were contemptible, yet chosen by David; because he had no skill to use other arms; because he had inward assurance of the victory, even by these weapons; and because such a conquest would be more honourable to God, and most shameful, and discouraging to the Philistines.

41. Drew near - Probably a signal was made, that his challenge was accepted.

42. Fair - Not having so much as the countenance of a martial person.

43. Dog - Dost thou think to beat me as easily as thou wouldst thy dog?

46. A God - Hebrew. that God, the only true God, is for Israel; or on Israel's side, and against you. Or, that Israel hath a God, a God indeed, one who is able to help them; and not such an impotent idol as you serve.

47. Saveth - That is, that he can save without these arms, and with the most contemptible weapons. The battle - That is, the events of war are wholly in his power. He will - David speaks thus confidently, because he was assured of it by a particular inspiration.

48. Drew nigh - Like a stalking mountain. Ran - So far was he from fear!

49. Forehead - Probably the proud giant had lift up that part of his helmet which covered his forehead; in contempt of David and his weapons, and by the singular direction of providence.

51. David took - Hence it appears, that David was not a little man, as many fancy; but a man of considerable bulk and strength, because he was able to manage a giant's sword. The stone threw him down to the earth, and bereaved him of sense and motion; but there remained some life in him, which the sword took away, and so compleated the work. God is greatly glorified, when his proud enemies are cut off with their own sword.

55. Whose son - David had been some considerable time dismissed from Saul's court, and was returned home. And therefore it is not strange, if Saul for the present had forgot David. Besides the distemper of Saul's mind might make him forgetful; and that David might be now much changed, both in his countenance and in his habit. I cannot tell - Abner's employment was generally in the camp, when David was at the court; and when Abner was there, he took little notice of a person so much inferior to him as David was.

XVIII

David becomes the friend of Jonathan, the constant attendant of Saul, and the favourite of all the people, ver. 1-5. Saul's envy raised, ver. 6-9. He seeks to kill David, ver. 10-11 Is afraid of him, ver. 12-16. Promises to give him his elder daughter, and gives him the younger, hoping to destroy him thereby, but in vain, ver. a 7-27. He is more feared by Saul and esteemed by the people, ver. 28-30.

1. Loved him - For his excellent virtues and endowments, which shone forth both in his speeches and actions; for the service he had done to God and to his people; and for the similitude of their age and qualities.

2. Took him, &c. - By which it appears, that before this David had not his constant residence at court.

5. Went - Upon military expeditions, of which that word is often used.

10. The evil spirit, &c. - His fits of frenzy returned upon him. The very next day after he conceived envy at David, the evil spirit was permitted by God to seize him again. Such is the fruit of envy and uncharitableness. Prophesied - That is, he used uncouth gestures, and signs, as the prophets often did.

11. And Saul cast the javelin - Being now quite under the power of that evil spirit. Twice - Once now, and another time upon a like occasion, chap. xix, 10.

12. Afraid - Lest as he had gained the favour of God and of all the people, he should also take away his kingdom.

13. Removed him from him - From his presence and court; which he did, because he feared lest David should find an opportunity to kill him, as he had designed to kill David; because his presence now made him more sad than ever his musick made him chearful: and principally, that hereby he might expose him to the greatest hazards.

18. What is my life - How little is my life worth, that by the exposing of that to some hazard, I should purchase a king's daughter! In these expressions David sheweth not only his humility, but also his wisdom, in discovering so deep a sense of his own meanness, that Saul might see how far he was from aspiring at the kingdom.

19. Adriel - The son of Bar-zillai, as he is called, 2 Sam. xxi, 8. This was an act of great injustice; and accordingly this marriage was accursed by God, and the children begotten in it, were, by God's appointment cut off, 2 Sam. xxi, 8, 9.

26. The days - That is, the time allowed by Saul to David for the execution of this exploit.

27. Two hundred - He doubled the number required; to oblige Saul the more to the performance of

his promise; and to shew his great respect and affection to Saul's daughter.

30. Went forth - To war against the Israelites, being provoked by their former losses, and especially by that act of David's.

XIX

Saul is pacified by Jonathan, ver. 1-7. Attempts again to kill David, ver. 8-10. Is deceived by Michal, who sends David away, ver. 11-17. David flies to Ramah, and Saul prophesies, ver. 18-24.

4. Spake good - Which he could not do without hazard to himself. Herein therefore he performed the duty of a true friend, and of a valiant man.

6. As the Lord, &c. - And without all doubt, he intended what he said, feeling a real change in himself for the present. "God," says Mr. Henry, "inclined the heart of Saul to hearken to the voice of Jonathan."

8. And David, &c. - So David continues his good service, tho' it was ill requited. They who are ill paid for doing good, yet must not be weary of well doing, remembering how bountiful a benefactor God is, even to the evil and unthankful.

9. The evil spirit - David's successes against the Philistines revived his envy, and the devil watched the opportunity, as he had done before.

13. Goats hair - Or, put great goats hair upon his bolster; upon the head and face of the image, which lay upon his bolster, that it might have some kind of resemblance of David's head and hair, at least in a sick man's bed, where there useth to be but a glimmering light. Covered it - Upon pretense of his being sick, and needing some such covering.

18. To Samuel - Both for comfort and direction in his distress; and for safety, supposing that Saul would be ashamed to execute his bloody designs in the presence of so venerable a person as Samuel.

20. Over them - To instruct and direct them in those holy exercises. For though they prophesied by Divine inspiration, yet they were both to prepare themselves for it before hand, and to make good improvement of it afterwards, in both which they needed Samuel's counsel and assistance. And whereas some might falsely pretend to those raptures; or the devil might transform himself into an angel of light, Samuel's presence and judgment was necessary to prevent and to detect such impostures. Besides, Samuel would by his present conjunction with them in those holy exercises, encourage them, and stir up others to the coveting of those gifts, and to the performance of such religious duties. Prophesied - Being inspired by God as Balaam was; that being wrapt up into such an extasy, their minds might be wholly taken off from their design of seizing David.

23. The spirit - It came upon him in the way; whereas it came not upon his messengers 'till they came to the place. Hereby God would convince Saul of the vanity of his designs against David, and that in them he fought against God himself.

24. Lay down - Hebrew. fell, down upon the earth; for his mind being in an extasy, he had not the use of his senses. God so ordering it, that David might have an opportunity to escape. Naked - That is, stript of his upper garments, as the word naked is often used; and it is here repeated to signify how long he lay in that posture. Day and night - So God kept him as it were in chains, 'till David was got out of his reach. Is Saul - The same proverb which was used before, is here revived, as an evidence of God's wonderful care over David; he made Saul in some sort a prophet, that he mightst make David a king.

XX

David complains to Jonathan; and desires his help, ver. 1-5. Jonathan promises to give him intelligence, and confirms his friendship, ver. 9-23. He finds his father implacable, ver. 24-34. He gives David notice of it, in the manner they had agreed on, ver. 35-42.

2. Is it not so - For Jonathan gave credit to his father's oath, chap. xix, 6.

3. David swear - The matter being of great moment, and Jonathan doubting the truth of it, he confirms his word with an oath, which follows in the end of the verse. Only he interposeth a reason why Saul concealed it from Jonathan.

5. To the third day - That is, unto the next day, but one after the new moon. His meaning is not, that he would hide himself in any certain place all the three days, but that he would secure himself either at Bethlehem with his friends, or in any other place 'till the third day.

6. Asked me - Who being the king's son and deputy, used to give license to military men to depart for a season upon just occasions.

8. Deal kindly - In giving me timely notice, and a true account of Saul's disposition and intention towards me. A covenant of the Lord - That is, a solemn covenant, not lightly undertaken, but seriously entered into, in the name and fear of God, and in his presence, calling him to be the witness of our

sincerity therein, and the avenger of perfidiousness in him that breaks it. Slay me - I am contented thou shouldst kill me. For why - Why shouldst thou betray me to thy father, by concealing his evil intentions from me?

12. O Lord God - Do thou hear and judge between us. It is an abrupt speech which is usual in great passions.

14. Kindness as the Lord - That kindness to which thou hast engaged thyself, in the covenant sworn between thee and me in God's presence. I die not - That thou do not kill me or mine, as princes of another line use to kill the nearest relations of the former line, from whom the kingdom was translated to them.

16. A covenant - The covenant which before was personal, he now extends to the whole house of David, expecting a reciprocal enlargement of it on David's side, which doubtless he obtained. Enemies - If either I or any of my house shall break this covenant, and shall prove enemies to David or to his house, let the Lord, the witness of this covenant, severely punish the violators of it.

17. Swear again - Hebrew. and Jonathan added or proceeded to make David swear; that is, having himself sworn to David or adjured David, in the foregoing verse, he here requires David's oath to him, by way of restipulation or confirmation. Loved him - Because he had a true friendship for David, he desired that the covenant might be inviolably observed through all their generations.

19. Was in hand - When this same business which now they were treating about, was in agitation formerly; namely, to discover Saul's mind and purpose towards him, chap. xix, 2, 3. Ezel - By that stone which directs travelers in the way; namely, in some cave, or convenient place, which was near it.

21. I will send - I will send him out before I shoot, to find out, and take up the arrows which I shall shoot. And I shall shoot them either short of him, or beyond him, as I shall see occasion.

23. Between - As a witness and a judge between us and our families forever, if on either side this league of friendship be violated.

24. Hid himself - Namely, at the time appointed: for it seems probable, that he went first to Bethlehem, and thence returned to the field, when the occasion required.

25. Arose - He rose from his seat where he was sat next the king, and stood at Abner's coming, to do honour to him, who was his father's cousin, and the general of the army.

26. Something - Some accident which has rendered him unclean, and so unfit to partake of this feast, which consisted in part of the remainders of the peace-offerings, according to the law, Levit vii, 20. Unfit also to come into any company, much more, into the king's company, lest he should pollute them also.

27. Son of Jesse - So he calls him in scorn, to note the meanness of his original; and as not deigning to call him by his proper name. To day - For the uncleanness which came by some chance, usually lasted but for one day.

30. Thy confusion - Men will conclude that thou hast no royal blood in thy veins, that canst so tamely give up thy crown to so contemptible a person.

33. To smite him - Saul seemed to be in great care, that Jonathan should be established in his kingdom: and now he himself aims at his life! What fools, what worse than savage beasts does anger make.

37. To - That is, near the place. For the words following shew, that he was not yet come thither.

40. Artillery - His bow, and arrows, and quiver.

XXI

David coming to Nob, takes the shew-bread, and Goliath's sword, ver. 1-9. Goes to Achish, and feigns himself mad, ver. 10- 13. Is dismissed by Achish, ver. 14, 15.

1. Nob - A city of priests, where the tabernacle now was. Hither David resorted, for a supply of his necessities, which he supposed he might receive here, without danger of being betrayed into Saul's hands: and principally, that in this great distress, he might receive comfort and counsel from the Lord. Ahimelech - The chief priest, brother to that Ahiah, chap. xiv, 3, and he being now dead, his successor in the priesthood, for they were both sons of Ahitub. Was afraid - Suspecting some extraordinary cause of his coming in such a manner. Alone - For though David had some servants as is manifest from ver. 4, 5, whom Jonathan probably had sent to a place appointed, yet they were left at another place: as David himself affirmeth, ver. 2. And David was now alone, as also he was when he fled to Achish. He who had been suddenly advanced to the highest honour, is as soon reduced to the desolate conditions of an exile. Such changes are there in this world, and so uncertain are its smiles.

2. The king, &c. - This seems to be a plain lie extorted from him, by fear. But it was pernicious to all the priests there. Whence David afterwards declares his repentance for this sin of lying, Psalm lxix, 29. To such a place - To a certain place which it not convenient now to mention; because the whole business requires concealment.

4. There is, &c. - Here in the tabernacle: though doubtless he had other provisions is his house; but David was in great haste, and in fear of Doeg whom he saw, and knew and therefore would not stay 'till any thing could be fetched thence. There was a double impediment to the giving this bread to them;

1. Its sacredness in itself; which the priest implies, and David answers ver. 5, and the priest was satisfied therein by David's great necessities.

2. The abstinence from all women, which he supposed should be in those that use it; concerning which he now inquires. And though he mentions this only concerning David's young men, and out of reverence forbears to name him; yet he is also included in the number, as David's answer shews.

5. Three days - As long as the law required, Exod. xix, 15. And so long David, and his men hid, it seems, hid themselves for fear of Saul, whereby they were kept both from women: and from food convenient for them. Vessels - That is, Either,

1. Their garments, or other utensils for their journey. Or

2. their bodies. The bread - Hebrew. and this bread; is in a manner common: that is, considering the time, and our necessity, this maybe used in a manner, like common bread. For though for a season while it is to stand before the Lord, it be so holy, that the priest himself might not eat it; yet afterwards it is eaten by the priest, and his whole family, and so it may be by us, in our circumstances. Tho' it were - But newly put into the vessel, it must give place to the great law of necessity, and charity; because God will have mercy preferred before sacrifice.

7. Detained - Not by force but by his choice; he fixed his abode there for that day; either because it was the sabbath-day; on which he might not proceed in his journey, or for the discharge of some vow. Before the Lord - That is, at the tabernacle. An Edomite - By birth, but he was proselyted to the Jewish religion.

9. Ephod - That is, behind that holy place allotted for the keeping of the sacred, or priestly garments; all which are here comprehended under the ephod; which, as the chief is put for all the rest. Here it was laid up as a sacred monument of God's power and goodness. None like it - Because it not only served him for his use, for he was a strong and tall man, and one that could wield that sword, but was also a pledge of God's favour to him. Whenever be looked upon it, it would be a support to his faith, by reminding him of what God had already done.

10. To Achish - A strange action; but it must be considered, that Saul's rage was so great, his power also, and diligence in hunting after him that he despaired of escaping any other way: and a desperate disease, produceth a desperate remedy. The king elect is here an exile: anointed to the crown, and yet forced to run his country. So do God's providences sometimes run counter to his promises, for the trial of our faith, and the glorifying his name in accomplishing his counsels, notwithstanding the difficulties that lie in the way.

11. King of the land - Of Canaan. They call him king, either more generally for the governor, the most eminent captain and commander, or, as the king elect, the person designed to be king: for, by this time, the fame of Saul's rejection, and David's destination to the kingdom, was got abroad among the Israelites, and from them, probably to the Philistines. Did they not sing, &c. - And therefore consider what to do; and now our great enemy is in thy hand, be sure thou never let him go alive.

12. Was afraid - Lest either their revenge or policy should prompt them to kill him. Perhaps he was the more apprehensive, because he wore Goliath's sword, which was probably well known at Gath. He now learned by experience what he afterward taught us, Psalm lxviii, 9. It is better to trust in the Lord, than to put any confidence in princes.

15. Mad men - It is highly probable, Achish was aware, that this madness was counterfeit. But being desirous to preserve David, he speaks as if he thought it real.

XXII

David escapes to the cave of Adullam, where many resort to him, ver. 1, 2. Lodges his parents with the king of Moab, ver. 3, 4. Comes to the forest of Hareth, ver. 5. Saul complains of his servants as unfaithful to him, ver. 6-8. On the information of Doeg, he orders the priests of Nob to be slain, and their city destroyed, ver. 9-19. David is informed of this by Abiathar, ver. 20-23.

2. Debt - Probably poor debtors, whom the creditors were obliged to spare, Exod. xxii, 25. And though their persons were with David, yet their lands and goods were liable to their creditors. Captain over them - He did not maintain any injustice or wickedness, which some of them possibly might be guilty of; but on the contrary, he instructed and obliged them to the practice of all justice and honesty.

3. 'Till I know, &c. - He expresses his hopes very modestly, as one that had entirely cast himself upon God, and committed his way to him, trusting not in his own arts or arms, but in the wisdom, power and goodness of God.

4. Hold - In holds; the singular number being put for the plural; as is frequent; that is, as long as David was forced to go from place to place, and from hold to hold, to secure himself: for it concerned

David to secure his father, and he did doubtless secure him for all that time; and not only while he was in the hold of Mizpeh, or of Adullam, which was but a little while.

5. Abide not - Do not shut up thyself here. Judah - Go and shew thyself in the land of Judah, that thou mayest publicly put in thy claim to the kingdom after Saul's death; and that thy friends may be invited and encouraged to appear on thy behalf. Hereby also God would exercise David's faith, and wisdom, and courage; and so prepare him for the kingdom.

6. Spear - It seems, as an ensign of majesty, for in old times kings carried a spear instead of a scepter.

7. Ye Benjamites - You that are of my own tribe and kindred, from whom David designs to translate the kingdom to another tribe. Will he distribute profits and preferments among you Benjamites, as I have done? Will he not rather prefer those of his own tribe before you?

8. That all, &c. - See the nature of jealousy, and its arts of wheedling to extort discoveries of things that are not.

10. He inquired - David chargeth him with the sin of lying, Psalm lii, 3, and it is not improbable, that he told many lies not here expressed; and withal, he was guilty of concealing part of the truth, which in this case he was obliged to declare for Ahimelech's just defense, namely, the artifice whereby David circumvented Ahimelech: making him believe, that he was then going upon the king's business, so that the service he did to David, was designed in honour to Saul.

11. The priests - Of the house of Eli, which God had threatened to cut off, chap. ii, 31.

14. And said - He doth not determine the difference between Saul and David; nor affirm what David now was: but only declared what David formerly had been, and what he was still, for anything he knew to the contrary.

15. Knew nothing of all this - Of any design against thee.

18. The Edomite - This is noted to wipe off the stain of this butchery from the Israelitish nation, and to shew, why he was so ready to do it, because he was one of that nation which had an implacable hatred against all Israelites, and against the priests of the Lord.

19. Both men, &c. - In all the life of Saul, there is no wickedness to be compared to this. He appears now to be wholly under the power of that evil spirit which had long tormented him. And this destruction could not but go to the heart of every pious Israelite, and make them wish a thousand times, they had been content with the government of Samuel.

20. Abiathar - Who by his father's death was now high-priest.

XXIII

David saves Keilah from the Philistines, ver. 1-6. His danger there, and deliverance from it, ver. 7-13. He remains in the wilderness of Ziph, and is visited by Jonathan, ver. 14-18. Saul pursues him, ver. 19-25. His narrow escape, ver. 26-29

1. The Philistines, &c. - Probably it was the departure of God and David from Saul, that encouraged the Philistines to make this inroad. When princes begin to persecute God's people and ministers, let them expect nothing but vexation on all sides.

4. Inquired again - Not for his own, but for his soldiers satisfaction.

6. Ephod - With the Ephod, the high-priest's Ephod, wherein were the Urim and the Thummim, which when Ahimelech and the rest of the priests went to Saul, were probably left in his hand. This gave him the opportunity both of escaping, whilst Doeg the butcher was killing his brethren, and of bringing away the Ephod, which Saul now was justly deprived of.

11. The Lord said - From this place it may appear that God's answer by Urim and Thummim, was not by any change in the colour or situation of the precious stones in the breast-plate of the Ephod, but by a voice or suggestion from God to the high-priest. He will - He purposeth to come, if thou continuest here. For still as David's question, so God's answer, is upon supposition.

16. And strengthened - He comforted and supported him against all his fears, by minding him of God's infallible promises made to him, and his singular providence which hitherto had and still would be with him.

17. Next to thee - Which he gathered either from David's generosity, and friendship to him; or from some promise made to him by David concerning it. So that the whole imports thus much; I do not look to be king myself (as by my birth I might expect,) but that thou shalt be king (God having so appointed) and I but in a secondary place inferior to thee.

18. Made a covenant - They then parted, and never came together again, that we find, in this world.

19. Ziphites - Who were of David's own tribe tho' for this their unnatural carriage to him, he calls them strangers, Psalm liv, 3.

25. A rock - That is, into a cave which was in the rock; where at first he might think to hide

himself, but upon farther consideration he removed from thence upon Saul's approach.

27. A messenger, &c. - The wisdom of God is never at a loss for ways, and means to preserve his people.

28. Called, &c. - That is, The rock of divisions, because there Saul was separated, and in a manner pulled asunder from David, who was now almost within his reach.

XXIV

Saul pursues David to Engedi, ver. 1, 2. David cuts off his skirt, ver. 3-7. He reasons with Saul, ver. 8-15. Saul owns his fault, and returns home, ver. 16-22

2. Rocks - Which the wild goats used to delight in and climb over. These very rocks are exceeding steep, and full of precipices, and dangerous to travelers, as an eye-witness hath left upon record. And yet Saul was so transported with rage, as to venture himself and his army here, that he might take David, who, as he thought, would judge himself safe, and therefore be secure in such inaccessible places.

3. Went in - To sleep there: Saul being a military man, used to sleep with his soldiers upon the ground. And it is not improbable, that being weary with his eager and almost incessant pursuit, first of David, then of the Philistines, and now of David again, he both needed and desired some sleep, God also disposing him thereto, that David might have this eminent occasion to demonstrate his integrity to Saul, and to all Israel. Of the cave - For that there were vast caves in those parts is affirmed, not only by Josephus, but also by Heathen authors; Strabo writes of one which could receive four thousand men.

4. Behold, &c. - Not that God had said these words, or made any such promise; but they put this construction upon those promises which God had made to him, of delivering him from all his enemies, and carrying him through all difficulties to the throne. This promise they conceived put him under an obligation of taking all opportunities which God put into his hand for their accomplishment.

10. Mine eye - The eye is said to spare, because it affects the heart with pity, and moves a man to spare.

12. Will avenge - If thou persistest in thy injuries and cruel designs against me.

13. Wickedness, &c. - That is, wicked men will do wicked actions, among which this is one, to kill their sovereign Lord and king; and therefore if I were so wicked a person as thy courtiers represent me, I should make no conscience of laying violent hands upon thee.

16. Thy voice - He knew his voice, though being at a great distance from him, he could not discern his face. Wept - From the sense of his sin against God, and his base carriage to David. He speaks as one quite overcome with David's kindness, and as one that relents at the sight of his own folly and ingratitude.

17. More righteous than I - He ingenuously acknowledges David's integrity, and his own iniquity.

19. The Lord reward thee - Because he thought himself not able to recompense so great a favour, he prays God to recompense it.

22. Unto the hold - Of En-gedi, ver. 1, for having had by frequent experience of Saul's inconstancy, he would trust him no more.

XXV

Samuel's death, ver. 1. The character of Nabal, ver. 2, 3. David's requests to him, ver. 4-9. His churlish answer, ver. 10-13. David's purpose to destroy him told to Abigail, ver. 13-17. She pacifies David, ver. 18-31. His answer, ver. 32-35. The death of Nabal, ver. 36-38. David marries Abigail and Ahinoam, ver. 39- 44.

1. Lamented him - Those have hard hearts, that can bury their faithful ministers with dry eyes, and are not sensible of the loss of them who have prayed for them, and taught them the way of the Lord.

2. Carmel - In some part of this wilderness Israel wandered, when they came out of Egypt. The place would bring to mind God's care concerning them, which David might now improve for his own encouragement.

3. Abigail - That is, the joy of his father: yet he could not promise himself much joy of her, when he married her to such an husband: it seems, in inquiring, (no unfrequent thing) more after his wealth, than after his wisdom. Caleb - This is added to aggravate his crime, that he was a degenerate branch of that noble stock of Caleb, and consequently of the tribe of Judah, as David was.

4. Shear sheep - Which times were celebrated with feasting.

6. Prosperity - By this expression David both congratulates Nabal's felicity, and tacitly minds him of the distress in which he and his men were.

7. We hurt not - This considering the licentiousness of soldiers, and the necessities David and his men were exposed to, was no small favour, which Nabal was bound both in justice, and gratitude, and

prudence to requite.

8. A good day - That is, in a day of feasting and rejoicing; when men are most chearful and liberal; when thou mayst relieve us out of thy abundance without damage to thyself; when thou art receiving the mercies of God, and therefore obliged to pity and relieve distressed and indigent persons.

17. Can not speak - But he flies into a passion.

18. Abigail took, &c. - This she did without his leave, because it was a case of apparent necessity, for the preservation of herself, and husband, and all the family from imminent ruin. And surely, that necessity which dispenseth with God's positive commands, might dispense with the husband's right, in this case. Bottles - Casks or rundlets.

22. Enemies of David - That is, unto David himself. But because it might seem ominous to curse himself, therefore instead of David, he mentions David's enemies. But is this the voice of David? Can he speak so unadvisedly with his lips? Has he been so long in the school of affliction, and learned no more patience therein? Lord, what is man? And what need have we to pray, lead us not into temptation.

24. And said, &c. - Impute Nabal's sin to me, and if thou pleasest, punish it in me, who here offer myself as a sacrifice to thy just indignation. This whole speech of Abigail shews great wisdom, by an absolute submitting to mercy, without any pretense of justification, of what was done, (but rather with aggravation of it) she endeavours to work upon David's generosity, to pardon it. And there is hardly any head of argument, whence the greatest orator might argue in this case, which she doth not manage to the best advantage.

25. Nabal is his name - Nabal signifies a fool.

26. As Nabal - Let them be as contemptible as Nabal is, and will be for this odious action; let them be as unable to do thee any hurt as he is; let them be forced to yield to thee, and implore thy pardon, as Nabal now doth by my mouth: let the vengeance thou didst design upon Nabal and his family fall upon their heads, who, by their inveterate malice against thee, do more deserve it than this fool for this miscarriage; and much more than all the rest of our family, who, as they are none of thine enemies, so they were in way guilty of this wicked action. And therefore spare these, and execute thy vengeance upon more proper objects.

27. Blessing - So a gift or present is called here, and elsewhere; not only because the matter of it comes from God's blessing; but also because it is given with a blessing, or with a good will. Unto the young men - As being unworthy of thine acceptance or use.

28. The trespass - That is, which I have taken upon myself, and which, if it be punished, the punishment will reach to me. Sure house - Will give the kingdom to thee, and to thy house forever, as he hath promised thee. And therefore let God's kindness to thee, make thee gentle and merciful to others; do not sully thy approaching glory with the stain of innocent blood; but consider, that it is the glory of a king, to profit by offenses: and that it will be thy loss to cut off such as will shortly be thy subjects. The battles - For the Lord, and for the people of the Lord against their enemies; especially, the Philistines. And as this is thy proper work, and therein thou mayest expect God's blessing; so it is not thy work to draw thy sword in thy own private quarrel against any of the people of the Lord; and God will not bless thee in it. Evil hath not, &c. - Though thou hast been charged with many crimes by Saul and others; yet thy innocency is evident to all men: do not therefore by this cruel act, justify thine enemies reproaches, or blemish thy great and just reputation.

29. A man - Saul though no way injured. Thy soul - To take away thy life. Bundle of life - Or, in the bundle: that is, in the society, or congregation of the living; out of which, men are taken, and cut off by death. The phrase is taken from the common usage of men, who bind those things in bundles, which they are afraid to lose. The meaning is, God will preserve thy life; and therefore it becomes not thee, unnecessarily to take away the lives of any; especially of the people of thy God. With the Lord - That is, in the custody of God, who by his watchful providence, preserves this bundle, and all that are in it; and thee in a particular manner, as being thy God in a particular way, and special covenant. The Jews understand this. not only of the present life, but of that which is to come, even the happiness of departed souls, and therefore use it commonly, as an inscription on their grave-stones. "Here we have laid the body, trusting the soul is bound up in the bundle of life with the Lord." Sling out - God himself will cut them off suddenly, violently, and irresistibly; and cast them far away; both from his presence, and from thy neighbourhood, and from all capacity of doing thee hurt.

31. No grief - The mind and conscience will be free from all the torment which such an action would cause in thee. By which, she intimates, what a blemish this would be to his glory, what a disturbance to his peace, if he proceeded to execute his purpose: and withal implies, how comfortable it would be to him to remember, that he had for conscience to God, restrained his passions. Causeless - Which she signifies would be done if he should go on. For though Nabal had been guilty of abominable rudeness, and ingratitude; yet he had done nothing worthy of death, by the laws of God or of man. And whatsoever he had done, the rest of his family were innocent. Avenged - Which is directly contrary to God's law, Levit xix, 18 Deut. xxxii, 35. Then - When God shall make thee king, let me find grace in thy sight.

32. *The Lord* - Who by his gracious providence so disposed matters, that thou shouldst come to me: He rightly begins at the fountain of his deliverance; and then proceeds to the instruments.

33. *From coming, &c.* - Which I had sworn to do. Hereby it plainly appears, that oaths whereby men bind themselves to any sin, are null and void: and as it was a sin to make them; so it is adding sin to sin to perform them.

35. *Accepted* - That is, shewed my acceptance of thy person, by my grant of thy request.

36. *A feast* - As the manner was upon those solemn occasions. Sordid covetousness, and vain prodigality were met together in him. *Told nothing* - As he was then incapable of admonition, his reason and conscience being both asleep.

37. *His heart died* - He fainted away through the fear and horror of so great a mischief though it was past. As one, who having in the night galloped over a narrow plank, laid upon a broken bridge, over a deep river; when in the morning he came to review it, was struck dead with the horror of the danger he had been in.

38. *Smote* - God either inflicted some other stroke upon him, or increased his grief and fear to such an height, as killed him.

39. *Blessed, &c.* - This was another instance of human infirmity in David. *David sent* - But this doubtless was not done immediately after Nabal's death, but some time after it; though such circumstances be commonly omitted in the sacred history; which gives only the heads, and most important passages of things.

XXVI

The Ziphites inform Saul of David, who pursues him again, ver. 1-3. David sends out spies, and views his camp, ver. 4, 5. Comes to him, being asleep, and takes his spear and cruse of water, ver. 6-12. Reasons with him upon it, ver. 13-20. Saul again owns his spirit, and promises to pursue him no more, ver. 21-25.

5. *The Ziphites* - Probably Saul would have pursued David no more, had not these wretches set him on.

6. *Zerujah* - David's sister. His father is not named either because he was now dead; or because he was an obscure person.

7. *Came* - That is, to Saul's host. It might seem a bold and strange attempt; but it may be considered:
1. That David had a particular assurance that God would preserve him to the kingdom.
2. That he had a special instinct from God, to this work; and possibly God might inform him, that he had cast them into a deep sleep, that he might have this second opportunity of manifesting his innocency towards Saul.

9. *Destroy him not, &c.* - Though Saul be a tyrant, yet he is our Lord and king; and I, though designed king, as yet am his subject; and therefore cannot kill him without sin, nor will I consent that thou shouldst do it.

11. *Take the spear* - Which will shew where we have been, and what we could have done.

13. *Afar off* - That his person might be out of their reach, and yet his voice might be heard; which in a clear air, and in the silence of the night might be heard at a great distance.

14. *Cried to the people* - It is probable this was early in the morning.

19. *The Lord* - If the Lord hath by the evil spirit which he hath sent, or by his secret providence, directed thy rage against me for the punishment of thine, or my sins. *An offering* - Let us offer up a sacrifice to God to appease his wrath against us. *Driven me* - From the land which God hath given to his people for their inheritance, and where he hath established his presence and worship. *Go serve* - This was the language of their actions. For by driving him from God's land, and the place of his worship, into foreign and idolatrous lands, they exposed him to the peril of being either ensnared by their counsels, or examples; or forced by their power to worship idols.

20. *Before the Lord* - Remember, if thou dost it, God the judge of all men seeth it, and will avenge it; though I will not avenge myself.

21. *My soul, &c.* - This second instance of David's tenderness wrought more upon Saul than the former. He owns himself melted and quite overcome by David's kindness to him. My soul was precious in thine eyes, which I thought had been odious. He acknowledges he had done very ill to persecute him: I have acted against God's law, I have sinned: and against my own interest, I have played the fool, in pursuing him as an enemy, who was indeed one of my best friends. And herein I have erred exceedingly, have wronged both thee and myself. Nothing can be more full and ingenuous than this confession: God surely now touched his heart. And he promises to persecute him no more: nor does it appear that he ever attempted it.

25. *Blessed, &c.* - So strong was his conviction now, that he could not forbear blessing him,

foretelling his success, applauding David, and condemning himself, even in the hearing of his own soldiers. And this, it seems, was their last interview. After this they saw each other no more.

XXVII

David retires to Gath, ver. 1-4. Achish gives him Ziklag, ver. 5-7. David destroys the Canaanites, ver. 8, 9. Persuades Achish he fought against Judah, ver. 10-12.

1. I shall perish - But this was certainly a very great fault in David: for
1. This proceeded from gross distrust of God's promise and providence; and that after such repeated demonstrations of God's peculiar care over him.
2. He forsakes the place where God had settled him, chap. xxii, 5, and given him both assurance and experience of his protection there.
3. He voluntarily runs upon that rock, which he cursed his enemies for throwing him upon, chap. xxvi, 19, and upon many other snares and dangers, as the following history will shew; and withal, deprives the people of the Lord of those succors which he might have given them, in case of a battle. But God hereby designed to withdraw David from the Israelites, that they might fall by the hand of the Philistines, without any reproach or inconvenience to David.
4. Sought no more for him - At their meeting Saul's heart was deeply wounded, and he had said, "Return, my son David, Be with me as in time past." Nor have we the least proof, that he would have sought for him again, with any other design.
5. Give me a place - A prudent desire. Hereby David designed to preserve his people, both from the vices, which conversation with the Philistines would have exposed them to; and from that envy, and malice, which diversity of religion might have caused. With thee - Which is too great an honour for me, and too burdensome to thee, and may be an occasion of offense to thy people.
6. Gave Ziklag - Not only to inhabit, but to possess it as his own. Which he did, to lay the greater obligations upon David, whom he knew so able to serve him. It was given to the tribe of Judah before, Josh. xv, 31, but the Philistines kept the possession of it 'till this time. And being given by them to David, it now belonged not to the tribe of Judah; but to the king of Judah, David and his heirs forever. To this day - This, and some such clauses seem to have been added, after the main substance of the several books was written.
8. Amalekites - The remnant of those whom Saul destroyed, chap. xv, 3-9, who retired into remote and desert places.
9. Let neither man, &c. - In that part where he came: but there were more of the Amalekites yet left in another part of that land.
10. David - These and the following words are ambiguous, and contrary to that simplicity which became David, both as a prince, and as an eminent professor of the true religion. The fidelity of Achish to him, and the confidence he put in him, aggravates his sin in thus deceiving him, which David seems penitently to reflect on, when he prays, Remove from me the way of lying.

XXVIII

The conference between Achish and David, ver. 1-2. The preparation of the Philistines, and the distress of Saul, ver. 3-6. He applies to a woman which had a familiar spirit, to raise Samuel, ver. 7-11. Samuel appears, and foretells his defeat and death, ver. 12-19. Saul faints, and is with difficulty persuaded to take any sustenance, ver. 20-25.

2. Can do - He speaks ambiguously, as he did before.
5. He trembled - Had he kept close to God, he needed not fear all the armies of the Philistines.
7. That hath, &c. - One that converseth with the devil, or dead men's ghosts, and by them can discover future things. See Isaiah viii, 19.
8. Disguised - Both because he was ashamed to be known, or thought guilty of this practice; and because he suspected, the woman, had she known him, would not practice her art before him.
11. Samuel - Whose kindness and compassion as he had formerly experienced, so now he expected it in his deep distress. This practice of divination by the dead, or the souls of dead persons, was very usual among all nations.
12. Saw Samuel - The words are express, the woman saw Samuel, instead of the spirit whom she expected to see, God ordering it so for his own glory. She cried with a loud voice - Terrified and astonished, and thence easily conjectured, whom she had been talking with.
13. Gods - That is, a God, and divine person, glorious, and full of majesty and splendour, exceeding not only mortal men, but common ghosts. She used the plural number, gods, either after the manner of the Hebrew language, which commonly uses that word of one person: or, after the language

and custom of the heathens.

14. A mantle - The usual habit of prophets, and particularly of Samuel, chap. xv, 27. If it was not Samuel, but an other spirit in his shape, it is not true, that Saul perceived it was Samuel. It seems Saul did not see him, so soon as the woman, which occasioned his asking those questions.

15. Called Samuel - Happy had it been, if he had called Samuel sooner, or rather the God of Samuel! It was now too late: destruction was at hand and God had determined, it should not be stayed.

17. To him - To David.

19. Tomorrow shalt thou and thy sons be with me: "What do these solemn words portend? A gleam of hope when life shall end. Thou and thy sons, tho' slain shall be Tomorrow in repose with me. Not in a state of health or pain If Saul with Samuel doth remain; Not in a state of damn'd despair, If loving Jonathan is there." Tho' these words may only mean, ye shall surely die, without any reference to the state of their souls after death. See note on "chap. xxxi, 8."

20. Fell - As if the Archers of the Philistines had already hit him, and there was no strength in him, to bear up against these heavy tidings: especially, as we cannot doubt, but all his past sins were now brought to his remembrance and what authority has any man to affirm, that he felt no contrition all this time? Altho' it did not seem good to the holy ghost, to leave it upon record?

21. Came to Saul - From whom she departed, when she had brought him and Samuel together, that they might more freely converse together.

24. Unleavened - Not having time to leaven it.

XXIX

The princes of the Philistines object against David's going with them to the battle, ver. 1-5. He is dismissed by Achish, ver. 6-11.

2. With Achish - As the life-guard of Achish. Achish being, as it seems, the general of the army.

3. The princes - The Lords of the other eminent cities, who were confederate with him in this expedition. These days or years - That is, did I say days? I might have said years. He hath now been with me a full year and four months, chap. xxvii, 7, and he was with me some years ago, chap. xxi, 10, and since their time hath been known to me. And it is not improbable, but David, after his escape from thence, might hold some correspondence with Achish, as finding him to be a man of a more generous temper than the rest of the Philistines, and supposing that he might have need of him for a refuge, in case Saul continued to seek his life. Since he fell - Revolted, or left his own king to turn to me.

4. Make this fellow - Herein the wise and gracious providence of God appeared, both in helping him out of these difficulties, out of which no human wit could have extricated him, but he must have been, an ungrateful person either to the one or the other side, and moreover in giving him the happy opportunity of recovering his own, and his all from the Amalekites, which had been irrecoverably lost, if he had gone into this battle. And the kindness of God to David was the greater, because it had been most just for God to have left David in those distresses into which his own sinful counsel had brought him. These men - That is, of these our soldiers, they speak according to the rules of true policy; for by this very course, great enemies have sometimes been reconciled together.

8. David said &c. - This was deep dissimulation and flattery, no way to be justified. None knows, how strong a temptation they are in to compliment and dissemble, which they are in who attend great men.

9. Angel of God - In whom nothing is blame-worthy. The Heathens acknowledged good spirits, which also they worshipped as an inferior sort of deities, who were messengers and ministers to the supreme God; Achish had learned the title of angels, from the Israelites his neighbours, and especially from David's conversation.

11. Rose up early - David did not then know, how necessary this was, for the relief of his own city. But God knew it well, and sent him thither accordingly. On how many occasions may he say, What I do thou knowest not now; but thou shalt know hereafter?

XXX

Ziklag plundered: David and his men distressed, ver. 1-6. Encouraged of God, he pursues them, ver. 7-10. He gains intelligence from a straggler, ver. 11-15. Routs the enemy, and recovers all they had taken, ver. 16-20. Makes an order for dividing the spoil, ver. 21-25. Sends presents to his friends, ver. 26-31.

1. The south - Namely, the southern part of Judah, and the adjacent parts.

4. Wept - It is no disparagement to the boldest, bravest spirits, to lament the calamities of friends or relations.

6. Stoning him - As the author of their miseries, by coming to Ziklag at first, by provoking the Amalekites to this cruelty, and by his forwardness in marching away with Achish, and leaving their wives and children unguarded. Encouraged himself - That is, in this that the all-wise, and all-powerful Lord, was his God by covenant and special promise, and fatherly affection, as he had shewed himself to be in the whole course of his providence towards him. It is the duty of all good men, whatever happens, to encourage themselves in the Lord their God, assuring themselves, that he both can and will bring light out of darkness.

7. The ephod - And put it upon thyself, that thou mayst inquire of God according to his ordinance, David was sensible of his former error in neglecting to ask counsel of God by the ephod, when he came to Achish, and when he went out with Achish to the Battle; and his necessity now brings him to his duty, and his duty meets with success.

8. He answered - Before, God answered more slowly and gradually, chap. xxiii, 11, 12, but now he answers speedily, and fully at once, because the business required haste. So gracious is our God, that he considers even the degree of our necessities, and accommodates himself to them.

10. Four hundred - A small number for such an attempt: but David was strong in faith, giving God the glory of his power and faithfulness.

12. Three days and nights - One whole day and part of two others, as appears from the next verse, where he saith, three days ago I fell sick, but in the Hebrew it is, this is the third day since I fell sick.

13. Egypt - God by his providence so ordering it, that he was not one of that cursed race of the Amalekites, who were to be utterly destroyed, but an Egyptian, who might be spared. Left me - In this place and condition: which was barbarous inhumanity: for he ought, and easily might have carried him away with the prey which they had taken. But he paid dear for this cruelty, for this was the occasion of the ruin of him and all their company. And God by his secret providence ordered the matter thus for that very end. So that there is no fighting against God, who can make the smallest accidents serviceable to the production of the greatest effects.

14. Cherethites - That is, the Philistines. Caleb - This is added by way of explication: that part of the south of Judah which belongs to Caleb's posterity.

15. Will bring thee - For his master had told him whither they intended to go, that he might come after them, as soon as he could.

16. Upon all the earth - Secure and careless, because they were now come almost to the borders of their own country, and the Philistines and Israelites both were otherwise engaged, and David, as they believed, with them. So they had no visible cause of danger; and yet then they were nearest to destruction.

17. Twilight - The word signifies both the morning and evening twilight. But the latter seems here intended, partly because their eating, and drinking, and dancing, was more proper work for the evening, than the morning; and partly, because the evening was more convenient for David, that the fewness of his forces might not be discovered by the day-light. It is probable, that when he came near them, he reposed himself, and his army, in some secret place, whereof there were many parts, for a convenient season; and then marched on so as to come to them at the evening time.

20. Other cattle - Before those that belonged to Ziklag. David's spoil - The soldiers, who lately were so incensed against David, that they spake of stoning him: now upon this success magnify him, and triumphantly celebrate his praise; and say concerning this spoil, David purchased it by his valour and conduct, and he may dispose of it as he pleaseth.

21. Saluted them - He spoke kindly to them, and did not blame them because they went no further with them.

23. My brethren -- he useth his authority to over-rule them; but manageth it with all sweetness, tho' they were such wicked and unreasonable men, calling them brethren; not only as of the same nation and religion with him, but as his fellow-soldiers. What God hath freely imparted to us, we should not unkindly and injuriously withhold from our brethren.

24. Part alike - A prudent and equitable constitution, and therefore practiced by the Romans, as Polybius and others note. The reason of it is manifest; because they were exposed to hazards, as well as their brethren: and were a reserve to whom they might retreat in case of a defeat; and they were now in actual service, and in the station in which their general had placed them.

26. Elders of Judah - Partly in gratitude for their former favours to him: and partly, in policy, to engage their affections to him.

XXXI

Israel overthrown, and Saul, his three sons, his armour-bearer and all his men slain, ver. 1-6. The Israelites forsake their cities, ver. 7. The camp plundered and the dead bodies insulted, ver. 8-10. But rescued by the men of Jabesh-Gilead, ver. 11-13.

2. Jonathan - David's dear friend; God so ordering it for the farther exercise of David's faith and patience; and that David might depend upon God alone for his crown, and receive it solely from him, and not from Jonathan; who doubtless, had he lived, would have speedily settled the crown upon David's head. There was also a special providence of God, in taking away Jonathan, (who of all Saul's sons, seems to have been the fairest for the crown) for preventing divisions, which might have happened amongst the people concerning the successor: David's way to the crown being by this means made the more clear. Abinadab - Called also Ishui, chap. xiv, 49. Ishbosheth was not here, being possibly at home for the management of affairs there.

8. Saul and his three sons - "The scripture, as Mr. Henry well observes, makes no mention of the souls of Saul and his sons, what became of them after they were dead: secret things belong not to us."

9. Cut off his head - As the Israelites did by Goliath, and fastened it in the temple of Dagon, 1 Chron. x, 10. Idols - To give them the glory of this victory. And by this respect shewn to their pretended deities, how do they shame those, who give not the honour of their achievements to the living God?

12. Took the body, &c. - This they did, not only out of a concern, for the honour of Israel, and the crown of Israel, but out of gratitude to Saul, for his zeal and forwardness to rescue them from the Ammonites.

13. Fasted - To testify their sorrow for the loss of Saul, and of the people of God; and to intreat God's favour to prevent the utter extinction of his people. But you must not understand this word of fasting strictly, as if they eat nothing for seven whole days; but in a more large sense, as it is used both in sacred and profane writers; that they did eat but little, and that but mean food, and drank only water for that time. This book began with the birth of Samuel, and ends with the death of Saul: The comparing these together will teach us to prefer the honour that comes from God, before all the honours of the world.

NOTES ON THE SECOND BOOK OF SAMUEL

THIS book is the history of the reign of David. It gives us an account of his triumphs and of his troubles.

I. His triumphs, over the house of Saul, chap. 1-4. Over the Jebusites and Philistines, chap. 5. In the bringing up of the ark, chap. 6, 7. Over the neighbouring nations, chap. 8-10.

II. His troubles; the cause of them, his sin in the matter of Uriah, chap. 11-12. The troubles themselves, from the sin of Amnon, chap. 13. The rebellion of Absolom, chap. 14-19. And of Sheba, chap. 20. From the famine, chap. 21. And the pestilence, for his numbering the people, chap. 24. His song we have, chap. 22. And his words and worthies, chap. 23. In many instances throughout this book, he appears as a great and a good man. Yet it must be confessed he had great vices: So that his honour shines brighter in his psalms than in his annals.

I

David receives an account of the death of Saul and Jonathan, ver. 1-10. He mourns over them, ver. 11, 12. Puts the man to death, who boasted he had killed Saul, ver. 13-16. His elegy upon Saul and Jonathan, ver. 17-27.

1. Ziklag - Which though burnt, yet was not so consumed by the fire, that David and his men could not lodge in it.

2. Third day - From David's return to Ziklag. With his clothes rent, &c. - As a mourner.

18. Judah - These he more particularly teacheth, because they were the chief, and now the royal tribe, and likely to be the great bulwark to all Israel against the Philistines, upon whose land they bordered; and withal, to be the most true to him, and to his interest. The bow - That is, of their arms, expressed, under the name of the bow, which then was one of the chief weapons; and for the dextrous use whereof Jonathan is commended in the following song: which may be one reason, why he now gives forth this order, that so they might strive to imitate Jonathan in military skill, and to excel in it, as he did. Jasher - It is more largely and particularly described in the book of Jasher.

19. Beauty - Their flower and glory. Saul and Jonathan, and their army. High places - Hebrew. upon thy high places; that is, those which belong to thee, O land of Israel. How - How strangely! How suddenly! How universally!

20. Tell it not - This is not a precept, but a poetical wish; whereby he doth not so much desire, that this might not be done, which he knew to be impossible; as, express his great sorrow, because it would be done, to the dishonour of God, and of his people. The daughters - He mentions these, because it was the custom of women in those times and places to celebrate those victories which their men obtained, with triumphant songs and dances.

21. Let there be, &c. - This is no proper imprecation; but a passionate representation of the horror which he conceived at this publick loss; which was such, as if he thought every person or thing which contributed to it, were fit to bear the tokens of divine displeasure, such as this is, when the earth wants the necessary influences of dew and rain. Fields of offerings - That is, fruitful fields, which may produce fair and goodly fruits fit to be offered to God. Vilely - Dishonourably: for it was a great reproach to any soldier, to cast away or lose his shield. Cast away - By themselves, that they might flee more swiftly as the Israelites did, and Saul with the rest. As though, &c. - As if he had been no more, than a common soldier: he was exposed to the same kind of death and reproach as they were.

22. Not back - Without effect: their arrows shot from their bow, and their swords did seldom miss, and commonly pierced fat, and flesh, and blood, and reached even to the heart and bowels. Returned not, &c. - But filled and glutted with blood: for the sword is metaphorically said to have a mouth, which we translate an edge; and to devour. And this their former successfulness is mentioned as an aggravation of their last infelicity.

23. Lovely - Amiable, and obliging in their carriage and conversation, both towards one another, and towards their people: for, as for Saul's fierce behaviour towards Jonathan, it was only a sudden passion, by which his ordinary temper was not to be measured; and for his carriage towards David, that was from that jealousy and reason of state which usually engageth even well- natured princes, to the

same hostilities. But it is observable, that David speaks not a word here of his piety; but only commends him for those things which were truly in him. A fit pattern for all preachers in their funeral commendations. Swifter, &c. - Expeditious in pursuing their enemies, and executing their designs; which is a great commendation in a prince, and in a soldier. Stronger, &c. - In regard of their bodily strength, and the courage of their mind.

24. Daughters - These he mentions; because the women then used to make songs both of triumph, and of lamentation, and, because they usually are most delighted with the ornaments of the body here following. Clothed you - This he did, because he procured them so much peace as gave them opportunity of enriching themselves: and, because he took these things as spoils from the enemies, and clothed his own people with them.

25. Thine - Which were in thy country, and (had not thy father disinherited thee by his sins) in thy dominions.

26. Distressed - That is, for the loss of thee. For, besides the loss of a true friend, which is inestimable; he lost him who both could, and undoubtedly would have given him a speedy, and quiet, and sure possession of the kingdom, whereas now, he met with long and troublesome interruptions. Of women - That is, that love wherewith they love their husbands, or children for their affections are usually more ardent than mens.

II

David goes up to Hebron and is crowned there, ver. 1-4. Thanks the men of Jabesh-gilead, ver. 5-7. Ishbosheth is set up in opposition to him, ver. 8-11. An encounter between David's men and Ishbosheth's, in which the latter are beaten, ver. 12-17. Asahel is killed by Abner, ver. 18-23. Joah sounds retreat by the advice of Abner, who retires to Mahanaim, ver. 24-29. The loss on each side, ver. 30-31. Asahel buried, ver. 32

1. Inquired - By Urim. Thus David begins at the right end, and lays his foundation in God's counsel and assistance. Shall I go - He asked not whether he should take the kingdom; for that was appointed before; and he would not offend God, nor dishonour his ordinance with unnecessary enquiries; but only where he should enter upon it; whether in Judah, as he supposed, because of his relation to that tribe, and his interest in it; or in some other tribe: for he doth not limit God, but resolves exactly to follow his counsels. Hebron - Which was next to Jerusalem (part whereof the Jebusites now possessed) the chief city of that tribe, and a city of the priests, and in the very center of that tribe, to which the whole tribe might speedily resort, when need required. And the sepulchres of the patriarchs adjoining to Hebron, would remind him of the ancient promise.

3. Dwelt in - That is, the cities or towns belonging to Hebron, which was the Metropolis. For in Hebron itself there was not space for them all, because it was filled with priests, and with David's court.

4. Anointed - This they did upon just grounds, because not only the kingdom was promised to that tribe, but David was designed and anointed by God, whose will both they and all Israel were obliged to obey. And they resolved not to neglect their duty, though they saw the other tribes would. Yet their modesty is observable, they make him king of Judah only, and not of all Israel. And therefore there was need of a third anointing to the kingdom over all Israel, which he had chap. v, 3, that first anointing; 1 Sam. xvi, 13, was only a designation of the person who should be king, but not an actual inauguration of him to the kingdom.

5. Kindness - This respect and affection. For as it is, an act of inhumanity to deny burial to the dead; so it is an act of mercy and kindness to bury them.

6. Kindness and truth - That is, true and real kindness; not in words only, but also in actions, as you have done to your king. I will requite - So far am I from being offended with you for this kindness to my late enemy.

7. Be valiant - Be not afraid lest the Philistines should punish you for this fact, but take good courage, I will defend you. For, &c. - Or, though your master Saul be dead, and so your hearts may faint, as if you were now sheep without a shepherd.

8. Abner - Tho' ambition and desire of rule, because he knew that Ishbosheth would have only the name of king, whilst he had the power.

9. Gilead - Largely so taken, for all the land of Israel beyond Jordan. Ashurites - That is, the tribe of Asher, as the Chaldee paraphrast and others understand it. Jezreel - A large and rich valley situate in the borders of the tribes of Zebulun, Issachar and Naphtali, and so put for them all. All Israel - Except Judah.

10. Two years - Namely, before the following war broke out, which continued five years.

12. Went out - To fight with David's army, and to bring back the rest of the kingdom to Saul's house.

13. Met - That is, met the opposite army, and put themselves in a posture for battle.

14. And play - That is, shew their prowess and dexterity in fighting together. He speaks like a vain-glorious and cruel man, and a soldier of fortune, that esteemed it a sport to see men wounding and killing one another. So this he designed, partly for their mutual recreation and trial of skill; and partly, that by this occasion they might be engaged in a battle. But he is unworthy the name of a man, who is thus prodigal of human blood.

16. By the head - By the hair of the head, which after their manner was of a considerable length. Helkath-kazzurim - Or, the field of rock; that is, of men who stood like rocks unmovable, each one dying upon the spot where he fought.

21. And take, &c. - If thou art ambitious to get a trophy or mark of thy valour, desist from me who am an old and experienced captain, and go to some young and raw soldier; try thy skill upon him, and take away his arms from him.

23. And died - So Asahel's swiftness, which he presumed on so much, only forwarded his fate! With it he ran upon his death, instead of running from it.

26. Bitterness - It will produce dreadful effects. Brethren - By nation and religion: whom therefore they should not pursue with so fierce a rage, as if they were pursuing the Philistines.

27. Unless, &c. - Unless thou hadst made the motion that they should fight, ver. 14. It was thou, not I, that gave the first occasion of this fight. Abner was the sole cause of this war; otherwise all things had been ended by an amicable agreement: which might have been made that very morning, if he had so pleased.

32. In Bethlehem - The rest they buried in the field of battle, but Asahel in the sepulchre of his father. Thus are distinctions made upon earth, even between the dust of some and of others! But in the resurrection no difference will be made but between good and bad; which will remain forever.

III

David's success and sons, ver. 1-5. Abner's quarrel with Isbosheth, ver. 6-11. His treaty with David, ver. 12-16. He undertakes to bring Israel over to David, ver. 17-21. Joab murders Abner, ver. 22-27. David's concern and mourning over him, ver. 28-39.

1. Long war - For five years longer: for it is probable, Isbosheth was made king presently upon Saul's death; and the other tribes did not submit to David before seven years were expired.

3. Geshur - A part of Syria, northward from the land of Israel. Her he married, as it may seem, in policy, that he might have a powerful friend and ally to assist him against Ishbosheth's party in the north, whilst himself opposed him in the southern parts. But he paid dear for making piety give place to policy, as the history of Absolom sheweth.

5. Eglah - This is added, either because she was of obscure parentage, and was known by no other title but her relation to David: or, because this was his first and most proper wife, best known by her other name of Michal, who, though she had no child by David after she scoffed at him for dancing before the ark, chap. vi, 23, yet might have one before that time. And she might be named the last, because she was given away from David, and married to another man. Six sons in seven years. Some have had as numerous an offspring, and with much more honour and comfort, by one wife. And we know not that any of the six were famous: but three were very infamous.

6. Strong - He used all his endeavours to support Saul's house: which is mentioned, to shew the reason of his deep resentment of the following aspersion.

12. Messengers - Who in his name might treat with David concerning his reconciliation with him. Thus God over-rules the passions of wicked men, to accomplish his own wise and holy purposes. And who then dare contend with that God who makes even his enemies to do his work, and destroy themselves? Whose, &c. - To whom doth this whole land belong, but to thee? Is it not thine by Divine right?

14. Ishbosheth - Whose consent was necessary, both to take her away from her present husband, and to persuade her to return to David. Hereby also David opened to him a door of hope for his reconciliation, lest being desperate he should hinder Abner in his present design. My wife - Who, though she was taken from me by force, and constrained to marry another, yet is my rightful wife. David demands her, both for the affection he still retained to her, and upon a political consideration that she might strengthen his title to the kingdom.

19. Benjamin - To these he particularly applies himself, because they might be thought most kind to Saul and his house, and most loath to let the kingdom go out of their own tribe; and therefore it was necessary that he should use all his art and power with them, to persuade them to a compliance with his design; and besides, they were a valiant tribe, and bordering upon Judah, and situate between them and the other tribes; and therefore the winning of them, would be of mighty concernment to bring in all the rest.

22. A troop - Of robbers, or Philistines, who taking advantage of the discord between the houses

of Saul and David, made inroads into Judah.

29. Let it, &c. - But would not a resolute punishment of the murderer himself have become David better, than this passionate imprecation on his posterity?

30. Abishai - For though Joab only committed the murder, yet Abishai was guilty of it, because it was done with his consent, and counsel, and approbation. In battle - Which he did for his own necessary defense; and therefore it was no justification of this treacherous murder.

31. Joab - Him he especially obliged to it, to bring him to repentance for his sin, and to expose him to public shame. Followed - That is, attending upon his corps, and paying him that respect which was due to his quality. Though this was against the usage of kings, and might seem below David's dignity; yet it was now expedient to vindicate himself from all suspicion of concurrence in this action.

33. As a fool - That is, as a wicked man. Was he cut off by the hand of justice for his crimes? Nothing less; but by Joab's malice and treachery. It is a sad thing to die as a fool dieth, as they do that any way shorten their own days: and indeed all they that make no provision for another world.

34. Not bound - Thou didst not tamely yield up thyself to Joab, to be bound hand and foot at his pleasure. Joab did not overcome thee in an equal combat, nor durst he attempt thee in that way, as a general or soldier of any worth would have done. Wicked men - By the hands of froward, or perverse, or crooked men, by hypocrisy and perfidiousness, whereby the vilest coward may kill the most valiant person.

36. Pleased them - They were satisfied concerning David's integrity.

38. Know ye not, &c. - But how little, how mean are they made by death, who were the terror of the mighty in the land of the living.

39. Weak - In the infancy of my kingdom, not well settled in it. The metaphor is taken from a young and tender child or plant. These men - Joab and Abishai, the sons of thy sister Zeruiah. Too hard - That is, too powerful. They have so great a command over all the soldiers, and so great favour with the people, that I cannot punish them without apparent hazard to my person and kingdom; especially, now when all the tribes, except Judah, are in a state of opposition against me. But although this might give some colour to the delay of their punishment, yet it was a fault that he did not do it within some reasonable time, both because this indulgence proceeded from a distrust of God's power and faithfulness; as if God could not make good his promise to him, against Joab and all his confederates; and because it was contrary to God's law, which severally requires the punishment of willful murderers. It was therefore carnal wicked policy, yea cruel pity that spared him. If the law had had its course against Joab, it is probable the murder of Ishbosheth, Ammon, and others, had been prevented. So truly was he in these, and some other respects, a bloody man, which may be observed to the glory of the Divine grace, in his forgiveness and conversion.

IV

Two of his servants murder Ishbosheth, and bring his head to David, ver. 1-8. He puts them to death, ver. 9-52.

4. Jonathan had a son - This history is inserted as that which encouraged these men to this wicked murder, because Saul's family was now reduced to a low ebb; and if Isbosheth was dispatched, there would be none left, but a lame child, who was altogether unfit to manage the kingdom, and therefore the crown must necessarily come to David by their act and deed; for which they promised themselves no small recompense. Jezreel - The place of that last and fatal fight.

6. Fetched wheat - Which was laid up in publick granaries in the king's house, and was fetched thence by the captains and commanders of the army for the pay of their soldiers, who, in those ancient times were not paid in money, but in corn. Upon this pretense they were admitted into the house, and so went from room to room, to the place where the king lay.

12. David commanded. &c.But what a disappointment to Baanah and Rechab, was the sentence which David passed upon them! And such they will meet with, who think to serve the Son of David, by cruelty or injustice: who under colour of religion, outrage or murder of their brethren, think they do God service. However men may now canonize such methods of serving the church and the catholic cause, Christ will let them know another day, that Christianity was not designed to destroy humanity. And they who thus think to merit heaven, shall not escape the damnation of hell.

V

David is anointed king by all the tribes, ver. 1-5. Takes the strong hold of Zion, ver. 6-10. David builds him an house; his kingdom is established, ver. 11, 12. Has more children, ver. 13- 16. Conquers the Philistines, ver. 17-25.

2. Shalt feed - That is, rule them, and take care of them, as a shepherd doth of his sheep, Psalm lxxviii, 70, 71. This expression, he useth to admonish David, that he was not made a king to advance his own glory, but for the good of his people; whom he ought to rule with all tenderness, and to watch over with all diligence.

3. A league - Whereby David obliged himself to rule them according to God's laws; and the people promised obedience to him.

6. Cannot come - They confided in the strength of their fortifications, which they thought so impregnable, that the blind and the lame were sufficient to defend them, against the most powerful assailant. And probably they set a parcel of blind and lame people, invalids or maimed soldiers, to make their appearance on the wall, in contempt of David and his men.

8. To the gutter - That is, whosoever scaleth the fort, or getteth up to the top of it, where the gutter was. That are hated - The Jebusites, and the lame, and the blind, Who had probably themselves insulted him, and blasphemed God. He shall be - These words are fitly supplied out of 1 Chron. xi, 6, where they are expressed. They said &c. - That is, whence it became a proverb, or a common saying, used by David, and others, the blind and the lame Jebusites, were set to keep the house, that is, the fort of Zion; and to keep others from coming into it; but now they are shut out of it, and none of them, either of the Jebusites, or of blind and lame persons, shall be admitted to come into it again. Which David might ordain, to keep up the memory of this great exploit, and of the insolent carriage of the Jebusites.

9. Millo - Which seems to have been the town-hall or, state-house, near the wall of the city of Zion.

12. King over Israel - That he might be a blessing to them, and they might be happy under his administration.

13. David took, &c. - This may well be reckoned amongst David's miscarriages, the multiplication of wives being expresly forbidden to the king, Deut. xvii, 17. It seems to have been his policy, that hereby he might enlarge his family, and strengthen his interest by alliances with so many considerable families. But all these did not preserve him from coveting his neighbour's wife. Rather they inclined him to it: for men who have once broke the fence, will wander carelessly.

17. The hold - To some fortified place to which his people might conveniently resort from all places, and where he might intrench his army, which lay towards the Philistines.

20. Baal-perazim-Whither the Philistines were come from the valley of Rephraim, 1 Chron. xiv, 11. Baal-perazim, signifies the master of the breaches: So he ascribes all to God. As waters - As floods or rivers of waters, which break the banks, and overflow a land, and overturn all that stands in their way.

21. Images - When the ark fell into the hand of the Philistines, it consumed them: but when these images fell into the hands of Israel, they could not save themselves from being consumed.

22. And spread themselves - The expression intimates, that they were very numerous, and made a very formidable appearance. So we read, Rev. xx, 9, of the church's enemies going up on the breadth of the earth. But the wider they spread themselves, the fairer mark they are for God's arrows.

23. Go up - Directly against them, as the following words explain it. Behind - Where they least expect thee; God's purposes and promises do not exclude men's endeavours.

24. The sound - A noise as it were of persons walking upon the tops of them, which I shall cause; and by this sign, both thou shalt be assured that I am coming to help thee; and the Philistines shall be affrighted, and not perceive the noise of thy army, until thou art upon them. Bestir - Fall upon them.

VI

The ark is brought from the house of Abinadab, ver. 1-5. Its progress stopped by the death of Uzzah, ver. 6-11. It is brought into the city of David with solemn rejoicings, ver. 12-19. David answers the reproof of Michal, ver. 20-23.

2. On which, &c. - That is, by, or before which, they were to present their prayers to God for counsel and succor upon all occasions. And this is mentioned here as the reason why David put himself and his people to so great trouble and charge, because it was to fetch up the choicest treasure which they had.

3. They set, &c. - Being taught, and encouraged to do so, by the example of the Philistines, who did so without any token of God's displeasure upon them for so doing. But they did not sufficiently consider, that God might wink at the Philistines, because they were ignorant of God's laws; and yet be

angry with them for the same thing, because they knew, or might have known the law of God, which commanded the priests to bear it upon their shoulders. But their present transports of joy of the happy change of their affairs, and their greedy desire of having the ark of God removed, made them inconsiderate. In Gibeah - Or, on the hill, as 1 Sam. vii, 1.

5. Played before the Lord - Public joy should always be as before the Lord, with an eye to him, and terminating in him. Otherwise it is no better than public madness, and the source of all manner of wickedness.

7. He died - This may seem very severe, considering his intention was pious, and his transgression not great. But, besides that, men are improper Judges of the actions of God; and that God's judgments are always just, though sometimes obscure: it is reasonable, God should make some present examples of his high displeasure against sins, seemingly small; partly, for the demonstration of his own exact and impartial holiness; partly, for the establishment of discipline, and for the greater terror and caution of mankind, who are very prone to have slight thoughts of sin, and to give way to small sins, and thereby to be led on to greater; all which is, or may be prevented by such instances of severity: and consequently there is more of God's mercy, than of his justice, in such actions, because the justice is confined to one particular person, but the benefit of it common to mankind in that, and all future ages.

8. Displeased - Or, grieved, both for the sin, and for God's heavy judgment; whereby their hopes were dashed, and their joys interrupted. Perez-uzzah - That is, the breach of Uzzah.

10. House of Obed-edom - Obed-edom knew what slaughter the ark had made among the Philistines and the Bethshemites. He saw Uzzah struck dead; yet invites it to his house, and opens his doors without fear, knowing it was a savour of death, only to them that treated it ill. "O the courage, says Bishop Hall, of an honest and faithful heart! Nothing can make God otherwise than amiable to him: even his justice is lovely."

11. The Lord blessed, &c. - The same hand that punished Uzzah's presumption, rewarded Obed-edom's humble boldness. None ever had, or ever shall have reason to say, that it is in vain to serve God. Piety is the best friend to prosperity. His household too shared in the blessing. It is good living in a family that entertains the ark; for all about it will fare the better for it.

14. Danced - To express his thankfulness to God by his outward carriage, according to the manner of those times. Linen ephod - The usual habit of the priests and Levites, in their sacred ministrations yet sometimes worn by others, as it was by the young child Samuel; and so David, who laid by his royal robes, and put on this robe to declare, that although he was king of Israel, yet he willingly owned himself to be the Lord's minister and servant.

16. Despised - As one of a base and mean spirit, that knew not how to carry himself with that majesty which became his place.

17. David had pitched - For Moses tabernacle was still at Gibeon, 1 Chron. xvi, 39; xxi, 29; 2 Chron. i, 3, which David left there, because he designed to build a temple at Jerusalem with all speed.

18. He blessed - That is, he heartily and solemnly prayed to God for his blessing upon them: which he did both as a prophet, and as their king, to whom by office it belongs, by all means, to seek his people's welfare.

20. Bless his household - Ministers must not think, that their public performances will excuse them from family worship: but when they have blessed the public assembly, they are to return and bless their own household. And none is too great to do this. It is the work of angels to worship God; and therefore certainly can be no disparagement to the greatest of men. Who uncovered - By stripping himself of his royal robes, that he might put on a Levitical ephod.

21. Before the Lord - In his presence and service, which though contemptible to thee, is, and ever shall be honourable in mine eyes. Who chose - Who took away the honour from him and his, and transferred it unto me, whereby he hath obliged me to love and serve him with all my might.

22. More vile than thus - The more we are vilified for well doing, the more resolute therein we should be, binding our religion the closer to us, for the endeavours of Satan's agents to shame us out of it. Be base - I will always be ready to abase myself before God, and think nothing to mean to stoop to for his honour. Be had in honour - So far will they be from despising me on this account, that they will honour me the more.

23. Therefore - Because of her proud and petulant speech and carriage to David, which God justly punished with barrenness. No child - After this time.

VII

Nathan approves David's design of building an house for God, ver. 1-3. God forbids it, but promises to bless him and his seed, ver. 4-17. His prayer and thanksgiving, ver. 18-29.

1. Sat - That is, was settled in the house which Hiram's men had built for him, then he reflected upon the unsettled state of the ark.

Wesley's Notes on the Bible - The Old Testament: First Samuel - Psalms

2. *Curtains* - That is, in a tent or tabernacle, ver. 6, composed of several curtains.

3. *Nathan said* - Pursue thy intentions, and build an house for the ark. The design being pious and the thing not forbidden by God, Nathan hastily approves it, before he had consulted God about it, as both he and David ought to have done in a matter of so great moment. And therefore Nathan meets with this rebuke, that he is forced to acknowledge his error, and recant it. For the holy prophets did not speak all things by prophetic inspiration, but some things by an human spirit.

4. *The word of the Lord came* - Because David's mistake was pious, and from an honest mind, God would not suffer him to lie long in it.

5. *Shalt thou* - That is, thou shalt not.

6. *Tent and tabernacle* - These two seem thus to be distinguished, the one may note the curtains and hangings within, the other the frame of boards, and coverings upon it.

8. *My servant* - Lest David should be too much discouraged, or judge himself neglected of God, as one thought unworthy of so great an honour, God here gives him the honourable title of his servant, thereby signifying that he accepted of his service, and good intentions.

10. *Appoint* - That is, I will make room for them, whereas hitherto they have been much distressed by their enemies. Or, I will establish a place for them, that is, I will establish them in their place or land. *My people* - Among the favours which God had vouchsafed, and would vouchsafe to David, he reckons his blessings to Israel, because they were great blessings to David; partly, because the strength and happiness of a king consists in the multitude and happiness of his people; and partly, because David was a man of a public spirit, and therefore no less affected with Israel's felicity than with his own. *Before time* - Namely in Egypt.

11. *And as since* - Nor as they did under the Judges. But all this is to be understood with a condition, except they should notoriously forsake God. *And have caused thee* - That is, and as until this time in which I have given thee rest. But these words, though according to our translation they be enclosed in the same parenthesis with the foregoing clauses, may be better put without it, and taken by themselves. For the foregoing words in this verse, and in ver. 10, all concern the people of Israel; but these words concern David alone, to whom the speechs returns after a short digression concerning the people of Israel. And they may be rendered thus. And I will cause thee to rest, &c. - More fully and perfectly than yet thou dost. *He will, &c.* - For thy good intentions to make him an house, he will make thee an house, a sure house, that is, he will increase and uphold thy posterity, and continue thy kingdom in thy family.

12. *And when, &c.* - When the time of thy life shall expire. This phrase implies, that his days shall be prolonged to the usual course of nature, and not cut off in the midst, by any violent or untimely death. *I will set* - I will set up in thy throne, thy posterity, first Solomon, and then others successively, and at last the Messiah. So the following words may be understood, part of his posterity in general, part of Solomon, and part of Christ only, according to the different nature of the several passages.

13. *He shall* - This is meant literally of Solomon, who alone did build the material house or temple; but ultimately of Christ, who is the builder of God's spiritual house or temple. *For my name* - That is, for my service, and glory. *For ever* - This is not meant of Solomon, for his kingdom was not forever. But it is to be understood of David's posterity, in general, and with special respect to Christ, in whose person the kingdom was to be lodged forever. 14. *His father* - I will carry myself towards him as a father, with all affection, and I will own him as my son. This is intended both of Solomon, as a type of Christ; and of Christ himself as is evident from Heb. i, 5. *If he commit* - This agrees only to Solomon and some others of David's posterity; but not to Christ, who never committed iniquity, as Solomon did, who therein was no type of Christ, and therefore this branch is terminated in Solomon; whereas in those things wherein Solomon was a type of Christ, the sense passes through Solomon to Christ. *Rod of men* - With such rods as are gentle and moderate, and suited to man's weakness.

15. *My mercy* - That is, Or, my kindness, that is, the kingdom which I have mercifully promised to thee and thine. *From Saul* - In regard of his posterity, for the kingdom was continued to his person during life.

16. *Before thee* - Thine eyes in some sort beholding it: for he lived to see his wise son Solomon actually placed in the throne, with reputation and general applause, which was in itself a good presage of the continuance of the kingdom in his family: and being considered, together with the infallible certainty of God's promise to him and his, (of the accomplishment whereof, this was an earnest,) gave him good assurance thereof; especially considering that he had his eyes and thoughts upon the Messiah, Psalm cx, 1, &c. whose day he saw by faith, as Abraham did, John viii, 56, and whom he knew that God would raise out of the fruit of his loins to sit on his throne, and that forever: and so the eternity of his kingdom is rightly said to be before him.

18. *In* - Into the tabernacle. *Sat* - He might sit for a season whilst he was meditating upon these things, and then alter his posture and betake himself to prayer. *Who am I, &c.* - How infinitely unworthy am I and my family of this great honour and happiness!

19. *This* - Which thou hast already done for me, that thou hast brought me hitherto, to that pitch of

honour, and peace, and prosperity, in which through thy favour I now stand. Was small - Though it was more than I deserved, or could expect, yet thou didst not think it enough for thee to give to me. A great while - For many future ages, and indeed to all eternity. Is this, &c. - Do men use to deal so kindly with their inferiors, as thou hast done with me? No: this is the prerogative of divine grace.

20. David say - Either in a way of gratitude and praise, words cannot express my obligations to thee, nor my sense of these obligations: Or in a way of prayer. What can I ask of thee more than thou hast freely done? Thou knowest - Thou knowest my deep sense of thy favours, and my obligations to thee. And my condition and necessities, what I do or may need hereafter; and as thou knowest this, so I doubt not thou wilt supply me.

21. Thy word's sake - That thou mightest fulfil thy promises made to me, and thereby demonstrate thy faithfulness. Own heart - Or thy own mere liberality and good pleasure, without any desert of mine. So far was David, though a very gracious man, from thinking his actions meritorious.

22. Great - Both in power and in goodness, as appears by the great and good things which thou hast done for me.

24. Confirmed - Partly, by thy promises, and that sure covenant which thou hast made with them: and partly, by thy glorious works wrought on their behalf, as it appears this day. Their God - In a peculiar manner, and by special relation and covenant: for otherwise he is the God and father of all things.

26. Let thy name - That is, do thou never cease to manifest thyself to be the God and governor of Israel.

27. This prayer, &c. - That prayer that is found in the tongue only will not please God. It must be found in the heart. That must be lifted up and poured out before God.

28. That God - That God who hast declared thyself to be Israel's God, and in particular my God.

29. Continue forever, &c. - When Christ forever sat down on the right-hand of God, and received all possible assurance, that his seed and throne should be as the days of heaven, then this prayer was abundantly answered.

VIII

David subdues the Philistines and Moabites, ver. 1-2. Smites Hadadezer, and the Syrians, ver. 3-8. Dedicates the presents he had received and the spoils to God, ver. 9-12. Conquers the Syrians again, and the Edomites, ver. 13, 14. His administration of justice and chief officers, ver. 15-18,

1. And David took - Gath and her towns, as it is expressed in the parallel place, 1 Chron. xviii, 1. Which are called Metheg-ammah, or the bridle of Ammah, Gath was situate in the mountain of Ammah; and because this being the chief city of the Philistines, and having a king, which none of the rest had, was the bridle which had hitherto kept the Israelites in subjection.

2. Moab - For although the king of Moab, out of hatred to Saul, gave protection to his parents, 1 Sam. xxii, 3, 4, yet the Moabites were perpetual and sworn enemies to the Israelites, who therefore were forbidden to admit them into the congregation of the Lord. And though God commanded them in their march to Canaan, to spare the Moabites, yet afterwards they proved fierce enemies to God and his people, and thereby provoked God to alter his carriage towards them. Measured them - That is, having conquered the land, he made an estimate of it, and distributed the towns and people into three parts. Casting down - Overthrowing their towns, and utterly destroying their people in manner following. And now that prophecy, Num. xxiv, 17, was accomplished.

3. As he went - David, remembering the grant which God had made to his people of all the land as far as Euphrates, and having subdued his neighbouring enemies, went to recover his rights, and stablish his dominion as far as Euphrates.

4. Seven hundred - Or, seven hundred companies of horsemen, that is, in all seven thousand; as it is 1 Chron. xviii, 4, there being ten in each company, and each ten having a ruler or captain. Houghed - That is, cut the sinews of their legs, that they might be useless for war.

5. Of Damascus - That is, who were subject to Damascus, the chief city of Syria.

7. On the servants - Or rather, which were with the servants, that is, committed to their custody, as being kept in the king's armoury: for it is not probable they carried them into the field.

8. From Betah, &c. - In 1 Chron. xviii, 8, it is, from Tibhath, and from Chun. Either therefore the same cities were called by several names, as is usual, the one by the Hebrew, the other by the Syrians, or those were two other cities, and so the brass was taken out of these four cities.

14. The Lord preserved, &c. - All David's victories were typical of the success of the gospel over the kingdom of Satan, in which the Son of David rode forth, conquering and to conquer, and will reign 'till he has brought down all opposing rule, principality and power.

16. Recorder - The treasurer, who examined all the accounts, and kept records of them.

17. Scribe - Or, secretary of state.

18. *Cherethites, &c.* - The Cherethites and Pelethites were undoubtedly soldiers, and such as were eminent for their valour and fidelity. Most probable they were the king's guards, which consisted of these two bands, who might be distinguished either by their several weapons, or by the differing time or manner of their service. They are supposed to be thus called either, first, from their office, which was upon the king's command to cut off or punish offenders, and to preserve the king's person, as their names in the Hebrew tongue may seem to imply. Or, secondly, from some country, or place to which they had relation. As for the Cherithites, it is certain they were ether a branch of the Philistines, or a people neighbouring to them, and so might the Pelethites be too, though that be not related in scripture. And these Israelites and soldiers of David might be so called, either because they went and lived with David when he dwelt in those parts or, for some notable exploit against, or victory over these people.

IX

David sends for Jonathan's son, Mephibosheth, ver. 1-6. Restores to him all the land that was Saul's, and appoints him to eat at his own table, ver. 7-13.

1. *Of Saul* - He saith not of the house of Jonathan, for he knew not of any son he had left, and therefore thought his kindness and obligation was to pass to the next of his kindred. As for Mephibosheth, he was very young and obscure, and possibly concealed by his friends, lest David should cut him off, as hath been usual among princes.

5. *Machir* - This Machir appears to have been a generous man, who entertained Mephibosheth out of mere compassion, not of disaffection to David: for afterwards we find him kind to David himself, when he fled from Absalom. David now little thought, that the time would come, when he himself should need his assistance. Let us be forward to give, because we know not what we ourselves may sometime want.

8. *Bowed himself* - It is good to have the heart humbled under humbling providences. If when divine providence brings our condition down, divine grace brings our spirits down, we shall be easy.

X

David's ambassadors are abused by Hanun, ver. 1-4. The Ammonites prepare for war and are routed, ver. 5-14. Their allies, the Syrians rally and are defeated again, ver. 15-19.

2. *David sent* - There had hitherto been friendship between David and him: and therefore the spoils of the children of Ammon are mentioned, chap. viii, 12, by way of anticipation, and with respect to the story here following.

4. *Shaved* - To fasten this is a reproach upon them, and to make them ridiculous and contemptible. *Cut off, &c.* - This was worse than the former, because the Israelites wore no breeches, and so their nakedness was hereby uncovered.

19. *And served them* - And thus at length was fulfilled the promise made to Abraham, and repeated to Joshua, that the borders of Israel should extend as far as the river Euphrates. The son of David sent his ambassadors, his apostles and ministers, to the Jewish church and nation. But they intreated them shamefully, as Hanun did David's, mocked them, abused them, slew them. And this it was that filled the measure of their iniquity, and brought upon them ruin without remedy.

XI

David commits adultery with Bathsheba, ver. 1-5. endeavours to father the child upon Uriah, ver. 6-13. Contrives the death of Uriah, ver. 14-25. Marries Bathsheba, ver. 26, 27.

1. *After* - When that year ended, and the next begun, which was in the spring time. *When kings* - Which is, when the ground is fit for the march of soldiers, and brings forth provision for man and beast. *Tarried at Jerusalem* - Had he been now in his post, at the head of his forces be had been out of the way of temptation.

2. *Arose from off his bed* - Where he had lain, and slept for some time. And the bed of sloth often proves the bed of lust. *Washing herself* - In a bath, which was in her garden. Probably from some ceremonial pollution.

3. *He inquired* - Instead of suppressing that desire which the sight of his eyes had kindled, he seeks rather to feed it; and first inquires who she was; that if she were unmarried, he might make her either his wife or his concubine.

4. *Took her* - From her own house into his palace, not by force, but by persuasion. *Lay with her* - See how all the way to sin is down hill! When men begin, they cannot soon stop themselves.

8. Go down - Not doubting but he would there converse with his wife, and so cover their sin and shame.

9. The servants - With the king's guard. This he did, by the secret direction of God's wise providence, who would bring David's sin to light.

10. Camest - Wearied with hard service and travel, nor did I expect or desire that thou shouldest now attend upon my person, or keep the watch.

11. The ark - This it seems, was now carried with them for their encouragement and direction, as was usual. Fields - In tents which are in the fields. His meaning is, now, when God's people are in a doubtful and dangerous condition, it becomes me to sympathize with them, and to abstain even from lawful delights.

15. He arose - So far is David from repenting, that he seeks to cover one sin with another. How are the beginnings of sin to be dreaded! For who knows where it will end? David hath sinned, therefore Uriah must die! That innocent, valiant, gallant man, who was ready to die for his prince's honour, must die by his prince's hand! See how fleshly lusts war against the soul, and what devastations they make in that war! How they blind the eyes, fear the conscience, harden the heart, and destroy all sense of honour and justice!

27. The mourning - Which was seven days. Nor could the nature of the thing admit of longer delay, lest the too early birth of the child might discover David's sin. Bare a son - By which it appears, That David continued in the state of impenitency for divers months together; and this notwithstanding his frequent attendance upon God's ordinances. Which is an eminent instance of the corruption of man's nature, of the deceitfulness of sin, and of the tremendous judgment of God in punishing one sin, by delivering a man up to another.

XII

Nathan delivers and applies his parable, ver. 1-12. David repents and is forgiven, but punished, ver. 13. 14. The sickness and death of the child, with David's behaviour on the occasion, ver. 15-23. The birth of Solomon, ver. 24-25. The taking of Rabbah, ver. 26-31.

1. The Lord sent - When the ordinary means did not awaken David to repentance, God takes an extraordinary course. Thus the merciful God pities and prevents him who had so horribly forsaken God. He said - He prudently ushers in his reproof with a parable, after the manner of the eastern nations, that so he might surprise David, and cause him unawares to give sentence against himself.

2. Many flocks - Noting David's many wives and concubines.

3. Bought - As men then used to buy their wives: or, had procured.

5. Is worthy to die - This seems to be more than the fact deserved, or than he had commission to inflict for it, Exod. xxii, 1. But it is observable, that David now when he was most indulgent to himself, and to his own sin, was most severe and even unjust to others; as appears by this passage, and the following relation, ver. 31, which was done in the time of David's impenitent continuance in his sin.

7. Thus saith the Lord God - Nathan now speaks, not as a petitioner for a poor man, but as an ambassador from the great God.

9. To be thy wife - To marry her whom he had defiled, and whose husband he had slain, was an affront upon the ordinance of marriage, making that not only to palliate, but in a manner to consecrate such villainies. In all this he despised the word of the Lord; (so it is in the Hebrew.) Not only his commandment in general, but the particular word of promise, which God had before sent him by Nathan, that he would build him an house: which sacred promise if he had had a due value for, he would not have polluted his house with lust and blood.

10. Never depart - During the residue of thy life.

11. Own house - From thy own children and family. Thine eyes - Openly, so that thou shalt know it as certainly as if thou didst see it, and yet not be able to hinder it. And give them - I shall by my providence, give him power over them. neighbour - To one who is very near thee. But God expresseth this darkly, that the accomplishment of it might not be hindered.

13. I have sinned - How serious this confession was, we may see, Psalm li, 1-19. Put away thy sin - That is, so far as concerns thy own life. Not die - As by thy own sentence, ver. 5, thou dost deserve, and may expect to be done by my immediate stroke.

16. Besought - Supposing the threatening might be conditional, and so the execution of it prevented by prayer. Went - Into his closet.

17. Elders - The chief officers of his kingdom and household. He would not - This excessive mourning did not proceed simply from the fear of the loss of the child; but from a deep sense of his sin, and the divine displeasure manifested herein.

18. Seventh day - From the beginning of the distemper.

20. And came - That is, to the tabernacle, to confess his sin before the Lord, to own his justice in

this stroke, to deprecate his just displeasure, to acknowledge God's rich mercy, in sparing his own life; and to offer such sacrifices as were required in such cases.

23. I fast - Seeing fasting and prayer cannot now prevail with God for his life. I shall go to him - Into the state of the dead in which he is, and into heaven, where I doubt not I shall find him.

24. His wife - Who was now much dejected, both for her former sin, and for the loss of the child. Loved him - That is, the Lord declared to David, that he loved his son, notwithstanding the just cause David had given to God to alienate his affections from him.

25. Jedidiah - That is, beloved of the Lord. Because - Either, because of the Lord's love to him, or because the Lord commanded him to do so.

26. Royal city - That is, that part of the city where was the king's palace; though now it seems he was retired to a strong fort.

27. Of waters - Rabbah was so called because it was encompassed with water.

28. Take it - For having taken one part of the city, he concluded the remaining part of it could not long stand out. Lest - Lest I have the honour of taking it.

30. The weight - Or rather, the price whereof, &c. For the same words both in Hebrew, Greek and Latin, are used, to signify either weight, or price. And the addition of precious stones, which are never valued by the weight of gold, makes this signification most probable. Moreover, the weight might seem too great either for the king of Ammon, or for David to wear it upon his head.

31. The people - The words are indefinite, and therefore not necessarily to be understood of all the people; but of the men of war, and especially of those who had been the chief actors of that villainous action against David's ambassadors, and of the dreadful war ensuing upon it; for which, they deserved severe punishments. Altho' indeed there seems to have been too much rigor used; especially, because these deaths were inflicted not only upon those counsellors, who were the only authors of that vile usage of the ambassadors; but upon some number of the people. And therefore it is probable, David exercised this cruelty whilst his heart was hardened, and impenitent; and when he was bereaved of that good spirit of God, which would have taught him more mercy. Saws - He sawed them to death of which punishment, we have examples both in scripture, and in other authors. Brick-kiln - Or, made them to pass through the furnace of Malchen: that is, of Moloch; punishing them with their own sin, and with the same kind of punishment which they had inflicted upon their own children.

XIII

Amnon ravishes Tamar, ver. 1-20. Absalom kills him, ver. 21-29. David mourns: Absalom flees to Geshur, ver. 30-39.

1. A sister - His sister by father and mother.

2. A virgin - And therefore diligently kept, so he could not get private converse with her.

5. My sister - So he calls her, to prevent the suspicion of any dishonest design upon so near a relation. At her hand - Pretending, his stomach was so nice, that he could eat nothing but what he saw dressed, and that by a person whom he much esteemed.

9. Out - Out of the frying-pan into the dish.

10. Chamber - Amnon lying upon his couch in one chamber where the company were with him, where also she made the cakes before him, first sends all out of that room, and then rises from his couch, and, upon some pretense, goes into another secret chamber.

12. Brother - Whom nature both teaches to abhor such thoughts and obliges to defend me from such a mischief with thy utmost hazard, if another should attempt it. Force - Thou shouldst abhor it, if I were willing; but to add violence, is abominable. Israel - Among God's people who are taught better things; who also will be infinitely reproached for such a base action.

13. Shame - How can I either endure or avoid the shame? Fools - That is, contemptible to all the people, whereas now thou art heir apparent of the crown. Withhold - This she spoke, because she thought her royal father would dispense with it, upon this extraordinary occasion, to save his first-born son's life:

15. Hated her - By the just judgment of God both upon Amnon and David, that so the sin might be made publick, and way for the succeeding tragedies.

16. No cause - For me to go. Greater thou the other - This she might truly say, because though the other was in itself a greater sin, yet this was an act of greater cruelty, and a greater calamity to her because it exposed her to publick infamy and contempt, and besides, it turned a private offense into a publick scandal, to the great dishonour of God and of his people, and especially of all the royal family.

18. Garment - Of embroidered work.

19. Put ashes - To signify her grief for some calamity which had befallen her, and what that was, concurring circumstances easily discovered. Head - In token of grief and shame, as if she were unable and ashamed to shew her face. Crying - To manifest her abhorrency of the fact, and that it was not done

by her consent.

20. Been with thee - Behold, and imitate the modesty of scripture expressions. Brother - Wherefore thou must forgive and forgot the injury; therefore thy disgracing of him will be a blot to us all; therefore thou wilt not get right from David against him, because he is as near and dear to him as thou; therefore thy dishonour is the less, because thou wast not abused by any mean person, but by a king's son; therefore this evil must be born, because it cannot be revenged: and thus he covers his design of taking vengeance upon him at the first opportunity. Regard not - So as to torment thyself. Desolate - Through shame and dejection of mind, giving her self up to solitude and retirement.

21. Wroth - With Amnon: whom yet he did not punish, at least so severely as he should either from the consciousness of his own guilt in the like kind; or, from that foolish indulgence which he often shewed to his children.

22. Spake - That is, he said nothing at all to him, about that business. He neither debated it with him, nor threatened him for it; but seemed willing to pass it by with brotherly kindness. If he had wholly forborne all discourse with him, it would have raised jealousies in Amnon and David.

23. Two years - This circumstance of time is noted, as an aggravation of Absalom's malice, which was so implacable: and as an act of policy, that both Amnon and David might more securely comply with his desires.

26. Let Amnon - For the king designed (as the following words shew) to keep him at home with him, as being his eldest son, and heir of his kingdom: otherwise Absalom would never have made particular mention of him; which now he was forced to do. Nor did this desire of Amnon's presence want specious pretenses, as that seeing the king would not, he who was next to him might, honour him with his company; and that this might be a publick token of friendship between him and his brother, notwithstanding the former occasion of difference.

27. Pressed him - It is strange that his urgent desire of Amnon's company raised no suspicion in so wise a king; but God suffered him to be blinded that he might execute his judgments upon David, and bring upon Amnon the just punishment of his lewdness.

28. Merry - When he least suspects, and will be most unable to prevent the evil. I - I who am the king's son, and, when Amnon is gone, his heir: who therefore shall easily obtain pardon for you, and will liberally reward you.

29. Commanded - Now the threatened sword is drawn in David's house, which will not depart from it. His eldest son falls by it, thro' his own wickedness, and his father by his connivance is accessory to it.

37. Talmai - His mother's father, that he might have present protection and sustenance from him; and that by his mediation he might obtain his father's pardon.

39. Go forth - And could not he recalled, to visit him, or to send for him. What amazing weakness was this! At first he could not find in his heart, to do justice to the ravisher of his sister! And now he can almost find in his heart to receive into favour the murderer of his brother? How can we excuse David from the sin of Eli; who honoured his sons more than God?

XIV

The story told David of the widow of Tekoah, ver. 1-20. Absalom is brought back to Jerusalem, but not to court, ver. 21- 24. An account of Absalom's person and children, ver. 21-27. He is at length introduced to David, ver. 28-33.

1. Was towards - He desired to see him, but was ashamed to shew kindness to one whom God's law and his own conscience obliged him to punish; he wanted therefore a fair pretense, which therefore Joab gave him.

2. Anoint - As they used to do when they were out of a mourning state.

5. Widow - One of them who most need thy compassion, and whom thou art by God's law obliged in a singular manner to relieve.

9. Be guiltless - If through thy forgetfulness or neglect of this my just cause, my adversaries prevail and destroy my son, my desire is, that God would not lay it to the king's charge, but rather to me and mine, so the king may be exempted thereby. Whereby she insinuates, that such an omission will bring guilt upon him; and yet most decently orders her phrase so as not to seem to blame or threaten the king. This sense seems best to agree with David's answer, which shew's that she desired some farther assurances of the king's care.

11. Remember - Remember the Lord, in whose presence thou hast made me this promise, and who will be a witness against thee, if thou breakest it.

13. Wherefore then - If thou shouldst not permit the avengers of blood to molest me, or to destroy my son, who are but two persons; how unreasonable is it that thou shouldest proceed in thy endeavours to avenge Amnon's blood upon Absalom, whose death would be grievous to the whole commonwealth

of Israel, all whose eyes are upon him as the heir of the crown, and a wise, and valiant, and amiable person, unhappy only in this one act of killing Amnon, which was done upon an high provocation, and whereof thou thyself didst give the occasion by permitting Amnon to go unpunished? Faulty - By thy word, and promise, and oath given to me for my son, thou condemnest thyself for not allowing the same equity towards thy own son. It is true, Absalom's case was widely different from that which she had supposed. But David was too well affected to him, to remark that difference, and was more desirous than she could be, to apply that favourable judgment to his own son, which he had given concerning hers.

14. We - We shall certainly die, both thou, O king, who art therefore obliged to take care of thy successor, Absalom; and Absalom, who, if he do not die by the hand of justice, must shortly die by the necessity of nature: and Amnon too must have died in the common way of all flesh, if Absalom had not cut him off. Respect - So far as to exempt him from this common law of dying. Not expelled - He hath given laws to this purpose, that the man-slayer who is banished should not always continue in banishment, but upon the High-priest's death return to his own city.

15. The people - The truth is, I was even forced to this bold address to thee by the disposition of thy people, who are discontented at Absalom's perpetual banishment, lest, if Absalom by his father-in-law's assistance invade the land, the people who have a great kindness for him, and think he is very hard used, should take up arms.

16. Hear - For I know the king is so wise and just, that I assure myself of audience and acceptation. Deliver - To grant my request concerning my son, and consequently the peoples petition concerning Absalom. My son - Implying that her life was bound up in the life of her son, and that she could not outlive his death; (and supposing that it might be David's case also, and would therefore touch him in a tender part, though it were not proper to say it expressly:) and thereby suggesting, that the safety and comfort of the people of Israel, depended upon Absalom's restitution. Inheritance - That is, out of that land which God gave to his people to be their inheritance, and in which alone God hath settled the place of his presence and worship: whereby she intimates the danger of Absalom's living in a state of separation from God, and his house, amongst idolaters.

17. Angel - In wisdom, and justice, and goodness. Therefore - Because thou art so wise and gracious to those who in strict justice deserve punishment, God will own and stand by thee in this thy act of grace: or God will prosper thee in thy enterprizes.

19. Of Joab - Hast thou not said and done this by Joab's direction. Said - It is even so, thou hast discovered the truth. These words - As to the substance of them, but not as to all the expressions; for these were to be varied as the king's answer gave occasion.

20. To fetch - That is, to propose his, and the peoples desire of Absalom's restitution in this parabolical manner. In the earth - Or, in this land, in all thy kingdom; all the counsels and devices of thy subjects.

22. Fulfilled - But it seems David had no power to dispense with God's laws, nor to spare any whom God appointed him to destroy: for the laws of God bound the kings and rulers, as well as the people of Israel. How justly did God make this man, whom he had so sinfully spared, a scourge to him?

24. Let him turn - Lest whilst be shewed some mercy to Absalom, he should seem to approve of his sin. Likewise by this means Absalom might be drawn to a more thorough humiliation and repentance.

25. Beauty - This is noted as the occasion of his pride, and of the people's affection to him.

26. Weighed - Others understand this not of the weight, but of the price of his hair.

27. Sons - All which died not long after they were born, as may be gathered from chap. xviii, 18, where it is said, that Absalom had no son.

32. Kill me - For it is better for me to die, than to want the sight and favour of my dear father. Thus he insinuates himself into his father's affections, by pretending such respect and love to him It seems that by this time Absalom having so far recovered his father's favour, began to grow upon him, and take so much confidence as to stand upon his own justification, as if what he had done, had been no iniquity, at least not such as to deserve death. See how easily wise parents may be imposed on by their children, when they are blindly fond of them.

33. Kissed - Did the bowels of a father prevail to reconcile him to an impenitent son? And shall penitent sinners question the compassion of him who is the Father of mercy? If Ephraim bemoan himself, God soon bemoans him, with all the expressions of fatherly tenderness. He is a dear son, a pleasant child.

XV

Absalom steals the hearts of the people, ver. 1-6. He conspires against David, ver. 7-12. David flies from Jerusalem, ver. 13-18. He confers with Ittai, and passes over Kidron, ver. 19- 23. Sends back Zadok with the ark, ver. 24-29. His prayer on this occasion, ver. 30, 31. He concerts with Hushai, ver. 32-37.

1. Prepared - As being the king's eldest son, now Amnon was dead; for Chileab, who was his eldest brother, chap. iii, 3, was either dead, or incapable of the government. And this course he knew would draw the eyes of the people to him, and make them conclude that David intended him for his successor.

2. Early - Thereby making a shew of solicitude for the good of the public, and of every private person. Called him - Preventing him with the offers of his assistance. And as if he were ready to make particular enquiry into the state of his cause.

3. See - Upon some very slight hearing of their cause, he approved it, that he might oblige all. No man - None such as will do thee justice. The other sons and relations of the king, and the rest of the Judges and rulers under him and them, are wholly corrupted; or, at least not careful and diligent as they should be: and my father being grown in years, is negligent of publick affairs. It is the way of turbulent, aspiring men, to reproach the government they are under. Even David himself, the best of kings, could not escape the worst of censures.

7. After forty years - From the change of the government, into a monarchy, which was about ten years before David began to reign. So this fell out about the thirtieth year of his reign.

9. Hebron - This place he chose as being an eminent city, and next to Jerusalem, the chief of the tribe of Judah, and the place where his father began his kingdom, which he took for a good omen. And where it is probable he had secured many friends. It was also at a convenient distance from Jerusalem.

11. Called - Such as Absalom had picked out as fit for his purpose; such as were of some reputation with the king and people, which would give a countenance to his undertaking, and give occasion to people at first to think that this was done by his father's consent, as being now aged, and infirm, and willing to resign the kingdom to him. It is no new thing, for good men to be made use of by designing men to put a colour upon ill practices.

12. Sacrifices - Which he did not in devotion to God; but merely that upon this pretense he might call great numbers of people together.

14. Let us flee - For though the fort of Zion was strong, and he might have defended himself there; yet he had not laid in provisions for a long siege; and, if he had been once besieged there, Absalom would have got speedy possession of his whole kingdom; whereas if he marched abroad, he might raise a considerable army for his defense. Besides, the greatest part of Jerusalem could not be well defended against him.

16. After him - Or, on foot, which the king chose to do, to humble himself under the hand of God; to encourage his companions in this hard and comfortless march; and to move compassion in his people towards him. Concubines - For he supposed that their sex would protect them, and their relation to David would gain them some respect, or at least, safety from his son.

17. Far off - At some convenient distance, tho' not very far.

18. Gittites - Or rather strangers, as Ittai their head is called, ver. 19, and they are called his brethren, ver. 20. Probably they were Philistines by birth, born in the city or territory of Gath, as the following words imply, who by David's counsel, and example, were won to embrace the true religion, and had given good proof of their military skill, and valour, and fidelity to the king.

19. Thy place - To Jerusalem, where thy settled abode now is. The king - With Absalom who is now made king. An exile - Not much concerned in our affairs, and therefore not fit to be involved in our troubles.

20. Brethren - Thy countrymen the Gittites, ver. 18. Mercy, &c. - Since I am now unable to recompense thy kindness and fidelity to me, my hearty prayer to God is, that he would shew to thee his mercy, in blessing thee with all sorts of blessings, and his faithfulness in making good all these promises which he had made, not to Israelites only, but to all true hearted proselytes, such as thou art.

21. Will thy servant be - He is a friend indeed, who loves at all times, and will cleave to us in adversity. Thus should we cleave to the Son of David, that neither life, nor death may separate us from his love.

22. Little ones - For being so deeply engaged for David, he durst not leave his little ones to Absalom's mercy.

23. Kidron - Or, Cedron, which was near Jerusalem. The very same brook that Christ passed over when he entered upon his sufferings, John xviii, 1. Wilderness - Which was between Jerusalem and Jericho.

24. Went up - From the ark to the city, which was on higher ground, that so he being high-priest,

might use his authority with the people, to persuade them to do their duty; and there he staid until all those whom he could persuade were gone forth.

25. Carry back - Out of care and reverence to the ark, which though it might be carried our to a certain place; yet he might justly think unfit to carry it from place to place he knew not whither, and out of respect to the priests, whom, by this means, he thought he should expose to the rage of Absalom, as he had before exposed them to Saul's fury. Habitation - That is, the tabernacle which David had lately built for it, chap. vi, 17, in which the ark, and God, by means hereof, ordinarily dwelt.

26. Let him do - That we may not complain of what is, let us see God's hand in all events. And that we may not be afraid of what shall be, let us see all events in God's hand.

27. A seer - A seeing, discerning, or observing man: for so the Hebrew verb raah is often used. And this suits well with David's mind: Thou art a wise man, and therefore fit to manage this great business, which requires prudence and secrecy.

30. Barefoot - In testimony of his deep sorrow, and humiliation and shame for his sins.

34. And say - That is, as faithful to thee, as I have been to thy father. David's suggesting this crafty counsel must be reckoned amongst his sins. Nevertheless God was pleased to direct this evil advice to a good end.

36. There - Not in Jerusalem, but in a place near it, to which they could easily send upon occasion.

37. Absalom came, &c. - How soon do royal cities and royal palaces change their masters? But we look for a kingdom which cannot be moved.

XVI

David is deceived by Ziba, ver. 1-4. And cursed by Shemei, ver. 5-14. Absalom receives Hushai, ver. 15-19. Lies with his father's concubines, ver. 20-23.

1. Bottle - A large bottle, or vessel proportionable to the other provisions.

4. Behold - A rash sentence, and unrighteous to condemn a man unheard, upon the single testimony of his accuser, and servant. Find grace - Thy favour is more to me, than this gift; which, as a token of thy favour, I accept with all thankfulness.

8. Of Saul - Either,

1. The blood of Abner and Ishbosheth; which he imputes to David, as if they had been killed by David's contrivance: or,

2. the death of Saul's seven sons, chap. xxi, 8, which, though related after this, seems to have been done before. Art taken - The same mischief thou didst bring upon others, is now returned upon thy own head.

10. What have I, &e. - In this matter I ask not your advice, nor will I follow it; nor do I desire you should at all concern yourselves in it. The Lord - God did not put any wickedness into Shimei's heart, for he had of himself an heart full of malignity against David; but only left him to his own wickedness; and brought David into so distressed a condition, that he might seem a proper object of his scorn. And this is ground enough for this expression, the Lord said, not by the word of his precept, but by the word of his providence, in respect whereof he is said to command the ravens, 1 Kings xvii, 4, and to send forth his word to senseless creatures, Psalm lxlvii, 15, 18. Who shall reproach God's providence for permitting this? Or, who shall restrain him from executing his just judgment against me?

11. My life - Which is a greater mischief, than to reproach me with words. Benjamites - Of that tribe and family from which God hast taken away the kingdom, and given it to me. Let him - Do not now hinder him violently from it, nor punish him for it. It is meet I should bear the indignation of the Lord, and submit to his pleasure.

14. Came - To the city of Bahurim.

17. Is this - Doth this action answer that profession of friendship which thou hast hitherto made to him? He speaks thus only to try him. And he saith, thy friend, by way of reflection upon David; as one who was a friend to Hushai, and to strangers but not to his own son, whom, by his severity he provoked to this course; and therefore he doth not vouchsafe to call him his father.

21. Go - This counsel he gave, partly to revenge the injury done to Bathsheba, the daughter of Eliam, chap. xi, 3, who was the son of Ahithophel, chap. xxiii, 34, and principally for his own, and the people's safety, that the breach between David and Absalom might be irreparable. For this would provoke David in the highest degree and cut of all hope of reconciliation, which otherwise might have been expected by some treaty between Absalom and his tender-hearted father. But in that case his followers, and especially Ahithophel, had been left to David's mercy, and therefore obliged to prosecute the war with all vigour, and to abandon all thoughts of peace: as knowing that his father, though he might dissemble, yet would never forgive so foul a crime. Be strong - They will fight with greater courage and resolution, when they are freed from the fear of thy reconciliation, which otherwise would make their hearts faint, and hands slack in thy cause. But by this we may see the character of Absalom's

party, and how abominably wicked they were, whom such a scandalous action tied the faster to him. And we may farther learn, how corrupt the body of the people was, how ripe for that judgment which is now hastening to them.

22. The top - Of the king's palace, the very place from whence David had gazed upon Bathsheba, chap. xi, 2, so that his sin was legible in the very place of his punishment. Went in - To one, or some of them. And by so doing did farther make claim to the kingdom; and, as it were, take possession of it. It being usual in the eastern countries to account the wives and concubines of the late king, to belong of right to the successor. Israel - Who saw him go into the tent; and thence concluded, that he lay with them, as he had designed to do. God had threatened by Nathan, that for his defiling Bathsheba, David's own wives should be defiled in the face of the sun. This is now fulfilled: the Lord is righteous; and no word of his shall fall to the ground.

23. The counsel, &c. - It was received by the people with equal veneration, and was usually attended with as certain success. Which is mentioned as the reason why a counsel which had so ill a face, should meet with such general approbation.

XVII

Ahithophel advises Absalom to dispatch, ver. 1-4 Hushai advises deliberation, and his advice is received, ver. 5-14. Intelligence is sent to David, ver. 15-21. David passes over Jordan, ver. 22. Ahithophel hangs himself, ver. 23. Absalom pursues David, ver. 24-26. David is supplied with necessaries, ver. 27-29.

2. And I will, &c. - That such a wretch as Absalom should aim at his father's throat is not strange. But that the body of the people, to whom David had been so great a blessing, should join with him in it, is amazing. But the finger of God was in it. Let not the best of parents, or the best of princes think it strange, if they are injured by those who should be their support and joy, when they (like David) have provoked God to turn against them.

5. Call Hushai - A wonderful effect of Divine Providence, influencing his heart, that he could not rest in Ahithophel's counsel, though it was so evidently wise, and approved by the general consent of his whole party; and that he should desire Hushai's advice, though neither his reputation for wisdom was equal to Ahithophel's, nor had he yet given anyone proof of his fidelity to Absalom. But there is no contending with that God who can arm a man against himself, and destroy him by his own mistakes and passions.

9. Pit - Having been often accustomed to that course, and well acquainted with in all hiding-places from Saul's time. In one of them, unknown to us, he will lurk with some of his chosen men, and lie in ambush for us; and, when they see a fit opportunity, they will suddenly come forth and surprize some of our men, when they least expect it, and probably at first put them to flight. Some - Namely, of Absalom's men sent against David. At the first - Implying, that their good success at first would mightily animate David's men to proceed vigourously in the fight, and intimidate Absalom's army, and consequently would be both a presage and an occasion of their total defeat.

11. I counsel - His pretense was, that they might make sure, though slow work: his design was to gain David time, that he might increase his army, and make better provision for the battle; and that the present heat of the people might be cooled, and they might bethink themselves of their duty, and return to their allegiance. Thou - For thy presence will put life and courage into thy soldiers, who will be ambitious to shew their skill and courage in defending thy person, when they know that all their actions are observed by him who hath the distribution of rewards and punishments in his hands. Besides, the glory of the victory will be wholly thine, which now Ahithophel seeks to get to himself.

12. As dew - That is, plenteously, suddenly, irresistibly, and on all sides; for so the dew falls.

13. Bring ropes - It is an hyperbolical expression, suited to the vain-glorious temper of this insolent young man: implying, that they would do so if they could not destroy him another way: or, that they should be enough to do so, if there were occasion. River - Adjoining to the city; it being usual to build cities near some river, both for defense, and for other accommodations.

14. Absalom and all, &c. - Be it observed, to the comfort of all that fear God, he turns all mans hearts as the rivers of water. He stands in the congregation of the mighty, has an over-ruling hand in all counsels, and a negative voice in all resolves, and laughs at mens projects against his children.

16. Lodge not - Lest the king's and people's mind's change, and Ahithophel persuade the king to pursue you speedily.

17. Enrogel - Or, the fullers well. A place near Jerusalem, Josh. xv, 7; xviii, 16. Wench - Pretending to go thither to wash some cloaths, or to draw water.

19. Spread corn - Under pretense of drying it by the sun: which shews it was summer-time.

20. Over the brook of water - That is, over Jordan. This was a manifest lie.

23. Hanged himself - See here contempt poured upon the wisdom of man! He that was more

renowned for policy than ever any man was, played the fool with himself more than ever any man did. See likewise honour done to the justice of God! The wicked is snared in the work of his own hands.

24. *Passed* - Not speedily, but when all the men of Israel were gathered together according to Hushai's counsel.

25. *Nahash* - Nahash is the name of Jesse's wife, by whom he had this Abigail, as he had Zeruiah by another wife; so they were sisters by the father, but not by the mother.

27. *Shobi* - Who, as it may seem, disliked and disowned that barbarous action to the ambassadors; and therefore, when the rest were destroyed, was left king or governor of the residue of the Ammonites. *Machir* - See above chap. ix, 4.

29. *In* - Having been in the wilderness. Thus God sometimes makes up to his people that comfort from strangers, which they are disappointed of in their own families.

XVIII

David prepares to engage the rebels, ver. 1-5. The total defeat of Absalom, ver. 6-8. His death and burial, ver. 9-18. The news brought to David, ver. 19-32. His lamentation over Absalom, ver. 33.

5. *Deal gently* - If you conquer (which be presaged they would by God's gracious answer to his prayer for the turning of Ahithophel's counsel into foolishness,) take him prisoner, but do not kill him. Which desire proceeded, from his great indulgence towards his children: from his consciousness that he himself was the meritorious cause of this rebellion, Absalom being given up to it for the punishment of David's sins; from the consideration of his youth, which commonly makes men foolish, and subject to ill counsels: and from his piety, being loth that he should be cut off in the act of his sin without any space for repentance. But "what means, says Bp. Hall, this ill-placed mercy? Deal gently with a traitor? Of all traitors with a son? And all this for thy sake, whose crown, whose blood he hunts after? Even in the holiest parents nature may be guilty of an injurious tenderness. But was not this done in type of that unmeasurable mercy, of the true King of Israel, who prayed for his murderers, Father, forgive them! Deal gently with them for my sake!" Yea, when God sends an affliction to correct his children, it is with this charge, deal gently with them for my sake: for he knows our frame.

8. *The wood* - More people died in the wood, either through hunger, and thirst, and weariness: or, by the wild beasts, whereof great numbers were there, which, though they were driven away from the place of the main battle, yet might easily meet with them when they fled several ways: or, by falling into ditches and pits, which were in that place, ver. 17, and probably were covered with grass or wood, so that they could not see them till they fell into them: and especially by David's men, who pursued them, and killed them in the wood: and the wood is rightly said to have devoured them, because it gave the occasion to their destruction, inasmuch as the trees, and ditches, and pits, entangled them, and stopped their flight, and made them an easy prey to David's men, who followed them, and slew them in the pursuit. *The sword* - In the main battle: the sword being put for the battle, by a common figure.

9. *The servants of David* - Who, according to David's command, spared him, and gave him an opportunity to escape. *His head* - In which probably he was entangled by the hair of the head, which being very long and thick, might easily catch hold of a bough, especially when the great God directed it. Either he wore no helmet, or he had thrown it away as well as his other arms, to hasten his flight. Thus the matter of his pride was the instrument of his ruin.

15. *Slew him* - The darts did not dispatch him, and therefore they smote him again, and killed him.

18. *A pillar* - To preserve his name; whereas it had been more for his honour if his name had been buried in perpetual oblivion.

24. *Gates* - For the gates of the cities then were, as now they are, large and thick; and for the greater security, had two gates, one more outward, the other inward. Here he sat, that he might hear tidings when any came into the city.

33. *Over the gate* - Retiring himself from all men and business, that he might wholly give up himself to lamentation. *My son* - This he might speak from a deep sense of his eternal state, because he died in his sins, and because David himself had by his own sins been the occasion of his death. But it seems rather to be the effect of strong passion, causing him to speak unadvisedly with his lips.

XIX

Joab prevails on David to refrain, ver. 1-8. He is brought back to his kingdom by the men of Judah, ver. 9-15. Pardons Shimei, ver. 16-23. Restores to Mephibosheth his estate, ver. 24- 30. Barzillai is dismissed, and his son taken into David's service, ver. 31-40. The Israelites expostulate with the men of Judah, ver. 41-43.

3. *By stealth* - Not openly and triumphantly, as conquerors use to do; but secretly, as if they were

John Wesley

afraid and ashamed, lest David should see them, and look upon them with an evil eye, as those that had an hand in killing of his beloved son.

5. Hast shamed - By disappointing their just hopes of praises and rewards, and by requiting them with contempt and tacit rebukes.

6. Pleased thee - This is not be understood as exactly true; but David's carriage gave too much colour to such a suggestion; and such sharpness of speech was in a manner necessary to awaken the king out of his lethargy, and to preserve him from the impendent mischiefs.

9. At strife - Quarrelling one with another as the authors or abettors of this shameful rebellion, and discoursing privately and publickly of David's high merits, which God, being now reconciled to David, brings afresh to their memories.

10. Now therefore - The people of Israel speak thus to the elders of Israel, as appears by comparing this verse with the next. Seeing their designs for Absalom disappointed, they now repented of that undertaking, and were willing to testify so much by their forwardness to bring back David, and re-establish him.

11. Judah - Who being the abettors of Absalom's rebellion, despaired of pardon, and therefore were backward to promote the king's restoration. His house - Even to Mahanaim, where now the king's house and family is.

13. Of Joab - Who, besides his other crimes, had lately exasperated the king by his murder of Absalom, contrary to David's express command. And therefore the king having now the opportunity of another person who had a greater interest than Joab, gladly complies with it, that so he might both chastise Joab for his faults, and rescue himself from the bondage in which Joab had hitherto held him.

14. He bowed - David by this prudent and kind message and his free offer of pardon.

17. With him - Whom he brought, partly to shew his interest in the people, and partly, as intercessors on his behalf, and as witnesses of David's clemency or severity, that in him they might see what the rest of them might expect. Ziba - Who, being conscious of his former abuse of David, and of his master Mephibosheth, which he knew the king would understand, designed to sweeten David's spirit towards him, by forwardness in meeting him.

20. House of Joseph - The house of Joseph is here put for all the tribes, except Judah, which are fitly distinguished from Judah, because the rights of the first-born were divided between Judah and Joseph, 1 Chron. v, 2. And though Benjamin, after the division of the kingdoms was fitly joined with Judah, because then they adhered to that tribe; yet before that time it was joined with Joseph, because they marched under the standard of the house of Joseph, or of Ephraim, Num. x, 22, 23, 24. Whence it is, that Ephraim, Benjamin, and Manasseh, are put together, Psalm lxxx, 2.

22. Adversaries - That is, that you put me upon things unfit for me to do, and contrary to my interest; for it was David's interest at this time to appease the people, and reconcile them to him, and not to give them any new distaste by acts of severity: for this would make others jealous, that he would watch an opportunity to be revenged on them. King - Is not my kingdom, which was in a manner wholly lost, just now restored and assured to me? And when God hath been so merciful to me in forgiving my sin, shall I shew myself revengeful to Shemei? Shall I sully the publick joy and glory of this day, with an act of such severity? Or, shall I alienate the hearts of my people from me, now they are returning to me?

24. The son - That is, the grandson, chap. vi, 3, 6. His feet - By washing his feet, which was usual in those hot climates, and very refreshing; and therefore now neglected, as becoming a mourner. Beard - But suffered it to grow very long, and disorderly, as was usual with persons in a forlorn, or mournful state. Clothes - His linen cloathes. This and the former were signs, that he was a true and obstinate mourner, and evidences of the falsehood of Ziba's relation concerning him, chap. xvi, 3.

25. Jerusalem - Probably he had continued near Jerusalem, because he could not go to meet him, as others did.

26. Deceived me - By carrying away the ass which I bid him saddle for me.

27. Angel - To distinguish between true reports and calumnies; See note on "chap. xiv, 20".

28. Before - Before thy tribunal: we were all at thy mercy: not my estate only but my life also was in thy power, if thou hadst dealt with rigor, and as earthly kings use to do with their predecessor's and enemies children. To cry - For the vindication of mine honour, and the restitution of my estate.

29. Divide - The land shall be divided between thee and him, as it was by my first order, chap. ix, 10, he and his sons managing it, and supporting themselves out of it, as they did before, and giving the rest of the profits thereof to thee.

35. I am, &c. - My senses are grown dull, and incapable of relishing the pleasures of a court. I am past taking pleasures in delicious tastes, or sweet musick, and other such delights. I am through age both useless and burdensome to others, and therefore most improper for a court life.

37. That I may die in mine own city - That my bones may with little ado, be carried to the place of their rest. The grave is ready for me: let me go and get ready for it, go and die in my nest.

40. Half - Whereas the men of Judah came entirely and unanimously to the king, the Israelites of

the other tribe came in but slowly, and by halves, as being no less guilty of the rebellion, than the tribe of Judah; but not encouraged to come in by such a gracious message as they were. And this is here mentioned as the occasion both of the contention here following, and of the sedition, chap. xx, 1-22.

41. All - Such as were present. Stolen - That is, conveyed thee over Jordan hastily, not expecting our concurrence. David's men - All thy officers, guards, and soldiers. This is mentioned as an aggravation of their fault, that they did not only carry the king over Jordan, but all his men too, without asking their advice.

42. Of kin - Of the same tribe with us, and therefore both oweth the more respect to us, and might expect more respect from us. Gifts - We have neither sought nor gained any advantage to ourselves hereby, but only discharged our duty to the king, and used all expedition in bringing him back, which you also should have done, and not have come in by halves, and so coldly as you have done.

43. Ten - They say but ten, though strictly there were eleven; either, because they accounted Joseph (which comprehends both Ephraim and Manasseh under it) for one tribe, or because Simeon, whose lot lay within the tribe of Judah, were joined with them in this action. More right - As in the general we have more right in the king and kingdom; so particularly, we have more right in David than you, because you were the first beginners, and the most zealous promoters of this rebellion; howsoever, as he is king, we justly claim a greater interest in him, than you; inasmuch as we are the far greatest part of his subjects. Fiercer - Instead of mollifying them with gentle words, they answered them with greater fierceness so that David durst not interpose in the matter.

XX

A new rebellion raised by Sheba, ver. 1, 2. David confines his ten concubines for life, ver. 3. Joab murders Amasa, ver. 4-12. Pursues Sheba to Abel, ver. 13-15. He is delivered up, ver. 16-22. David's great officers, ver. 23-26.

1. Happened - His presence was casual in itself, though ordered by God's providence. No part - The tribe of Judah have monopolized the king to themselves, and will not allow us any share in him; let them therefore enjoy him alone, and let us seek out a new king. The son of Jesse - An expression of contempt, implying that he was no more to be owned as their king, but as a private person, as the son of Jesse. To his tents - Let us all desist from this unthankful office, of bringing the king back, and go each to our homes, that we may consider, and then meet together to chuse a new king.

2. Every man - That is, the generality of those Israelites who were present.

5. Tarried - Either, because the people being wearied out by the late war, were not forward to engage in another: or because the soldiers had more affection to Joab, than to their new general.

6. Abishai - Not to Joab; lest by this means he should recover his place, and Amasa be discontented, and David's fidelity in making good his promise to Amasa be questioned.

7. Joab's men - The remainders of Joab's army who were there present, with whom also Joab might go as a reformade, watching an opportunity to do what he designed.

8. Amasa went - Having gathered some forces, and given due orders for the rest to follow him, he returned to Jerusalem, and by the king's command went after those mentioned ver. 7, and being come up to them at the place where they waited for him, he put himself in the head of Joab's men, and the Cherethites and the Pelethites, and such as he had brought along with him, and marched before them as their general. Girded - After the manner of travelers and soldiers. Went forth - To meet and salute Amasa, who was coming towards him to do him honour. It fell - Things having (it is likely) been so contrived by Joab, that upon the least motion of his body, his sword should drop out, and he might take it up without raising Amasa's suspicion.

9. Beard - As the manner of ancient times was, when they saluted one another.

10. The sword - Which falling out, as it seemed, casually, he supposed that Joab intended only to put it into its scabbard, and therefore took no care to defend himself against the stroke. So Joab - Who now boldly resumed his former place, and marched in the head of the army. It is not strange, that Amasa's soldiers did not fight to revenge his death; partly, because not many of them were yet come up, as the following verses shew; and partly, because Joab's interest and authority with the military-men was very great; especially, with David's guards, who were here present, and who had no kindness for Amasa, as having been the general of the rebellious army; and, as they might think, not fit to be put into a place of so great trust.

11. One - Left there on purpose to deliver the following message. favoureth Joab - He that would have Joab to be general, rather than such a perfidious rebel as Amasa. For David - He that wisheth David good success against Sheba, and against all rebels.

12. Stood still - Wondering at the spectacle, and enquiring into the author and occasion of it. Removed - Perceiving, that it both incensed them against Joab and hindered the king's service. Cast a cloth upon him - But the covering of blood with a cloth cannot stop its cry to God for vengeance.

14. He - Sheba, who marched from tribe to tribe to stir them up to sedition. Abel - Unto Abel-beth-maachah, as this place is called here in the Hebrew text, ver. 15, to distinguish it from other Abels; and to signify, that this was that Abel which was in the northern border of Canaan towards that part of Syria called Maachah, chap. x, 8. Berites - Such as lived in the city, or territory of Beeroth of Benjamin, Josh. xviii, 25, who being of the same tribe, if not city with Sheba, adhered to him, and followed him through all the tribes of Israel. They - The tribes of Israel; that is, a considerable number of them; as might well be expected, when the discontents were so high and general.

15. They - That is, Joab and his army. A bank - From whence they might either batter the wall, or shoot at those who defended it. It stood - The bank stood in, or near to the trench, or the wall of the city; so that the city was in great danger of being taken.

16. Then cried a wise woman - It seems none of all the men of Abel, offered to treat with Joab: no, not when they were reduced to extremity: but one wise woman saved the city. Souls know no difference of sex: many a manly heart is lodged in a female breast. Nor is the treasure of wisdom the less valuable, for being lodged in the weaker vessel.

18. Ask counsel - This city which thou art about to destroy, is no mean and contemptible one, but so honourable and considerable for its wisdom, that when any differences arose among any of the neighbours, they used proverbially to say, We will ask the opinion and advice as the men of Abel about it, and we will stand to their arbitration; and so all parties were satisfied, and disputes ended.

19. A mother - Great cities are commonly called mothers; as lesser towns or villages subject to them, and depending upon them, are called their daughters. Inheritance - That is, a considerable part of, that land which God hath chosen for his particular possession. The destruction which thou art about to bring upon us, is an injury to Israel, and to the God of Israel.

21. Ephraim - Probably mount Ephraim was a place in Benjamin so called, either because it was upon the borders of Ephraim or for some notable action or event of the Ephraimites in that place. His head - Which she undertook, because she knew the present temper of the citizens, and soldiers too. And it is not unlikely, that this woman might be a governess in that city. For though this office was commonly performed by men; yet women were sometimes employed in the government: as we see in Deborah, who judged Israel, Judg. iv, 4.

22. Wisdom - Prudently treated with them about it, representing to them the certainty and nearness of their ruin, if they did not speedily comply with her desires, and certain deliverance if they did.

23 Over all the host - The good success of this, and of the former expedition, under the conduct of Joab, had so fixed his interest in the army, and others of David's fastest friends, that the king could not without danger displace him.

XXI

A famine, caused by Saul's killing the Gibeonites, ver. 1-3. Seven of his family put to death, ver. 4-9. Care taken of their dead bodies, and of the bones of Saul, ver. 10-14. Battles with the Philistines, ver. 15-22.

1. Then - The things related here and chap. xxiv, 1-25, are by the best interpreters conceived to have been done long before Absalom's rebellion. And this opinion is not without sufficient grounds: first, this particle, then, is here explained, in the days, that is, during the reign of David: which general words seem to be added as an intimation that these things were not done after the next foregoing passages, for then the sacred writer would rather have added, after these things, as it is in many other places. Secondly, here are divers passages which it seems improbable to ascribe to the last years of David's reign: such as first, that Saul's sin against the Gibeonites should so long remain unpunished. And indeed that this was done, and Saul's seven sons hanged by David's order before that time, seems to be intimated by that passage, chap. xvi, 8, where he is charged with the blood of the house of Saul: for which there was not the least colour 'till this time. Secondly, that David should not remove the bones of Saul and Jonathan to their proper place, 'till that time. Thirdly, that the Philistines should wage war with David again and again, ver. 15, &c. so long after he had fully subdued them, chap. viii, 1, and that David in his old age should attempt to fight with a Philistine giant, or that his people should suffer him to do so. Fourthly, that David should then have so vehement a desire to number his people, chap. xxiv, 1, which being an act of youthful vanity, seems not at all to agree with his old age, nor with that state of deep humiliation in which he then was. And the reason why these matters are put here out of their proper order, is plainly this, because David's sin being once related, it was very convenient that David's punishments should immediately succeed: this being very frequent in scripture-story, to put those things together which belong to one matter, though they happened at several times. He flew - Which was not only an act of cruelty, but also of perfidiousness, because it was a public violation of that solemn oath given to them by Joshua and the princes, in the name of all the Israelites, of that and succeeding generations. "But why did not God punish Saul whilst he was alive for this, but his children, and the

Israelites of this age?" First, God did severely punish Saul for this and his other sins. Secondly, as God may justly inflict temporal punishments upon any offender, either in his person, or in his posterity, when he pleaseth; so it is meet he should take his own time for it; and it is folly in us to quarrel with God for so doing. Thirdly, the Israelites might sundry ways make themselves guilty of Saul's sin, tho' it be not particularly mentioned, advising or encouraging him to it; or, assisting him in the execution of it. And whereas many of the people were probably innocent of that crime, yet they also were guilty of many other sins, for which God might punish them, though he took this occasion for it.

2. Sought - That is, he sought how he might cut them off with some colour of justice, aggravating their faults, and punishing them worse than they deserved; oppressing them with excessive labours, and intending by degrees to wear them out.

6. I will - Having doubtless consulted God in the matter; who as he had before declared Saul's bloody house to be the causes of this judgment, so now commanded that justice should be done upon it, and that the remaining branches of it should be cut off; as sufficiently appears from hence, that God was well pleased with the action; which he would not have been, if David had done it without his command; for then it had been a sinful action of David's, and contrary to a double law of God, Deut. xxi, 23; xxiv, 16.

7. Spared - For the Gibeonites desiring only such a number, it was at David's choice whom to spare. Of Jonathan - This is added, to distinguish him from the other Mephibosheth, ver. 8.

10. Spread it - As a tent to dwell in: being informed that their bodies were not to be taken away speedily, as the course of the law was in ordinary cases, but were to continue there until God was intreated, and removed the present judgment. On the rock - In some convenient place in a rock, near adjoining. Until water - Until they were taken down: which was not to be done 'till God had given rain as a sign of his favour, and a mean to remove the famine, which was caused by the want of it. Thus she let the world know, that her sons died not for any sin of their own, not as stubborn and rebellious sons, whose eye had despised their mother: but for their father's sin, and therefore her mind could not be alienated from them by their hard fate.

11. David - Who heard it with so much approbation, that he thought fit to imitate her piety, being by her example provoked to do what hitherto he had neglected, to bestow an honourable interment on the remains of Saul and Jonathan, and, with them, upon those that are now put to death, that the honour done to them herein, might be some comfort to this disconsolate widow.

13. The bones - Having first burnt off the flesh which remained upon them when they were taken down. Compare 1 Sam. xxxi, 10, &c.

14. After that - After those things were done which were before related; that is, after they were hanged up: for by that God was pacified, and not by their burial.

18. After this - After the battle last mentioned.

22. Born to the giant in Gath - These giants were probably the remains of the sons of Anak, who, tho' long feared, fell at last.

XXII

This chapter is inserted among the Psalms, No. 18, with some little variation. It is here as it was composed for his own closet; there, as it was delivered to the chief musician for public service. The inspired writer having largely related David's deliverances in this and the foregoing book, thought fit to record this sacred poem, as a memorial of all that had been before related

XXIII

The last words of David, ver. 1-7. An account of his mighty men, the first three, ver. 8-12. Two of the next three, ver. 13-23. And the thirty, ver. 24-39.

1. Last words - Not simply the last that he spoke, but the last which he spake by the spirit of God, assisting and directing him in an extraordinary manner. When we find death approaching, we should endeavour both to honour God, and to profit others with our last words. Let those who have had experience of God's goodness, and the pleasantness of the ways of wisdom, when they come to finish their course, leave a record of those experiences, and bear their testimony to the truth of the promise. Raised - Advanced from an obscure estate, to the kingdom. Whom, God singled out from all the families of Israel, and anointed to be king. Psalmist - He who was eminent among the people of God, for composing sweet and holy songs to the praise of God, and for the use of his church in after ages: these seem not to be the words of David, but of the sacred penman of this book.

2. His word - The following words, and consequently the other words and Psalms composed and uttered by me upon the like solemn occasions, are not to be looked upon as human inventions, but both the matter and the words of them are suggested by God's spirit, the great teacher of the church.

John Wesley

3. Rock - He who is the strength, and defense, and protector of his people; which he manifests by directing kings and rulers so to manage their power as may most conduce to their comfort and benefit. Ruleth - Here are the two principal parts of a king's duty, answerable to the two tables of God's law, justice towards men, and piety towards God, both which he is to maintain and promote among his people.

4. Shall be - These words are a farther description of the king's duty, which is not only to rule with justice and piety, but also with sweetness, and gentleness, and condescension to the infirmities of his people; to render his government as acceptable to them, as is the sun-shine in a clear morning, or the tender grass which springs out of the earth by the warm beams of the sun after the rain.

5. Altho' - Although God knows, that neither I, nor my children have lived and ruled as we should have done, so justly, and in the fear of the Lord; and therefore have not enjoyed that uninterrupted prosperity which we might have enjoyed. Covenant - Notwithstanding all our transgressions whereby we have broken covenant with God, yet God, to whom all my sins were known, was graciously pleased to make a sure covenant, to continue the kingdom to me, and to my seed forever, chap. vii, 16, until the coming of the Messiah who is to be my son and successor, and whose kingdom shall have no end. Ordered - Ordained in all points by God's eternal counsel; and disposed by his wise and powerful providence which will over-rule all things, even the sins of my house so far, that although he punished them for their sins, yet he will not utterly root them out, nor break his covenant made with me and mine. Sure - Or, preserved, by God's power and faithfulness in the midst of all oppositions. For this - Or, in this is, that is, it consists in, and depends upon this covenant. Salvation - Both mine own eternal salvation, and the preservation of the kingdom to me and mine. Tho' - Although God as yet hath not made my house or family to grow; that is, to increase, or to flourish with worldly glory as I expected; yet this is my comfort, that God will inviolably keep this covenant. But this refers also to the covenant of grace made with all believers. This is indeed an everlasting covenant, from everlasting, in the contrivance of it, and to everlasting, in the continuance and the consequence of it. It is ordered, well ordered in all things; admirably well, to advance the glory of God and the honour of the mediator, together with the holiness and happiness of believers. It is sure, and therefore sure, because well-ordered: the promised mercies are sure, on the performance of the conditions. It is all our salvation: nothing but this will save us, and this is sufficient. Therefore it should be all our desire. Let me have an interest in this covenant, and I have enough, I desire no more.

6. But - Having in the foregoing verses described the nature, and stability of that kingdom which God had by a sure covenant settled upon him and his seed; and especially, upon the Messiah, who was to be one of his posterity; he now describes the nature and miserable condition, of all the enemies of this holy and blessed kingdom. As thorns - Which men do not use to handle, but thrust them away. And so will God thrust away from himself, and from his people, and kingdom, all those who shall either secretly or openly set themselves against it.

7. Fenced - He must arm himself with some iron weapon, whereby he may cut them down; or, with the staff of a spear, or some such thing, whereby he may thrust them away from himself, that they do him no hurt. Burnt - Or, if they do not cut them down or thrust them away they will burn and consume them. The place - Or, in their place, where they grow or stand.

8. These - But this catalogue, though placed here, was taken long before, as is manifest from hence, that Asahel and Uriah are named here. And whereas there are some difference between this list, and that, 1 Chron. xi, 10-47, most of them are easily reconciled by these two considerations;

1. that nothing is more common than for one person to have divers names.

2. That as some of the worthies died, and others came in their stead; this must needs cause some alteration in the latter catalogue, 1 Chron. xi, 10-47, from this which was the former. Learn hence, how much religion tends to inspire men with true courage. David both by his writings and example greatly promoted piety among the grandees of the kingdom. And when they became famous for piety, they became famous for bravery. Adino - This was his proper name. Lift up - Which words are fitly supplied out of 1 Chron. xi, 11, where they are expressed. One time - In one battle, which though it be strange, yet cannot seem incredible, supposing him to be a person of extraordinary strength and activity, and his enemies to be discouraged, and fleeing away.

9. Gone away - That is, fled away, 1 Chron. xi, 13, being dismayed at the approach of their enemies.

11. Lentiles - Or barley, as it is 1 Chron. xi, 13. For both might grow in the same field, in divers parts of it. And this fact is ascribed to Eleazar, 1 Chron. xi, 12, but it is implied, that he had some partner or partners in it; for it is there said, 1 Chron. xi, 14 they set themselves, &c. So Eleazar might fight in that part where the barley was and Shammah where the lentiles were.

12. Lord wrought - How great soever the bravery of the instruments is, the praise of the achievement is to be given to God. These fought, but God wrought the victory.

15. Said - Being hot and thirsty, he expresses how acceptable a draught of that water would be to

him; but was far from desiring, or expecting that any of his men should hazard their lives to procure it.

16. Would not - Lest by gratifying himself upon such terms, he should seem either to set too high a price upon the satisfaction of his appetite, or too low a price upon the lives of his soldiers. Poured it - As a kind of drink offering, and acknowledgment of God's goodness in preserving the lives of his captains in so dangerous an enterprize; and to shew, that he esteemed it as a sacred thing, which it was not fit for him to drink.

17. These three - Jointly: then two of them are mentioned severally.

19. Attained not - He fell short of them in strength and valour.

21. Pit - Where he put himself under a necessity, either of killing, or being killed. Of snow - When lions are most fierce, both from the sharpness of their appetite in cold seasons, and from want of provisions.

25. Harodite - In 1 Chron. xi, 27, Shammoth the Harorite. Concerning which, and other changes of the names, which will be observed, by comparing this catalogue with that, it will be sufficient to suggest,

1. that the same names of persons, or places, are differently pronounced according to the different dialects of divers places or ages.

2. That one man had often two names.

3. That David had more worthies than those here mentioned; and as some of these were slain in the former part of David's reign, as Asahel was; so others came up in their stead; and some were added to this number, as appears from 1 Chron. xi, 10-47, where they are named, but not numbered, as they were here; and where there is a greater number than is here expressed.

John Wesley

NOTES ON THE FIRST BOOK OF KINGS

THE two books of Samuel are an introduction to the two books of Kings, as they relate the original of the royal government in Saul, and of the royal family in David. These two books give us an account of David's successor, Solomon, the division of his kingdom, and the several kings of Israel and Judah, down to the captivity. And in these special regard is had to the house of David, from which Christ came. Some of his sons trod in his steps, and their reigns were usually long, whereas those of the wicked kings were usually short: so that the state of Judah (in Israel all the kings were wicked) was not so bad as it would otherwise have been. In this first book we have, The death of David, chap. 1, 2. The glorious reign of Solomon, chap. 3-10. His defection, chap. 11. The division of the kingdom between Rehoboam and Jeroboam, chap. 12-14. The reigns of Abijah and Asa over Judah, of Basha and Omni over Israel, chap. 15, 16. The history of Elijah, chap. 17-19. Ahab's success, wickedness, and death, chap. 20-22.

I

David declines in health, ver. 1-4. Adonijah aspires to the kingdom, ver. 5-10. Nathan and Bathsheba procure an order for the succession of Solomon, ver. 11-31. The anointing of Solomon, and the peoples joy, ver. 32-40. The dispersion of Adonijah's party, ver. 41-49. Solomon dismisses Adonijah, ver. 50-53.

1. Old - Being in the end of his seventieth year. No heat - Which is not strange in a person who had been exercised with so many hardships in war, and with such tormenting cares, and fears, and sorrows, for his own sins (as divers of his Psalms witness) and for the sins and miseries of his children and people. Besides, this might be from the nature of his bodily distemper.

2. Servants - His physicians. Virgin - Whose natural heat is fresh and wholesome, and not impaired with bearing or breeding of children. The same counsel doth Galen give for the cure of some cold and dry distempers. Stand - That is, minister unto him, or wait upon him, in his sickness, as occasion requires. Lie in his bosom - As his wife: for that she was so, may appear by divers arguments. First, otherwise this had been a wicked course; which therefore neither his servants durst have prescribed, nor would David have used, especially being now in a dying condition. Secondly, it appears from this phrase of lying in his bosom, which is everywhere in scripture mentioned as the privilege of a wife. Thirdly, this made Adonijah's crime in desiring her to wife, so heinous in Solomon's account, because he saw, that by marrying the king's wife he designed to revive his pretense to the kingdom.

4. Knew her not - Which is mentioned to note the continuance and progress of the king's malady.

5. Then - Upon notice of the desperateness of the king's disease, and the approach of his death. Exalted - Entertained high thoughts and designs. I will - As the right of the kingdom is mine, ver. 6, so I will now take possession of it. Prepared - As Absalom had done upon the like occasion, chap. xv, 1.

6. Displeased him - This is noted as David's great error, and the occasion of Adonijah's presumption. Saying - He neither restrained him from, nor reproved him for his miscarriages: which David well knew was a great sin. Goodly man - This was a second ground of his confidence, because his great comeliness made him amiable in the peoples eyes.

7. They helped - Either because they thought the right of the crown was his: or to secure and advance their own interest. It seems God left them to themselves, to correct them for former miscarriages, with a rod of their own making.

10. Called not - Because he knew they favoured Solomon his competitor.

11. Nathan spake - Being prompted to it both by his piety in fulfilling the will of God declared to him, concerning Solomon's succession, 2 Sam. vii, 13, and by his prudence, knowing that Adonijah hated him for being the principal instrument of Solomon's advancement. Bathsheba - Who being retired and private in her apartment, was ignorant of what was done abroad: and, who was likely to be most zealous in the cause, and most prevalent with David.

26. But me - Whom he knew to be acquainted with thy mind, and with the mind of God in this matter: and therefore his neglect of me herein gives me cause to suspect that this is done without thy privity.

27. Shewed thy servant - Who, having been an instrument in delivering God's message to thee concerning thy successor, might reasonably expect that if the king had changed his mind, thou wouldest have acquainted me with it, as being both a prophet os the Lord, and one whom thou hast always found faithful to thee.

28. Call Bathsheba - Who, upon Nathan's approach to the king had modestly withdrawn.

29. Out of all distress - The words contain a grateful acknowledgement of the goodness of God to him, in bringing him safe through the many difficulties, which had lain in his way, and which he now mentions to the glory of God, (as Jacob when he lay a dying) thus setting to his seal, from his own experience that the Lord redeemeth the souls of his servants.

31. Live forever - Though I desire thy oath may be kept, and the right of succession confirmed to my son, yet I am far from thirsting after thy death, and would rather rejoice, if it were possible for thee to live and enjoy the crown forever. 33. My mule - As a token that the royal dignity is transferred upon Solomon, and that by my consent. Gihon - A river near Jerusalem, on the west side. Adonijah was inaugurated on the east side. This place David chose, either, as remote from Adonijah and his company, that so the people might be there without fear of tumults or bloodshed; or, to shew that Solomon was chosen king in opposition to Adonijah: or, because this was a place of great resort, and fit to receive and display that numerous company, which he knew would follow Solomon thither.

34. Anoint - As they used to do where there was any thing new or extraordinary in the succession. And this unction signified both the designation of the persons to the office, and the gifts and graces which were necessary for their office, and which, they, seeking them sincerely from God, might expect to receive.

35. My stead - My deputy and vice-king whilst I live, and absolutely king when I die. And Judah - This is added, lest the men of Judah, who were in a special manner invited by Adonijah, ver. 9, might think themselves exempted from his jurisdiction.

47. Bowed himself - Adoring God for this great mercy, and thereby declaring his hearty consent to this action.

48. Blessed, &c. - It is a great satisfaction to good men, when they are going out of the world, to see their children rising up in their stead, to serve God and their generation: and especially to see peace upon Israel, and the establishment of it.

51. His servants - He owns Solomon as his king, and himself as his servant and subject; and being sensible of his guilt, and of the jealousy which kings have of their competitors, could not be satisfied without Solomon's oath.

53. Go to thine house - Lead a private life, without noise and numerous attendants, and meddle not with the affairs of the kingdom.

II

David's charge to Solomon ver. 1-9. His death and burial, with the beginning of Solomon's reign, ver. 10-12. He puts Adonijah to death, ver. 13-25. Deposes Abiathar from the high-priesthood, ver. 26, 27. Puts Joab to death, ver. 28-35. Confines Shimei, to Jerusalem, ver. 36-38. Puts him to death, ver. 39-46.

2. I go the way, &c. - Even the sons and heirs of heaven, must go the way of all the earth, of all who dwell thereon. But they walk with pleasure in this way, thro' the valley of the shadow of death. Prophets, yea kings must go this way to brighter light and honour than prophecy or sovereignty. Be strong - For, to govern his people according to the law of God, requires great fortitude, or strength of mind. And a man - In manly wisdom, and courage, and constancy, though thou art but young in years.

3. The law - Which the prince was enjoined to transcribe and read, Deut. xvii, 11, that be might govern his own and his peoples actions by it. Mayest profit - Or, behave thyself prudently. Hereby he intimates, that religion is the truest reason of state, and that all true wisdom and good success depend upon piety.

4. Confirm his word - Fulfil his promise, the condition upon which it was suspended, being performed.

5. To me - That is, against me; in what he did against Abner and Amasa: whose death was a great injury to David, as it was a breach of his laws and peace; a contempt of his person and government; a pernicious example to his subjects, and a great scandal to him, as if Joab had been only David's instrument, to affect what he secretly designed. And shed - He slew them as if they had been in the state of war, when there was not only a cessation of arms, but also a treaty of peace. Put the blood - This is added to note his impenitency, that although by his perfidious manner of killing them when he pretended to embrace them, he stained his own garments with their blood, yet he was not ashamed of it, but gloried in it, and marched boldly along with the army, with the same girdle and shoes which were sprinkled with their blood.

6. Do therefore - That is, what in reason and justice thou seest fit. For tho' I was forced to forbear him, yet I never forgave him; punish him according to his demerits.

7. For so - With such kindness.

8. I will not, &c. - The words are, The king said unto Shimei, thou shalt not die: and the king swear unto him, 2 Sam. xix, 23. The oath, we see, was absolute. It was not, "I will not put thee to death now." or, "I will not put thee to death with the sword." But who can reconcile his charge to Solomon with this oath? Surely, considering the time of that charge, this next to the matter of Uriah, is the greatest blemish in all David's life.

25. Benaiah - For the execution of justice was not then committed to obscure persons, as now it is; but to persons of great honour and authority. It is far from clear, that Solomon did right herein, or that Adonijah had any ill design in asking Abishag.

26. Because, &c. - Thus Solomon shews respect to his sacred function. He mixes mercy with justice, and requites Abiathar's former kindness to David; hereby teaching princes, that they should not write injuries in marble, and benefits in sand, as they have been so often observed to do.

27. Which he spake - Concerning the translation of the priesthood from the house of Eli, and of Ithamar, to that of Eleazar: which being threatened eighty years ago, is now executed. So divine vengeance, though sometimes it be slow, is always sure.

30. He said, Nay, &c. - For he supposed, either, that Solomon would not defile that place with his blood, but would spare him for his respect to it, as he had done Adonijah: or, he had a superstitious conceit, that his dying there might give his guilty and miserable soul some advantage.

31. Do, &c. - Kill him, though he be there; take him from that place, and then kill him: for, Exod. xxi, 14, doth not command the ruler to kill the murderer there, but to remove him thence, to take him from the altar, that he may die.

34. Wilderness - Places which have but few houses and inhabitants, are often so called in scripture. He was buried privately, like a criminal, not pompously, like a general.

36. Go not forth - This Solomon ordered, both for his own security; and as a penalty for his former wickedness.

37. Kidron - A brook nigh Jerusalem, which he particularly names, because that was the way to Bahurim, his former habitation: but this is not all, for the restraint was general, that he should not go forth thence any whither. Thy blood - The blame and guilt of thy blood shall lie upon thyself only.

38. Is good - Thy sentence is more merciful than I expected, or deserved.

39. Achish - A king, but subject and tributary, to Solomon. Permitted to enjoy the title and honour of a king, but not the full power; whence it was, that Achish could not keep these servants though they had fled to him for protection; but suffered Shimei to take them away from his royal city.

40. To seek his servants - By "seeking his servants, says Bp. Hall, he lost himself. These earthly things either are, or should be our servants. How commonly do we see men run out of the bounds set by God's laws, to hunt after them, till their souls incur a fearful judgment."

44. Thine heart - For which thine own conscience accuseth thee, and there is no need of other witnesses. The Lord - God hath punished thee for thy former wickedness, by suffering thee to expose thyself to thy deserved death.

III

Solomon marries Pharaoh's daughter, ver. 1. His religion, ver. 2-4. His prayer for wisdom, and the answer, ver. 5-15. He decides the dispute between the two harlots, ver. 16-28.

1. Pharaoh - As being a powerful neighbour, whose daughter doubtless was first instructed in, and proselyted to the Jewish religion. It seems, this was designed by God to be a type of Christ, calling his church to himself, and to the true religion, not only out of the Jews, but even out of the Gentile world. City of David - Into David's palace there. The wall - Which though in some sort built by David, yet Solomon is here said to build, either because he made it higher, and stronger, in which sense Nebuchadnezzar is said to have built Babylon, Dan. iv, 30, or because he built another wall besides the former, for after this time Jerusalem was encompassed with more walls than one.

2. Only - This particle is used here, and ver. 3, as an exception to Solomon's integrity and as a blemish to his government, That he himself both permitted and practiced this which was expressly forbidden, Levit xvii, 3, 4 Deut. xii, 13, 14. High places - Which were groves, or other convenient places upon hills, in which the patriarchs used to offer up their sacrifices to God; and from them this custom was derived both to the Gentiles and the Jews: and in them the Gentiles sacrificed to idols, the Hebrew to the true God. Because, &c. - Which reason was not sufficient, for there was a tabernacle, to which they were as much confined as to the temple, Exod. xl, 34-38, &c.

3. Yet - Although he miscarried in the matter of high places, yet in the general, his heart was right with God. Statutes - According to the statutes or commands of God, which are here called the statutes of

David; not only because they were diligently practiced by David, but also because the observation of them was so earnestly pressed upon Solomon, and fortified with David's authority and command.

6. Truth - In the true worship of God, in the profession, belief, practice and defense of the true religion. So truth here contains all duties to God, as righteousness doth his duties to men, and uprightness the right manner of performing both sorts of duties. With thee - That is, in thy judgment, to whom he often appealed as the witness of his integrity.

7. Child - So he was in years: not above twenty years old; and withal (which he principally intends) he was raw and unexperienced, as a child, in state affairs. Go out, &c. - To govern my people, and manage affairs.

8. In the midst - Is set over them to rule and guide them. A metaphor from the overseer of divers workmen, who usually is in the midst of them, that he may the better observe how each of them discharges his office. Chosen - Thy peculiar people, whom thou takest special care of, and therefore wilt expect a more punctual account of my government of them.

9. An understanding heart - Whereby I may both clearly discern, and faithfully perform all the parts of my duty: for both these are spoken of in scripture, as the effects of a good understanding; and he that lives in the neglect of his duties, or the practice of wickedness, is called a fool, and one void of understanding. Discern - Namely in causes and controversies among my people; that I may not through mistake, or prejudice, or passion, give wrong sentences, and call evil good, or good evil. Absalom, that was a fool, wished himself a judge: Solomon, that was a wise man, trembles at the undertaking. The more knowing and considerate men are, the more jealous they are of themselves.

13. All thy days - Whereby he signifies that these gifts of God were not transient, as they were in Saul, but such as should abide with him whilst he lived.

14. And if - This caution God gives him, lest his wisdom should make him proud, careless, or presumptuous.

15. A dream - Not a vain dream, wherewith men are commonly deluded; but a divine dream, assuring him of the thing: which he knew, by a divine impression after he was awakened: and by the vast alteration which he presently found within himself in point of wisdom and knowledge. The ark - Which was there in the city of David, 2 Sam. vi, 17, before which he presented himself in a way of holy adoration. Burnt offerings - Chiefly for the expiation of his and his peoples sin, through the blood of Christ, manifestly signified in these sacrifices. Peace offerings - Solemnly to praise God for all his mercies, and especially for giving him quiet possession of the kingdom, and for his glorious appearance to him in the dream, and for the promise therein made to him, and the actual accomplishment of it.

16. Harlots - Or, victuallers: for the Hebrew words signifies both. Yet that they are unmarried persons, seems probable, both because there is no mention of any husbands, whose office it was, if there were any such, to contest for their wives; and because they lived a solitary life in one house.

19. Overlaid it - And so smothered it: which she justly conjectures, because there were evidences of that kind of death, but no appearance of any other cause thereof.

25. Said - Though with a design far above the reach of the two women, or of the people present, who probably with horror expected the execution of it.

27. She is the mother - As is evident from her natural affection to the child, which she had rather have given away from her, than destroyed.

28. Wisdom of God - Divine wisdom with which God had inspired him for the government of his people.

IV

Solomon's ministers of state, ver. 1-6. The purveyors of his household, ver. 7-19. The number of his subjects, and extent of his kingdom, ver. 20, 21. The provision for his table, ver. 22, 23. The peace of his subjects, ver. 24, 25. His stables, ver. 26-28. His wisdom, ver. 29-34.

1. All Israel - This is spoken with respect to his successors, who were kings only over a part, and that the smallest part of it.

2. Princes - That is, the chief rulers or officers. The son - Or the grand-son. The priest - The second priest, or the priest that attended upon Solomon's person in holy offices and administrations.

3. Scribes - That is, secretaries of state. He chose two, whereas David had but one: either, because he observed some inconveniences in trusting all those matters in one hand: or, because he had now much more employment than David had, this being a time of great peace and prosperity, and his empire enlarged.

4. Priests - That is, the high-priests, successively, first Abiathar, and then Zadok.

5. Officers - Over those twelve Officers, named ver. 7, &c. who were all to give up their accompts to him. Nathan - The prophet, who had been so highly instrumental in Solomon's establishment in the throne. Principal officer - Possibly, president of the king's council. Friend - His confident, with whom

he used to communicate his most secret counsels.

6. Abiathar was - Steward of the king's household. Tribute - The personal tribute, or the levy of men, as appears by comparing this with chap. v, 13, 14, it being very fit that there should be some one person to whom the chief conduct of that great business was committed.

8. The son, &c. - This and others of them are denominated from their fathers, because they were known and famous in their generation.

10. Hepher - In Judah.

19. Country of Gilead - That is, in the remaining part of that land of Gilead, which was mentioned above. The only officer - In all Gilead, excepting the parcels mentioned before, in all the territories of Sihon and Og; which because they were of large extent, and yet all committed to this one man, it is here noted concerning him as his privilege above the rest.

21. The river - Euphrates: for so far David, having conquered the Syrians, extended his empire, which Solomon also maintained in that extent. And so God's promise concerning the giving the whole land, as far as Euphrates, to the Israelites, was fulfilled. And, if the Israelites had multiplied so much that the land of Canaan would not suffice them, having God's grant of all the land as far as Euphrates, they might have seized upon it whensoever occasion required. The land of the Philistines - Which is to be understood inclusively; for the Philistines were within Solomon's dominion. The border of Egypt - Unto the river Sihor, which was the border between Egypt and Canaan. And served - By tribute, or other ways, as he needed and required.

22. Measures - Hebrew. Cors: each of which contained ten ephahs. So this provision was sufficient for near three thousand persons. Meal - Of a coarser sort for common use.

23. Fat - Fatted in stalls. Out of pastures - Well fleshed, tender and good, though not so fat as the former.

24. Tiphsah - Either that Tiphsah, 2 Kings xv, 16, which was in the kingdom of Israel within Jordan; or, rather, another place of that name upon Euphrates, even that eminent city which is mentioned by Ptolemy, and Strabo, and Pliny, called Thapsarum. And this best agrees with the following: Azzah, which was the border of Canaan in the south and west, as Tiphsah was in the north and east. And so his dominion is described by both its borders. All kings - Who owned subjection, and paid tribute to him.

25. Under his vine - Enjoying the fruit of his own labour with safety and comfort. Under these two trees, which were most used and cultivated by the Israelites, he understands all other fruit-bearing trees, and all other comforts. And they are brought in as fitting or dwelling under these trees, partly for recreation or delight in the shade; and partly, for the comfort or advantage of the fruit; and withal, to note their great security, not only in their strong cities, but even in the country, where the vines and fig-trees grew, which was most open to the incursions of their enemies.

26. Forty thousand - In 2 Chron. ix, 25, it is but four thousand. But it is not exactly the same Hebrew word which is here and there, though we translate both stalls; and therefore there may well be allowed some difference in the signification, the one signifying properly stables, of which there were four thousand, the other stalls or partitions for each horse, which were forty thousand. Chariots - Both for his military chariots, which seem to be those fourteen hundred, chap. x, 26, and for divers other uses, as about his great and various buildings, and merchandises, and other occasions, which might require some thousands of other chariots. Horsemen - Appointed partly for the defense of his people in peace; and partly for attendance upon his person, and for the splendour of his government.

27. The officers - Named above. They lacked - Or rather, they suffered nothing to be lacking to any man that came thither, but plentifully provided all things necessary.

29. Largeness of heart - Vastness of understanding, a most comprehensive knowledge of all things both Divine and human.

30. East country - The Chaldeans, Persians, and Arabians, who all lay eastward from Canaan, and were famous in ancient times for their wisdom and learning. Egypt - The Egyptians, whose fame was then great for their skill in the arts and sciences, which made them despise the Grecians as children in knowledge.

31. All men - Either of his nation; or, of his time: or, of all times and nations, whether of the east or any other country excepting only the first and second Adam. Ethan, &c. - Israelites of eminent wisdom, probably the same mentioned, 1 Chron. ii, 6; xv, 19; xxv, 4 Psalm 8viii, 1(title,) Psalm lxxxix, 1(title). Chalcol, &c. - Of whom see 1 Chron. ii, 6.

32. Proverbs - That is, short, and deep, and useful sentences, whereof a great part are contained in the books of Proverbs and Ecclesiastes. Songs - Whereof the chief and most divine are in the Canticles.

33. Trees - That is, of all plants, of their nature and qualities: all which discourses are lost, without any impeachment of the perfection of the holy scriptures; which were not written to teach men philosophy or physick, but only to make them wise unto salvation. From the cedar, &c. - That is, from the greatest to the least.

34. All kings - All the neighbouring kings; a restriction grounded upon the following words, where

this is limited to such as heard of Solomon's wisdom. Let those who magnify the modern learning above that of the ancients, produce such a treasury of learning, anywhere in these later ages, as that was, which Solomon was master of. Yet this puts an honour upon human learning, that Solomon is praised for it, and recommends it to the great ones of the earth, as well worthy their diligent search. In all this Solomon was a type of Christ, in whom are hid all the treasures of wisdom and knowledge.

V

Hiram congratulates Solomon on his accession, and agrees to furnish him with workmen and timber for the temple, ver. 1-9. The work is well done, and the workmen paid, ver. 10-18.

6. They - That is, thy servants. And this assistance which these Gentiles gave to the building of Solomon's temple, was a type of the calling of the Gentiles, and that they should be instrumental in building and constituting Christ's spiritual temple. Cedar-trees - Which for their soundness, and strength, and fragrancy, and durableness, were most proper for his design. Of these David had procured some, but not a sufficient number. Lebanon - Which was in Solomon's jurisdiction: and therefore he doth not desire that Hiram would give him the cedars, because they were his own already; but only that his servants might hew them for him; which the ingenious Tyrians well understood. With thy servants - Either to be employed therein as they shall direct; or to receive the cedars, from their hands, and transmit them to me. Hire - Pay them for their labour and art. Sidonians - Or Tyrians: for these places and people being near, are promiscuously used one for another.

7. Rejoiced - Being a faithful friend to David and his house, and tho' it is not probable he was a sincere proselyte, yet he had sufficient information concerning the nature and excellency of the God of Israel, and had honourable thoughts of him.

9. The sea - The mid-land sea. Floats - Or, rafts. It is thought the timber were tied together in the water, as now is usual, and so by the help of boats or ships, conveyed to the appointed place, which was at no great distance. Household - My family and court, which most properly is called his house.

11. Measures - Hebrew. twenty cors pure oil; but in 2Chr ii, 10, it is twenty thousand baths of oil. To which there is added twenty thousand measures of barley, and twenty thousand baths of wine. Either therefore, first, he speaks of several things. Or, secondly, he speaks there of what Solomon offered: for it runs thus, I will give; and here of what Hiram accepted. Or, thirdly, the barley, and wine, and twenty thousand baths of common oil, mentioned 2 Chron. ii, 10, must be added to the twenty thousand measures of wheat, and the twenty measures of pure oil here expressed, and the whole sum is to be made up from both places; that book of Chronicles being written to supply and compleat the histories of the books of Samuel, and of the Kings. Gave Hiram - Either, first, for sustenance to the workmen, during the years wherein they were employed in the cutting down and hewing of timber. Or, for the yearly support of the king's house, during the said time. Thus by the wise disposal of providence, one country has need of another, and is benefited by another, that there may be a mutual correspondence and dependence, to the glory of God our common Parent.

13. The levy - Which were to be employed in the most honourable and easy parts of the work relating to the temple; and these were Israelites; but those fifteen hundred thousand mentioned ver. 15, were strangers. If it seem strange, that so many thousands should be employed about so small a building as the temple was; it must be considered,

1. that the temple, all its parts being considered, was far larger than men imagine;

2. that it is probable, they were employed by turns, as the thirty thousand were, ver. 14, else they had been oppressed with hard and uninterrupted labours.

3. that the timber and stone hewed and carried by them, was designed, not only for the temple, but also for Solomon's own houses, and buildings; because we read of no other levy of men, nor of any care and pains taken after the building of the temple, for the procurement, or preparation of materials for his own houses, or his other buildings; nay, that this very levy of men was made and employed for the building of the Lord's house, and Solomon's house, and Millo, and the wall of Jerusalem, and Hazor, and Megiddo, and Gezer, is expressed chap. ix, 15.

16. Three thousand &c. - Whereof three thousand were set over the fifteen hundred thousand, expressed ver. 15, each of these, over fifty of them, and the odd three hundred were set over these three thousand, each of these to have the oversight of ten of them, to take an account of the work for them. But in 2 Chron. ii, 18, these overseers are said to be thirty-six hundred. The three thousand added in 2 Chron. ii, 2, might be a reserve, to supply the places of the other three thousand: yea, or of the thirty-three hundred, as any of them should be taken off from the work by death, or sickness, or weakness, or necessary occasions; which was a prudent provision, and not unusual in like cases. And so there were thirty-six hundred commissioned for the work, but only thirty-three hundred employed at one time; and therefore both computations fairly stand together.

17. Great and costly - Marble and porphyry, or other stones of great size and value. The

foundation - Where they could not afterward be seen: and therefore that this was done, is mentioned only as a point of magnificence, except it was intended for a type, or mystical signification of the preciousness of Christ, who is the foundation of the true temple, the church of God.

18. Stone-squarers - Hebrew. the Giblites, the inhabitants of Gebel, a place near Zidon, famous for artificers and architects, Josh. xiii, 5. These are here mentioned apart, distinct from the rest of Hiram's builders, as the most eminent of them.

VI

The time when the temple was built, ver. 1. The dimensions of it, ver. 2, 3. The windows, chambers, materials, doors, ver. 4-10. God's message to Solomon, ver. 11-13. The walls and flooring, ver. 14-18. The oracle and cherubim, ver. 19-30. The doors and inner court, ver. 31-36. How long it was building, ver. 37-38.

1. Four hundred and four score, &c. - Allowing forty years to Moses, seventeen to Joshua, two hundred ninety-nine to the Judges, forty to Eli, forty to Samuel and Saul, forty to David, and four to Solomon before he began the work, we have just the sum of four hundred and eighty. So long it was before that holy house was built, which in less than four hundred and thirty years was burnt by Nebuchadnezzar. It was thus deferred, because Israel by their sins, made themselves unworthy of this honour: and because God would shew how little he values external pomp and splendour in his service. And God ordered it now, chiefly to be a shadow of good things to come.

2. The house - Properly so called, as distinct from all the walls and buildings which were adjoining to it; namely, the holy, and most holy place. Length - From east, to west. And this and the other measures may seem to belong to the inside from wall to wall. Cubits - Cubits of the sanctuary. Height - Namely, of the house: for the porch was one hundred and twenty cubits high, 2 Chron. iii, 4. So that all the measures compared each with other were harmonious. For sixty to twenty (the length to the breadth) is triple: or as three to one: and sixty to thirty (the length to the height) is double, or as two to one: and thirty to twenty (the height to the breadth) is one and an half, as three to two. Which are the proportions answering to the three great concords in music, commonly called, a twelfth, an eighth, and a fifth. Which therefore must needs be a graceful proportion to the eye, as that in music is graceful to the ear.

3. The porch - In the front of, or entrance into the house, 2 Chron. iii, 4, being a portico, a walk or gallery, at one end of the building (from side to side.) And the measures of this were harmonious also. For twenty to ten (the length of the portico to the breadth of it) is double, or as two to one. And, if the height within, be the same with that of the house, that is thirty; it will be to the length of it, as three to two; and to its breadth, as three to one. Or, if we take in the whole height mentioned, 2 Chron. iii, 4, which is one hundred and twenty; there is in this no disproportion: being to its length as six to one; and to its breadth as twelve to one; especially when this height was conveniently divided into several galleries, one over another, each of which had their due proportions.

4. Narrow - Narrow outward, to prevent the inconveniences of the weather; widening by degrees inward, that so the house might better receive, and more disperse the light.

5. Against the wall - The beams of the chambers were not fastened into the wall, but leaned upon the buttresses of the wall. Chambers - For the laying the priests garments, and other utensils belonging to the temple, therein. Round about - On all the sides except the east, where the porch was; and except some very small passages for the light. And yet these lights might be in the five uppermost cubits of the wall, which were above all these chambers, for these were only fifteen cubits high, and the wall was twenty cubits high. Chambers - Galleries which encompassed all the chambers; and which were necessary for passage to them.

6. Broad - On the inside, and besides the galleries mentioned above. Narrowed rests - Or, narrowings: as in our buildings the walls of an house are thicker, or broader at the bottom, and narrower towards the top: only these narrowings were in the outside of the wall, which at each of the three stories was a cubit narrower than that beneath it. And this is mentioned, as the reason of the differing breadth of the chambers; because the wall being narrower, allowed more space for the upper chambers. Not fastened - That there might be no holes made in the wall for fastening them; and that the chambers might be removed, if occasion were, without any inconvenience to the house.

7. Made ready - Hewed, and squared, and fitted exactly according to the direction of the architect. Neither hammer, &c. - So it was ordered, partly for the ease and conveniency of carriage: partly, for the magnificence of the work, and commendation of the workmen's skill and diligence: and partly, for mystical signification. And as this temple was a manifest type both of Christ's church upon earth, and of the heavenly Jerusalem: so this circumstance signified as to the former, that it is the duty of the builders and members of the church, as far as in them lies, to take care that all things be transacted there with perfect peace and quietness; and that no noise of contention, or division, or violence, be heard in that sacred building: and for the latter, that no spiritual stone, no person, shall bear a part in that heavenly

temple, unless he be first hewed, and squared, and made meet for it in this life.

8. The door - That is, by which they entered to go up to the middle chamber or chambers; such as were in the middle story. Right side - That is, in the south-side, called the right side; because when a man looks towards the east, the south is on his right hand. There was another door on the left, or the north-side, leading to the chambers on that side. Winding stairs - Without the wall, leading up to the gallery out of which they went into the several chambers. Middle chamber - Or rather, into the middle story, or row of chambers; and so in the following words, out of the middle story: for these stair's could not lead up into each of the chambers; nor was it needful, but only into the story, which was sufficient for the use of all the chambers.

10. Built chambers - The Hebrew words may be properly rendered, He built a roof, a flat and plain roof, over all the house, according to the manner of the Israelitish buildings. The inner roof was arched, ver. 9, that it might be the more beautiful, but the outward roof was flat. Five cubits - Above the walls of the temple: that it might be a little higher than the arched roof, which it was designed to cover and secure. They rested - Hebrew. it rested, namely, the roof. Timber of cedar - Which rested upon the top of the wall, as the chambers, ver. 5, rested upon the sides of the wall.

12. If - God expresses the condition upon which his promise and favour is suspended; and by assuring him thereof in case of obedience, he plainly intimates the contrary upon his disobedience. Thus he was taught, that all the charge he and the people were at, in erecting this temple, would neither excuse them from obedience to the law of God, nor shelter them from his judgments in case of disobedience.

15. Walls - The name of a wall is not appropriated to stone or brick, because we read of a brazen wall, Jer. xv, 20, and a wall of iron, Ezek iv, 3. And that wall into which Saul smote his javelin, 1 Sam. xix, 10, seems more probably to be understood of wood, than of stone; especially, considering that it was the room where the king used to dine. By this periphrasis, from the floor of the house, unto the walls of the ceiling, he designs all the side-walls of the house. Them - The side-walls of the house. Wood - With other kind of wood, even with fir; as appears from 2 Chron. iii, 5, wherewith the floor is here said to be covered. Floor - This is spoken only concerning the floor, because there was nothing but planks of fir; whereas there was both cedar and fir in the sides of the house, the fir being either put above, or upon the cedar; or intermixed with, or put between the boards or ribs of cedar: as may be gathered from, 2 Chron. iii, 5.

16. House - That is, the most holy place, which contained in length twenty cubits, which may be said to be on the sides Of the house, because this part took off twenty cubits in length from each side of the house, and was also twenty cubits from side to side, so it was twenty cubits every way. The oracle- the most holy place - The last words are added, to explain what he means by the word oracle, which he had not used before.

17. House - That is, the holy place. Temple - This is added, to restrain the signification of the word house, which otherwise notes the whole building. It - The oracle.

18. Cedar - Cedar is here named, not to exclude all other wood, but stone only; as the following words shew.

19. Prepared - That is, adorned and fitted it for the receipt of the ark. Solomon made every thing new, but the ark. That with its mercy seat was still the same that Moses made. This was the token of God's presence, which is with his people, whether they meet in tent or temple, and changes not with their condition.

20. Forepart - Which was in the inner part of the house, called in Hebrew, the forepart; not because a man first enters there, but because when a man is entering, or newly entered into the house, it is still before him. Covered - With gold, chap. vii, 48; 1 Chron. xxviii, 18. The altar - The altar of incense.

21. House - Or, that house, the oracle. Partition - He made a veil, which was a farther partition between the holy, and the most holy; which veil did hang upon these golden chains. Before the oracle - In the outward part of the wall, or partition, which was erected between the oracle and the holy place; which is properly said to be before the oracle, there the veil was hung; and there the chains or bars, or whatsoever it was which fastened the doors of the oracle, were placed. It - The partition; which he here distinguisheth from the house, or the main walls of the house, which he had in the former part of this verse told us were overlaid with gold; and now he affirms much as of the partition.

22. Whole house - Not only the oracle, but all the holy place. The altar - the altar of incense, which was set in the holy place close by the doors of the oracle. With gold - As before he overlaid it with cedar.

23. Cherubim - Besides those two made by Moses, Exod. xxv, 18, which were of gold, and far less than these. The Heathens set up images of their gods, and worshipped them. These were designed to represent the servants and attendants of the God of Israel, the holy angels, not to be worshipped themselves, but to shew how great he is whom we worship.

29. Cherubim - As signs of the presence and protection of the angels vouch-safed by God to that

place. Palm-trees - Emblems of that peace and victory over their enemies, which the Israelites duly serving God in that place might expect. Within and without - Within the oracle and without it, in the holy place.

31. Fifth part - That is, four cubits in height or breadth, whereas the wall was twenty cubits.

36. Inner court - The priests court, 2 Chron. iv, 9, so called, because it was next to the temple which it compassed. Cedar beams - Which is understood, of so many galleries, one on each side of the temple, whereof the three first were of stone, and the fourth of cedar, all supported with rows of pillars: upon which there were many chambers for the uses of the temple, and of the priests.

38. Seven years - It is not strange that this work took up so much time: for,

1. The temple properly so called, was for quantity the least part of it, there being very many and great buildings both above ground in the several courts, (for though only the court of the priests be mentioned, yet it is thereby implied, that the same thing was proportionably done in the others) and under ground.

2. The great art which was used here, and the small number of exquisite artists, required the longer time for the doing it. And if the building of Diana's temple employed all Asia for two hundred years; and the building of one pyramid employed three hundred and sixty thousand men, for twenty years together; both which, Pliny affirms: no reasonable man can wonder that this temple was seven years in building. Now let us see what this temple typifies.

1. Christ himself is the true temple. He himself spoke of the temple of his body: and in him dwelt all the fulness of the godhead. In him all the Israel of God meet, and thro' him have access with confidence to God.

2. Every believer is a living temple, in whom the spirit of God dwelleth. We are wonderfully made by the Divine Providence, but more wonderfully made anew by the Divine grace. And as Solomon's temple was built on a rock, so are we built on Christ.

3. The church is a mystical temple, enriched and beautified, not with gold and precious stones, but with the gifts and graces of the spirit. Angels are ministering spirits, attending the church and all the members of it on all sides.

4. Heaven is the everlasting temple. There the church will be fixt, and no longer moveable. The cherubim there always attend upon the throne of glory. In the temple there was no noise of axes or hammers: every thing is quiet and serene in heaven. All that shall be stones in that building, must here be fitted and made ready for it; must be hewn and squared by the Divine grace, and so made meet for a place in that temple.

VII

Solomon builds several other houses, ver. 1-12. He furnishes the temple with two pillars, ver. 13-22. With a molten sea, ver. 23-26. With ten bases and ten lavers of brass, ver. 27-39. With all other utensils, and the things David had dedicated, ver. 40-51.

1. House - The royal palace for himself, and for his successors. Thirteen years - Almost double the time to that in which the temple was built; because neither were the materials so far provided and prepared for this, as they were for the temple: nor did either he or his people use the same diligence in this, as in the other work; to which they were quickened by God's express command.

2. Of the forest of Lebanon - An house so called, because it was built in the forest of Lebanon, for a summer-seat, whither Solomon, having so many chariots and horses, might at any time retire with ease. The length - Of the principal mansion; to which doubtless other buildings were adjoining. Pillars - Upon which the house was built, and between which there were four stately walks. Beams - Which were laid for the floor of the second story.

3. Fifteen - So in this second story were only three rows of pillars, which was sufficient for the ornament of the second and for the support of the third story.

4. Against light - One directly opposite to the other, as is usual in well-contrived buildings. In ranks - One exactly under another.

5. Windows - He speaks, of smaller windows or lights, which were over the several doors.

6. A porch - Supported by divers pillars, for the more magnificent entrance into the house; upon which also it is thought there were other rooms built, as in the house. The porch - Now mentioned which is said to be before them; before the pillars on which the house of Lebanon stood. Pillars - Or, and pillars; That is, fewer and lesser pillars for the support of the lesser porch. Beam - Which was laid upon these pillars, as the others were ver. 2.

7. A porch - Another porch or distinct room without the house. The other - The whole floor; or, from floor to floor, from the lower floor on the ground, to the upper floor which covered it.

8. Another court - That is, between the porch and the house, called therefore the middle court, chap. 2 Kings xx, 4. Like this - Not for form or quantity, but for the materials and workmanship, the

rooms being covered with cedar, and furnished with like ornaments.

9. These - Buildings described here and in the former chapter. The measures - Hewed in such measure and proportion as exact workmen use to hew ordinary stones. Within, &c. - Both on the inside of the buildings which were covered with cedar, and on the outside also. To the coping - From the bottom to the top of the building. And so on - Not only on the outside of the front of the house, which being most visible, men are more careful to adorn; but also of the other side of the house, which looked towards the great court belonging to the king's house.

11. Above - That is, in the upper part; for this is opposed to the foundation. Stones and cedars - Intermixed the one, and the other.

12. The court - Namely, of Solomon's dwelling-house mentioned, ver. 8.

14. In brass - And Of gold, and stone, and purple, and blue, 2 Chron. ii, 14. But only his skill in brass is here mentioned, because he speaks only of the brasen things which he made.

16. Five cubits - The word chapter is taken either more largely for the whole, so it is five cubits; Or, more strictly, either for the pommels, as they are called, 2 Chron. iv, 12, or for the cornice or crown, and so it was but three cubits, to which the pomegranates being added make it four cubits, as it is below, ver. 19, and the other work upon it took up one cubit more, which in all made five cubits.

17. The chapiters - Which those nets and wreathes encompass, either covering, and as it were receiving and holding the pomegranates, or being mixed with them.

18. Two rows - Either of pomegranates, by comparing this with ver. 20, or of some other curious work.

19. Lilly work - Made like the leaves of lillies. In the porch - Or, as in the porch; such work as there was in the porch of the temple, in which these pillars were set, ver. 21, that so the work of the tops of these pillars might agree with that in the top of the porch.

20. The belly - So he calls the middle part of the chapiter, which jetted farthest out. Two hundred - They are said to be ninety and six on a side of a pillar; in one row and in all an hundred, Jer. lii, 23, four great pomegranates between the several checker-works being added to the first ninety six. And it must needs be granted, that there were as many on the other side of the pillar, or in the other row, which makes them two hundred upon a pillar, as is here said, and four hundred upon both pillars, as they are numbered, 2 Chron. iv, 13.

21. Jachin - Jachin signifies he; That is, God shall establish, his temple, and church, and people: and Boaz signifies, in it, or rather, in him (to answer the he in the former name) is strength. So these pillars being eminently strong and stable, were types of that strength which was in God, and would be put forth by God for the defending and establishing of his temple and people, if they were careful to keep the conditions required by God on their parts.

23. A Sea - He melted the brass, and cast it into the form of a great vessel, for its vastness called a sea, which name is given by the Hebrew to all great collections of waters. The use of it was for the priests to wash their hands and feet, or other things as occasion required, with the water which they drew out of it.

24. Knops - Carved or molten figures: for this word signifies figures or pictures of all sorts. Ten, &c. - So there were three hundred in all. Cast - Together with the sea; not carved. Two rows - It seems doubtful whether the second row had ten in each cubit, and so there were three hundred more; or, whether the ten were distributed into five in each row.

25. Oxen - Of solid brass, which was necessary to bear so great a weight.

26. Baths - Which amounts to five hundred barrels, each bath containing about eight gallons; the bath being a measure of the same bigness with an ephah.

27. Bases - Upon which stood the ten lavers mentioned below, ver. 38, in which they washed the parts of the sacrifices.

28. Borders - Broad brims, possibly for the more secure holding of the lavers.

29. Base above - So he calls the upper-most part of the base: for though it was above, yet it was a base to the laver, which stood upon it. Additions - Either as bases for the feet of the said lions and oxen: or, only as farther ornaments.

30. Wheels - Whereby the bases and lavers might be removed from place to place as need required. Under-setters - Hebrew. shoulders; fitly so called, because they supported the lavers, that they should not fall from their bases, when the bases were removed together with the lavers.

31. The mouth - So he calls that part in the top of the base which was left hollow, that the foot of the laver might be let into it. The chapiter - Within the little base, which he calls the chapiter, because it rose up from, and stood above the great base. Above - Above the chapiter; for the mouth went up, and grew wider like a funnel. A cubit - In height, ver. 35, whereof half a cubit was above the chapiter or little base, and the other half below it. A cubit and half - In compass. Four square - So the innermost part, called the mouth, was round, but the outward part was square, as when a circle is made within a quadrangle.

33. Molten - And cast together with the bases.

34. *Of the base* - Not only of the same matter, but of the same piece, being cast with it.

36. *The proportion* - Or, empty place, that is, according to the bigness of the spaces which were left empty for them, implying that they were smaller than those above mentioned.

39. *Right side* - In the south side, not within the house, but in the priests court, where they washed either their hands or feet, or the parts of the sacrifices. *Left side* - On the north side. *The south* - In the southeast part, where the offerings were prepared.

45. *The pots* - To boil those parts of the sacrifices which the priests, &c. were to eat.

48. *Vessels* - Such as Moses had made only these were larger, and richer, and more. *Table of gold* - Under which, are comprehended both all the utensils belonging to it, and the other ten tables which he made together with it.

49. *Candlesticks* - Which were ten, according to the number of the tables, whereas Moses made but one: whereby might be signified the progress of the light of sacred truth, which was now grown clearer than it was in Moses's time, and should shine brighter and brighter until the perfect day of gospel light. *Pure gold* - Of massy and fine gold. *The oracle* - In the holy place. *Flowers* - Wrought upon the candlesticks, as it had formerly been.

51. *Silver and gold* - So much of it as was left. *And vessels* - Those which David had dedicated, and with them the altar of Moses, and some other of the old utensils which were now laid aside, far better being put in the room of them.

VIII

The chief men of Israel called together, ver. 1, 2. The ark fixt in the most holy place, ver. 3-9. God takes possession of it by a cloud, ver. 10-12. Solomon tells the people the occasion of their meeting, ver. 13-21. The prayer of dedication, ver. 22-53. He dismisses the assembly with a blessing and an exhortation, ver. 54-61. Offers abundance of sacrifices, ver. 62-66.

1. *Elders* - The senators, and Judges, and rulers. *Heads* - For each tribe had a peculiar governor. *Chief* - The chief persons of every great family in each tribe. *Jerusalem* - Where the temple was built. *Bring the ark* - To the top of Moriah, upon which it was built; whither they were now to carry the ark in solemn pomp. *City of David* - Where David had placed the ark, which is called Zion, because it was built upon that hill.

2. *All Israel* - Not only the chief men, but a vast number of the common people. *The feast* - The feast of the dedication, to which Solomon had invited them. *Seventh month* - Which time he chose with respect to his peoples convenience, because now they had gathered in all their fruits, and were come up to Jerusalem, to celebrate the feast of tabernacles. But the temple was not finished till the eighth month, chap. vi, 38, how then could he invite them in the seventh month? This was the seventh month of the next year. For although the house in all its parts was finished the year before, yet the utensils of it were not then fully finished: and many preparations were to be made for this great and extraordinary occasion.

3. *The priests* - For although the Levites might do this, Num. iv, 15, yet the priests did it at this time, for the greater honour of the solemnity; and because the Levites might not enter into the holy-place, much less into the holy of holies, where it was to be placed, into which the priests themselves might not have entered, if the high-priest alone could have done it.

4. *The tabernacle* - That made by Moses, which doubtless before this time had been translated from Gibeon to Zion, and now together with other things, was put into the treasuries of the Lord's house, to prevent all superstitious use of it, and to oblige the people to come up to Jerusalem, as the only place where God would now be worshipped.

5. *Sacrificing* - When the ark was seated in its place: for although they might in the way offer some sacrifices, as David did; yet that was not a proper season to offer so many sacrifices as could not be numbered. This is more particularly related below, ver. 62, 63, 64, which is here signified by way of anticipation.

6. *Cherubim* - Of Solomon's new made cherubim, not of the Mosaic cherubim, which were far less, and unmovably fixed to the ark, Exod. xxxvii, 7, 8, and therefore together with the ark, were put under the wings of these cherubim.

8. *Drew out* - Not wholly, which was expressly forbidden, Exod. xxv, 15, Num. iv, 6, but in part. *Seen out* - In the most holy place, which is oft called by way of eminency, the holy place, and the Hebrew words rendered before the oracle, may be as well rendered, within the oracle. And these staves were left in this posture, that the high-priest might hereby be certainly guided to that very place where he, was one day in a year to sprinkle blood, and to offer incense before the ark, which otherwise he might mistake in that dark place, where the ark was wholly covered with the wings of the great cherubim, which stood between him and the ark when he entered in.

9. *Nothing* - Strictly and properly: but in a more large sense, the pot of manna, and Aaron's rod

were also in it, Heb. ix, 4, that is, by it, in the most holy place, before the ark of the testimony, where God commanded Moses to put them.

10. *The cloud* - The usual token of God's glorious presence. *Filled* - In testimony of his gracious acceptance of this work, and their service; and to beget an awe and reverence in them, and in all others, when they approach to God.

12. *Then spake* - Perceiving both priests and people struck with wonder at this darkness, he minds them, that this was no sign of God's disfavour, as some might possibly imagine; but a token of his approbation, and special presence among them. *Said* - He hath declared, that he would manifest his presence with, and dwelling among his people, by a dark cloud, in which he would appear.

14. *Turned* - From the temple to the body of the congregation. *Stood* - In token of reverence, and of their readiness to receive the blessing.

16. *Since, &c.* - Until David's time; for then he did chuse Jerusalem. *That my name* - That my presence, and grace, and worship, and glory, might be there. *Chose David* - And in and with him the tribe of Judah, of which he was, and Jerusalem where he dwelt.

21. *The covenant* - The tables of the covenant, wherein the conditions of God's covenant with Israel are written.

22. *Stood* - Upon a scaffold set up for him in the court of the people, 2 Chron. vi, 13.

24. *Hast kept* - That branch of thy promise concerning the building of this house by David's son.

25. *Keep* - Make good the other branch of thy promise.

27. *But will* - Is it possible that the great, and high, and lofty God should stoop so low, as to take up his dwelling amongst men? *The heaven* - All this vast space of the visible heaven. *And heaven, &c.* - The third and highest, and therefore the largest heaven, called the heaven of heavens for its eminency and comprehensiveness. *Contain* - For thy essence reacheth far beyond them, being omnipresent. *Much less* - This house therefore was not built as if it were proportionable to thy greatness, or could contain thee, but only that therein we might serve and glorify thee.

28. *Yet* - Tho' thou art not comprehended within this place, yet shew thyself to be graciously present here, by accepting and granting my present requests here tendered unto thee.

29. *Open* - To behold with an eye of favour. *My name* - My presence, and glory and grace. *This place* - This temple, to which Solomon did now look, and towards which, the godly Israelites directed their looks in their prayers.

30. *In heaven* - Which he adds to direct them in their addresses to God in this temple, to lift up their eyes above it, even to heaven, where God's most true, and most glorious dwelling-place is. *Forgive* - The sins of thy people, praying, and even of their prayers; which, if not pardoned, will certainly hinder the success of all their prayers, and the course of all thy blessings.

31. *Trespass* - If he be accused of a trespass. *Laid on him* - Either by the judge, or by the party accusing him, or by the accused person himself: which was usual, when there were no witnesses. *Thine altar* - For here God, who was appealed to as witness, was especially present. Hence the Heathens used to swear at their altars.

32. *His way* - The just recompence of his wicked action. *Give him, &c.* - To vindicate him, and manifest his integrity.

33. *Confess* - Give glory to thy name, by acknowledging their sins, and by justice; and by accepting the punishment of their iniquity; and by trusting to thy power and goodness alone, for their deliverance.

35. *Heaven* - The lower heaven in which the clouds are. *Shut up* - Heaven is compared to a great store-house in God's keeping, out of which nothing can be had, so long as it is close shut up.

36. *Good way* - The way, of their duty, which is good in itself; and both delightful and profitable, to those that walk in it. *Give rain* - The order of Solomon's prayer is very observable; first and chiefly, he prays for their repentance and forgiveness, which is the chief blessing, and the only solid foundation of all other mercies: and then he prays for temporal mercies; thereby teaching us what to desire principally in our prayers; which also Christ hath taught us in his perfect prayer; wherein there is but one petition for outward, and all the rest are for spiritual blessings.

38. *The plague* - His sin, which may be called the plague of his heart, in opposition to the other plagues here mentioned; so the sense is, who, by their afflictions are brought to a true and serious sense of their worse and inward plague of their sins, which are most fitly called the plague of the heart, because that is both the principal seat of sin, and the fountain from whence all actual sins flow.

39. *Thou knowest* - Not only the plagues of their hearts, their several wants and burdens, (these he knows! but he will know them from us,) but the desire and intent of the heart, the sincerity or hypocrisy of it.

41. *A stranger* - A proselyte. *But cometh* - That he may worship, and glorify thy name.

43. *Calleth for* - Agreeable to thy will and word. It is observable, that his prayer for the strangers is more large, and comprehensive, than for the Israelites; that thereby he might both shew his public-spiritedness, and encourage strangers to the worship of the true God. Thus early were the indications of

God's favour, toward the sinners of the Gentiles. As there was then one law for the native and for the stranger, so there was one gospel for both.

44. To battle - In a just cause, and by thy warrant or commission. Shall pray - Whereby he instructs them, that they should not trust, either to the strength or justice of their arms, but only to God's help and blessing. Chosen - For thy dwelling-place, and the seat of thy temple. Towards the house - For to it they were to turn their faces in prayer; to profess themselves worshippers of the true God, in opposition to idols; and to strengthen their faith in God's promises and covenant, the tables whereof were contained in that house. Soldiers in the field must not think it enough that others pray for them: they must pray for themselves. And they are here encouraged to expect a gracious answer. Praying should always go along with fighting.

48. And return - Sincerely, universally, and steadfastly.

49. Their course - Hebrew. their right, against their invaders and oppressors. For they had forfeited all their rights to God only, but not to their enemies; whom tho' God used as scourges to chastise his peoples sins, yet they had no pretense of right to their land.

55. He stood - He spoke this standing, that he might be the better heard, and because he blessed as one having authority. Never were words more pertinently spoken: never was a congregation dismissed, with that which was more likely to affect them, and to abide with them.

56. Blessed, &c. - This discharge he gives in the name of all Israel, to the everlasting honour of the Divine faithfulness, and the everlasting encouragement of all those that build upon the Divine promises.

58. Incline - That he may not only bless us with outward prosperity, but especially, with spiritual blessings: and that as he hath given us his word to teach and direct us, so he would by his holy Spirit, effectually incline us to obey it.

61. Perfect - Let your obedience be universal, without dividing; upright, without dissembling; and constant, without declining.

63. Offered - Not all in one day, but in the seven, or it may be in the fourteen days, mentioned ver. 65.

64. Middle of the court - Of the priests court, in which the great altar was. This he consecrated as he did the great altar, by sacrifices; but with this difference, that he consecrated that for perpetual use: but this only for the present occasion, being warranted to do so both by the necessity of it for God's service, and for the present solemn work, for which the brazen altar was not sufficient; and by the direction of God's spirit, wherewith Solomon was endowed, as being a prophet, as well as a king. Here therefore he suddenly reared up divers altars, which, after this solemnity were demolished.

65. Seven - Seven for the dedication of the temple, or altar; and the other seven for the feast of tabernacles. And it seems to be expressed in this manner, to intimate, that these fourteen days of rejoicing, were not altogether, but that there was some interval between them, which indeed was necessary, because the day of atonement was on the tenth day of this month, Lev. xxiii, 27. And because these fourteen days ended on the twenty-second day, 2 Chron. vii, 10, it may seem most probable, that the feast of the dedication was kept before the tenth day: and the feast of tabernacles some days after it.

66. He sent - Solomon having joined with the people in the solemn assembly, which was kept on the eighth day; in the close of that day took his solemn farewell, and dismissed them with his blessing; and the next morning when the heads and elders with divers of the people came to take their leave of the king, he sent them away.

IX

God in a vision answers Solomon's prayer, ver. 1-9. The mutual presents of Solomon and Hiram, ver. 10-14. His workmen and buildings, ver. 15-24. His devotion, ver. 25. His navy, ver. 26- 28.

3. For ever - As long as the Mosaic dispensation lasts; whereas hitherto my worship has been successively in several places. Eyes - My watchful and gracious providence. Heart - My tender affection. Shall be there - Shall be towards this place and people.

5. Then - Upon that condition; for my promise to David was conditional.

8. High - Glorious and renowned. Astonished - At its unexpected and wonderful ruin. Hiss - By way of contempt and derision.

11. Galilee - Or, near the land of Galilee, bordering upon it; in those parts which were near, and adjoining to Hiram's dominions: with the cities, understand the territories belonging to them. These cities, though they were within those large bounds which God fixed to the land of promise, Gen. xv, 18 Josh. i, 4, yet were not within those parts which were distributed by lot in Joshua's time. It is probable they were not inhabited by Israelites, but by Canaanites, or other Heathens; who being subdued, and extirpated by David or Solomon, those cities became a part of their dominions; and afterwards were reckoned a part of Galilee, as Josephus notes.

13. Cabul - That is, of dirt, as most interpret it. Because, though the land was very good, yet being

a thick and stiff clay, and therefore requiring great pains to manure it, it was very unsuitable to the disposition of the Tyrians, who were delicate, and lazy, and luxurious, and wholly given to merchandise. And on his returning them, there is no doubt but Solomon gave him an equivalent more to his taste.

14. Sent - And this seems to be here added, both to declare the quantity of the gold sent, which had been only named before, ver. 11, and as the reason why he resented Solomon's action, because so great a sum required a better recompense.

15. Raised - Both the levy of men; of which, chap. v, 13, and the levy of money upon his people and subjects. He raised this levy, both to pay what he owed to Hiram, and to build the works following.

21. Those - He used them as bondmen, and imposed bodily labours upon them. "But why did not Solomon destroy them as God had commanded, when now it was fully in his power to do so?" The command of destroying them, Deut. vii, 2, did chiefly, if not only, concern that generation of Canaanites, who lived in, or, near the time of the Israelites entering into Canaan. And that command seems not to be absolute, but conditional, and with some exception for those who should submit and embrace the true religion, as may be gathered both from Josh. xi, 19, and from the history of the Gibeonites. For if God's command had been absolute, the oaths of Joshua, and of the princes, could not have obliged them, nor dispensed with such a command.

25. Three times - That is, at the three solemn feasts: and undoubtedly at all other appointed times.

26. Made - Not now, but in the beginning of his reign.

27. Knowledge of the sea - For which the Tyrians were famous. He sent also ships to join with Solomon's, not from Tyre, the city of Phoenicia; but from an island in the Red-sea, called Tyre, because it was a colony of the Tyrians, as Strabo notes.

28. Ophir - A place famous for the plenty and fineness of the gold there. It is agreed, that it was a part of the East-Indies, probably Ceylon, which though very remote from us, yet was far nearer the Red-sea, from whence they might easily sail to it in those ancient times, because they might (according to the manner of those first ages) sail all along near the coast, though the voyage was thereby more tedious, which was the reason why three years were spent in it. And here, and here only were to be had all the commodities which Solomon fetched from Ophir, chap. x, 22. Fetched - In all there came to the king four hundred and fifty talents, whereof it seems thirty talents were allowed to Hiram and his men, and so there were only four hundred and twenty that came clear into the king's treasury.

X

The queen of Sheba's interview with Solomon, ver. 1-10. His riches, ver. 11-15. Targets, ivory throne, vessels, ver, 16-23. Presents, chariots and horses, tribute, ver. 24-29.

1. Sheba - Of that part of Arabia, called Shabaea, which was at great distance from Jerusalem, bordering upon the Southern Sea; for there, much more than in Ethiopia, were the commodities which she brought, ver. 2, 10. Name of the Lord - That is, concerning God; the name of God being often put for God; concerning his deep knowledge in the things of God. For it is very probable she had, as had divers other Heathens, some knowledge of the true God, and an earnest desire to know more concerning him. Questions - Concerning natural, and civil, and especially, Divine things.

2. All her heart - Of all the doubts and difficulties wherewith her mind was perplexed.

4. House - Or, the houses, the temple and the king's house, in both which there were evidences of singular wisdom.

5. Sitting - The order and manner in which his courtiers, or other subjects (who all were his servants in a general sense) sat down at meals, at several tables in his court. Attendance - Upon the king, both at his table, and in his court; and when he went abroad to the temple or other places. Apparel - Both the costliness of it, and especially the agreeableness of it to their several places and offices. Went up - From his own palace. See 2 Kings xvi, 18, but the ancients, and some others, translate the words thus, and the burnt-offerings which he offered up in the house of the Lord; under which, is the chief, all other sacrifices are understood: when she saw the manner of his offering sacrifices to the Lord; which doubtless she would not neglect to see; and in the ordering of which she might discern many characters of excellent wisdom, especially when she had so excellent an interpreter as Solomon was, to inform her of the reasons of all the circumstances of that service. No spirit - She was astonished, and could scarcely determine whether she really saw these things, or whether it was only a pleasant dream.

8. Happy, &c. - With much more reason may we say this of Christ's servants: Blessed are they that dwell in thy house: they will be always praising thee.

14. Six hundred, &c. - Which amounts to about three millions of our money. And this gold did not come from Ophir in India, or Tharshish; but from Arabia and Ethiopia, which then were replenished with gold, though exhausted by the insatiable avarice of succeeding Ages.

15. Merchant-men - Hebrew. of the searchers; either merchants, who use to search out

commodities: or, the gatherers of the king's revenues, who used to search narrowly into all wares, that the king might not be defrauded of his rights. Spice-merchants - Or rather, of the merchants in general, as the word is often used. So this and the former particular contain both the branches of the king's revenue, what he had from the land, and what he had from the merchants and traders. Kings - Of those parts of Arabia which were next to Canaan, which were either conquered by David, or submitted to pay tribute to Solomon. But we must not think all these to be kings of large dominions; many of them were only governors of cities, and the territories belonging to them, such as were formerly in Canaan, and were anciently called kings. The country - Or, of the land; the land of Arabia: whereof some parts were so far conquered, that he had governors of his own over them, who were each of them to take care of the king's revenue in his jurisdiction; and part only so far, that they still had kings of their own, but such as were tributaries to him.

16. Targets - For pomp and magnificence, and to be carried before him, by his guard, when he went abroad. The Roman magistrates had rods and axes carried before them, in token of their power to correct the bad: but Solomon shields and targets, to shew he took more pleasure in his power to defend and protect the good.

17. Shields - Smaller than targets.

19. Round - Made like the half of a circle.

21. Nothing - Comparatively. Such hyperbolical expressions are frequent both in scripture and other authors. But if gold in abundance, would make silver seem so despicable, shall not wisdom and grace, and the foretastes of heaven, make gold seem much more so?

22. Tharshish - Ships that went to Tharshish. For Tharshish was the name of a place upon the sea, famous for its traffick with merchants, and it was a place very remote from Judea, as appears from the three years usually spent in that voyage. But whether it was Spain, where in those times there was abundance of gold and silver, as Strabo and others affirm; or, some place in the Indies, it is needless to determine.

24. All the earth - That is, all the kings of the earth, (as it is expressed 2 Chron. ix, 23,) namely of those parts of the earth.

28. Horses, &c. - The two chief commodities of Egypt. Price - Solomon received them from Pharaoh at a price agreed between them, and gave this privilege to his merchants, for a tribute to be paid out of it.

29. Chariot - This is not to be understood of the chariots and horses themselves, but for the lading of chariots and horses, which consisting of fine linen and silk, were of great value: and the king's custom, together with the charges of the journey, amounted to these sums. Hittites - A people dwelling principally in the northern and eastern parts of Canaan, Josh. i, 4, whom the Israelites, contrary to their duty, suffered to live amongst them, Judg. iii, 5, who afterwards grew numerous and potent, and, it may be, sent out colonies (after the manner of the ancient times) into some parts of Syria and Arabia. And possibly, these kings of the Hittites may be some of those kings of Arabia, ver. 15.

XI

Solomon's many wives turn his heart from God, ver. 1-8. God reproves and threatens him, ver. 9-13. Stirs up Hadad and Rezon against him, ver. 14-25. An account of Jeroboam, ver. 26-40. Solomon's death and burial, ver. 41-43.

3. Seven hundred wives, &c. - God had particularly forbidden the kings to multiply either horses or wives, Deut. xvii, 16, 17, we saw chap.

chap. x, 29, how he broke the former law, multiplying horses: and here we see, how he broke the latter, multiplying wives. David set the example. One ill act of a good man may do more mischief than twenty of a wicked man. Besides, they were strange women, of the nations which God had expressly forbidden them to marry with. And to compleat the mischief, he clave unto these in love; was extravagantly fond of them, Solomon had much knowledge. But to what purpose, when he knew not how to govern his appetites?

4. Was old - As having now reigned nigh thirty years. When it might have been expected that experience would have made him wiser: then God permitted him to fall so shamefully, that he might be to all succeeding generations an example of the folly, and weakness of the wisest and the best men, when left to themselves. Turned his heart - Not that they changed his mind about the true God, and idols, which is not credible; but they obtained from him a publick indulgence for their worship, and possibly persuaded him to join with them in the outward act of idol-worship; or, at least, in their feasts upon their sacrifices, which was a participation of their idolatry.

5. Milcom - Called also Moloch.

6. Did evil - That is, did not worship God wholly, but joined idols with him.

7. An high place - That is, an altar upon the high place, as the manner of the Heathens was. The

hill - In the mount of olives, which was nigh unto Jerusalem, 2 Sam. xv, 30, and from this act was called the mount of corruption, 2 Kings xxiii, 13. As it were, to confront the temple.

8. And sacrificed, &c. - See what need those have to stand upon their guard, who have been eminent for religion. The devil will set upon them most violently: and if they miscarry, the reproach is the greater. It is the evening that commends the day. Let us therefore fear, lest having run well, we come short.

12. Fathers sake - For my promise made to him, 2 Sam. vii, 12-15.

13. One tribe - Benjamin was not entirely his, but part of it adhered to Jeroboam, as Bethel, chap. xii, 29, and Hephron, 2 Chron. xiii, 19, both which were towns of Benjamin.

15. In Edom - By his army, to war against it. To bury - The Israelites who were slain in the battle, 2 Sam. viii, 13, 14, whom he honourably interred in some certain place, to which he is said to go up for that end. And this gave Hadad the opportunity of making his escape, whilst Joab and his men were employed in that solemnity. Had smitten - Or, and he smote, as it is in the Hebrew: which is here noted as the cause of Hadad's flight; he understood what Joab had done in part, and intended farther to do, even to kill all the males and therefore fled for his life.

18. Midian - He fled at first with an intent to go into Egypt, but took Midian, a neighbouring country, in his way, and staid there a while, possibly 'till he had by some of his servants tried Pharaoh's mind, and prepared the way for his reception. Paran - Another country in the road from Edom to Egypt, where he hired men to attend him, that making his entrance there something like a prince, he might find more favour from that king and people. Land - To support himself and his followers out of the profits of it.

19. Found favour - God so disposing his heart, that Hadad might be a scourge to Solomon for his impieties.

21. Joab - Whom he feared as much as David himself. Own country - Whither accordingly he came; and was there, even from the beginning of Solomon's reign. And it is probable, by the near relation which was between his wife and Solomon's; and, by Pharaoh's intercession, he obtained his kingdom with condition of subjection and tribute to be paid by him to Solomon; which condition he kept 'till Solomon fell from God, and then began to be troublesome, and dangerous to his house and kingdom.

23. Who fled - When David had defeated him. Zobah - A part of Syria, between Damascus and Euphrates.

24. A band - Of soldiers, who fled upon that defeat, 2 Sam. x, 18, and others who readily joined them, and lived by robbery; as many Arabians did. Damascus - And took it, whilst Solomon was wallowing in luxury.

25. All adversity - He was a secret enemy, all that time; and when Solomon had forsaken God, he shewed himself openly. Beside - This infelicity was added to the former; whilst Hadad molested him in the south, Rezon threatened him in the north. But what hurt could Hadad or Rezon have done, to so powerful a king as Solomon, if he had not by sin made himself mean and weak? If God be on our side, we need not fear the greatest adversary. But if he be against us, he can make us fear the least: yea, the grasshopper shall be a burden. Syria - Over all that part of Syria, enlarging his empire the more, and thereby laying a foundation for much misery to Solomon's kingdom.

28. Charge - The taxes and tributes.

29. Went - Probably to execute his charge. Were alone - Having gone aside for private conference; for otherwise it is most likely that he had servants attending him, who, though they hear not the words, yet might see the action, and the rending of Jeroboam's coat; and thus it came to Solomon's ears, who being so wise, could easily understand the thing by what he heard of the action, especially when a prophet did it.

39. For this - For this cause, which I mentioned ver. 33. Not forever - There shall a time come when the seed of David shall not be molested by the kingdom of Israel, but that kingdom shall be destroyed, and the kings of the house of David shall be uppermost, as it was in the days of Asa, Hezekiah and Judah. And at last the Messiah shall come, who shall unite together the broken sticks of Judah and Joseph, and rule over all the Jews and Gentiles too.

40. Solomon - To whose ears this had come. Shishak - Solomon's brother-in-law, who yet might be jealous of him, or alienated from him, because he had taken so many other wives to his sister, might cast a greedy eye upon the great riches which Solomon had amassed together, and upon which, presently after Solomon's death, he laid violent hands, 2 Chron. xii, 9.

41. The book - In the publick records, where the lives and actions of kings were registered from time to time, so this was only a political, not a sacred book.

42. Forty years - His reign was as long as his father's, but not his life; sin shortened his days.

43. Slept - This expression is promiscuously used concerning good and bad; and signifies only, that they died as their fathers did. But did he repent before he died? This seems to be put out of dispute by the book of Ecclesiastes; written after his fall; as is evident, not only from the unanimous testimony

of the Hebrew writers, but also, from the whole strain of that book, which was written long after he had finished all his works, and after he had liberally drunk of all sorts of sensual pleasures, and sadly experienced the bitter effects of his love of women, Eccles vii, 17, &c. which makes it more than probable, that as David writ Psalm li, 1-19. So Solomon wrote this book as a publick testimony and profession of his repentance.

XII

Rehoboam succeeds and Jeroboam returns out of Egypt, ver. 1, 2. The peoples petition to Rehoboam, and his answer, ver. 3-15. Ten tribes revolt and make Jeroboam king, ver. 16-20. God forbids Rehoboam to make war upon them, ver. 21-24. Jeroboam sets up two golden calves, ver. 25-33.

1. Were come - Rehoboam did not call them thither, but went thither, because the Israelites prevented him, and had pitched upon that place, rather than upon Jerusalem, because it was most convenient for all, being in the center of the kingdom; and because that being in the potent tribe of Ephraim, they supposed there they might use that freedom of speech, which they resolved to use, to get there grievances redressed. So out of a thousand wives and concubines, he had but one son to bear his name, and he a fool! Is not sin an ill way of building up a family?

3. They sent - When the people sent him word of Solomon's death, they also sent a summons for him to come to Shechem. That the presence and countenance of a man of so great interest and reputation, might lay the greater obligation upon Rehoboam to grant them ease and relief.

4. Grievous - By heavy taxes and impositions, not only for the temple and his magnificent buildings, but for the expenses of his numerous court, and of so many wives and concubines. And Solomon having so grossly forsaken God, it is no wonder if he oppressed the people.

7. This day - By complying with their desires, and condescending to them for a season, till thou art better established in thy throne. They use this expression, fore-seeing that some would dissuade him from this course, as below the majesty of a prince. And answer - Thy service is not hard, it is only a few good words, which it is as easy to give as bad ones.

8. Young men - So called, comparatively to the old men: otherwise they were near forty years old.

10. Shall be thicker - Or rather, is thicker, and therefore stronger, and more able to crush you, if you proceed in these mutinous demands, than his loins, in which is the principal seat of strength.

15. From the Lord - Who gave up Rehoboam to so foolish and fatal a mistake, and alienated the peoples affections from him; and ordered all circumstances by his wise providence to that end.

16. In David - In David's family and son; we can expect no benefit or relief from him, and therefore we renounce all commerce with him, and subjection to him. They named David, rather than Rehoboam; to signify, that they renounced not Rehoboam only, but all David's family. Son of Jesse - So they call David in contempt; as if they had said, Rehoboam hath no reason to carry himself with such pride and contempt toward his people; for if we trace his original, it was as mean and obscure as any of ours. To your tents - Let us forsake him, and go to our own homes, there to consider, how to provide for ourselves.

17. Judah - The tribe of Judah; with those parts of the tribes of Levi, and Simeon, and Benjamin, whose dwellings were within the confines of Judah.

18. Sent Adoram - Probably to pursue the counsel which he had resolved upon, to execute his office, and exact their tribute with rigor and violence, if need were.

19. Rebelled - Their revolt was sinful, as they did not this in compliance with God's counsel, but to gratify their own passions.

20. Was come - From Egypt; which was known to them before who met at Shechem, and now by all the people. Was none - That is, no entire tribe.

24. From me - This event is from my counsel and providence, to punish Solomon's apostasy.

25. Shechem - He repaired, and enlarged, and fortified it; for it had been ruined long since, Judg. ix, 45. He might chuse it as a place both auspicious, because here the foundation of his monarchy was laid; and commodious, as being near the frontiers of his kingdom. Penuel - A place beyond Jordan; to secure that part of his dominions.

26. Said, &c. - Reasoned within himself. The phrase discovers the fountain of his error, that he did not consult with God, who had given him the kingdom; as in all reason, and justice, and gratitude he should have done: nor believed God's promise, chap. xi, 38, but his own carnal policy.

27. Will turn - Which in itself might seem a prudent conjecture; for this would give Rehoboam, and the priests, and Levites, the sure and faithful friends of David's house, many opportunities of alienating their minds from him, and reducing them to their former allegiance. But considering God's providence, by which the hearts of all men, and the affairs of all kingdoms are governed, and of which he had lately seen so eminent an instance; it was a foolish, as well as wicked course.

28. Calves - In imitation of Aaron's golden calf, and of the Egyptians, from whom he was lately

come. And this he the rather presumed to do, because he knew the people of Israel were generally prone to idolatry; and that Solomon's example had exceedingly strengthened those inclinations; and therefore they were prepared for such an attempt; especially, when his proposition tended to their own ease, and safety, and profit, which he knew was much dearer to them, as well as to himself, than their religion. Too much - Too great a trouble and charge, and neither necessary, nor safe for them, as things now stood. Behold thy gods - Not as if he thought to persuade the people, that these calves were that very God of Israel, who brought them out of Egypt: which was so monstrously absurd and ridiculous, that no Israelite in his right wits could believe it, and had been so far from satisfying his people, that this would have made him both hateful, and contemptible to them; but his meaning was, that these Images were visible representations, by which he designed to worship the true God of Israel, as appears, partly from that parallel place, Exod. xxxii, 4, partly, because the priests and worshippers of the calves, are said to worship Jehovah; and upon that account, are distinguished from those belonging to Baal, chap. xviii, 21, xxii, 6, 7, and partly, from Jeroboam's design in this work, which was to quiet the peoples minds, and remove their scruples about going to Jerusalem to worship their God in that place, as they were commanded: which he doth, by signifying to them, that he did not intend any alteration in the substance of their religion; nor to draw them from the worship of the true God, to the worship of any of those Baals, which were set up by Solomon; but to worship that self-same God whom they worshipped in Jerusalem, even the true God, who brought them out of Egypt; only to vary a circumstance: and that as they worshipped God at Jerusalem, before one visible sign, even the ark, and the sacred cherubim there; so his subjects should worship God by another visible sign, even that of the calves, in other places; and as for the change of the place, he might suggest to them, that God was present in all places, where men with honest minds called upon him; that before the temple was built, the best of kings, and prophets, and people, did pray, and sacrifice to God in divers high places, without any scruple. And that God would dispense with them also in that matter; because going to Jerusalem was dangerous to them at this time; and God would have mercy, rather than sacrifice.

29. Beth-el, &c. - Which two places he chose for his peoples conveniency; Beth-el being in the southern, and Dan. in the northern parts of his kingdom.

30. A sin - That is, an occasion of great wickedness, not only of idolatry, which is called sin by way of eminency; nor only of the worship of the calves, wherein they pretended to worship the true God; but also of the worship of Baal, and of the utter desertion of the true God; and of all sorts of impiety. To Daniel - Which is not here mentioned exclusively, for they went also to Beth-el, ver. 32, 33, but for other reasons, either because that of Daniel was first made, the people in those parts having been long leavened with idolatry, Judg. xviii, 30, or to shew the peoples readiness and zeal for idols; that those who lived in, or near Beth-el, had not patience to stay 'till that calf was finished, but all of them were forward to go as far as Daniel, which was in the utmost borders of the land, to worship an idol there; when it was thought too much for them to go to Jerusalem to worship God.

31. An house - Houses, or chapels, besides the temples, which are built at Daniel and Beth-el; he built also for his peoples better accommodation, lesser temples upon divers high places. Of the lowest - Which he might do, either,

1. because the better sort refused it, or,

2. because such would be satisfied with mean allowances; and so he could put into his own purse a great part of the revenues of the Levites, which doubtless he seized upon when they forsook him, and went to Jerusalem, 2 Chron. xi, 13, 14, or,

3. because mean persons would depend upon his favour, and therefore be pliable to his humour, and firm to his interest, but the words in the Hebrew properly signify, from the ends of the people; which may be translated thus, out of all the people; promiscuously out of every tribe. Which exposition seems to be confirmed by the following words, added to explain these, which were not of the sons of Levi; though they were not of the tribe of Levi. And that indeed was Jeroboam's sin; not that he chose mean persons, for some of the Levites were such; and his sin had not been less, if he had chosen the noblest and greatest persons; as we see in the example of Uzziah. But that he chose men of other tribes, contrary to God's appointment, which restrained that office to that tribe. Levi - To whom that office was confined by God's express command.

32. A feast - The feast of tabernacles. So he would keep God's feast, not in God's time, which was the fifteenth day of the seventh month, and so onward, Levit xxiii, 34, but on the fifteenth day of the eighth month. And this alteration he made, either,

1. to keep up the difference between his subjects, and those of Judah as by the differing manners, so by the distinct times of their worship. Or,

2. lest he should seem directly to oppose the God of Israel, (who had in a special manner obliged all the people to go up to Jerusalem at that time,) by requiring their attendance to celebrate the feast elsewhere, at the same time. Or,

3. to engage as many persons as possibly he could, to come to his feast; which they would more willingly do when the feast at Jerusalem was past and all the fruits of the earth were perfectly gathered

in. Fifteenth day - And so onward till the seven days ended. Like that in Judah - He took his pattern thence, to shew, that he worshipped the same God, and professed the same religion for substance, which they did: howsoever he differed in circumstances. He offered - Either,

 1. by his priests. Or, rather,

 2. by his own hands; as appears from chap. xiii. 1, 4, which he did, to give the more countenance to his new-devised solemnity. Nor is this strange; for he might plausibly think, that he who by his own authority had made others priests might much more exercise a part of that office; at least, upon an extraordinary occasion; in which case, he knew David himself had done some things, which otherwise he might not do. So he did - He himself did offer there in like manner, as he now had done at Dan.

 33. Devised - Which he appointed without any warrant from God.

XIII

 A prophet threatens Jeroboam's altar, and gives a sign, which immediately comes to pass, ver, 1-5. He restores Jeroboam's withered hand, and leaves Bethel, ver. 6-10. The old prophet deceives and entertains him, ver. 11-19. He is threatened with death, ver. 20-23. Slain by a lion and buried, ver. 24-32. Jeroboam is hardened in his idolatry, ver. 33, 34.

 1. Man of God - An holy prophet. By the word, &c. - By Divine inspiration and command.

 2. The altar - And consequently, against all that worship. O altar - He directs his speech to the altar, because the following signs were wrought upon it. Josiah - Which being done above three hundred years after this prophecy, plainly shews the absolute certainty of God's providence; and fore-knowledge even in the most contingent things. For this was in itself uncertain, and wholly depended upon man's will, both as to the having of a child, and as to the giving it this name. Therefore God can certainly and effectually over-rule man's will which way he pleaseth; or else it was possible, that this prediction should have been false; which is blasphemous to imagine. The priests - The bones of the priests, 2 Kings xxiii, 15, 16, whereby the altar should be defiled. How bold was the man, that durst attack the king in his pride, and interrupt the solemnity he was proud of? Whoever is sent on God's errand, must not fear the faces of men. It was above three hundred and fifty years ere this prophecy was fulfilled. Yet it is spoken of as sure and nigh at hand. For a thousand years are with God as one day.

 3. Gave a sign - That is, he then wrought a miracle, to assure them of the truth of his prophecy.

 4. Put forth, &c. - To point out the man whom he would have the people lay hands on. The altar - Where it was employed in offering something upon it. Dried up - Or, withered, the muscles and sinews, the instruments of motion, shrunk up. This God did, to chastise Jeroboam for offering violence to the Lord's prophet: to secure the prophet against farther violence: and, that in this example God might shew, how highly he resents the injuries done to his ministers, for the faithful discharge of their office.

 6. Thy God - Who hath manifested himself to be thy God and friend, in a singular manner; and therefore will hear thy prayers for me, though he will not regard mine, because I have forsaken him and his worship. Besought - To assure Jeroboam, that what he had said, was not from ill-will to him, and that he heartily desired his reformation, and not his ruin. Restored - Because he repented of that violence, which he intended against that prophet, for which God inflicted it: and that this goodness of God to him, might have led him to repentance; or, if he continued impenitent, leave him without excuse.

 9. For so, &c. - My refusal of thy favour, is not from any contempt, or hatred of thy person; but in obedience to the just command of my God, who hath forbidden me all father converse or communication with thee. Eat nor drink - In that place, or with that people. Whereby God declares, how detestable they were in God's eyes; because they were vile apostates from the true God, and embraced this idol-worship, against the light of their own consciences, merely to comply with the king's humour and command. Nor turn - That by thy avoiding the way that led thee to Beth-el as execrable, although thou wentest by my special command, thou mightest teach all others, how much they should abhor that way, and all thoughts of going to that place, or to such people, upon any unnecessary occasion.

 11. A prophet - One to whom, and by whom God did sometimes impart his mind; as it is manifest from ver. 20, 21, and one that had a respect to the Lord's holy prophets, and gave credit to their predictions: but whether he was a good man, may be doubted, seeing we find him in a downright lie, ver. 18. And altho' an holy prophet may possibly have continued in the kingdom of Israel, he would never have gone from his own habitation, to dwell at Beth- el, the chief seat of idolatry, unless with design to preach against it: which it is evident he did not; his sons seem to have been present at, and, and to have joined with others in that idolatrous worship.

 21. Cried - With a loud voice, the effect of his passion, both for his own guilt and shame, and for the prophet's approaching misery.

 22. Shall not, &c. - Thou shalt not die a natural, but a violent death; and that in this journey, before thou returnest to thy native habitation. But is it not strange that the lying prophet escapes, while the man of God is so severely punished? Certainly there must be a judgment to come, when these things shall be

called over again, and when those who sinned most and suffered least in this world, will receive according to their works.

23. *Saddled for him* - But, it is observable, he doth not accompany him; his guilty conscience making him fear to be involved in the same judgment with him.

24. *Slew him* - "But why doth God punish a good man so severely for so small an offense?" His sin was not small, for it was a gross disobedience to a positive command. And it cannot seem strange if God should bring his deserved death upon him in this manner, for the accomplishment of his own glorious designs, to vindicate his own justice from the imputation of partiality; to assure the truth of his predictions, and thereby provoke Jeroboam and his idolatrous followers to repentance; and to justify himself in all his dreadful judgments which he intended to inflict upon Jeroboam's house, and the whole kingdom of Israel.

28. *He found, &c.* - Here was a concurrence of miracles: that the ass did not run away from the lion, according to his nature, but boldly stood still, as reserving himself to carry the prophet to his burial; that the lion did not devour its prey, nor yet go away when he had done his work, but stood still, partly to preserve the carcase of the prophet from other wild beasts or fowls, partly, as an evidence that the prophet's death was not casual, nor the effect of a lion's ravenous disposition, but of God's singular and just judgment; and consequently, that his prediction was divine, and should be infallibly accomplished in its proper time; and partly, as a token of God's favour to the deceased prophet, of whose very carcase he took such special care: thereby signifying, that although for wise and just reasons he thought fit to take away his life, yet his remains was precious to him.

30. *His grave* - So that threatening, ver. 22, was fulfilled; and withal, the memory of his prophecy was revived and preserved among them, and his very carcase resting there, might be a witness of their madness and desperate wickedness, in continuing in their abominable idolatry, after such an assurance of the dreadful effects of it. *They* - The old prophet and his sons, and others, whom common humanity taught to lament the untimely death of so worthy a person. *Alas, &c.* - Which was an usual form of expression in funeral-Lamentations.

31. *When I am dead, &c.* - Tho' he was a lying prophet, yet he desired to die the death of a true prophet. Gather not my Soul with the sinners of Beth-el, but with this man of God: Because what he cried against the altar of Beth-el, shall surely come to pass. Thus by the mouth of two witnesses was it established, if possible to convince Jeroboam.

32. *Samaria* - That is, of the kingdom of Samaria; as it was called, though not when this fact was done, yet before these books were written. Samaria was properly this name of one city, chap. xxi, 1, but from hence the whole kingdom of Israel was so called.

33. *After this* - That is, after all these things: the singular number put for the plural; after so many, and evident, and successive miracles. *Made again* - He abated not so much as a circumstance in his idolatrous worship. *Whosoever* - Without any respect to tribe or family, or integrity of body, or mind, or life; all which were to be regarded in the priesthood.

34. *Sin* - Either, an occasion of sin, and means of hardening all his posterity in their idolatry: or, a punishment, for so the word sin is often used. This his obstinate continuance in his idolatry, after such warnings, was the utter ruin of all his family. They betray themselves effectually, who endeavour to support themselves by any sin.

XIV

Jeroboam sends to the prophet, to inquire concerning his sick son, ver. 1-6. The destruction of Jeroboam's household told, ver. 7-16. The death of his child, ver. 17, 18. The conclusion of his reign, ver. 19, 20. The declension of Rehoboam's house and kingdom, ver. 21-28. The conclusion of his reign, ver. 28-31.

1. *At that time* - Presently after the things described in the former chapter; which, though related in the beginning of his reign, yet might be done a good while after it, and so Ahijah the prophet might be very old, as he is described to be ver. 4. It is probable he was his eldest son.

2. *His wife* - Because she might without suspicion inquire concerning her own child; and because she would inquire exactly, and diligently, and faithfully acquaint him with the truth. *Disguise* - Change thy habit, and voice, and go like a private and obscure person. This caution proceeded: first, from the pride of his heart, which made him loth to confess his folly in worshipping such helpless idols, and to give glory to the God whom he had forsaken. Secondly, from jealousy and suspicion, lest the prophet knowing this, should either give her no answer, or make it worse than indeed it was. Thirdly, from policy, lest his people should by his example be drawn to forsake the calves, and to return to the God of Judah.

3. *And take* - A present, after the manner, but mean, as became an ordinary country woman, which she personated. It had been more pious to inquire, why God contended with him.

6. Thou wife - By which discovery he both reproves their folly, who thought to conceal themselves from God, and withal gives her assurance of the truth, and certainty of that message which he was to deliver. 8. David - Who though he fell into some sins, yet, first, he constantly persevered in the true worship of God; from which thou art revolted. Secondly, he heartily repented of, and turned from all his sins whereas thou art obstinate and incorrigible.

9. Above all - Above all the former kings of my people, as Saul, and Solomon, and Rehoboam. Images - Namely the golden calves: not as if they thought them to be other gods in a proper sense; for it is apparent they still pretended to worship the God of their fathers, but because God rejected their whole worship, and, howsoever they accounted it, he reckoned it a manifest defection from him, and a betaking themselves to other gods, or devils, as they are called, 2 Chron. xi, 15, whom alone they served and worshipped therein, whatsoever pretenses they had to the contrary. To provoke - Whereby thou didst provoke me. For otherwise this was not Jeroboam's design in it, but only to establish himself in the throne. Hast cast - Despised and forsaken me, and my commands, and my worship, as we do things which we cast behind our backs.

10. Shut up - Those who had escaped the fury of their enemies invading them, either because they were shut up in caves, or castles, or strong towns, or, because they were left, over-looked or neglected by them, or spared as poor, impotent, helpless creatures. But now, saith he, they shall be all searched out, and brought to destruction. Dung - Which they remove, as a loathsome thing, out of their houses, and that throughly and universally.

11. Eat - So both sorts shall die unburied.

12. When, &c. - Presently upon thy entrance into the city; when thou art gone but a little way in it, even as far as to the threshold of the king's door, ver. 17, which possibly was near the gates of the city. And by this judge of the truth of the rest of my prophecy.

13. Shall mourn - For the loss of so worthy and hopeful a person, and for the sad calamities which will follow his death, which possibly his moderation, and wisdom, and virtue, might have prevented. So they should mourn, not simply for him, but for their own loss in him. Grave - Shall have the honour of burial. Some good - Pious intentions of taking away the calves, and of permitting or obliging his people to go up to Jerusalem to worship, if God gave him life and authority to do it, and of trusting God with his kingdom. In the house - Which is added for his greater commendation; he was good in the midst of so many temptations and wicked examples; a good branch of a bad flock.

14. A king - Baasha, chap. xv, 28. That day - When he is so raised; in the very beginning of his reign, chap. xv, 29. But what? - But what do I say, he shall raise, as it were a thing to be done at a great distance of time: the man is now in being if not in power, who shall do this: this judgment shall be shortly executed. Sometimes God makes quick work with sinners. He did so with the house of Jeroboam. It was not twenty four years from his first elevation, to the final extirpation of his family.

15. Is shaken - Hither and thither, with every wind. So shall the kingdom and people of Israel be always in an unquiet and unsettled posture, tossed to and fro by foreign invasions and civil wars; by opposite kings and factions, and by the dissensions of the people. The river - Euphrates, so called by way of eminency, this was accomplished in part 2 Kings xv, 29, and more fully, 2 Kings xvii, 6. Groves - For the worship of their idols, God having before condemned the making and worshipping of the calves, by which they pretended to worship the true God; he now takes notice that they were not contented with the calves, but (as it is in the nature of idolatry, and all sin, to proceed from evil to worse) were many of them fallen into a worse kind of idolatry, even their worship of the heathenish Baals, which they commonly exercised in groves.

16. Who made, &c. - By his invention, and making the occasion of their sin, the calves; by his example, encouraging those and only those that worshipped the calves; and by his authority requiring and compelling them to do it. This is mentioned as a monstrous aggravation of his wickedness, that he was not content with his own sin, but was the great author of drawing others into sin, and of corrupting and undoing the whole kingdom, which therefore God would never forgive him, but upon all occasions mentions him with this eternal brand of infamy upon him.

17. Tirzah - An ancient and royal city, in a pleasant place, where the kings of Israel had a palace, whither Jeroboam was now removed from Shechem, either for his pleasure, or for his son's recovery, by the healthfulness of the place. The threshold - Of the king's house, which probably was upon, or by the wall of the city, and near the gate.

18. Mourned - And justly: not only for the loss of an hopeful prince, but because his death plucked up the floodgates, at which an inundation of judgments broke in.

19. The chronicles - not that canonical book of chronicles; for that was written long after this book: but a book of civil records, the annals, wherein all remarkable passages were recorded by the king's command from day to day; out of which the sacred penman by the direction of God's spirit, took those passages which were most useful for God's honour, and mens edification.

21. Forty one years - Therefore he was born a year before Solomon was king, as appears from chap. xi, 42, this is noted as an aggravation of Rehoboam's folly, that he was old enough to have been

wiser. **An Ammonitess** - A people cursed by God, and shut out of the congregation of his people forever. This is observed as one cause both of God's displeasure in punishing Solomon with such a son, and of Rehoboam's apostacy after his three first years, 2 Chron. xi, 17. None can imagine how fatal and how lasting are the consequence of being unequally yoked with an unbeliever.

22. **In the sight of the Lord** - In contempt and defiance of him, and the tokens of his special presence. **Jealousy** - As the adulterous wife provokes her husband, by breaking the marriage covenant.

23. **They also** - Followed the example of the Israelites, although they were better instructed, and had the temple in their kingdom, and liberty of access to it, and the privilege of worshipping God in his own way, and the counsels, and sermons, and examples of the priests and Levites, and the dreadful example of Israel's horrid apostacy, to caution and terrify them. **High places** - Which was unlawful, and, now especially when the temple was built, and ready to receive them; unnecessary, and therefore expressed a greater contempt of God and his express command. **Groves** - Not only after the manner of the Heathens and Israelites, but against a direct and particular prohibition. **Under every green tree** - The people were universally corrupted: which is prodigious, all things considered, and is a clear evidence of the greatness and depth of the original corruption of man's nature.

24. **Abomination** - They dishonoured God by one sin, and then God left them to dishonour themselves by another.

25. **Fifth year** - Presently after his and his people's apostacy, which was not 'till his fourth year: while apostate, Israel enjoyed peace and some kind of prosperity, of which difference, two reasons may be given: first, Judah's sins were committed against clearer light, and more powerful means and remedies of all sorts, and therefore deserved more severe and speedy judgments. Secondly, God discovered more love to Judah in chastizing them speedily, that they might be humbled, reformed, and preserved, as it happened; and more anger against Israel, whom he spared to that total destruction which he intended to bring upon them. **Sishak** - He is thought to be Solomon's brother-in-law. But how little such relations signify among princes, when their interest is concerned, all histories witness. Besides Rehoboam was not Solomon's son by Pharaoh's daughter and so the relation was in a manner extinct. **Came up** - Either, from a desire to enlarge his empire: or, by Jeroboam's instigation: or from a covetous desire of possessing those great treasures which David and Solomon had left: and above all, by God's providence, disposing his heart to this expedition for Rehoboam's punishment.

26. **He took** - First the city: which may seem strange, considering the great strength of it, and how much time it took Nebuchadnezzar and Titus to take it. But, first, it might cost Shishak also a long siege though that be not here related. Secondly, it is probable David and Solomon in their building and altering the city, had more respect to state and magnificence than to its defense, as having no great cause to fear the invasion of any enemies. And it is certain, that after the division between Judah and Israel, the kings of Judah added very much to the fortifications of it.

27. **Brazen shields** - This was an emblem of the diminution of his glory. Sin makes the gold become dim, it changes the most fine gold and turns it into brass.

28. **To the house, &c.** - By which it seems the affliction had done him some good, and brought him back to the worship of God, which he had forsaken.

30. **Was war** - Not an invasive war with potent armies, which was forbidden, chap. xii, 24, and not revived 'till Abijam's reign, 2 Chron. xiii, 1-3, but a defensive war from those hostilities which by small parties and skirmishes they did to one another.

31. **An Ammonitess** - This is repeated as a thing very observable.

XV

The reigns of Abijam and Asa over Judah, ver. 1-24. Of Nadab and Baasha over Israel, ver. 25-34.

1. **Abijam reigned** - So his reign began with Jeroboam's eighteenth year, continued his whole nineteenth year, and ended within his twentieth year, in which also Asa's reign began. And thus one and the same year may be attributed to two several persons.

2. **Three years** - That is, part of three years. **Abishalom** - Or, of Absalom, as he is called 2 Chron. xi, 21. And because he is here mentioned as a known person, without any addition of his kindred or quality, some conceive that this was Absalom's daughter, called properly Tamar, 2 Sam. xiv, 27, and from her royal grandmother, 2 Sam. iii, 3, Maacah.

4. **A lamp** - A son and successor to perpetuate his name and memory, which otherwise had gone into obscurity. **Jerusalem** - That he might maintain that city, and temple, and worship, as a witness for God, in the world, against the Israelites and heathen world.

5. **Save only** - This and the like phrases are not to be understood as exclusive of every sinful action, but only of an habitual and continued apostasy from God, as the very phrase of turning aside from God, or from his commands, doth constantly imply. And thus it is most true. For David's other sins were either sudden and transient acts, soon repented of and blotted out, as in the cases of Nabal and

Achish; or, mistakes of his judgment, which was not fully convinced of the sinfulness of such actions: whereas that which concerned Uriah's wife was a designed and studied sin, long continued in, defended with a succession of other sins, presumptuous, and scandalous to his government, and to the true religion.

6. War between, &c. - Upon Jeroboam's invading him with a great army: acting then in his own defense, he totally routed Jeroboam, so that he was quiet the rest of his reign.

10. Mother's - That is, his grandmother's, as appears from ver. 2, who is called his mother, as David is called Abijam's father, ver. 3. And his grand-mother's name may be here mentioned, rather than his mother's, because his mother was either an obscure person, or was dead, or unwilling to take care of the education of her son, and so he was educated by the grand-mother, who, though she poisoned his father Abijam with her idolatrous principles, ver. 12, yet could not infect Asa, nor withhold him from prosecuting his good purposes of reforming religion.

11. Right - As to the government of his kingdom, and the reformation, and establishment of God's worship. That is right indeed which is so in God's eyes. Those are approved whom he commendeth.

12. Sodomites - All whom he could find out; but some escaped his observation, as appears from chap. xxii, 46. Idols, &c. - And if his father had made them, he had the more need to remove them, that he might cut off the entail of the curse.

13. He removed - He took from her either the name and authority of queen regent, which she, having been Rehoboam's wife, and Abijam's mother, took to herself during Asa's minority; or, the dignity of the queen mother, and those guards, or instruments of power, which she had enjoyed and misemployed. An Idol - Hebrew. a terror, or horror, that is, an horrible idol; which it may be so called, because it was of a more terrible shape than ordinary, and not to be seen without horror. Kidron - That when it was burnt to powder, it might be thrown into the water, and be unfit for any use.

14. High places - 2 Chron. xiv, 3. He took away the altars of the strange gods, and the high places where they were worshipped: but as for those high places where the true God was worshipped he did not take them away; partly, because he thought there was no great evil in them, which had been used by David and Solomon, and other good men; partly, because he thought the removal of them might do more hurt than their continuance, by occasioning the total neglect of God's worship by many of the people, who either could not, or, through want of faith and zeal, would not go up to Jerusalem to worship, now especially, when the Israelites, formerly their friends, were become their enemies, and watched all opportunities to invade or molest them. Was perfect - That is, he sincerely and constantly adhered to the worship of God. Though he could not hinder the people from using the high places, yet he entirely devoted himself to the worship of God in the manner and place prescribed by him.

15. His father - Abijam, when he was in distress, and going to fight with Jeroboam, 2 Chron. xiii, 1-3, though afterwards he did not perform his vows, nor bring in what he had devoted; probably he was prevented by death.

17. Built - That is, repaired and fortified.

18. Were left - What either Shishak had left, or Abijam, or Asa, or others, both of Israel or Judah had dedicated; which probably was not inconsiderable, because Asa had got great spoils from Zerah, 2 Chron. xiv, 9-15, and he and his numerous and prosperous people, did at this time express a great zeal for the house and worship of God. Sent them - Wherein he committed three great faults, amongst many others, first, he alienated things consecrated to God, without necessity. Secondly, he did this out of distrust of that God whose power and goodness he had lately experienced. Thirdly, he did this for an ill intent, to hire him to the breach of his league and covenant with Baasha, ver. 19, and to take away part of that land which by right, and the special gift of God, belonged to the Israelites.

21. Tirzah - Now the royal city of Israel. There he abode to defend his own kingdoms, and durst not return to oppose Asa, lest the Syrian king should make a second invasion. So Asa met with success in this ungodly course as good men sometimes meet with disappointment in a good cause and course. So there is no judging of causes by events.

22. None, &c. - All sorts of persons were obliged to come, except those who were disabled by age, or infirmity, or absence, or by the public service of the king and kingdom in other places. Built - Repaired and strengthened them, for they were built before.

23. Nevertheless - Notwithstanding the great things which he had done, and the glory and prosperity which he enjoyed, he felt the effects of human infirmity, and of his own sins.

25. Two years - Not compleat, as appears from ver. 28, 33.

26. In his sin - In the worship of the calves which his father had made.

28. Even, &c. - It was threatened, chap. xiv, 15, that Israel should be as a reed shaken in the water. And so they were, when, during the single reign of Asa, their government was in seven or eight different hands. Jeroboam was upon the throne at the beginning of his reign, and Ahab at the end of it: between whom were Nadab, Baashah, Elah, Zimri, Tibni, and Omri, undermining and destroying one another. This they got by deserting the house both of God and of David.

29. Any - Any of the males of that family. According, &c. - So God overruled Baasha's ambition

and cruelty, to fulfil his own prediction.

30. *Because* - So that same wicked policy which he used to establish the kingdom in his family, proved his and their ruin: which is very frequently the event of ungodly counsels.

XVI

The ruin of Baasha's family foretold, ver. 1-7. And executed by Zimri, ver. 8-14. Zimri's short reign, ver. 15-20. The struggle between Omri and Tibni, and Omri's reign, ver. 21-28. The beginning of Ahab's reign, ver. 29-33.

1. *Hanani* - He was sent to Asa, king of Judah. But the son, who was young and more active, was sent on this longer and more dangerous expedition to Baasha, king of Israel.

2. *I made thee* - Though that invading the kingdom was from himself, and his own wicked heart; yet the translation of the kingdom from Nadab to Baasha simply considered, was from God, who by his providence disposed of all occasions, and of the hearts of the soldiers and people, so that Baasha should have opportunity of executing God's judgment upon Nadab; nay, the very act of Baasha, the killing his master Nadab, was an act of divine justice. And if Baasha had done this in obedience to God's command, and with a single design, to execute God's vengeance threatened against him, it had been no more a sin, than Jehu's act in killing his master king Jehoram, upon the same account, 2 Kings ix, 24. But Baasha did this, merely to gratify his own pride, or covetousness, or malice, ver. 7.

7. *Came, &c.* - The meaning is, the message which came from the Lord to Jehu, ver. 1, &c. was here delivered by the hand, the ministry of Jehu, unto Baasha. Jehu did what God commanded him in this matter, tho' it was not without apparent hazard to himself.

8. *Two years* - One compleat, and part of the other, ver. 10.

9. *Chariots* - Of all his military chariots, and the men belonging to them: the chariots for carriage of necessary things, being put into meaner hands. *Tirzah* - Whilst his forces were elsewhere employed, ver. 15, which gave Zimri advantage to execute his design.

11. *Kinfolks* - Hebrew. avengers; to whom it belonged to revenge his death.

13. *Vanities* - Idols called vanities; because they are but imaginary deities, and mere nothings; having no power to do either good or hurt.

15. *Gibbethon* - Which had been besieged before, but, it seems, was then relieved, or afterwards recovered by the Philistines; taking the advantage of the disorders and contentions which were among their enemies.

19. *For his sins* - This befell him for his sins. *In walking, &c.* - This he might do, either before his reign, in the whole course of his life, which is justly charged upon him, because of his impenitency: or during his short reign; in which, he had time enough to publish his intentions, about the worship of the calves; or to sacrifice to them, for his good success.

21. *Were divided* - Fell into a civil war: yet neither this, nor any other of God's dreadful judgments could win them to repentance.

22. *Prevailed* - Partly, because they had the army on their side; and principally, by the appointment of God, giving up the Israelites to him who was much the worst, ver. 25, 26. *Died* - A violent death, in the battle: but not till after a struggle of some years. But why in all these confusions of the kingdom of Israel, did they never think of returning to the house of David? Probably because the kings of Judah assumed a more absolute power than the kings of Israel. It was the heaviness of the yoke that they complained of, when they first revolted from the house of David. And it is not unlikely, the dread of that made them averse to it ever after.

23. *Twelve years* - That is, and he reigned twelve years, not from this thirty-first year of Asa, for he died in his thirty-eighth year, ver. 29, but from the beginning of his reign, which was in Asa's twenty-seventh year, ver. 15, 16. So he reigned four years in a state of war with Tibni, and eight years peaceably.

24. *Two talents* - Two talents is something more than seven hundred pounds.

26. *Did worse* - Perhaps he made severer laws concerning the calf worship; whence we read of the statutes of Omri, Micah vi, 16.

31. *A light thing* - The Hebrew runs, was it a light thing,&c., that is, was this but a small sin, that therefore he needed to add more abominations? Where the question, as is usual among the Hebrew, implies a strong denial; and intimates, that this was no small sin, but a great crime; and might have satisfied his wicked mind, without any additions. *Jezebel* - A woman infamous for her idolatry, and cruelty, and sorcery, and filthiness. *Eth-baal* - Called Ithbalus, or Itobalus in heathen writers. So she was of an heathenish and idolatrous race. Such as the kings and people of Israel were expressly forbidden to marry. *Baal* - The idol which the Sidonians worshipped, which is thought to be Hercules. And this idolatry was much worse than that of the calves; because in the calves they worshipped the true God; but in these, false gods or devils.

34. In his days - This is added,

1. as an instance of the certainty of divine predictions, this being fulfilled eight hundred years after it was threatened; and withal, as a warning to the Israelites, not to think themselves innocent or safe, because the judgment threatened against them by Ahijah, chap. xiv, 15, was not yet executed. Or,

2. as an evidence of the horrible corruption of his times, and of that high contempt of God which then reigned. The Bethelite - Who lived in Bethel, the seat and sink of idolatry, wherewith he was throughly leavened. He laid, &c. - That is, in the beginning of his building, God took away his first-born, and others successively in the progress of the work, and the youngest when he finished it. And so he found by his own sad experience, the truth of God's word.

XVII

Elijah foretells the drought, ver. 1. Is fed by ravens, ver. 2-7. By a widow, whose meal and oil are multiplied, ver. 8-16. He raises her dead son, ver. 17-24

1. Elijah - The most eminent of the prophets, who is here brought in, like Melchisedek, without any mention of his father, or mother, or beginning of his days; like a man dropt out of the clouds, and raised by God's special providence as a witness for himself in this most degenerate time that by his zeal, and courage and miracles, he might give some check, to their various and abominable idolatries, and some reviving to that small number of the Lord's prophets, and people, who yet remained in Israel. He seems to have been naturally of a rough spirit. And rough spirits are called to rough services. His name signifies, my God Jehovah is he: he that sends me, and will own me, and bear me out. Said to Ahab - Having doubtless admonished him of his sin and danger before; now upon his obstinacy in his wicked courses, he proceeds to declare, and execute the judgment of God upon him. As the Lord, &c. - I Swear by the God of Israel, who is the only true and living God; whereas the gods whom thou hast joined with him, or preferred before him, are dead and senseless idols. Before whom - Whose minister I am, not only in general, but especially in this threatening, which I now deliver in his name and authority. There shall not, &c. - This was a prediction, but was seconded with his prayer, that God would verify it, James v, 17, And this prayer was truly charitable; that by this sharp affliction, God's honour, and the truth of his word (which was now so horribly and universally contemned) might be vindicated; and the Israelites (whom impunity had hardened in their idolatry) might be awakened to see their own wickedness, and the necessity of returning to the true religion. Those years - That is, These following years, which were three and an half, Luke iv, 25 James v, 17. My word - Until I shall declare, that this judgment shall cease, and shall pray to God for the removal of it.

3. Hide thyself - Thus God rescues him from the fury of Ahab and Jezebel, who, he knew, would seek to destroy him. That Ahab did not seize on him immediately upon these words must be ascribed to God's over-ruling providence.

4. Have commanded - Or, I shall command, that is, effectually move them, by instincts which shall be as forcible with them, as a law or command is to men. God is said to command both brute creatures, and senseless things; when he causeth them to do the things which he intends to effect by them. The ravens - Which he chuseth for this work; to shew his care and power in providing for the prophet by those creatures, which are noted for their greediness, that by this strange experiment he might be taught to trust God in those many and great difficulties to which he was to be exposed. God could have sent angels to minister to him. But he chose winged messengers of another kind to shew he can serve his own purposes as effectually, by the meanest creatures as by the mightiest. Ravens neglect their own young, and do not feed them: yet when God pleaseth, they shall feed his prophet.

6. And flesh - Not raw, but boiled by the ministry of some angel or man, and left in some place 'till the ravens came for it: in all which, there is nothing incredible, considering the power and providence of God.

7. A while - Hebrew. at the end of days; that is, of a year; for so the word days is often used. Dried - God so ordering it, for the punishment of those Israelites who lived near it, and had hitherto been refreshed by it: and for the exercise of Elijah's faith, and to teach him to depend upon God alone.

9. Zarephath - A city between Tyre and Sidon, called Sarepta by St. Luke iv, 26, and others. Zidon - To the jurisdiction of that city, which was inhabited by Gentiles. And God's providing for his prophet, first, by an unclean bird, and then by a Gentile, whom the Jews esteemed unclean, was a presage of the calling of the Gentiles, and rejection of the Jews. So Elijah was the first prophet of the Gentiles. Commanded - Appointed or provided, for that she had as yet no Revelation or command of God about it, appears from ver. 12.

12. She said - Therefore though she was a Gentile, yet she owned the God of Israel as the true God. Two sticks - A few sticks, that number being often used indefinitely for any small number. And die - For having no more provision, we must needs perish with hunger. For though the famine was chiefly in the land of Israel, yet the effects of it were in Tyre and Sidon, which were fed by the corn of

that land. But what a poor supporter was this likely to be? who had no fuel, but what she gathered in the streets, and nothing to live upon herself, but an handful of meal and a little oil! To her Elijah is sent, that he might live upon providence, as much as he had done when the ravens fed him.

13. But make, &c. - This he requires as a trial of her faith, and obedience, which he knew God would plentifully reward; and so this would be a great example to encourage others to the practice of the same graces.

14. The barrel, &c. - The meal of the barrel So the cruse of oil for the oil of the cruse.

15. Many days - A long time, even above two years, before the following event about her son happened. And surely the increase of her faith to such a degree, as to enable her thus to deny herself and trust the promise, was as great a miracle in the kingdom of grace, as the increase of her oil in the kingdom of providence. Happy are they who can thus against hope believe and obey in hope.

16. Wasted not - See how the reward answered the service. She made one cake for the prophet and was repaid with many for herself and her son. What is laid out in charity is set out to the best interest, an upon the best securities.

17. No breath - That is, he died. We must not think it strange, if we meet with sharp afflictions, even when we are in the way of eminent service to God.

18. She said - Wherein have I injured thee? Or, why didst thou come to sojourn in my house, if this be the fruit of it? They are the words of a troubled mind. Art thou come - Didst thou come for this end, that thou mightest severely observe my sins, and by thy prayers bring down God's just judgment upon me, as thou hast brought down this famine upon the nation? To call, &c. - To God's remembrance: for God is said in scripture, to remember sins, when he punisheth them; and to forget them, when he spares the sinner.

19. Into a loft - A private place, where he might more freely pour out his soul to God, and use such gestures as he thought most proper.

20. He cried - A prayer full of powerful arguments. Thou art the Lord, that canst revive the child: and my God; and therefore wilt not, deny me. She is a widow, add not affliction to the afflicted; deprive her not of the support and staff of her age: she hath given me kind entertainment: let her not fare the worse for her kindness to a prophet, whereby wicked men will take occasion to reproach both her, and religion.

21. Come into him - By which it is evident, that the soul was gone out of his body, this was a great request; but Elijah was encouraged to make it; by his zeal for God's honour, and by the experience which he had of his prevailing power with God in prayer.

22. Into him again - This plainly supposes the existence of the soul in a state of separation, and consequently its immortality: probably God might design by this miracle to give an evidence hereof, for the encouragement of his suffering people.

XVIII

Elijah sends notice to Ahab of his coming, ver. 1-16. His interview with Ahab, ver. 17-19. His interview with all Israel upon mount Carmel, ver. 21-39. He slays the prophets of Baal, ver. 40. Obtains rain, and runs before Ahab to Jezreel, ver. 41-46.

1. The third year - Either,
1. From the time when he went to hide himself by the brook Cherith; six months before which time the famine might begin. And so this being towards the end of the third year, it makes up these three years and six months, James v, 17. Or,
2. From the time of his going to Sarepta, which probably was a year after the famine begun; So this might be in the middle of the third year, which also makes up the three years and six months. Go to Ahab - To acquaint him with the cause of this judgment, and to advise him to remove it, and upon that condition to promise him rain. Will send - According to thy word and prayer, which thou shalt make for it. Thus God takes care to maintain the honour of his prophet, and in judgment remembers mercy to Israel, for the sake of the holy seed yet left among them, who suffered in this common calamity.

2. Elijah went - Wherein he shews a strong faith, and resolute obedience, and invincible courage, that he durst at God's command run into the mouth of this raging lion.

3. Obadiah - Being valued by Ahab for his great prudence and fidelity, and therefore indulged as to the worship of the calves and Baal. "But how could he and some other Israelites be said to fear the Lord, when they did not go up to Jerusalem to worship, as God had commanded?" Although they seem not to be wholly excusable in this neglect, yet because they worshipped God in spirit and truth, and performed all moral duties to God and their brethren, and abstained from idolatry, being kept from Jerusalem by violence, God bares with their infirmity herein.

4. Prophets - This name is not only given to such as are endowed with an extraordinary spirit of prophecy, but to such ministers as devoted themselves to the service of God in preaching, praying, and

praising God. And fed - With the hazard of his own life, and against the king's command; as wisely considering, that no command of an earthly prince could over-rule the command of the king of kings. Bread and water - With meat and drink. See how wonderfully God raises up friends for his ministers and people where one would least expect them!

7. And fell - By this profound reverence, shewing his great respect and love to him.

8. Thy Lord - Ahab: whom, though a very wicked man, he owns for Obadiah's Lord and king; thereby instructing us, that the wickedness of kings doth not exempt their subjects from obedience to their lawful commands.

9. He said - Wherein have I offended God, and thee, that thou shouldest expose me to certain ruin.

10. No nation - Near his own, where he could in reason think that Elijah had hid himself. It does not appear, that Ahab sought him, in order to put him to death: but rather in hopes of prevailing upon him, to pray for the removal of the drought.

12. Carry thee - Such transportations of the prophets having doubtless been usual before this time, as they were after it. Slay me - Either as one that hath deluded him with vain hopes: or, because I did not seize upon thee, and bring thee to him. But I, &c. - He speaks not these words, in a way of boasting; but that he might move the prophet to spare him, and not put him upon that hazardous action.

17. Ahab said - Have I at last met with thee, O thou disturber of my kingdom, the author of this famine, and all our calamities?

18. He answered - These calamities are not to be imputed to me, but thine and thy father's wickedness. He answered him boldly, because he spoke in God's name, and for his honour and service. Ye - All of you have forsaken the Lord, and thou in particular, hast followed Baalim.

19. Send - Messengers, that this controversy may be decided, what is the cause of these heavy judgments. All Israel - By their heads, or representatives, that they may be witnesses of all our transactions. Carmel - Not that Carmel, in Judah, but another in Issachar by the midland sea, which he chose as a convenient place being not far from the center of his kingdom, to which all the tribes might conveniently resort, and at some distance from Samaria, that Jezebel might not hinder. Prophets of Baal - Who were dispersed in all the parts of the kingdom. Of the groves - Who attended upon those Baal's or idols that were worshipped in the groves, which were near the royal city, and much frequented by the king and the queen.

20. Ahab sent - He complied with Elijah's motion; because the urgency of the present distress made him willing to try all means to remove it; from a curiosity of seeing some extraordinary events; and principally, because God inclined his heart.

21. And said - Why do you walk so lamely and unevenly, being so unsteady in your opinions and practices, and doubting whether it is better to worship God or Baal? If the Lord - Whom you pretend to worship. Follow - Worship him, and him only, and that in such place and manner as he hath commanded you. If Baal - If Baal can prove himself to be the true God. Answered not - Being convinced of the reasonableness of his proposition.

22. I only - Here present, to own the cause of God. As far the other prophets of the Lord, many of them were slain, others banished, or hid in caves.

23. Let then, &c. - To put this controversy to a short issue.

24. By Fire - That shall consume the sacrifice by fire sent from heaven; which the people knew the true God used to do. It was a great condescension in God, that he would permit Baal to be a competitor with him. But thus God would have every mouth to be stopped, and all flesh become silent before him. And Elijah doubtless had a special commission from God, or he durst not have put it to this issue. But the case was extraordinary, and the judgment upon it would be of use not only then, but in all ages. Elijah does not say, The God that answers by water, tho' that was the thing the country needed, but that answers by fire, let him be God; because the atonement was to be made, before the judgment could be removed. The God therefore that has power to pardon sin, and to signify that by consuming the sin-offering, must needs be the God that can relieve us against the calamity.

25. Dress it first - And I am willing to give you the precedency. This he did, because if he had first offered, and God had answered by fire, Baal's priests would have desisted from making the trial on their part; and because the disappointment of the priests of Baal, of which he was well assured, would prepare the way for the people's attention to his words, and cause them to entertain his success with more affection; and this coming last would leave the greater impression upon their hearts. And this they accepted, because they might think, that if Baal answered them first, which they presumed he would, the people would be so confirmed and heightened in their opinion of Baal, that they might murder Elijah before he came to his experiment.

26. Dressed - Cut it in pieces, and laid the parts upon the wood. From morning - From the time of the morning sacrifice; which advantage Elijah suffered them to take. They leapt upon - Or, beside the altar: or, before it. They used some superstitious and disorderly gestures, either pretending to be acted by the spirit of their God, and to be in a kind of religious exstasy; or, in way of devotion to their God.

27. Mocked them - Derided them and their gods, which had now proved themselves to be

ridiculous and contemptible things.

28. Cut themselves - Mingling their own blood with their sacrifices; as knowing by experience, that nothing was more acceptable to their Baal (who was indeed the devil) than human blood; and hoping thereby to move their God to help them. And this indeed was the practice of divers Heathens in the worship of their false gods.

29. Prophesied - That is, prayed to, and worshipped their God.

30. The altar - This had been built by some of their ancestors for the offering of sacrifice to the God of Israel, which was frequently done in high places. Broken down - By some of the Baalites, out of their enmity to the true God, whose temple, because they could not reach, they shewed their malignity in destroying his altars.

31. Twelve stones - This he did, to renew the covenant between God and all the tribes, as Moses did, Exod. xxiv, 4, to shew, that he prayed and acted in the name, and for the service of the God of all the Patriarchs, and of all the tribes of Israel, and for their good: and, to teach the people, that though the tribes were divided as to their civil government, they ought all to be united in the worship of the same God. Israel - Jacob was graciously answered by God when he prayed to him, and was honoured with the glorious title of Israel, which noted his prevalency with God and men. And I, calling upon the same God, doubt not of a like gracious answer; and if ever you mean to have your prayers granted, you must seek to the God of Jacob.

33. With water - This they could quickly fetch, either from the river Kishon; or, if that was dried up, from the sea; both were at the foot of the mountain. This he did to make the miracle more glorious, and more unquestionable.

36. The evening sacrifice - This time he chose, that he might unite his prayers with the prayers of the godly Jews at Jerusalem, who at that time assembled together to pray. Lord God of, &c. - Hereby he shews faith in God's ancient covenant, and also reminds the people, of their relation both to God and to the patriarchs. Done these things - Brought this famine, gathered the people hither, and done what I have done, or am doing here; not in compliance with my own passions, but in obedience to thy command.

37. Hast turned - Let them feel so powerful a change in their hearts, that they may know it is thy work. Back again - Unto thee, from whom they have revolted.

38. Consumed - Solomon's altar was consecrated by fire from heaven; but this was destroyed, because no more to be used.

39. They fell - In acknowledgment of the true God. He is God - He alone; and Baal is a senseless idol. And they double the words, to note their abundant satisfaction and assurance of the truth of their assertion.

40. Elijah said - He takes the opportunity, whilst the peoples hearts were warm with the fresh sense of this great miracle. The brook Kishon - That their blood might be poured into that river, and thence conveyed into the sea, and might not defile the holy land. Slew them - As these idolatrous priests were manifestly under a sentence of death, passed upon such by the sovereign Lord of life and death, so Elijah had authority to execute it, being a prophet, and an extraordinary minister of God's vengeance. The four hundred prophets of the groves, it seems, did not attend, and so escaped, which perhaps Ahab rejoiced in. But it proved, they were reserved to be the instruments of his destruction, by encouraging him to go up to Ramoth-Gilead.

41. Get up - From the river, where he had been present at the slaughter of Baal's priests, to thy tent: which probably was pitched on the side of Carmel. Eat, &c. - Take comfort, and refresh thyself: for neither the king, nor any of the people could have leisure to eat, being wholly intent upon the decision of the great controversy. For there is, &c. - The rain is as certainly coming, as if you heard the noise which it makes.

42. The top of Carmel - Where he might pour out his prayers unto God; and whence he might look towards the sea. He had a large prospect of the sea from hence. The sailors at this day call it cape Carmel. Between his knees - That is, bowed his head so low, that it touched his knees; thus abasing himself in the sense of his own meanness, now God had thus honoured him.

43. Go - While I continue praying. Elijah desired to have timely notice of the first appearance of rain, that Ahab and the people might know that it was obtained from Jehovah by the prophet's prayers, and thereby be confirmed in the true religion.

44. Like a man's hand - Great blessings often rise from small beginnings, and showers of plenty from a cloud of a span long. Let us therefore never despise the day of small things, but hope and wait for greater things from it.

46. The hand, &c. - God gave him more than natural strength, whereby he was enabled to outrun Ahab's chariot, for so many miles together. He girded, &c. - That his garments, which were long, might not hinder him. Ran before Ahab - To shew how ready he was to honour and serve the king, that by this humble and self-denying carriage, it might appear, what he had done was not from envy or passion, but only from a just zeal for God's glory: that by his presence with the king and his courtiers, he might

animate and oblige them to proceed in the reformation of religion: and, to demonstrate, that he was neither ashamed of, nor afraid for what he had done, but durst venture himself in the midst of his enemies.

XIX

Elijah flees from Jezebel, ver. 1-3. Is fed by an angel, ver. 4- 8. God manifests himself and directs him, ver. 9-18. He calls Elisha, ver. 19-21.

1. All the prophets - Of Baal.

2. Jezebel sent - She gives him notice of it before hand: partly, out of the height of her spirit, as scorning to kill him secretly: partly, out of her impatience, till she had breathed out her rage: and principally, from God's all-disposing providence, that so he might have an opportunity of escaping. Do to me, &c. - So far was she from being changed by that evident miracle, that she persists in her former idolatry, and adds to it a monstrous confidence, that in spight of God she would destroy his prophet.

3. Left his servant - Because he would not expose him to those perils and hardships which he expected: and because he desired solitude, that he might more freely converse with God.

4. Into the wilderness - The vast wilderness of Arabia. He durst not stay in Judah, tho' good Jehosaphat reigned there, because he was allied to Ahab, and was a man of an easy temper, whom Ahab might circumvent, and either by force or art seize upon Elijah. It is enough - I have lived long enough for thy service, and am not like to do thee any more service; neither my words nor works are like to do any good upon these unstable and incorrigible people. I am not better - That I should continue in life, when other prophets who have gone before me, have lost their lives.

7. Angel of the Lord, &c. - He needed not to complain of the unkindness of men, when it was thus made up by the ministration of angels. Wherever God's children are, they are still under their father's eye.

8. And went - He wandered hither and thither for forty days, 'till at last he came to Horeb, which in the direct road was not above three or four days journey. Thither the spirit of the Lord led him, probably beyond his own intention, that he might have communion with God, in the same place that Moses had.

9. Unto a cave - Perhaps the same wherein Moses was hid when the Lord passed before him, and proclaimed his name.

10. I have been, &c. - I have executed my office with zeal for God's honour, and with the hazard of my own life, and am fled hither, not being able to endure to see the dishonour done to thy name by their obstinate idolatry and wickedness. I only - Of all thy prophets, who boldly and publickly plead thy cause: for the rest of thy prophets who are not slain, hide themselves, and dare not appear to do thee any service. They seek my life - I despair of doing them any good: for instead of receiving my testimony, they hunt for my life. It does by no means appear, that he was at all to blame, for fleeing from Jezebel. If they persecute you in one city flee into another. Besides, the angels feeding and preparing him for his journey, and the peculiar blessing of God upon that food, indicated the divine approbation.

11. And behold - This is a general description of the thing, after which the manner of it is particularly explained. Strong wind - Whereby he both prepares Elijah to receive this discovery of God with greatest humility, reverence, and godly fear; and signifies his irresistible power, to break the hardest hearts of the Israelites, and to bear down all opposition that was or should be made against him in the discharge of his office. The Lord was not - The Lord did not vouchsafe his special and gracious presence to Elijah in that wind, which possibly was to teach him not to wonder if God did not accompany his terrible administration at mount Carmel with the presence of his grace, to turn the hearts of the Israelites to himself.

12. A still voice - To intimate, that God would do his work in and for Israel in his own time, not by might or power, but by his own spirit, Zech iv, 6, which moves with a powerful, but yet with a sweet and gentle gale.

13. He wrapped, &c. - Through dread of God's presence, being sensibly that he was neither worthy nor able to endure the sight of God with open face. And stood, &c. - Which God commanded him to do; and as he was going towards the mouth of the cave, he was affrighted and stopped in his course, by the dreadful wind, and earthquake, and fire; when these were past, he prosecutes his journey, and goeth on to the mouth of the cave.

16. The son, &c. - That is, his grand-son, for he was the son of Jehosaphat, 2 Kings ix, 2. This was intended as a prediction that by these God would punish the degenerate Israelites, plead his own cause among them, and avenge the quarrel of his covenant.

17. Shall Elisha slay - One or other of these should infallibly execute God's judgments upon the apostate Israelites. Elisha is said to slay them, either, because he slew those forty two children, 2 Kings ii, 24, besides others whom upon like occasions he might destroy; or, because he by God's appointment inflicted the famine, 2 Kings viii, 1, or rather, by the sword which came out of his mouth: the prophets

being said to pull down and to destroy what they declare and foretel shall be pulled down. Hazael began to slay them before Jehu was king, though his cruelty was much increased afterward. Jehu destroyed those whom Hazael did not, as king Joram himself, and Ahaziah, and all the near relations of Ahab.

18. I have left - Or, I have reserved to myself; I have kept from the common contagion: therefore thou art mistaken to think that thou art left alone. Seven thousand - Either, definitely so many: or rather, indefinitely, for many thousands; the number of seven being often used for a great number. Kissed him - That is, all those who have not worshipped Baal, nor professed reverence or subjection to him: which idolaters did to their idols, by bowing the knee, and by kissing them.

19. Was plowing - Who had twelve ploughs going, whereof eleven were managed by his servants, and the last by himself; according to the simplicity of those ancient times, in which men of good estate submitted to the meanest employments. Cast his mantle - By that ceremony conferring upon him the office of a prophet, which God was pleased to accompany with the gifts and graces of his spirit.

20. He ran - Being powerfully moved by God's spirit to follow Elijah, and wholly give up himself to his function. Let me kiss - That is, bid them farewell. Go - And take thy leave of them, and then return to me again. For what, &c. - Either first, to hinder thee from performing that office. That employment to which I have called thee, doth not require an alienation of thy heart from thy parents, nor the total neglect of them. Or, secondly, to make such a change in thee, that thou shouldst be willing to forsake thy parents, and lands, and all, that thou mayest follow me. Whence comes this marvelous change? It is not from me, who did only throw my mantle over thee; but from an higher power, even from God's spirit, which both changed thy heart, and consecrated thee to thy prophetical office: which therefore it concerns thee vigorously to execute, and wholly to devote thyself to it.

21. From him - From Elijah to his parents; whom when he had seen and kissed, he returned to Elijah. The instruments - That is, with the wood belonging to the plow, &c. to which more was added, as occasion required. But that he burned, to shew his total relinquishing of his former employment. And gave - That is, he made thereof a feast for his servants who had been ploughing with him, and for him, and his other friends and neighbours who came to take their leave of him. Hereby he shewed how willingly and joyfully he forsook all his friends, that he might serve God in that high and honourable employment. It is of great advantage to young ministers, to spend some time under the direction of those that are aged and experienced; and not to think much, if occasion be, to minister unto them. Those who would be fit to teach, must have time to learn; those should first serve, who may hereafter rule.

XX

Ben-hadad's invasion of Israel and insolent demand, ver. 1- 12. Ahab, encouraged by a prophet, overthrows him twice, ver. 13-30. Makes a covenant with him, ver. 31-34. Is reproved and threatened by a prophet, ver. 35-43.

1. Gathered his host - To war against Israel: wherein his design was to enlarge the conquest which his father had made, but God's design was to punish Israel for their apostacy and idolatry.

3. Thy silver, &c. - I challenge them as my own, and expect to have them forthwith delivered, if thou expect peace with me.

4. The king said - I do so far comply with thy demand, that I will own thee for my Lord, and myself for thy vassal, and will hold my wives, and children, and estate, as by thy favour, and with an acknowledgment.

5. Saying, &c. - Although I did before demand not only the dominion of thy treasures, and wives, and children, as thou mayst seem to understand me, but also the actual portion of them; wherewith I would then have been contented.

6. Yet, &c. - Yet now I will not accept of those terms, but together with thy royal treasures, I expect all the treasures of thy servants or subjects; nor will I wait 'till thou deliver them to me, but I will send my servants into the city, and they shall search out and take away all thou art fond of, and this to prevent fraud and delay; and then I will grant thee a peace.

7. Seeketh mischief - Though he pretended peace, upon these terms propounded, it is apparent by those additional demands, that he intends nothing less than our utter ruin. I denied not - I granted his demands in the sense before mentioned.

10. And said, &c. - If I do not assault thy city with so numerous an army, as shall turn all thy city into an heap of dust, and shall be sufficient to carry it all away, though every soldier take but one handful of it.

11. Let not him, &c. - Do not triumph before the victory, for the events of war are uncertain.

13. And behold, &c. - God, though forsaken and neglected by Ahab, prevents him with his gracious promise of help: that Ahab and the idolatrous Israelites, might hereby be fully convinced, or left without excuse, that Ben-hadad's intolerable pride, and contempt of God, and of his people, might be punished: and that the remnant of his prophets and people who were involved in the same calamity

with the rest of the Israelites, might be preserved and delivered. I am the Lord - And not Baal, because I will deliver thee, which he cannot do.

14. He said, &c. - Not by old and experienced soldiers, but by those young men; either the sons of the princes, and great men of the land, who were fled thither for safety; or their pages, or servants that used to attend them: who are bred up delicately, and seem unfit for the business. Thou - Partly to encourage the young men to fight courageously, as being the presence of their prince: and partly, that it might appear, that the victory was wholly due to God's gracious providence, and not to the valour or worthiness of the instruments.

15. All Israel - All that were fit to go out to war; all, except those whom their age, or the same infirmity excused.

18. Take them - He bids them not fight, for he thought they needed not to strike one stroke; and that the Israelites could not stand the first brunt.

20. His man - Him who came to seize upon him, as Ben-hadad had commanded. Fled - Being amazed at the unexpected and undaunted courage of the Israelites, and struck with a divine terror.

21. The king went - Proceeded further in his march. Smote the chariots - The men that fought from them.

22. Mark, and see - Consider what is necessary for thee to do by way of preparation. The enemies of the children of God, are restless in their malice and tho' they may take some breathing time for themselves, they are still breathing out slaughter against the church. It therefore concerns us always to expect our spiritual enemies, and to mark and see what we do.

23. Said to him - They suppose that their gods were no better than the Syrian gods and that there were many gods who had each his particular charge and jurisdiction; which was the opinion of all heathen nations; that some were gods of the woods, other of the rivers, and others of the mountains; and they fancied these to be the latter, because the land of Canaan was a mountainous land, and the great temple of their God at Jerusalem, stood upon an hill, and so did Samaria, where they had received their last blow: it is observable, they do not impute their ill success to their negligence, and drunkenness, and bad conduct, nor to the valour of the Israelites; but to a divine power, which was indeed visible in it. In the plain - Wherein there was not only superstition, but policy; because the Syrians excelled the Israelites in horses, which are most serviceable in plain ground.

24. Take the kings away - Who being of softer education, and less experienced in military matters, were less fit for service; and being many of them but mercenaries, and therefore less concerned in his good success, would be more cautions in venturing themselves. Captains - That is, experienced soldiers of his own subjects, who would faithfully obey the commands of the general (to which the kings would not so readily yield) and use their utmost skill and valour for their own interest and advancement.

27. And went - Being encouraged by the remembrance of their former success, and an expectation of assistance from God again. And pitched - Probably upon some hilly ground, where they might secure themselves, and watch for advantage against their enemies; which may be the reason why the Syrians durst not assault them before the seventh day, ver. 29. Little flocks - Few, and weak, being also for conveniency of fighting, and that they might seem to be more than they were, divided into two bodies.

30. The wall - Or, the walls (the singular number, for the plural) of the city; in which they were now fortifying themselves. This might possibly happen thro' natural causes; but most probably, was effected by the mighty power of God, sending some earthquake, or violent storm which threw down the walls upon them; or doing this by the ministry of angels. And if ever miracle was to be wrought, now seems to have been the proper season for it; when the blasphemous Syrians denied the sovereign power of God, and thereby in some sort obliged him, to give a proof of it; and to shew, that he was the God of the plains, as well as of the mountains; and that he could as effectually destroy them in their strongest holds, as in the open fields; and make the very walls, to whose strength they trusted for their defense, to be the instruments of their ruin. But it may be farther observed, that it is not said, that all these were killed by the fall of this wall; but only that the wall fell upon them, killing some, and wounding others.

31. He will save thy life - This encouragement have all poor sinners, to repent and humble themselves before God. The God of Israel is a merciful God; let us rend our hearts and return to him.

32. My brother - I do not only pardon him, but honour and love him as my brother. What a change is here! From the height of prosperity, to the depth of distress. See the uncertainty of human affairs! Such turns are they subject to, that the spoke of the wheel which is uppermost now, may soon be the lowest of all.

33. Thy brother - Understand, Liveth: for that he inquired after, ver. 32.

34. Streets - Or, Markets, &c. places where thou mayest either receive the tribute which I promise to pay thee, or exercise judicature upon my subjects in case of their refusal. So he made, &c. - He takes no notice of his blasphemy against God; nor of the injuries which his people had suffered from him.

35. In the word - In the name, and by the command of God, whereof doubtless he had informed him. Smite me - So as to wound me, ver. 37. He speaks what God commanded him, though it was to his own hurt; by which obedience to God, he secretly reproacheth Ahab's disobedience in a far easier

matter. And this the prophet by God's appointment desires, that looking like a wounded soldier, he might have the more free access to the king. Refused - Not out of contempt of God's command, but probably, in tenderness to his brother.

36. Slew him - We cannot judge of the case; this man might be guilty of many other heinous sins unknown to us but known to God; for which, God might justly cut him off: which God chose to do upon this occasion, that by the severity of this punishment of a prophet's disobedience, proceeding from pity to his brother, he might teach Ahab the greatness of his sin, in sparing him through foolish pity, whom by the laws of religion, and justice, and prudence, he should have cut of.

38. With ashes - Or, with a cloath, or band; (as the Hebrew doctors understand the word) whereby he bound up his wound, which probably was in his face; for it was to be made in a conspicuous place, that it might be visible to Ahab and others.

39. He said - This relation is a parable; an usual way of instruction in the eastern parts, and most fit for this occasion wherein an obscure prophet was to speak to a great king; impatient of a down-right reproof, and exceeding partial in his own cause. A man - My commander as the manner of expression sheweth.

40. Thy judgment - Thy sentence; thou must perform the condition. Either suffer the one, or do the other.

42. Thy life - "What was the great sin of Ahab in this action, for which God so severely punisheth him?" The great dishonour hereby done to God, in suffering so horrid a blasphemer, to go unpunished, which was contrary to an express law, Lev. xxiv, 16. And God had delivered him into Ahab's hand, for his blasphemy, as he promised to do, ver. 28, by which act of his providence, compared with that law, it was most evident, that this man was appointed by God to destruction, but Ahab was so far from punishing this blasphemer, that he doth not so much as rebuke him, but dismisseth him upon easy terms, and takes not the least care for the reparation of God's honour, and the people were punished for their own sins, which were many, and great; though God took this occasion to inflict it.

XXI

Ahab covets Naboth's vineyard, ver. 1-4. Jezebel procures Naboth to be stoned, ver. 5-14. Ahab goes to take possession, ver. 15, 16 Elijah meets him, and denounces the judgment of God, ver. 17-24. Upon his humiliation a reprieve is granted, ver. 25-29.

3. The Lord forbid - For God had expressly, and for divers weighty reasons forbidden the alienation of lands from the tribes and families to which they were allotted. And although these might have been alienated 'till the jubilee, yet he durst not sell it to the king for that time; because he supposed, if once it came into the king's hand, neither he, nor his posterity, could ever recover it; and so he should both offend God, and wrong his posterity.

7. Dost thou govern - Art thou fit to be king, that hast not courage to use thy power.

9. A fast - To remove all suspicion of evil design in Ahab, and to beget a good opinion of him amongst his people, as if he were grown zealous for God's honour, and careful of his people's welfare, and therefore desirous to inquire into all those sins which provoked God against them. On high - On a scaffold, or high- place, where malefactors were usually placed, that they might be seen, and heard by all the people.

10. Blaspheme God and the king - Indeed his blaspheming God would only be the forfeiture of his life, not his estate. Therefore he is charged with treason also, that his estate may be confiscated, and so Ahab have his vineyard.

13. Stoned him - And it seems his sons too, either with him or after him. For God afterward says, (2 Kings ix, 26) I have seen the blood of Naboth and the blood of his sons. Let us commit the keeping of our lives and comforts to God; for innocence itself will not always be our security.

19. Saying - Thou hast murdered an innocent man; and instead of repenting for it, hast added another piece of injustice and violence to it, and art going confidently and cheerfully to reap the fruit of thy wickedness. Thy blood - The threatening was so directed at first; but afterwards, upon his humiliation, the punishment was transferred from him to his son, as is expressed, ver. 29, yet upon Ahab's returning to sin, in the next chapter, he brings back the curse upon himself, and so it is no wonder if it be in some sort fulfilled in him also.

20. Hast thou found - Dost thou pursue me from place to place? Wilt thou never let me rest? Art thou come after me hither with thy unwelcome messages? Thou art always disturbing, threatening, and opposing me. I have - The hand of God hath found and overtaken thee. Sold thyself - Thou hast wholly resigned up thyself to be the bondslave of the devil, as a man that sells himself to another is totally in his master's power. To work evil, &c. - Impudently and contemptuously. Those who give themselves up to sin will certainly be found out, sooner or later, to their unspeakable amazement.

23. By the wall - Or, in the portion, as it is explained 2 Kings ix, 36.

24. Him that dieth, &c. - Punishments after death are here most insisted on. And these, tho' lighting on the body only, yet undoubtedly were designed as figures of the soul's misery in an after state.

25 Was none - None among all the kings of Israel which had been before him. Whom Jezebel - This is added to shew, that temptations to sin are no excuse to the sinner.

27. Softly - Slowly and silently, after the manner of mourners, or those who are under a great consternation.

29. Humbleth himself - His humiliation was real, though not lasting, and accordingly pleasing to God. This discovers the great goodness of God, and his readiness to shew mercy. It teaches us to take notice of that which is good, even in the worst of men. It gives a reason why wicked persons often prosper: God rewards what little good is in them. And it encourages true penitents. If even Ahab goes to his house reprieved, doubtless they shall go to their houses justified.

XXII

Ahab invites Jehoshaphat to join in recovering Ramoth- gilead, ver. 1-4. His false prophets promise him success, ver. 5, 6. He sends for Micaiah, ver. 7-10. Farther promises, ver. 11, 12. Micaiah's uprightness and prediction, ver. 13-23. He is abused and imprisoned, ver. 24-28. An account of the battle, wherein Ahab is slain, ver. 29-40. The good reign of Jehoshaphat, ver. 41-50. The wicked reign of Ahaziah, ver. 51-53.

2. Came down, &c. - It is strange, that so good a man would be so closely connected with a king revolted from the worship of God! But he appears to have been of too easy a temper, which betrayed him to many inconveniencies.

3. Is ours - Belongeth to us by right. both by God's donation, and by our last agreement with Ben-hadad, chap. xx, 34, which yet he refuseth to deliver up.

5. Inquire - A good man, wherever he goes, will take God along with him, will acknowledge him in all his ways, and look to him for success. And wherever he goes, he ought to take his religion along with him: and not be ashamed to own it, even among those who have no kindness for it.

6. The prophets - Doubtless his own false prophets, or the priests of the groves; who yet gave in their answer in the name of Jehovah; either, in compliance with Jehoshaphat, or by Ahab's direction, that Jehoshaphat might be deceived by them, into a good opinion of the war.

8. One man - In this place, for whom I can speedily send: for there were also other prophets elsewhere in the kingdom, but these were not at hand. Micaiah - Not one of the twelve prophets, who lived about a hundred and fifty years after this time, but another of that name. Let not, &c. - Let us neither hate his person, nor despise his message; but first hear it, and then do as we see cause.

9. Micaiah - It seems, he had imprisoned him; for ver. 26, he bids the officer carry him back, namely to the place where he was before. Probably this was he that had reproved him, for letting Ben-hadad go: And for that, had lain in prison three years. But this did not make him less confident, or less faithful in delivering his message.

14. Said - What answer God shall put in to my mouth. Bravely resolved! And as became one who had an eye to a greater king than either of these.

15. Go - Using the very words of the false prophets, in way of derision. Micaiah's meaning is plainly this, because thou dost not seek to know the truth, but only to please thyself, go to the battle, as all thy prophets advise thee, and try the truth of their prediction by thy own experience.

17. I saw - In the spirit, or in a vision. The hills - Upon the mountains of Gilead, nigh Ramoth, where they lay encamped by Ahab's order. As sheep - As people who have lost their king. Return - Discharged from the war: which was fulfilled, ver. 26.

18. Evil - Nay, but what evil was it, to tell him, what would be the event, if he proceeded in his expedition, while it was in his own power, whether he would proceed, or no? The greatest kindness we can do to one that is walking in a dangerous way, is to tell him of his danger.

19. He said - I will give thee a distinct and true account of the whole matter, in God's name and presence. I saw - By the eyes of my mind: for he could not see the Lord with bodily eyes. The Host - The angels, both good and bad, the one possibly on his right, the other on his left hand. Nor is it strange that the devils are called the host of heaven; if you consider, first, that their original seat was in heaven. Secondly, that the name of heaven is often given to all that part of the world which is above the earth, and among the rest, to the air, and where the devil's residence and dominion lies, Eph. ii, 2, and that both Michael and his angels, and the Dragon and his angels, are said to be, and to wage war in heaven, Rev. xii, 7, either the air, or the church.

20. Who shall - This is not to be grossly understood, as if God were at a loss to find out an expedient to accomplish his own will; but only to bring down divine things to our shallow capacities, and to express the various means which God hath to execute his own designs.

21. A spirit - An evil spirit came, and presented himself before the throne.

22. He said - I will inspire a lie into the minds and mouths of his prophets. Thou shalt - I will give them up into thy hands, and leave them to their own ignorance and wickedness. Go - This is not a command, but only a permission.

24. Zedekiah - The chief of the false prophets, who was much in the king's favour. Which way - In what manner went it? Forasmuch as I and my brethren have consulted the Lord, and have the same spirit which thou pretendest to have.

25. Hide thyself - Probably he went with Ahab to the battle, after which he was glad to shelter himself where he could.

27. Bread, &c. - With a very course and sparing diet, whereby he may be only supported to endure his torment.

31. Save only - This he ordered, truly supposing this to be the best way to put an end to the war: and by the providence of God, which disposeth the hearts of kings as he pleaseth; and inclined them to this course, that they might, though ignorantly, accomplish his counsel. Perhaps Ben-hadad only designed to have taken him prisoner, that he might now give him as honourable a treatment, as he had formerly received from him.

34. The joints - Where the several parts of his armour were joined together. The only place about him where this arrow of death could find entrance. No armour is proof against the darts of divine vengeance. Case the criminal in steel, and it is all one: he that made him, can make his sword approach him. And that which to us seems altogether casual, comes by the determinate counsel of God.

37. Died - Finding too late the truth of Micaiah's words; and Zedekiah's horns of iron, pushing not the Syrians, but himself, into destruction.

39. Ivory house - Not that it was made of solid ivory, but because the other materials were covered, or inlaid with ivory.

41. Of Ahab - Who reigned twenty two years; therefore he reigned about eighteen years with Ahab.

43. High places - He took them away, but not fully; or not in the beginning of of his reign.

44. Made peace - With Ahab first, and then with his son. This is noted as a blemish in his government, 2 Chron. xix, 2, and proved of most mischievous consequence to his posterity.

47. A deputy - Sent, and set over them by the kings of Judah, from the time of David, until the days of Jehoram, 2 Chron. xxi, 8.

49. Would not - He did join with Ahaziah before this time, and before the ships were broken: for the breaking of the ships mentioned here, is noted to be the effect of his sin, in joining with Ahaziah, 2 Chron. xx, 37. And Jehoshaphat being warned and chastised by God for this sin, would not be persuaded to repeat it.

51. Ahaziah, &c. - Ahaziah was made king by his father, and reigned in conjunction with him a year or two before Ahab's death, and as long after it; even as Jehoram the son of Jehoshaphat was made king by his father in his life-time, which possibly was done in compliance with Ahab's desire upon marriage of his daughter to Jehoshaphat's son; and it may be Ahab, to induce him to do so, give him an example of it, and made his son his partner in the kingdom.

52. In the way - Which seems added, to shew, how little the example of parents, or ancestors, is to be valued where it is opposed to the will and word of God.

53. His father, &c. - Most unhappy parents, that thus help to damn their own children's souls!

NOTES ON THE SECOND BOOK OF KINGS

THE former book of Kings had an illustrious beginning in the glory of the kingdom of Israel. This has a melancholy conclusion, in the desolations of the kingdom of Israel first, and then of Judah. Here is Elijah fetching fire from heaven, and ascending in fire to heaven, chap. 1, 2. Elisha working many miracles, chap. 3-7. Hazael anointed, for the correction of Israel, Jehu, for the destruction of the house of Ahab and of Baal, chap. 8-10. The reigns of several kings, both of Judah and Israel, chap. 11-16. The captivity of the ten tribes, chap. 17. The glorious reign of Hezekiah, chap. 18-20. The wicked reign of Manasseh, and the good one of Josiah, chap. 21-23. The destruction of Jerusalem by the king of Babylon, chap. 24, 25.

I

The rebellion of Moab, ver. 1. The message of Ahaziah to Baal-zebub, ver.

2. God's message to him, ver. 3-8. The destruction of the men sent to seize Elijah, ver. 9-12. He spares the third messenger, and goes to the king, ver. 13-16. Ahaziah's death, ver. 17; 18.

1. Moab - This had been subdued by David, as Edom was; and upon the division of his kingdom, Moab was adjoined to that of Israel, and Edom to that of Judah, each to that kingdom upon which it bordered. But when the kingdoms of Israel and Judah were weak and forsaken by God, they took that opportunity to revolt from them; Moab here, and Edom a little after.

2. Chamber - In which, the lattess might be left to convey light into the lower room. But the words may be rendered, through the battlements (or through the lattess in the battlements) of the roof of the house. Where, standing and looking through, and leaning upon this lattess, it broke, and he fell down into the court or garden. Baal-zebub - Properly, the God of flies; an idol so called, because it was supposed to deliver those people from flies; Jupiter and Hercules were called by a like name among the Grecians. And it is evident, both from sacred and prophane histories, That the idol-gods, did sometimes through God's permission, give the answers; though they were generally observed, even by the Heathens themselves, to be dark and doubtful.

3. And say - Dost thou not cast contempt on the God of Israel, as if he were either ignorant of the event of thy disease, or unable to give thee relief; and as if Baal-zebub had more skill and power than he?

5. Why, &c. - Before you have been at Ekron: which he knew by their quick return.

8. An hairy man - His garment was rough and hairy, such as were worn by eminent persons in Greece, in ancient times; and were the proper habit of the prophets. Girdle - As John the baptist also had. That by his very outward habit, he might represent Elijah, in whose spirit and power he came.

9. Man of God - So he calls him by way of scorn. Come - The king commands thee to come to him: which if thou refusest, I am to carry thee by force.

10. Let fire, &c. - Elijah did this, not to secure himself, he could have done that some other way: nor to revenge himself, for it was not his own cause that he acted in: but to prove his mission, and to reveal the wrath of God from heaven against the ungodliness and unrighteousness of men.

11. And said - He discovers more petulancy than the former; and shews, how little he was moved by the former example.

13. Besought - Expressing both reverence to his person, and a dread of God's judgments. There is nothing to be got by contending with God: if we would prevail with him, it must be by supplication. And those are wise who learn submission from the fatal consequences of obstinacy in others.

16. He said - To his very face. Nor durst the king lay hands upon him, being daunted with the prophet's presence, and confidence; and affrighted by the late dreadful evidence of his power with God.

17. Jehoram - His brother. The son of Jehoshaphat - Jehoshaphat, in his seventeenth year, when he went to Ahab, and with him to Ramoth-Gilead, appointed his son Jehoram his vice-roy, and (in case of his death) his successor. In the second year from that time, when Jehoram was thus made vice-king in his father's stead; this Jehoram, Ahab's son, began to reign: and in the fifth year of the reign of this Jehoram son of Ahab, which was about the twenty-fourth year of Jehoshaphat's reign, Jehoram son of Jehoshaphat was made king of Judah, together with his father.

II

Elisha keeps close to Elijah, and walks with him through Jordan, ver. 1-8. Elijah is taken up, and Elisha laments the loss of him, ver. 9-12. He divides Jordan, ver. 13, 14. Is acknowledged by the sons of the prophets, ver. 15. Who send to seek Elijah, ver. 16-18. Elisha heals the unwholesome waters, ver. 19-22. Destroys the mocking children, ver. 23-25

1. About to take, &c. - It is supposed, (tho' not expressly revealed) that Elijah flourished about twenty years, before he was translated, body and soul, to heaven, only undergoing such a change, as was necessary to qualify him for being an inhabitant in that world of Spirits. By translating him, God gave in that dark and degenerate age, a very sensible proof of another life, together with a type of the ascension of Christ, and the opening of the kingdom of heaven to all believers.

2. Tarry here - This he desires, either,

1. That being left alone, he might better prepare himself for his great change. Or,

2. Out of indulgence to Elisha, that he might not be overwhelmed with grief at so sad a sight. Or,

3. That he might try his love, and whet his desire to accompany him; it being highly convenient for God's honour, that there should be witnesses of so glorious a translation. To Beth-el - Which was truth, tho' not the whole truth: for he was to go a far longer journey. But he was first to go to Beth-el, as also to Jericho, to the schools of the prophets there, that he might comfort, and strengthen their hearts in God's work, and give them his dying counsels.

3. And said - This was revealed to some of the sons of the prophets, and by them to the whole college. In the kingdom of Judah they had priest and Levites, and the temple service. The want of these in the kingdom of Israel, God graciously made up by these colleges, where men were trained up and employed, in the exercises of religion, and whither good people resorted, to solemnize the appointed feasts, with prayer and hearing, tho' they had not conveniencies for sacrifice. From thy head - Hebrew. from above thy head: which phrase may respect, either, the manner of sitting in schools, where the scholar sat at his master's feet. Or, the manner of Elijah's translation, which was to be by a power sent from heaven, to take him up thither. Hold you your peace - Do not aggravate my grief, nor divert me with any unseasonable discourses. He speaks as one that was himself, and would have them calm and sedate, and with awful silence waiting the event.

7. To view - To observe this great event, Elijah's translation to heaven, which they expected every moment: and whereof they desired to be spectators, not to satisfy their own curiosity, but that they might be witnesses of it to others.

8. Smote the waters - These waters of old yielded to the ark, now to the prophet's mantle; which to those that wanted the ark, was an equivalent token of God's presence. When God will take his children to himself, death is the Jordan, which they must pass through. And they find a way thro' it, a safe and comfortable way. The death of Christ has divided those waters, that the ransomed of the Lord may pass over.

9. A double portion - Or, rather double to what the rest of the sons of the prophets receive at thy request. He alludes to the double portion of the first-born, Deut. xxi, 17. But though Elisha desired no more, yet God gave him more than he desired or expected; and he seems to have had a greater portion of the gifts of God's Spirit, than even Elijah had.

10. A hard thing - A rare and singular blessing, which I cannot promise thee, which only God can give; and he gives it only when, and to whom he pleaseth. If thou seest - This sign he proposed, not without the direction of God's Spirit, that hereby he might engage him more earnestly to wait, and more fervently to pray for this mercy.

11. A chariot of fire - In this form the angels appeared. The souls of all the faithful, are carried by an invisible guard of angels, into the bosom of Abraham. But Elijah being to carry his body with him, this heavenly guard appeared visibly: Not in an human shape, tho' so they might have born him in their arms, but in the form of a chariot and horses, that he may ride in state, may ride in triumph, like a prince, like a conqueror. See the readiness of the angels to do the will of God, even in the meanest services for the heirs of salvation! Thus he who had burned with holy zeal for God and his honour, was now conveyed in fire into his immediate presence.

12. My father - So he calls him for his fatherly affection to him, and for his fatherly authority which he had over him, in which respect the scholars of the prophets are called their sons. He saw his own condition like that of a fatherless child, and laments it accordingly. The chariot, &c. - Who by thy example, and counsels, and prayers, and power with God, didst more for the defense and preservation of Israel than all their chariots and horses. The expression alludes to the form of chariots and horses which he had seen.

13. Which fell - God so ordering it for Elisha's comfort, and the strengthening of his faith, as a pledge, that together with Elijah's mantle, his Spirit should rest upon him. And Elijah himself was gone to a place, where he needed not the mantle, either to adorn him, or to shelter him from weather, or to

wrap his face in.

14. The Lord - Who at Elijah's request divided these waters, and is as able to do it again.

15. Bowed themselves - They had been trained up in the schools: Elisha was taken from the plough. Yet, when they perceive, that God is with him, and that this is the man whom he delights to honour, they readily submit to him as their head and father, as the people to Joshua when Moses was dead. "Those that appear to have God's Spirit and presence with them, ought to have our esteem and best affections, notwithstanding the meanness of their extraction and education."

16. Strong men - Able to take such a journey. Lest, &c. - They thought, either that God had not finally taken him away from them, but only for a time; or that God had only taken away his soul, and that his body was cast down into some place, which they desired to seek, that they might give it an honourable burial.

17. Was ashamed - That is, to deny them any longer, lest they should think his denial proceeded from a neglect of his master, or a contempt of them.

19. Barren - Either it was so originally, at least, as to that part of the city where the college of the prophets was: or, it became so from the curse of God inflicted upon it, when Hiel rebuilt it. However, upon the prophet's care, it grew exceeding fruitful, and therefore is commended for its fertility in later writers.

20. A new cruse - That there might be no legal pollution in it which might offend God, and hinder his miraculous operation. Put salt - A most improper remedy; for salt naturally makes waters brackish, and lands barren. Hereby therefore he would shew, that this was effected solely by the Divine power, which could work either without means, or against them.

21. Death - Hurt, or danger, to man or beast, by drinking of it.

23. To Beth-el - To the other school of prophets, to inform them of Elijah's translation, and his succession to the same office; and to direct, and comfort, and stablish them. Children - Or, young men: as this Hebrew word often signifies. It is more than probable they were old enough to discern between good and evil. The city - Beth-el was the mother-city of idolatry, where the prophets planted themselves, that they might bear witness against it, and dissuade the people from it; though, it seems, they had but small success there. Mocked him - With great petulancy and vehemency, as the word signifies; deriding both his person and ministry, and that from a prophane contempt of the true religion, and a passionate love to that idolatry which they knew he opposed. Go up - Go up into heaven, whither thou pretendest Elijah is gone. Why didst not thou accompany thy friend and master to heaven? Bald-head - So they mock his natural infirmity, which is a great sin. The repetition shews their heartiness and earnestness, that it was no sudden slip of their tongue, but a scoff proceeding from a rooted impiety and hatred of God and his prophets. And very probably it was their usual practice, to jeer the prophets as they went along the streets, that they might expose them to contempt, and if possible drive them out of their town. Had the abuse done to Elisha been the first offense of the kind, they might not have been so severely punished. But mocking the messengers of the Lord, was one of the crying sins of Israel.

24. Cursed them - Nor was this punishment too great for the offense, if it be considered, that their mocking proceeded from a great malignity of mind against God; that they mocked not only a man, and an ancient man, whose very age commanded reverence; and a prophet; but even God himself, and that glorious work of God, the assumption of Elijah into heaven; that they might be guilty of many other heinous crimes, which God and the prophet knew; and were guilty of idolatry, which by God's law deserved death; that the idolatrous parents were punished in their children; and that, if any of these children were more innocent, God might have mercy upon their souls, and then this death was not a misery, but a real blessing to them, that they were taken away from that education which was most likely to expose them not only to temporal, but eternal destruction. In the name - Not from any revengeful passion, but by the motion of God's Spirit, and by God's command and commission. God did this, partly, for the terror and caution of all other idolaters and prophane persons who abounded in that place; partly, to vindicate the honour, and maintain the authority of his prophets; and particularly, of Elisha, now especially, in the beginning of his sacred ministry. Children - This Hebrew word signifies not only young children, but also those who are grown up to maturity, as Gen. xxxii. 22, xxxiv, 4, xxxvii, 30, Ruth i, 5.

III

The character of Jehoram, ver. 1-3. He and his allies invade Moab, ver. 4-8. Their distress and relief, ver. 9-20. Their success, ver. 21-25. The king of Moab sacrifices his son, and they retire, ver. 26, 27.

3. The sins - The worship of the calves: which all the kings of Israel kept up as a wall of partition between their subjects and those of Judah. So that altho' he had a little religion, yet he had not enough to over-rule this policy.

4. A sheep-master - A man of great wealth (which in those times and places consisted much in cattle) which enabled and emboldened him to rebel against his sovereign.

7. He said - He joins with him in this war; because the war was just in itself, and convenient for Jehoshaphat, both in the general, that revolters should be chastised: lest the examples should pass into his dominions, and the Edomites be encouraged to revolt from him, as they did from his son; and in particular, that the Moabites should be humbled, who had invaded his land before this time, 2 Chron. xx, 1, and might do so again if they were not brought low; for which a fair opportunity now offered.

9. King of Edom - That is, the vice-roy under Jehoshaphat, 1 Kings xxii, 47, here called king: because that word is sometimes used for any prince or chief ruler. Seven days - Because they made a great army, which could move but slowly; and they fetched a greater compass than was usual, for some advantage which they expected by it. No water - A frequent want in those parts; and now, it seems, increased by the extraordinary heat and dryness of the season.

11. Is there not, &c. - This he should have asked before, when they first undertook the expedition, as he did in a like case, 1 Kings xxii, 5, and for that neglect he now suffers; but better late than never: his affliction brings him to the remembrance of his former sin, and present duty. Poured water - Who was his servant; this being one office of a servant: and this office was the more necessary among the Israelites, because of the frequent washings which their law required. Probably it was by a special direction from God, that Elisha followed them, unasked, unobserved. Thus does God prevent us with the blessings of his goodness; and provide for those who provide not for themselves.

12. The word, &c. - He is a true prophet. Which Jehoshaphat might easily understand, because being a good man, many would be ready to inform him of. Went - To his tent; which was either in the camp, or not far from it: they did not send for him, but went to him, that by giving him this honour, they might engage him to give them his utmost assistance.

13. What have I, &c. - I desire to have no discourse with thee. Get thee - To the calves, which thou after thy father's example dost worship; and to the Baals which thy mother yet worshippeth by thy permission; let these idols whom thou worshippest in thy prosperity, now help thee in thy distress.

14. Jehoshaphat - Whom I reverence and love for his piety. It is good being with those who have God's favour, and the love of his people. Wicked men often fare the better, for the friendship and society of good men.

15. Minstrel - One that can sing and play upon a musical instrument. This he requires, that his mind which had been disturbed at the sight of wicked Jehoram, might be composed, and that he might be excited to more fervent prayer whereby he was prepared to receive the prophetic inspiration. Those that desire communion with God must keep their spirits quiet and serene. All hurry of spirit, and all turbulent passions, make us unfit for divine visitations. The hand, &c. - The spirit of prophecy, so called, to note that it was no natural nor acquired virtue inherent in him; but a singular gift of God, given to whom and when he pleased.

19. Ye shall smite - And if this command seem severe, it must be considered, that the Moabites were a very wicked people, perfidious, cruel, implacable enemies to God's people upon all occasions, and now in a state of rebellion.

20. The meal-offering - That is, the morning sacrifice: which doubtless was attended with the solemn prayers of God's people. At this time Elisha joined his prayers with the prayers of God's people, especially those at Jerusalem. And this time God chose to answer their prayers, and to work this miracle, that thereby he might determine the controversy between the Israelites and the Jews, about the place and manner of worship, and give a publick testimony from heaven for the Jews, and against the Israelites. God that commands all the waters both above and beneath the firmament, sent them abundance of water on a sudden.

21. The border - Of their country, to defend the passage.

25. Kir-haraseth - This was the royal city of the Moabites, into which the remnant of the Moabites were gathered, where also their king was with them. The stones - The walls and buildings of this city only were left; their whole country being destroyed. The slingers - Such as slung great stones against the walls to break them down, according to the manner of those times. Made breaches in the walls, by which they might enter the city, and take it.

26. To break thro' - That he might make an escape: which he chose to do on the king of Edom's quarter; because he thought his was the weakest side.

27. His son - Or rather, his own son: whom he sacrificed; partly, to obtain the favour of his God, according to the manner of the Phoenicians and other people in publick calamities; and partly, to oblige the Israelites to quit the siege out of compassion; or, as despairing to conquer (at least without greater loss of men than it was worth) him who was resolved to defend the city to the utmost extremity. On the wall - That the besiegers might see it, and be moved by it. There was, &c. - Or, great trouble or repentance upon Israel, the Israelitish king and people (who was the first cause of the war, and had brought the rest into confederacy with him) were greatly grieved for this barbarous action, and resolved to prosecute the war no farther.

IV

Elisha multiplies the widow's oil, ver. 1-7. Obtains a son for the Shunamite, ver. 8-17. Raises him again to life, ver. 18-37. Heals the deadly pottage, ver. 38-41. Feeds an hundred men with twenty small loaves, ver. 42-44.

1. Prophets - Who, though they were wholly devoted to sacred employment, were not excluded from marriage, any more than the priests and Levites. Fear the Lord - His poverty therefore was not procured by his idleness, or prodigality; but by his piety, because he would not comply with the king's way of worship, and therefore lost all worldly advantages. Bondmen - Either, to use them as his slaves, or to sell them to others, according to the law.

2. What shall I - How shall I relieve thee, who am myself poor?

7. Unto her son - To one of them: for she had two, ver. 1. The oil stayed - To teach us, that we should not waste any of his good creatures; and that God would not work miracles unnecessarily. We are never straiten'd in God, and in his power and bounty, and the riches of his grace. All our straitness is in ourselves. It is our faith that fails, not his promise. Were there more vessels, there is enough in God to fill them, enough for all, enough for each.

8. Great - For estate, or birth and quality.

9. This is - A prophet, and that of eminent holiness: by our kindness to whom, we shall procure a blessing to ourselves.

10. On the wall - That he may be free from the noise of family business, and enjoy that privacy, which, I perceive, he desireth for his prayers and meditations. A bed, &c. - He will not be troublesome or chargeable to us: he cares not for rich furniture or costly entertainment, and is content with bare necessaries.

12. She stood - The relation seems to be a little perplexed, but may be thus conceived. It is in this verse recorded in the general, that the prophet sent Gehazi to call her, and that she came to him upon that call: then follows a particular description of the whole business, with all the circumstances, first, of the message with which Gehazi was sent when he went to call her, and of her answer to that message, ver. 13, and of Gehazi's conjecture thereupon, ver. 14, and then of her coming to the prophet at his call: which is there repeated to make way for the following passages.

13. I dwell - I live among my kindred and friends; nor have I any cause to seek relief from higher powers.

14. He said - Hast thou observed any thing which she wants or desires? For the prophet kept himself much in his chamber, whilst Gehazi went more freely about the house, as his occasions led him.

16. Do not lie - Do not delude me with vain hopes. She could not believe it for joy.

17. Time of life - See note on Gen. xviii. 10.

21. Bed of the man of God - Being apt to believe, he that so soon took away what he had given, would restore what he had taken away. By this faith women received their dead raised to life. In this faith she makes no preparation for the burial of her child, but for his resurrection.

23. New moon, &c. - Which were the usual times in which they resorted to the prophets for instruction. It shall be well - My going will not be troublesome to him, nor prejudicial to thee or me.

26. It is - So it was in some respects, because it was the will of a wise and good God, and therefore best for her. When God calls away our dearest relations by death, it becomes us to say, it is well both with us and them. It is well, for all is well that God doth: all is well with them that are gone, if they are gone to heaven. And all is well with us that stay behind, if by the affliction we are furthered in our way thither.

27. The feet - She fell at his feet and touched them, as a most humble and earnest supplicant. Withal, she intimated, what she durst not presume to express in words, that she desired him to go along with her. Let her alone - Disturb her not, for this gesture is a sign of some extraordinary grief. Hid it - Whereby he signifies, that what he knew or did, was not by any virtue inherent in himself, but from God, who revealed to him only what and when he pleased.

28. She said - This child was not given to me upon my immoderate desire, for which I might have justly been thus chastised, but was freely promised by thee in God's name, and from his special favour. Deceive me - With vain hopes of a comfort that I should never have. And I had been much happier if I had never had it, than to lose it so quickly.

29. Gird up - Tie up thy long garments about thy loins for expedition. If thou meet, &c. - Make no delay nor stop by the way, neither by words nor actions.

30. Will not leave thee - Until thou goest home with me. For she had no great confidence in Gehazi, nor was her faith so strong as to think that the prophet could work so great a miracle at this distance.

31. Neither voice - Neither speech, nor sense, nor any sign of life, in the child. This disappointment might proceed from hence, that Elisha having changed his mind, and yielded to her

importunity to go with her, did alter his course, and not join his fervent prayers with Gehazi's action. Not awaked - Not revived.

33. Shut the door - Upon himself and the dead child, that he might pray to God without distraction, and might more freely use those means which he thought fit.

34. And put - One part upon another successively; for the disproportion of the bodies would not permit it to be done together. Grew warm - Not by any external heat, which could not be transmitted to the child's body by such slight touches of the prophet's body; but from a principle of life, which was already infused into the child, and by degrees enlivened all the parts of his body.

35. He walked - He changeth his postures for his own necessary refreshment, and walked to and fro, exercising his mind in prayer to God. And went - Repeating his former actions, to teach us not to be discouraged in our prayers, if we be not speedily answered. Opened his eyes - So the work begun in the former verse is here perfected. Although miracles were for the most part done in an instant, yet sometimes they were done by degrees.

36. Unto him - To the door.

40. Death - That is, some deadly thing.

41. Into the pot - Together with the pottage which they had taken out of it.

42. First fruits - Which were the priests due, Num. xviii, 12, but these, and probably the rest of the priests dues, were usually brought by the pious Israelites, according to their ability and opportunity, to the Lord's prophets, because they were not permitted to carry them to Jerusalem.

V

Naaman hears of Elisha, ver. 1-4. The king of Syria sends him to the king of Israel, ver. 5-7. He goes to Elisha and is healed, ver. 8-14. His grateful acknowledgment to Elisha, ver. 15-19. Gehazi follows him, and receives gifts from him, ver. 20-24. The leprosy of Naaman entailed on Gehazi's family, ver. 25-27.

5. Go to, &c. - It was very natural for a king to suppose, that the king of Israel could do more than any of his subjects.

10. Elisha sent - Which he did, partly, to exercise Naaman's faith and obedience: partly, for the honour of his religion, that it might appear he sought not his own glory and profit, but only God's honour, and the good of men.

11. Was wroth - Supposing himself despised by the prophet.

12. Are not, &c. - Is there not as great a virtue in them to this purpose? But he should have considered, that the cure was not to be wrought by the water, but by the power of God.

13. My father - Or, our father. So they call him, to shew their reverence and affection to him.

16. He refused - Not that he thought it unlawful to receive presents, which he did receive from others, but because of the special circumstances of the case; this being much for the honour of God that the Syrians should see the generous piety, and kindness of his ministers and servants, and how much they despised all that worldly wealth and glory, which the prophets of the Gentiles so greedily sought after.

17. Two mules burden of earth - So he seems to farm the money which he brought with him, to express how little value he now set upon it. Ten talents (above three thousand five hundred pounds) in silver, with six thousand pieces of gold, (beside ten changes of raiment) were a burden for several mules. Shall I not give this to thy servant, Gehazi, if thou thyself will accept of nothing? This seems a more probable interpretation than the common one, that he wanted to build an altar therewith. For what altar could be built of the earth which two mules could carry into Syria? Unless they were as large and as strong as Elephants.

18. Rimmon - A Syrian idol, called here by the LXX, Remman, and Acts vii, 43, Remphan. My hand - Or, arm, upon which, the king leaned, either for state, or for support.

20. Gehazi - One would expect Elisha's servant should have been a saint: but we find him far otherwise. The best men, the best ministers, have often had those about them, that were their grief and shame. This Syrian - A stranger, and one of that nation who are the implacable enemies of God's people. As the Lord - He swears, that he might have some pretense for the action to which he had bound himself by his oath; not considering, that to swear to do any wicked action, is so far from excusing it, that it makes it much worse.

23. Urged him - Who at first refused it upon a pretense of modesty.

26. Olive yards, &c. - Which Gehazi intended to purchase with this money: and therefore the prophet names them, to inform him, that he exactly knew, not only his outward actions, but even his most secret intentions. What a folly is it, to presume upon sin in hopes of secrecy? When thou goest aside into any bye-path, doth not thy own conscience go with thee? Nay, doth not the eye of God go with thee? What then avails the absence of human witnesses?

27. For ever - That is, for some generations; as that word is often used and as may be thought by comparing this with Exod. xx, 55. (?) White - Which is the worst kind of leprosy, and noted by physicians to be incurable. Those who get money by any way displeasing to God, make a dear purchase. What was Gehazi profited by his two talents, when he lost his health, if not his soul, forever?

VI

Elisha causes iron to swim, ver. 1-7. Discloses to the king of Israel the secret counsels of the king of Syria, ver. 8-12. Saves himself out of the hands of those who were sent to apprehend him, ver. 13-23. Samaria is besieged by the Syrians, and reduced to extremity, ver. 24-33.

2. Jordan - To the woods near Jordan. A beam - A piece of timber for the building. Hence it may be gathered, that although the sons of the prophets principally devoted themselves to religious exercises, yet they sometimes employed themselves about manual arts.

10. Sent - Soldiers to secure the place and passage designed.

16. They - Angels, unspeakably more numerous, God, infinitely more powerful.

17. He saw, &c. - Fire is both dreadful and devouring: that power which was engaged for Elisha, could both terrify and consume the assailants. Elijah gave a specimen of Divine justice, when he called for flames of fire on the heads of his persecutors to consume them. Elisha gives a specimen of Divine mercy, in heaping coals of fire on the heads of his persecutors to melt them.

22. Wouldest thou smite - It is against the laws of humanity, to kill captives, though thou thyself hast taken them with thy own sword and bow; which might seem to give thee some colour to destroy them; but much more unworthy will it be in cold blood to kill these, whom not thy arms, but God's providence hath put into thy hands. Set bread - Give them meat and drink, which may refresh and strengthen them for their journey. This was an action of singular piety and charity, in doing good to their enemies, which was much to the honour of the true religion; and of no less prudence, that hereby the hearts of the Syrians might be mollified towards the Israelites.

23. No more - For some considerable time.

24. Ben-hadad - He whom Ahab wickedly spared, now comes to requite his kindness, and to fulfil that Divine prediction. Ben-hadad was a name very frequent among the kings of Syria, if not common to them all.

25. Famine in Samaria - Probably the siege was so sudden, that they had no time to lay in provisions. Pieces - Supposed to be shekels; and the common shekel being valued at fifteen pence of English money, this amounts to five pounds. A vast price, especially for that which had on it so little meat, and that unwholesome and unclean. A kab - A measure containing twenty-four eggs. Dung - This Hebrew word is of a doubtful signification, and no where else used, probably it means a sort of pease, which in the Arabick language (near a-kin to the Hebrew) is called doves dung: for this was a food much in use amongst the poorer Israelites, and was a very coarse food, and therefore fit to be joined with the asses head: and a kab was the usual measure of all sorts of grains and fruits of that sort.

27. Whence shall I help thee - Dost thou ask of me corn or wine, which I want for myself? If God does not, I cannot help thee. Creatures are helpless things without God. Every creature is all that, and only that which God makes it to be.

29. We boiled - A dreadful judgment threatened to them in case of their apostacy, Deut. xxviii, 56, 57, in which they were now deeply plunged.

31. God do so, &c. - Because he had encouraged them to withstand the Syrians, by promising them help from God.

32. He said - Being admonished by God of his danger. This son - The genuine son of that wicked Ahab the murderer of the Lord's prophets. This expression may seem very harsh and unfit; nor is it to be drawn into imitation by others: but it must be considered, that he was an extraordinary prophet, intrusted with a power in some sort superior to that of Joram, and had authority to control and rebuke him in the name of the king of kings. Hold him - That he may not break in upon me, and take away my life, before the king comes.

33. He said - Or, the king, who, though not here named, may be presumed to be present, both by the prophet's prediction of his speedy coming, and by the presence of the Lord, on whose hand the king leaned, chap. vii, 2. This evil - This dreadful famine, which is now so extreme, that women are forced to eat their own children. The Lord - Hath inflicted it, and (for ought I see) he will not remove it. All penal evil is of the Lord, as the first cause and sovereign judge. And this we ought to apply to particular cases: if all evil, then this evil which we are groaning under. Whoever are the instruments, God is the principal agent. What should I, &c. - Thou bidst me wait upon God for help: but I perceive I may wait long enough before deliverance comes: I am weary with waiting, I can wait no longer.

VII

Elisha foretells plenty, and the death of the unbelieving Lord, ver. 1, 2. Four lepers discover that the Syrians are fled, and bring the news into the city, ver. 3-11. The king sends messengers in order to be assured of the truth, ver. 12-15. Sudden plenty and the death of the unbelieving Lord, ver. 16-20.

1. Measure - Hebrew. Seah, a measure containing six cabs, or about a peck and pottle of our measure.
2. Windows - Through which he could rain down corn, as once he did Manna.
6. Hittites - Under which name (as elsewhere under the name of the Amorites) he seems to understand all the people of Canaan. For though the greatest number of that people were destroyed, yet very many of them were spared, and many of them upon Joshua's coming, fled away, some to remote parts, others to the lands bordering upon Canaan, where they seated themselves, and grew numerous and powerful. Kings - Either the king of Egypt, the plural number being put for the singular, or, the princes and governors of the several provinces in Egypt.
7. Fled - None of them had so much sense as to send scouts to discover the supposed enemy, much less, courage enough to face them. God can when he pleases, dispirit the boldest, and make the stoutest heart to tremble. They that will not fear God, he can make them fear at the shaking of a leaf. Perhaps Gehazi was one of these lepers, which might occasion his being taken notice of by the king, chap. viii, 4.
13. Behold, &c. - The words may be rendered, Behold, they are of a truth (the Hebrew prefix, Caph, being not here a note of similitude, but an affirmation of the truth and certainty of the things, as it is taken Num. xi, 1 Deut. ix, 10,) all the multitude of the horses of Israel that are left in it: behold, I say, they are even all the multitude of the horses of the Israelites, which (which multitude) are consumed, reduced to this small number, all consumed except these five. And this was indeed worthy of a double behold, to shew what mischief the famine had done both upon men and beasts, and to what a low ebb the king of Israel was come, that all his troops of horses, to which he had trusted, were shrunk to so small a number.
20. And so it fell out, &c. - See how heinously God resents our distrust of his power, providence and promise! Whenever God promises the end, he knows where to provide the means.

VIII

Elisha's advice to the Shunamite, ver. 1, 2. The king restores her land, ver. 3-6. Elisha's prophecy to Hazael, and the death of Ben-hadad, ver. 7-15. The reign of Jehoram, ver. 16-24. Succeeded by Ahaziah, ver. 25-29.

1. Sojourn - In any convenient place out of the land of Israel. The Lord, &c. - Hath appointed to bring a famine. This expression intimates, that all afflictions are sent by God, and come at his call or command. Seven years - A double time to the former famine under Elijah, which is but just, because they were still incorrigible under all the judgments of God, and the powerful ministry of Elisha.
3. Her house - Which having been forsaken by her, were possessed by her kindred.
4. Gehazi the servant - Formerly his servant. The law did not forbid conversing with lepers, but only dwelling with them.
8. Inquire of the Lord, &c. - In his health he bowed down in the house of Rimmon; but now he tends to inquire of the God of Israel. Among other instances of the change of mens minds by affliction or sickness, this is one; that it often gives them other thoughts of God's ministers, and teacheth them to value those whom they before hated and despised.
9. Thy son - He who before persecuted him as an enemy, now in his extremity honours him like a father.
10. Howbeit - Here is no contradiction: for the first words contain an answer to Benhadad's question, shall I recover? To which the answer is, thou mayest, notwithstanding thy disease, which is not mortal. The latter words contain the prophet's addition to that answer, which is, that he should die, not by the power of his disease, but by some other cause.
11. He settled - The prophet fixed his eyes upon Hazael. Until - 'Till Hazael was ashamed, as apprehending the prophet discerned something of an evil and shameful nature in him.
13. A dog - So fierce, barbarous, and inhuman. King - And when thou shalt have power in thy hand, thou wilt discover that bloody disposition, and that hatred against God's people, which now lies hid from others, and possibly from thyself.
15. Spread it - So closely, that he choaked him therewith.
16. Jehoram - Jehoram was first made king or vice-roy, by his father divers years before this time, at his expedition to Ramoth-Gilead, which dominion of his, ended at his father's return. But now

Jehoshaphat, being not far from his death, and having divers sons and fearing some competition among them, makes Jehoram king the second time, as David did Solomon upon the like occasion.

18. He walked - After his father's death. The daughter - Athaliah. This unequal marriage, though Jehoshaphat possibly designed it as a means of uniting the two kingdoms under one head, is here and elsewhere noted, as the cause both of the great wickedness of his posterity, and of those sore calamities which befel them. No good could be reasonably expected from such an union. Those that are ill matched are already half-ruined.

19. Alway - Until the coming of the Messiah: for so long, and not longer, this succession might seem necessary for the making good of God's promise and covenant made with David. But when the Messiah, was once come, there was no more need of any succession, and the scepter might and did without any inconvenience depart from Judah, and from all the succeeding branches of David's family, because the Messiah was to hold the kingdom forever in his own person, though not in so gross a way as the carnal Jews imagined. A light - A son and successor.

29. Ramah - The same place with Ramoth, or Ramoth-Gilead.

IX

A prophet commissions Jehu to take upon him the government, and destroy the house of Ahab, ver. 1-10. Jehu communicates this to his captains, ver. 11-15. Marches to Jezreel, ver. 16-20. Kills Joram, ver. 21-26. Ahaziah, ver. 27-29. And Jezebel, ver. 30-37.

1. Ramoth - The kings of Israel and Judah were both absent, and Jehu, as it seems, was left in chief command.

7. I may avenge,&c. - That they were idolaters was bad enough: yet that is not mentioned here: the controversy God has with them, is for being persecutors. Nothing fills the measure of the iniquity of any prince so as this doth, nor brings a surer or sorer ruin.

11. Mad fellow - They perceived him to be a prophet by his habit, and gestures, and manner of speech. And these prophane soldiers esteemed the prophets mad-men. Those that have no religion, commonly speak of those that are religious with disdain, and look upon them as crack-brained. They said of our Lord, He is beside himself; of St. Paul, that much learning had made him mad. The highest wisdom is thus represented as folly, and they that best understand themselves, as men beside themselves.

13. They hasted - God putting it into their hearts thus readily to own him. Under him - Under Jehu. A ceremony used in the eastern parts towards superiors, in token of reverence to his person, that they would not have his feet to touch the ground, and that they put themselves and their concerns under his feet, and into his disposal. The stairs - In some high and eminent place, whence he might be seen and owned by all the soldiers, who were called together upon this great occasion.

21. Portion of Naboth - The very sight of that ground was enough to make Jehu triumph and Joram tremble. The circumstances of events are sometimes so ordered by Divine providence, as to make the punishment answer the sin, as face answers face in a glass.

22. Whoredoms, &c. - This may be understood, either literally; spiritual whoredom, which is idolatry, being often punished with corporal: and witchcraft was often practiced by idolaters: or spiritually, of her idolatry, which is often called whoredom, because it is a departing from God, to whom we are tied by many obligations; and witchcraft, because it doth so powerfully bewitch men's minds; and because it is a manifest entering into covenant with the devil. He mentions not Joram's, but his mother's sins; because they were more notorious and infamous: and because they were the principal cause why God inflicted, and he was come to execute these judgments. The way of sin can never be the way of peace.

24. The arrow - It was one of God's arrows, which he ordained against the persecutor.

27. He died - The history is briefly and imperfectly described here, and the defects supplied in (the book of Chronicles, is great part written for that end, to supply things omitted in the book of Kings) out of both it may be thus compleated: he fled first to Megiddo, and thence to Samaria, where he was caught, and thence brought to Jehu, and by his sentence was put to death at Megiddo.

31. Had Zimri - Remember thy brother traitor Zimri had but a very short enjoyment of the benefit of his treason.

34. And said - It seems he had forgot the charge given him above, ver. 10. A king's daughter - He doth not say, because she was a king's wife, lest he should seem to shew any respect to that wicked house of Ahab, which God had devoted to utter destruction.

X

Jehu cuts off all Ahab's sons, ver. 1-10. And kindred, ver. 11- 14. Takes Jehonadab with him, ver. 11-17. Slays the worshippers of Baal, ver. 18-25. Abolishes his worship, ver. 26-28. Yet retains the worship of the Calves, ver. 29-31. Which God punishes by Hazael, ver. 32-33. Jehu's death, ver. 34-37

5. The house - The chief governor of the kings palace. City - The chief magistrate or military governor.

7. Sent them - Jehu justly required this, because the sovereign Lord of all mens lives commanded it, but the Samaritans wickedly obeyed it, without any knowledge of, or regard to God's command.

11. Left none - In that place and kingdom; for he did leave some of the royal seed of Judah.

15. Rechab - A Kenite, 1 Chron. ii, 55, and a man of singular prudence and piety. Coming - To congratulate with him, for the destruction of that wicked family; and to encourage him to proceed in fulfilling the will of God. Him - Jehu saluted Jehonadab. Is, &c. - Dost thou heartily approve of me, and my present proceedings.

18. Jehu said - The words being manifestly false, and spoken with a design to deceive, cannot be excused, this being an unmovable principle, That we must not do the least evil, that the greatest good may come.

25. City - To some buildings belonging to this house of Baal, which may be here called the city; because they were very numerous and capacious. For as there were divers chambers and rooms built without the temple, belonging to it, for the use of the priests, and Levites. So it may probably be conceived, That this famous temple of Baal had many such buildings; in some of which, the priests of Baal, or of the groves, (whereof there were great numbers belonging to the king's court, 1 Kings xviii, 19,) peradventure might dwell; and others of them might be for divers uses belonging to the house, and service of Baal.

27. Draught-house - A sink or common shore.

29. Jehu departed not - So that it is plain, his religion was but superficial: otherwise it would not have given way to his policy.

30. Done well - In part, and so far as is here expressed.

31. Took no heed - Sin, clearly shewed that his heart was not right with God.

XI

Athaliah usurps the government and destroys all the seed royal; only Joash escapes, ver. 1-3. He is made king, ver. 4-12. Athaliah is slain, ver. 13-16. Joash reigns well, ver. 17-21.

1. She destroyed - This was the fruit of Jehoshaphat's marrying his son to a daughter of that idolatrous house of Ahab. And this dreadful judgment God permitted upon him and his, to shew how much he abhors all such affinities.

2. They hid - Jehosheba and her husband Jehoiada. Bed-chamber - Which was in the house of the Lord. So that it was one of those chambers adjoining to the temple, that were for the uses of the priests and Levites only: which made it more proper for this purpose. Now was the promise made to David bound up in one life. And yet it did not fail. Thus to the Son of David will God, according to his promise, secure a spiritual seed: which tho' sometimes reduced to a small number, brought very low, and seemingly lost, yet will be preserved to the end of time. It was a special providence that Joram tho' a king, a wicked king, married his daughter to Jehoiada, a priest, an holy priest. This some might think a disparagement to the royal family; but it saved the royal family from ruin. For Jehoiada's interest in the temple, gave her an opportunity to preserve the child: and her interest in the royal family, gave him an opportunity of setting him on the throne. See what blessings they lay up in store for their families who marry their children to those that are wise and good.

4. The house - Into the courts of that house, for into the house none but the priests or Levites might enter.

5. Of you - Levites, who were distributed into twenty four courses, to minister in turns, each course consisting of about a thousand men for a week. Enter in - That come into the temple to attend your ministry. King's house - Of that part which lead to the king's palace, which Athaliah now possessed.

6. Sur - The chief gate of the temple. The guard - Either,

1. the king's guard. Or,

2. the guard of the temple; this gate was in the south-side. So, &c. - So you shall guard all the gates or entrances into the temple that neither Athaliah nor any of her soldiers may break in.

7. That go, &c. - Who having finished their course, should have gone home, but were detained, 2 Chron. xxiii, 8. Shall keep - While the rest guard the entrances into the temple; these shall have a special

care of the king's person.

8. Ranges - Or, fences, the wall wherewith the courts of the temple were environed.

12. Testimony - The book of the law, which he put into the king's hand, to mind him of his duty at his entrance upon his kingdom, which was to read and write out that holy book, Deut. xvii, 18, and to govern himself and his kingdom by it: the law of God being frequently and most properly called a testimony, because it is a witness of God's will, and man's duty.

15. Host - Of these companies of Levites, who are elsewhere called the Lord's host, and now were the king's host.

17. A covenant - A sacred covenant whereby he solemnly engaged both the king, and people, that they should be the Lord's people; that they should renounce, and root out all idolatry, and set up and maintain God's true worship. Between the king - This was a civil covenant, whereby the king engaged himself to rule them justly, and in the fear of God; and the people obliged themselves to defend and obey him.

XII

Jehoash reigns well while Jehoiada lives, ver. 1-3. Repairs the temple, ver. 4-16. Compounds with Hazael, ver. 17, 18. Dies ingloriously, ver. 19-21.

3. Burnt incense - To the true God.

4. And Jehoash said, &c. - Remembering that he owed his preservation and restoration to the temple, and that he was made by God the guardian of his temple, he now takes care to repair it. Dedicated things - The money which had been either formerly or lately vowed or dedicated to the service of God and of his house. That is brought - Or rather, that shall be brought: for though the people might vow to bring it thither in convenient time, yet it is not likely they would bring much money thither in the tyrannical and idolatrous reign of Athaliah. The money - The half shekel, which was paid for every one that was numbered from twenty years old and upward. Is set at - Hebrew. the money of souls, or persons according to his taxing, the money which every man that had vowed his person to God, paid according to the rate which the priest put upon him. That cometh - All that shall be freely offered.

15. Faithfully - For they perceived by many experiments that they were faithful.

20. And slew Joash - We are told, in the Chronicles, that his murdering the prophet, Jehoiada's son, was the provocation. In this, how unrighteous so ever they were, yet the Lord was righteous. And this was not the only time, that he let even kings know, it was at their peril, if they touched his anointed, or did his prophets any harm. Thus fell Joash, who began in the spirit, and ended in the flesh. And indeed God usually sets marks of his displeasure upon apostates, even in this life.

XIII

The reign of Jehoahaz, ver. 1-9. A general account of the reign of Joash, ver. 10-13. Elisha falls sick, encourages Joash and dies, ver. 14-19. A dead body is raised by touching his bones, ver. 20-21. Hazael oppresses Israel, and dies, ver. 22-24. Joash beats the Syrians, ver. 25.

6. The grove - Which Ahab had planted for the worship of Baal, and which should have been destroyed, Deut. vii, 5.

7. He - The king of Syria. People - Of his army, or men of war.

8. His might - For though his success was not good, he shewed much personal valour. Which is noted to intimate, that the Israelites were not conquered, because of the cowardice of their king, but merely from the righteous judgment of God, who was now resolved to reckon with them for their apostacy.

14. Fallen sick, &c. - He lived long: for it was sixty years since he was first called to be a prophet. It was a great mercy to Israel and especially to the sons of the prophets, that he was continued so long, a burning and a shining light. Elijah finished his testimony, in a fourth part of that time. God's prophets have their day set them, longer or shorter, as infinite wisdom sees fit. But all the latter part of his time, from the anointing of Jehu, which was forty five years before Joash began his reign, we find no mention of him, or of any thing he did, 'till we find him here upon his death bed. Yet he might be useful to the last, tho' not so famous as he had sometimes been.

17. Eastward - Toward Syria, which lay northeastward, from the land of Israel: this arrow is shot against the Syrians, as a token what God intended to do against them.

18. Smite - The former sign portended victory, this was to declare the number of the victories.

20. Moabites invaded - The mentioning this immediately on the death of Elisha intimates, that the removal of God's faithful prophets, is a presage of judgments approaching.

21. He revived - Which miracle God wrought, to do honour to that great prophet, and that by this seal he might confirm his doctrine, to strengthen the faith of Joash, and of the Israelites, in this promise of their success against the Syrians; and in the midst of all their calamities to comfort such Israelites as were Elisha's followers, with the hopes of eternal life, whereof this was a manifest pledge, and to awaken the rest of that people to a due care and preparation for it.

23. Had compassion - The slowness of God's process against sinners even when they remain impenitent must be construed to the advantage of his mercy, not the impeachment of his justice.

XIV

The good character of Amaziah, ver. 1-4. He avenges his father's death, ver. 5, 6. Overthrows the Edomites, ver. 7. Is defeated by Joash, ver. 8-14. The death and burial of Joash, ver. 15, 16. Amaziah is killed by conspirators, ver. 17-20. The beginning of Azariah's reign, ver. 21, 22. The reign and death of Jeroboam, ver. 23-29.

4. High places - It is hard to get clear of those corruptions, which by long usage have gained prescription.

6. Slew not - Wherein he shewed faith and courage, that he would obey this command of God, though it was hazardous to himself, such persons being likely to seek revenge for their father's death.

7. Joktheel - Which signifies, the obedience of God, that is, given him by God as a reward of his obedience to God's message by the prophet, 2 Chron. xxv, 8, 9.

8. Sent - This challenge he sent, from self-confidence, and a desire of advancing his glory. But he that is fond either of fighting or going to law, will probably be the first that repents it.

9. Saying, &c. - By the thistle, a low and contemptible, yet troublesome shrub, he understands Amaziah; and by the cedar, himself, whom he intimates to be far stronger than he, and out of his reach. Trod down - And with no less ease shall my soldiers tread down thee and thy forces.

10. Glory - Content thyself with that glory, and let not thine ambition betray thee to ruin.

12. Tents - Josephus says, when they were to engage, they were struck with such a terror, that they did not strike a stroke, but every man made the best of his way.

13. Ahaziah - Amaziah's pedigree comes in somewhat abruptly, the son of Joash, the son of Ahaziah: Probably because he now smarted, for the iniquity of his ancestors.

20. On horses - Or, with horses, in a chariot.

21. Azariah - This Azariah is called Uzziah, chap. xv, 30, both names signifying the same thing for substance; that, God's help; and this, God's strength. But this was not done till twelve years after his father's death: so long the government was in the hands of protectors.

25. The sea - Unto the dead sea, once a goodly plain, Gen. xiii, 10, which was their southern border.

26. Was bitter - Whereby he was moved to pity and help them, though they were an unworthy people. Nor any left - Both towns and country were utterly laid waste.

27. Said not - Not yet; he had not yet declared this, as afterwards he did by the succeeding prophets.

29. Jeroboam - It was in the reign of this Jeroboam, that Hosea began to prophesy, and he was the first that wrote his prophecies. At the same time Amos prophesied, soon after Micah, and then Isaiah in the days of Ahaz and Hezekiah. Thus God never left himself without witness, but in the darkest ages of the church, raised up some to be burning and shining lights, to their own age, by their preaching and living; and a few by their writings to reflect light upon us, on whom the ends of the world are come.

XV

The reign of Azariah, ver. 1-7. Of Zachariah, ver. 8-12. Of Shallum, ver. 13-15. Of Menahem, ver. 16-22. Of Pekahiah, ver. 23-26. Of Pekah, ver. 27-31. Of Jotham, ver. 32-38.

1. To reign - Solely and fully to exercise his regal power.

5. A leper - The cause whereof see 2 Chron. xxvi, 16.

8. Six months - After the throne had been vacant several years, thro' the dissentions that were in the kingdom.

13. Full moon - That dominion seldom lasts long, which is founded in blood and falsehood.

30. Twentieth year - The meaning is, that he began his reign in the twentieth year after the beginning of Jotham's reign; or, which is the same thing, in the fourth year of Ahaz, son of Jotham.

33. To reign - Alone: for he had reigned before this, as his father's deputy.

35. Gate - Not of the temple, but of one of the courts of the temple, probably that which led to the king's palace.

XVI

The idolatry of Ahaz, ver. 1-4. He hires the king of Assyria to invade Syria and Israel, ver. 5-9. He erects a new altar in the temple, ver. 10-16. Spoils the temple, ver. 17-18. Dies, ver. 19, 20.

3. Pass - By way of oblation, so as to be consumed for a burnt- offering, which was the practice of Heathens, and of some Israelites, in imitation of them.

5. Could not overcome - Because God of his own mere grace, undertook his protection, and disappointed the hopes of his enemies.

7. Sent messengers, &c. - But was it because there was no God in Israel, that he sent to the Assyrian for help? The sin itself was its own punishment; for tho' it served his present turn, yet he made but an ill bargain, seeing he not only impoverished himself, but enslaved both himself and his people.

12. Offered - A sacrifice, and that not to God, but to the Syrian idols, to whom that altar was appropriated.

13. Peace-offerings - For the Heathens; and Ahaz, in imitation of them, offered the same sorts of offerings to their false gods, which the Israelites did to the true.

14. Brazen altar - Of burnt-offerings, made by Solomon, and placed there by God's appointment. From between, &c. - His new altar was at first set below the brazen altar, and at a farther distance from the temple. This he took for a disparagement to his altar; and therefore impiously takes that away, and puts his in its place. And put, &c. - So he put God's altar out of its place and use! A bolder stroke than the very worst of kings had hitherto given to religion.

15. Great altar - This new altar; which was greater than Solomon's. Sacrifice - Whatsoever is offered to the true God, either in my name (for possibly he did not yet utterly forsake God, but worshipped idols with him) or on the behalf of the people, shall be offered on this new altar. Inquire by - That shall be reserved for my proper use, to inquire by; at which I may seek God, or inquire of his will, by sacrifices joined with prayer, when I shall see fit. Having thrust it out from the use for which it was instituted, which was to sanctify the gifts offered upon it, he pretends to advance it above its institution, which it is common for superstitious people to do. But to overdo is to underdo. Our wisdom is, to do just what God has commanded.

18. The covert - The form and use whereof is now unknown. It is generally understood of some building, either that where the priests after their weekly course was ended, abode until the next course came; which was done upon the sabbath-day: or that in which the guard of the temple kept their station; or that under which the king used to sit to hear God's word, and see the sacrifices; which is called, the covert of the sabbath, because the chief times in which the king used it for those ends, was the weekly sabbath, and other solemn days of feasting, or fasting (which all come under the name of sabbaths in the Old Testament) upon which the king used more solemnly, to present himself before the Lord, than at other times. The entry - By which the king used to go from his palace to the temple.

XVII

The reign of Hoshea, ver. 1, 2. The king of Assyria imprisons him, and carries Israel captive, ver. 3-6. The cause of this captivity, ver. 7-23. The strange nations transplanted into Canaan are plagued with lions, ver. 24-26. An Israelitish priest is sent to them, ver. 27-28. The mongrel religion which followed, ver. 29-41.

1. To reign - He usurped the kingdom in Ahaz's fourth year; but either was not owned as king, by the generality of the people; or was not accepted and established in his kingdom, 'till Ahaz's twelfth year. Nine - After his confirmation and peaceable possession of his kingdom: for in all, he reigned seventeen, or eighteen years; twelve with Ahaz, who reigned sixteen years, and six with Hezekiah.

2. But not, &c. - For he neither worshipped Baal, as many of his predecessors did; nor compelled the people to worship the calves; (one of them, that of Daniel, being destroyed, or carried away before, as the Hebrew writers affirm;) nor, as some add, hindered those by force, who were minded to go to Jerusalem to worship. And yet, the measure of the Israelites sins, being now full, vengeance comes upon them without remedy.

3. Shalmaneser - The son, or successor of Tiglath-pileser. The ancient Hebrew writers made him the same with Sennacherib, who eight years after this time, invaded the kingdom of Judah; it being very frequent in the Eastern parts, for one man to be called by several names. Josephus affirms, that he met with his name in the annals of the Tyrians, which were extant in his days. He came against him, either because he denied the tribute which he had promised to pay; or that he might make him tributary.

6. Carried Israel away, &c. - There, we have reason to think, after some time, they were so mingled with the nations, that they were lost, and the name of Israel was no more in remembrance. They

that forgot God, were themselves forgotten, and they that studied to be like the nations, were buried among them. Thus ended Israel as a nation. When we read their entry into Canaan, under Hoshea the son of Nun, who would have thought, that such would be their exit, under Hoshea, the son of Elah? Yet we find St. James writing to the twelve tribes scattered abroad. So that tho' we never read of the return of those that were carried captive, nor have any ground to believe, that they still remain a distinct body in some remote corner of the world, yet a remnant of them did escape, and will remain 'till all Israel shall be saved.

9. Did secretly - This belongs, either,

1. To their gross idolatries, and other abominable practices, which they were ashamed to own before others; or,

2. to the worship of calves: and so the words are otherwise rendered; they covered things that were not right towards the Lord: they covered their idolatrous worship of the calves, with fair pretenses of necessity, the two kingdoms being now divided, and at enmity; and of their honest intention of serving the true God, and retaining the substance of the Jewish religion. City - In all parts and places, both in cities, and in the country; yea, in the most uninhabited parts, where few or none dwell, beside the watchmen, who are left there in towers, to preserve the cattle and fruits of the earth, or to give notice of the approach of enemies.

13. Seers - To whom he declared his mind, by Revelations and visions, and by whom he published it, bearing witness, from heaven to their doctrine by eminent and glorious miracles.

14. Hardened, &c. - Refused to submit their neck to the yoke of God's precepts. A metaphor from stubborn oxen, that will not bow to the yoke.

15. Vanity - Idols; so called because of their nothingness, impotency, and unprofitableness; and by the long worship of idols, they were made like them, vain, sottish, and senseless creatures.

16. Left all - They grew worse and worse; from a partial disobedience to some of God's laws, they fell by degrees to a total apostacy from all. The host - The stars, as Saturn, Jupiter, Mars, Venus.

18. Judah only - And the greatest part of the tribe of Benjamin, with those of the tribes of Simeon and Levi who were incorporated with them.

19. Judah kept not - Judah's idolatry and wickedness are here remembered, as an aggravation of the sin of the Israelites, which was not only evil in itself, but mischievous to their neighbour, who by their examples were instructed in their wicked arts, and provoked to an imitation of them.

20. All Israel - All the tribes of Israel: first, one part of them, and now the rest. But this extends not to every individual person of these tribes; for many of them removed into the kingdom of Judah, and were associated with them.

21. They made - Which action is here ascribed to the people, because they would not tarry 'till God by his providence, had invested Jeroboam with the kingdom which he had promised him; but rashly, and rebelliously, rose up against the house of David, to which they had so great obligations; and set him upon the throne without God's leave or advice. Drave - He not only dissuaded, but kept then, by force from God's worship at Jerusalem, the only place appointed for it. A great sin - So the worship of the calves is called, to meet with that idle conceit of the Israelites, who esteemed it a small sin, especially when they were forced to it by severe penalties; which yet he shews did not excuse it from being a sin, and a great sin too.

25. Therefore - For their gross neglect, and contempt of God, which was contrary to the principles and practices of the Heathens, who used to worship the gods of the nations where they lived, and gave that honour to their false Gods, which here they denied to the true. Hereby also God asserted his own sovereignty over that land, and made them to understand, that neither the Israelites were cast out, nor they brought in by their valour, or strength, but by God's providence, who as he had cast the Israelites out for their neglect of God's service; so both could, and would in his due time, turn them out also, if they were guilty of the same sins.

28. Taught them - The manner of God's worship, as it was practiced in Israel; as may be gathered both from the quality of this person, who was an Israelitish priest; and from the place of his residence, Beth-el, a place infamous for the worship of the calves, and from the manner of their making priests by this man's direction.

32. Sacrificed - Unto the true God: for as to the worship of their own gods, they needed no instruction, and would not permit a person of another religion to minister therein.

33. They feared - They worshipped God externally in that way which the Israelites used. But every nation made gods of their own besides.

34. Unto this day - That is, till the time when this book was written, above three hundred years in all, till the time of Alexander the Great, when they were prevailed upon to call away their idols. Former manners - As the Israelites before their captivity, gave these nations an ill example, in serving the Lord, and Baal together; so, or after their former manner, they do unto this day, in the land of their captivity. They fear not - Though they pretended to fear, and serve both the Lord and idols, yet in truth they did not, and do not fear or worship the Lord, but their own calves, or other vain inventions: and God will

not accept that mongrel and false worship, which they pretend to give to the true God. Statutes - God's law delivered to their fathers, and to them, as their inheritance, Psalm 1xix, 111. This is alleged as an evidence, that they did not fear the Lord, whatsoever they pretended, because they lived in the constant breach of his statutes. Israel - A name, signifying his special interest in God, and power with him, which was given to him, not only for himself, but for his posterity also, whom God frequently honours with that name. And by this great favour he aggravates their sin.

41. So - In like manner, and after their example. These - Who came in their stead.

XVIII

Hezekiah reforms his kingdom, ver. 1-6. Prospers in all his undertakings, even at the time the ten tribes are led captive, ver. 7- 12. Yet is invaded, and his country put under contribution by Sennacherib, ver. 13-16. Jerusalem is besieged, ver. 17. The virulent speech of Rabshakeh, ver. 18-25. He incites the people to revolt, ver. 26-37.

2. To reign - It is not certain that Ahaz lived only thirty six years, for those sixteen years which he reigned, may be computed, not from the first beginning of his reign, when he reigned with his father; which was at the twentieth year of his age, but from the beginning of his reigning alone.

4. Serpent - The most of them, or such as the people most frequented: for all were not taken away, chap. xxiii, 13, 14, tho' his own father had set them up. We must never dishonour God, in honour to our earthly parents. Brazen serpent - Which had been hitherto kept as a memorial of God's mercy; but being now commonly abused to superstition, was destroyed. To it - Not doubtless as to a God, but only as to an instrument of God's mercy, by and through which, their adoration was directed to God, and given to that only for God's sake. Nehushtan - He said, this serpent, howsoever formerly honoured, and used by God as a sign of his grace, yet now it is nothing but a piece of brass which can do you neither good nor hurt.

5. Trusted - Without calling in foreign succors to establish or help him; which his father Ahaz did; and before him Asa. Before him - Of the kings of Judah only; for David and Solomon were kings of all Israel. The like is said of Josiah, chap. xxiii, 25. Each of them, excelled the other in several respects. Hezekiah in this, that he fell upon this work in the beginning of his reign, which Josiah did not, and with no less resolution, undertaking to do that which none of his predecessors durst do, even to remove the high places, wherein Josiah did only follow his example.

7. Rebelled - He shook off that yoke of subjection, to which his father had wickedly submitted, and reassumed that full and independent sovereignty which God had settled in the house of David. And Hezekiah's case differs much from that of Zedekiah, who is blamed for rebellion against the king of Babylon, both because he had engaged himself by a solemn oath and covenant, which we do not read of Ahaz; and because he broke the covenant which he himself had made; and because God had actually given the dominion of his own land and people to the king of Babylon, and commanded both Zedekiah and his people to submit to him. And whereas Hezekiah is here said to rebel; that word implies, only a defection from that subjection which had been performed to another; which sometimes may be justly done, and therefore that word doth not necessarily prove this to be a sin. And that it was not a sin in him, seems certain, because God owned and assisted him therein; and did not at all reprove him for it, in that message which he sent to him by Isaiah, nor afterwards, though he did particularly reprove him, for his vain-glory, and ostentation, 2 Chron. xxxii, 25, 26.

13. Them - Many of them; universal particles being frequently so used both in scripture, and other authors; and this success God gave him; to lift him up to his own greater and more shameful destruction: to humble and chastise his own people for their manifold sins, and, to gain an eminent opportunity to advance his own honour by that miraculous deliverance which he designed for his people.

14. Three hundred talents, &c. - Above two hundred thousand pounds.

17. Sent - Having received the money, upon which he agreed to depart from Hezekiah and his land, he breaks his faith with Hezekiah, thereby justifying his revolt, and preparing the way for his own destruction.

19. Thus saith, &c. - But what are the greatest men when they come to compare with God, or when God comes to contend with them?

21. This broken reed - Whoever trusts in man, leans on a broken reed: but God is the rock of ages.

22. Is not, &c. - Thus boldly he speaks of the things which he understood not, judging of the great God, by their petty gods; and of God's worship by the vain fancies of the Heathens, who measured piety by the multitude of altars.

25. Am I, &c. - He neither owned God's word, nor regarded his providence; but he forged this, to strike a terror into Hezekiah and the people.

27. To the men - To tell them to what extremities and miseries he will force them.

28. *Jews language* - The tradition of the Jews is, that Rabshaketh was an apostate Jew. If so, his ignorance of the God of Israel was the less excusable, and his enmity the less strange: for apostates are usually the most bitter and spiteful enemies.

31. *A present* - Upon which terms, I will give you no disturbance; but quietly suffer each of you to enjoy his own possession.

XIX

Hezekiah sends to Isaiah to desire his prayers, ver. 1-5. And receives from him an answer of peace, ver. 6, 7. Sennacherib sends a threatening letter to Hezekiah, ver. 8-13 Who recommends his case to God, ver. 14-19. God by Isaiah sends him a comfortable message, ver. 20-34. The army of the Assyrians is destroyed, ver. 35-37

1. *Rent his cloaths, &c.* - Great men must not think it any disparagement to them, to sympathize with the injured honour of the great God.

3. *The children* - We are like a poor travailing woman in great extremity, having no strength left to help herself, and to bring forth her infant into the world. We have attempted to deliver ourselves from the Assyrian yoke; and had carried on that work to some maturity, and as we thought, brought it to the birth; but now we have no might to finish. We have begun an happy reformation, and are hindered by this insolent Assyrian, from bringing it to perfection.

4. *For the remnant* - For Judah, which is but a remnant, now the ten tribes are gone: for Jerusalem, which is but a remnant, now the defensed cities of Judah are taken.

8. *Returned* - To the king, to give him an account of the treaty; leaving behind him the army under the other commanders.

15. *O Lord God of Israel, &c.* - He calls him the God of Israel, because Israel was his peculiar people; but yet the God of the whole earth, not as Sennacherib fancied, the God of Israel only. Let them say what they will, thou art sovereign Lord, the God of gods, even thou alone: Universal Lord of all the kingdoms of the earth; and rightful Lord; for thou hast made heaven and earth. Being creator of all, by an incontestable title thou art owner and ruler of all.

16. *Him* - Rabshakeh: he would not do him the honour to name him.

21. *Virgin* - So he calls Zion, or Jerusalem; because she was pure in good measure from that gross idolatry wherewith other people were defiled, which is called spiritual whoredom: and to signify, that God would defend her from the rape which Sennacherib intended to commit upon her with no less care than parents do their virgin daughters from those who seek to force and deflower them.

23. *Mountains* - I have brought up my very chariots to those mountains which were thought inaccessible by my army. *Lebanon* - An high hill, famous for cedars and fir-trees. *Cut down* - I will cut down the trees that hinder my march, and plane the way for my numerous army and chariots. *Lodgings* - Those cities (which he calls lodgings in way of contempt) which are in his utmost borders. I am come into the land of Canaan at one border, Lebanon, and I resolve to march on to the other border, and so destroy the whole country, from one border to the other. *Carmel* - The forest of mount Carmel, which may seem to be another inaccessible place, like Lebanon.

24. *Strange waters* - Such as were never discovered by others. *Dried up* - And as I can furnish my army with water digged out of the earth; so I can deprive my enemies of their water, and can dry up their rivers, and that with the sole of my feet; with the march of my vast and numerous army, who will easily do this, either by marching through them, and each carrying away part with them: or by making new channels, and driving the waters of the river into them.

25. *Hast thou not, &c.* - Hast thou not long since learned, that which some of thy philosophers could teach thee; that there is a supreme and powerful God, by whose decree and providence all these wars and calamities were sent, and ordered; whose mere instrument thou art, so that thou hast no cause for these vain boastings? This work is mine, not thine. I have, &c. - I have so disposed of things by my providence, that thou shouldest be a great and victorious prince, and that thou shouldest be so successful as thou hast hitherto been, first against the kingdom of Israel, and now against Judah.

26. *Therefore* - Because I had armed thee with my commission and strength, and taken away their spirit and courage.

27. *I know* - Though thou dost not know me, yet I throughly know thee, and all thy designs and actions, all thy secret contrivances in the place of thy abode, in thy own kingdom and court; and the execution of thy designs abroad, what thou intendest in thy going out, and with what farther thoughts thou comest in, or returnest to thy own land.

28. *My hook, &c.* - What a comfort is it, that God has a hook in the nose and a bridle in the jaws of all his and our enemies?

29. *A sign* - Of the certain accomplishment of the promises here made: that God will not only preserve the city from his present fury, but also, bless his people with a durable prosperity, ver. 30, 31.

The third year - This was an excellent sign; especially, considering the waste and havock which the Assyrians had made in the land; and that the Jews had been forced to retire into their strong hold, and consequently to neglect their tilling, and sowing, and reaping; and yet this year they should have sufficient provision from those fruits of the earth which the Assyrians left; and the second year, which was the year of release, in which they might neither sow, nor reap, from such fruits as the earth brought forth of its own accord; and so in the third year. And eat - You shall not sow, and another reap, as lately you did; but you shall enjoy the fruit of your own labours.

30. The remnant, &c. - They shall be well fixt and provided for themselves, and then do good to others.

31. Go forth - That handful of Jews who were now gathered together, and shut up in Jerusalem, shall go out of their several habitations, and by my singular blessing increase exceedingly. The zeal - Although when you reflect upon yourselves, and consider either your present fewness, and weakness, or your great unworthiness, this may seem too great a blessing for you to expect; yet God will do it from the zeal which he hath, both for his own name, and for the good of his undeserving people.

32. He shall not - The army sent with Rabshaketh did not form a close siege against it, but only disposed themselves so as to block it up at some distance; possibly waiting 'till the king of Assyria had taken Libnah and Lachish, (which they presumed he would speedily do.)

35. Angel - Such an angel as destroyed the first-born of Egypt. Arose - The few that were left alive: all their companions were dead.

36. So Sennacherib, &c. - The manner of the expression intimates the great disorder and distraction of mind he was in.

37. Was worshipping, &c. - The God of Israel had done enough to convince him, that he was the only true God. Yet he persists in his idolatry. Justly then is his blood mingled with his sacrifices, who will not be convinced by so dear-bought a demonstration, of his folly in worshipping idols.

XX

Hezekiah's sickness and recovery, ver. 1-7. The sign given him, ver. 8-11. He shews the Babylonians all his treasures, ver. 12-13. The Babylonish captivity foretold, ver. 14-19. He dies, ver. 20, 21

1. Those days - In the year of the Assyrian invasion. Set, &c. - Make thy will, and settle the affairs of thy family and kingdom. Not live - Such threatenings, though absolutely expressed, have often secret conditions.

2. Turned his face - As he lay in his bed. He could not retire to his closet, but he retired as well as he could, turned from the company, to converse with God.

3. In truth - Sincerely with an honest mind. I am not conscious to myself of any gross exorbitances, for which thou usest to shorten mens days. Wept - For that horror of death which is and was common to men, especially, in the times of the Old Testament, when the grace of God in Christ was not so fully manifested, as now it is: and, for the distracted condition in which the church and state were then likely to be left, through the uncertainty of the succession to the crown.

4. Court - Of the king's palace. This is noted to shew God's great readiness to hear the prayers of his children.

5. God of, &c. - I am mindful of my promise made to David and his house, and will make it good in thy person. Shalt go - To give me solemn praise for this mercy.

6. Fifteen years - We have not an instance of any other, who was told before-hand just how long, he should live. God has wisely kept us at uncertainties, that we may be always ready.

10. Go down - In an instant: for that motion of the sun is natural for the kind of it, though miraculous for the swiftness of it; but the other would be both ways miraculous.

11. Degrees - These degrees were lines in the dial: but whether each of these lines or degrees noted an hour, or half an hour, or a quarter of an hour, is uncertain. But the sun itself went back, and the shadow with it. This miracle was noted by the Babylonians, who, having understood that it was done for Hezekiah's sake, sent to inquire into the truth and manner of it, 2 Chron. xxxii, 31. Of Ahaz - Which Ahaz had made in the king's palace. This dial he mentions, because the truth of the miracle might be best and soonest discovered there, this dial possibly being visible out of the king's chamber, and the degrees being most distinct and conspicuous in it.

12. Berodach-baladan - He seems to have been the king of Assyria's vice-roy in Babylon, and upon that terrible slaughter in the Assyrian host, and the death of Sennacherib, and the differences among his sons, to have usurped absolute sovereignty over Babylon. And either himself or his son destroyed the Assyrian monarchy, and translated the empire to Babylon. Sent - Partly, for the reasons mentioned, 2 Chron. xxxii, 31, and partly, to assure himself of the assistance of Hezekiah against the Assyrians, their common enemy.

13. His treasures - For though his country had lately been harassed by the Assyrians, yet he had reserved all his treasures and precious things, which he and his fathers had gathered in Jerusalem. Besides, he had considerable spoils out of the Assyrian camp. Also he had many presents sent to him, 2 Chron. xxxii. 23. Shewed - Which he did through pride of heart, 2 Chron. xxxii, 25, 26, being lifted up by the great honour which God had done him, in working such glorious miracles for his sake, and by the great respects rendered to him from divers princes, and now by this great Babylonian monarch. So hard a matter is it even for a good man to be high and humble.

17. Behold - This judgment is denounced against him for his pride; for his ingratitude, whereby he took that honour to himself which he should have given entirely to God; and for his carnal confidence in that league which he had now made with the king of Babylon, by which, it is probable, he thought his mountain to be so strong, that it could not be removed.

18. Thy sons - Of thy grand-children. Eunuchs - They shall be servants to that heathen monarch, whereby both their bodies will be subject to slavery, and their souls exposed to the peril of idolatry, and all sorts of wickedness.

19. Good is, &c. - I heartily submit to this sentence, as being both just, and merciful. True penitents, when they are under divine rebukes, call them not only just, but good. Not only submit to, but accept of the punishment of their iniquity. So Hezekiah did, and by this it appeared, he was indeed humbled for the pride of his heart.

XXI

The wicked reign of Manasseh, ver. 1-9. Judgment denounced against him and Jerusalem, ver. 10-16. His death, ver. 17, 18. The wicked reign of Amon, ver. 19-22. He is slain, and succeeded by Josiah, ver. 23-26.

1. Reigned - In which time the years of his imprisonment are comprehended.

3. He built, &c. - Trampling on the dust and affronting the memory of his worthy father. All the host of heaven - The sun, moon and stars.

6. Through the fire - Between two fires, by which he dedicated him to Molock, in contempt of the seal of circumcision by which he had been dedicated to God. Times - Lucky, or unlucky days according to the superstitious practice of the heathens.

7. An image - The image of that Baal which was worshipped in the grove.

9. More evil - Partly, because they were not contented with those idols which the Canaanites worshipped, but either invented, or borrowed from other nations many new idols, and partly, because as their light was far more clear, their obligations to God infinitely higher, and their helps against idolatry much stronger than the Canaanites had; so their sins, though the same in kind, were unspeakably worse in respect of these dreadful aggravations.

13. The line - She shall have the same measure, the same judgments which Samaria had. The line is often put for one's lot or portion, because mens portions or possessions used to be measured by lines. A dish - As men do with a dish that hath been used, first wholly empty it of all that is in it, then throughly cleanse and wipe it; and lastly, turn it upside down, that nothing may remain in it; so will I deal with Jerusalem, throughly empty and purge it from all its wicked inhabitants. Yet the comparison intimates, that this should be in order to the purifying, not the final destruction of Jerusalem. The dish shall not be broken in pieces, or wholly cast away, but only wiped.

15. Since, &c. - This forejudgment, though it was chiefly inflicted for the sins of Manasseh and his generation, yet had a respect unto all their former sins.

16. Blood - The blood of those prophets and righteous men who either reproved his sinful practices, or refused to comply with his wicked commands. His sin - His idolatry, which is called sin, by way of eminency. The tradition of the Jews is, that he caused Isaiah in particular to be sawn asunder.

18. Garden - Not in the sepulchre of the kings; probably, by his own choice and command, as a lasting testimony of his sincere repentance and abhorrence of himself for his former crime.

21. He walked, &c. - He revived that idolatry which Manasseh in the latter end of his reign had put down. Those who set bad examples, if they repent themselves, cannot be sure that they whom their example has drawn into sin will repent. It is often otherwise.

XXII

The general character of Josiah, ver. 1, 2. He repairs the temple, ver. 3-7. The high-priest brings him the original book of the law, ver. 8-10. He sends to consult Huldah the prophetess, ver. 11-14. The destruction of Jerusalem foretold, ver. 15-20.

3. The scribe - The secretary of state.

8. The book - That original book of the law of the Lord, given or written by the hand of Moses, as it is expressed, 2 Chron. xxxiv, 14, which by God's command was put beside the ark, Deut. xxxi, 26, and probably taken from thence and hid, by the care of some godly priest, when some of the idolatrous kings of Judah persecuted the true religion, and defaced the temple, and (which the Jewish writers affirm) burnt all the copies of God's law which they could find. It was now found among the rubbish, or in some secret place.

11. The words - The dreadful comminations against them for the sins still reigning among the people. If Josiah had seen and read it before, which seems more probable, yet the great reverence which he justly bare to the original book, and the strange, and remarkable, and seasonable finding of it, had awakened and quickened him to a more serious and diligent consideration of all the passages contained in it. And what a providence was this, that it was still preserved! Yea, what a providence, that the whole book of God is preserved to us. If the holy scriptures had not been of God, they had not been in being at this day. God's care of the bible, is a plain proof of his interest in it. It was a great instance of God's favour, that the book of the law was thus seasonably brought to light, to direct and quicken that blessed reformation, which Joash had begun. And it is observable, they were about a good work, repairing the temple, when it was found. They that do their duty according to their knowledge, shall have their knowledge increased.

13. Inquire - What we shall do to appease his wrath, and whether the curses here threatened must come upon us without remedy, or whether there be hope in Israel concerning the prevention of them.

14. Huldah - The king's earnest affection required great haste; and she was in Jerusalem, which is therefore noted in the following part of the verse, when Jeremiah might at this time be at Anathoth, or in some more remote part of the kingdom; and the like may be said of Zephaniah, who also might not be a prophet at this time, though he was afterward, in the days of Josiah. College - Where the sons of the prophets, or others, who devoted themselves to the study of God's word, used to meet and discourse of the things of God, and receive the instructions of their teachers.

15. The man - She uses no compliments. Tell the man that sent you - Even kings, though gods to us, are men to God, and shall be so dealt with: for with him there is no respect of persons.

17. The works - Gods made with hands.

19. Tender - He trembled at God's word. He was grieved for the dishonour done to God by the sins of his people. He was afraid of the judgments of God, which he saw coming on Jerusalem. This is tenderness of heart.

20. In peace - That is, in a time of public peace: for otherwise he died in battle. Besides, he died in peace with God, and was by death translated to everlasting peace.

XXIII

Josiah reads the law to all the people, ver. 1, 2. Renews the covenant between God and them, ver. 3. Cleanses the temple, ver. 4. Roots out idolatry, ver. 5-20. Keeps a solemn passover, ver. 21- 23. Clears the land of witches, ver. 24. A general commendation of him, ver. 25. His untimely death, ver. 26-30. The reigns of Jehoahaz and Jehoiakim, ver. 31-37.

2. Prophets - Either Jeremiah, Zephaniah, Urijah: or, the sons of the prophets. It seems he read it himself. Josiah did not think it beneath him, to be a reader, any more than Solomon did to be a preacher, and David to be even a door keeper in the house of God. All people are concerned to know the scripture, and all in authority, to spread the knowledge of it.

3. Stood - They declared their consent to it, and their concurrence with the king in that act, which possibly they did by standing up, as the king himself stood when he took it. It is of good use, with all possible solemnity, to oblige ourselves to our duty. And he that bears an honest heart, does not startle at assurances.

4. Second order - Either those two who were next in degree to the high-priest, and in case of sickness were to manage his work: or the heads of the twenty four courses which David had appointed. The grove - The image of the grove: it being most frequent to call images by the names of the persons or things which they represent. The fields - Adjoining to the brook of Kidron. To Beth- el - To shew his abhorrence of them, and that he would not give the ashes of them a place in his kingdom: and to pollute and disgrace that place which had been the chief seat and throne of idolatry.

5. Priests - Hebrew. the Chemarim; the highest rank of priests, employed in the highest work, which was to burn incense.

6. The people - Of that people, those idolatrous people, as it is explained, 2 Chron. xxxiv, 4.

7. Sodomites - Sodomy was a part of idol-worship, being done to the honour of some of their idols, and by the appointment of those impure and diabolical spirits, which were worshipped in their idols. Hangings - Or, curtains, either to draw before the idols which were worshipped in the grove, to preserve them from defilement, or to gain more reverence for them: Or, garments for the service of the

grove, for the idols or the priests belonging to them. Hebrew. houses, that is, either little chappels made of woven work, like those which were made of silver, Acts xix, 24, within which there were some representations of their grove-idols: or rather, tents made of those curtains for the use above- mentioned.

8. Priests - Belonging to the high-places following, whether such as worshipped idols; or such as worshipped God in those forbidden places. Defiled - By burning dead mens bones upon them, or by putting them to some other unclean use. From Geba - The northern border of the kingdom of Judah. Beer-sheba - The southern border, from one end to the other. Gates - Which were erected by the gates of the city here mentioned, to the honour of their tutelary gods, whom after the manner of the heathen they owned for the protectors of their city and habitations. The governor - This circumstance is noted to shew Josiah's great zeal and impartiality, in rooting out all monuments of idolatry, without any respects unto those great persons who were concerned in them.

9. The priest - Who worshipped the true God there. In Jerusalem - Were not suffered to come thither to the exercise of their priestly function; as a just punishment for the corruption of God's worship, and the transgression of so plain and positive a law of God, Deut. xii, 11, which was much worse in them who had more knowledge to discern the will of God, and more obligations to observe it. Did eat - Of the meal-offerings, allotted to the priests, wherein there was to be no leaven, Lev. ii, 4, 5, 10, 11, and consequently of other provisions belonging to the priests, which are contained under this one kind. Thus their spiritual blemish puts them into the very same state which corporal blemishes brought them, Lev. xxi, 17, &c. And thus he mitigates their punishment: he shuts them out from spiritual services, but allows them necessary provisions.

10. Topheth - Very near Jerusalem, where was the image of Molech, to whom some sacrificed their children, burning them in the fire, others dedicated them, making them pass between two fires. It is supposed to be called Topheth, from toph, a drum; because they beat drums at the burning of the children, that their shrieks might not be heard.

11. Horses - Such the eastern nations used to consecrate to the sun, to signify the swiftness of his motion. The sun - Either, to be sacrificed to the sun: or, to draw those chariots in which the kings, or some other in their stead, went forth every morning to worship the rising sun: for both these were the customs of the Armenians and Persians, as Xenophon testifies. Entering in - By the gate of the outward court of the temple. Chamberlain - Or, officer, to whom the care of these horses were committed. Suburbs - Of the temple: in certain outward buildings belonging to the temple. Chariots - Which were made for the worship of the sun.

12. The top - Upon the roof of the king's house. They were so mad upon their idols, that they were not content with all their publick high places and altars, but made others upon their house-tops, for the worship of the heavenly bodies. Cast - To shew his detestation of them: and to abolish the very remembrance of them.

13. Corruption - The mount of olives, called the mount of corruption, for the gross idolatry there practiced. Which - Not the same individual altars; which doubtless either Solomon upon his repentance, or some other of Josiah's predecessors had taken away, but other altars built by Manasseh or Amon, which because erected by Solomon's example, and for the same use, and in the same place, are called by his name: this brand is left by the Holy Ghost upon his name and memory, as a just punishment of that abominable practice, and a mean to deter others from the like. Abomination - The idol, so called, because it was abominable, and made them abominable to God.

14. Men - Of the idolatrous priests, which he caused to be taken out of their graves, ver. 18. As he carried the ashes of the images to the graves, to mingle them with dead mens bones, so he carried dead mens bones to the places where the images had been, that both ways idolatry might be rendered loathsome. Dead men and dead gods were indeed much alike, and fittest to go together.

15. Beth-el - Probably this city was now under the kingdom of Judah, to which it was added by Abijah long since. And it is probable, since the ten tribes were carried away, many cities had put themselves under the protection of Judah. The golden calf, it seems, was gone; but Josiah would leave no remains of that idolatry.

16. Himself - Josiah's care and zeal was so great, that he would not trust his officers with these things, but would see them done with his own eyes. These words - Three hundred years before it was done.

20. The priests - By this relation it appears, that after the departure of the king of Assyria, divers of the Israelites who had retired to other parts, and kept themselves out of the conqueror's hands, returned together with their priests to their own land, and to their old trade, worshipping idols; to whom, peradventure, they ascribed this their deliverance from that judgment which Jehovah had brought upon them. And burnt - According to that famous prophecy, 1 Kings xiii, 1, 2.

22. Such a passover - Celebrated with such solemn care, and great preparation, and numerous sacrifices, and universal joy of all good men; which was much the greater, because of their remembrance of the former wicked and miserable times under Manasseh, and Amon; and the good hopes they now had of the happy establishment of their nation, and the true religion; and of the

prevention of God's judgments denounced against them. Judges - Or, from the days of Samuel, the last of the Judges; as it is expressed 2 Chron. xxxv. 18. None of the kings had taken such care to prepare themselves, the priests, and people, and accurately to observe all the rites, and diligently to purge out all uncleanness, and to renew their covenant with God. And undoubtedly God was pleased to recompense their zeal in destroying idolatry with uncommon tokens of his presence and favour. All this concurred to make it such a passover as had not been, even in the days of Hezekiah.

24. Images, &c. - Three words noting the same thing, to shew, That all the instruments and monuments of idolatry were destroyed, as God had commanded. Spied - All that were discovered; not only such as were in the place of worship, but such as their priests or zealots had removed, and endeavoured to hide.

25. No king - For his diligent study in God's law, and his exact care, and unwearied industry, and fervent zeal, in rooting out idolators, and all kinds and appearances of idolatry, not only in Judah, but in Israel also; and in the establishment of the true religion in all his dominions, and in the conforming of his own life, and his peoples too, (as far as he could) to the holy law of God: though Hezekiah might excel him in some particulars.

26. Notwithstanding - Because though the king was most hearty in his repentance and acceptable to God, and therefore the judgment was delayed for his time; yet the people were in general corrupt, and secretly averse from Josiah's pious reformation, as appears from the complaints of the prophets, especially Jeremiah and Zephaniah, against them: and by the following history, wherein we see, that as soon as ever Josiah was gone, his children, and the princes, and the people, suddenly and greedily returned to their former abominations. Because - The sins of Manasseh, and for the men of his generation; who concurred with him in his idolatrous and cruel practices, are justly punished in this generation: because of God's sovereign right of punishing sinners when he sees fit: because of that publick declaration of God, that he would visit the iniquity of the fathers upon the children: and principally, because these men had never sincerely repented of their own, nor of their fathers sins.

27. I said - Upon the conditions in sundry places expressed, which they broke, and therefore God justly made them to know his breach of promise.

29. The king, &c. - The king of Babylon, who having formerly rebelled against the Assyrian had now conquered him; as appears by the course of the sacred, and the concurrence of the prophane history; and therefore is here and elsewhere called the Assyrian, and the king of Assyria, because now he was the head of that empire. Euphrates - Against Carchemish by Euphrates, as it is expressed, 2 Chron. xxxv, 20, which the Assyrian had taken from Pharaoh's confederates, who therefore sends forces against the Assyrian, that he might both help them, and secure himself. Josiah went - Either to defend his own country from Pharaoh's incursions; or to assist the king of Babylon, with whom he seems to have been in league. Slew - Gave him his death wound there; though he died not 'till he came to Jerusalem. Seen him - When he fought with him, or in the first onset. It does not appear, that Josiah had any clear call to engage in this war; possibly he received his death wound, as a punishment of his rashness.

30. Dead - Mortally wounded. Jehoahaz - Who was younger than Jehoiakim, yet preferred by the people before the elder brother; either because Jehoiakim refused the kingdom for fear of Pharaoh, whom he knew he should hereby provoke. Or because Jehoahaz was the more stout and warlike prince; whence he is called a lion, Ezek xix, 3.

32. His fathers - His grand-parents, Manasseh, and Amon. He restored that idolatry which his father had destroyed. Jerusalem saw not a good day, after Josiah was laid in his grave; but one trouble came after another, 'till within two and twenty years it was destroyed.

33. In bands - Either, because he presumed to take the kingdom without his consent: or because he renewed the war against Pharaoh.

34. Jehoiakim - The giving of names was accounted an act of dominion; which therefore parents did to their children, and conquerors to their vassals or tributaries.

XXIV

Judah severely punished, ver. 1-4. Jehoiakim dies, ver. 5-6. Nebuchadnezzar's conquests, ver. 7. The wicked reign of Jehoiachin, ver. 8, 9. Nebuchadnezzar takes Jerusalem and carries the people captive, ver. 10-16. The wicked reign of Zedekiah, ver. 17-20

2. Bands - For Nebuchadnezzar's army was made up of several nations, who were willing to fight under the banner of such a puissant and victorious emperor.

3. The sins - Properly and directly for their own sins, and occasionally for the sins of Manasseh, which had never been charged upon them, if they had not made them their own by their repetition of them.

6. With his fathers - But it is not said, he was buried with them. No doubt the prophecy of

Jeremiah was fulfilled, that he should not be lamented as his father was, but buried with the burial of an ass.

7. Came not - In this king's days. He could not now come to protect the king of Judah, being scarce able to defend his own kingdom.

8. To reign - In his eighth year he began to reign with his father, who made him king with him as divers other kings of Israel and Judah had done in times of trouble; and in his eighteenth year he reigned alone.

12. Went out - Yielded up himself and the city into his hands; and this by the counsel of Jeremiah, and to his own good. His reign - Of Nebuchadnezzar's reign; as appears by comparing this with chap. xxv, 8, and because Jehoiachin reigned not half a year. Had he made his peace with God, and taken the method that Hezekiah did in the like case, he needed not to have feared the king of Babylon, but might have held out with courage, honour and success. But wanting the faith and piety of an Israelite, he had not the resolution of a man.

13. Vessels - The most and choicest of them, by comparing this with chap. xxv, 14, 15. Solomon made - Though the city and temple had been rifled more than once both by the kings of Egypt and Israel, and by the wicked kings of Judah; yet these golden vessels were preserved from them, either by the case of the priests, who hid them; or by the clemency of the conquerors, or by the special providence of God, disposing their hearts to leave them. Or, if they had been taken away by any of these kings, they might afterwards be recovered good, at the cost of the kings of Judah.

14. All - Not simply all, but the best and most considerable part, as the following words explain it. Captives - Which are more particularly reckoned up, ver. 16, where there are seven thousand mighty men, and a thousand smiths; and those mentioned ver. 15, make up the other two thousand. Craftsmen and smiths - Who might furnish them with new arms, and thereby give him fresh trouble.

17. Zedekiah - That he might admonish him of (what this name signifies) the justice of God, which had so severely punished Jehoiakim for his rebellion; and would no less certainly overtake him, if he should be guilty of the same perfidiousness.

20. Came to pass - Thus the peoples sins were the true cause why God gave them wicked kings, whom he suffered to do wickedly, that they might bring the long-deserved, and threatened punishments upon themselves and their people.

XXV

Jerusalem is taken, ver. 1-4. Zedekiah taken and sentenced, ver. 5-7. Nebuzaradan burns the city, breaks down the walls, and carries away the spoils, with most of the people, ver. 3-17. The chief officers are put to death, ver. 18-21. The very remnant of the people is scattered, ver. 22-26. Jehoiachin is countenanced, after thirty seven years imprisonment, ver. 27-30.

1. Came - To chastise Zedekiah for his rebellion and perjury. Built - To keep all supplies of men or provisions from entering into the city: and that from thence they might shoot darts, or arrows, or stones.

3. The people - For the common people, but only for the great men. Now they eat their own children for want of food, Lam. iv, 3, &c. Jer. in this extremity, earnestly persuaded the king to surrender; but his heart was hardened to his destruction.

6. Riblah - Where Nebuchadnezzar staid, that he might both supply the besiegers with men, and military provisions, as their occasions required; and have an eye to Chaldea, to prevent or suppress any commotions which might happen there in his absence. They - The king's officers appointed thereunto, examined his cause, and passed the following sentence against him.

7. Slew, &c. - Tho' they were but children, that this spectacle, the last he was to behold, might leave a remaining impression of grief and horror upon his spirit. And in slaying his sons they in effect declared, that the kingdom was no more, and that he nor any of his breed were fit to be trusted: therefore not fit to live. Babylon - Thus two prophecies were fulfilled, which seemed contrary one to the other, that he should go to Babylon, Jer. xxxii, 5, xxxiv, 3, and that he should never see Babylon: which seeming contradiction, because Zedekiah the false prophet could not reconcile, he concluded both were false, and it seems Zedekiah the king might stumble at this difficulty.

8. Months, &c. - So the Chaldeans did not put all to fire and sword, as soon as they had taken the city: but about a month after, orders were sent, to compleat the destruction of it. This space God gave them to repent after all the foregoing days of his patience. But in vain; they still hardened their hearts: and therefore execution is awarded to the utmost.

9. Burnt the house of the Lord - One of the apocryphal writers tells us, that Jeremiah got the ark out of the temple, and conveyed it to a cave in mount Nebo, 2Macc ii, 4, 5. But this is like the other tales of that author, who has no regard either to truth or probability. For Jeremiah was at this time a close prisoner. By the burning of the temple God would shew, how little he cares for the outward pomp

of his worship, when the life and power of religion are gone. About four hundred and thirty years the temple of Solomon had stood. And it is observed by Josephus, that the second temple was burnt by the Romans, the same month, and the same day of the month, that the first temple was burnt by the Chaldeans.

11. People - Whom neither the sword nor famine had destroyed, who were eight hundred and thirty two persons, Jer. lii, 29, being members and traders of that city: for it is likely, there were very many more of the country people fled thither, who were left with others of their brethren to manure the land. Multitude - Of the inhabitants of the country.

12. Left of the poor - So while the rich were prisoners in a strange land, the poor had liberty and peace in their own country! Thus providence sometimes humbles the proud, and favours them of low degree.

21. Out of the land - This compleated their calamity, about eight hundred and sixty years after they were put in possession of it by Joshua.

22. Gedaliah - A righteous and good man, and a friend to the prophet Jeremiah.

24. Swear - Assured them by his promise and oath, that they should be kept from the evils which they feared. This he might safely swear, because he had not only the king of Babylon's promise but also God's promise deliver'd by Jeremiah. And it might seem, a fair prospect was opening again. But how soon was the scene changed! This hopeful settlement is quickly dashed in pieces, not by the Chaldeans, but by some of themselves.

25. Came - Moved with envy to see so mean a person advanced into their place. Ten men - Ten captains or officers, and under each of them many soldiers.

26. Egypt - And here they probably mixt with the Egyptians by degrees, and were heard of no more as Israelites.

27. Seven and twentieth - Or, on the twenty fifth day, as it is, Jer. lii, 31. For then the decree was made, which was executed upon the twenty seventh day.

30. All the days of his life - Let none say, they shall never see good again, because they have long seen little but evil. The most afflicted know not what blessed turn providence may yet give to their affairs.

NOTES ON THE FIRST BOOK OF CHRONICLES

THE chief design of these books is, to compleat the history of the kings of Judah; to gather up fragments of sacred history, which were omitted in the books of Samuel and Kings; to explain some passages there mentioned, and to give an exact account of the genealogies. This was then a work of great necessity, to preserve the distinction of the tribes and families; that it might appear, Christ came of that nation, tribe and family, of which he was to be born. And this account, having been hitherto neglected, is most seasonably mentioned in these books, compiled by Ezra after the captivity, because this was to be, in a manner, the last part of the Sacred history of the Old Testament. If many things herein are now obscure to us, they were not so to the Hebrew. And all the persons here named were known to them, by those exact genealogies, which they kept in their several families, and in public registers. In this first book we have a collection of Sacred genealogies, from Adam to David, with several histories inserted, chap. 1-9. An account of the translation of the kingdom from Saul to David, and of David's reign, chap. 10-21. An account of the settlement of ecclesiastical affairs by David, and of his preparations for building the temple, chap. 22-29. These are words of days as the Hebrew title runs, of the best days of the Old Testament Church. But now He is come, for whose sake the registers were preserved, the Jews have lost all their genealogies, even that of the priests, so that there is not any man in the world, that can seasonably prove himself of the house of Aaron.

I

The descents from Adam to Noah and his sons, ver. 1-4. The posterity of Japheth and Ham, ver. 5-16. Of Shem to Abraham, ver. 17-27. Abraham's posterity by Ishmael, ver. 28-31. By Keturah, ver. 32, 33. The posterity of Isaac by Esau, ver. 34-54.

1. *Sheth* - Adam begat Sheth: and so in the following particulars. For brevity sake he only mentions their names; but the rest is easily understood out of the former books. This appears as the peculiar glory of the Jewish nation, that they alone were able to trace their pedigree from the first man that God created, which no other nation pretended to, but abused themselves and their posterity with fabulous accounts of their originals: the people of Thessaly fancying that they sprang from stones, the Athenians, that they grew out of the earth.

5. *The sons of Japheh* - The historian repeating the account of the replenishing the earth by the sons of Noah, begins with those that were strangers to the church, the sons of Japheth, who peopled Europe, of whom he says little, as the Jews had hitherto little or no dealings with them. He proceeds to those that had many of them been enemies to the church, and thence hastens to the line of Abraham, breaking off abruptly from all the other families of the sons of Noah, but that of Arphaxad, from whom Christ was to come. The great promise of the Messiah was transmitted from Adam to Seth, from him to Shem, from him to Eber, and so to the Jewish nation, who were intrusted above all nations with that sacred treasure, 'till the promise was performed, and the Messiah was come: and then that nation was made not a people.

14. *The Jebusite* - The names which follow until ver. 17, are not the names of particular persons, but of people or nations. And all these descended from Canaan, though some of them were afterwards extinct or confounded with others of their brethren by cohabitation or mutual marriages, whereby they lost their names: which is the reason why they are no more mentioned, at least under these names.

17. *The sons* - Either the name of sons is so taken here as to include grandsons, or, these words, the children of Aram, are understood before Uz, out of Gen. x, 23, where they are expressed.

18. *Begat* - Either immediately, or mediately by his son Cainan, who is expressed, Luke iii, 35.

19. *Divided* - In their languages and habitations.

24. *Arphaxad* - Having given a brief and general account of the original of the world and the people in it, he now returns to a more large and particular account of the genealogy of Shem, from whom the Jews were descended.

28. *The sons of Abraham* - All nations but the seed of Abraham are already shaken off from this genealogy. Not that we conclude, no particular persons of any other nation but this found favour with God. Multitudes will be brought to heaven out of every nation, and we may hope there were many, very

many people in the world, whose names were in the book of life, tho' they did not spring from the loins of Abraham.

36. Timna - There is another Timna, the concubine of Eliphaz, Gen. xxxvi, 12, but this was one of his sons, though called by the same name; there being some names common both to men and women in the Hebrew and in other languages.

38. Seir - One of another nation, prince of the Horims; whose genealogy is here described, because of that affinity which was contracted between his and Esau's posterity; and those who were not united and incorporated with them, were destroyed by them. See Deut. ii, 12.

54. These are the dukes of Edom - Let us, in reading these genealogies, think of the multitudes that have gone thro' the world, have successively acted their parts in it, and retired into darkness. All these and all theirs had their day; many of them made a mighty noise in the world; until their day came to fall, and their place knew them no more. The paths of death are trodden paths. How soon are we to tread them?

II

The sons of Jacob, ver. 1-2. Of Judah, to Jesse, ver. 3-12. Of Jesse, ver. 13-17. Of Caleb, the son of Hezron, ver. 18-20. Of Hezron, ver. 21-24. Of Jerahmeel down to Elishama, ver. 25-41. Another branch of Caleb's posterity, ver. 42-49. The sons of Caleb, the son of Hur, ver. 50-55.

3. Judah - Whom he puts first, because the best part of the right of the firstborn, namely, the dominion, was conferred upon him, Gen. xlix, 8, and because the Messiah was to come out of his loins.

6. Dara - If these be the same who are mentioned as the sons of Machol, 1 Kings iv, 31, either the same man had two names, Zerah and Machol, as was usual among the Hebrew: or, one of these was their immediate father, and the other their grand-father. These are named, because they were the glory of their father's house. When the Holy Ghost would magnify the wisdom of Solomon, he saith, he was wiser than these four men. That four brothers should be so eminent, was a rare thing.

7. Carmi - Who is here mentioned, because he was the son of Zimri, who is also called Zabdi, Josh. vii, 1. Achar - Called Achan, Josh. vii, 1, and here Achar, with a little variation for greater significancy: for Achar signifies a troubler.

13. Eliab - Called also Elihu, chap. xxvii, 18, unless that was another person, and the word brother be taken more largely for a kinsman, as it is frequently.

15. Seventh - He had eight sons, 1 Sam. xvi, 10, but probably one of them died presently after that time.

17. Ishmaelite - By birth or habitation, but by profession an Israelite, 2 Sam. xvii, 25.

18. Her sons - The sons of Azubah, who is by way of distinction called his wife, when Jerioth probably was only his concubine, and, it may seem, barren: therefore upon Azubah's death he married another wife. And those other sons of this Caleb mentioned, ver. 42, are his sons by some other wife distinct from all these.

21. Gilead - Of a man so called: a man of noted valour, and the great champion in those parts.

23. Sons of Machir - Partly to his own sons, and partly to his son-in-law Jair, who by reason of that dear affection which was betwixt them, and his forsaking his own tribe and kindred to fight for them and to dwell with them, is here reckoned as his own son.

24. Tekoa - A known place whose father he is called, because he was either the progenitor of the people inhabiting there: or, their prince and ruler: or, the builder of the city.

31. The sons - An expression often used in prophane authors too, where there is but one son.

35. Jarha - Probably he was not only a proselyte, but an eminent man: else an Israelite would not have given him his only daughter.

45. Beth-zur - A place in Judah.

49. Madmannah - This, and divers other following names are the names of places in Judah.

51. Bethlehem - That is, the inhabitants of Bethlehem.

55. Scribes - Either civil, who were public notaries, that wrote and signed legal instruments: or ecclesiastical. And these were either Levites, or Simeonites, or rather Kenites, and are here mentioned not as if they were of the tribe of Judah, but because they dwelt among them, and probably were allied to them by marriages, and so in a manner incorporated with them.

III

The sons of David, ver. 1-9. His successors in the throne, ver. 10-16. The remains of his family in and after the captivity, ver. 17-24.

3. *His wife* - Possibly so called because she was his first, and therefore most proper wife, though her son was born after all the rest before mentioned, and therefore she and her son are put in the sixth place, the wive being here named only for the sons sake.

5. *Four* - All David's children by her, as the text positively affirms: and therefore Solomon is called her, only son, Prov. iv, 3, because she loved him as if he had been so. Ammiel - Called also Eliam, 2 Sam. xi, 3.

6. *Eliphelet* - And he had two other sons called by the same names, ver.

8, probably they were by different wives: and probably they were then distinguished by some additional clause or title, which is here omitted, because the two first were dead before the two second were born, and therefore the names of the deceased were given to these to preserve their memory.

8. *Nine* - There are but seven mentioned, 2 Sam. v, 14. Two of them are omitted there, because they died very early, and here we have all the sons of David, which clause is not added 2 Sam. v, 13-16.

15. *Shallum* - Which most conceive to be the same who is called Jehoahaz, 2 Kings xxiii, 30.

16. *Zedekiak* - This was another Zedekiah. How seldom has a crown gone in a direct line, from father to son, as it did here, for seventeen generations! This was the recompense of David's piety. About the captivity the lineal descent was interrupted, and the crown went from a nephew to an uncle, a presage of the glory's departing from that house.

17. *Assir* - Or, of Jechoniah the captive, which is added to shew that he begat his son when he was captive in Babylon.

18. *Pedaiah* - The sentence seems to be short and imperfect, as is frequent in the Hebrew language, and something is here understood, as, the sons also of Salathiel were Malchiram and Pedaiah, &c. as they gather from hence that the same Zerubbabel is called the son of Pedaiah, ver. 19, and the son (that is, the grandson) of Salathiel, Matt. i, 12.

19. *Their sister* - Sister to the two last named sons of Zerubbabel, namely, by both parents; and therefore named before the other five, ver.

20, who were her brethren by the father, but not by the mother.

21. *Shechaniah* - All these both parents and their sons blended together, are mentioned as the sons of Hananiah, and branches of the royal stock.

22. *Six* - Including the father. But the Hebrew word, Shisha, which is rendered six, may be the proper name of one of the sons of Shemaiah.

IV

The prosperity of Shobal, ver. 1-4. Of Ashur, ver. 5-8. The character and prayer of Jabez, ver. 9, 10. The posterity of Chelah and others, ver. 11-20. Of Shelah, ver. 21-23. The posterity, cities and victories of Simeon, ver. 24-43.

1. *The sons* - The posterity: for only Pharez was his immediate son. But they are all mentioned here only to shew Shobal's descent from Judah.

9. *honourably* - For courage, and for fervent piety. She records this, that it might be a memorandum to herself, to be thankful to God as long as she lived, for bringing her through that sorrow: and a memorandum to him, that she bore him into a vale of tears, in which he might expect few days and full of trouble. And the sorrow in his name might serve to put a seriousness upon his spirit.

10. *Called* - When he was undertaking some great and dangerous service. Enlarge - Drive out these Canaanites, whom thou hast commanded us to root out. Grieve - That it may not oppress and overcome me: more is understood than is expressed. He useth this expression in allusion to his name, which signifies grief. And God granted, &c. - Prospered him remarkably in his undertakings, in his studies, in his worldly business, and in his conflicts with the Canaanites.

12. *Rechab* - From these are sprung the present inhabitants of Rechab, a town not elsewhere mentioned.

14. *Father* - Of the inhabitants of the valley.

21. *Shelah* - Having treated of the posterity of Judah by Pharez, and by Zara, he now comes to his progeny by Shelah.

22. *Had dominion* - Which they ruled in the name and for the use of the kings of Judah, to whom Moab was subject from David's time. Ancient things - The sense is those blessed times are long since past. Our ancestors had the dominion over the Heathen, but their degenerate posterity are slaves in Chaldea, were they are employed as potters or gardeners, or in other servile works.

23. There are - He seems to oppose their present servitude to their former glory, and to shew their mean spirits that had rather tarry among the Heathen to do their drudgery, than return to Jerusalem to serve God and enjoy their freedom. The king - Of Babylon: esteeming it a greater honour to serve that earthly monarch in the meanest employments, than to serve the king of kings in his temple.

27. Of Judah - The tribe of Simeon did not increase proportionably to the tribe of Judah in which they dwelt; as appears by those two catalogues, Num. i, 22; xxvi, 14, which is to be ascribed to God's curse upon them, delivered by the mouth of holy Jacob, Gen. xlix, 5-7, and signified by Moses's neglect of them when he blessed all the other tribes.

31. Their cities - Several of these cities though given to Simeon by Joshua, yet through the sloth or cowardice of that tribe, were not taken from the Philistines, until David's time, who took some of them; and, the Simeonites having justly forfeited their right to them by their neglect, gave them to his own tribe. For it is evident concerning Ziklag, one of them, that it was in the Philistines hands in David's time, and by them given to him, and by him annexed to the tribe of Judah, 1 Sam. xxvii, 6.

40. Fat pasture, &c. - Those who thus dwelt (as we do) in a fruitful country, and whose land is wide and quiet and peaceable, have reason to own themselves indebted to that God, who appoints the bounds of our habitation. Of Ham - The Canaanites, who descended from Ham. And accordingly these words contain a reason, why they went and possessed this place, because it was not in the hands of their brethren of Judah, but in the possession of that people which they had authority to expel.

V

The genealogies of Reuben, ver. 1-10. Of Gad, ver. 11-17. Joined together they conquer the Hagarites, ver. 18-22. Of the half tribe of Manasseh, ver. 23, 24. They are led captive by the king of Assyria, ver. 26, 26.

1. Sons of Israel - This is added emphatically, because they were treated as if they had been the immediate sons of Jacob. Not reckoned - This is the second reason, which sheweth both why Reuben's genealogy was not first mentioned; and if another tribe was to be ranked before it, why that was Judah, and not Joseph, because the order of their genealogy was not to be ruled by the birthright, but by an higher privilege, which was given to Judah.

2. Judah - Not the person, but the tribe of Judah. Prevailed - Excelled the other tribes, especially in the following privilege.

9. Euphrates - From Jordan and the wilderness beyond it unto Euphrates. Or, of the wilderness, which lies towards or reacheth to the river Euphrates, namely, the great wilderness of Kedemoth, Deut. ii, 26, which was extended far and wide towards Euphrates: for that was the eastern border of Reuben's possession, and not Euphrates, to which their habitation never reached. Multiplied - Which forced them to enlarge their habitation as far as they could towards Euphrates.

10. They made war - Thus God did for his people, as he promised them. He cast out the enemy from before them by little and little, and gave them their land as they had occasion for it.

14. These - These seven last named.

20. Helped - By God, ver. 22, who gave them extraordinary courage and success.

22. Was of God - Undertaken in his fear, and carried on in a dependence on him. Then we may expect to prosper in any enterprize, and then only, when we take God along with us.

VI

The first fathers of the tribe of Levi, ver. 1-3. The line of the priests from Aaron to the captivity, ver. 4-15. Of some other families, ver. 16-30. The work of the Levites, ver. 31-48 Of the priests, ver. 49-53. The cities of the priests and Levites, ver. 54- 81.

10. The priest's office - So did all the rest, but it is implied that he did it worthily, he filled his place, and valiantly discharged his office in Uzziah's time. Solomon built - In Solomon's temple; so called to distinguish it from the second temple which was built or in building when these books were written.

44. Ethan - Called also Jeduthun, chap. ix, 16; 2 Chron. xxxv, 15, and in the titles of divers psalms.

54. Castles - So called, not only because, walled and well guarded by the country; but because they and their possessions were in a particular manner the care of divine providence. As God was their portion, so God was their protector. And a cottage will be a castle to those that abide under the shadow of the Almighty. The lot - Or, the first lot.

66. Coasts - Or, of their borders, of their country contained within its borders.

VII

The prosperity of Issachar, ver. 1-5. Of Benjamin, ver. 6-12. Of Naphtali, ver. 13. Of Manasseh, ver. 14-19. Of Ephraim, ver. 20-29. Of Asher, ver. 30-40.

6. Three - They were ten, Gen. xlvi, 25, and five of them are named, chap. chap. viii, 1, but here only three are mentioned, either because these were most eminent; or because the other families are now extinct.

7. Heads - Each of them head of that family to which he belonged. For it may seem by comparing this with chap. viii, 3, &c. that these were not the immediate sons of Belah, but his Grand- children descended each from a several father.

14. She - His wife; his concubine is here opposed to her.

15. Second - Of the second son or grandson of Machir; for so Zelophehad was. Had daughters - Only daughters, and no sons.

17. These - Ashriel and Zelophehad, named ver. 14, 15, the relative being here referred to the remoter antecedent; as is frequent in the Hebrew.

18. His - Gilead's sister. Mahalah - Understand, and Shemida, out of the next verse.

21. Slew - This history is not recorded else where in scripture, but it is in the ancient Hebrew writers. The Philistines (one of whose cities Gath was) and the Egyptians were next neighbours; and in those ancient times it was usual for such to make inroads one into another's country, and to carry thence what prey they could take. And as the Philistines had probably made such inroads formerly into Egypt, and particularly into the land of Goshen, which was the utmost part of Egypt bordering upon the Philistines land; so the Israelites might requite them in the like kind: and particularly the children of Ephraim, to their own loss. And this seems to have happened a little before the Egyptian persecution, and before the reign of that new king mentioned Exod. i, 8. And this clause, that were born in that land, may be added emphatically, as the motive which made them more resolute in their fight with the Ephraimites, because they fought in, and for their own land, wherein all their wealth and concerns lay.

23. Bare a son - Thus the breach was in some measure repaired, by the addition of another son in his old age. When God thus restores comfort to his mourners, he makes glad according to the days wherein he afflicted, setting the mercies over against the crosses, we ought to observe the kindness of his providence. Yet the joy that a man was born into his family could not make him forget his grief. For he gives a melancholy name to his son, Beriah, that is, in trouble: for he was born when the family was in mourning. It is good to have in remembrance the affliction and the misery which are past, that our souls may be humbled within us.

VIII

Some of the heads of the tribe of Benjamin, ver. 1-32. The family of Saul, ver. 33-40.

6. These - These following, ver. 7, because he here speaks of them who were removed. He describes the sons of Benjamin by the places of their habitation, without an exact account of their parents; because their genealogies were broken by that almost total extirpation of this tribe, Judg. xx, 29-48.

28. Heads of the fathers, &c. - Particular notice is taken of these, that others, at their return from captivity, might be induced to settle there too, which it seems few were willing to do, because it was the post of danger. Many great and mighty nations were then upon earth, and many illustrious men in them, whose names are buried in perpetual oblivion, while the names of multitudes of the Israel of God, are here carefully preserved in everlasting remembrance: a figure of God's writing the names of his spiritual Israel, in the Lamb's book of life.

40. Archers - Hebrew. that tread the bow; for the bows of steel, which these used, required great strength to bend them; which therefore they did by treading the bow with their feet, and pulling the string with both their hands.

IX

The chief of Judah, Benjamin. Ephraim and Manasseh, who returned from captivity and dwelt at Jerusalem, ver. 1-9. The priests, ver. 10-13. The Levites, ver. 14-16. Their various offices in the temple, ver. 17-34. The family of Saul, ver. 35-44.

1. The book - In the publick records, wherein there was an account of that kingdom, and of the several families in it.

2. The first - After the return from Babylon. Dwelt - That took possession of their own lands and

cities, which had been formerly allotted them; but of late years had been taken from them for their sins, and possessed by other people. Israelites - The common people of Judah and Israel, called here by the general name of Israelites, which was given them before that unhappy division of the kingdoms, and now is restored to them when the Israelites are united with the Jews in one and the same commonwealth, that so all the names and signs of their former division might be blotted out. And though the generality of the ten tribes were yet in captivity, yet divers of them upon Cyrus's general proclamation, associated themselves, and returned with those of Judah and Benjamin. Levites - These took possession of the cities belonging to them, as they had need and opportunity. Nethinims - A certain order of men, either Gibeonites or others joined with them, devoted to the service of God, and of his house, and of the priests and Levites; who, that they might attend upon their work without distraction, had certain places and possessions given to them; which they are now said to repossess.

4. Ammihud - That there is so great a diversity of names between this catalogue and that of Nehem xi, 4-36, may be ascribed to two causes:

 1. to the custom of the Hebrew, who used frequently to give several names to one person: and,

 2. to the change of times; for here they are named who came up at the first return but many of those in Nehemiah might be such as returned afterward, and came and dwelt either instead of the persons here named, or with them.

9. And fifty-six - They are reckoned but nine hundred and twenty- eight in Neh. xi, 8, either because there he mentions only those that were by lot determined to dwell at Jerusalem, to whom he here adds those who freely offered themselves to it; or because some of the persons first placed there were dead, or removed from Jerusalem upon some emergent occasion.

11. The ruler - Or, a ruler in the house of God: not the high-priest, who was Ezra, Ezra iii, 8, but a chief ruler under him.

13. Able men - Hebrew. mighty men of valour: which is here noted as an excellent qualification for their place; because the priests might meet with great opposition in the discharge of their office, in the execution of the censures upon all impure persons without exception, and in preserving sacred things from violation by the touch of forbidden hands.

17. Porters - Whose office it was to keep all the gates of the temple, that no unclean person or thing might enter into it.

18. King's gate - In the east-gate of the temple, which was so called, because the kings of Judah used to go to the temple through that gate. Under this gate he comprehends all the rest, which also were guarded by these porters. Companies - Or, according to the courses. They kept the gates successively, according to that method into which the Levites were distributed, for the more convenient management of their several offices; among which this of the porters was one.

19. Tabernacle - Namely, in time past, when the tabernacle was standing, before the temple was built. Fathers - The Kohathites. Host - When the Israelites were in the wilderness, encamped in a military manner round about the tabernacle, with whom these were then placed. Entry - Of the veil by which they entered into the tabernacle; which he calls the entry because then there were no gates. The meaning is, that all things were now restored to their primitive order; and the several persons took those offices upon them, which their ancestors had before them.

21. Was - In the time of David, as the following verse sheweth. Porter - Chief porter. The door - Of the door which led out of the priests court into the tabernacle, in which the ark was placed. Before the temple was built, they had a mean and moveable tent, which they made use of in the mean time. They that cannot yet have a temple, let them be thankful for a tabernacle, and make the best use of it. Never let God's work be left undone, for want of a place to do it in.

22. Villages - Where their usual residence was, and whence they came to Jerusalem in their courses. Ordain - In the times of the Judges there was much disorder both in the Jewish state and church, and the Levites came to the tabernacle promiscuously, and as their inclinations or occasions brought them. But Samuel observing they were greatly increased, began to think of establishing order in their ministration. And these intentions of his probably were communicated to David, who after his own peaceable settlement in his throne, revived and perfected Samuel's design, and took care to put it in execution.

23. The oversight - Namely, in David's time. Tabernacle - This is added to explain what he means by the house of the Lord, not that tabernacle which David had set up for the ark; but that more solemn tabernacle, which Moses had made by God's express command; which in David's time was at Gibeon; in which God was worshipped until the temple was built. Wards - By turns or courses.

25. To come - From their several villages to the place of worship. Seven days - Every seventh day the courses were changed, and the new comers were to tarry 'till the next sabbath day. With them - To be with them, with the chief porters, who alway's abode in the place of God's worship.

26. Set office - These were constantly upon the place, in the execution of their office, that they might oversee the inferior porters in their work. Treasuries - In which the sacred utensils and other treasures belonging to the temple, were kept.

30. *The ointment* - This is added to shew, that though the Levites were intrusted with the keeping of this ointment, yet none but the priests could make it.

31. *The pans* - Was to take care that fine flour might be provided, that when occasion required they might make cakes in pans.

33. *These* - Others of the Levites; of whose several offices he had spoken before. *Are* - Or rather, *were*; which is understood, all along in the foregoing and following verses. *Chambers* - That they might be ready to come whensoever they were called to the service of God in the tabernacle. *Free* - From all trouble and employment, that they might wholly attend upon the proper work. *That work* - Either composing or ordering sacred songs; or actually singing; or teaching others to sing them. *Day and night* - Continually, and particularly in the morning and evening, the two times appointed for solemn service. Thus was God continually praised, as it is fit he should be, who is continually doing us good.

34. *Jerusalem* - Upon their return from Babylon they were not suffered to chuse their habitations in the country, as others were, but were obliged to settle themselves at Jerusalem, that they might constantly attend upon God's service there.

35. *Maachah* - In this and the following verses, he repeats Saul's genealogy, that he might make way for the following history.

X

The overthrow and death of Saul, ver. 1-7. The triumph of the Philistines, ver. 8-10. The men of Jabesh-gilead take down and bury the bodies of Saul and his sons, ver. 11, 12. The reason of Saul's death, ver. 13, 14.

1. *The men of Israel fled, &c.* - Thus princes sin and the people suffer for it. No doubt there was enough in them to deserve it. But that which divine justice had chiefly an eye to, was the sin of Saul. Great men should in an especial manner, take heed of provoking God's wrath. For if they kindle that fire, they know not how many may be consumed by it for their sakes.

6. *His house* - All his children, then present with him, namely, his three sons, for Ishbosheth and Mephiboshieth were not slain.

10. *Temple of Dagon* - If we give not God the glory of our successes, even Philistines will rise up in judgment with us and condemn us. Shall Dagon have so great a place in their triumphs, and the true God be forgotten in ours?

12. *Seven days* - Every day 'till evening, after the manner of the Jewish fasts.

13. *The word* - Against God's express command: which is a great aggravation of any sin. *Familiar spirit* - Which also was contrary to a manifest command, Levit xix, 31.

14. *Inquired not* - He did in some sort, but not in a right manner, not humbly and penitently, not diligently and importunately, not patiently and perseveringly. Nor 'till he was brought to the last extremity. And then it was too late.

XI

David is made king, ver. 1-3. He takes the castle of Zion, ver. 4-9. A catalogue of his mighty men, ver. 10-47.

6. *Chief* - Before this he was one of David's chief captains: but now he is made captain-general of all the forces of Israel and Judah.

10. *Mighty men* - Yet David ascribed his success, not to the hosts he had, but to the Lord of hosts: not to the mighty men that were with him, but to the mighty God, whole presence with us is all in all.

11. *Slain* - By his own hand, five hundred more being slain by others then joining with him, who pursued the victory, both which sums make up the eight hundred, numbered 2 Sam. xxiii, 8. The slaughter of all is justly ascribed to him, because it was the effect of his valour.

18. *Would not drink of it* - That water which he thought too precious for his own drinking, he poured out to the Lord for a drink-offering. If we have any thing better than other, let God be honoured with it, who is the best and should have the best.

19. *Shall I drink the blood, &c.* - It put him into the utmost confusion, to think three brave men should hazard their lives, to fetch water for him. In his account, it turns the water into blood. It is to the honour of great men, not to be prodigal of the blood of those they employ.

21. *Attained not* - He did not equal them.

41. *Uriah* - The last of that catalogue in 2 Sam. xxiii, 39. But here some others are added to the number, because though they were not of the thirty, yet they were men of great valour and renown amongst David's commanders.

42. *Thirty* - Thirty captains who were under him as their colonel.

XII

The companies that came to David at Ziklag, ver. 1-22. The armies that came to him at Hebron, ver. 23-40.

2. Even - Of Saul's own tribe: who were moved hereto by God's spirit, by the conscience of their duty to David; and by their observation of God's departure from Saul, and of his special presence with David.

4. Thirty - Who came attended with thirty valiant Benjamites, and was their commander.

17. The God of our fathers - He calls God, the God of our fathers, both his fathers and theirs; thus he minds them, not to deal ill with him; for they were both descendents from the same patriarchs, and servants of the same God. And thus he encourages himself to believe, that God would right him, if he was abused. For he was the God of his fathers; therefore a blessing was entailed upon him: and a God to all Israel in particular, as well as a Judge to all the earth.

18. The Spirit - Not only saving graces, but other heroical and generous motions are ascribed to God's spirit, which here stirred up in him a more that ordinary greatness of mind and resolution.

20. As - As he returned from the camp of the Philistines to Ziklag.

21. Against - Against the Amalekites who had taken and burnt Ziklag, whom David and his six hundred men were now pursuing.

22. That time - While he was at Ziklag, and in his march to Hebron, and principally at Hebron. Like - Innumerable, like the stars or angels, both which are called God's hosts.

24. Six thousand, &c. - Who came hither in the name of their brethren; for that whole tribe stuck to David.

27. Jehoida - Not the high-priest, for that was Abiathar, 1 Sam. xxiii, 6, but one of eminent place under him.

29. Kept the ward - endeavoured to keep the crown in Saul's family.

31. Manasseh - Which was within Jordan: for of the other half beyond Jordan he speaks, ver. 37. By name - Who were not ashamed publickly to own David by putting their names to some paper presented to them for that purpose.

32. The times - They understood public affairs, the temper of the nation, and the tendencies of the present events. And they shewed their wisdom at this time; for as they had adhered to Saul while he lived, as knowing the time was not yet come for David to take possession of the kingdom: and as they could not join David, while Abner lived, and had the command of the other tribes wherewith they were encompassed, so as soon as he was dead, and they had opportunity to declare themselves, they owned David for their king.

33. Double heart - They were sincerely loyal, and did not dissemble with David, pretending to be for him, while in their hearts they favoured Saul's family. And none had any separate interests, but all were for the public good.

XIII

David brings up the ark from Kirjath-jearim, ver. 1-8. Uzza being smitten, it is left at the house of Obed-edom, ver. 9-14.

2. David said - After this was proposed by the king and accepted by the people, this great assembly was dismissed, only some of them David reserved to go with him against Jerusalem, which accordingly he did, and succeeded in his enterprize. But before this resolution could be executed, the Philistines came and fought twice with David, as is related 2 Sam. v, 17, 22, &c. and here chap. chap. xiv, 8, &c. And after they were repulsed with great loss and shame, David sets upon the execution of what he had resolved, and in order to it calls another general assembly of the people. Of the Lord - If this translation of the ark be pleasing to God. Are left - After the great desolations and destructions which God for their sins had made among them.

3. For, &c. - The ark was then neglected; and the generality of the people contented themselves with going to Gibeon and offering sacrifices there, not caring, though the ark, the soul of the tabernacle, was in another place. As soon as David had power in his hand, he would use it for the advancement of religion. It ought to be the first care of those that are enriched or preferred, to honour God with their honours, and to serve him and the interests of his kingdom among men, with their wealth and power.

6. That is - The same city was called by both names.

10. Put his hand, &c. - Let the case of Uzza warn us, to take heed of presumption or rashness with regard to holy things; and not to think, that a right intention will justify a wrong action.

11. Perez-uzza - That is, the breach of Uzza. Let David's displeasure on this occasion caution us, to watch over our spirit, lest when God reproves us, instead of submitting to God, we quarrel with him.

If God be angry with us, shall we dare to be angry with him?

14. And the Lord blessed,&c. - Let this encourage us to welcome God's ordinance into our houses, believing the ark is a guest no body shall lose by. Nor let it be the less precious to us, for its being to others a rock of offense.

XIV

David is confirmed in his kingdom, ver. 1, 2. His wives and children, ver. 3-7. His victories over the Philistines, ver. 8-17.

XV

David prepares to bring up the ark, ver. 1-24. It is brought up, ver. 25-28. Michal despises him, ver. 29.

1. Houses - A palace consisting of many houses or apartments for his several wives and children. A tent - He did not fetch the tabernacle of Moses from Gibeon, because he intended forthwith to build the temple.

5. The sons - Of Amram or Izhar, Kohath's sons, Num. iii, 27, otherwise Elizaphan, ver. 8, and Hebron, ver. 9, and Uzziel, ver. 10, were Kohath's children.

11. The Priests - Abiathar the high-priest, and Zadok the second priest.

18. Second degree - The first rank of sacred musicians being those three famous persons named ver. 17, next to whom were these here named. Porters - who were to keep the doors of the tabernacle and courts, but with all were instructed in musick, that when these were free from attendance upon their proper office, they might not be idle nor unprofitable in God's house.

20. Alamoth - Or, with Alamoth which is thought to be the name of an instrument of musick; or of a certain tune, or note, or part in musick. The certain signification of it is not now known; and the like may be said of Sheminith, ver. 21.

21. To excel - Which word may be added to note the excellency of that instrument, or part of musick; or that there was a greater extension or elevation of the voice than in the former. This way of praising God by musical instruments, had not hitherto been in use. But David instituted it by divine direction, and added it to the other ordinances of that dispensation.

22. For song - He was the moderator of the musick, instructing them when and how to lift up their voices, or change their notes, or make their stops.

23. Door-keepers - They were appointed to keep the door of the tent in which the ark was to be kept, that no unallowed person might press in and touch it; and in like manner they were to attend upon the ark in the way, and to guard it from the press and touch of prophane hands; for which end these two went before the ark, is their other two brethren mentioned in the close of ver. 24, came after it.

26. Helped - Encouraging them in their work with some comfortable sign of his presence with them. In all our religious exercises, we must derive help from heaven. God's ministers that bare the vessels of the Lord, have special need of divine help in their ministrations, that God may be glorified thereby, and the people edified.

27. Linen - With a linen ephod. This circumstance is repeated, because it was an unusual thing for one, who was no Levite, to wear a Levitical garment.

XVI

David's sacrifices and alms, ver. 1-3. He appoints Levites to minister before the ark, ver. 4-6. His psalm of thanksgiving, ver. 7-36. Ministers and others are appointed to attend the ark continually, ver. 37-43.

4. To thank, and praise - All our rejoicings should express themselves in thanksgivings to him, from whom all our comforts are received.

7. First - Hereby it is implied, that after this he delivered many other psalms into their hands, to be sung by them to the praise of God in his public service. We shall find it in the same words, in Psalm cv, 1-15 and Psalm 9vi, 1-11, all but the three last verses.

35. From the Heathen - This psalm or prayer was made by David for the use of the church, not only in that present time, but in future ages, in which David foresaw by the spirit of prophecy, the Israelites would forsake God, and for their apostacy be dispersed among the Heathens. In the midst of our praises, we must not forget to pray for those servants of God that are in distress. When we are rejoicing in God's favours, we should remember our afflicted brethren, and pray for their deliverance as our own. We are members one of another.

37. He left - He appointed them their work and station there. Indeed no incense was burnt there, nor sacrifices offered, because the altars were not there. But David's prayers were directed as incense, and the lifting up of his hands as an evening sacrifice. So early did spiritual worship take place of ceremonial.

39. Zadok - The chief-priest at Gibeon, where the tabernacle and altar made by Moses still were, where also the ordinary sacrifices were offered, and the stated worship of God was performed, as the extraordinary worship was before the ark upon great occasions, as when God was consulted, which was to be done before the ark and by the high-priest, who was Abiathar.

40. Which he commanded Israel - These must be kept up; because however in their own nature they were inferior to prayer and praise, yet as they were types of the mediation of Christ, the observance of them was of mighty importance.

42. Of God - Appropriated to the worship of God; not such as they used on other occasions. Between common mirth and holy joy, there is a vast difference: and the limits and distances between them must be carefully kept up.

XVII

God forbids David's building him an house, ver. 1-10. Gives him a gracious promise, ver. 11-15. David's prayer, ver. 16-27.

1. Now - This whole chapter is explained, 2 Sam. vii, 1-29, where the same things are recorded with little variation.

10. Furthermore, &c. - Must he think, that his purpose was in vain, and that he should lose the reward of it? No: it being God's act that prevented the execution of it, he shall be as fully recompensed as if it had been done.

14. Settle him - In the temple, this expression agrees but imperfectly with Solomon, or his successors, but strictly and properly with Christ, to whom alone that promise also of an everlasting establishment in this kingdom belongs. Kingdom - In God's kingdom in a large and general sense. And this, as well as the former phrase, singularly belongs to the Messiah, who was not only to be the king of Israel, but also of all nations. This is an intimation of that great mystery which is more fully revealed in the new testament, namely, that Christ, is the head, or king of all God's church, consisting of Jews and Gentiles, and of all nations, and indeed of all creatures, all which is God's kingdom, and by him given to his son our blessed Lord.

16. Who am I, &c. - We have here David's solemn address to God, in answer to his gracious message. How humbly does he here abase himself, and acknowledge his own unworthiness! How highly does he advance the name of God, and admire his condescending favour? With what devout affections does he magnify the God of Israel: with what assurance build upon the promise! What an example is this of believing, fervent prayer! The Lord enable us all thus to seek him!

18. The honour of thy servant - The honour God puts upon his servants, by taking them into covenant and communion with himself, is so great, that they need not, they cannot desire to be more highly honoured.

19. Servant's sake - In 2 Sam. vii, 21, it is, for thy words sake, for the sake of thy promise made to thy servant.

24. A God - He is really to his people that which he hath styled himself, their God, having taken such care of them, and shewed such mercy and truth to them, as fully answered that title.

27. Blessed forever - David's prayer concludes, as God's promise did, ver. 14, with that which is forever. God's word looks at things eternal. And so should our desires and hopes.

XVIII

David conquers the Philistines, the Moabites, the king of Zobah and the Syrians, ver. 1-8. Makes the king of Hamath and the Edomites pay tribute, ver. 9-13. His court and kingdom flourish, ver. 14-17.

XIX

David's friendly message to king Hanun, ver. 1, 2. Hanun's base usage of his ambassadors, ver. 3-5. The Ammonites prepare for war, ver. 6, 7. David overthrows them and the Syrians, ver. 8- 19.

7. Chariots - Thirty two thousand men, who fought partly from chariots, and partly on foot with chariots, or attending upon the chariots, as the ancient manner of fighting was.

19. His servants - Let those who have in vain stood it out against God, be thus wise for themselves. Let them become his servants; for they are undone, if they remain his enemies.

XX

Rabbah is taken, ver. 1-3. The Philistine giants are slain, ver. 4-8.

2. To weigh a talent - Or, to be worth a talent, that is, five thousand four hundred and seventy five pounds.

8. They fell,&c. - We need not fear great men against us, while we have the great God for us.

XXI

David causes Joab to number the people, ver. 1-6. He repents, ver. 7, 8. God gives him his choice of three judgments, and he chuses the pestilence, ver. 9-13. The havock made thereby: Jerusalem spared, ver. 14, 15. David's prayer, ver. 16, 17. His sacrifice and staying of the plague, ver. 18-30.

1. Satan stood - Before the Lord and his tribunal to accuse David and Israel, and to beg God's permission to tempt David. Standing is the accusers posture before men's tribunals; and consequently the holy scripture (which useth to speak of the things of God, after the manner of men, to bring them down to our capacities) elsewhere represent Satan in this posture.

3. Why, &c. - Or, why should this be a cause of trespass, or an occasion of punishment to Israel? God commonly punishes the people for the sins of their rulers, because they are for the most part guilty of their sins in one kind or other; or at least God takes this occasion to punish people for all their sins.

6. Counted not - Partly for the following reason; and principally by God's gracious providence to Levi, because they were devoted to his service; and to Benjamin, because they were the least of all the tribes, having been almost extinct, Judg. xxi, 6, and because God foresaw that they would be faithful to the house of David in the division of the tribes, and therefore he would not have them diminished. And Joab also presumed to leave these two tribes unnumbered, because he had specious pretenses for it; for Levi, because they were no warriors, and the king's command reached only of those that drew sword. And for Benjamin, because they, being so small a tribe, and bordering upon Jerusalem, might easily be numbered afterward.

7. Displeased - Because this was done without any colour of necessity, and out of mere curiosity, and ostentation.

14. There fell, &c. - He was proud of the number of his people, but God took a course to make them fewer. Justly is that we are proud of so, taken from us, or embittered to us.

16. Sackcloth - In mourning garments, humbling themselves before God for their sins, and deprecating his wrath against the people.

18. Set up an altar, &c. - The commanding of David to build an altar, was a blessed token of reconciliation. For if God had been pleased to kill him, he would not have commanded, because he would not have accepted a sacrifice at his hands.

20. Hid themselves - Because of the glory and majesty in which the angel appeared, which mens weak natures are not able to bear; and from the fear of God's vengeance which now seemed to be coming to their family.

25. Six hundred - We read, 2 Sam. xxiv, 24, he gave fifty shekels of gold: that is, he gave in gold the value of six hundred shekels of silver. 26. By fire - Hebrew. by fire sent from heaven: which was the sign of God's acceptance. The fire that might justly have fastened on the sinner, fastened upon the sacrifice and consumed it. Thus Christ was made sin and a curse for us, and it pleased the Lord to bruise him, that through him God might be to us, not a consuming fire, but a reconciled Father.

28. Sacrificed - When he perceived that his sacrifice was acceptable to God, he proceeded to offer more sacrifices in that place.

30. Afraid - When he saw the angel stand with his drawn sword over Jerusalem, he durst not go away to Gibeon, lest the angel in the mean time should destroy Jerusalem: for the prevention whereof he thought it proper to worship God in that place, which he had consecrated by his special presence and acceptance.

XXII

David prepares for building the temple, ver. 1-5. Instructs Solomon concerning the work, ver. 6-16. Commands the princes to assist him therein, ver. 17-19.

1. Said - Thro' the instinct and direction of God's spirit, by which as he is said to have had the pattern of the house, porch, altar, &c. chap. xxviii, 11, 12, 19, so doubtless he was instructed as to the place where the house should be built. This - This is the place appointed by God for the building of his temple and altar.

5. *Prepared, &c.* - And good reason, because it was intended for the honour of the great God, and was to be a type of Christ, in whom all fulness dwells, and in whom are hid all treasures.

8. *Shed blood* - Not that wars are simply unlawful, but to teach us that the church (whereof the temple was an illustrious type) should be built by Christ, the prince of peace, Isaiah ix, 6, and that it should be gathered and built up, not by might or power but by God's spirit, Zech iv, 6, and by the preaching the Gospel of peace. David therefore was less fit for that service, than one who had not been called to such bloody work. Likewise by setting him aside for this reason, God shewed how precious human life is to him.

14. *Trouble* - This he alleges as a reason why he could do no more, because of the many wars, whereby much of his treasures were exhausted. *Talents* - A talent of Gold in the first constitution was three thousand shekels, as may be gathered from Exod. xxxviii, 24, 25, 26, and so this amounts to a vast sum, yet not impossible for David to get, considering how many and great conquests he made, and what vast spoils and presents he got; and that he endeavoured by all honourable ways to get as much as he could, out of zeal for God's house. And whereas some object, that this quantity of gold and silver was sufficient, tho' the whole fabrick of the temple had consisted of massy gold and silver, it is to be considered, that all this treasure was not spent upon the materials of the temple, but a great part of it upon the workmen, who were nigh two hundred thousand, whereof a great number were officers, and what was not employed in the building of the temple, was laid up in the sacred treasures.

16. *Be doing* - When thou shalt come to the throne. The sense of God's presence must not slacken our endeavours; because he is with us, we must rise and be doing. Then he will be with us even to the end. Work out your salvation, and God will work in you.

XXIII

David declares Solomon his successor, ver. 1. Numbers the Levites and appoints them their several offices, ver. 2-5. Takes an account of the families of the Levites, ver. 6-23. Reckons them from twenty years old, and appoints them their work, ver. 24-32.

2. *Gathered, &c.* - To declare God's mind and his own will, that Solomon should be his successor: and to acquaint them with those directions which he had received from God by the spirit.

3. *Upwards* - Not only 'till fifty, as it was appointed, Num. iv, 2, 3, but even 'till their death: for that was but a temporary law grounded upon a special reason, because the Levites were employed in carrying the tabernacle and sacred vessels from place to place; and therefore God would have them freed from those burdens when they came to feel the infirmities of age: which reason wholly ceasing upon the building of the temple, their work being far easier than it had been, and their service being more a privilege than a burden, their time of service is justly prolonged.

4. *Officers* - To take care that all the work of the temple about sacrifices should be punctually performed, either by themselves or others: which they were not to do all at once, but by courses, a thousand at a time. *Judges* - Not in the affairs of the temple; there the priests presided; but in several parts of the kingdom, where they assisted the princes and elders of every tribe, in the administration of justice.

13. *Sanctify* - That he might keep them from pollution: for these most holy things were polluted when they were touched by any other person. *He and his* - Not only his eldest sons the high-priests successively, but all his posterity or all the priests; for the works here following were not peculiar to the high-priest, but common to all the priests.

14. *Levi* - They were accounted only as common Levites, and were not priests: which is mentioned for the honour of Moses, and the demonstration of his eminent piety and self-denial, who willingly left the government to Joshua, and the priesthood to Aaron, and was content to have his posterity reduced to a private and mean condition.

24. *Twenty years* - As the Levites were anciently numbered from two several times, from the twenty fifth year of their age, and from the thirtieth, Num. iv, 3; viii, 24. In like manner they are here numbered both from their twentieth year, when they were solemnly prepared for, and instructed, and by degrees exercised in some parts of their work; and from their thirtieth year, when they were admitted to the full exercise of their office. And the reason why they were now sooner admitted to service than they had been formerly, is given in the next verses because now their work was more easy, being wholly discharged from that burdensome work of carrying the tabernacle. Besides the people of Israel were multiplied: therefore more hands were necessary, that every Israelite who brought an offering, might find a Levite ready to assist him.

28. *Holy things* - Holy places, and garments, and vessels, and sacrifices, which were to be washed and cleansed from any filthiness that might cleave to them.

29. *All measure* - All measures used either in sacred or civil things, the publick standards whereof were kept in the temple; and therefore the care of keeping them inviolable and producing them upon

occasion, musts needs belong to the priests, and under them to the Levites, who were to examine other measures and all things by them, as occasion required; that so the priests might be at leisure for their higher and greater employments.

30. Morning and even - The two solemn times of offering sacrifices: which work was attended with publick prayer and thanksgiving.

32. Charge - What the priests should commit to their charge, or command them to do.

XXIV

The distribution of the priests, ver. 1-19. Of the Levites, ver. 20-31.

1. Divisions - The several branches into which that family was divided.
2. Therefore, &c. - Were the only persons to whom the execution of that office was committed.
3. Distributed - Allotting to each of them several times, wherein they should by turns have the government of holy ministrations.
5. By lot - That the disposal thereof might be of the Lord, and so all contention be prevented, as no man could be charged with partiality, nor could any say, they had wrong done them. In like manner Matthias was chosen to the apostleship by lot with prayer. "And I know not, says Mr. Henry, but it might be still used in faith, in parallel cases, as an instituted ordinance." Of God - Or rather, of the things of God, that is, of all persons ministering in the sanctuary, and of all holy ministrations done in it, and of all other matters of the Lord, as they are called by way of distinction from, the king's matters, 2 Chron. xix, 11.
6. One, &c. - Or, the chief of one house of the fathers was taken (by lot) for Eleazar (out of his family) and that which was taken after it was taken for Ithamar, out of his family. So the first lot fell to Eleazar, and the second to Ithamar, the third to Eleazar, and the fourth to Ithamar, so successively, 'till all the families of Ithamar had received their lots. And afterwards all the lots came forth to the rest of Eleazar's families, which were double in number to those of Ithamar.
7. Came - Out of the vessel in which all the lots were put together, and out of which they were severally taken.
19. These, &c. - In this order and method they were to come to perform the offices of the temple. To come - To come into the temple every sabbath-day, and to continue there 'till the next sabbath, when they were relieved by others. Aaron - Under the direction of the high-priests, whom he calls Aaron, because he represented his person and executed his office, and their father, because of the authority which by God's appointment he had over them.
31. Over against - Answerable for number and order to those of the priests, so that there should be a course of the Levites for each course of the priests.

XXV

The person's that were to be employed in singing, ver. 1-7. The order in which they were to attend determined by lot, ver. 8- 31.

1. And captains - All the princes of Israel, with the priests and the Levites, whom David gathered together, chap. xxiii, 2, for this very end, that with their approbation and consent, all these things might be established; who are here fitly called the captains of the host; for the princes were, under David, the chief captains of the militia of the kingdom; and as the Levites are called an host, and the Lord's host, because of their number and order in holy ministrations; so these priests and Levites were the captains and governors of the rest. Separated - Distributed them into their several ranks: which, tho' chiefly done by David as a prophet, and by Divine direction, yet is imputed in part to the captains of the host, because it was done with their concurrence and approbation. The service - To the service of God under the conduct of these persons. Prophecy - Praise God by singing the psalms of David, and other sacred songs made by themselves, who were prophets, or by other prophets or holy men of God. Workmen - Of the persons employed in this sacred work. This good work it seems Samuel revived, but did not live to bring it to perfection. Let each in his day do what he can for God, tho' he cannot carry it so far as he would. When we are gone, God can raise up others to build on our foundation, and bring forth the top-stone.
2. Of Asaph - Under his direction. Of the king - In such manner and order as David appointed.
3. Six - Jeduthun their father being included in that number: or Shimei, mentioned ver. 17.
5. The king's seer - He is called the king's seer, either because the king took special delight in him; or because he frequently attended the king in his palace, executing his sacred office there, while the rest were employed in the tabernacle. In the words - To sing Divine songs as were inspired by God to the prophets or holy men of God. The horn - To praise God with the sound of a trumpet or some other

musical instrument made of horn, which being a martial kind of music, might be most grateful to David's martial spirit: tho' he was also skilled in other instruments of music which he used in the house of God.

7. Cunning - Who were so skilful that they were able to teach others; and together with their scholars, made up the four thousand mentioned chap. xxiii, 5.

8. Ward - A course of Levites answerable to one of the priests, upon whom the Levites were to wait in their holy ministrations, chap. xxiii, 28. The scholar - Without any respect to their different ages or abilities.

9. To Joseph - For the family of Asaph, of which Joseph was. Here that clause, he, his sons, and his brethren were twelve, is to be understood, as it is expressed in all the following verses, otherwise they do not make up that number of two hundred and eighty-eight mentioned ver. 7.

XXVI

The Levites that were appointed to be porters, ver. 1-19. Those that were appointed to be treasurers and store-keepers, ver. 20-28. Those that were officers and Judg. in the country, ver. 29- 32.

5. Blessed him - With a numerous posterity and other blessings, for his respect and affection to the ark. The increase and building up of families, is owing to the Divine blessing. And a great blessing it is to have many children, when they are like these, eminent in the service of God.

6. Of valour - This clause is divers times mentioned, because their office required both strength and courage: for they were to shut the doors of the temple, one whereof was so great and weighty, that in the second temple it required twenty men to open and shut it. They were also to keep the guard, to keep out all unclean or forbidden persons, to prevent or suppress any tumults or disorders which might happen in the temple or in its courts, to keep the treasures of the temple, ver. 20, 22, 24, 26, to be officers and Judges over Israel, ver. 29, and to manage every matter pertaining to God, and the affairs of the king, ver. 32.

10. Made him the chief - Not in inheriting the estate; (this was forbidden by the law) but in this service, for which he was better qualified than his elder brother.

12. Wards - Hebrew. having wards answerably to their brethren the other Levites, who were divided into twenty-four courses, as the priests also and the porters were.

13. Cast lots - Determining the times and places of their service not by age or dignity, but merely by lot. Every gate - That it might be known to whom the care of each gate was more especially committed.

15. Asuppim - Or, of gatherings, probably so named from the assembly of the elders, who met there to consult about the affairs of the temple.

16. Shallecheth - A gate of the court so called, as some think, because the ashes and filth of the temple were cast out on that side, which was the most convenient for that purpose, because that was a private quarter, the great ways to the temple lying on the other sides. Going up - By which causeway they went up towards the temple. Ward against ward - As one gate was over against another, the west against the east, and the north against the south, so one ward was over against another.

17. Six - For that being the chief gate of the temple required a better guard.

20. Treasures - There seem to be two different kinds of treasures, the former containing the sacred vessels and other treasures, which by God's command were appropriated to the maintenance of the house; the latter only those things which had been freely given or dedicated to God.

23. The Amramites - The persons following were of these, or the most of these families. Only here is none of the family of the Uzzielites; either because that family was now extinct, whence it is that we read no more of them in the scripture, but only in this place, and Num. iii, 27, or because there was none of them fit to be employed and trusted in these matters.

24. Ruler - The chief over all the treasures, mentioned before or afterward, as his title shews, which is peculiarly given to him and to none of the rest.

27. Maintain - Or repair it.

29. Judges - Judges over the people, in the several cities and towns, to determine questions and controversies which might arise among them. And the reason why the Levites were intrusted with these matters was, because the common law of Israel, by which they had and held all their rights was no other than the law of God, whereof the priests and Levites being the established interpreters, must needs be the most proper Judges of things depending thereon.

30. Of the Lord - In all things which concerned the house or worship of God; to take care that such monies as were given towards building the temple, or towards the sacrifices and other holy ministrations should be gathered and received, and faithfully sent up to Jerusalem; and to see to the execution of all the laws of God among the people. Service of, &c. - They served the king in the execution of his decrees, by which the several rights of the king and people were established. And as the king was the

principal person intrusted with the execution of God's laws, so these Levites chiefly were his eyes by which he saw his people's transgressions, and his hands by which he inflicted due censures upon them for their miscarriages.

31. Fortieth year - His last year, in which he made all the orders of families and officers recorded in these chapters. We should be so much the more diligent in doing good, as we see the day approaching. If we live not to enjoy the fruit of our labours, let us not grudge it to them that come after us.

XXVII

The captains for every month of the year, ver. 1-15. The princes of the several tribes, ver. 16-24. The officers of the court, ver. 25-34.

1. Officers - The standing militia of Israel as it was settled under their several officers. Of courses - In all the business wherein the king had occasion for these persons who were to attend him by turns. Came in, &c. - who being armed and mustered, and to wait upon the king, at Jerusalem or other places, as the king should see fit. By this order near three hundred thousand of his people were instructed and exercised in the use of their arms, and fitted for the defense of their king and kingdom when it should be needful, and in the mean time sufficient provision was made against any sudden tumults or irruptions of enemies. And this monthly course was contrived that the burden of it might be easy and equally distributed among the people.

16. The ruler - These were the princes of the tribes, the constant rulers of the tribes; who seem to have had a superior power to these twenty four captains, and therefore are named before them, being probably the king's chief counsellors and assistants in the great affairs of his kingdom.

22. Tribes - Of the most of the tribes, not of all: for Gad is omitted, probably because that tribe was joined with the Reubenites under one prince.

23. Because - And therefore to number them all both above and under twenty years old, had been both an infinite trouble and a tempting of God, or a questioning the truth of his promises.

27. Vineyards - Over the workmen and labourers in the vineyards; as the next officer is over the fruit of the vineyards. In like manner, one man was over the labourers in the fields, ver. 26, and another over the fruits of the fields put into stores.

31. All these - It is observable, here are no officers for state, none for sport, no master of the ceremonies, or of the bounds, but all for substance, agreeable to the simplicity and plainness of those times. David was a great soldier, a great scholar, and a great prince; and yet a great husband of his estate. Those magistrates who would have their subjects industrious, must themselves be examples of application to business.

32. A scribe - Either one learned in the laws of God, which were also the laws of the land, or, the king's secretary. King's sons - As their tutor or governour.

33. Counsellor - The person whose counsel in matters of state the king most prized and followed. Companion - Or his friend, 2 Sam. xv, 37, the person whom he trusted with his secrets, and whose conversation was most pleasant and acceptable to him. Observe, A cunning man was his counsellor: but an honest man was his friend.

34. After Ahithophel - After his death, these were his chief counsellors.

XXVIII

David declares to the general assembly, that God had appointed Solomon to succeed him and to build the temple, ver. 1- 7. Exhorts the people and Solomon, to cleave to God, ver. 8-10. Delivers to him the model and materials for the temple, ver. 11- 19. Encourages him to begin and finish the work, ver. 20, 21.

1. And David assembled, &c. - A great deal of business David had done in his day. And the nearer he comes to his end, the more busy he is, still endeavouring to do his work with all his might. He is now recovered from the weakness mentioned 1 Kings i, 1. He therefore improves his recovery, as giving him an opportunity of doing God and his country a little more service.

2. Stood - Out of reverence to God and respect to this great and honourable assembly. Brethren - So he calls the princes and chief rulers, both because they had a share with him, though under him in the government; and in compliance with the Divine command, that the king should not be lifted up above his brethren; Deut. xvii, 20. Of rest - A place where it might be fixed, and no more removed from place to place, as it had been. Foot-stool - An house for the ark is here styled an house for the foot-stool of our God. Heaven is his throne: the earth and the most magnificent temples thereon are but his foot-stool. So much difference is there between the manifestations of his glory, in the upper and in the lower world!

6. My house, &c. - So was he a figure of him that was to come, who is both the founder and the foundation of the gospel-temple.

7. At this day - As he hath begun. This promise is absolute with regard to the Messiah, but conditional, with regard to Solomon. If we are constant in our duty, then and not otherwise, we may expect the continuance of his favour.

8. Of our God - I exhort and charge you every one, calling God who is here present, and this congregation wherein all Israel are present by their representatives, or witness against you, if you do not follow my counsel. Keep and seek - Keep those commands which you know, and seek for, or search into what you are yet ignorant of, that you may distinctly understand the whole will of God, and seriously give yourselves to the practice of it. God's commandments cannot be kept without great care.

9. Know - So as to love and serve him. Words of knowledge in scripture-use commonly imply affection and practice. Or, acknowledge him, as thy God, by loving and obeying him. Searcheth - If thou dost only put on a profession of religion to please me, or if thy obedience to God be unsincere, thou mayest indeed deceive me, but thou canst not deceive him, for he searcheth the motions of thy heart. Cast thee off - Notwithstanding all his promises to me and to my seed, and that great honour and favour which he hath shewed thee.

10. The sanctuary - For the ark to dwell in. Be strong - Take courage to break through all difficulties. Without this, we can do no work of God as we ought.

11. The porch - Of the temple. The houses - The houses of the temple, namely, the holy place, and the holy of holies. Parlors - Those rooms which were made against the wall of the house round about, 1 Kings vi, 5. The place - In what particular part of the holy of holies it was to be placed.

12. By the spirit - All the particulars of the tabernacle built by Moses were suggested to him by God's spirit, and it is not credible that God would use less care and exactness in the building of this far more glorious and durable work. All this, it seems, was given him in writing, probably by the ministry of an angel. The temple was to be a sacred thing, a type of Christ, of his church, and of heaven. Therefore it was not to be contrived by man's invention, but to be framed by divine institution. So Christ, the true temple, the church, the gospel-temple, and heaven, the everlasting temple, are all framed according to the divine counsels, and the plan laid before the world began. It is supposed, the tabernacle of Moses, with all its utensils, being wanted no more, was laid up here.

15. According, &c. - Whether they were fixed in one place, whereof there were ten in the holy place, or to be carried from place to place.

16. The tables - There were divers tables to be used about the shew-bread; but one of them seems to have been of more eminency than the rest, and therefore it is commonly called the table of the shew-bread in the singular number.

18. Refined gold - Purer than any of the rest. For that was typical of the intercession of Christ, than which nothing can be more pure and perfect. The cherubim - Which Solomon was to make, (for those which were fastened to the mercy-seat were made by Moses long before) which he fitly compares to a chariot, because within them God is said to sit and to dwell. And because a chariot is made to carry a person from place to place, this expression may be used to intimate that God was not so fixed to them by the building of this temple, but that he would remove from them if they forsook him. Covered - Not above it, for that was done by Moses's cherubim, but before it, to keep it from the eyes of the high-priest, when he entered into the most holy place.

19. In writing - God revealed this to some man of God, who put it into writing, and by him to David. Or, God did, as it were, by his own hand, (where-with he wrote the Ten Commandments) write these things upon the table of his mind.

20. My God - Whom I have chosen and served, who has all along been with me and prospered me, I recommend thee to him; he will be with thee, to strengthen, direct and prosper thee. The God that owned our fathers, and carried them thro' the services of their day, will, in like manner, if we are faithful to him, go along with us in our day, and will never fail us. God never leaves any, unless they first leave him.

XXIX

David exhorts them to contribute toward building and furnishing the temple, ver. 1-5. They do contribute accordingly, ver. 6-9. He offers up solemn prayers, praises and sacrifices to God, ver. 10-21. Solomon is enthroned, ver. 22-25. David finishes his course, ver. 26-30.

2. My might - Work for God must be done with all our might, or we shall bring nothing to pass in it.

4. Of Ophir - The best and purest gold. The walls - The walls of the temple with God, and of the rooms adjoining to it, with silver beaten out into plates.

5. To consecrate - To offer an offering, as I have done. Hebrew. To fill his hand unto the Lord.

Wesley's Notes on the Bible - The Old Testament: First Samuel - Psalms

They that engage themselves in the service of God, will have their hands full: there is work enough for the whole man in that service.

9. Rejoiced - Because this was both an effect of God's grace in them, an eminent token of God's favour to them, and a pledge that this long-desired work, would receive a certain and speedy accomplishment. Great joy - To see the work, which his heart was so much set upon, likely to go on. It is a great reviving to good men when they are leaving the world, to see those they leave behind zealous for the work of God.

10. Blessed, &c. - David was now full of days, and near his end, and it well becomes the aged children of God, to have their hearts much enlarged in praise and thanksgiving. The nearer we come to the land of everlasting praise, the more we should speak the language, and do the work of that world.

14. To offer - That thou shouldest give us both riches to make such an offering, and a willing heart to offer them, both which are the gifts and the fruits of thy good grace and mercy to us. Of thine - We return only what we have received, and therefore only pay a debt to thee. The more we do for God, the more we are indebted to him; for the honour of being employed in his service, and for grace enabling us in any measure to serve him.

15. Strangers - For the land which we possess is thine, not ours; we are not the proprietors but only thy tenants: and as our fathers once were mere strangers in it, even before men, so we at this day are no better before thee, having no absolute right in it, but only to travel through it, and sojourn in it for the short time that we live in the world. None abiding - We only give thee what we must shortly leave, and what we cannot keep to ourselves: and therefore it is a great favour that thou wilt accept such offerings. David's days had as much of substance in them as most men: for he was upon the whole a good man, an useful man, and now an old man. And yet he puts himself in the front of those who must acknowledge, that their days on the earth are as a shadow: which speaks of our life as a vain life, a dark life, a transient life, and a life that will have its period, either in perfect light or perfect darkness.

16. All thine own - In like manner we ought to acknowledge God in all spiritual things: referring every good thought, good desire, and good work to his grace.

18. Of Abraham, &c. - A God in covenant with them, and with us for their sakes. Keep forever - Since it is from thy grace that thy people have such willing minds, continue that grace to them, that they may persist in the same generous disposition towards thee and thy worship. Prepare - Or, rather, confirm, thou who hast begun a good work, confirm and carry it on by thy grace.

20. Worshipped - The Lord with religious, and the king with civil worship.

22. The second time - The first time, was when he was made king during Adonijah's conspiracy. And Zadok - It must be remembered that the high-priest had his viceregent who might officiate in his stead. So that this action of theirs, the anointing Zadok, did not, actually constitute him high-priest, but only settled the reversion of it upon him and his line after Abiathar's death; even as David's making Solomon king, and their anointing Solomon to be the chief governor here, did not put him into actual possession of the kingdom, but only gave him a right to it after the present king's death: hence, notwithstanding this anointing, Abiathar continued to exercise his office 'till Solomon thrust him out, 1 Kings ii, 27.

24. Of the Lord - On the throne of Israel, which is called the throne of the Lord, because the Lord himself was in a peculiar manner the king and governor of Israel. He had the founding, he had the filling of their throne, by immediate direction.

26. Thus, &c. - This sacred writer having mentioned the anointing of Solomon and upon that occasion proceeded to give a farther account of Solomon's actual settlement in his kingdom, returns to his main business, to give an account of the close of David's reign and life. He here brings him to the end of his day, leaves him asleep, and draws the curtains about him.

28. Riches and honour - That is, he had enough of this world, and of the riches of honour of it; and he knew when he had enough. He was satisfied with it, and very willing to go to a better place.

29. The book - In the chronicles of the kingdom, which were written by Nathan and Gad, who were not only prophets, but historiographers out of which either they or some other prophets took by the direction of God's spirit such passages, as were most important and useful for the church in succeeding ages.

30. The times - The changes which befel him; both his troubles, and his successes, the word time or times being often put for things done or happening in them. The countries - Bordering upon the land of Canaan.

John Wesley

NOTES ON THE SECOND BOOK OF CHRONICLES

THIS book begins with the reign of Solomon, continues the history of the kings of Judah to the captivity, and concludes with the fall of that illustrious monarchy and the destruction of the temple. That monarchy, as it was prior in time, so it was in dignity to the four which Nebuchadnezzar dreamed of. The Babylonian began in Nebuchadnezzar himself, and lasted about seventy years: the Persian monarchy, in several families, about an hundred and thirty: the Grecian, in its several branches, about three hundred: and three hundred more went far with the Roman. Whereas the monarchy of Judah continued considerable in a lineal descent, between four and five hundred years. We had the story of the house of David before intermixt with that of the kings of Israel: but here we have its entire, much is repeated here which we had before: yet many passages are enlarged on, and divers added which we had not before, especially relating to religion: the reign of Solomon we have, chap. 1-9. That of Rehoboam, chap. 10-12. The short reign of Ahijah, chap. 13. The long rein of Asa, chap. 14-16. The reign of Jehoshaphat, chap. 17-20. Of Jehoram and Ahaziah, chap. 21, 22. Of Joash and Amaziah, chap. 23-25. Of Uzziah, chap. 26. Of Jotham, chap. 27. Of Ahaz, chap. 28. Of Hezekiah, chap. 29-32. Of Manasseh and Amon, chap. 33. Of Josiah, chap. 34, 35. Of his sons, chap. 36.

I

Solomon's sacrifices, ver. 1-6. His prayer and God's answer, ver. 7-12. The strength, wealth, and trade of Israel, ver. 13-17.

2. Spake - Concerning his intention of going to Gibeon, and that they should attend him thither.

4. The ark - He separated the ark from the tabernacle, and brought it to Jerusalem, where he intended to build a more noble and lasting habitation for it.

5. Sought - Sought the Lord and his favour by hearty prayers and sacrifices in the place which God had appointed.

8. To reign, &c. - Give me the spirit of my father David, that Israel may not suffer by the change. The eminency of those that went before us, and the obligation that lies upon us, to keep and carry on the good work they were engaged in, should quicken our prayers for wisdom and grace, that we may do the work of God in our day, as faithful as they did in theirs.

12. Neither &c. - Those that make this world their end, come short of the other, and frequently of this too. But those who make the other world their end, shall not only obtain that, but shalt have as much as is convenient of this world in their way.

II

Solomon appoints men to build the temple and his own house, ver. 1-2. His message to Huram, ver. 3-10. Huram's obliging answer, ver. 11-16.

1. His kingdom - A royal palace for himself and his successors.

5. Great - For though the temple strictly so called, was but small, yet the buildings belonging to it, were large and numerous.

6. Contain - When I speak of building an house for our great God, let none think I mean to comprehend God within it, for he is infinite. To sacrifice - To worship him there where he is graciously present.

12. Made heaven and earth - It seems Huram was not only a friend to the Jewish nation, but a proselyte to their religion, and that he worshipped Jehovah, the God of Israel, (who was now known by that name to the neighbour-nations) as the God that made heaven and earth, and the fountain of power as well as of being.

14. Of Daniel, &c. - A good omen of uniting Jew and Gentile in the gospel-temple.

17. The strangers - For David had not only numbered his own people, but afterward the strangers, that Solomon might have a true account of them, and employ them about his buildings. Yet Solomon numbered them again, because death might have made a considerable alteration among them since

David's numbering.

18. Hewers in the mountains - He would not employ the free-born Israelites in this drudgery, but the strangers that were proselytes, who having no lands, applied themselves to trades, and got their living by their industry or ingenuity.

III

The place and time of his building the temple, ver. 1, 2. The dimension and ornaments of it, ver. 3-9. The cherubim in the most holy place, ver. 10-13. The veil, ver. 14. The two pillars, ver. 15- 17.

1. Moriah - It was the belief of the ancient Jews, that the temple was built on that very place, where Abraham offered up Issac.
3. Instructed - By David, and by the Spirit of God. The measure - According to the measure which was first fixed.
4. The height - This being a kind of turret to the building.
5. Greater house - The holy place, which was thrice as large as the holy of holies.
9. Nails - Each of the nails, screws, or pins, by which the golden plates were fastened to the walls, weighed, or rather was worth, fifty shekels, workmanship and all. Upper chambers - Rather, the roof.
10. Image work - Or, of moveable work, not fixed to the mercy- seat, as the Mosaical cherubim, but in a moving posture. It seems, they were designed to represent the angels, who attend the Divine Majesty.
13. Inward - Hebrew. towards the house, that is, the most holy house.
14. The veil - The inner veil before the most holy place. This denoted the darkness of that dispensation and the distance at which the worshippers were kept. But at the death of Christ this veil was rent; for thro' him we are brought nigh, and have boldness, or liberty, not only to look, but to enter into the holiest.
17. Jachin - That is, He shall establish. Boaz - That is, In it is strength.

IV

The brazen altar, sea and lavers, ver. 1-5. The golden candlesticks and tables, ver. 7, 8. The doors overlaid with brass, the vessels of the altar, and other brass work, ver. 9-18. The golden altar of incense with its appurtenances, ver. 19-22.

7. Their form - The old form which God prescribed to Moses.
8. Ten tables - Whereon the shew-bread was set, ver. 19. Perhaps each of these had twelve loaves on it. As the house was enlarged, so was the provision.
16. His father - He is so called because Solomon usually called him by that name out of that great respect which he bare to him for his excellent art and service which he did for him: it being usual to call great artists and inventors of things by this name.
20. The manner - According to the prescription of God to Moses.
22. Of gold - In part; they were made of wood, but covered with golden plates.

V

Solomon brings the dedicated treasures into the house, and the ark into the sanctuary, ver. 1-10. While the priests and Levites sing praise, the glory of God fills the house, ver. 11-14.

1. The gold - The remainder of those vast sums mentioned, 1 Chron. xxii, 14.
5. The ark - The ark was a type of Christ, and a token of the presence of God. That gracious promise, Lo, I am with you always, even unto the end of the world, does in effect bring the ark into our religious assemblies, if we claim it by faith and prayer. And this we should be earnest for: the temple itself, if Christ leave it, is a desolate place. Those &c. - As many of them as were fit for use, it is probable, were still used. The rest were carefully laid up, as monuments of antiquity.
9. To this day - When this history was first written; not when it was reviewed by Ezra: for after the return from Babylon, neither staves nor ark were any more seen.
11. By course - According to David's appointment, 1 Chron. xxiv, 1-31, xxv, 1-22, which was only for the ordinary service, but in extraordinary solemnities, such as this, they all came together.
14. Glory of the Lord - And this beautified it more than all the gold with which it was overlaid, or the precious stones with which it was garnished. Yet even that was no glory, in comparison of the glory of the gospel-dispensation.

VI

Solomon declares his intent in building the house, ver. 1-11. His prayer of dedication, ver. 12-42.

1. Thick darkness - He has indeed made darkness his pavilion. But let this house be the residence of that darkness. It is in the upper world that he dwells in light, such as no eye can approach.

9. But thy son, &c. - Thus one sows, and another reaps. And let not the wisest of men, think it any disparagement to pursue the good designs which those that went before them had laid.

14. O Lord, &c. - By this prayer the temple of Solomon is made a figure of Christ, the great Mediator thro' whom we are to offer up all our prayers, and to expect all God's favours, and to whom we are to have an eye in everything wherein we have to do with God.

21. And when they shall, &c. - He asks not, that God would help them without their praying for themselves, but that God would help them, in answer to their prayers. Even Christ's intercession does not supersede, but encourage our supplications.

41. Arise - O thou that sittest in the heavens, arise from the throne of thy glory, and come down into this place, which thou hast appointed for thy constant habitation, from which thou wilt not remove, as formerly thou hast done, from place to place. And the ark - Thou in the ark. Thy strength - Which is the sign and instrument of thy great power put forth from time to time on the behalf of thy people. Salvation - Let them be encompassed on every side with thy protection and benediction.

42. Thine anointed - Of me, who by thy command was anointed the king and ruler of thy people: do not deny my requests, nor send me from the throne of thy grace with a dejected countenance. The mercies - Those which thou hast promised to David and to his house for ever. And thus may we plead, with an eye to Christ, who is called David, Hosea iii, 5. Lord, remember his merits, and accept of us, on the account of them. Remember the promises of the everlasting covenant, which are called the sure mercies of David, Isaiah lv, 3. This must be all our desire, all our hope, all our prayer, and all our plea; for it is all our salvation.

VII

God answers by fire, the people worship, ver. 1-3. Solomon's sacrifices, ver. 4-7. After keeping the feast he sends the people away, ver. 8-11. God appears to him in a vision, ver. 12-22.

1. The fire &c. - In token of God's acceptance of his prayer. The surest evidence of God's acceptance of our prayers is the descent of his holy fire upon us. As a farther token that God accepted Solomon's prayer, the glory of the Lord filled the house; the heart that is filled with an holy awe and reverence of the divine glory, to which God manifests his greatness, and (which is no less his glory) his goodness, is thereby owned as a living temple.

3. With their faces - Thus expressing their awful dread of the Divine Majesty, their chearful submission to the Divine authority, and the sense they had of their utter unworthiness to enter into his presence. Upon - The cloud first came down upon the house, and then entered into the house, and was seen both within it by the priests, and without it by the people.

6. David praised - For David composed the Psalms or hymns, and appointed them to be sung by the Levites, and instrumental music to be joined to their voices.

16. This house - There will I make myself known, and there will I be called upon.

VIII

Solomon's buildings, ver. 1-6. His workmen and officers, ver. 7-10. He settles his wife, ver. 11. Fixes the method of the temple service, ver. 12-16. His trade, ver. 17, 18.

11. The house - He built this house for her; because the ark was now in the house of David, which therefore ought to be kept pure and free from the very danger and appearance of pollution.

14. Man of God - A prophet inspired by God in these matters, whose commands therefore are the commands of God.

16. Prepared - All the materials were procured, and in all points fitted and compleated beforehand.

IX

The queen of Sheba visits Solomon, ver. 1-12. The riches and splendour of his court, ver. 13-28. The conclusion of his reign, ver. 29-31.

8. *For the Lord* - In the Lord's name and stead, in a special manner, because he sat in God's own throne, and ruled over God's peculiar people, and did in an eminent manner maintain the honour of God in his land, and in the eyes of all the world. Those mercies are doubly sweet, in which we can taste the kindness and good will of God as our God.

12. *Besides* - Besides what he gave her of his royal bounty, as is expressed, 1 Kings x, 13, which was in compensation for her presents.

23. *And all the kings of the earth sought the presence of Solomon* - All in those parts of the world.

29. *Iddo* - This, and the other prophets mentioned, were also historians, and wrote annals of their times; out of which these sacred books were taken, either by these, or other prophets.

31. *And Solomon slept* - We have here Solomon in his throne, and Solomon in his grave; for the throne could not secure him from the grave. Here is he stripped of his pomp, and leaving all his wealth and power, not to one whom he knew not whether he would be a wise man or a fool; but one he knew would be a fool! This was not only vanity, but vexation of spirit.

X

The people request Rehoboam to ease their grievances, ver. 1-5. Rehoboam rejecting the old mens counsel, by the advice of the young men answers them roughly, ver. 6-15. Ten tribes revolt, ver. 16-19.

4. *Grievous* - It is probable, when Solomon had declined from God, that God left him to himself to act thus impolitically.

7. *If thou be kind, &c.* - Moderate counsels are generally best. Gentleness will do what violence will not do. Good words cost nothing but a little self-denial, and yet they purchase great things.

16. *See to thine own house* - When public affairs are in a ferment, violent proceedings do but make ill worse. Many have been driven to the mischief they did not intend, by being too severely dealt with.

XI

Rehoboam is forbidden to fight against Israel, ver. 1-4. He secures the two tribes, ver. 5-12. The priests and Levites resort to him, ver. 13-17. His wives and children, ver. 18-23.

3. *Son of Solomon* - Intimating, that this was determined for the sin of Solomon, and therefore could not be reversed.

5. *Built* - Repaired, enlarged, and fortified them. They were built before.

14. *Cast them off* - They would not suffer them to instruct the Israelites in the worship of God, nor to go up to Jerusalem to worship in their courses: and these priests would not join with them in the worship of the calves, as they were commanded to do; and therefore, willingly forsook all their patrimonies and possessions for God's sake. No secular advantages whatsoever should detain us there, where we are in danger of making shipwreck of faith and a good conscience.

15. *High places* - Or, for the high places, both for the devils (the Baals, or false gods, which divers of his people worshipped, whom he encouraged to do so, giving them liberty to do anything but to serve God at Jerusalem) and for the calves. So he erected two sorts of high places, some for Baal, and some for the true God, whom be pretended to worship, in and by the calves.

16. *Set their heart* - Such as loved and feared God in truth.

17. *So they strengthened the kingdom of Judah* - Not only by the addition of so many persons to it: but by their piety and prayers they procured a blessing upon the kingdom which was a sanctuary to them. They made him strong three years; for so long he served God; but when he forsook God, none could strengthen him. We retain our strength as long as we cleave to God and our duty, and no longer. *And Solomon* - This honourable mention of Solomon, as a pattern of piety, is a considerable evidence of his true repentance before his death.

22. *Ruler* - He declared him his successor, and gave him the dominion over, his brethren.

23. *Dispersed* - Lest his other sons should after his death unite together against Abijah, he wisely dispersed them into distant places.

John Wesley

XII

Rehoboam forsaking God is oppressed by Shishak, ver. 1-4. He humbles himself, and is preserved in his kingdom, but spoiled of his treasures, ver. 6-12. His character and death, ver. 13-16.

1. And all Israel - So called, because they forsook God, as Israel had done.
2. Fifth year - Presently after the apostacy of the king and people, which was in the fourth year.
3. Lubims - A people of Africk bordering upon Egypt. Sukkiims - A people living in tents, as the word signifies; and such there were not far from Egypt, both in Africk and in Arabia. Ethiopians - Either those beyond Egypt, or the Arabians.
7. Some deliverance - I will give some stop to the course of my wrath, which was ready to be poured forth upon them to their utter destruction. Those who acknowledge God is righteous in afflicting them, shall find him gracious.
8. May know - That they may experimentally know the difference between my yoke and the yoke of a foreign and idolatrous prince.
12. Went well - The began to recruity themselves, and regain some degree of their former prosperity.
14. Did evil - Or, settled not, although he humbled himself, for a season, yet he quickly relapsed into sin, because his heart was not right with God.

XIII

Abijah sets the battle in array against Jeroboam, ver. 1-3. He declares the justice of his cause, ver. 4-12. Trusts in God and gains the victory, ver. 13-20. His wives and children, ver. 21. 22.

5. Of salt - By a perpetual covenant.
8. Golden calves - There is that among you which may damp your confidence: you worship those images which God abhors.
9. Consecrate - To make himself a priest.
10. The Lord - Hebrew. Jehovah, the only true God. We - Maintain his worship which you have rejected.
11. Pure table - Made of pure gold, Exod. xxv, 23, 24, he saith table and candlestick, though there were ten of each, because ordinarily there was but one of each used at a time for those uses. We keep - Perhaps he flattered himself, that his keeping up the external worship of God would make satisfaction for the errors of his life.
12. Trumpets - Upon the sounding whereof God hath solemnly promised to assist his people, Num. x, 9. The Lord - You have not only us for your enemies, but God, even the God whom your fathers served. It is folly to fight against the God of almighty power: but it is treachery and base ingratitude, to fight against your father's God.
13. Jeroboam - While Abijah was discoursing, Jeroboam takes the advantage of it to lay an ambush. It does not appear that he made any answer to all that Abijah said. The longest sword he thinks will determine the matter, not the better cause.
15. Gave a shout - It is unspeakable comfort, that no stratagem or ambush can cut off our communication with heaven. To the cry of prayer they added the shout of faith, and so became more than conquerors.
20. The Lord struck him - He escaped the sword of Abijah: but God struck him: there is no escaping his sword.
21. Married - Not after this victory, for he died presently after it, but in the whole time of his life.

XIV

The piety of Asa, ver. 1-5. His policy, ver. 6-8. His victory over the Ethiopians, ver. 9-15.

1. Quiet - There was no open war, but there were private hostilities between his and Baasha's subjects.
6. The land had rest - Those have rest indeed, to whom God gives rest; peace indeed, to whom Christ gives peace. We find by experience, it is good to seek the Lord. While we pursue the world, we meet with nothing but vexation.
7. Before us - In our power.
9. Ethiopian - Or, the Arabian, as the Hebrew word Cush is commonly used: these being much nearer to Asa than the Ethiopians.
11. Let not man prevail - If he prevails against us, he prevails, as it were, against thee; because

thou art our God. And we rest on thee, and go forth in thy name, which thou hast encouraged us to do.

12. Smote - With terror, and an unaccountable consternation.

14. Smote the cities - because they had joined, with Zerah in this war.

XV

God's message to Asa, ver. 1-7. Idols removed and the spoil dedicated to God, ver. 8-11. Judah makes a covenant with God, ver. 12-15. Asa removes his mother, destroys her idol, and brings the dedicated things into the temple, ver. 16-18. He has great peace, ver. 19.

1. Spirit of God - Both to instruct him what to say, and to enable him to say it plainly and boldly.

3. Now Israel - They have long lived without the found knowledge and worship of the true God. Israel is here understood of the whole nation of Israel in former times, and especially in the times of the Judges: for then many times they were in a great measure, without God and his law, and teaching priests, as plainly appears from the book of the Judges; they were brought to all the exigencies and calamities following; and they sometimes turned to the Lord, and he was found of them.

5. In those times - When Israel lived in the gross neglect of God and his law. No peace - Men could not go abroad about their private occasions without great danger; as it was in the days of Shamgar, Judg. v, 6.

6. And nation, &c. - One part of the people of Israel destroyed the other by civil wars. As all Israel are called a nation, so the several tribes of them are sometimes called nations.

7. Be strong - Go on resolutely to maintain God's worship and to root out idolatry, as you have begun to do; for this is the only method of preserving yourselves from such calamities as your predecessors have felt.

8. Of Oded - Of Azariah, ver. 1, who was also called by his father's name Oded.

12. Into covenant - The matter of this covenant was nothing but what they were before obliged to. And tho' no promise could lay any higher obligation upon them, than they were already under, yet it would help to increase their sense of the obligation, and to arm them against temptations. And by joining all together in this, they strengthened the hands of each other

15. Rejoiced at the oath - The times of renewing our covenant with God, should be times of rejoicing. It is an honour and happiness to be in bonds with God. And the closer, the better.

XVI

Asa hires the Syrians to invade Israel, ver. 1-6. Puts the prophet who reproved him for it in prison, ver. 7-10. His sickness, death and burial, ver, 11-14.

1. Of the reign - Or, of the kingdom of Asa, that is, of the kingdom of Judah, which was now Asa's kingdom; or from the time of the division of the two kingdoms. Rehoboam reigned seventeen years, Abijah three years, Asa had now reigned fifteen years, all which put together, make up the thirty five years mentioned chap. xv, 19, and in the next year Baasha wars against him; and the ground of the war was the defection of many of his subjects to Asa, chap. xv, 9.

7. Escaped - And so reserved to be a scourge to thy kingdom and posterity: whereas if he had joined with Baasha against thee, thou shouldst have overthrown them both, and prevented all that mischief which that monarch will do to thy family.

8. Lubims - Either, the Lybians in Africa; or another people, possibly descended from them, but now seated in some part of Arabia.

9. Done foolishly - It is a foolish thing to lean on a broken reed, when we have the rock of ages to rely upon. Perfect - Upright and sincere, as thine is not. He was sincere in the general course of his life, but some particulars, whereof this is one, his heart did not perfectly cleave to God.

12. Sought not - He did not humble himself before God, but put his confidence in the skill and faithfulness of his physicians. His making use of physicians was his duty, but his trusting in them, and expecting that from them, which was to be had from God only, was his sin and folly. The help of every creature must be used, with an eye to the creator, and in dependence on him, who makes every creature that to us which it is, without whom the most skilful and faithful are physicians of no value.

14. Burning - Of precious spices; thereby testifying their respect to him notwithstanding his miscarriages.

John Wesley

XVII

Jehoshaphat is established in his kingdom, ver. 1-3. His piety, ver. 4-6. He sends Levites to teach Judah, ver. 7-9. His influence over his neighbours, ver. 10, 11. His greatness, captains and armies, ver. 12-19.

3. Sought not, &c. - It is true, he recovered from that fall. "Yet perhaps, says Mr. Henry, he never, while he lived, fully retrieved the spiritual strength he lost by it."

5. Brought presents - As subjects in those times used to do to their kings, as a token of their respect and subjection to them.

6. Lifted up - Above all discouragements, and fears. He was valiant and resolute for God and his ways. Groves - Those wherein idols were worshipped, and though Asa had done this before, yet either he did not do it thoroughly; or the Jews (who were many of them mad upon their idols) had secretly made new ones, in the latter part of his reign, when he grew more infirm in body, and more remiss in God's cause.

7. To teach - To inform the people of their duty, and of the king's pleasure, as Judges teach or instruct the people in the laws of the land, when they deliver their charges upon the bench; so did these princes in the king's name admonish and require the people to observe and obey the laws of God, which were the municipal laws of that land: the particular explication and enforcement whereof, they left to the Levites and priests here following, who were sent for this end, and accordingly taught the people, ver. 9.

9. And they taught, &c. - And these itinerant Judges and itinerant preachers together, Mr. Henry observes were instrumental to diffuse a blessed light throughout the cities of Judah.

10. Fear fell - Justly concluding from his singular piety that God would eminently appear for him, for even the Heathens could not but observe, that the kings of Judah were either prosperous or unhappy, according as they served God or forsook him.

13. Business - To repair and fortify them, and furnish them with provisions: and to purge out all their relicks of idolatry and injustice.

19. Waited - These above-mentioned were the trained bands or auxiliaries: whose chief officers waited on the king to receive his commands, and to raise, and bring in all, or part of their forces, to the service of the king as need required. A vast number for so small a compass of ground, to furnish out and maintain. But we may consider, that God had promised to make the seed of Abraham like the sand of the sea for number; that there had now been a long peace; that many were come to them from the kingdom of Israel and that Jehoshaphat was under a special blessing of God. They were doubtless dispersed all the country over, every one residing on his own land: only they were ready at call, whenever there was occasion.

XVIII

Jehoshaphat joins affinity with Ahab, and consents to go with him to Ramoth-gilead, ver. 1-3. The false prophets promise them success, ver. 4-11. Micaiah foretells the death of Ahab, ver. 6-27. Jehoshaphat hardly escapes, ver. 28-32. Ahab slain, ver. 33, 34.

1. With Ahab - For Joram's eldest son married Athaliah, Ahab's daughter.

4. Inquire, &c. - This we should do, whatever we undertake, by particular, believing prayer, by an unbiased consulting of the scriptures and our own consciences, and by a close regard to the hints of providence.

22. Lying spirit, &c. - See the power of Satan! One lying spirit can make four hundred lying prophets. And thus he frequently becomes a murderer by being a liar, and destroys men by deceiving them.

26. This fellow, &c. - How frequently has this been the lot of faithful ministers, to be hated and ill treated, merely for being true to God: and just and kind to the souls of men! But that day will declare who is in the right, and who is in the wrong, when Christ appears to the unspeakable consolation of the persecuted, and the everlasting confusion of their persecutors.

31. Cried out - He cried out, either to his friends to help, or to his enemies, to let them know, he was not the king of Israel: or to God, and not in vain; for he moved the captains to depart from him. Many are moved in a manner unaccountable both to themselves and others; but an invisible power moves them.

34. He died - What can hurt those whom God will protect? And what can shelter those whom God will destroy? Jehoshaphat is saved in his robes; Ahab is killed in his armour!

XIX

Jehoshaphat is reproved by a prophet, ver. 1-3. He reforms the kingdom, ver. 4. Gives instructions to the itinerant Judges, ver. 5-7. And to the supreme court at Jerusalem, ver. 8-11.

2. *Therefore* - Therefore God will chastise thee for this miscarriage. Which he did partly by stirring up the Moabites, and others to invade him, chap. xx, 1, partly by permitting his eldest son Jehoram to kill all his brethren, chap. xxi, 4, and principally by bringing that almost general destruction upon his grand- children by Jehu, 2 Kings ix, 27; x, 13, 14, which was the fruit of his alliance with Ahab.

3. *Good things* - Good marks proceeding from an honest heart; which God more regards than this particular error: and therefore though he will chasten thee, yet he will not utterly destroy thee.

4. *Through* - Through the whole kingdom, whereof these were the two bounds. *And brought* - Such of them as had revolted from God to idols, he reclaimed by his counsel and example, and by the instructions of the Levites and priests, whom he carried with him. Many, probably, had revolted to idolatry, when they saw their king so intimate with idolaters. Therefore he thought himself doubly obliged to do all he could to reduce them. If we truly repent of sin, we shall do our utmost to repair the damage we have done to religion, or the souls of others.

6. *The Lord* - You represent God's person to whom judgment belongeth, you have your commission from God, and not from man only; and your administration of justice is not only for man's good, but also for God's honour and service. *With you* - Both to observe your carriage, and to defend you against all those enemies whom the impartial exercise of justice may provoke.

7. *Wherefore* - And therefore you who are in God's stead, and do his work, and must give an account to him, must imitate God herein.

8. *The fathers* - Persons of other tribes eminent for their dignity, ability and integrity. But whether these persons made up one court, called the Sanhedrim, by which all causes ecclesiastical and civil were decided; or there were two distinct courts, the one ecclesiastical, consisting of the priests and Levites; the other civil, consisting of the chief of the fathers of Israel, it is not easy to determine. *The Lord* - For matters concerning the laws and worship, of God. *Controversies* - For matters of difference between man and man. *When* - When Jehoshaphat and his company were returned to Jerusalem, he made this order concerning establishing Judges there.

10. *Blood* - This refers to Deut. xvii, 8, between the blood of the person slain, and the blood of the man-slayer. All the cities of refuge, except Hebron, now belonged to the kingdom of Israel, so that the man-slayer now usually fled to the courts of the temple, or the horns of the altar. And therefore the trial of these, was reserved for the court at Jerusalem. *Law, &c.* - When any debates shall arise about the meaning of any of God's laws. *Warn* - Ye shall not only give a righteous sentence for what is past, but ye shall admonish the offender, and others, to take better heed for the future.

11. *Over you* - Shall be your president. *Matters of the Lord* - In Spiritual, or ecclesiastical matters. *Ruler* - The prince, or chief ruler, under the king, of the tribe of Judah. *The king's matters* - For civil causes, or controversies either between the king and his people; or between subject and subject, which may be called the king's matters, because it was a principal part of his office to see them justly decided. *The Levites* - Shall be at your command to see your just sentences executed; which work was fitly committed to the Levites, as persons who might add their instructions to the corrections, and might work the guilty to an acknowledgement of their fault and a submission to their punishment. *The Lord* - Shall protect and bless good Judges.

XX

The land being invaded, Jehoshaphat and all the people seek God by fasting and prayer, ver. 1-13. They thankfully receive the promise of victory given by a prophet, ver. 14-19. Their enemies are overthrown, ver. 20-25. Their thanksgiving, ver. 25-30. The conclusion of his reign, ver. 31-37.

2. *The sea* - The dead sea, beyond which mount Seir lay. *Syria* - Largely so called, and so it includes the Moabites and Ammonites. And it may be thus expressed, to intimate that they came by the instigation of the Syrians, to revenge themselves of Jehoshaphat for joining with Ahab against them.

5. *The house* - Largely so called, in the court of the people, upon that brazen scaffold which Solomon had erected. *New court* - Before the priests court: which is called the new court, because it had lately been renewed when the altar was renewed.

7. *Abraham* - To whom thou hast engaged thyself by covenant to be his friend, and the friend of his seed forever. 9. *The sword* - Or rather, the sword of judgement or of vengeance, that is, war, whereby thou punisheth thy people for their sins.

12. *Wilt thou not judge* - Wilt thou not give sentence against them, and execute it upon them? The

justice of God is the refuge of those that are wronged. No might - Though he had great armies, yet he seems to have been surprized by these men, before his forces were in readiness to oppose them.

13. Little ones - Whom they used to present before the Lord in times of great distress, to stir up themselves to more fervent prayers, their eyes being upon their harmless and tender children, and to move God to compassion, because God hath declared, that he will be prevailed with, by such methods as these.

15. But God's - God will fight for you, and he alone will do the work, you need not strike a stroke.

16. Go down - From Jerusalem, where he and his army now were; which stood upon high ground.

19. Stood up - By Jehoshaphat's appointment. On high - With heart and voice lifted up: whereby they shewed their full assurance of the victory.

20. Believe - God's promise delivered to us by this prophet, and consequently all other predictions of the prophet.

21. Consulted - Jehoshaphat called a counsel of war, and it was resolved, to appoint singers to go out before the army, who had nothing to do, but to praise God, to praise his holiness, which is his beauty, to praise him as they did in the temple, that beauty of holiness. By this strange advance to the field of battle, Jehoshaphat shewed his firm reliance on the word of God, which enabled him to triumph before the battle, to animate his own men and confound the enemy.

22. To sing - So acceptable are the fervent prayers of God's people to God, and so terrible to their enemies. Ambushments - Or, liers in wait, either

1. the holy angels, who appeared in the shape of men, and possibly put on the appearances and visages of the Moabites or Ammonites, and in that shape slew the rest, who supposing this slaughter to be done by a part of their own army, fell upon them, and so broke forth into mutual slaughters. Or,

2. God raised jealousies and animosities among themselves, which broke forth, first into secret ambushments, which one party laid for another, and then into open hostilities to their utter destruction. So vain are all mens attempts against God, who needs none to destroy his enemies but themselves, and their own mistakes, and passions, which he can, when he pleaseth, arm against them.

24. The watch tower - Which stood upon the cliff of Ziz, mentioned ver. 16, and looked toward the wilderness, where their enemies lay encamped, whose numbers, and order, and condition, they could descry from thence.

25. Jewels - Which they brought with them to corrupt any of Jehoshaphat's officers as they saw occasion: to procure necessaries for their vast army from time to time: and because they came as to triumph rather than to fight, being confident of the victory because of their numbers, and especially because they thought to surprize Jehoshaphat ere he could make any considerable preparations against them; God also permitting them to be puffed up to their own destruction.

26. Berachah - Hebrew. of blessing; so called from their solemn blessings and praises given to God in it upon this occasion.

28. To the house - To renew their praises in the court of the temple, the proper and usual place for it. Praising God must not be the work of a day only, but our praises when we have received mercy, must be often repeated, as our prayers were, when we where in pursuit of it. Every day we must bless God: as long as we live, and while we have any being, we must praise him, spending our time in that work, in which we hope to spend our eternity.

33. Not taken - Not universally; the fault was not in Jehoshaphat, but in the people, who, though they did worship the true God, yet would not be confined to the temple, but for their own conveniency, or from their affection to their ancient custom chose to worship him in the high-places.

35. After this - This is mentioned as an aggravation of his sin, after so great an obligation laid upon him by God; and after he had been so singularly reproved by a prophet yet he relapsed into the same sin which proceeded partly from that near relation which was contracted between the two families, and partly from the easiness of Jehoshaphat's temper, which could not resist the solicitations of others, in such things as might seem indifferent. For he did not join with him in war, as he did with Ahab, but in a peaceable way only, in a matter of trade and commerce. And yet God reproves and punisheth him for it, ver. 37, to shew his great dislike of all familiar conversation of his servants and people with professed enemies of God and of religion, as Ahaziah was. Very wickedly - Or who did industriously, and maliciously, and constantly work wickedness, as the Hebrew phrase implies, giving himself up to idolatry and all wickedness.

XXI

Jehoram succeeds, ver. 1-3. His wickedness, ver. 4-7. Edom and Libnah revolt and Jehoram is still more wicked, ver. 8-11. The prophecy of Elijah against him, ver. 12-15. The success of his enemies, ver. 16, 17. His sickness and death, ver. 18-20.

2. Azariah - Two sons called by the same name, though doubtless distinguished by some

additional title: which is not mentioned here, because it did not concern succeeding ages to know it. Of Israel - So he is called either,

1. Because he was so by right: or

2. Because he was king not only of Judah and Benjamin, but of a great number of Israelites, who had come and settled in his kingdom.

4. Strengthened himself - He hardened his heart, as that word sometimes signifies. Princes - The chief of those Israelites, who out of love to God and the true religion, had forsaken their estates in the kingdom of Israel, and were now incorporated with the kingdom of Judah: because he thought these would be most zealous for that religion which he was resolved to oppose.

10. Libnah - Libnah seems to have set up for a free state. And the reason is here given, both why God permitted it, and why they did it, because Jehoram was become an idolater. While he adhered to God, they adhered to him; but when he cast God off, they cast him off. Whether this would justify them in their revolt or no, it justified God's providence which suffered it.

11. High places - Not to the Lord, but to Baals or false gods. And caused - Not only by his counsel and example, but by force, by threats, and penalties.

12. From Elijah - By this it appears, that Jehoram came to the throne before Elijah's translation. It is true, we find Elisha attending Jehoshaphat; but that might be, while Elijah was yet on earth: for we read of Jehoram's coming to the crown, before we read of Elijah's translation, 1 Kings xxii, 50. We may suppose, the time of his departure was at hand, so that he could not go in person to Jehoram. But he left this writing, probably with Elisha, to be sent the first opportunity. The message is sent in the name of the Lord God of David his father, upbraiding him with his relation to David, as that which was no more his honour, but an aggravation of his degeneracy.

15. People - Because the generality of them sinned, in complying with his wicked and idolatrous commands. Wives - Whose lives shall go for the lives of thy brethren, ver. 4.

16. Philistines - A people fully subdued and dispirited: but God now raises their spirits and courage to do his work. Ethiopians - A people in Arabia, so called, either for their likeness in complexion to the Ethiopians, or because the one of these people were a colony of the other.

17. His wives - Whom also they slew, chap. xxii, 1, except Ahaziah and Athaliah; who possibly were hidden in some secret place. Left him - Blood for blood. He had slain all his brethren; they slay all his sons, but one. And he had not escaped, had be not been of the house of David; which must not be extirpated, like that of Ahab: because a blessing was in it; no less a blessing than that of the Messiah.

20. Desired - This is an emphatical expression, because it is usual with men to desire the deaths of some persons, whom afterward they lament, and heartily wish they were alive again. But for this ungodly and unhappy prince, his people did not only in his life time wish his death, but afterwards did not repent of those desires.

XXII

Ahaziah's wicked reign, ver. 1-4. Being confederate with Joram, he is slain by Jehu, ver. 5-9. Athaliah destroys the seed royal, and usurps the kingdom, ver. 10-12.

2. Forty two years - Some acknowledge an error in the transcribers of the present Hebrew copies, in which language the numeral letters for 22 and

42 are so like, that they might easily be mistaken. For that it was read 22 here, as it is in the book of Kings, in other Hebrew copies, they gather from hence, that it is at this day so read in divers ancient Greek copies, as also in those two ancient translations, the Syriack and the Arabick, and particularly in that most ancient copy of the Syriack which was used by the church of Antioch in the primitive times, and to this day is kept in the church of Antioch. The daughter - Of Ahab, Omri's Son. Grand-children are often called sons and daughters.

4. His father - Who, while he lived, seduced his son himself, and made other evil counsellors unnecessary.

9. Ahaziah - Who, tho' wounded, had made an escape, 2 Kings ix, 27.

XXIII

Jehoiada prepares the people and crowns the king, ver. 1- 11. Athaliah is slain, ver. 12-15. The kingdom is reformed, ver. 16-21.

5. Foundation - At the east gate, so called because it stood lower than the rest of the doors at the foot of the steps, by which they went up from the king's house to the temple.

11. His sons - And Zechariah among the rest, whom afterwards he ungratefully slew, chap. xxiv, 21.

13. Rejoiced - To see a rod sprung out of the stem of Jesse! To see what they despaired of ever seeing, a king of the house of David.

16. Him - The Lord, as is expressed, 2 Kings xi, 17.

18. Appointed - Or, as it is in the Hebrew, put the offices of the house of the Lord into the hand, that is, he restored the priests and Levites to the exercise of their office.

21. Rejoiced, &c. - The generality of the people rejoiced, the rest were quiet and made no opposition. When the Son of David is enthroned in the soul, all therein is quiet, and springs of joy are opened.

XXIV

Joash takes care to repair the temple, ver. 1-14. After Jehoiada's death, he sets up the worship of Baal again, tho' warned, ver. 15-19. He puts Zechariah to death, ver. 20-22. Is invaded by the Syrians, ver. 23, 24. Struck with sore diseases and slain, ver. 25-27

6. The chief - It is observable, that he is not called the chief priest, or high-priest, but only the chief, or the head, which he might be in many other respects, either by reason of his near relation to the royal family: or because he was the chief of one of the twenty- four families.

7. The sons - Ahaziah, and his brethren before they were carried away captive, chap. xxi, 17, who did this by her instigation, as this phrase implies. Broke up - Both broke up the treasuries, and defaced the house itself.

14. Vessels - Because Athaliah and her sons had taken the old ones away, ver. 7.

15. An hundred and thirty years old - By which it appears, that he was born in Solomon's time, and had lived six entire reigns before this. They buried him among the kings, with this honourable encomium, (perhaps inscribed upon his grave-stone) that he had done good in Israel. But the little religion that Joash had, was all buried in his grave. See how great a judgment to any prince or people, the death of holy, useful men is!

16. Israel - In Judah, which was an eminent part of Israel, and the only part of it which owned God, or was owned by God as his Israel, to whom therefore he often appropriates this name.

17. Made obeisance - In that posture presenting their requests to him, that they might not be confined to troublesome journeys to Jerusalem, but might have the liberty, which their fore-fathers enjoyed, os worshipping God in the high-places. This liberty once obtained, they knew they could worship idols without disturbance: which was the thing at which they aimed. And for the prevention of such abuses, God obliged all to worship him in one place.

18. Left, &c. - The king and princes that awhile ago so zealously repaired the temple, now forsook the temple! So inconstant a thing is man! So little confidence is to be put in him!

20. Who stood - The people were assembled in the court of the temple, which they had not quite forsook, when Zechariah stood up in some of the desks that were in the court of the priests, and plainly told them their sin, and the consequences of it.

21. Stoned him - They stoned him immediately, without even colour of law; as horrid a piece of wickedness, as any we read of in all the history of the kings. That ever such a villainy should be committed, by men, by Israelites, in contempt and violation of everything that is just, honourable, and sacred! The Jews say, there were seven transgressions in one: They killed a priest, a prophet, a judge; they shed innocent blood; polluted the court of the temple, the Sabbath, and the day of expiation: for on that day, their tradition says, this happened.

22. Require it - Make inquisition for innocent blood. But the words may be rendered, The Lord will look upon it, and require it, will require satisfaction from you for it.

23. The year - So soon did God hear the cry of his holy prophet's blood, and revenge it. The princes - That it might appear they were sent and directed by God to single out to destruction the first beginners of this general apostacy.

25. Son - By which it seems, he slew not only Zechariah, but his brothers also. Perhaps they that slew him intended to take vengeance for that innocent blood. However that was it, which God intended, in permitting them to do it.

27. Burdens - The great judgments of God upon him, both by the Syrians, ver. xxiv, 23, and by great diseases, ver. 25.

XXV

Amaziah revenges his father's death, ver. 1-4. Obeys the command of God and dismisses the Israelites, 5-10. Conquers the Edomites, ver. 11-13. Turns idolater and despises reproof, ver. 14- 16. Challenges the king of Israel and suffers for it, ver. 17-24. Ends his days ingloriously, ver. 25-28.

2. But not, &c. - He was not an enemy to religion, but a cool and indifferent friend. He was not a man of serious piety; for his heart was not whole with God.

7. Let not, &c. - It is comfortable to employ those, who we have reason to hope, have an interest in heaven, but dangerous associating with those from whom the Lord is departed.

8. Do it - It is an ironical concession like that, go, and prosper.

10. Anger kindled - Because they were both disgraced by this rejection, and disappointed of that spoil which they hoped to gain, whereas now they are sent away empty; for the hundred talents probably were given to their officers only to raise men for this service.

13. Cities of Judah - Thus God chastised those cities of Judah for their idolatries which were found most in the parts next to Israel. The men of Israel had corrupted them, and now are a plague to them.

16. Art thou, &c. - Who art thou that presumest to direct my affairs, without my commission? The secure sinner perhaps values himself on having silenced his reprovers and monitors. But what comes of it? It is a plain indication he is marked out for ruin. They that are deaf to reproof, are ripening apace for destruction.

17. Advice - About the injury which the Israelites had done to his people, and how he should repair it. He took advice. But with whom? Not with the prophet, but with his flattering statesmen. It is good to take advice: but it should be of them who are fit to advise us.

20. Of God - Who gave him up to his own error and passion, in order to his ruin.

24. Obed-edom - With Obed-edom's posterity, to whom the custody of the sacred treasures was committed.

XXVI

Uzziah reigns well, ver. 1-5. Prospers in his wars, building, and the affairs of his kingdom, ver. 6-15. Invading the priest's office, is struck with a leprosy, ver. 16-20. Is confined to his death, ver. 21-23.

10. Towers - To guard his cattle from the inroads which the Arabians were accustomed to make: and to give notice of the approach of any enemy.

16. Into Jerusalem - Into the holy place, where the altar of incense stood, and into which none but the priests might enter, much less offer incense.

18. Withstood - Hebrew. stood up against Uzziah, not by force, or laying hands upon him to restrain him, for in the next verse you still find the censer in his hand; but only by admonition and reproof, which follows. Neither, &c. - Expect that God will punish thee, or put some brand of infamy upon thee for this presumption. But this they express modestly, because they considered that he to whom they spake, though an offender, was their sovereign.

19. His forehead - So that he could not hide his shame: though it is probable it was also in the rest of his body. From beside - By a stroke from an invisible hand coming from the altar; that he might be assured this was the effect of God's displeasure.

20. Thrust - Not by force, which needed not, for he voluntarily hasted away, as it follows; but by vehement persuasions and denunciations of God's farther judgments upon him, if he did not depart.

21. His death - God would have this leprosy to be incurable, as a lasting monument of his anger against such presumptuous invaders of the priest's office. Dwelt, &c. - As he was obliged to do by law, which he durst not now resist, being under the hand of God, and under the fear of worse plagues, if he did not so. For - He dwelt in a several house, because he might not come into the temple or courts, nor consequently into any publick assembly. So the punishment answered the sin, as face does to face in a glass. He thrust himself into the temple of God, whether the priests only had admission: and for that was thrust out of the very courts of the temple, into which the meanest of, his subjects might enter. He invaded the dignity of the priesthood, to which he had no right, and is for that deprived of the royal dignity, to which he had an undoubted right.

John Wesley

XXVII

Jotham reigns well and prospers, ver. 1-6. The conclusion of his reign, ver. 7-9.

2. He did - He did according to all that his father Uzziah did; except in his miscarriages. We must not imitate those we have the greatest esteem for, any farther than we do well; but their failings must be warnings to us, to walk more circumspectly.
3. Built - Repaired it: for it was built before, chap. xi, 5.

XXVIII

Ahaz reigns ill, ver. 1-4. Is smitten by the Syrians and Israelites, ver. 5-8. who send back the captives they had taken, ver. 9-15. Ahaz sends for help to the king of Asyria, but in vain, ver. 16-21. Yet he continues in idolatry, ver. 22-25. and dies, ver. 26, 27.

5. His God - God was his God, tho' not by special relation, (which Ahaz had renounced) yet by his sovereign dominion over him: for God did not forfeit his right by Ahaz's denying it.
6. Forsaken - Ahaz walked in the ways of the kings of Israel, and God chose the king of Israel for his scourge: it is just with God, to make them a plague to us, whom we have made our patterns, or partners in sin.
9. A rage - An unbounded rage, which cries to God for vengeance, against such bloody men.
10. To keep under - It ill becomes sinners to be cruel. Shew mercy to them, for you are undone, unless God shew you mercy.
14. Left the captives - And herein they shewed a more truly heroic bravery, than they did in taking them. It is true honour for a man to yield to reason and religion even in spite of interest.
15. Were expressed - Who were appointed to take care about the management of this business.
16. Kings - Princes, who may be called kings in a more general signification of the word.
19. Low - As high as they were before in wealth and power. They that will not humble themselves under the word of God will be humbled by his judgments. Naked - Taking away their ornament and their defense and strength, namely their treasures, which he sent to the Assyrian to no purpose; their frontier towns, and other strong holds, which by his folly and wickedness were lost; their religion, and the Divine protection, which was their great and only firm security.
20. Distressed - Or, straitened him, by robbing him of his treasures. Strengthened not - A most emphatical expression: for tho' he weakened his present enemy the Syrian, yet all things considered, he did not strengthen Ahaz and his kingdom, but weaken them; for by removing the Syrian, who, tho' a troublesome neighbour, was a kind of bulwark to him, he smoothed the way for himself, a far more dangerous enemy, as appears in the very next king's reign.
22. That Ahaz - That monster and reproach of mankind, that unteachable and incorrigible prince, whom even grievous afflictions made worse, which commonly make men better. This is he, whose name deserves to be remembered and detested forever.

XXIX

Hezekiah's exhortation to the priests and Levites, ver. 1-11. The care of the Levites to cleanse the temple and put things into order, ver. 12-19. A solemn revival of God's ordinances, ver. 20- 36.

4. And he brought in,&c. - He found Judah low and naked, yet did not make it his first business to revive the civil interests of his kingdom, but to restore religion to a good posture. Those that begin with God, begin at the right end of their work; and it will prosper accordingly.
5. Filthiness - That filthy altar, which Ahaz had put in the place of God's altar, 2 Kings xvi, 11, and the idols, or other abominable things which were there.
6. Turned, &c. - They have wilfully and obstinately forsaken God and his worship; that posture being a signification of contempt.
7. They - He saith not, my father, because it became him as a son, to be as tender as might be of his father's name: and because his father would not have done all this, if their fathers had not neglected their duty.
8. Hissing - To such calamities as all that see and hear of, shall be astonished at, and hiss at those, who by their own sin and folly have brought such miseries upon themselves. When we are under the rebukes of God's providence, it is good for us to inquire, Whether we have not neglected God's ordinances, and whether that be not the controversy he has with us?
9. Captivity - Tho' they were presently released, chap. xxviii, 5, 14, 15.
11. Sons - So he calls them, though many of them were elder than himself, because he was by his

tender love and affection, as he was by his office obliged to be, a nursing father to them. Negligent - In sanctifying yourselves and the temple, ver. 5, and in quickening and preparing yourselves and the people for God's service.

15. To cleanse - From the dirt it had contracted, while it was so long shut up; from dust, cobwebs, and the rust of the vessels. Much more from the idols, and idolatrous altars which had been set up therein.

17. The first day - A happy beginning of the new year! Thus should every year begin with the reformation of what is amiss, and the purging away of all the defilements contracted the foregoing year.

19. Sanctified - Tho' the vessels of the sanctuary may be profaned for a while, God will find a time and a way to sanctify them. Neither his ordinances nor his obedient people, shall be suffered to fail forever.

21. Seven - The number seven is customary in sacred matters, and is here used in regard of the vast numbers and various kinds of sins, the guilt whereof yet lay upon the kingdom, which was now to be expiated. Indeed, in case of one particular sin of ignorance done by the people, there was but one bullock to be offered, but here the sins were many and presumptuous. Kingdom - To make atonement for the sins of the king and the royal family, and the court. Sanctuary - For all the idolatry and uncleanness wherewith the temple had been polluted. They thought it not enough to lament and forsake their sins, but they brought a sin-offering. Even our repentance and reformation will not obtain pardon, but thro' Christ, who was made sin, that is, a sin-offering for us.

23. They laid - The king and the elders of the congregation in the name of the whole congregation.

27. The song - The psalms composed by David and Asaph. Even sorrow for sin must not put us out of tune for praising God. By faith we must even then rejoice in the Lord our righteousness, and our prayers and praises must attend with his offering, to be accepted only in the virtue of it.

31. Consecrated - Now that you have reconciled yourselves and the house to God, and that he is willing and ready to accept your sacrifices. Burnt-offerings - Wherein there was more generosity than in the other sacrifices, because they were wholly burnt and offered to God.

33. Consecrated things - All the offerings consecrated to God, besides the burnt-offerings already mentioned.

34. Too few - Such as were sanctified and fit for their work, as the following words shew: for otherwise the number of the priests was more than sufficient for this employment. Burnt-offerings - And much less all the other sacrifices, which were more numerous; the slaying whereof was the priests proper work. The Levites - Necessity excusing their deviation from the rule.

36. Rejoiced - It was, as a very great, so a sudden change, that the people, who but the other day were so ready to comply with wicked Ahaz in his idolatrous presumptions, were now so free and forward in God's service: whereby it plainly appeared to be the work of God, changing their hearts by his Holy Spirit.

XXX

The king and people resolve to keep the passover, ver. 1-5. He invites Judah and Israel to it, ver. 6-12. The joyful celebration of it, ver. 13-27.

1. Israel - All the persons of the ten tribes, who were settled in his kingdom. Ephraim, &c. - To all the remainder of the ten tribes, ver. 5, here expressed by the names of Ephraim and Manasseh, as elsewhere by the name of Ephraim only. But he names these two tribes, because they were nearest to his kingdom, and a great number of them had long since, and from time to time joined themselves to the kingdom of Judah, chap. xv, 8, 9. At Jerusalem - Admonishing them of their duty to God, and persuading them to comply with it.

2. Second month - Which was against the common rule, but the doing of this in its proper time, namely, the fourteenth day of the first month was impossible, because the temple was not cleansed, nor they prepared. As there was a proviso in the law, that particular persons who were unclean in the first month, might keep the passover the fourteenth day of the second month, he doubted not but that might be extended by the whole congregation.

3. They kept - Not in the same manner as they had done the former, V. 3. Sufficiently - In such manner as was fit, nor in such numbers as but in the solemn worship of God, by sacrifices, and prayers, and praise, were necessary for the slaying and offering of so many thousands of and publick instruction of that great congregation in the good knowledge paschal-offerings, as appears, because they were not sufficient for of the Lord; which was most necessary for the people after so long and those offerings, which were comparatively few, chap. xxix, 32, 33, 34. dismal a night of ignorance, superstition and idolatry.

10. They - The generality of the ten tribes; who by long want of meat had now lost their appetite to God's ordinances, for which they paid dear. For about six years after their refusal of this offer of grace

they were all carried away captive, 2 Kings xviii, 1, 10.

12. The hand of God - God by the power of his grace inclined their hearts to an unanimous compliance with God's and the king's will. And this is mentioned as the reason of this wonderful change wrought in these men, who had lately been given up to idolatry.

15. Ashamed - Their negligence and remissness being upbraided by the general forwardness of the people. The zeal which we observe in others, should make us ashamed of our own coldness, and quicken us not only to do our duty, but to do it with our might.

19. The sanctuary - With that purification which was required of them that came in God's sanctuary. So he calls it to distinguish from that internal purity which they are here acknowledged to have. The great thing required in our attendance on God's ordinances is, that we prepare our heart to seek him; that the inward man be engaged, that we make heart work of it. All is nothing without this.

20. Healed - That is, pardoned this their sin, and accepting them and their services, as if they had been clean.

22. Spoke comfortably - Encouraged them to a cheerful and diligent attendance upon their holy ministrations. Princes and magistrates by encouraging faithful and labourious preachers, greatly promote the kingdom of God. That taught - Who by their office were to instruct and build up the people in the knowledge and fear of God: which is mentioned as the cause of his respect and kindness to them.

24. Did give - First to God, to whom the parts appointed were offered in a way of thanksgiving; and then to the people, who feasted upon the relicks, as the offerer used to do in peace- offerings: and Hezekiah, who was the offerer, gave away his right in the remains of the sacrifices to the people. Which generosity is the more considerable, because it was in the beginning of his reign, when he found the exchequer empty; and when he had been at great expense about cleansing and refitting the temple, and making preparations for this great feast.

27. The Levites - Those of the Levites who were priests also; for to them only this work belonged.

XXXI

The remains of idolatry are destroyed, ver. 1. Hezekiah provides work and maintenance for the priests and Levites, ver. 2- 4. The people bring in their dues abundantly, ver. 5-10. Officers are appointed to dispose of them, ver. 11-19. Hezekiah's sincerity, ver. 20, 21.

1. Manasseh - By the special impulse and direction of God's spirit. And he knew Hoshea contented himself with the worship of the calves, and did not practice that great idolatry which his predecessors had used, and therefore would patiently suffer the breaking of the images of Baal, and the things belonging to them.

2. The tents - Within the gates of the house of the Lord: which is here called tents, because the host of the Lord, the priests and Levites, encamped there. And perhaps to intimate, that it was shortly to be removed.

3. Of his substance - Which had hitherto been taken out of the treasures of the temple, but that he might ease the people in their present poverty, which his predecessor had brought upon them, and engage them to a more cheerful attendance upon God's service, he took the burden upon himself.

4. Encouraged - Freed them from worldly cares and distractions, and enabled to give up themselves entirely to the serious study of God's law, and to the instruction, and direction, and quickening of the people.

5. Came abroad - As Soon as the king extended that command to all the parts of his kingdom, which, ver. 4, was confined to them that dwelt in Jerusalem. Honey - Or, dates, as the Hebrew writers generally, understand this word, which were given to them, because of the sweetness of their taste in some sort resembling honey. For the law requires no tithes, but of the fruits of trees, or of the earth, or of beasts.

6. By heaps - What the priests and the Levites had occasion for, they made use of, and the overplus was laid in heaps.

7. Third month - Of the sacred year, in which their harvest began. Seventh - In which their harvest ended and the feast of tabernacles was kept.

8. Blessed the Lord - Both for giving such plentiful provisions to his land and for giving his people such liberal hearts. And they praised the people for their forwardness and faithfulness in it.

9. Questioned - How it came to pass that no more of their provision was spent and that there yet remained such great heaps of it.

14. Most holy things - The remainders of the freewill-offering, the sin-offering, and trespass-offering, and the shew-bread; to see that all had a competent maintenance for themselves and their families.

15. And next, &c. - These were intrusted with receiving and distributing the several portions belonging to the priests who abode in their several cities, whilst their brethren came up to Jerusalem.

18. *For, &c.* - This is alleged as a reason why their wives and children were provided for out of the holy things, because they sequestered themselves from worldly affairs, by which they might otherwise have provided for their families.

XXXII

Sennacherib invading Judah, Hezekiah fortifies himself, ver. 1-8. The insolent letters and messages sent by Sennacherib, ver. 9-19. The destruction of his army, ver. 20-23. Hezekiah's sickness, riches, and death, ver. 24-33.

1. *After, &c.* - An emphatical preface, signifying, that notwithstanding all his zeal for God, God saw fit to exercise him with a sore trial. And God ordered it at this time, that he might have an opportunity of shewing himself strong, on the behalf of his returning people. It is possible, we may be in the way of our duty, and yet meet with trouble and danger. God permits this, for the trial of our confidence in him, and the manifestation of his care over us.
3. *To stop* - And withal to draw the waters by secret pipes underground to Jerusalem.
21. *The Lord sent an angel* - The Jewish comment says the word of the Lord sent Gabriel to do this execution, and that it done with lightning, and in the passover night, the same night wherein the first-born in Egypt were slain.
25. *Lifted up* - For that prodigious victory over the Assyrians, for his miraculous restoration from sickness, and for the honour since done him by an embassy from the great king of Babylon. All which probably raised in him too great an opinion of himself, as if these things were done for his piety and virtues.
29. *Provided* - He repaired, fortified, and beautified them for the honour and safety of his kingdom.
30. *Stopped, &c.* - A rivulet near Jerusalem consisting of two streams, the upper which was brought into one pool, called the upper pool, Isaiah vii, 3, and the lower which was brought into another, called the lower pool, Isaiah xxii, 9. The former he diverted and brought by pipes into Jerusalem, which was a work of great art and labour.
31. *Wonder that was done* - Either the destruction of the Assyrians, or the going back of the sun. These miracles were wrought to alarm and awaken a stupid, careless world, and to turn them from dumb and lame idols to the living God. *God left him* - To himself, and suffered Satan to try him; that he might know he had infirmities and sins as well as virtues. O what need have great men, and good men, and useful men, to study their own follies and infirmities, and to beg earnestly of God, that he would hide pride from them!
33. *Did him honour* - It is a debt we owe to those who have been eminently useful, to do them honour at their death, when they are out of the reach of flattery, and we have seen the end of their conversation.

XXXIII

The wicked reign of Manasseh, ver. 1-10. His captivity, prayer, and reformation, ver. 11-17. The conclusion of his reign, ver. 18-20. The wicked reign and death of Amon, ver. 21-25.

11. *To Babylon* - The king of Babylon is here called the king of Assyria, because he had added Assyria to his empire, who having been informed by his ambassadors of the great riches which were in Hezekiah's treasures at Jerusalem, and being assured of Manasseh's degeneracy from the piety of his father, and from that God whose power alone made Hezekiah formidable, he thought this a fit season to invade Manasseh's kingdom. The Jews say, in the twenty second year of his reign.
12. *Besought* - It becomes sinners to humble themselves before that God, whom they have offended. It becomes sufferers to humble themselves before him that corrects them, and to accept of the punishment of their iniquity.
17. *Still* - Manasseh could not carry the reformation so far as he had carried the corruption. It is an easy thing to debauch men's manners; but not so easy to reform them again.
18. *Of Israel* - Of Judah, often called Israel, he speaks not of the book of Kings, for these things are not mentioned there, but of their publick records, whence the most important things were taken by the prophets, and put into those canonical books.
19. *Hosai* - A writer so called.

XXXIV

The general character of Josiah, ver. 1, 2. He roots out idolatry, ver. 3-7. Repairs the temple, ver. 8-13. Rends his clothes on hearing the book of the law, and sends to inquire of God, ver. 14-22. Huldah foretells the destruction of Jerusalem, ver. 23-28. Josiah and the people renew their covenant with God, ver. 29-33.

3. Young - In the sixteenth year of his age; when he was entering into the age of temptation, and had the administration of his kingdom wholly in his own power, and none to restrain him; even then he begins to be religious in good earnest.

6. Naphtali - Which was in the utmost borders of the kingdom of Israel. For it must be remembered, that the ten tribes were now gone into captivity; and those who were come in their stead were weak and few, and not able to withstand the power of Josiah.

8. The house - The house of God, called the house by way of eminency.

11. Houses - The chambers joining to the temple.

12. Musick - All these here named, were skilful in instruments of musick. Which may be here mentioned, to intimate, that as they were skilful, so they were exercised in both employments, and did successively oversee the work, and praise God with their voices and instruments.

19. Rent his clothes - Were the things contained in scripture new to us, as they were here to Josiah, surely they would make deeper impressions upon us than they commonly do. But they are not the less weighty, and therefore should not be the less regarded, because they are well known.

32. To stand to it - He caused them to engage by an oath or covenant, that they would observe the laws of God, as his predecessors had formerly done, and which indeed they were before obliged to do.

33. Even to serve - The repetition shews, that this was the only thing his heart was set upon. He aimed at nothing in all he did, but to engage them to God and their duty.

XXXV

Josiah keeps a solemn passover, ver. 1-19. He goes against Pharaoh-necho, and is slain, ver, 20-24. He is bitterly lamented, ver. 25-27.

3. The house - In the holy of holies. Whence, it may seem, it had been removed, by some of the wicked kings of Judah, possibly by Josiah's father Amon. A burden - Or, that it might not be a burden, so these words are to be joined with the former, as the reason why Solomon built this house, that the ark might have a constant and fixed habitation, and not need to be carried from place to place upon their shoulders, as it had been done while it was in the tabernacle. Ministers must look upon themselves as servants both to Christ, and to the people, for his sake. They must take care and take pains, and lay themselves out to the utmost, both for the honour and glory of God, and for the benefit of his people, not as having dominion over their faith, but as helpers of their holiness and joy.

5. Stand - Or, minister, (as that word is frequently used) in the court of the priests. According - According to the several families both of the people, whom he calls their brethren, lest they should despise them, or grudge to serve them, and of the Levites. For the passover was to be eaten by the several families according to their numbers, and therefore he commands these persons, that when the paschal lambs were brought to them to be killed, they might so order the matter, that they might be distributed to the several families whether of the Levitical or other tribes.

8. Princes - Not the political, but ecclesiastical princes, or the chief of the priests and Levites, whose names here follow. Levites - For the use of any of the families of them, as need should be. For they supposed the thirty thousand which the king had given were not sufficient for all the families.

12. Removed - Some of the lesser cattle; for these also might be offered as burnt-offerings, Lev. i, 10, and hence it may seem that all these small cattle were not given for paschal-lambs, but were to be offered as burnt-offerings for the people. And these they put apart lest they should be confounded with them which were for another use; and, that they might not be hindered from that which was their present work, that they might give, the paschal-lambs or kids. To offer - These words may belong to the last words, and to the paschal-lambs, which they were first to offer to the Lord, by killing them and sprinkling the blood, and then to give to the people; though the giving be here mentioned before the offering, such transpositions being usual in scripture. Oxen - As they did with the lesser cattle; they removed those oxen which were to be offered as burnt-offerings, from those which were to be offered as peace-offerings.

18. Like to that - The whole solemnity was performed exactly according to the law, whereas in Hezekiah's passover there were several irregularities: likewise Josiah furnished the whole congregation with beasts for sacrifice at his own charge, which no king ever did before him.

20. After all - When he and his people hoped that God was reconciled, and the foundation of a

lasting happiness laid, their hopes were quickly blasted. So much are men often mistaken in their judgments about the designs of God's providence.

21. The house - Against the house of the king of Assyria, between whom and me there is war. It is at thy peril, if thou engage against one who has both a better army, and a better cause and God on his side.

22. Hearkened not - How can we think to prosper in our ways, if we do not acknowledge God in them!

25. To this day - In all their succeeding Lamentations for their publick calamities, they remembered Josiah's death as their first and fatal blow, which opened the flood-gates to all their following miseries.

XXXVI

The wicked reign of Jehoahaz, ver. 1-4. Jehoiakim, ver. 5-8. Jehoiachin and Zedekiah, ver. 9-13. The wickedness of the people, ver. 14-16. Jerusalem destroyed, Judah laid waste, the people slain or led away captive, according to God's word, ver. 17-21. The proclamation of Cyrus, ver. 22, 23.

8. Found in him - That crime of rebellion against the king of Babylon, which for a time he kept in his own breast, but when he saw fit, discovered it, and was convicted of it.

10. Expired - Hebrew. at the return of the year: at the beginning of the next year, according to the sacred account of the Hebrew, at the spring of the year, the time when kings go forth to battle, as is elsewhere said, when Nebuchadnezzar, among others, went forth to settle and enlarge his conquests. His brother - Largely so called, for this was his uncle, or his father's brother, being the son of Josiah.

13. By God - Who had required him to swear fealty and constant obedience to him by the true God, whom he called upon to be a witness against him if he broke his oath. So his rebellion was aggravated with perjury, and horrid contempt of God.

15. Rising - Sending them early and diligently, as a careful house-holder, who rises betimes about his business. God sent them many prophets and messages, some at the very beginning of their apostacy, and others afterward, 'till the very day of their captivity.

16. No remedy - Because the people would not repent, and God would not pardon them.

17. Chaldees - Abraham was called out of Ur of the Chaldees, when God took him into covenant with himself. And now his degenerate seed are carried into that country again, to signify that they had forfeited all that kindness wherewith they had been loved for their father's sake, and the benefit of the covenant into which he was called.

21. Sabbaths - Had rested from the labour of the husbandman in plowing and harrowing it; the people that should have managed it being destroyed. Many a time had they ploughed and sowed their land in the seventh year, when it should have rested: and now it lay unploughed and unsown for ten times seven years. Yet even this might encourage them to hope, that they should in due time return to it again. Had others come and taken possession of it, they might have despaired of ever recovering it. But while it lay desolate, it, as it were, waited for them, and refused to acknowledge any other owners.

John Wesley

NOTES ON THE BOOK OF EZRA

THE history of this book is the accomplishment of Jeremiah's prophecy, concerning the return of the Jews out of Babylon, at the end of seventy years, and a type of the accomplishment of the prophecies in the Revelation, touching the deliverance of the Gospel Church from Spiritual Babylon. Ezra preserved the records of that great revolution, and transmitted them to the church in this book. It gives us an account of the Jews return from their captivity, chap. 1, 2. Of the building of the temple, notwithstanding the opposition it met with, chap. 3-6. Of Ezra's coming to Jerusalem, chap. 7, 8. Of his obliging those that had married strange wives to put them away, chap. 9, 10.

I

The proclamation of Cyrus, for the release of the Jews, and building of the temple, ver. 1-4. The return of many of them, ver. 5, 6. Orders given for restoring the vessels of the temple, ver. 7- 11.

1. Fulfilled - Nebuchadnezzar carried many of the Jews into captivity in the first year of his reign (the fourth of Jehoiakim). He reigned forty-five years, his son Evil-merodach twenty-three, and his grandson Belshazzar, three years, which make up the seventy years foretold by Jeremiah. First year - Of his reign in Babylon: for he had been king of Persia for many years.

2. All, &c. - In those parts of the world; all that vast empire formerly under the Assyrians and Babylonians. The gift of which he ascribes to the great God; by that express prophecy of Isaiah concerning him, Isaiah xliv, 28; xlv, 1, 13, so long before he was born; which prophecy the Jews had doubtlessly shewed him, which also carried a great evidence with it, especially to him who was so highly encouraged by it: or by a special illumination which God vouchsafed to him, as he did to Nebuchadnezzar and Darius, and some other Heathen princes.

5. Then rose up, &c. - These being a new generation, went out like their father Abraham, from this land of the Chaldees, not knowing whither they went.

6. Strengthened their hands - God can, when he pleases, incline the hearts of strangers to be kind to his people; yea, make those strengthen their hands, who formerly weakened them.

8. Sheshbazzar - Zerubbabel; the Chaldeans called him Sheshbazzar, that is, Joy in tribulation, but among his own people he was called Zerubbabel, a stranger in Babylon. So he looked upon himself, tho' (Josephus says) he was captain of the life- guard.

II

The leaders that returned, ver. 1, 2. The people, ver. 3-35 The priests, Levites and retainers to the temple, ver. 36-63. The sum total and their substance, ver. 64-67. Their offerings, ver. 68-70.

1. The province - Of Judah, called a province, chap. v, 8. And he calls it thus emphatically to mind himself and his brethren of that sad change which their sins had made among them, that from an illustrious, independent, and formidable kingdom, were fallen to be an obscure, servile, and contemptible province, first under the Chaldeans, and now under the Persians.

2. Who came, &c. - This catalogue, differs in some names and numbers from that Neh. vii, 6-64, which might be because several names were given to the same persons; and because of the many changes which might happen in the same families between the time of the first making of this catalogue by Ezra, and the making it anew so many years after.

3. The children - The posterity, as that word is constantly taken in this catalogue. Of Parosh - That descend either from Parosh, or from that family whereof Parosh was the chief. And so for the rest.

5. Seven hundred, &c. - In Neh. vii, 10, they were only six hundred and fifty two, it seems seven hundred and seventy five marched out of Babylon, but some of them died, others were hindered by sickness, or other casualties, and so there came only six hundred and fifty two to Jerusalem. And the like is to be said in the like differences: which it suffices to hint once for all.

21. Beth-lehem - And so these were the remainders of the inhabitants of that city. (And the like may be said of the two following names, Netophah and Anathoth, or others of the like nature.) So little

was Beth-lehem among the thousands of Judah! Yet thence must the Messiah arise.

39. *Harim* - The head of one of the twenty four courses which David appointed, 1 Chron. xxiv, 8, of all which courses, some observe here are not above four or five that returned. There is another Harim mentioned above, ver. 32, but that was no priest, as this was ver. 36.

43. *Nethinims* - Persons devoted to the inferior services of the priests and Levites. Commonly supposed to be the Gibeonites, given, (so their name signifies) by Joshua first, and again by David, when Saul had expelled them, to the priests and Levites, for those services.

55. *Servants* - Who had lived in Solomon's family, and after his death, called themselves and their families by that name, esteeming it a great honour that they had been servants to so great a prince.

62. *Genealogy* - The Jews were generally very exact in their genealogies from their own choice and interest, that they might preserve the distinctions of the several tribes and families, which was necessary both to make out their titles to offices or inheritances, and to govern themselves thereby in the matter of marriages, and from the special providence of God, that so it might be certainly known of what tribe and family the Messiah was born.

63. *Tirshatha* - The governor, Zerubbabel. With Urim, &c. - That this point which could not be found out by human skill, might be determined by Divine direction. Hereby it appears that the Urim and Thummim were lost in the destruction of the city and temple, tho' the Jews fed themselves with hopes of recovering them, but in vain. And by the want of that oracle, they were taught to expect the great oracle, the Messiah.

64. *The whole, &c.* - The particular sums here recited, come only to twenty and nine thousand eight hundred and eighteen. Unto whom are added in this total sum twelve thousand five hundred and forty two. Which, either were of the other tribes beside Judah and Benjamin: or were such as were supposed to be Israelites, but could not prove their pedigree by their genealogies.

65. *Women* - For women as well as men were employed in this exercise in the temple-service.

68. *The house* - That is, to the ruins of the house; or to the place were it stood.

69. *Sixty one thousand drams* - Sixty one thousand drams of gold amount to something more than so many pounds of our money. So bishop Cumberland, who likewise supposes five thousand pounds of silver, to be about thirty seven thousand pounds sterling.

70. *And all Israel in their cities* - And they dwelt in peace, in perfect harmony, a blessed presage of their settlement, as their discord in the latter times of that state, was of their ruin.

III

They set up the altar, offer sacrifices thereon, and keep the feasts, ver. 1-6. They contribute, and lay the foundation of the temple, ver. 7-13.

1. *Seventh month* - This was a sacred kind of month wherein there were divers festivals, for which the people had been preparing themselves, and now came to Jerusalem to the celebration of them.

2. *Altar* - Which was of more present necessity than the temple, both to make atonement to God for all their sins, and to obtain God's assistance for the building of the temple, and to strengthen their own hearts and hands in that great work.

3. *For fear* - So they made the more haste, lest they should be hindered. Apprehension of dangers should quicken us in our duty. Have we many enemies? We have the more need to have God for our friend and to keep up our correspondence with him.

4. *Tabernacles* - This seems to be mentioned for all the solemnities of this month, whereof this was the most eminent, otherwise it is not probable, that they would neglect the day of atonement which was so severely enjoined, Lev. xxiii, 27-29, and was so exceeding suitable to their present condition.

5. *Offering* - The morning and evening, sacrifice. The law required much; but they offered more; for tho' thy had little wealth, they had much zeal. Happy they that bring with them out of the furnace of affliction, such a holy heat as this!

6. *Burnt-offerings* - And the other sacrifices which were to be offered with them upon that day, being the feast of trumpets. Burnt-offerings are often put for all sacrifices.

9. *Joshua* - Not the high-priest so called, but a Levite, of whom see chap. ii, 40. To set forward - To encourage them to a vigourous prosecution of the work.

11. *Sung* - That everlasting hymn, which will never be out of date, and to which our tongue should never be out of tune, the burden of Psalm lxxxvi, 1-26. Whatever our condition is, let it be owned, that God is good, and whatever fails, that his mercy fails not.

12. *Had seen* - Which divers of them might well do; because it was destroyed not sixty years ago. Wept - Because of the poor preparations made for this, in comparison of what was made for the other temple: because this was destitute of those things which were the principal glory of the former temple, namely, the ark, and the Urim and Thummim; because these foundation-stones were far inferior to the former, both for quantity and price, 1 Kings vii, 9, 10, and because these foundations were of a far

narrower compass than the former: for although the foundations of this house of the Lord, strictly so called, were of equal largeness with those of the former, yet the foundations of the whole building belonging to the first temple, were far larger than these.

13. Could not discern - The mixture of sorrow and joy here, is a representation of this world. In heaven all are singing and none sighing; in hell all are wailing, and none rejoicing: but here on earth we can scarce discern the shouts of joy from the noise of the weeping, let us learn to rejoice with them that rejoice, and weep with them that weep. Meantime let us ourselves rejoice as though we rejoiced not, and weep as though we wept not.

IV

THE adversaries, not being allowed to build with them, endeavour to hinder the work, ver. 1-5. They falsely accuse them to Artaxerxes, ver. 6-16. Who thereupon orders the work to be stopt, ver. 17-22. It is stopt, ver. 23, 24.

1. The adversaries - The Samaritans. The relicks of the ten tribes, and the foreigners who had joined with them.
2. With you - This they spake not sincerely, but that by this conjunction with them, they might pry into their counsels, and thereby find some matter of accusation against them. We seek - For so they did, though in a mongrel way, 2 Kings xvii. 26, &c. Esarhaddon - Son of Sennacherib, and after him king of Assyria, who brought or sent these persons hither, either,
   1. in the day's of Salmanasar, who reigned in Assyria but eight years before Esarhaddon; and so Esarhaddon might be one of his commanders, and the man by whom that colony was sent. Or,
   2. in the reign of Esarhaddon, who sent this second colony to strengthen the first.
3. With us - As being of another nation and religion, and therefore not concerned in Cyrus's grant, which was confined to the Israelites. Take heed, whom you go partners with, and on whose hand you lean. While we trust God with an absolute confidence, we must trust men with a prudent caution.
5. Cyrus - For though Cyrus still favoured the Jews, yet he was then diverted by his wars, and his son Cambyses was left his vice-roy, who was a wicked prince, and an enemy to the Jews. Until - Hebrew. and until, &c. not only in the reign of Cyrus but also of Cambyses, and of the magician, after whom was Darius.
6. Ahasuerus - A common name to divers kings of Persia. Cambyses the son and successor of Cyrus, was known to be no friend to the Jewish nation.
7. Artaxerxes - Cambyses, called by his Chaldee name, Ahashuerus, ver. 6, and here by his Persian name, Artaxerxes: by which he is here called in the inscription of this letter, because so he was called by himself, and others in the letters written either by him; or to him. Interpreted - It was written in the Chaldee or Syrian language, and in the Syrian character: for sometimes the Chaldee or Syrian words are written in the Hebrew character.
10. Asnapper - Either Esarhaddon, or some other person of eminency, who was captain of this colony, and conducted them hither. The river - Euphrates. Time - The date of the epistle was particularly expressed therein, but here it was sufficient to note it in general.
12. Be it known, &c. - This is a mere fiction, which being confidently affirmed, they thought would easily find belief with a king whose heart and ears they possessed by their hired counsellors.
23. To cease. &c. - As they abused the king by their misinformations, in the obtaining of this order, so they abused him in the execution of it; for the order was only to prevent the walling of the city. But having power in their hands, they, on this pretense, stopt the building of the temple. See what need we have to pray, not only for kings, but for all in authority under them: because the quietness of our lives depends much on the integrity and wisdom of inferior magistrates as well as the supreme.
24. Darius - Darius the son of Hystaspes, successor of Cambyses.

V

Zerubbabel encouraged by Haggai and Zechariah, sets the work forward again, ver. 1, 2. Their adversaries oppose them again, ver. 3-5. Write to Darius, ver. 6-17.

1. The son - His grand-child; for he was the son of Baraciah. Prophesied - Commanding them from God to return to building the temple, with a promise of his favour and assistance.
2. Helping - Encouraging the people to work by their presence, and assurance of success. It is supposed, the work had stopt about fifteen years. The first chapter of Haggai is the best comment on these two verses.
3. Shethar-boznai - Not Rehum and Shimshai, &c. who were either dead, or removed from their office by Darius.

4. **We** - Jews. **Accordingly** - According to what they asked. **That made this building** - That were the undertakers and encouragers of it.

8. **Great God** - And indeed, thus far the greater part of the Samaritans agreed with them.

17. **Now therefore. &c.** - If the case had been so fairly stated to Artaxerxes, he would hardly have hindered the work. The people of God could not be persecuted, if they were not belied.

VI

Darius's answer, ver. 1-7. His decree, ver. 8-12. The temple is finished, ver. 13-15. The dedication of it, ver. 16-18. The passover kept, ver. 19-22.

1. **A decree** - To search the rolls in Babylon, where search was first made; but not finding the edict there, they searched in Achmetha, or Ecbatana, and found it.

2. **Achmetha** - The royal city of the Medes and Persians.

3. **Cubits** - Those proportions differ from those of Solomon's temple, which was but thirty cubits high, only the porch was a hundred and twenty cubits high, and but twenty cubits in breadth. Either therefore Solomon's cubits were sacred cubits, which were larger than the other, and these but common cubits. Or, the sixty cubits of height are meant only for the porch. And the word rendered breadth, may be rendered the extension or the length of it; it being improbable that the king should give orders about the breadth, and none about the length of it.

12. **Destroy** - Tho' this temple was at length most justly destroyed by the righteous hand of God, yet perhaps the Romans, who were the instruments of that destruction, felt the effects of this curse. For that empire sensibly declined ever after, 'till it was wholly destroyed.

14. **Through the prophesying** - This is a seasonable intimation that this great and unexpected success was not to be ascribed to chance, or to the kindness or good humour of Darius, but unto God only, who by his prophets had required and encouraged them to proceed in the work, and by his mighty power disposed Darius's heart to such kind and noble purposes.

21. **Children of Israel** - Probably some out of each of the twelve tribes.

22. **Joyful** - He had given them both cause to rejoice, and hearts to rejoice. God is the fountain whence all the streams of true joy flow. **Of Assyria** - Of the king of Persia, who was now king of Assyria also, here so called emphatically, to note the great power and goodness of God in turning the hearts of these great monarchs, whose predecessors had been the chief persecutors and oppressors of God's people.

VII

An account of Ezra and his expedition to Jerusalem, ver. 1-10. The commission which Artaxerxes gave him, ver. 11-26. His thankfulness to God for it, ver. 27, 28.

1. **Artaxerxes** - The same of whom he speaks, chap. vi, 14. **The son** - His grand-son. Here are divers persons omitted for brevity sake, which may be supplied out of 1 Chron. vi, 1-xi, 47. Ezra was not himself the high priest; but he was nearly related to him.

6. **Went** - With the king's consent and commission. **Scribe** - A learned and expert doctor. The Jews say, he collected and collated all the copies of the law, and published an accurate edition of it, with all the books that were given by Divine inspiration, and so made up the canon of the Old Testament. Moses in Egypt, and Ezra in Babylon, were wonderfully fitted for eminent service to the church. **According, &c.** - By the favour of God so disposing the heart of the king.

10. **To teach** - The order of things in this verse is very observable; first he endeavours to understand God's law and word, and that not for curiosity or ostentation, but in order to practice: next he consciously practices what he did understand, which made his doctrine much more effectual: and then he earnestly desires and labours to instruct others, that they also might know and do it.

11. **Words** - The phrase seems emphatical, noting that he explained both the words and the things: for the Jews in the land of their captivity had in a great measure lost both the language, and the knowledge of God's commands, and therefore Ezra and his companions instructed them in both.

14. **According, &c.** - To make inquiry into all abuses and deviations from your law, and to redress them. **Which** - Which is now and always in thine hand, being the matter of thy daily study.

16. **Find** - Procure, as that word is used, Gen. vi, 8; xxvi, 12 Psalm 8iv, 3. Whatsoever thou canst get of my subjects by way of free gift. **The people** - Of Israel.

25. **The wisdom** - Which God hath put into thy heart, and appears in the works of thy hand. All that professed the Jewish religion, were to be under the jurisdiction of these Judges.

26. **Let judgment** - What could David himself, as king, have done more, for the honour of God, and the furtherance of religion?

27. Blessed, &c. - Ezra cannot proceed in his story, without inserting this thankful acknowledgment of God's goodness to him and the people.

28. As the hand, &c. - If God gives us his hand, we are bold and chearful: if he withdraws it, we are weak as water. Whatever service we are enabled to do for God and our generation, God must have all the glory of it.

VIII

The company that went up with Ezra, ver. 1-15. He sends for the Levites, ver. 16-20. Proclaims a fast, ver. 21-23. Delivers the treasure he brought to the priests and Levites, ver. 24-30. Goes on to Jerusalem, ver. 31, 32. The treasure delivered in there, ver. 33, 34. The people offer, ver. 35. The king's commissions delivered to his lieutenants, ver. 36.

3. Males - Though the males only be expressed yet doubtless they carried the women along with them, as they did the little ones.

13. Whose names are, &c. - It seems the rest came before; so that now all the sons of that family returned.

15. Of Levi - None who were simple Levites, and not the priests. And therefore the Levites mentioned, chap. vii, 7, by anticipation were not yet come to him.

18. By the good hand - If where ministers have been wanting, the vacancies are well supplied, let us ascribe it to the good hand of God, qualifying them for the service, inclining them to it, and opening a door for them.

21. A fast - For public mercies. Publick prayers must be made, that all who are to share in the comfort, may share in the requests for it. Afflict ourselves - For our sins; and so be qualified for the pardon of them. When we are entering on any new condition of life, our care should be to bring into it none of the guilt of the sins of our former condition. When we are in any imminent danger, let us make our peace with God, and then nothing can hurt us. Right way - A safe and prosperous journey; such a way and course as might be best for us.

23. Intreated - He gave us an assurance of his gracious answer to our request.

35. Sin offering - For it is the atonement that secures every mercy to us, which will not be truly comfortable, unless iniquity be taken away, and our peace made with God. They offer twelve bullocks, twelve he-goats, and ninety six rams, (eight times twelve) signifying the union of the two kingdoms. They did not any longer go two tribes one way, and ten tribes another; but all the twelve met by their representatives at the same altar.

IX

Ezra is troubled at the marriages with strange women, ver. 1-4. His solemn confession to God, ver. 5-15.

3. I rent - Both mine inner and my upper garment.

4. Evening sacrifice - When the people used to assemble together. All good people ought to own those that appear and act for God against vice and profaneness. Everyone that fears God, ought to stand by them, and do what he can to strengthen their hands.

5. Heaviness - From that mournful posture, and put myself into the posture of a petitioner. He did this at the time of the evening sacrifice, because then devout people used to come into the courts of the temple, that hearing his confession, they likewise might be made sensible of the sins of the people. And he had an eye to that great propitiation, of which that sacrifice was a peculiar type.

6. Our - He includes himself in the number of the transgressors, because he himself was guilty of many sins; and because the princes and priests, and so many of the people having done this, the guilt was now become national.

7. Have we been - We are not purged from the guilt of our fathers sins, but we are still feeling the sad effects of them; yea, and are repeating the same sins.

8. A little space - It is but a little while since God hath delivered us, and yet we are already returned to our sin. A remnant - The far greatest part of the Israelitish nation were yet in captivity. A nail - Some kind of settlement; whereas before we were tossed and removed from place to place as our masters pleased. It is a metaphor from tents, which are fastened by cords and nails, or pins. Holy place - In Jerusalem, called the holy city, Neh. xi, 1, 18 Dan. ix, 24, which is peculiarly mentioned, because of the temple, which was the nail that fastened their tents and gave them some hopes of continuing in their land. To lighten - That he might revive and comfort our hearts. For as darkness is often put for a state of sorrow and affliction, so light is put for joy and comfort. In bondage - For we are not quite delivered, being even here in subjection to our former lords.

9. A wall - The favour of the kings of Persia whose edicts were their security against all those enemies wherewith they were encompassed: and the gracious providence of God, which had planted them in their own land, and watched over them from time to time.

11. It is unclean - This land is as corrupt as any of the rest of the heathen nations.

12. Strong - Although you may fancy making leagues and marriages with them, as the only way to establish you, yet I assure you, it will weaken and ruin you, and the contrary course will make you strong.

15. We are - We are here in thy presence, and so are all our sins; we are arraigning ourselves before thy tribunal, acknowledging thee to be just, if thou destroy us. Before thee - In judgment, as that word is often used, we must needs fall and perish at thy presence.

X

The people mourn, ver. 1. Shechaniah encourages Ezra to put away the strange wives, ver. 2-4. All Israel swear to do it, ver. 5. Ezra, mourning assembles the people, ver. 6-9 They all, on his exhortation, agree to the reformation, ver. 10-14. They perform it, ver. 15-17. The names of them that had married strange wives, ver. 18-44.

1. There assembled - The account of his grief, and publick expressions thereof in the court before the temple, being in an instant dispersed over all the city, brought a great company together. See what an happy influence the example of great ones may have upon their inferiors!

2. We - He saith, we, in the name of the people, and their several families, and his own amongst the rest. For this man's name is not in the following catalogue, but there we have his father, Jehiel, and his father's brethren, five other sons of his grandfather, Elam, ver. 26. It was therefore an evidence of his great courage, and good conscience, that he durst so freely discharge his duty, whereby he shewed, that he honoured God more than his nearest and dearest relations. Hope - In case of our repentance, and reformation.

3. Such as are born - These children were only cast out of the common-wealth of Israel, but were not utterly forsaken; probably care was taken by authority, that they should have provision made for them.

6. Went - That with the princes and elders, he might consult about the execution of their resolution. Thither - 'Till he saw something done.

9. Of Judah - Not only of these two tribes, as appears from the following catalogue, where there are priests and Levites; but all the Israelites, ver. 25, who are thus described, because the greatest part of them were of these tribes, though others were mixed with them: and because they all now dwelt in that land, which formerly was appropriated to those tribes. The street - In that street of the city, which was next the temple, and within the view of it, that so they might be as in God's presence, whereby they might be awed to a more faithful and vigourous prosecution of their work. And this place they might chuse rather than the court of the people, because they thought it might be polluted by the delinquents, who were all to come thither. Great rain - Which they took for a token of God's displeasure against them.

14. Our rulers - Let the great council, called the Sanhedrim, be settled, and meet to determine of all particular causes. Judges - Who are best able to inform the great council of the quality of the persons, and all matters of fact and circumstances. Until - Until the thing be done, and God's wrath thereby removed.

15. Employed - To take care that the business should be executed in the manner proposed, that the officers and delinquents of every city should come successively in convenient time and order, as these should appoint, to keep an exact account of the whole transaction, and of the names of the cities and persons whose causes were dispatched, to give notice to others to come in their turns, and to prepare the business for the hearing of the Judges. These two were priests, as their helpers were Levites; that so they might inform the persons concerned, in any matter of doubt.

16. Separated - Sequestered themselves from all other business, and gave themselves wholly to this.

25. Of Israel - Of the people of Israel, distinguished from the priests and Levites hitherto named.

44. Had children - This implies that most of their wives were barren. Which came to pass by God's special providence, to manifest his displeasure against such matches, and that the putting them away might not be encumbered with too many difficulties. One would think this grievance altogether removed. Yet we meet with it again, Neh. xiii, 22. Such corruptions are easily and insensibly brought in, tho' not easily purged out. The best reformers can but do their endeavour. It is only the Redeemer himself, who when he cometh to Sion, will effectually turn away ungodliness from Jacob.

NOTES ON THE BOOK OF NEHEMIAH

THIS book continues the history of the children of the captivity, the Jews lately returned out of Babylon. We have a full account of Nehemiah's labours for them, in these his commentaries: wherein he records not only the works of his hands, but the very workings of his heart, inserting many devout reflections and ejaculations, which are peculiar to his writing. Twelve years he was the tirshatha, or governor of Judea, under the same Artaxerxes that gave Ezra his commission. This book relates his concern for Jerusalem and commission to go thither, chap. 1, 2. His building the wall of Jerusalem, notwithstanding much opposition, chap. 3, 4. His redressing the grievances of the people, chap. 5. His finishing the wall, chap. 6. The account he took of the people, chap. 7. His calling the people to read the law, fast and pray, and renew their covenant, chap. 8-10. He peoples Jerusalem and settles the tribe of Levi, chap. 11, 12. He reforms divers abuses, chap. 13. This was the last historical book that was written, as Malachi, the last prophetical book of the old testament.

I

Nehemiah is informed of the deplorable state of the Jews at Jerusalem, ver. 1-3. He fasts and prays, ver. 4-11

1. The words - Or rather, the acts, as the word often signifies. Chisleu - Which is the ninth month, containing part of November, and part of December. Year - Of Artaxerxes. Shushan - The royal city of Persia.
3. The province - In Judea, now a province under the Persian monarchs. The wall, &c. - The walls and gates continue as Nebuchadnezzar left them; the Jews not being in a condition to rebuild them, nor having commission from the kings of Persia to do so.
4. The God of heaven - Who seeth in secret; secret; having no opportunity of doing it openly.
6. Which I pray, &c. - He refers to all the prayers, which he had for some time been putting up.
11. To fear thy name - Those who truly desire to fear his name, shall be graciously accepted of God. This man - The king: who is but a man and therefore his heart is wholly at thy disposal. favour with men is then comfortable, when we see it springing from the mercy of God. Cup-bearer - Whereby I had opportunity to speak to him, and some favour with him.

II

Artaxerxes sends Nehemiah to Jerusalem, with a commission to build the wall, ver. 1-8. He comes thither, to the grief of his enemies, ver. 9-11. He secretly views the ruins of it, ver. 12-16. He informs the rulers of his commission, ver. 17, 18. Answers them that derided him, ver. 19, 20.

1. Nisan - Four months after he had heard those sad tidings. The reason of this long delay might be either that his turn of attending upon the king did not come 'till that time: or that 'till then he wanted a fit opportunity to move it to him.
2. Sad - His fasting joined with inward grief had made a sensible change in his countenance. Afraid - It was an unusual and ungrateful thing to come into the king of Persia's presence with any token of sorrow. And he feared a disappointment, because his request was great and invidious, and odious to most of the Persian courtiers.
3. Why should, &c. - All the grievances of the church, but especially its desolations, ought to be matter of grief to all good people, to all that have a concern for God's honour, and are of a public spirit.
4. Let, &c. - My sadness comes not from any disaffection to the king, for whom my hearty prayers are that he may live forever; but from another cause. Sepulchres - Which by all nations are esteemed sacred and inviolable. He saith not a word of the temple as he spake before a Heathen king who cared for none of these things. I prayed - To direct my thoughts and words, and to incline the king's heart to grant my request.
6. The queen - Which is here noted, as an unusual thing; for commonly the kings of Persia dined alone, and perhaps because the queen expressed some kindness to him, and promoted his request. How

long - This question shewed the king's affection to him, and that he was not willing to want his attendance longer than was necessary. A time - He built the walls in fifty two days, chap. vi, 15, and probably not long after returned to the king, by whom he was sent a second time with a more ample commission.

8. King's forest - Of the forest of Lebanon, famous for choice trees. Palace - Of the king's palace, which was adjoining to the house of God. Enter - That I shall build to dwell in while I am there.

10. Horonite - So called either, from the place of his birth or rule, which is supposed to be Horonaim, an eminent city of Moab. The servant - So called probably from the condition from which he was advanced to his present power and dignity: which also may be mentioned as one reason why he now carried himself so insolently, it being usual for persons suddenly raised from a low state, so to demean themselves.

12. Night - Concealing both his intentions as long as he could, knowing that the life of his business lay in secrecy and expedition. Beast - To prevent noise.

13. I went - The footmen who accompanied him directing and leading him in the way. His design was to go round the city, to observe the compass and condition of the walls and gates, that he might make sufficient provisions for the work.

14. No place - The way being obstructed with heaps of rubbish.

16. That did - Or, were to do, whom he intended to employ in it.

18. Rise up - Let us do it with vigour, and diligence, and resolution, as those that are determined to go through with it. Their hands - Their own and one anothers.

20. No portion - You have no authority over us, nor interest in our church and state, but are aliens from the common-wealth of Israel. Memorial - No testimony, or monument, either of your relation to us by birth or religion, or of your kindness to us, or to this place.

III

The names of those who presided over the builders, and the parts which each company built, ver. 1-32.

1. Eliashib - Grand-child of Joshua, the first high-priest after their return from Babylon. Rose - Began the work. Ministers should be foremost in every good work, animating others by their example as well as doctrine. Sheep-gate - Which was next to the temple; so called, because the sheep were brought thro' it to be sacrificed. Sanctified - Or, they prepared or repaired it: for so the word sometimes signifies. But our translation seems best, both because that use of the word is most common, and because this is spoken only of this gate, which being built by the priests, and nighest to the temple, and with a special eye to the service of the temple, for which both men and things were most commonly brought in this way, and being also the first part of the building, might be in a peculiar manner sanctified by solemn prayer and sacrifice, whereby it was dedicated to God's service.

5. Their nobles - Did not submit to it, would not further it, either through sloth or covetousness, or secret compliance with the enemies of the Jews. Of their Lord - Of God, whom they owned for their Lord, whose work this was, because it had proceeded thus far by his singular providence: and because it was done for the defense of the city, and people, and temple of God. And therefore they are branded to all posterity. Let not nobles think any thing beneath them, by which they may benefit their country. What is their nobility good for, but that it places them in an higher and larger sphere of usefulness?

7. The throne - Unto the place where the governor of the country on this side Euphrates, under the Persian kings, sometimes had a palace or throne.

8. Fortified - It is not said, they repaired, but they fortified it, either because this part of the wall was less demolished than the other, and therefore they needed not to repair it, but only to make it stronger: or, to note their extraordinary care and diligence, that they would not only repair it, but make it stronger than ever.

9. Half part - As Rome was anciently divided into several quarters or regions, so was Jerusalem; and especially into two parts, whereof one was in the tribe of Benjamin, and nearest the temple, the other in the tribe of Judah, these accordingly had two several rulers, this man and the other, ver. 12, but both under the chief governor of the city.

12. His daughters - Who were either heiresses or rich widows, and caused part to be done at their charges.

14. Beth-haccerem - A town or territory, the government whereof was divided between two persons.

16. Made - By Hezekiah, 2 Kings xx, 20. Whereby it is distinguished from that pool which was natural. Mighty - Or, of the valiant: which possibly was formerly appointed for the receipt of those chief captains that should attend upon the king in their courses.

20. Earnestly - Did his work with eminent diligence and fervency: which is here noted to his

commendation. And it is probable, this good man's zeal provoked many, to take the more pains, and make the more haste.

21. The door - Therefore the door was not in the middle of the house, as now they commonly are, but at one end of it.

27. Tekoites - The same spoken of before, who having dispatched their first share sooner than their brethren, freely offered to supply the defects of others, who, as it seems, neglected that part of the work which had been committed to them. And this their double diligence is noted both for the greater shame of their nobles, who would not do any part of it, and for their own honour, who were so far from being corrupted by that bad example, that they were quickened to greater zeal and industry in this pious work.

30. The sixth son of Zalaph - It seems, his five elder brethren, laid not their hands to the work. But in doing that which is good, we need not stay to see our betters go before us.

IV

The enemies scoff, but Nehemiah prays, and continues the work, ver. 1-6. To frustrate their design, he prays and sets a guard, ver. 7-13. He encourages the workmen, and directs them how to proceed, ver. 14-18. His farther directions, ver. 19-23.

2. In a day - Do they intend to begin, and finish the work, all in one day? For if they spend any long time about it, they cannot think that we will suffer them to do it. The stones - Will they pick up their broken stones out of the ruins, and patch them together. Burnt - Which stones were burnt, and broken, by the Chaldeans when they took the city.

4. A prey - Give them for a prey to their enemies, and let these carry them into the land of captivity.

5. Cover not - Let their wickedness be in thy sight, so as to bring down judgments upon them, that either they may be reformed, or others may be warned by their example. God is said to cover or hide sin when he forbears to punish it. Provoked thee - They have not only provoked us builders, but thee also.

6. The half - Unto half its height.

10. Judah - The Jews now dwelling in Judah, some of them being partly terrified by their enemies, and partly wearied with continual labour. Rubbish - More than we are able suddenly to remove. Not able - Being forced to spend our time in removing the rubbish, and therefore we must desist for a season.

12. By them - Or, among them: whereby they came to the knowledge of their counsels. Tho' these had not zeal enough to help in the work, yet they had some concern for their brethren. Ten tribes - Very often, a certain number for an uncertain. Be upon you - They will invade you every way, by which we can come to you, or you to us; therefore keep watches on every side.

13. Behind - Within the walls where they were not yet raised to their due height, and therefore most liable to the enemies assault. Higher - Upon the tops of the walls where they were finished, and the towers which were built here and there upon the wall; whence they might shoot arrows, or throw stones.

14. Looked - He looked up, engaged God for him, and put himself and his cause under the Divine protection. That was his way, and should be ours: all his cares, all his griefs, all his fears he spread before God. Great and terrible - You think your enemies are great and terrible. But what are they in comparison of God? Especially in opposition to him?

16. From that time forth - Lest our enemies should repeat their enterprize. My servants - Of my domestick servants, and of my guards. Held, &c. - All their weapons: they stood in their arms prepared for battle. Were behind - To encourage them in their work, sometimes to assist with their own hands: and to direct and command them in case of an assault. Judah - The Jews who were upon the wall.

17. A Weapon - This is to be taken figuratively; being a proverbial speech, as when they say of a man pretending kindness, he carries bread in one hand, and a stone in another. Thus must we work out our salvation, with the weapons of our warfare in our hands. For in every duty we must expect opposition from our spiritual enemies.

18. Sounded - To call the people together, when, and where it was necessary.

23. Washing - When they were to wash and cleanse themselves from some impurity, which might befall them or their garments.

V

The poor complain of being oppressed by the rich, ver. 1-5. Nehemiah removes the oppression, ver. 6-13. He sets an example of compassion on the poor, ver. 14-19.

2. Many - Which is in itself a blessing, but to us is turned into a curse. Take up - We are forced to take up corn, upon unreasonable terms.

3. The dearth - Which might happen, both from the multitude of the people in and near Jerusalem, from their work, which wholly took them up, and kept them from taking care of their families, and from the expectation of their enemies invasion, which hindered them from going abroad to fetch provision, and the people round about from bringing it to them.

5. Our flesh - We are of the same nature, and religion with them, though they treat us as if we were beasts or Heathens. Bondage - We are compelled to sell them for our subsistence. Daughters - Which was an evidence of their great necessity, because their daughters were more tender, and weak, and unfit for bond-service, and more exposed to injuries than their sons. Redeem - Which we are allowed to do, Exod. xxi, 7-11, but have not wherewith to do it.

7. Exact - Which was against the plain and positive law of God, Deut. xxiii, 19, 20, especially in this time of publick calamity. I set - I called a publick congregation, both of the rulers and people, the greatest part whereof were free from this guilt, and therefore more impartial Judges of the matter, and represented it to them, that the offenders might be convinced, and reformed; if not for fear of God, or love of their brethren, yet at least for the publick shame and the cries of the poor. Ezra, and Nehemiah were both good and useful men; but of how different tempers? Ezra was a man of a mild tender spirit, and when told of the sin of the rulers, rent his clothes and wept: Nehemiah forced them to reform, being of a warm and eager spirit. So God's work may be done, and yet different methods taken in doing it; which is a good reason why we should not arraign the management of others, nor make our own standard.

8. We - I, and my brethren, and predecessors, have used our utmost interest and power, both with the kings of Persia, that our brethren might be redeemed from bondage, and with particular persons in Babylon, and Persia, whose bond-slaves the Jews were, and who would not part with them without a price. Be sold - Do you expect that we should pay you a price for them, as we did to the Babylonians?. Or, must we use as much importunity to solicit you for their redemption, as we did to their enemies?

9. Reproach - Who are round about you, and observe all your actions, and will reproach both you for such barbarous usage of your brethren, and religion for your sakes.

10. Brethren - In office; these who are employed with me in the government of this people. Servants - In my name, and for my use. Exact - As a just recompense for our pains and care for the publick good, to which we wholly devote ourselves, even to the neglect of all our private concerns. But I freely remit my own right, and therefore you also ought to do so, seeing I lay no burden upon you, but what I am willing to bear a part of upon my own shoulders.

11. Also - Also require not: which is to be supplied out of the next verse, where it is expressed in their grant of this desire. Hundredth part - Which they required every month for the use of their monies or goods, according to the custom then used.

12. Require - For the hundredth part. Priests - As witnesses; that the oath being taken before the priests, who acted in God's name, the oath might make the more deep and durable impression upon their consciences.

13. My lap - The extreme parts of my garment, which I first folded together, and then shook it and scattered it asunder. This was a form of swearing then in use.

14. Twelve years - Not that he continued so long together at Jerusalem, but he so long governed Jerusalem by himself when present, and in his absence, by a deputy. The bread - That allowance which by the laws of God and nations, and of the king of Persia, the governors might require.

15. The former - Not Ezra, who was no governor, nor Zerubbabel, but others between him and Nehemiah, whom he forbears to name. Beside, &c. - Which they required of the people every day to defray their other expenses. Their servants - Ruled them with rigor and cruelty; which fault of the servants is charged upon their masters, because they did not restrain them. He had an awe of God's mercy, and a fear of offending him. Those that truly fear God, will not dare to do any thing cruel or unjust. And this is not only a powerful, but an acceptable principle both of justice and charity.

16. I continued - Overseeing, directing, and encouraging the workmen, which was my whole business; and this at my own cost. Bought - Of our poor brethren, whose necessities gave abundant opportunity of enriching myself with good bargains.

17. Rulers - Not only Jews of the inferior sort, for whom meaner provisions might suffice, but also their rulers, for whom better provision was fit; who resorted to him upon all occasions, to give him notice of the enemies designs; or to receive his orders.

18. Required not - But bore it out of my own estate: which was very considerable, his office in the Persian court being a place of great profit.

19. According - As I have done thy people good for thy sake, so do me good for thine own sake; for thou art pleased, and hast promised graciously to reward us according to our works, and to mete to men the same measure which they meet to others.

VI

Nehemiah's answer to his enemies, courting him to an interview, ver. 1-4. To their charge of rebellion, ver. 5-9. To Shemaiah's false prophecy, ver. 10-14. Notwithstanding the treachery of some of the nobles, the work is finished, ver. 15-19

1. The doors - Not all of them.

2. Meet - To consult about the common service of our master the king of Persia, or to make a friendly accommodation.

4. Four times, &c. - We must never be overcome by the greatest importunity, to do anything ill or imprudent: but when we are attacked with the same temptation, still resist it with the same reason and resolution.

5. Open letter - As speaking of a thing commonly known.

7. A king - We have now a king of our nation. Counsel - That we may impartially examine the matter, that thy innocency may be cleared.

9. Strengthen my hands - A good prayer, when we are entering on any particular services or conflicts in our Christian warfare.

10. Shut up - In his chamber adjoining to the temple, upon pretense of singular devotion, and communion with God, and withal upon pretense of certain knowledge, by the Spirit of God concerning their approaching danger, from which thy could be safe nowhere but in the temple. For if Nehemiah had done this, the people would have left their work, and every one have shifted for his own safety.

11. As I - I the chief governor, upon whose presence, the very life of the whole city and nation in a great measure depends: I who have professed such resolution, and courage, and confidence in God. I, who have had such eminent experience of God's assistance, of his calling me to this employment, and carrying me through it when our danger was greater than now it is. Shall I now dishonour God and religion, and betray the people and city of God by my cowardice? Go in - Tho' his life depended upon it.

13. And sin - By going into a place forbidden to me, and that in such a manner, which would have been both sinful and shameful. Reproach - As a coward, and conscious of my own guilt, that they might make me contemptible and odious both to my own people, and to the king of Persia.

14. My God, &c. - This prayer we are not to imitate.

15. Elul - Answering part to our August, and part to September.

VII

Nehemiah appoints persons to keep the city, ver. 1-4. Reviews the people, ver. 5-7.

3. Hot - 'Till it be clear and broad day; when the people will be ready in case of an assault. They - The watches appointed to that end. Watches - Nehemiah was now about to return to the court, and left the charge of the city to these in his absence.

5. God put it into mine heart - Whatever good motion is in our minds, we must acknowledge it to come from God. What is done by human prudence is to be ascribed to the direction of Divine Providence.

7. Tirshatha - Nehemiah. So it is no wonder that the number of the monies, and other things here contributed, differ from that Ezra ii, 68, 69, because this is another collection.

VIII

The solemn reading and expounding of the law, ver. 1-8. The joy of the people, ver. 9-12. The keeping of the feast of tabernacles, ver. 13-18.

2. First day - This was the feast of trumpets, which is called a sabbath, and on which they were to have an holy convocation, Lev. xxiii, 24. And it was on this day, the altar was set up, after their return from captivity; in remembrance of which they had probably kept it ever since, with more than ordinary solemnity.

7. Understand - As well the words, which being Hebrew, now needed to be translated into the Chaldee or Syriack language, now, the common language of that people, who together with their religion, had also in a great part lost their language; as also the meaning of them: they expounded the mind and will of God in what they read, and applied it to the peoples present condition. Place - That is, In their several places and stations into which the company seems to have been distributed for conveniency of hearing; it not being likely that so vast a congregation could distinctly hear one man's voice. Or, by their stations, that is, by the several stations of the Levites, and persons last named; who seem to have had several scaffolds, by comparing this with chap. ix, 4, upon which thy stood, as Ezra

did upon his pulpit, ver. viii, 4.

8. They - Ezra and his companions successively. Sense - The meaning of the Hebrew words, which they expounded in the common language. Thy gave - So they gave them both a translation of the Hebrew words into the Chaldee, and an exposition of the things contained in them.

9. Wept - Out of a sense of their guilt and danger by reason of it.

10. Eat - Feast before the Lord. Send - For the relief of your poor brethren. Holy - Being the feast of trumpets, and the beginning of this joyful month, wherein so many days of thanksgiving were to be observed. Strength - Rejoicing in God in serving him with chearfulness, and thankfulness, which is your duty always, but now especially, will give you that strength both of mind and body, which you greatly need, both to perform all the duties required of you, and to oppose all the designs of your enemies.

13. Levites - Chusing rather to confess their ignorance than vainly to pretend to more knowledge than they had: wherein they shew both humility, and serious godliness, that they were more careful to learn their duty than to preserve their reputation.

15. Mount - The Mount of Olives, which was next Jerusalem, and stored with olive-branches, and probably with the rest: for these trees seem to have been planted hereabouts principally, for the use of the city in this very feast, which, though, long neglected, should have been celebrated every year. And this place seems to be here designed as the most eminent place, being put for any place near to the several cities of Judah, where these branches were to be procured.

17. Done so - So, as to the manner and circumstances. They never kept this feast so joyfully, having not only the same causes of rejoicing which they formerly had, but special causes to increase their joy; they never kept it so solemnly and religiously: for whereas at other times, only the first and last day of that feast were celebrated with an holy convocation, now there was an holy convocation, and the people assembled, and attended upon the reading of the law, every day of this feast.

IX

The people keep a solemn fast, ver. 1-3. The Levites bless God for his goodness to them and their fathers, ver. 4-8. In Egypt and in their journey out of it, ver. 9-12. On Mount Sinai, ver. 13, 14. And their journey toward Canaan, ver. 15-18. In the wilderness, ver. 19-21. In driving out the Canaanites, ver. 22-26. In hearing their prayer when in trouble, ver. 27-31. They confess their sin, ver. 32-37. And seal a covenant with God, ver. 38.

1. Now - The next day, but one after the feast of tabernacles, which begun on the fourteenth day, and ended on the twenty second, for their consciences having been fully awakened and their hearts filled with grief for their sins, which they were not allowed to express in that time of publick joy; now they resume their former thoughts, and recalling their sins to mind, set apart a day for solemn fasting and humiliation.

2. Separated - From all unnecessary society with the Heathens, and particularly from those strange women whom some of them had married. For though Ezra had done this formerly, yet, it seems, there were some criminals, without his knowledge, or, these were some new delinquents, that since that time had fallen into the same error, and shewed the truth of their repentance by forsaking their beloved sins, and dearest relations.

3. Book of the law - As they did before, giving them the sense of what they read. Fourth part - For three hours; there were twelve hours in their day, probably they began after the morning sacrifice, and continued their work till the evening sacrifice. The work of a fast-day is good work. We should endeavour to make a day's work, a good day's work of it.

4. Stairs - Upon such stairs, or pulpits, as the Levites used to stand upon, when they taught the people. But they stood upon several pulpits, each of them teaching that part of the congregation which was allotted him, or praying, or blessing God with them. Loud voice - Thereby testifying their deep sense of their sins and miseries, and their servant, and importunate desire of God's mercy.

13. Good statutes - The moral and judicial precepts were all founded on natural equity. And even the ceremonial were tokens of God's goodness, being types of gospel-grace.

17. Made - Designed, and resolved to do so, Num. xiv, 4, and therefore they are said to do so, as Abraham is said to have offered up Isaac, Heb. xi, 17, because he intended to do it.

22. Divide - The Heathen nations, whom God in a great measure destroyed, and the remainders of them he dispersed into corners; that whereas before the Israelites came, they had large habitations, now they were cooped up, some in one town, and some in another, in the several corners of their land, while the Israelites dwelt in a large place, and had the possession of their whole land, some few and small parcels excepted.

32. Mercy - He adds mercy, because the covenant in itself was not a sufficient ground of hope, because they had so basely broken it. God was discharged from keeping it, and therefore they fly to God's free and rich mercy for relief.

33. Thou art just. &c. - It becomes us, when we are under the rebukes of providence, be they ever so sharp, or ever so long continued, still to justify God, and to own we are punished less than our iniquities deserve.

37. Yieldeth much, &c. - We plow, and sow, and labour, and thou givest thy blessing to our endeavours; and yet in a great measure this is not for ourselves, as formerly it was, but for our kings, to whom we pay heavy tributes. Dominion - Pressing or forcing both us and our beasts to go and to do what they please.

38. Sure covenant, &c. - It was sealed and left upon record, that it might be a witness against them, if they dealt deceitfully.

X

The names of those who set their seal to the covenant, ver. 1- 27. An account of those who consented thereto, ver. 28-31. They engage to adhere to the temple service, ver. 32-39.

1. Sealed - Both in their own names, and in the name of all the rest. It may seem strange that Ezra doth not appear among them. But that might be because he was prevented, by some sickness, or other extraordinary impediment. It is true, we meet with Ezra after this, at the dedication of the wall of Jerusalem, chap. xii, 36, and therefore he was then freed from this impediment, whatsoever it was.

29. Their nobles - The commonality agreed with the nobles in this good work, great men never look so great, as when they encourage religion and are examples of it: and they would by that, as much as any thing, make an interest in the most valuable of their inferiors, who would cleave to them closer than they can imagine. Observe their nobles are called their brethren; for in the things of God, rich and poor, high and low meet together. They cleave - They ratified what the others had done in their names, declaring their assent to it.

31. People of the land - The Heathens. On the sabbath - They that covenant to keep all the commandments of God, must particularly covenant to keep the sabbath holy. For the profanation of this is a sure inlet to all manner of profaneness.

XI

The rulers and men drawn by lot dwell at Jerusalem, ver. 1, 2. Their names, numbers and families, ver. 3-19. The cities and villages that were peopled by the rest, ver. 20-36.

1. To dwell - That the buildings of the city might be compleated, and the safety of it better provided for.

2. Blessed - Because they denied themselves, and their own safety and profit for the publick good; for this city was the butt of all the malicious plots of their enemies; and for the present it was rather chargeable than beneficial to its inhabitants.

3. Province - Of Judea, which was now made a province. Israel - The generality of the people of Israel, whether of Judah, or Benjamin, or any other tribe. These he calls Israel rather than Judah, because there were many of the other tribes now incorporated with them; and because none of the tribes of Israel, except Judah and Benjamin, dwelt in Jerusalem.

9. Overseer - The captain of their thousand.

16. Outward - For those things belonging to the temple and its service, which were to be done without it, or abroad in the country, as the gathering in of the voluntary contributions, or other necessary provision out of the several parts of the land.

17. To begin - In the publick and solemn prayers and praises, which were constantly joined with the morning and evening sacrifice, at which the singers were present, and praised God with a psalm or hymn which, this man began.

21. The Nethinims dwelt in Ophel - Which was upon the wall of Jerusalem, because they were to do the servile work of the temple: therefore they were to be posted near it, that they might be ready to attend.

24. Was, &c. - Or, on the king's part, to determine civil causes and controversies between man and man, by the laws of that kingdom; between the king and people; as in matters of tribute, or grievances.

36. Divisions - Or, for the Levites (those who were not settled in Jerusalem) there were divisions, places appointed for them, and distributed among them. Thus were they settled free and easy, tho' few and poor. And they might have been happy, but for that general lukewarmness, with which they are charged by the prophet Malachi, who prophesied about this time and in whom prophecy ceased for some ages, 'till it revived in the great prophet.

XII

The chief of the priests and Levites that came up with Zerubbabel, ver. 1-9. The succession of the chief-priests, ver. 10- 21. The eminent Levites, ver. 22-26. The wall dedicated, ver. 27- 43. The offices of the priests and Levites settled, ver. 44-47.

1. Priests - The chief of the priests, the heads of those twenty four courses which David appointed by divine direction, 1 Chron. xxiv, 1-19. And whereas there were twenty four, and here but twenty-two, and ver.

12, &c. only twenty, the reason of this difference may be, because two of the twenty four courses were extinct in Babylon, and two of the persons here named, ver. 2, 5, Hattush, and Maadiah, may be omitted in the account of the posterity of these, ver. 12, &c. because they had no posterity. Ezra - Either this was another Ezra, or if it were the same mentioned Ezra vii, 1, he lived to a great age; which may well be supposed, considering his great sobriety, and his great piety to which God promised long life, and withal the special providence of God continuing him so long in such a season, wherein the church of God did greatly need his help and counsel.

8. Moreover, &c. - He was to see, that the Psalms of thanksgiving were continually sung in the temple, in due time and manner.

10. Jeshua - Here follows a catalogue of the Jewish high-priests; which was the more necessary, because their times were now to be measured, not by the years of their kings as formerly, but by their high-priests.

12. Priests - As their fathers were priests in the days of Joshua, so in the days of Joiakim the son of Joshua, the sons of those persons executed the priesthood in their father's steads, some of their fathers probably being yet living, and many of them dead.

22. Darius - Darius Noehus; and so this Jaddua might be father to him who was in the days of Darius Codomanus, and of Alexander the Great.

27. The wall - Of the city itself, which is here dedicated to God, and to his honour and service, not only upon a general account, by which we ought to devote ourselves, and all that is ours, to God; but upon a more special ground, because this was a place which God himself had chosen, and sanctified by his temple and gracious presence, and therefore did of right belong to him; whence it is often called the holy city. And they restored it to God by this dedication, withal imploring the presence, and favour, and blessing of to this city by solemn prayers, and praises, and sacrifices, wherewith this dedication was accompanied. Places - To which they were now retired after that great and general assembly, chap. 8, 9, & 10. chap. viii, 1 &c.

30. Purified themselves - They that would be instrumental to sanctify others, must sanctify themselves, and set themselves apart for God, with purity of mind and sincerity of intention.

31. Princes - And half of the people with them. The wall - For the wall was broad and strong, and so ordered that men might conveniently walk upon it. Right hand - Towards the south and east.

39. Stood still - Waiting, as also their brethren did, that they might go together in due order into God's house, there to perfect the solemnity.

43. The children rejoiced - And their hosanna's were not despised, but are recorded to their praise. All that share in public mercies, ought to join in public thanksgivings.

44. Rejoiced - For the eminent gifts and graces which they observed in many of them: for the great benefit which they had now received by their ministry: and for the competent provision which hereby was made for them, that so they might wholly wait upon their office. The sure way for ministers to gain an interest, in the affections of their people, is to wait on their ministry, to spend their whole time, and thought, and strength therein.

45. The ward - That ward, or charge, which God had prescribed to them. And in particular the charge of purification, of taking care that no unclean person or thing should enter into the house or courts of the Lord.

47. Sanctified - They set apart the first-fruits and tithes from their own share, and devoted them to the use of the Levites. And so did the Levites by the tithe of the tithes. Thus they all conscientiously paid their dues, and did not profane those things which God had sanctified, nor take them into their own common use. When what is contributed for the support of religion, is given with an eye to God, it is sanctified, and will cause the blessing to rest upon the house, and all that is therein.

XIII

John Wesley

The Israelites are separated from the mixt multitude, ver. 1-3. Nehemiah cleansed the chambers of the temple, ver. 4-9. He recovers and secures the portion of the priests and Levites, ver. 10-14. Contends with the nobles concerning the sabbath, and takes care for the due observance of it, ver. 15-22. Restrains them from marrying strange wives, ver. 23-31.

1. That day - Not presently after the dedication of the wall and city, but upon a certain day, when Nehemiah was returned from the Persian court to Jerusalem, from which he had been absent for some considerable time, in which some errors and abuses had crept in. Not come - Not be incorporated into the common-wealth of Israel, nor be joined with any Israelite in marriage.

3. Multitude - All the heathenish people with whom they had contracted alliance.

4. Eliashib - The high-priest. Chamber - Of the chambers, the high-priest having the chief power over the house of God, and all the chambers belonging to it. Tobiah - The Ammonite, and a violent enemy to God's people.

5. Prepared - By removing the things out of it, uniting divers small chambers into one, and furnishing it for the use of Tobiah when he came to Jerusalem: whom he seems to have lodged there, that he might have more free communication with him.

6. But, &c. - Eliashib took the occasion of my absence to do these things. Came I - From Jerusalem; where he had been once and again.

8. Grieved me - That so sacred a place should be polluted by one who in many respects ought not to come there, being no priest, a stranger, an Ammonite, and one of the worst of that people; and that all this should be done by the permission and order of the high-priest.

10. Not given - Which might be either,

1. from this corrupt high-priest Eliashib, who took their portions, as he did the sacred chambers, to his own use, or employed them for the entertainment of Tobiah, and his other great allies. Or,

2. from the people, who either out of covetousness reserved them to themselves, contrary to their own solemn agreement, or were so offended at Eliashib's horrid abuse of sacred things, that they abhorred the offering and service of God, and therefore neglected to bring in their tithes, which they knew would be perverted to bad uses. Fled - To his possession in the country, being forced to do so for a livelihood.

11. Contended - I sharply reproved those priests to whom the management of those things was committed, for neglect of their duty, and breach of their late solemn promise. Why, &c. - You have not only injured men in with-holding their dues, but you have occasioned the neglect of God's house and service. Gathered - To Jerusalem from their several country possessions. Set - Restored them to the exercise of their office.

12. Bought - Out of the respect which they had to Nehemiah, and because they saw they would now be applied to their proper uses.

13. Faithful - By the consent of those who knew them. Such he now sought out the more diligently, because he had experience of the perfidiousness of the former trustees.

16. Jerusalem - The holy city, where God's house was; and where the great judicatories of the nation were. So this is added as an aggravation of their sin, that it was done with manifest contempt of God and man.

17. Nobles - Their chief men and rulers; whom he charges with this sin, because though others did it, it was by their countenance or connivance: probably too by their example. If the nobles allowed themselves in recreations, in idle visits and idle talk on the sabbath day, the men of business would profane it by their worldly employments, as the more justifiable of the two.

19. At the gates - Out of a diffidence in those, to whom the keeping of the gates was committed.

22. Cleanse - Because the work they now were set upon, though common in its nature, yet was holy in design of it, and had respect unto the sabbath: and, because the day in which they were to do this was the sabbath-day, for the observation whereof they were obliged to purify themselves. Gates - The gates of the city; not daring to trust the common porters, he commits the charge of them upon the sabbath-days, to the Levites, to whom the care of sanctifying the sabbath did properly belong. Mercy - Whereby he intimates, that though he mentioned his good-works, as things wherewith God was well-pleased, and which he had promised to reward, yet he neither did, nor durst trust to their merit, or his own worthiness, but, when he had done all, he judged himself an unprofitable servant, and one that needed God's infinite mercy to pardon all his sins, and particularly those infirmities and corruptions which adhered to his good deeds.

25. Cursed - Caused them to be excommunicated and cast out of the society of God's people. This and the following punishments were justly inflicted upon them, because this transgression was contrary both to a plain law of God, and to their own late solemn covenants. Smote - I caused to be beaten with stripes, according to the law, Deut. xxv, 2, such whose faults were most aggravated; to whom he added

this punishment over and above the former. Plucked off - Or, shaved them. The hair was an ensign of liberty among the eastern nations; and baldness was a disgrace, and token of slavery and sorrow.

28. And one, &c. - Said by Josephus to be that Manasses, who by Sanballat's interest procured liberty to build the Samaritan temple in mount Gerizim; to which those priests who had married strange wives, or been otherwise criminal, betook themselves, and with, or after them, others of the people in the same or like circumstances. Chased - From my presence and court, from the city and temple, and from the congregation and church of Israel.

31. For good - This may well be the summary of our petitions. We need no more to make us happy but this.

John Wesley

NOTES ON THE BOOK OF ESTHER

BOTH Jews and Christians have generally supposed Mordecai to be the writer of this book, which shews the care of God even over those Israelites, who were still scattered among the Heathens. It is the narrative of a plot to cut off all the Jews, disappointed by a wonderful concurrence of providences. The name of God is not found in this book: but the, finger of God is, directing so many minute events for the deliverance of his people. The particulars are very encouraging to God's people, in the most difficult and dangerous times. Here we are told how Esther came to be queen, and Mordecai to be great at court, chap. 1, 2. How Haman obtained an order for the destruction of the Jews, chap. 3. The distress of the Jews thereupon, chap. 4. The defeating of Haman's plot against Mordecai, chap. 5-7. The defeating of his plot against the Jews, chap. 8. The care taken to perpetuate the memory of this, chap. 9, 10.

I

Ahasuerus feasts his great men, ver. 1-9. Sends for his queen, who refuses to come, ver. 10, 11. He divorces her, ver. 12-22.

1. Ahasuerus - Many suppose this to be Darius Hystapas, for his kingdom was thus vast, and he subdued India, as Herodotus reports: and one of his wives was called Atossa, differing little from Hadassah, which is Esther's other name, Esth ii, 7. Provinces - So seven new provinces were added to those hundred and twenty mentioned, Dan. vi, 1.

2. Sat - Was settled in the peaceable possession of it. Shushan - The chief or royal city. Shushan might be the proper name of the palace, which thence was given to the whole city. Here the kings of Persia used to keep their courts in winter, as at Exbatana in summer.

4. Many days - Making every day a magnificent feast, either for all his princes, or for some of them, who might come to the feast successively, as the king ordered them to do. The Persian feasts are much celebrated in authors, for their length and luxury.

6. Beds - For in those eastern countries, they did not then sit at tables as we do, but rested or leaned upon beds or couches.

8. The law - According to this law which the king had now made, that none should compel another to drink more than he pleased. How does this Heathen prince shame many, that are called Christians, who think they do not make their friends welcome, unless they make them drunk, and under pretense of sending the health round, send the sin round, and death with it!

9. Women - While the king entertained the men. For this was the common custom of the Persians, that men and women did not feast together.

12. Refused - Being favoured in this refusal by the law of Persia, which was to keep mens wives, and especially queens, from the view of other men.

13. The times - The histories of former times, what princes have done in such cases as this was.

14. Saw - Who had constant freedom of access to the king, and familiar converse with him: which is thus expressed, because the Persian kings were very seldom seen by their subjects. Sat - Who were his chief counsellors and officers.

18. Contempt - Contempt in the wives, and thereupon wrath in the husbands; and consequently strife in families.

II

The virgins of the kingdom are gathered together, ver. 1-4. And Esther with the rest, ver. 5-8. She finds favour with the king's chamberlain, ver. 9-11. The manner of preparing the virgins, and bringing them to the king, ver. 12-14. Esther pleases him, who makes her queen, ver. 15-20. Mordecai discovers a conspiracy against the king, ver. 21-23.

3. Keeper - Of all the women, both virgins and concubines: only the virgins he himself took care of, as requiring more care and caution, and the concubines be committed to Shaashgaz, ver. 14, his deputy. Purification - That is, to cleanse them from all impurities, to perfume, and adorn, and every way

prepare them for the king: for the legal purification of the Jews he never regarded.

7. Esther - Hadassah was her Hebrew name before her marriage; and she was called Esther by the king after it.

9. Pleased - Because she was very beautiful, therefore he supposed she would be acceptable to the king; and by the Divine power, which moveth the hearts of men which way he pleaseth.

10. Shew it - Lest the knowledge hereof should either make her contemptible, or bring some inconvenience to the whole nation; but there was also an hand of God in causing this to be concealed, for the better accomplishment of that which he designed, though Mordecai was ignorant of it.

13. Desired - For ornament, or by way of attendance. And it should be observed, that every one whom the king took to his bed, was his wife of a lower rank, as Hagar was Abraham's, so that it would have been no sin or dishonour to Esther, though she had not been made queen.

19. Sat - By office, as one of the king's guards or ministers; being advanced to this place by Esther's favour.

III

Haman offended at Mordecai, resolves to destroy all the Jews, ver. 1-6. He obtains an order from the king, to have them all slain on one day, ver. 7-11. This order is sent throughout the kingdom, ver. 12-15.

1. Agagite - An Amalekite of the royal seed of that nation, whose kings were successively called Agag. All the princes - Gave him the first place and seat, which was next to the king.

2. But, &c. - Probably the worship required was not only civil, but Divine: which as the kings of Persia arrogated to themselves, so they did sometimes impart this honour to some of their chief favourites, that they should be adored in like manner. And that it was so here, seems more than probable, because it was superfluous, to give an express command to all the kings servants, to pay a civil respect to so great a prince, which of course they used, and therefore a Divine honour must be here intended. And that a Jew should deny this honour, is not strange, seeing the wise Grecians did positively refuse to give this honour to the kings of Persia themselves, even when they were to make their addresses to them: and one Timocrates was put to death by the Athenians for worshipping Darius in that manner.

4. To see - What the event of it would be. For, &c. - And therefore did not deny this reverence out of pride, but merely out of conscience.

6. Scorn - He thought that vengeance was unsuitable to his quality. Destroy - Which he attempted, from that implacable hatred which, as an Amalekite, he had against them; from his rage against Mordecai; and from Mordecai's reason of this contempt, because he was a Jew, which as he truly judged, extended itself to all the Jews, and would equally engage them all in the same neglect. And doubtless Haman included those who were returned to their own land: for that was now a province of his kingdom.

7. They cast - The diviners cast lots, according to the custom of those people, what day, and what month would be most lucky, not for his success with the king (of which he made no doubt) but for the most effectual extirpation of the Jews. Wherein appears likewise both his implacable malice, and unwearied diligence in seeking vengeance of them with so much trouble to himself; and God's singular providence in disposing the lot to that time, that the Jews might have space to get the decree reversed.

11. The silver - Keep it to thy own use; I accept the offer for the deed.

15. The city - Not only the Jews, but a great number of the citizens, either because they were related to them, or engaged with them in worldly concerns; or out of humanity and compassion toward so vast a number of innocent people, appointed as sheep for the slaughter.

IV

The Jews fast and mourn, ver. 1-3. Esther is informed of the design, ver. 4-9, Mordecai presses her to intercede with the king, ver. 10-14. She desires all the Jews to keep a solemn fast, ver. 15- 19.

1. Cry - To express his deep sense of the mischief coming upon his people. It was bravely done, thus publickly to espouse a just cause though it seemed to be a desperate one.

2. Sackcloth - Lest it should give the king any occasion of grief and trouble. But what availed, to keep out the badges of sorrow unless they could have kept out the causes of sorrow too? To forbid sackcloth to enter unless they could likewise forbid sickness, and trouble, and death?

4. To clothe - That so he might be capable of returning to his former place, if not of coming to her to acquaint her with the cause of his sorrow.

11. Inner court - Within which, the king's residence and throne was. Not called - This was decreed,

to maintain both the majesty, and the safety of the king's person; and by the contrivance of the greater officers of state, that few or none might have access to the king but themselves and their friends. I have not been called, &c. - Which gives me just cause to fear that the king's affections are alienated from me, and that neither my person nor petition will be acceptable to him.

14. From another place - This was the language of strong faith, against hope believing in hope. Who knoweth - It is probable God hath raised thee to this honour for this very season. We should every one of us consider, for what end God has put us in the place where we are? And when an opportunity offers of serving God and our generation, we must take care not to let it slip.

16. Fast - And pray; so as you use to do, leave off your common dinners by day, and suppers at night, and eat and drink no more than mere necessity requires; that so you may give yourselves to constant and fervent prayers. Maidens - Which she had chosen to attend upon her person, and were doubtless either of the Jewish nation, or Proselytes. Which is not, &c. - Which may belong, either

    1. to the thing only, that as they did fast, so she would. Or, rather,

    2. to the time of three days and three nights; for so she might do, though she went to the king on the third day. For the fast began at evening, and so she might continue her fast three whole nights, and two whole days, and the greatest part of the third; a part of a day being reputed a day in the account of scripture, and other authors: of which see on Matt. xii, 40. Yea, she might fast all that day too: for it is probable she went not to the king 'till he had dined; when she supposed she might find him in the most mild and pleasant humour, and then returned to her apartment, where she fasted 'till the evening.

V

Esther finding favour with the king, invites him and Haman to a banquet, ver. 1-5. She invites them to a second, ver. 6-8. Haman makes a gallows for Mordecai, ver. 9-14.

2. Held out - In testimony that he pardoned her presumption, and was ready to grant her petition. Touched - In token of her thankful acceptance of the king's favour, and of her reverence and submission.

3. It shall be given - God in his providence often prevents the fears and outdoes the hopes of his servants. To the half of the kingdom - A proverbial expression: that is, nothing in reason shall be denied.

4. Haman - Whom she invited, that by shewing such respect to the king's great favourite, she might insinuate herself the more into the king's affection; and, that if she saw fit, she might then present her request to the king.

6. Of wine - So called, because it consisted not of meats, which probably the king had plentifully eaten before, but of fruits and wines; which banquets were very frequent among the Persians.

8. Tomorrow - I will acquaint thee with my humble request. She did not present her petition at this time, but delayed it 'till the next meeting; either because she was a little daunted with the king's presence, or, because she would farther engage the king's affection to her, and would also intimate to him that her petition was of a more than ordinary nature: but principally by direction of Divine providence, which took away her courage of utterance for this time, that she might have a better opportunity for it the next time, by that great accident which happened before it.

9. Nor moved - To shew how little he feared him, and that he had a firm confidence in his God, that he would deliver him and his people in this great exigency.

10. Refrained - From taking present vengeance upon Mordecai, which he might easily have effected, either by his own, or any of his servants hands, without any fear of inconveniency to himself. But herein God's wise and powerful providence appeared, in disposing Haman's heart, contrary to his own inclination, and making him, as it were, to put fetters upon his own hands.

12. Am I - Thus he makes that matter of glorying which was the occasion of his utter ruin. So ignorant are the wisest men, and subject to fatal mistakes, rejoicing when they have most cause of fear, and sorrowing for those things which tend to joy and comfort.

13. Availeth - Gives me no content. Such torment did his envy and malice bring upon him. Sitting - Enjoying that honour and privilege without disturbance, and denying me the worship due to me by the king's command. Thus tho' proud men have much to their mind, if they have not all to their mind, it is nothing. The thousandth part of what Haman had, would give a modest, humble man, as much happiness as he expects to receive from anything under the sun. And Haman as passionately complains, as if he was in the lowest depth of poverty!

14. Fifty cubits - That it may be more conspicuous to all, and thereby be more disgraceful to Mordecai, and strike all Haman's enemies with a greater dread of despising or opposing him.

VI

Providence recommends Mordecai to the king's favour, ver. 1- 3. Haman is constrained publickly to honour him thro' the city, ver. 4-11. His friends foretell his doom, ver. 12, 13, He goes to the banquet, ver. 14.

1. Sleep - How vain are all the contrivances of foolish man against the wise and omnipotent God, who hath the hearts and hands of kings and all men perfectly at his disposal, and can by such trivial accidents (as they are accounted) change their minds, and produce such terrible effects. Were read - His mind being troubled he knew not how, nor why, he chuses this for a diversion, God putting this thought into him, for otherwise he might have diverted himself, as he used to do, with his wives or concubines, or voices and instruments of musick, which were far more agreeable to his temper.

3. Nothing - He hath had no recompence for this great and good service. Which might either happen through the king's forgetfulness; or through the envy of the courtiers; or because he was a Jew, and therefore odious and contemptible.

4. Haman - Early in the morning, because his malice would not suffer him to sleep; and he was impatient 'till he had executed his revenge; and was resolved to watch for the very first opportunity of speaking to the king, before he was engaged in other matters. Outward court - Where he waited; because it was dangerous to come into the inner court without special license, chap. iv, 11.

6. Man - He names none, because he would have the more impartial answer. And probably knew nothing of the difference between Haman and Mordecai. Thought - As he had great reason to do, because of the favour which the king had shewed to him above all others.

8. Royal apparel - His outward garment, which was made of purple, interwoven with gold, as Justin and Cartius relate.

12. Gate - To his former place; shewing that as he was not overwhelmed by Haman's threats, so he was not puffed up with this honour. Cover'd - In token of his shame and grief for his unexpected disappointment, and for the great honour done to his abhorred adversary, by his own hands, and with his own public disgrace.

13. Wise men - The magicians, whom after the Persian manner he had called together to consult upon this strange emergency.

14. To bring - Who was now slack to go thither, by reason of the great dejection of his own mind.

VII

Esther petitions for her life, and the lives of her people, ver. 1- 4. She tells the king that Haman is the man who designed her ruin, ver. 5, 6. By the king's order, he is hanged on the gallows he had prepared for Mordecai, ver. 7-10.

3. My life - It is my only request, that thou wouldst not give me up to the malice of that man who designs to take away my life. Even a stranger, a criminal, shall be permitted to petition for his life. But that a friend, a wife, a queen, should have occasion to make such a petition, was very affecting.

4. Sold - By the cruelty of that man who offered a great sum to purchase our destruction. Countervail - His ten thousand talents would not repair the king's loss, in the customs and tributes which the king receives from the Jews, within his dominions.

5. Who, &c. - The expressions are short and doubled, as proceeding from a discomposed and enraged mind. Durst - That is, to circumvent me, and procure a decree, whereby not only my estate should be so much impaired, and so many of my innocent subjects destroyed, but my queen also involved in the same destruction. We sometimes startle at that evil, which we ourselves are chargeable with. Ahasuerus is amazed at that wickedness, which he himself was guilty of. For he consented to the bloody edict. So that Esther might have said, Thou art the man!

6. Afraid - And it was time for him to fear, when the queen was his prosecutor, the king his judge, his own conscience a witness against him. And the surprising turns of providence that very morning, could not but increase his fear.

7. Went - As disdaining the company and sight of so audacious a person: to cool and allay his troubled and inflamed spirits, and to consider what punishment was fit to be inflicted upon him. He saw - By the violent commotion of the king's mind.

8. Bed - On which the queen sat at meat. Force - Will he attempt my queen's chastity, as he hath already attempted her life! He speaks not this out of real jealousy, but from an exasperated mind, which takes all occasions to vent itself against the person who gave the provocation. They - The king's and queen's chamberlains attending upon them. Covered - That the king might not be offended or grieved with the sight of a person whom he now loathed: and because they looked upon him as a condemned person; for the faces of such used to be covered.

John Wesley

VIII

The estate of Haman is given to Esther, ver. 1, 2. Esther petitions the king, to reverse the edict against the Jews, ver. 3-6. They are authorized to defend themselves, ver. 7-14. The Jews and their friends rejoice, ver. 15-17.

1. The house - With all his goods and estate, which being justly forfeited to the king, he no less justly bestows it upon the queen, to compensate the danger to which Haman had exposed her. Came - Was by the queen's desire admitted into the king's presence, and family, and, as it seems, made one of the seven princes. Had told - How nearly he was related to her: which 'till this time she had wisely concealed.

2. Ring - That ring which he had formerly given to Haman he now gives to Mordecai, and with it that power whereof this ring was a sign, making him, as Haman had been, the keeper of his signet. Set - As her steward, to manage that great estate for her as he thought fittest.

3. To put - To repeal that cruel decree.

5. If &c. - She uses various expressions, that she might confirm the king's favour, by such a full submission to his good pleasure. Haman - She prudently takes off the hatefulness of the action from the king, and lay's it upon Haman, who had for his own ends contrived the whole business, and circumvented the king in it.

8. Reverse - For this reason he could not recall the former letters, because they were irrevocable by the law of the Medes and Persians. How much more prudent is our constitution, that no law whatever can be established as to be unrepealable? It is God's prerogative, not to repent, and to say what can never be altered.

9. Then - Which was above two months after the former decree. All which time God suffered the Jews to lie under the error of this dreadful day, that they might be more throughly humbled for, and purged from those many and great sins under which they lay; that they might be convinced of their great sin and folly in the many offers they had had of returning to their native country, by which means being dispersed in the several parts of this vast dominion, they were like to be a very easy prey to their enemies, whereas their brethren in Judea were in a better capacity to preserve themselves: and for the greater illustration of God's glorious power, and wisdom, and goodness, in giving his people such an admirable and unexpected deliverance.

10. Riders - Which were not employed in sending the former letter: but this coming later required more care and speed, that the Jews might be eased from their present fears, and have time to provide for their own defense.

11. To stand - To fight for the defense of their lives against all that should seek to destroy them. The power - Either governors or governed, without any exception either of age, dignity, or sex, Both little ones and women - Which is here added, to strike the greater terror into their enemies; and according to the laws and customs of this kingdom; whereby children were punished for their parents offenses: yet we read nothing in the execution of this decree of the slaughter of women or children, nor is it probable, they would kill their innocent children, who were so indulgent to their families, as not to meddle with the spoil.

15. Great crown - Which the chief of the Persian princes were permitted to wear but with sufficient distinction from the king's crown. The city - Not only Jews, but the greatest number of the citizens, who by the law of nature abhorred bloody counsels, and had a complacency in acts of mercy.

16. Joy - This explains the former metaphor by two words expressing the same thing, to denote the greatness of the joy. honour - Instead of that contempt under which they had lain.

IX

The Jews slay their enemies, ver. 1-11. A second day is granted them, ver. 12-19. A yearly feast is instituted, in memory of this great deliverance, ver. 20-32

2. No man - Their enemies, though they did take up arms against them, yet were easily conquered and destroyed by them.

6. Shushan - In the city so called. Slew - Whom they knew to be such as would watch all opportunities to destroy them; which also they might possibly now attempt to do.

10. But, &c. - Because they would leave it to their children, that it might appear what they did was not done out of malice, or covetousness, but out of mere necessity, and by that great law of self-preservation.

12. What - In which doubtless many more were slain. So that I have fully granted thy petition. And yet, if thou hast any thing farther to ask, I am ready to grant it.

13. Let it, &c. - To kill their implacable enemies. For it is not improbable that the greatest and

worst of them had hidden themselves for that day; after which, the commission granted to the Jews being expired, they confidently returned to their homes. Hanged - They were slain before; now let their bodies be hanged on their father's gallows, for their greater infamy, and the terror of all others who shall presume to abuse the king in like manner, or to persuade him to execute such cruelties upon his subjects.

26. Pur - This Persian word signifies a lot, because Haman had by lot determined this time to be the time of the Jews destruction.

27. As joined - Gentile Proselytes; who were obliged to submit to other of the Jewish laws, and therefore to this also; the rather because they enjoyed the benefit of this day's deliverance; without which the Jewish nation and religion had been in a great measure, if not wholly, extinct. According - According to that writing which was drawn up by Mordecai, and afterwards confirmed by the consent of the Jews.

29. Wrote - The former letter, ver. 20, did only recommend but this enjoins the observation of this solemnity: because this was not only Mordecai's act, but the act of all the Jews, binding themselves and posterity.

30. Peace - With peace, friendship and kindness to his brethren, and truth, sincerity.

31. Cry - For those great calamities which were decreed to all the Jews, and for the removing of which, not only Esther, and the Jews in Shushan, but all other Jews in all places, did doubtless fly to God by fasting, and strong cries.

32. Either - Who had received authority from the king. The book - In the records which the Jews kept of their most memorable passages.

X

The greatness of Ahasuerus, and of Mordecai, ver. 1-3.

2. Chronicles, &c. - These are lost long since, and buried in oblivion, while the sacred writings remain throughout the world. When the kingdoms of men, monarchs and their monarchies are destroyed, and their memorial is perished with them, the kingdom of God among men, and the records of that kingdom, shall remain as the days of heaven.

John Wesley

NOTES ON THE BOOK OF JOB

THE preceding books of scripture are, for the most part, plain and easy narratives, which he that runs may read and understand: but in the five poetical books, on which we are now entering, Job, Psalms, Proverbs, Ecclesiastes, and Solomon's Song, are many things hard to be understood. These therefore require a more close application of mind, which yet the treasures they contain will abundantly recompence. The former books were mostly historical: these are doctrinal and devotional. And they are wrote in verse, according to the ancient rules of versifying, tho' not in rhythm, nor according to the rules of latter tongues. Job is a kind of heroic poem; the book of Psalms a collection of sacred odes, Solomon's song, a Divine pastoral. They are all poetical, yet serious and full of majesty. They have a poetic force and flame, without poetic fury, move the affections, without corrupting the imagination; and while they gratify the ear, improve the mind, and profit the more by pleasing. We have here much of God, his infinite pefections, and his government both of the world, and of the church. And we have much of Christ, who is the spring, and soul, and center of revealed religion. Here is what may enlighten our understandings, and acquaint us with the deep things of God. And this divine light may bring into the soul a divine fire, which will kindle and inflame devout affections, on which wings we may soar upwards, until we enter into the holiest. We are certain that the book of Job is a true history. That there was such a man as Job, undeniably appears, from his being mentioned by the prophet, together with Noah and Daniel, Ezek xiv, 14, and the narrative we have of his prosperity and piety, his strange afflictions and exemplary patience, the substance of his conferences with his friends, and God's discourse with him out of the whirlwind, with his return to a prosperous condition, are no doubt exactly true. We are sure also this book is very ancient, probably of equal date with the book of Genesis itself. It is likely, Job was of the posterity of Nahor, Abraham's brother, whose first-born was Uz, and in whose family religion was kept up, as appears Gen. xxxi, 53, where God is called not only the God of Abraham, but the God of Nahor. He lived before sacrifices were confined to one altar, before the general apostacy of the nations, and while God was known by the name of God Almighty, more than by the name of Jehovah: for he is called Shaddai, the Almighty, above thirty times in this book. And that he lived before (probably very little before) the deliverance of the children of Israel out of Egypt, we may gather from hence, that there is no allusion at all to that grand event throughout the whole book. In this noble poem we have,

1. A monument of primitive theology;
2. A specimen of Gentile piety: for Job was not of the promised seed, no Israelite, no proselyte:
3. An exposition of the book of providence, and a clear solution of man difficult passages therein:
4. A great example of patience and close adherence to God in the deepest calamities: and
5. An illustrious type of Christ, emptied and humbled, in order to his greater glory. In this book we have, an account of Job's sufferings, chap. 1, 2, Not without a mixture of human frailty, chap. 3. A dispute between him and his three friends, chap. 4-31. The interposal of Elihu, and of God himself, chap. 32-41. The end of all in Job's prosperity, chap. 42.

I

Job's piety, children, substance, ver. 1-5. Satan obtains leave to try him, ver. 6-12. His oxen, sheep, camels and servants destroyed, ver. 13-17. His sons and daughters killed, ver. 18, 19. His patience and piety, ver. 20-22.

1. Uz - Part of Arabia. Perfect - Not legally or exactly, but as to his sincere intentions, hearty affections, and diligent endeavours to perform all his duties to God and men. Upright - Hebrew. right, exact and regular in all his dealings, with men; one of an unblameable conversation. Feared - One truly pious, and devoted to God. Eschewed - Carefully avoiding all sin against God or men.

3. Camels - Camels in these parts were very numerous, and very useful, both for carrying burdens in these hot and dry countries, as being able to endure thirst much better than other creatures, and for service in war. Asses - He-asses also may be included in this expression, because the greatest part of them (from which the denomination is usually taken) were she asses. The greatest - That lived in those

parts. The account of his piety and prosperity comes before the account of his afflictions, to shew that neither of these will secure us from the common, no, nor from the uncommon calamities of human life.

4. Feasted - To testify and maintain their brotherly love. His day - Each his appointed day, perhaps his birth-day, or the first day of the month.

5. When - When each of them had had his turn. Satisfied - He exhorted them to examine their own consciences, to repent of any thing, which had been amiss in their feasting, and compose their minds for employments of a more solemn nature. Early - Thereby shewing his ardent zeal in God's service. May be - His zeal for God's glory, and his true love to his children, made him jealous. Cursed - Not in a gross manner, which it is not probable either that they should do, or that Job should suspect it concerning them, but despised or dishonoured God; for both Hebrew and Greek words signifies cursing, are sometimes used to note only, reviling or setting light by a person. Hearts - By slight and low thoughts of God, or by neglecting to give God the praise for the mercies which they enjoyed. Thus - It was his constant course at the end of every feasting time, to offer a sacrifice for each. Parents should be particular in their addresses to God, for the several branches of their family; praying for each child, according to his particular temper, genius and disposition.

6. A day - A certain time appointed by God. The sons - The holy angels, so called, chap. xxxviii, 7 Dan. iii, 25, 28, because of their creation by God, for their resemblance of him in power, and dignity, and holiness, and for their filial affection and obedience, to him. Before - Before his throne, to receive his commands, and to give him an account of their negotiations. But you must not think that these things are to be understood literally; it is only a parabolical representation of that great truth, that God by his wise and holy providence governs all the actions of men and devils: It being usual with the great God to condescend to our shallow capacities, and to express himself, as the Jews phrase it, in the language of the sons of men. And it is likewise intimated, that the affairs of earth are much the subject of the counsels of the unseen world. That world is dark to us: but we lie open to it.

9. For nought - Out of pure love and respect to thee? No. It is policy, not piety, that makes him good; he doth not serve thee, but serveth himself of thee, serving thee for his own ends.

12. Behold, &c. - It seems strange, that, God should give Satan such a permission as this. But he did it for his own glory, for the honour of Job, for the explanation of providence, and the encouragement of his afflicted people in all ages.

14. Messenger, &c. - One messenger immediately followed another; Satan so ordering by God's permission, that there might seem to be more than ordinary displeasure of God against him in his troubles, and that he might not have leisure to recollect himself, but be overwhelmed by a complication of calamities.

15. Sabeans - A people of Arabia, who led a wandering life, and lived by robbery and spoil. I - Whom Satan spared, that Job might have speedy and certain intelligence of his calamity.

16. The fire of God - As thunder is the voice of God, so lightning is his fire. How terrible then were the tidings of this destruction, which came immediately from the hand of God! And seemed to shew, That God was angry at his very offerings, and would receive no more from his hands.

17. Chaldeans - Who also lived upon spoil, as Xenephon and others observe.

19. The young men - This was the greatest of Job's losses, and therefore Satan reserved it to the last, that if the other provocations failed, this might make him curse God. They died by a wind of the devils raising, but which seemed to be the immediate hand of God. And they were taken away, when he had the most need of them, to comfort him under all his other losses. Such miserable comforters are creatures: in God we have a constant and sufficient help.

20. Shaved - Caused his hair to be shaved or cut off, which was then an usual ceremony in mourning. Worshipped - Instead of cursing God, which Satan said he would do, he adored him, and gave him the glory of his sovereignty, of his justice, and of his goodness also, in this most severe dispensation.

21. Naked - I brought none of these things with me, when I came out of my mother's womb into the world, but I received them from the hand of God, who hath now required his own again. Return thither - I shall be as rich when I die as I was when I was born, and therefore have reason to be contented with my condition, which also is the common lot of all men. Into the lap of our common mother, the earth, as the weary child lays its head in its mother's bosom. We go out of the world naked; the body doth, tho' the sanctified soul goes clothed. (2Cor v, 3.) Death strips us of all our enjoyments: clothing can neither warm nor adorn a dead body. Taken - He hath taken away nothing but his own, and what he so gave that he reserved the supreme disposal of in his own hand. And what is it to me, by what hand he that gives, resumes what he gave?

22. Charged - Hebrew. not imputed folly to God; so far was he from blaspheming God, that he did not entertain any dishonourable thought of God, as if he had done anything unworthy of his infinite wisdom, or justice, or goodness, but heartily acquiesced in his good pleasure, and in his righteous though sharp proceedings against him. Discontent and impatience do in effect impute folly to God. Against the workings of these we should carefully watch, acknowledging that God has done well, but

we have done foolishly.

II

Satan moves for another trial of Job, which God permits, ver. 1- 6. Satan smites him with boils from head to foot, ver. 7, 8. He is tempted by his wife, but resists the temptation, ver. 9, 10 His friends come to comfort him, ver. 11-13.

3. Still - Notwithstanding all his afflictions, and thy suggestion to the contrary. Movedst - This, as the rest of this representation, is not to be understood literally: But the design is to signify both the devil's restless malice in promoting man's misery and God's permission of it for wise and holy ends.

4. Skin, &c. - The sense is, this is so far from being an evidence of Job's sincere and generous piety, that it is only an act of mere self- love; he is contented with the loss of his estate, and children too, so long as he sleeps in a whole skin; and he is well pleased, that thou wilt accept of these a ransom in his stead; and it is not true patience which makes him seem to bear his crosses so submissively, but policy, that he may appease thy wrath against him, and prevent those farther plagues, which, for his hypocrisy, he fears thou wilt otherwise bring upon his own carcase.

6. In thine hand - If God did not chain up the roaring lion, how soon would he devour us! As far as he permits the wrath of Satan and wicked men, to proceed against his people, he will make it turn to his praise and theirs, and the remainder thereof he will restrain. Job, in being thus maligned of Satan, was a type of Christ. He had permission to bruise his heel, to touch his bone and his flesh; yea, and his life also; because by dying he was to do what Job could not do, to destroy him that had the power of death.

7. Boils - Like those inflicted upon the Egyptians, which are expressed by the same word, and threatened to apostate Israelites, Deut. xxviii, 27, whereby he was made loathsome to himself, and to his nearest relations, and filled with consuming pains in his body, and no less torments and anguish in his mind.

8. Scrape - This he did not with soft linen clothes, either because he had not now a sufficient quantity of them; or because therein he must have had the help of others who abhorred to come near him. Nor with his own hands or fingers, which were also ulcerous, and so unfit for that use; but with potsherds, either because they were next at hand, and ready for his present use; or in token of his deep humiliation under God's hand, which made him decline all things that favoured of tenderness and delicacy. Hebrew. in dust or ashes, as mourners used to do. If God lay him among the ashes, there he will contentedly sit down. A low spirit becomes low circumstances, and will help to reconcile us to them.

9. Then said his wife - Whom Satan spared, to be a troubler and tempter to him. It is his policy, to send his temptations by the hands of those that are dear to us. We must therefore carefully watch, that we be not drawn to any evil, by them whom we love and value the most. Die - I see thou art set upon blessing of God, thou blessest God for giving, and thou blessest God for taking away, and thou art still blessing God for thy loathsome diseases, and he rewards thee accordingly, giving thee more and more of that kind of mercy for which thou blessest him. Go on therefore in thy generous course, and bless God, and die as a fool dieth.

10. Shall we - Shall we poor worms give laws to our supreme Lord, and oblige him never to afflict us? And shall not those great and manifold mercies, which from time to time God hath given us, compensate these short afflictions? Ought we not to bless God for those mercies which we did not deserve; and contentedly bear those corrections which we do deserve. And if we receive so much good for the body, shall we not receive some good for our souls? That is, some affliction, whereby we may be made partakers of his holiness? Let murmuring therefore, as well as boasting, be forever excluded. Sin with his lips - By any reflections upon God, by any impatient or unbecoming expression.

11. They - Who were persons eminent for birth and quality, for wisdom and knowledge, and for the profession of the true religion, being probably of the posterity of Abraham, a-kin to Job, and living in the same country. Eliphaz descended from Teman, the grandson of Esau, Gen. xxxvi, 11. Bildad probably from Shuah, Abraham's son by Keturah, Gen. xxv, 2. Zophar is thought to be same with Zepho, (Gen. xxxvi, 11.) a descendant from Esau. The preserving of so much wisdom and piety among those who were not children of the promise, was an happy presage of God's grace to the Gentiles, when the partition wall should be taken down.

13. Upon the ground - In the posture of mourners condoling with him. Seven days - Which was the usual time of mourning for the dead, and therefore proper both for Job's children, and for Job himself, who was in a manner dead, while he lived: not that they continued in this posture so long together, which the necessities of nature could not bear; but they spent the greatest part of that time in sitting with him, and silent mourning over him. None spake - About his afflictions and the causes of them. The reason of this silence was the greatness of their grief for him, and their surprize and astonishment at his condition; because they thought it convenient to give him time to vent his own

sorrows, and because as yet they knew not what to say to him: for though they had ever esteemed him to be a truly good man, and came with full purpose to comfort him, yet the prodigious greatness of his miseries, and that hand of God which they perceived in them, made them now question his sincerity, so that they could not comfort him as they had intended, and yet were loth to grieve him with reproofs.

III

We have here Job cursing his birth day, and complaining that he was born, ver. 1-10. Complaining that he did not die as soon as he was born, ver. 11-19. Complaining that his life was continued, now he was in misery, ver. 20-26.

1. His day - His birth-day, in vain do some endeavour to excuse this and the following speeches of Job, who afterwards is reproved by God, and severely accuseth himself for them, chap. xxxviii. 2; xl, 4; xiii, 3, 6. And yet he does not proceed so far as to curse God, but makes the devil a liar: but although he does not break forth into direct reproaches of God, yet he makes indirect reflections upon his providence. His curse was sinful, both because it was vain, being applied to a thing, which was not capable of blessing and cursing, and because it cast a blame upon God for bringing that day, and for giving him life on that day.

3. Let the day - Let the remembrance of that day be utterly lost.

4. Darkness - I wish the sun had never risen upon that day, or, which is all one, that it had never been; and whensoever that day returns, I wish it may be black, and gloomy, and uncomfortable. Regard - From heaven, by causing the light of the sun which is in heaven to shine upon it.

5. Death - A black and dark shadow like that of the place of the dead, which is a land of darkness. Slain - Take away its beauty and glory. Terrify - That is, men in it. Let it be always observed as a frightful and dismal day.

6. Darkness - Constant and extraordinary darkness, without the least glimmering of light from the moon or stars. Be joined - Reckoned as one, or a part of one of them.

8. The day - Their birth-day: when their afflictions move them to curse their own birth-day, let them remember mine also, and bestow some curses upon it. Mourning - Who are full of sorrow, and always ready to pour out their cries, and tears, and complaints.

9. The stars - Let the stars, which are the glory and beauty of the night, be covered with thick darkness, and that both in the evening twilight, when the stars begin to shine; and also in the farther progress of the night, even 'till the morning dawns. Look - Let its darkness be aggravated with the disappointment of its expectations of light. He ascribes sense or reasoning to the night, by a poetical fiction, usual in all writers. Dawning - Hebrew. the eye-lids of the day, the morning-star which ushers in the day, and the beginning, and progress of the morning light, let this whole natural day, consisting of night and day, be blotted out of the catalogue of days.

10. It - The night or the day: to which those things are ascribed which were done by others in them, as is frequent in poetical writings. Womb - That it might never have brought me forth. Nor hid - Because it did not keep me from entering into this miserable life, and seeing, or experiencing, these bitter sorrows.

12. The knees - Why did the midwife or nurse receive and lay me upon her knees, and not suffer me to fall upon the bare ground, 'till death had taken me out of this miserable world, into which their cruel kindness hath betrayed me? Why did the breasts prevent me from perishing through hunger, or supply me that should have what to suck? Thus Job unthankfully despises these wonderful mercies of God towards poor helpless infants.

14. Kings - I had then been as happy as the proudest monarchs, who after all their great achievements and enjoyments, go down into their graves. Built - Who to shew their wealth and power, or to leave behind them a glorious name, rebuilt ruined cities, or built new cities and palaces, in places where before there was mere solitude and wasteness.

16. Hidden - Undiscerned and unregarded. Born before the due time. Been - In the land of the living.

17. There - In the grave. The wicked - The great oppressors and troublers of the world cease from their vexations, rapins and murders. Weary - Those who were here molested and tired out with their tyrannies, now quietly sleep with them.

18. The oppressor - Or, taskmaster, who urges and forces them to work by cruel threatenings and stripes. Job meddles not here with their eternal state after death, of which he speaks hereafter, but only their freedom from worldly troubles, which is the sole matter of his present discourse.

19. Small and great - Persons of all qualities and conditions. Are there - In the same place and state, all those distinctions being forever abolished. A good reason, why those who have power should use it moderately, and those that are in subjection should take it patiently.

20. Light - The light of life. Bitter - Unto those to whom life itself is bitter and burdensome. Life is

called light, because it is pleasant and serviceable for walking and working; and this light is said to be given us, because it would be lost, if it were not daily renewed to us by a fresh gift.

21. Dig - Desire with as much earnestness as men dig for treasure: but it is observable, Job durst not do anything to hasten or procure his death: notwithstanding all his miseries, he was contented to wait all the days of his appointed time, 'till his change came, chap. xiv, 14.

22. Glad, &c. - To be thus impatient of life, for the sake of the trouble we meet with, is not only unnatural in itself, but ungrateful to the giver of life, and shews a sinful indulgence of our own passion. Let it be our great and constant care, to get ready for another world: and then let us leave it to God, to order the circumstances of our removal thither.

23. Hid - From him; who knows not his way, which way to turn himself, what course to take to comfort himself in his miseries. Hedged in - Whom God hath put as it were in a prison, so that he can see no way or possibility of escape.

24. Before, &c. - Hebrew. before the face of my bread, all the time I am eating, I fall into sighing and weeping, because I am obliged to eat, and to support this wretched life, and because of my uninterrupted pains of body and of mind, which do not afford me one quiet moment. Roarings - My loud outcries, more befitting a lion than a man. Poured out - With great abundance, and irresistible violence, and incessant continuance, as waters flow in a river, or as they break the banks, and overflow the ground.

25. Feared - Even in the time of my prosperity, I was full of fears, considering the variety of God's providences, the changeableness of this vain world, God's justice, and the sinfulness of all mankind. And these fears of mine, were not in vain, but are justified by my present calamities.

26. Quiet - I did not misbehave myself in prosperity, abusing it by presumption, and security, but I lived circumspectly, walking humbly with God, and working out my salvation with fear and trembling. Therefore in this sense also, his way was hid, he knew not why God contended with him.

IV

Eliphaz owns Job's former usefulness, but infers from his present state and behaviour, that he was an hypocrite, ver. 1-6. He affirms that God never afflicts man, but for his wickedness, ver. 7-11. He confirms his assertion, by the words he heard in a vision, ver. 12-21. By all this he aims to make Job both penitent and patient under his sufferings.

2. If we, &c. - He speaks with great modesty. He will not undertake the cause alone, but joins his friends with him. He will not promise much, but only assay, or try if he could propose any thing pertinent to Job's case. Withhold - When he hears such words from such a person as thou art.

4. Feeble knees - Such as were weak hearted, and fainting under their trials.

6. Thy fear - We now plainly see what was the nature of thy fear of God, thy confidence in him, the uprightness of thy ways, and thy hope in God's mercy. Thy present carriage discovers that it was but mere talk and appearance.

7. Innocent - Therefore thou art guilty of some great, though secret crimes, and thy sin hath now found thee out. Cut off - By the sickle of Divine vengeance before his time, which is like to be thy case. Eliphaz here advances another argument to prove Job an hypocrite; taken not only from his impatience under afflictions, but from his afflictions themselves.

8. Even - As thou hast never seen any example of a righteous man cut off, so I have seen many of wicked men cut off for their wickedness. They - They that designedly work wickedness, first preparing themselves for it, and then continuing to execute it, as husbandmen first plow the ground, and then cast in the feed. Reap - The fruit of their iniquity, the just punishment of it.

9. The blast - Of his nostrils, as it follows; by his anger, which in men shews itself, in the nostrils, by hot and frequent breathings there, by a secret, but mighty judgment of God, they are blown away as chaff by the wind.

10. The roaring - Nor can they escape, even were they strong as lions, yea, as the strongest and fiercest of them. Broken - Which is true literally; the lions when taken having most commonly their teeth broken, as ancient and modern writers relate. But this is meant of powerful tyrants, who are fitly compared to lions, Ezek xxxii, 2; xxxviii, 13, who though for a time they persecute and oppress other men, yet in due time they are restrained, and broken, and crushed in pieces by the mighty power of God. Possibly he may secretly accuse Job, or his children, that being persons of great wealth and power, they had abused it to ruin their neighbours, and therefore were justly cut off.

11. Scattered - Gone from their dens several ways to hunt for prey, and can find none.

12. Now - To convince Job of the sin and folly of impatience, Eliphaz relates a vision he had had, perhaps since he came to him. Which in that age and state of the church, before the holy scriptures were written, was the usual way of God's discovering his mind to those that sought him. A thing - Hebrew. a word, from God, a message. Secretly - Hebrew. was stolen, or brought by stealth unto me, privately and

secretly, as the word of God used to come to the prophets, being spoken in their ear, as it was to Samuel, with a low and still voice. He does not pretend to have understood it fully; but something of it he perceived. How little a portion is heard of God! How little do we know of him in this world.

13. In thoughts - These thoughts arose from the visions of the night, which it is probable he had seen before. Visions differed from dreams herein, that God imparted his mind to men in dreams when asleep, but in visions, when they were awake. And these visions sometimes happened by day, but most frequently by night. Sleep - In the dead of the night, when men usually are in a deep sleep; though Eliphaz was not now asleep.

15. A spirit - An angel in visible shape, otherwise he could not have discerned it. Stood up - Through that excessive horror caused by so glorious, unusual, and terrible a presence.

16. Stood - Having passed by him to, and again, he made a stand, and addressed himself to speak. The form - Exactly and distinctly. An image - I saw some visible resemblance, though in a confused manner. Silence - The spirit, which possibly had made some noise with his motion, now standing still made no noise; all other persons and things about me were silent, and I also kept in my voice and breath, that I might distinctly hear. In the Hebrew, the words run thus, silence and a voice I heard.

17. More just - Pretend more strictly to observe the laws of justice? Shall (enosh) mortal, miserable man (so the word signifies) be thus insolent? Nay, shall geber, the strongest and most eminent man, stand in competition with God? Those that find fault with the directions of the Divine law, the dispensations of the Divine grace, or the disposal of the Divine providence, do make themselves more just and pure than God: who being their maker, is their Lord and owner: and the author of all the justice and purity that is in man.

18. Servants - They are called his servants by way of eminency, that general name being here appropriated to the chief of the kind, to intimate that sovereign dominion which the great God hath over the angels, and much more over men. With folly - Without all doubt, this refers to those angels who foolishly and wickedly fell from God.

19. How, &c. - The sense is, what strange presumption then is it for a foolish and mortal man, to make himself more just than God. In them - Who though they have immortal spirits, yet those spirits dwell in mortal bodies, which are great clogs, and incumbrances, and snares to them. These are called houses, (because they are the receptacles of the soul, and the places of its settled abode) and houses of clay, because they were made of clay, or earth, and to note their great frailty and mutability; whereas the angels are free spirits, unconfined to such carcasses, and dwell in celestial, and glorious, and everlasting mansions. Whose - Whose very foundation, no less than the rest of the building, is in the dust; had their original from it, and must return to it. We stand but upon the dust: some have an higher heap of dust to stand upon than others. But still it is the earth that stays us up, and will shortly swallow us up. Before - Sooner than a moth is crushed, which is easily done by a gentle touch of the finger. Or, at the face of a moth. No creature is so contemptible, but one time or other it may have the body of man in its power.

20. Destroyed - All the day long, there is not a moment wherein man is not sinking towards death and corruption. Perish - In reference to this present worldly life, which when once lost is never recovered. Regarding - Hebrew. without putting the heart to it, this is so common a thing for all men, though never so high and great, to perish in this manner, that no man heeds it, but passes it by as a general accident not worthy of observation.

21. Excellency - Whatsoever is by common estimation excellent in men, all their natural, and moral, and civil accomplishments, as high birth, great riches, power and wisdom, these are so far from preserving men from perishing, that they perish themselves, together with those houses of clay in which they are lodged. Without wisdom - Even without having attained that only wisdom for which they came into the world. Shall such mean, weak, foolish, sinful, dying creatures as this, pretend to be more just than God, more pure than his maker? No: instead of quarrelling with his afflictions, let him admire that he is out of hell.

V

Sin occasions destruction, ver. 1-5. Affliction is the common lot of mankind, ver. 6-7. In affliction we should fly to God, who is both able and willing to help, ver. 8-16. He will deliver them that trust in him, ver. 17-27.

1. Call - Call them all as it were by their names: will not every good man confirm what I say? If - Try if there be any one saint that will defend thee in these bold expostulations with God. Thou mayst find fools or wicked men, to do it: but not one of the children of God.

2. Killeth - A man's wrath, and impatience, preys upon his spirit, and so hastens his death; and provokes God to cut him off. The foolish - The rash and inconsiderate man, who does not weigh things impartially. Envy, &c. - I perceive thou art full of envy at wicked men, who seem to be in a happier condition than thou, and of wrath against God; and this shews thee to be a foolish and weak man. For

those men, notwithstanding their present prosperity, are doomed to great and certain misery. I have myself seen the proof of this.

3. Foolish - The wicked man. Root - Not only prosperous for the present, but, as it seemed, firm and secure for the future. Suddenly - In a moment, beyond mine, and his own, and all other mens expectation. Cursed - I saw by the event which followed his prosperity, that he was a man accursed of God.

4. Children - Whose greatness he designed in all his enterprizes, supposing his family would be established forever. Safely - Are exposed to dangers and calamities, and can neither preserve themselves, nor the inheritance which their fathers left them. There is no question but he glances here, at the death of Job's children.

5. Harvest - Which they confidently expect to reap after all their cost and labour, but are sadly and suddenly disappointed. The hungry - The hungry Sabeans eat it up. Thorns - Out of the fields: in spite of all dangers or difficulties in their way.

6. The dust - It springs not up by merely natural causes, as herbs grow out of the earth: but from God. Eliphaz here begins to change his voice, as if he would atone for the hard words he had spoken.

7. Is born - He is so commonly exposed to various troubles, as if he were born to no other end: affliction is become natural to man, and is transmitted from parents, to children, as their constant inheritance; God having allotted this portion to mankind for their sins. And therefore thou takest a wrong course in complaining so bitterly of that which thou shouldest patiently bear, as the common lot of mankind. As - As naturally, and as generally, as the sparks of fire fly upward. Why then should we be surprized at our afflictions as strange, or quarrel with them, as hard?

8. I would - If I were in thy condition. Seek - By prayer, and humiliation, and submission, imploring his pardon, and favour.

9. Who, &c. - Here Eliphaz enters upon a discourse of the infinite perfection of God's nature and works; which he doth as an argument to enforce the exhortation to seek and commit his cause to God, ver. 8, because God was infinitely able either to punish him yet far worse, if he continued to provoke him; or to raise him from the dust, if he humbly addressed himself to him: and that by a representation of God's excellency and glory, and of that vast disproportion which was between God and Job, he might convince Job of his great sin in speaking so boldly and irreverently of him. marvelous - Which (though common, and therefore neglected and despised, yet) are matter of wonder to the wisest men. The works of nature are mysteries: the most curious searches come far short of full discoveries: and the works of Providence are still more deep and unaccountable.

10. Rain - He begins with this ordinary work of God, in which he implies that there is something wonderful, as indeed there is in the rise of it from the earth, in the strange hanging of that heavy body in the air, and in the distribution of it as God sees fit; and how much more in the hidden paths of Divine Providence?

11. To set up - That is, he setteth up. Another example of God's great and wonderful works. He gives this instance to comfort and encourage Job to seek to God, because he can raise him out of his greatest depths.

13. The wise - Men wise to do evil, and wise in the opinion of the world, he not only deceives in their hopes and counsels, but turns them against themselves. Froward - Or, wrestlers: such as wind and turn every way, as wrestlers do, and will leave no means untried to accomplish their counsels. Is carried - Is tumbled down and broken, and that by their own precipitation.

14. Meet - In plain things they run into gross mistakes, and chuse those courses which are worst for themselves. Darkness often notes misery, but here ignorance or error. Grope - Like blind men to find their way, not knowing what to do.

15. Mouth - Which was ready to swallow them up.

16. So - So he obtains what he hoped for from God, to whom he committed his cause. Iniquity - Wicked men. Stoppeth - They are silenced and confounded, finding that not only the poor are got out of their snares, but the oppressors themselves are ensnared in them.

17. Behold - Eliphaz concludes his discourse, with giving Job a comfortable hope, if he humbled himself before God. Happy - Hebrew. Blessednesses (various and great happiness) belong to that man whom God rebukes. The reason is plain, because afflictions are pledges of God's love, which no man can buy too dear; and are necessary to purge out sin, and thereby to prevent infinite and eternal miseries. Without respect to this, the proposition could not be true. And therefore it plainly shews, that good men in those ancient times, had the belief, and hope of everlasting blessedness. Despise not - Do not abhor it as a thing pernicious, refuse it as a thing useless, or slight it as an unnecessary thing. But more is designed than is exprest. Reverence the chastening of the Lord: have an humble, aweful regard to his correcting hand, and study to answer the design of it. The Almighty - Who is able to support and comfort thee in thy troubles, and deliver thee out of them: and also to add more calamities to them, if thou art obstinate and incorrigible.

18. For he, &c. - God's usual method is, first to humble, and then to exalt. And he never makes a

wound too great, too deep for his own cure.

19. Deliver - If thou seekest to him by prayer and repentance. Here he applies himself to Job directly. Six - Manifold and repeated. Touch - So as to destroy thee. Thou shalt have a good issue out of all thy troubles, though they are both great and many.

20. He shall - These things he utters with more confidence, because the rewards or punishments of this life, were more constantly distributed to men in the Old Testament according to their good or bad behaviour, than they are now: and because it was his opinion, that great afflictions were the certain evidences of wickedness; and consequently, that great deliverances would infallibly follow upon true repentance.

22. Laugh - With a laughter of joy and triumph, arising from a just security and confidence in God's watchful and gracious providence.

23. League - Thou shalt be free from annoyance thereby, as if they had made an inviolable league with thee. This is a bold metaphor, but such as are frequent both in scripture and other authors. This is an addition to the former privilege; they shall not hurt thee, ver. 22, nay, they shall befriend thee, as being at peace with thee. Our covenant with God is a covenant with all the creatures, that they shall do us no hurt, but serve and be ready to do us good.

24. Know - By certain experience.

25. Know - By assurance from God's promises, and the impressions of his Spirit; and by experience in due time.

26. Full age - In a mature and old, but vigourous age, as the word implies. It is a great blessing, to live to a full age, and not to have the number of our years cut short. Much more, to be willing to die, to come cheerfully to the grave: and to die seasonably, just in the bed-time, when our souls are ripe for God.

27. Searched - This is no rash or hasty conceit, but what both I and my brethren have learned by deep consideration, long experience, and diligent observation. Know thou - Know it for thyself; (So the word is) with application to thy own case. That which we thus hear and know for ourselves, we hear and know for our good.

VI

Job shews that he has reason to complain, ver. 1-7. He compassionately wishes for death, ver. 8-13. Reproves his friends for their uncharitable censures, ver. 14-30.

2. My grief - The cause of my grief. Weighed - Were fully understood, and duly considered. O that I had an equal judge! that would understand my case, and consider whether I have not cause for complaints. Together - Together with any other most heavy thing to be put into the other scale.

3. Sea - Which is heavier than dry sand. Swallowed - My voice and spirit fail me. I cannot find, or utter words sufficient to express my sorrow or misery.

4. Arrows - So he fitly calls his afflictions, because, like arrows, they came upon him swiftly and suddenly one after another, immediately shot by God into his spirit. Poison - Implying that these arrows were more keen than ordinary, being dipped in God's wrath, as the barbarous nations used to dip their arrows in poison, that they might not only pierce, but burn up and consume the vital parts. Drinketh - Exhausteth and consumeth my soul. In array - They are like a numerous army, who invade me on every side. This was the sorest part of his calamity, wherein he was an eminent type of Christ, who complained most of the sufferings of his soul. Now is my soul troubled. My soul is exceeding sorrowful. My God, my God, why hast thou forsaken me? Indeed trouble of mind is the sorest trouble. A wounded spirit who can bear.

5. Doth, &c. - Even the brute beasts, when they have convenient food, are quiet and contented. So it is no wonder that you complain not, who live in ease and prosperity, any more than I did, when I wanted nothing.

6. Can, &c. - Do men use to eat unsavoury meats with delight, or without complaint? Men commonly complain of their meat when it is but unsavoury, how much more when it is so bitter as mine is?

7. The things, &c. - The sense may be, those grievous afflictions, which I dreaded the very thought of, are now my daily, though sorrowful bread.

9. Destroy - To end my days and calamities together.

10. Harden - I would bear up with courage under all my torments, with the hopes of death, and blessedness after death. Spare - Not suffer me to live any longer. Concealed - As I have steadfastly believed them, and not wilfully departed from them, so I have not been ashamed, nor afraid, boldly to profess and preach the true religion in the midst of Heathens. And therefore I know if God doth cut me off, I shall be a gainer by it.

11. Strength - My strength is so spent, that it is vain for me to hope for such restitution as thou hast

promised me, chap. v, 22. End - What is death to me? It is not terrible, but comfortable. That - Then why should I desire to prolong my life. But as desirous of death as Job was, yet he never offered to put an end to his own life. Such a thought will never be entertained by any, that have the least regard to the law of God and nature. How uneasy soever the soul's confinement in the body may be, it must by no means break the prison, but wait for a fair discharge.

12. Is, &c. - I am not made of stone or brass, but of flesh and blood, as others are, therefore I am unable to endure these miseries longer, and can neither hope for. nor desire the continuance of my life.

13. What, &c. - If my outward condition be helpless and hopeless? Have I therefore lost my understanding, cannot I judge whether it is more desirable for me to live or to die, whether I be an hypocrite or no, whether your words have truth and weight in them; whether you take the right method in dealing with me?

14. To him - Hebrew. to him that is melted or dissolved with affections. But. &c. - But thou hast no pity for thy friend; a plain evidence that thou art guilty of what thou didst charge me with, even of the want of the fear of God. The least which those that are at ease can do for them that are pained, is to pity them, to feel a tender concern for them, and to sympathize with them.

15. Brethren - Friends; for though Eliphaz only had spoken, the other two shewed their approbation of his discourse. Deceitfully - Adding to the afflictions which they said they came to remove. And it is no new thing, for even brethren to deal deceitfully. It is therefore our wisdom to cease from man. We cannot expect too little from the creature, or too much from the creator.

16. Which - Which in winter when the traveler neither needs nor desires it, are full of water congealed by the frost. Snow - Under which the water from snow, which formerly fell, and afterward was dissolved, lies hid. So he speaks not of those brooks which are fed by a constant spring, but of them which are filled by accidental falls of water or snow.

17. Warm - When the weather grows milder. Hot - In the hot season, when waters are most refreshing and necessary.

18. Perish - They are gone out of their channel, flowing hither and thither, 'till they are quite consumed.

19. Tema - This place and Sheba were both parts of the hot and dry country of Arabia, in which waters were very scarce, and therefore precious and desirable, especially to travelers. Companies - Men did not there travel singly, as we do, but in companies for their security against wild beasts and robbers.

20. Hoped - They comforted themselves with the expectation of water. Ashamed - As having deceived themselves and others. We prepare confusion for ourselves, by our vain hopes: the reeds break under us, because we lean upon them.

21. Nothing - You are to me as if you had never come to me; for I have no comfort from you. Afraid - You are shy of me, and afraid for yourselves, lest some further plagues should come upon me, wherein you for my sake, should be involved: or, lest I should be burdensome to you.

22. Did I say - Give me something for my support or relief. You might have at least given me comfortable words, when I expected nothing else from you.

23. Deliver - By the force of your arms, as Abraham delivered Lot. Redeem - By price or ransom.

24. Teach - Convince me by solid arguments. I will - I will patiently hear and gladly receive your counsels.

25. Forcible - The words of truth have a marvelous power. Reprove - But there is no truth in your assertions or weight in your arguments.

26. Words - Do you think it is sufficient to quarrel with some of my words, without giving allowance for human infirmity, or extreme misery. Desperate - Of a poor miserable, hopeless and helpless man. As wind - Which pass away and are forgotten.

27. Overwhelm - You load with censures and calumnies. Desolate - Me who am deprived of all my children, my estate, and my friends. I spoke all I thought, as to my friends, and you thence occasion to cast me down.

28. Look - Consider my cause better than you have done, that you may give a more righteous judgment. Evident - You will plainly discover it.

29. Return - Turn from your former judgment. Iniquity - Or, there shall be no iniquity, in my words. Righteousness - In this cause or matter between you and me; and you will find the right to be on my side.

30. Is there - Consider if there be any untruth or iniquity in what I have already said, or shall farther speak. Taste - My judgment, which judgeth of words and actions, as the palate doth of meats.

VII

Job bemoans himself to his friends, ver. 1-6. To God, ver. 7- 16. Begs for pardon and death, ver. 17-21.

1. Is there not - Job is here excusing what he cannot justify, his passionate longing for death. A time - Is there not a time limited by God, wherein man shall live in this sinful, and miserable world? And is it a crime in me, to desire that God would bring me to that joyful period? Our time on earth is limited and short, according to the narrow bounds of this earth. But heaven cannot be measured, nor the days of heaven numbered. Hireling - Whose time is short, being but a few years, or days, whose condition is full of toil and hardship.

2. Shadow - That is, the sun-set, the time allotted for his rest.

3. So - This so respects not so much the desire of an hired servant, as the ground of it, his hard toil and service. Possess - God, hath given me this as my lot and inheritance. Months - So he calls them rather than days, to note the tediousness of his affliction. Vanity - Empty and unsatisfying. Nights - He mentions nights, because that is the saddest time for sick and miserable persons; the darkness and solitude of the night being of themselves uncomfortable, and giving them more opportunity for solemn and sorrowful reflections.

5. Worms - Which were bred out of Job's corrupted flesh and sores. Dust - The dust of the earth upon which he lay. Broken - By ulcers in all parts of it.

6. Swifter - The time of my life hastens to a period. Shuttle - Which passes in a moment from one end of the web to the other. Hope - Of enjoying any good day here.

7. O - He turns his speech to God. Perhaps observing, that his friends grew weary of hearing it. If men will not hear us, God will: if men cannot help us, he can: for his arm is not shortened, neither is his ear heavy.

8. No more - In this mortal state: I shall never return to this life again. Am not - If thou cast one angry look upon me, I am not; thou canst look me into eternity.

9. No more - Never until the general resurrection. When we see a cloud which looked great, as if it would eclipse the sun, of a sudden dispersed and disappearing, say, Just such a thing is the life of man, a vapor that appears for a while and then vanisheth away.

10. Any more - He shall no more be seen and known in his former habitation. It concerns us to secure a better place when we die: for this will own us no more.

11. Therefore - Since my life is so vain and short, and when once lost, without all hopes of recovery. I will plead with God for pity before I die; I will not smother my anguish within my breast, but will ease myself by pouring out my complaints.

12. A sea - Am I as fierce and unruly as the sea, which, if thou didst not set bounds to it, would overwhelm the earth? Or, am I a vast and ungovernable sea-monster? Which thou must restrain by thy powerful providence. That, &c. - That thou shouldest guard and restrain me with such heavy and unexampled miseries? We are apt in affliction to complain of God, as if he laid more upon us than there is occasion for: whereas we are never in heaviness, but when there is need, nor more than there is need.

17. What, &c. - What is there in that poor, mean, creature called man, miserable man, as this word signifies, which can induce thee to take any notice of him, or to make such account of him? Man is not worthy of thy favour, and he is below thy anger; that thou shouldest concern thyself so much about him, as one near and dear to thee?

18. And try, &c. - What is man that vain, foolish creature, that thou shouldest magnify or regard, or visit him, (with thy mercy and blessings, that thou shouldest so far honour and regard him, as by thy visitation to preserve his spirit, or hold his soul in life) and try him, which God doth not only by afflictions, but also by prosperity and both inward and outward blessings? That thou shouldst observe his motions every moment, as in care for him, and jealous over him?

19. How long - How long will it be ere thou withdraw thy afflicting hand? Swallow - That I may have a breathing time: a proverbial expression.

20. Sinned - Although I am free from those crying sins, for which my friends suppose thou hast sent this judgment upon me, yet, I freely confess I am a sinner, and therefore obnoxious to thy justice. What, &c. - To satisfy thy justice, or regain thy favour? Who dost know and diligently observe all mens inward motions, and outward actions; and therefore, if thou shalt be severe to mark mine iniquities, I have not what to say or do unto thee. My case is singular, none is shot at as I am.

21. Pardon - Seeing thou art so gracious to others, why may not I hope for the same favour from thee? Dust - If thou dost not speedily help me, it will be too late. But I shall not be - It will be to late to shew me favour.

VIII

Bildad affirms, that Job had spoken amiss, ver. 1-3. That if he would sincerely seek to God, God would help him, ver. 4-7. That it is usual with God, to destroy the hypocrite, ver. 8-19. The joy of the upright, ver. 20-22.

2. *Strong wind* - Boisterous and violent.

3. *Doth God* - Hebrew. The might God, as this word signifies, the Almighty, or All-sufficient God, as the next name of God implies. These names are emphatically used, to prove that God cannot deal unjustly or falsely with men, because he hath no need of it, nor temptation to it, being self-sufficient for his own happiness, and being able by his own invincible power to do whatsoever pleaseth him. *Pervert* - Judge unrighteously? No, this is inconsistent with God's nature, and with his office of governor of the world.

4. *If* - If thou wast innocent, thy children, upon whom a great part of these calamities fell, might be guilty; and therefore God is not unrighteous in these proceedings.

5. *Betimes* - Hebrew. rise early to seek him, if thou wouldest seek him speedily, early and diligently.

6. *Habitation* - The concerns of thy house and family; which thou hast got and managed with righteousness.

8. *Search* - Seriously and industriously search the ancient records.

9. *We, &c.* - But lately born, and therefore have but little knowledge and experience. We live not so long as they did, to make observations on the methods of Divine Providence.

10. *Utter* - Not partially, but sincerely, speaking their inward thoughts; not rashly, but from deep consideration; not by hearsay, but their own knowledge.

11. *Can, &c.* - The hypocrite cannot build his hope, without some false, rotten ground or other, any more than the rush can grow without mire, or the flag without water.

12. *Greenness* - Whereby it promises long continuance. Tho' no man cut it down, it withers of itself, sooner than other herbs.

13. *Paths* - Of wicked men. By their paths he doth not understand their manner of living, but the events which befall them, God's manner of dealing with them.

14. *Hope* - Whose wealth and outward glory, the matter of his hope, and trust, shall be cut off suddenly and violently taken away from him. *Web* - Which tho' it be formed with great art and industry, is easily swept down, or pulled in pieces.

15. *House* - He shall trust to the multitude of his children and servants, and to his wealth, all which come under the name of a man's house in scripture. *Hold it* - To uphold himself by it. But his web, that refuge of lies, will be swept away, and he crushed in it.

16. *He* - The secure and prosperous sinner may think himself wronged, when he is compared to a rush or flag. Compare him then to a flourishing and well-rooted tree. Yet even then shall he be suddenly cut off. *Green* - Flourisheth in the world. *Before the sun* - Publickly and in the view of all men. *Branch* - His children, who are here mentioned as additions not only to his comfort, but also to his strength and safety. *Garden* - A place where it is defended from those injuries to which the trees of the field are subject, and where, besides the advantages common to all trees, it hath peculiar helps from the art and industry of men. So he supposes this man to be placed in the most desirable circumstances.

17. *Heap* - Of stones. This circumstance is added, to signify its firmness and strength, that it was not in loose and sandy ground, which a violent wind might overthrow, but in solid ground, within which were many stones, which its numerous and spreading roots embrace, folding and interweaving themselves about them. *Seeth* - The tree reacheth thither, takes the advantage of that place for the strengthening of itself.

18. *He* - God, who is the saviour of good men, and the destroyer of the wicked. *It* - The place; to which denying him, and seeing him, are here ascribed figuratively. *Not seen* - He shall be so utterly extirpated and destroyed, that there shall be no memorial of him left.

19. *Behold* - This is the issue of the flourishing state. This all his joy comes to. *And, &c.* - Out of the same earth or place shall another tree grow.

20. *Behold* - God who will not help the evildoer, will not cast away a good man, tho he may be cast down. Yet it may be, he will not be lifted up in this world: and therefore Bildad could not infer, that if Job was not restored to temporal prosperity, he was not a good man. Let us judge nothing before the time, but wait 'till the secrets of all hearts are revealed, and the present difficulties of providence solved, to universal and everlasting satisfaction.

21. *'Till, &c.* - And what I have said in general of good men, shall be made good to thee, if thou art such: God will not forsake thee, nor desist from doing thee good, 'till he give thee abundant matter of rejoicing.

IX

God's justice, wisdom, power and sovereignty, ver. 1-13. Job condemns himself, as not able to contend with God, ver. 14-21. Shews that we cannot judge men by their outward condition, ver. 22-24. And complains of the greatness of his troubles, and the loss he was at, what to say or do, ver. 25-35.

2. I know - That God is just in all his ways, that he doth ordinarily bless the righteous, and punish the wicked. Before God - And I know that no man is absolutely just, if God be severe to mark what is amiss in him.

3. One - One accusation among a thousand which God shall produce against him.

4. He - He is infinitely wise, and searcheth all mens hearts and ways, and discovers a multitude of sins which mens short sighted- eyes cannot see; and therefore can charge them with innumerable evils, where they thought themselves innocent, and sees far more malignity than men could discern in their sins. Mighty - So that whether men contend with God by wisdom or by strength: God will be conqueror. Hardened himself - Obstinately contended with him. The devil promised himself that Job in the day of his affliction, would curse and speak ill of God. But instead of that, he sets himself to honour God, and speak highly of him. As ill pained as he is, and as much as he is taken up with his own miseries, when he has occasion to mention the wisdom and power of God, he forgets his complaints and expatiates with a flood of eloquence on that glorious subject.

5. Who - He proceeds to give evidence of the Divine power and wisdom. Removeth - Suddenly and unexpectedly. They - The mountains, to which he ascribes sense and knowledge figuratively. In anger - In token of his displeasure with the men that live upon them.

6. The earth - Great portions of it, by earthquakes, or by removing islands. Pillars - The deep and inward parts of it, which like pillars supported those parts that appear to our view.

8. Who. &c. - A farther description of a black and tempestuous season, wherein the heavens seem to be brought down nearer to the earth. Treadeth - Represseth and ruleth them when they rage and are tempestuous: for treading upon any thing, signifies in scripture using power and dominion over it.

9. Ordereth - Disposeth them, governeth their rising and setting, and all their influences. These he names as constellations of greatest eminency; but under them he seems to comprehend all the stars, which as they were created by God, so are under his government. Arcturus is a northern constellation, near that called the Bear. Orion is a more southerly constellation, that rises to us in December. The Pleiades is a constellation not far from Orion, which we call the seven stars: by the chambers, (or inmost chambers, as the word signifies) of the south, he seems to understand those stars and constellations which are toward the southern pole, which are called inward chambers, because they are for the most part hid and shut up from these parts of the world.

10. Doth great things, &c. - Job here says the same that Eliphaz had said, chap. v, 9, and in the original, in the very same words, with design to shew his full agreement with him, touching the Divine perfections.

11. Goeth - He works by his providence in ways of mercy or judgment. Passeth - He goeth from place to place: from one action to another: he speaks of God after the manner of men.

12. Taketh - If he determines to take away from any man his children or servants, or estate, who is able to restrain him from doing it? Or who dare presume to reprove him for it? And therefore far be it from me to quarrel with God, whereof you untruly accuse me.

13. Helpers - Those who undertake to uphold and defend one another against him. Stoop - Fall and are crushed by him.

14. How shall I - Since no creature can resist his power, and no man can comprehend his counsels and ways; how can I contend with him? Answer his allegations and arguments, produced against me.

15. Tho' - Though I were not conscious to myself of any sin. Would not - I durst not undertake to plead my cause against him; or maintain my integrity before him, because he knows me better than I know myself. Supplication - That he would judge favourably of me and my cause, and not according to the rigor of his justice.

16. Yet - I could not believe that God had indeed granted my desire, because I am still full of the tokens of his displeasure; and therefore should conclude that it was but a pleasant dream, and not a real thing.

17. Breaketh - Unexpectedly, violently, and irrecoverably. Cause - Not simply without any desert of his, but without any special cause of such singular afflictions; and peculiar and extraordinary guilt, such as his friends charged him with.

18. Breath - My pains are continual, and I have not so much as a breathing time free from them.

19. If - If my cause were to be decided by power. Is Strong - Stronger than I. Judgment - If I would contend with him in a way of right. Who - There is no superior judge that can summon him and me together.

20. Justify - If I plead against God mine own righteousness and innocency.

21. Perfect - If I should think myself perfect, yet I would not know, not acknowledge, my soul; I could not own nor plead before God the integrity of my soul, but would only make supplication to my judge, I would abhor, or condemn my life, I would not trust to the integrity either of my soul and heart, or of my life, so as to justify myself before the pure and piercing eyes of the all-seeing God.

22. This - In the other things which you have spoken of God's greatness, and justice, I do not contend with you, but this one thing I do, and must affirm against you. He - God sends afflictions promiscuously upon good and bad men.

23. Suddenly - If some common judgment come upon a people. Laugh - God will be well pleased, to see how the same scourge, which is the perdition of the wicked, is the trial of the innocent, and of their faith, which will be found unto praise and honour and glory.

24. The earth - The dominion over it. Into - Into their power. As good men are frequently scourged, so the wicked are advanced. Faces - Meantime he covers the faces of wise and good men, fit to be Judges, and buries them alive in obscurity, perhaps suffers them to be condemned, and their faces covered as criminals, by those to whom the earth is given. This is daily done: if it be not God that doth it, where and who is he that doth?

25. Now - What he had said of the calamities which God frequently inflicts upon good men, he now exemplifies in himself. My days - The days of my life. Post - Who rides upon swift horses. See - I enjoy no good in them. Seeing is often put for experiencing either good or evil.

26. Eagle - Which flies swiftly, especially when in the sight of his prey. See here how swift the motion of time is! It is always upon the wing, hastening to its period. What little need have we of past-times! What great need to redeem time, which runs out, runs on so fast toward eternity! And how vain are the enjoyments of time, which we may be deprived of, even while time continues! Our day may be longer than our sunshine: and when that is gone, it is as if it had never been.

28. Afraid - I find all such endeavours vain; for if my griefs be suspended for a time, yet my fears continue. Will not - I plainly perceive thou, O God, (to whom he makes a sudden address, as he afflictions which make them judge me guilty of some great crime. Words proceeding from despair and impatience.

29. I shall - I shall be used like a wicked man still. Why - Why then should I comfort myself with vain hopes of deliverance, as thou advisest me.

30. If - If I clear myself from all imputations, and fully prove my innocency before men.

31. Yet - God would prove him to be a most guilty creature, notwithstanding all his purity before men. Abhor - I shall be so filthy, that my own clothes, if they had any sense in them, would abhor to touch me.

32. A man - But one infinitely superior to me in majesty, and power, and wisdom, and justice. That - That I should presume to debate my cause with him. Come - Face to face, to plead upon equal terms.

33. Days-man - Or, umpire. Lay his hand - Order and govern us in pleading; and oblige us to stand to his decision. Our Lord Jesus is now the blessed days-man, who has mediated between heaven and earth, has laid his hand upon us both: to him the father hath committed all judgment. But this was not made so clear then, as it is now by the gospel, which leaves no room for such a complaint as this.

34. Fear - The fear and dread of his majesty and justice. Let him not deal with me according to his perfect justice, but according to his grace and clemency.

35. Then - I would speak freely for myself, being freed from that dread, which takes away my spirit and courage. It is not - I am not free from his terror, and therefore cannot plead my cause with him.

X

Job complains of the hardships he was under, ver. 1-7. Pleads with God, that he is his workmanship, ver. 8-13. Complains again, that God deals severely with him, ver. 14-17. Comforts himself with the thoughts of death, ver. 18-22.

1. Shall I - Shall I give over complaining?

2. Condemn - Or, pronounce me not to be a wicked man, neither deal with me as such, as I confess thou mightest do in rigorous justice: O discover my integrity by removing this stroke, for which my friends condemn me. Wherefore - For what ends and reasons, and for what sins; for I am not conscious to myself of any peculiar sins by which I have deserved to be made the most miserable of all men. When God afflicts, he contends with us: when he contends with us, there is always a reason for it. And it is desirable to know, what that reason is, that we may forsake whatever he has a controversy with us for.

3. Good - Dost thou take any pleasure in it? Far be it from Job, to think that God did him wrong. But he is at a loss to reconcile his providences with his justice. And so other good men have often been,

and will be, until the day shall declare it.

4. Eyes of faith - No. Eyes of flesh cannot see in the dark: but darkness hideth not from God. Eyes of flesh are but in one place at a time, and can see but a little way. But the eyes of the Lord are in every place, and run to and fro thro' the whole earth. Eyes of flesh will shortly be darkened by age, and shut up by death. But the eyes of God are ever the same, nor does his sight ever decay. As man - Man sees the outside only, and Judges by appearances: but thou seest mine heart.

5. Man's - Man's time is short and uncertain, and therefore he must improve it, and diligently search out the crimes of malefactors, lest by death he lose the opportunity of doing justice: but thou art eternal, and seest at one view all mens hearts, and all their actions present and to come; and therefore thou dost not need to proceed with me in this manner, by making so long a scrutiny into my heart and life.

6. Searchest - Keeping me so long upon the rack, to compel me to accuse myself.

7. Wicked - An hypocrite, as my friends account me. Deliver - But thou art the supreme ruler of the world; therefore I must wait thy time, and throw myself on thy mercy, in submission to thy sovereign will.

9. Clay - As a potter makes a vessel of clay; so this may note both the frailty of man's nature, which of itself decays and perishes, and doth not need such violent shocks to overthrow it; and the excellency of the Divine artifice commended from the meanness of the materials; which is an argument why God should not destroy it. Again - I must die by the course of nature, and therefore while I do live, give me some ease and comfort.

10. As milk - Thus he modestly and accurately describes God's admirable work in making man out of a small and liquid, and as it were milky substance, by degrees congealed and condensed into that exquisite frame of man's body.

11. Clothed - Covered my inward and more noble parts; which are first formed. So he proceeds in describing man's formation gradually. Bones - The stay and strength of the body; and some of them, as the skull and ribs, enclose and defend its vital parts.

12. Life - Thou didst not only give me a curious body, but also a reasonable soul: thou didst at first give me life, and then maintain it in me; both when I was in the womb (which is a marvelous work of God) and afterward when I was unable to do anything to preserve my own life. favour - Thou didst not give mere life, but many other favours, such as nourishment by the breast, education, knowledge, and instruction. Visitation - The care of thy providence watching over me for my good, and visiting me in mercy. Preserved - My life, which is liable to manifold dangers, if God did not watch over us every day and moment. Thou hast hitherto done great things for me, given me life, and the blessings of life, and daily deliverances: and wilt thou now undo all that thou hast done? And shall I who have been such an eminent monument of thy mercy, now be a spectacle of thy vengeance.

13. Hid - Both thy former favours and thy present frowns. Both are according to thy own will, and therefore undoubtedly consistent, however they seem. When God does what we cannot account for, we are bound to believe, there are good reasons for it hid in his heart. It is not with us, or in our reach to assign the cause; but I know this is with thee.

14. Markest - If I am a wicked man, I cannot hide it from thee; and thou wilt punish me for it.

15. Wicked - An hypocrite, as my friends esteem me. Righteous - An upright man; so whether good or bad, all comes to one. Yet - Yet I have no comfort, or hopes of any good. Confusion - I am confounded within myself, not knowing what to say or do. Let my extremity move thee to pity, and help me.

16. Lion - Which hunteth after his prey with great eagerness, and when he overtakes it, falls upon it with great fury. Returnest - The lion tears its prey speedily, and so ends its torments; but thou renewest my calamities again and again, and makest my plagues wonderful both for kind and extremity, and continuance.

17. Witnesses - Thy judgments, which are the evidences both of my sins, and of thy wrath. Indignation - My miseries are the effects of thine anger. Army - Changes may denote the various kinds, and an army the great number of his afflictions.

20. Cease - My life is short, and of itself hastens to an end, there is no need that thou shouldest grudge me some ease for so small a moment.

XI

Zophar charges Job with falsehood and pride, ver. 1-4. Wishes that God would convince him of his wisdom, justice, and unsearchable perfections, ver. 5-9. Of his sovereignty, power and the cognisance he takes of men, ver. 10-12. He assures him, that on his repentance, God would restore him to prosperity, but that the wicked should perish, ver. 13-20.

1. Then answered - How hard is it, to preserve calmness, in the heat of disputation! Eliphaz began

modestly: Bildad was a little rougher: But Zophar falls upon Job without mercy. "Those that have a mind to fall out with their brethren, and to fall foul upon them, find it necessary, to put the worst colours they can upon them and their performances, and right or wrong to make them odious."

2. Answered - Truly, sometimes it should not. Silence is the best confutation of impertinence, and puts the greatest contempt upon it.

3. Lies - Both concerning thy own innocency, and concerning the counsels and ways of God. Mockest - Our friendly and faithful counsels, chap. vi, 14, 15, 25, 26.

4. Doctrine - Concerning God and his providence. Clean - I am innocent before God; I have not sinned either by my former actions, or by my present expressions. But Zophar perverts Job's words, for he did not deny that he was a sinner, but only that he was an hypocrite.

5. Speak - Plead with thee according to thy desire: he would soon put thee to silence. We are commonly ready with great assurance to interest God in our quarrels. But they are not always in the right, who are most forward, to appeal to his judgment, and prejudge it against their antagonists.

6. Secrets - The unsearchable depths of God's wisdom in dealing with his creatures. Double - That they are far greater (the word double being used indefinitely for manifold, or plentiful) than that which is manifested. The secret wisdom of God is infinitely greater than that which is revealed to us by his word or works: the greatest part of what is known of God, is the least part of those perfections that are in him. And therefore thou dost rashly in judging so harshly of his proceedings with thee, because thou dost not comprehend the reasons of them, and in judging thyself innocent, because thou dost not see thy sins; whereas the all-knowing God sees innumerable sins in thee, for which he may utterly destroy thee.

7. Find out - Discover all the depths of his wisdom, and the reasons of his actions?

10. Cut off - A person or family. Shut - Its a prison, or in the hands of an enemy. Gather - Whether it pleaseth God to scatter a family, or to gather them together from their dispersions. Hinder - Or, who can contradict him, charge him with injustice in such proceedings?

11. Knoweth - Though men know but little of God, yet God knows man exactly. He knoweth that every man in the world is guilty of much vanity and folly, and therefore seeth sufficient reason for his severity against the best men. Wickedness - He perceiveth the wickedness of evil men, though it be covered with the veil of religion. Consider - Shall he only see it as an idle spectator, and not observe it as a judge to punish it?

12. Man - That since the fall is void of all true wisdom, pretends to be wise, and able to pass a censure upon all God's ways and works. Colt - Ignorant, and dull, and stupid, as to divine things, and yet heady and untractable.

13. Heart - To seek God; turning thy bold contentions with God into humble supplications.

15. Lift up - Which denotes chearfulness, and holy boldness. Without spot - Having a clear and unspotted conscience. Steadfast - Shall have a strong and comfortable assurance of God's favour.

16. As waters - Thou shalt remember it no more, than men remember a land-flood, which as it comes, so it goes away suddenly.

17. Shine - Light in scripture commonly signifies prosperity and glory. Thy comfort, like the morning-light shall shine brighter and brighter, until the perfect day.

18. Secure - Thy mind shall be quiet and free from terrors, because thou shalt have a firm and well-grounded confidence in God. Dig - Either to fix thy tents, which after the manner of the Arabians were removed from place to place: or to plough the ground, as he had done, chap. i, 14, or to make a fence about thy dwelling.

20. Fail - Either with grief and tears for their sore calamities: or with long looking for what they shall never attain. Their hope - They shall never obtain deliverance out of their distresses, but shall perish in them. Ghost - Shall be as vain and desperate as the hope of life is in a man, when he is at the very point of death.

XII

Job blames his friends for their self-conceit and unkind behaviour, ver. 1-5. Shews that the wicked often prosper, ver. 6-11. Confirms and enlarges upon what had been said, of the wisdom, power and providence of God, ver. 12-25.

2. Ye - You have engrossed all the reason of mankind; and each of you has as much wisdom as an whole people put together. All the wisdom which is in the world, lives in you, and will be utterly lost when you die. When wise and good men die, it is a comfort to think that wisdom and goodness do not die with them: it is folly to think, that there will be a great, irreparable loss of us when we are gone, since God has the residue of the spirit, and can raise up others more fit to do his work.

3. But - In these things, which he speaks not in a way of boasting, but for the just vindication both of himself, and of that cause of God, which for the substance of it he maintained rightly, as God himself attests, chap. xlii, 7. Such things - The truth is, neither you nor I have any reason to be puffed up with

our knowledge of these things: for the most barbarous nations know that God is infinite in wisdom, and power, and justice. But this is not the question between you and me.

4. Upon God - Even by my religious neighbours, by those who call upon God, and not in vain; whose prayers therefore I covet, not their reproaches. The just - I, who, notwithstanding all their hard censures dare still own it, that through God's grace I am an upright man.

5. Slip with his feet - And fall into trouble; tho' he had formerly shone as a lamp, he is then looked upon as a lamp going out, as the snuff of a candle, which we throw to the ground and tread upon; and accordingly is despised in the thought of him that is at ease.

6. Are secure - Job's friends had all supposed, that wicked men cannot prosper long in the world. This Job opposes, and maintains, that God herein acts as sovereign, and reserves that exact distribution of rewards and punishments for the other world.

7. But - If thou observest the beasts, and their properties and actions, and events, from them thou mayst learn this lesson: that which Zophar had uttered with so much pomp and gravity, chap. xi, 7, 8, 9, concerning God's infinite wisdom, saith Job, thou needest not go into heaven or hell to know. but thou mayst learn it even from the beasts.

9. Lord - This is the only time that we meet with the name Jehovah in all the discourses between Job and his friends. For God in that age was more known by the name of Shaddai, the Almighty.

11. Doth not - This may be a preface to his following discourse; whereby he invites them to hear and judge of his words candidly and impartially; that they and he too might agree in disallowing what should appear to be false, and owning of every truth.

12. Wisdom - These words contain a concession of what Bildad had said, chap. viii, 8, 9, and a joining with him in that appeal; but withal, an intimation that this wisdom was but imperfect, and liable to many mistakes; and indeed mere ignorance and folly, if compared with the Divine wisdom, and therefore that antiquity ought not to be received against the truths of the most wise God.

14. No opening - Without God's permission. Yea, he shuts up in the grave, and none can break open those sealed doors. He shuts up in hell, in chains of darkness, and none can pass that great gulf.

15. The waters - Which are reserved its the clouds, that they may not fall upon the earth. They - The waters upon the earth, springs, and brooks, and rivers. As at the time of the general deluge, to which here is a manifest allusion.

16. With him - The same thing he had said before, ver. 13, but he repeats it here to prepare the way for the following events, which are eminent instances, both of his power and wisdom. Are his - Wholly subject to his disposal. He governs the deceiver and sets bounds to his deceits, how far they shall extend; he also over-rules all this to his own glory, and the accomplishment of his righteous designs of trying the good, and punishing wicked men, by giving them up to believe lies. Yet God is not the author of any error or sin, but only the wise and holy governor of it.

17. Spoiled - The wise counsellors or statesmen, by whom the affairs of kings and kingdoms are ordered, he leadeth away as captives in triumph, being spoiled either of that wisdom which they had, or seemed to have; or of that power and dignity which they had enjoyed. Fools - By discovering their folly, and by infatuating their minds, and turning their own counsels to their ruin.

18. Looseth - He freeth them from that wherewith they bind their subjects to obedience, their power and authority, and that majesty which God stamps upon kings, to keep their people in awe. Girdeth - He reduces them to a mean and servile condition; which is thus expressed, because servants did use to gird up their garments (that after the manner of those parts were loose and long) that they might be fitter for attendance upon their masters: he not only deposes them from their thrones, but brings them into slavery.

20. The speech - By taking away or restraining the gift of utterance from them. Or, by taking away their understanding which should direct their speech. Trusty - Of those wise and experienced counsellors, that were trusted by the greatest princes.

22. Darkness - The most secret counsels of princes, which are contrived and carried on in the dark.

23. Nations - What hitherto he said of princes, he now applies to nations, whom God does either increase or diminish as he pleases.

25. Grope - Thus are the revolutions of kingdoms brought about by an overruling providence. Heaven and earth are shaken: but the Lord remaineth a king forever.

XIII

Job sharply reproves his friends, ver. 1-13. Professes his faith, ver. 14-16. Desires to be heard, ver. 17-19. Expostulates with God, ver. 20-28.

1. Lo - All this which either you or I have discoursed concerning the infinite power and wisdom of God. I know, both by seeing it, by my own observation and experience, and by hearing it from my ancestors.

3. Surely - I had rather debate the matter with God than with you. I am not afraid of presenting my person and cause before him, who is a witness of my integrity.

8. Accept - Not judging according to the right of the cause, but the quality or the person.

12. Remembrance - Mouldering and coming to nothing. And the consideration of our mortality should make us afraid of offending God. Your mementos are like unto ashes, contemptible and unprofitable.

14. Wherefore - And this may be a reason of his desire of liberty of speech, because he could hold his tongue no longer, but must needs tear himself to pieces, if he had not some vent for his grief. The phrase having his life in his hand, denotes a condition extremely dangerous.

17. Hear - He now comes more closely to his business, the foregoing verses being mostly in way of preface.

18. Behold - I have seriously considered the state of my case, and am ready to plead my cause.

19. The ghost - My grief would break my heart, if I should not give it vent.

21. Withdraw - Suspend my torments during the time of my pleading with thee, that my mind may be at liberty. Do not present thyself to me in terrible majesty, neither deal with me in rigorous justice.

22. Then - This proposal savoured of self-confidence, and of irreverence towards God; for which, and the like speeches, he is reproved by God, chap. xxxviii, 2, 3; xl, 2.

23. My sin - That I am a sinner, I confess; but not that I am guilty of such crimes as my friends suppose, if it be so, do thou, O Lord, discover it.

25. Leaf - One that can no more resist thy power, than a leaf, or a little dry straw can resist the wind or fire.

26. Writest - Thou appointest or inflictest. A metaphor from princes or Judges, who anciently used to write their sentences.

28. He - He speaks of himself in the third person, as is usual in this and other sacred books. So the sense is, he, this poor frail creature, this body of mine; which possibly he pointed at with his finger, consumeth or pineth away.

XIV

Man's life is but short, sorrowful, and sinful; on which consideration he pleads for mercy, ver, 1-6. Other creatures revive, but man does not, ver. 7-12. Various wishes and complaints, ver. 13-22.

1. Man - A weak creature, and withal corrupt and sinful, and of that sex by which sin and all other calamity was brought into the world.

2. Flower - The flower is fading, and all its beauty soon withers and is gone. The shadow is fleeting, and its very being will soon be lost in the shadows of night. Of neither do we make any account, in neither do we put any confidence.

4. Not one - No man. This is the prerogative of thy grace, which therefore I humbly implore.

5. Determined - Limited to a certain period. With thee - In thy power and disposal. Thou hast appointed a certain end of his days, beyond which he cannot prolong his life.

6. Turn - Withdraw thine afflicting hand from him, that he may have some present ease. 'Till - He come to the period of his life, which thou hast allotted to him, as a man appoints a set time to an hired servant.

8. Die - To outward appearance.

9. Scent - By means of water. Scent or smell, is figuratively ascribed to a tree.

10. Man - Two words are here used for man. Geber, a mighty man, tho' mighty, dies. Adam, a man of earth, returns to it. Before death, he is dying daily, continually wasting away. In death, he giveth up the ghost, the spirit returns to God that gave it. After death, where is he? Not where he was: his place knows him no more. But is he nowhere? Yes, he is gone to the world of spirits, gone into eternity, gone, never to return to this world!

11. As - So it is with man. Or thus, as when the waters fail from the sea, when the sea forsakes the place into which it used to flow, the river which was fed by it, decayeth and drieth up without all hopes of recovery.

12. Lieth - In his bed, the grave. 'Till - Until the time of the general resurrection, when these visible heavens shall pass away.

13. The grave - The grave is not only a resting-place, but an hiding-place to the children of God. He hides them in the grave, as we hide our treasure in a place of secrecy and safety. Hide me there, not only from the storms of this life, but for the glory of a better. Until thy wrath be past - As long as our bodies lie in the grave, there are some fruits of God's wrath against sin: until the set time comes, for their being remembered, as Noah was remembered in the ark, Gen. viii, 1. Our bodies shall not be forgotten in the grave, there is a time set for their being inquired after.

14. Shall he live? - He shall not in this world. Therefore I will patiently wait 'till that change

comes, which will put a period to my calamities.

15. Answer thee - Thou shalt call my soul to thyself: and I will cheerfully answer, Here I am: knowing thou wilt have a desire to the work of thy hands - A love for the soul which thou hast made, and new-made by thy grace.

16. Numbereth - Thou makest a strict enquiry into all my actions.

17. Sealed - As writings or other choice things, that they may all be brought forth upon occasion, and not one of them forgotten. Thou keepest all my sins in thy memory. But herein Job speaks rashly.

18. And - As when a great mountain falls, by an earthquake or inundation, it moulders away like a fading leaf, (as the Hebrew word signifies) and as the rock, when by the violence of winds or earthquakes it is removed out of its place, and thrown down, is never re-advanced: and as the waters by continual droppings, wear away the stones, so that they can never be made whole again: and as thou wastest away, by a great and violent inundation, the things which grow out of the dust of the earth, herbs, and fruits, and plants, which once washed away are irrecoverably lost; in like manner, thou destroyest the hope of man: when man dies, all hope of his living again in this world is lost.

20. Prevailest - When once thou takest away this life, it is gone forever. Sendest - To his long home.

21. Knoweth not - Either is ignorant of all such events: or, is not concerned or affected with them. A dead or dying man minds not these things.

XV

Eliphaz reproves Job for justifying himself, ver. 1-13. Persuades him to humble himself before God, ver. 14-16. Describes the misery of wicked men, ver. 17-35.

2. Fill - Satisfy his mind and conscience. East wind - With discourses not only unprofitable, but also pernicious both to himself and others; as the east-wind was in those parts.

4. Castest off - Hebrew. thou makes void fear; the fear of God, piety and religion, by thy unworthy speeches of God, and by those false and pernicious principles, that God makes no difference between good and bad in the course of his providence, but equally prospers or afflicts both: thou dost that which tends to the subversion of the fear and worship of God. Restrainest prayer - Thou dost by thy words and principles, as far as in thee lies, banish prayer out of the world, by making it useless and unprofitable to men.

5. Uttereth - Thy words discover the naughtiness of thy heart. Crafty - Thou speakest wickedly, and craftily: thou coverest thy impious principles with fair pretenses of piety.

11. Are - Are those comforts, which we have propounded to thee on condition of thy repentance, small and contemptible in thine eyes? Secret - Hast thou any secret and peculiar way of comfort which is unknown to us, and to all other men?

12. Why - Why dost thou suffer thyself to be transported by the pride of thine heart, to use such unworthy expressions? Wink - Why dost thou look with such an angry, supercilious, and disdainful look?

13. Against God - Eliphaz here does in effect give the cause on Satan's side, and affirms that Job had done as he said he would, Curse God to his face.

15. Saints - In his angels, chap. iv, 18, who are called his saints or holy ones, Deut. xxxiii, 2 Psalm ciii, 20. Who though they were created holy, yet many of them fell. Heavens - The angels that dwell in heaven; heaven being put for its inhabitants. None of these are pure, simply and perfectly, and comparatively to God. The angels are pure from corruption, but not from imperfection.

16. Who - Who besides his natural proneness to sin, has contracted habits of sinning; and sins as freely, as greedily and delightfully, as men, especially in those hot countries, drink up water.

17. I - I will prove what I have affirmed, that such strokes as thine are peculiar to hypocrites. Seen - I speak not by hear-say, but from my own experience.

18. Hid - They judged it to be so certain and important a truth, that they would not conceal it in their own breasts.

19. To whom - By the gracious gift of God: this he alleges to make their testimony more considerable, because these were no obscure men, but the most worthy and famous men in their ages; and to confute what Job had said, chap. ix, 24, that the earth was given into the hand of the wicked. By the earth he means the dominion and possession of it. Stranger - No person of a strange nation and disposition, or religion. Passed - Through their land, so as to disturb, or spoil them, as the Sabeans and Chaldeans did thee. God watched over those holy men so, that no enemy could invade them; and so he would have done over thee, if thou hadst been such an one.

20. Pain - Lives a life of care, and fear, and grief, by reason of God's wrath, the torments of his own mind, and his outward calamities. Hidden - He knows not how short the time of his life is, and therefore lives in continual fear of losing it. Oppressor - To the wicked man: he names this one sort of

them, because he supposed Job to be guilty of this sin, in opposition of what Job had affirmed of the safety of such persons, chap. xii, 6, and because such are apt to promise themselves a longer and happier life than other men.

21. A sound - Even when he feels no evil, he is tormented with perpetual fears. Come upon him - Suddenly and unexpectedly.

22. Believeth not - When he falls into trouble, he despairs of deliverance, by reason of his guilty conscience. Waited for - Besides the calamity which is upon him, he is in constant expectation of greater; the sword is used for any grievous affliction.

23. Knoweth - From his own guilty conscience.

25. For - Now he gives the reason of all the fore-mentioned calamities, which was his great wickedness. Against God - He sinned against God with an high hand. The Almighty - Which aggravates the madness of this poor worm that durst fight against the omnipotent God.

26. He - The wicked man. Neck - As a stout warrior who cometh close to his adversary and grapples with him. He acts in flat opposition to God, both to his precepts and providences. Bosses - Even where his enemy is strongest.

27. Because - This is mentioned as the reason of his insolent carriage towards God, because he was fat, rich, potent, and successful, as that expression signifies, Deut. xxxii, 15 Psalm lxxviii, 31 Jer. xlvi, 21. His great prosperity made him proud and secure, and regardless of God and men. Fat - His only care is to pamper himself.

28. But - This is fitly opposed to the prosperity last mentioned, and is the beginning of the description of his misery.

29. Substance - What he had gotten shall be taken from him.

30. Depart - His misery shall have no end. Flame - God's anger and judgment upon him. Branches - His wealth, and power, and glory, wherewith he was encompassed, as trees are with their branches. His mouth - And this expression intimates, with how much ease God subdueth his enemies: his word, his blast; one act of his will is sufficient. Go - Hebrew. go back: that is, run away from God faster than he ran upon him, ver. 26. So it is a continuation of the former metaphor of a conflict between two persons.

31. Vanity - In the vain and deceitful things of this world, he subjoins a general caution to all men to take heed of running into the same error and mischief. Vanity - Disappointment and dissatisfaction, and the loss of all his imaginary felicity. Recompence - Hebrew. his exchange; he shall exchange one vanity for another, a pleasing vanity for a vexatious vanity.

32. Accomplished - That vanity should be his recompence. Before - When by the course of nature, and common providence he might have continued much longer.

XVI

Job upbraids his friends with unkindness, ver. 1-5. Bemoans himself, ver. 6-16. Appeals from their censure to the righteous judgment of God, ver. 17-22.

2. Such things - These things are but vulgar and trivial. And so are all creatures, to a soul under deep conviction of sin, or the arrest of death.

3. End - When wilt thou put an end to these impertinent discourses? He retorts upon him his charge, chap. xv, 2, 3.

7. He - God, as appears by the following words. Weary - Either of complaining, or, of my life. Desolate - Hast turned my society into desolation, by destroying my children and servants.

9. Eyes - Looks upon me with a fierce, and sparkling eye, as enraged persons use to do.

10. They - My friends. Gaped - Opened their mouths wide against me. In all this Job was a type of Christ. These very expressions are used in the predictions of his sufferings, Psalm xxii, 13. They gaped upon me with their mouths, and Micah v, 1. They shall smite the judge of Israel upon the check.

11. The wicked - And thus Christ was delivered into wicked hands, by the determinate counsel of God.

12. Shaken - As a mighty man doth with some stripling, when he wrestleth with him. Mark - That he may shoot all his arrows in me.

13. His archers - Whoever are our enemies, we must look on them as God's archers, and see him directing the arrow.

15. I have - So far am I from stretching out my hand against God, chap. xv, 25, that I have humbled myself deeply under his hand. I have not only put on sackcloth, but sewed it on, as being resolved to continue my humiliation, as long as my affliction continues. Defiled my horn - I have willingly parted with all my wealth, and power, and glory (as the horn often signifies in scripture,) and been content to lie in the dust.

17. Not - And all this is not come upon me for any injurious dealing, but for other reasons known

to God only. *Pure* - I do not cast off God's fear and service, chap. xv, 4. I do still pray and worship God, and my prayer is accompanied with a sincere heart.

18. *Earth* - The earth is said to cover that blood, which lies undiscovered and unrevenged: but saith Job, if I be guilty of destroying any man, let the earth disclose it; let it be brought to light. *Cry* - Let the cry of my complaints to men, or prayers to God, find no place in the ears or hearts of God or men, if this be true.

19. *Witness* - Besides the witness of my conscience, God is witness of my integrity.

22. *Go* - To the state and place of the dead, whence men cannot return to this life. The meaning is, my death hastens, and therefore I earnestly desire that the cause depending, between me and my friends, may be determined, that if I be guilty of these things, I may bear the shame of it before all men, and if I be innocent, that I may see my own integrity, and the credit of religion, (which suffers upon this occasion) vindicated. How very certainly, and how very shortly are we likewise to go this journey.

XVII

Job still bemoans himself, ver. 1-7. Encourages good men to hold on their way, ver. 8, 9. Declares he looks for no ease but in the grave, ver. 10-16. Job in this chapter suddenly passes from one thing to another as is usual for men in much trouble.

1. *The graves* - He speaks of the sepulchres of his fathers, to which he must be gathered. The graves where they are laid, are ready for me also. Whatever is unready, the grave is ready for us: it is a bed soon made. And if the grave be ready for us, it concerns us, to be ready for the grave.

2. *Are not* - Do not my friends, instead of comforting, mock me? Thus he returns to what he had said, chap. xvi, 20, and intimates the justice of his following appeal.

3. *Surety* - These words contain, an humble desire to God that he would be his surety, or appoint him a surety who should maintain his righteous cause against his opposers. *Strike hands* - Be surety to me; whereof that was the usual gesture.

4. *Hid* - Thou hast blinded the minds of my friends: therefore I desire a more wise and able judge. *Therefore* - Thou wilt not give them the victory over me in this contest, but wilt make them ashamed of their confidence.

7. *As a shadow* - I am grown so poor and thin, that I am not to be called a man, but the shadow of a man.

8. *Astonied* - At the depth and mysteriousness of God's judgments, which fall on innocent men, while the worst of men prosper. *Yet* - Notwithstanding all these sufferings of good men, and the astonishment which they cause, he shall the more zealously oppose those hypocrites, who make these strange providences of God an objection to religion.

10. *Come* - And renew the debate, as I see you are resolved to do.

11. *My days* - The days of my life. I am a dying man, and therefore the hopes you give me of the bettering of my condition, are vain. *Purposes* - Which I had in my prosperous days, concerning myself and children.

12. *They* - My thoughts so incessantly pursue and disturb me, that I can no more sleep in the night, than in the day. *The light* - The day-light, which often gives some comfort to men in misery, seems to be gone as soon as it is begun. *Darkness* - Because of my grievous pains and torments which follow me by day as well as by night.

13. *Wait* - For deliverance, I should be disappointed; for I am upon the borders of the grave, I expect no rest but in the dark grave, for which therefore I prepare myself. I endeavour to make it easy, by keeping my conscience pure, by seeing Christ lying in this bed, (so turning it into a bed of spices) and by looking beyond it to the resurrection.

14. *Corruption* - Hebrew. to the pit of corruption, the grave. *Father* - I am near a-kin to thee, and thou wilt receive and keep me in thy house, as parents do their children.

15. *Hope* - The happiness you would have me expect.

16. *They* - My hopes, of which he spake in the singular number, ver. 15, which he here changes into the plural, as is usual in these poetical books. *Bars* - Into the innermost parts of the pit: my hopes are dying, and will be buried in my grave. We must shortly be in the dust, under the bars of the pit, held fast there, 'till the general resurrection. All good men, if they cannot agree now will there rest together. Let the foresight of this cool the heat of all contenders, and moderate the disputers of this world.

John Wesley

XVIII

Bildad sharply reproves Job, as proud and impatient, ver. 1- 4. And enlarges on the misery of the wicked, ver. 5-12.

2. Ye - Thou, O Job; of whom he speaks here, as also ver. 3, in the plural number, as was a common idiotism of the Eastern language, to speak thus of one person, especially where he was one of eminency. Mark - Consider the matter better.

3. Beasts - Ignorant, and stupid men, chap. xvii, 4, 10.

4. He - Job. Thou art thy own tormentor. Forsaken - Shall God give over the government of the earth for thy sake, to prevent thy complaints and clamours? Shall the counsels of God, which are more immoveable than rocks, and the whole course of his providence be altered to comply with thy humours?

7. Steps - His strong steps, by a vulgar Hebraism: his attempts and actions; such of them as seem to be contrived with greatest strength of understanding, and carried on with greatest resolution. Straitened - Shall be hindered and entangled. He shall be cast into difficulties and perplexities, so that he shall not be able to proceed, and to accomplish his enterprizes.

8. Feet - By his own designs and actions.

13. First-born - A terrible kind of death. The first-born was the chief of his brethren, and therefore this title is given to things eminent in their kind.

14. Confidence - All the matter of his confidence, his riches, and children. Terrors - To death, which even Aristotle called, The most terrible of all terribles. And this it will do, either because it will expose him to his enemies, who will kill him; or because the sense of his disappointments, and losses, and dangers, will break his heart.

15. It - Destruction, expressed ver. 12, shall fix its abode with him. Because - Because it is none of his own, being got from others by deceit or violence. Brimstone - It shall be utterly destroyed, as it were, by fire and brimstone. He seems to allude both to the destruction of Sodom, which happened not long before these times, and to the judgment which befell Job, chap. i, 16.

18. Darkness - From a prosperous life to disgrace and misery, and to the grave, the land of darkness.

20. Astonied - At the day of his destruction. They shall be amazed at the suddenness, and dreadfulness of it. Before - Before the persons last mentioned. Those who lived in the time and place where this judgment was inflicted.

21. The place - The condition.

XIX

Job complains of the wicked usage of his friends, ver. 1-7. Of the shyness and strangeness of his relations and intimates, ver. 8-19. Pleads for pity, ver. 20-22. Testifies his firm belief of the resurrection, ver. 23-27. Cautions his friends against persisting in their hard censures, ver. 28, 29.

3. Ten - Many times. A certain number for an uncertain. Strange - That you carry yourselves like strangers to me, and condemn me as if you had never known my integrity.

4. Erred - If I have sinned, I myself suffer for my sins, and therefore deserve your pity rather than reproaches.

7. Cry - Unto God. Wrong - That I am oppressed by my friends.

9. Glory - Of my estate, children, authority, and all my comforts. Crown - All my power, and laid my honour in the dust.

10. Every side - In all respects, my person, and family, and estate. Gone - I am a lost and dead man. Hope - All my hopes of the present life, but not of the life to come. Tree - Which being once plucked up by the roots, never grows again. Hope in this life is a perishing thing. But the hope of good men, when it is cut off from this world, is but removed like a tree, transplanted from this nursery to the garden of God.

12. Troops - My afflictions, which are God's soldiers marching under his conduct. Raise - Cast up a trench round about me.

13. Estranged - As we must eye the hand of God, in all the injuries we receive from our enemies, so likewise in all the slights and unkindnesses we receive from our friends.

15. Maids - Who by reason of their sex, commonly have more compassionate hearts than men.

18. Arose - From my seat, to shew my respect to them, though they were my inferiors.

19. Inward - My intimates and confidants, to whom I imparted all my thoughts and counsels.

20. Skin - Immediately, the fat and flesh next to the skin being consumed. As - As closely as it doth to these remainders of flesh which are left in my inward parts.

21. Touched me - My spirit is touched with a sense of his wrath, a calamity of all others the most

grievous.

22. As God - As if you had the same infinite knowledge which God hath, whereby you can search my heart and know my hypocrisy, and the same sovereign authority to say and do what you please with me. Not satisfied - Are like wolves or lions that are not contented with devouring the flesh of their prey, but also break their bones.

23. My words - The words which I am now about to speak. And that which Job wished for, God granted him. His words are written in God's book; so that wherever that book is read, there shall this glorious confession be declared, for a memorial of him.

24. Lead - Anciently they used to grave the letters in a stone with an iron tool, and then to fill up the cuts with lead, that the words might be more plainly seen.

25. For - This is the reason of his confidence in the goodness of his cause, and his willingness to have the matter depending between him and his friends, published and submitted to any trial, because he had a living and powerful Redeemer to plead his cause, and to give sentence for him. My Redeemer - In whom I have a particular interest. The word Goel, here used; properly agrees to Jesus Christ: for this word is primarily used of the next kinsman, whose office it was to redeem by a price paid, the sold or mortgaged estate of his deceased kinsman; to revenge his death, and to maintain his name and honour, by raising up seed to him. All which more fitly agrees to Christ, who is our nearest kinsman and brother, as having taken our nature upon him; who hath redeemed that everlasting inheritance which our first parents had utterly lost, by the price of his own blood; and hath revenged the death of mankind upon the great contriver of it, the devil, by destroying him and his kingdom; and hath taken a course to preserve our name, and honour, and persons, to eternity. And it is well observed, that after these expressions, we meet not with such impatient or despairing passages, as we had before; which shews that they had inspired him with new life and comfort. Latter day - At the day of the general resurrection and judgment, which, as those holy patriarchs well knew and firmly believed, was to be at the end of the world. The earth - The place upon which Christ shall appear and stand at the last day. Hebrew. upon the dust; in which his saints and members lie or sleep, whom he will raise out of it. And therefore he is fitly said to stand upon the dust, or the grave, or death; because then he will put that among other enemies under his feet.

26. Though - Though my skin is now in a great measure consumed, and the rest of it, together with this body, shall be devoured by the worms, which may seem to make my case desperate. Flesh - Or with bodily eyes; my flesh or body being raised from the grave, and re-united to my soul. God - The same whom he called his Redeemer, ver. 25, who having taken flesh, and appearing in his flesh or body with and for Job upon the earth, might well be seen with his bodily eyes. Nor is this understood of a simple seeing of him; but of that glorious and beatifying vision of God, which is promised to all God's people.

27. See - No wonder he repeats it again, because the meditation of it was most sweet to him. For - For my own benefit and comfort. Another - For me or in my stead. I shall not see God by another's eyes, but by my own, and by these self-same eyes, in this same body which now I have. Though - This I do confidently expect, tho' the grave and the worms will consume my whole body.

28. Therefore - Because my faith and hope are in God. The root - The root denotes, a root of true religion. And the root of all true religion is living faith.

29. Sword - Of some considerable judgment to be inflicted on you which is called the sword, as Deut. xxxii, 41, and elsewhere. That - This admonition I give you, that you may know it in time, and prevent it. A judgment - God sees and observes, and will judge all your words and actions.

XX

Zophar, after a short preface, asserts, that the prosperity, of the wicked is short, and his ruin sure, ver. 1-9. He describes his misery in many particulars, ver. 10-29.

2. Therefore - For this thy severe sentence. Make haste - I speak sooner than I intended. And possibly interrupted Job, when he was proceeding in his discourse.

3. The check - Thy opprobrious reproofs of us. Understanding - I speak, not from passion, but certain knowledge.

4. This - Which I am now about to say. Since - Since the world was made.

6. Though - Though he be advanced to great dignity and authority.

11. Bones - His whole body, even the strongest parts of it. The sin - Of the punishment of it.

12. Mouth - To his taste; though it greatly please him for the present. Hide - As an epicure doth a sweet morsel, which he keeps and rolls about his mouth, that he may longer enjoy the pleasure of it.

14. Turned - From sweet to bitter. Gall of asps - Exceeding bitter and pernicious. Gall is most bitter; the gall of serpents is full of poison; and the poison of asps is most dangerous and within a few hours kills without remedy.

15. Vomit - Be forced to restore them. God, &c. - If no man's hand can reach him, God shall find

him out.

17. See - Not enjoy that abundant satisfaction and comfort, which good men through God's blessings enjoy.

18. Swallow - So as to hold it. He shall not possess it long, nor to any considerable purpose. Yea, he shall be forced to part with his estate to make compensations for his wrongs. So that he shall not enjoy what he had gotten, because it shall be taken from him.

20. Belly - He shall have no peace in his mind. Desired - Any part of his desirable things, but shall forfeit and lose them all.

21. Therefore - It being publickly known that he was totally ruined, none of his kindred shall trouble themselves about any relicks of his estate.

22. In, &c. - In the height of prosperity he shall be distressed. Hand, &c. - So his wickedness shall be punished by those as wicked as himself.

23. Rain - This phrase denotes both the author of his plagues, God, and the nature and quality of them, that they shall come upon him like rain; with great vehemency, so that he cannot prevent or avoid it. Eating - As it fell upon thy sons.

24. Flee - From the sword or spear; and so shall think himself out of danger.

25. It - The arrow, which had entered into his body, and now was drawn out of it either by himself or some other person; having in general said, that it came out of his body, he determines also the part of the body, the gall; which shews that the wound was both deep and deadly. Terrors - The terrors of death; because he perceived his wound was incurable.

26. Darkness - All sorts of miseries. Hid - Or, laid up; by God for him. It is reserved and treasured up for him, and shall infallibly overtake him. Secret - In those places where he confidently hopes to hide himself from all evil: even there God shall find him out. Not blown - By man, but kindled by God himself. He thinks by his might and violence to secure himself from men, but God will find him out. With him - With his family, who shall inherit his curse as well as his estate.

27. Heaven - God shall be a swift witness against him by extraordinary judgments; still he reflects upon Job's case, and the fire from heaven. Earth - All creatures upon earth shall conspire to destroy him. If the God of heaven and earth be his enemy, neither heaven nor earth will shew him any kindness, but all the host of both are, and will he at war with him.

28. Increase of his house - His estate. Depart - Shall be lost. Flow - Like waters, swiftly and strongly, and so as to return no more. His - Of God's wrath.

29. Heritage - Hebrew. the heritage; so called, to denote the stability and assurance of it, that it is as firm as an inheritance to the right heir; and in opposition to that inheritance which he had gotten by fraud and violence.

XXI

Job's preface to his answer, ver. 1-6. He describes the prosperity of wicked men, ver. 7-13. Hardening them in their impiety, ver. 14-16. He foretells their final ruin, ver. 17-21. He observes a great variety in the ways of God, ver. 22-26. He shews, that tho' sinners are always punished in the other world, they often escape in this, ver. 27-34.

2. Hear, &c. - If you have no other comfort to administer, at least afford me this. And it will be a comfort to yourselves in the reflection, to have dealt tenderly with your afflicted friend.

3. Speak - without interruption. Mock - If I do not defend my cause with solid arguments, go on in your scoffs.

4. Is - I do not make my complaint to, or expect relief from you, or from any men, hut from God only: I am pouring forth my complaints to God. If - If my complaint were to man, have I not cause?

5. Mark - Consider what I am about to say concerning the prosperity of the worst of men, and the pressures of some good men, and it is able to fill you with astonishment. Lay, &c. - Be silent.

6. Remember - The very remembrance of what is past, fills me with dread and horror.

13. Moment - They do not die of a lingering and tormenting disease.

14. Therefore - Because of their constant prosperity. Say - Sometimes in words, but commonly in their thoughts and the language of their lives.

16. Lo - But wicked men have no reason to reject God, because of their prosperity, for their wealth, is not in their hand; neither obtained, nor kept by their own might, but only by God's power and favour. Therefore I am far from approving their opinion, or following their course.

17. Often - I grant that this happens often though not constantly, as you affirm. Lamp - Their glory and outward happiness.

19. Layeth up - In his treasures, Rom. ii, 5. Iniquity - The punishment of his iniquity; he will punish him both in his person and in his posterity.

20. See - He shall be destroyed; as to see death, is to die.

21. For, &c. - What delight can ye take in the thoughts of his posterity, when he is dying an untimely death? When that number of months, which by the course of nature, he might have lived, is cut off by violence.

22. Teach - How to govern the world? For so you do, while you tell him that he must not afflict the godly, nor give the wicked prosperity. That he must invariably punish the wicked, and reward the righteous in this world. No: he will act as sovereign, and with great variety in his providential dispensations. High - The highest persons, on earth, he exactly knows them, and gives sentence concerning them, as he sees fit.

25. Another - Another wicked man. So there is a great variety of God's dispensations; he distributes great prosperity to one, and great afflictions to another, according to his wise but secret counsel.

26. Alike - All these worldly differences are ended by death, and they lie in the grave without any distinction. So that no man can tell who is good, and who is bad by events which befall them in this life. And if one wicked man die in a palace, and another in a dungeon, they will meet in the congregation of the dead and damned; and the worm that dieth not, and the fire that is not quenched will be the same to both: which makes those differences inconsiderable, and not worth perplexing ourselves about.

27. Me - I know that your discourses, though they be of wicked, men in general, yet are particularly levelled at me.

29. Them - Any person that passes along the high-way, every one you meet with. It is so vulgar a thing, that no man of common sense is ignorant of it. Tokens - The examples, or evidences, of this truth, which they that go by the way can produce.

30. They - He speaks of the same person; only the singular number is changed into the plural, possibly to intimate, that altho' for the present only some wicked men were punished, yet then all of them should suffer. Brought - As malefactors are brought forth from prison to execution.

31. Declare - His power and splendour are so great, that scarce any man dare reprove him.

32. And - The pomp of his death shall be suitable to the glory of his life. Brought - With pomp and state, as the word signifies. Grave - Hebrew. to the graves; to an honourable and eminent grave: the plural number being used emphatically to denote eminency. He shall not die a violent but a natural death.

33. Valley - Of the grave, which is low and deep like a valley. Sweet - He shall sweetly rest in his grave. Draw - Hebrew. he shall draw every man after him, into the grave, all that live after him, whether good or bad, shall follow him to the grave, shall die as he did. So he fares no worse herein than all mankind. He is figuratively said to draw them, because they come after him, as if they were drawn by his example.

34. How - Why then do you seek to comfort me with vain hopes of recovering my prosperity, seeing your grounds are false, and experience shews, that good men are often in great tribulation, while the vilest of men prosper.

XXII

Eliphaz, checks Job for his complaints of God, ver. 1-4. Charges miseries on his sins, ver, 5-14. Compares his case to that of the old world, ver. 15-20. Assures him, that if he would return to God, he would shew him mercy, ver. 21-30.

2. Can, &c. - Why dost thou insist so much upon thy own righteousness, as if thou didst oblige God by it.

3. Is it - Such a pleasure as he needs for his own ease and contentment. Nay, God needs not us, or our services. We are undone, forever undone without him: but he is happy, forever happy without us.

4. Reprove - Punish thee. Because he is afraid, lest if he should let thee alone, thou wouldst grow too great and powerful for him: surely no. As thy righteousness cannot profit him, so thy wickedness can do him no hurt.

5. Evil - Is not thy evil, thy affliction, are not thy calamities procured by, and proportionable to thy sins.

6. Surely - He speaks thus by way of strong presumption, when I consider thy unusual calamities, I conclude thou art guilty of all, or some of these crimes. Brother - Of thy neighbour. Nought - Without sufficient and justifiable cause. Stripped - By taking their garment for a pledge, or by robbing them of their rights, all other injuries being comprehended under this.

8. Dwelt - Either by thy sentence or permission, he had a peaceable and sure possession of it, whether he had right to it, or no.

9. Arms - Their supports, and rights.

11. Or - Either thou art troubled with fear of further evils or with the gross darkness of thy present state of misery. Waters - Variety of sore afflictions, which are frequently compared to water.

12. Heaven - And from that high tower looketh down upon men, to behold, and govern, and recompense all their actions, whether good or bad. How high - Yet God is far higher than they, and from thence can easily see all things.

14. Walketh - His delight is in heaven, which is worthy of his care, but he will not burden himself with the care of earth: which was the opinion of many Heathen philosophers, and, as they fancied, was Job's opinion also.

15. Old way - Hebrew. the way of antiquity, of men living in ancient times, their end or success.

16. Out of - Before their time. A flood - Who, together with their foundation, the earth and all their supports and enjoyments in it, were destroyed by the general deluge.

17. Who - He repeats Job's words, chap. xxi, 14, 15, but to a contrary purpose. Job alleged them to shew that they prospered notwithstanding their wickedness; and Eliphaz produces them to shew that they were cut off for it.

18. Yet - Yet it is true, that for a time God did prosper them, but at last, cut them off in a tremendous manner, But - He repeals Job's words, chap. xxi, 16, not without reflection: thou didst say so, but against thy own principle, that God carries himself indifferently towards good and bad; but I who have observed God's terrible judgments upon wicked men, have much more reason to abhor their counsels.

20. Because - Because when wicked men are destroyed, they are preserved. He should have said their substance; but he changes the person, and saith, our substance; either as including himself in the member of righteous persons, and thereby intimating that he pleaded the common cause of all such, while Job pleaded the cause of the wicked, or because he would hereby thankfully acknowledge some eminent and particular preservation given to him amongst other righteous men. Remnant - All that was left undestroyed in the general calamity. Fire - Sodom and Gomorrah. As if he had said, thou mayest find here and there an instance, of a wicked man dying in peace. But what is that to the two great instances of the final perdition of ungodly men, the drowning the whole world, and the burning of Sodom and Gomorrah.

21. Him - With God, renew thy acquaintance with God by prayer, and repentance for all thy sins, and true humiliation under his hand, and hearty compliance with all his commands, and diligent care to serve and enjoy him. It is our honour, that we are made capable of this acquaintance, our misery that by sin we have lost it; our privilege, that through Christ we may return to it; and our unspeakable advantage, to renew and cultivate it. And be at peace - At peace with God, and at peace with thyself, not fretful or uneasy. Good shall come unto thee - All the good thou canst desire, temporal, spiritual, eternal.

22. Receive - Take the rule whereby thou governest thy thoughts, and words, and whole life, not from thy own imaginations or passions, but from God, from his law, which is written in thy own mind, and from the doctrines and instructions of the holy men of God. And do not only hear them with thine ears, but let them sink into thy heart.

23. If - The Hebrew phrase is emphatical, and implies a thorough turning from sin, to God, so as to love him, and cleave to him, and sincerely devote a man's self to his fear and service. Built - God will repair thy ruins, and give thee more children, and bless thee with prosperity. Thou shalt - It is either,

1. a spiritual promise, if thou dost sincerely repent, God will give the grace effectually to reform thyself and family: or,

2. a temporal promise, thou shalt put away iniquity, or the punishment of thy sins; as iniquity is very often used: far from thy tabernacles; from all thy dwellings, and tents, and possessions.

26. Lift up - Look up to him, with chearfulness and confidence.

27. Make - The word is, thou shalt multiply thy prayer. Under all thy burdens, in all thy wants, cares and fears, thou shalt send to heaven for wisdom, strength and comfort. Pay - Thou shalt obtain those blessings for which thou didst make vows to God, and therefore, according to thy obligation, shalt pay thy vows to him.

28. Established - Thy purposes shalt not be disappointed, but ratified by God. And in all thy counsels, and actions, God shall give thee the light of his direction and governance, and of comfort and success.

29. Cast down - All round about thee, in a time of general calamity. There is - God will deliver thee. He - God.

30. He, &c. - God will have so great a respect to thy innocency, that for thy sake he will deliver those that belong to thee, or live with thee, or near thee, thought in themselves they be ripe for destruction. Their hands - By thy prayers proceeding from a pure heart and conscience. So Eliphaz and his two friends, who in this matter were not innocent, were delivered by the pureness of Job's hands, chap. xlii, 8.

XXIII

Here seems to be a struggle throughout this chapter between nature and grace, Job complains of his condition, yet with an assurance of God's clemency, ver. 1-7. He cannot understand God's dealings, nor hope for relief, yet holds fast his integrity, ver. 8-14. He is in deep trouble, ver. 15-17.

2. Today - Even at this time, notwithstanding all your pretended consolations. Stroke - The hand or stroke of God upon me. Groaning - Doth exceed my complaints.

3. O - I desire nothing more than his acquaintance and presence; but alas, he hides his face from me. Seat - To his throne or judgment-seat to plead my cause before him.

5. Know - If he should discover to me any secret sins, for which he contendeth with me, I would humble myself before him, and accept of the punishment of mine iniquity.

6. No - He would not use his power against me, but for me; by enabling me to plead my cause, and giving sentence according to that clemency, which he uses towards his children.

7. There - At that throne of grace, where God lays aside his majesty, and Judges according to his wonted clemency. Dispute - Humbly propounding the grounds of their confidence. So - Upon such a fair and equal hearing. Delivered - From the damnatory sentence of God. This and some such expressions of Job cannot be excused from irreverence towards God, for which God afterwards reproves him, and Job abhorreth himself.

8. Is not - As a judge to hear and determine my causes, otherwise he knew God was essentially present in all places.

10. Gold - Which comes out of the furnace pure from all dross.

11. Steps - The steps or paths which God hath appointed men to walk in.

14. Performeth - Those calamities which he hath allotted to me. And - There are many such examples of God's proceeding with men.

16. Soft - He hath bruised, and broken, or melted it, so that I have no spirit in me.

17. Because - God did not cut me off by death. Before - These miseries came upon me. Covered - By hiding me in the grave.

XXIV

Job shews that open sinners are often prosperous, ver. 1-12. That secret sinners often pass undiscovered, ver. 13-18. That God punishes such by secret judgments, and reserves them for future judgment, ver. 19-25.

1. Why - Why (how comes it to pass) seeing times, (the fittest seasons for every, action, and particularly for the punishment of wicked men,) are not hidden from, or unknown to the Almighty God, (seeing all times, and men that live, and things that are done, or to be done in their times and seasons, are exactly known to God) do they that know him, (who love and obey him) not see (whence is it that they cannot discern) his (that is, God's) days? His times and seasons which he takes for the punishment of ungodly men; which if they were constant and fixed in this life, they would not be unknown to good men, to whom God uses to reveal his secrets.

3. Pledge - Contrary to God's law, first written in mens hearts, and afterwards in holy scripture, Exod. xxii, 26, 27.

4. Way - Out of the path or place in which these oppressors walk and range. They labour to keep out of their way for fear of their farther injuries. Hide - For fear of these tyrants.

5. Wild asses - Which are lawless, and fierce, and greedy of prey. Desert - Which is the proper habitation of wild asses. They - The oppressors. Go - To spoil and rob.

6. They - The oppressors. Wicked - Of such as themselves: so they promiscuously robbed all, even their brethren in iniquity.

7. Naked - Those whom they stripped of their garments and coverings.

8. Wet - With the rain-water, which runs down the rocks or mountains into the caves, to which they fled for shelter. Rock - Are glad when they can find a cleft of a rock in which they may have some protection against the weather.

9. They - The oppressors. Pluck - Out of covetousness; they will not allow the mother time for the suckling of her infant.

10. The sheaf - That single sheaf which the poor man had got with the sweat of his brow to satisfy his hunger.

11. Walls - Within the walls of the oppressors for their use. Suffer - Because they are not permitted to quench their thirst out of the wine which they make.

12. Groan - Under grievous oppressions. Soul - The life or blood of those who are wounded to death, as this word properly signifies, crieth aloud to God for vengeance. Yet - Yet God doth not punish

them.

13. Light - As well the light of reason and conscience, as the light of Divine Revelation, which was then in good measure imparted to the people of God, and shortly after committed to writing. Know not - They do not approve, nor love, or chuse them.

14. Poor - Where he finds nothing to satisfy his covetousness, he exercises his cruelty.

16. They - The robber: having on that occasion inserted the mention of the adulterer as one who acted his sin in the same manner as the night-thief did, he now returns to him again.

17. Is - Terrible and hateful.

18. Swift - That is, he quickly passeth away with all his glory, as the waters which never stay in one place, but are always hasting away. Portion - His habitation and estate which he left behind him. He - He shall never more see or enjoy his vineyards, or other pleasant places and things, which seem to be comprehended under this particular.

20. Womb - His mother that bare him in her womb. Wickedness - The wicked man. Broken - Broken to pieces, or violently broken down, as the word signifies. Tree - Which being once broken down never grows again.

21. He - He here returns to the declaration of his farther wickednesses, the cause of these judgments. Barren - Barrenness was esteemed a curse and reproach; and so he added affliction to the afflicted.

22. Draweth - Into his net.

23. Yet - Yet his eyes are upon their ways: although God gives them such strange successes, yet he sees and observes them all, and will in due time punish them.

24. The way - Out of this world. Other - They can no more prevent or delay their death, than the meanest men in the world. Corn - In its greatest height and maturity.

XXV

Bildad teaches us, to think highly and honourably of God, and to think meanly of ourselves, ver. 1-6.

1. Answered - Not to that which Job spake last, but to that which seemed most reprovable in all his discourses; his censure of God's proceedings with him, and his desire of disputing the matter with him. Perhaps Bildad and the rest now perceived that Job and they did not differ so much as they thought. They owned that the wicked might prosper for a while. And Job owned, they would be destroyed at the last.

2. Dominion - Sovereign power over all persons and things. Fear - Terror, that which justly makes him dreadful to all men, and especially to all that undertake to dispute with him. He - This clause, as well as the following verse, seems to be added to prove God's dominion and dreadfulness: he keepeth and ruleth all persons and things in heaven, in peace and harmony. The angels, though they be very numerous, all own his sovereignty, and acquiesce in his pleasure. The stars, tho' vast in their bulk, and various in their motions: exactly keep the order which God hath appointed them: and therefore it is great folly for thee to quarrel with the methods of God's dealings with thee.

3. Armies - Of the angels, and stars, and other creatures, all which are his hosts. Light - The light of the sun is communicated to all parts of the world. This is a faint resemblance, of the cognisance and care which God takes of the whole creation. All are under the light of his knowledge: all partake of the light of his goodness: his pleasure is to shew mercy: all the creatures live upon his bounty.

4. Man - The word signifies man that is miserable, which supposes him to be sinful; and shall such a creature quarrel with that dominion of God, to which the sinless, and happy, and glorious angels submit? God - Before God's tribunal, to which thou dost so boldly appeal.

5. Moon - The moon, tho' bright and glorious, if compared with the Divine Majesty, is without any lustre or glory. By naming the moon, and thence proceeding to the stars, the sun is also included.

6. Worm - Mean, and vile, and impotent; proceeding from corruption, and returning to it. The son - For miserable man in the last branch he here puts the son of any man, to shew that this is true even of the greatest and best of men. Let us then wonder at the condescension of God, in taking such worms into covenant and communion with himself!

XXVI

Job observes, that Bildad's discourse was foreign to the matter, ver. 1-4. Enlarges on the power and greatness of God, which yet are unsearchable, ver. 5-14.

4. *To whom* - For whose instruction hast thou uttered these things? For mine? Dost thou think I do not know, that which the meanest persons are not unacquainted with; that God is incomparably greater and better than his creatures? *Whose spirit* - Who inspired thee with this profound discourse of thine?

5. *Dead things* - Job having censured Bildad's discourse, proceeds to shew how little he needed his information in that point. Here he shews that the power and providences of God reaches not only to the things we see, but also to the invisible parts of the world, not only to the heavens above and their inhabitants, and to men upon earth, of which Bildad discoursed, chap. xxv, 2, 3, but also to such persons or things as are under the earth, or under the waters; which are out of our sight and reach; yet not out of the ken of Divine providence. These words may be understood; either,

1. of dead, or lifeless things, such as amber, pearl, coral, metals, or other minerals, which are formed or brought forth; by the almighty power of God, from under the waters; either in the bottom of the sea, or within the earth, which is the lowest element, and in the scripture and other authors spoken of as under the waters; this being observed as a remarkable work of God's providence, that the waters of the sea, which are higher than the earth, do not overwhelm it. Or,

2. of dead men, and of the worst of them, such as died in their sins, and after death were condemned to farther miseries; for of such this very word seems to be used, Prov. ii, 18; ix, 18, who are here said to mourn or groan from under the waters; from the lower parts of the earth, or from under those subterranean waters, which are supposed to be within and under the earth; Psalm xxxiii, 7, and from under the inhabitants thereof; either of the waters or of the earth, under which these waters are, or with the other inhabitants thereof; of that place under the waters, namely, the apostate spirits. So the sense is, that God's dominion is over all men, yea, even the dead, and the worst of them, who though they would not own God, nor his providence, while they lived, yet now are forced to acknowledge and feel that power which they despised, and bitterly mourn under the sad effects of it in their infernal habitations.

6. *Hell* - Is in his presence, and under his providence. Hell itself, that place of utter darkness, is not hid from his sight. *Destruction* - The place of destruction.

7. *North* - The northern part of the heavens, which is put for the whole visible heaven, because Job and his friends lived in a northern climate. *Nothing* - Upon no props or pillars, but his own power and providence.

9. *Holdeth* - From our view, that his glory may not dazzle our sight; he covereth it with a cloud. *Throne* - The heaven of heavens, where he dwelleth.

11. *Pillars* - Perhaps the mountains which by their height and strength seem to reach and support the heavens. *Astonished* - When God reproveth not them, but men by them, manifesting his displeasure by thunders, or earthquakes.

14. *Parts* - But small parcels, the outside and visible work. *Portion* - Of his power and wisdom, and providence. *His Power* - His mighty power, is aptly compared to thunder; in regard of its irresistible force, and the terror which it causes to wicked men.

XXVII

Job protests his integrity, ver. 1-6. And his dread of hypocrisy, ver. 7-10. Shews the miserable end of the wicked, notwithstanding their long prosperity, ver. 11-23.

1. *Parable* - His grave and weighty discourse.
2. *Who* - Though he knows my integrity, yet doth not plead my cause against my friends.
6. *Reproach* - With betraying my own cause and innocency.
7. *Let* - I am so far from practicing wickedness, that I abhor the thoughts of it, and if I would wish to be revenged of my enemy, I could wish him no greater mischief than to be a wicked man.
8. *Though* - Though they prosper in the world. God, as the judge takes it away, to be tried, and determined to its everlasting state. And what will his hope be then? It will be vanity and a lie; it will stand him in no stead.
10. *Delight* - When he has nothing else to delight in? No: his delight is in the things of the world, which now sink under him. And those who do not delight in God, will not always, will not long, call upon him.
12. *Have seen* - I speak what is confirmed by your own, as well as others experiences. *Vain* - To condemn me for a wicked man, because I am afflicted.
15. *Remain* - Who survive that sword and famine. *Widows* - For they had many wives. *Weep* -

Because they also, as well as other persons, groaned under their tyranny, and rejoice in their deliverance from it.

16. As clay - In great abundance.

18. A moth - Which settleth itself in a garment, but is quickly and unexpectedly dispossessed of its dwelling, and crushed to death. A booth - Which the keeper of a garden or vineyard suddenly rears up in fruit-time, and as quickly pulls down again.

19. Lie down - In death. Not gathered - Instead of that honourable interment with his fathers, his carcase shall lie like dung upon the earth. One openeth his eyes - That is, while a man can open his eyes, in the twinkling of an eye. He is as if he had never been, dead and gone, and his family and name extinct with him.

20. Terrors - From the sense of approaching death or judgment. Waters - As violently and irresistibly, as a river breaking its banks, or deluge of waters bears down all before it. A tempest - God's wrath cometh upon him like a tempest, and withal unexpectedly like a thief in the night.

21. East-wind - Some terrible judgment, fitly compared to the east-wind, which in those parts was most vehement, and pernicious. Carrieth him - Out of his palace wherein he expected to dwell forever; whence he shall be carried either by an enemy, or by death.

22. Cast - His darts or plagues one after another. Would flee - He earnestly desires to escape the judgments of God, but in vain. Those that will not be persuaded to fly to the arms of Divine grace, which are now stretched out to receive them, will not be able to flee from the arms of Divine wrath, which will shortly be stretched out to destroy them.

23. Clap - In token of their joy at the removal of such a publick pest, by way of astonishment: and in contempt and scorn, all which this gesture signifies in scripture use. His - In token of detestation and derision.

XXVIII

The wisdom of God in the works of nature, ver. 1-11. A wisdom like this cannot be found in man, neither can it be bought at any price, ver. 12-21. Death makes a report concerning it, ver. 22. It is hid in God, ver. 23-27. To fear God is man's wisdom, ver. 28.

1. Surely - Job having in the last chapter discoursed of God's various providences toward wicked men, and shewed that God doth sometimes, for a season, give them prosperity, but afterwards calls them to a sad account, and having shewed that God doth sometimes prosper the wicked all their days, so they live and die without any visible token of God's displeasure, when on the contrary, good men are exercised with many calamities; and perceiving that his friends were, scandalized at these methods of Divine providence, and denied the thing, because they could not understand the reason of such dispensations: in this chapter he declares that this is one of the depths of Divine wisdom, not discoverable by any mortal man, and that although men had some degree of wisdom whereby they could search out many hidden things, as the veins of silver, and gold, yet this was a wisdom of an higher nature, and out of man's reach. The caverns of the earth he may discover, but not the counsels of heaven.

3. Perfection - Whatever is deeply wrought in the deepest caverns. Stones of darkness - The precious stones which lie hid in the dark bowels of the earth, where no living thing can dwell.

4. Breaketh out - While men are searching, water breaks in upon them. Inhabitants - Out of that part of the earth which the miners inhabit. Forgotten - Untrodden by the foot of man. Dried up - They are dried up, (or, drawn up, by engines made for that purpose) from men, from the miners, that they may not be hindered in their work.

5. Fire - Coals, and brimstone, and other materials of fire. Unless this refer, as some suppose, to a central fire.

6. Sapphires - Of precious stones; the sapphire, is one of the most eminent, being put for all the rest. In some parts of the earth, the sapphires are mixed with stones, and cut out of them and polished. Hath - The earth continueth. Dust - Distinct from that gold which is found in the mass, both sorts of gold being found in the earth.

7. A path - In the bowels of the earth. Vulture's eye - Whose eye is very quick, and strong, and searcheth all places for its prey.

8. Lion - Which rangeth all places for prey. The birds and beasts have often led men to such places as otherwise they should never have found out; but they could not lead them to these mines, the finding out of them is a special gift of God.

9. He, &c. - This and the two next verses mention other eminent works of God, who overturneth rocks, and produceth new rivers.

10. Seeth - Even those which no human art or industry was ever able to discover. 12. That wisdom - Man hath one kind of wisdom, to discover the works of nature, and to perform the operations of art;

but as for that sublime wisdom which consists in the knowledge of God and ourselves, no man can discover this, but by the special gift of God.

13. Found - Among men upon earth, but only among those blessed spirits that dwell above.

14. The depth - This is not to be found in any part of the sea, though a man may dig or dive ever so deep to find it, nor to be learned from any creature.

20. Whence, &c. - By a diligent inquiry, we find at length, that there is a twofold wisdom; one hid in God, which belongs not to us, the other revealed to man, which belongs to us and to our children.

21. Hid - The line and plummet of human reason, can never fathom the abyss of the Divine counsels. Who can account for the maxims, measures and methods of God's government? Let us then be content, not to know the future events of providence, 'till time discover them: and not to know the secret reasons of providence, 'till eternity brings them to light.

22. Death - The grave, the place of the dead, to 'which these things are here ascribed, as they are to the depths, and to the sea, by a common figure. Though they cannot give an account of it themselves yet there is a world, on which these dark regions border, where we shall see it clearly. Have patience, says death: I will fetch thee shortly to a place where even this wisdom shall be found. When the veil of flesh is rent, and the interposing clouds are scattered, we shall know what God doth, though we know not now.

23. God - God alone. The way - The methods which he takes in the management of all affairs, together with its grounds and ends in them. The place - Where it dwells, which is only in his own mind.

24. For - He, and he only knows it, because his providence, is infinite and universal, reaching to all places, and times, past, present, and to come; whereas the most knowing men have narrow understandings, and the wisdom, and justice, and beauty of God's works are not fully seen 'till all the parts of them be laid together.

25. Winds - God managed them all by weight, appointing to every wind that blows, its season, its proportion, its bounds, when, and where, and how much, and how long each shall blow. He only doth all these things, and he only knows why he doth them. He instanceth in some few of God's works, and those which seem to be most trivial, and uncertain, that thereby he might more strongly imply that God doth the same in other things which are more considerable, that he doth all things in the most exact order, and weight, and measure. The waters - Namely, the rain-waters, which God layeth up in his store-houses, the clouds, and thence draws them forth, and sends them down upon the earth in such times and proportions as he thinks fit. Measure - For liquid things are examined by measure, as other things are by weight: and here is both weight and measure to signify with what perfect wisdom God governs the world.

26. When - At the first creation, when he settled that course and order which should be continued. A decree - An appointment and as it were a statute law, that it should fall upon the earth, in such times, and places, and proportions.

27. It - Wisdom, which is the subject of the present discourse. This God saw within himself; he looked upon it in his own mind, as the rule by which he would proceed in the creation and government of all things. Declare - Or reveal it. Prepared - He had it in readiness for doing all his works, as if he had been for a long time preparing materials for them. So it is a speech of God after the manner of men. Searched - Not properly; for so searching implies ignorance, and requires time and industry, all which is repugnant to the Divine perfections; but figuratively, he did, and doth, all things with that absolute and perfect wisdom, so exactly, and perfectly, as if he had bestowed a long time in searching, to find them out.

28. Man - Unto Adam in the day in which he was created. And in him, to all his posterity. Said - God spake it, at first to the mind of man, in which he wrote this with his own finger, and afterwards by the holy patriarchs, and prophets, and other teachers, whom he sent into the world to teach men true wisdom. Behold - Which expression denotes the great importance of this doctrine, and withal man's backwardness to apprehend it. The fear of the Lord - True religion. Wisdom - In man's wisdom, because that, and that only, is his duty, and safety, and happiness, both for this life and for the next. Evil - From sin, which is called evil eminently, as being the chief evil, and the cause of all other evils. Religion consists of two branches, doing good, and forsaking evil; the former is expressed in the former clause of this verse, and the latter in these words; and this is the best kind of knowledge or wisdom to which man can attain in this life. The design of Job in this close of his discourse, is not to reprove the boldness of his friends, in prying into God's secrets, and passing such a rash censure upon him, and upon God's carriage towards him; but also to vindicate himself from the imputation of hypocrisy, which they fastened upon him, by shewing that he had ever esteemed it to be his best wisdom, to fear God, and to depart from evil.

XXIX

Job, after pausing a little while, shews, what comfort he formerly had in his house and family, ver. 1-6. What honour and power he had in his country, ver. 7-10. What good he did as a magistrate, ver. 11-17. And what a prospect he had of the continuance of his prosperity, ver. 18-25

2. Preserved - From all those miseries which now I feel.

3. Darkness - I passed safely through many difficulties, and dangers, and common calamities.

7. Seat - When I caused the seat of justice to be set for me. By this, and several other expressions, it appears that Job was a magistrate. Street - In that open place, near the gate, where the people assembled for the administration of justice.

10. Cleaved - It lay as still as if he had done so.

11. Witness - Gave testimony to my pious, and just, and blameless conversation.

14. Put on, &c. - Perhaps he did not wear these: but his steady justice was to him instead of all those ornaments.

18. Multiply - See how apt even good men are, to set death at a distance from them!

20. Glory - My reputation was growing every day. Bow - My strength which is signified by a bow, Gen. xlix, 24; 1 Sam. ii, 4, because in ancient times the bow and arrows were the principal instruments of war.

22. Dropped - As the rain, which when it comes down gently upon the earth, is most acceptable and beneficial to it.

24. Laughed - Carried myself so familiarly with them, that they could scarce believe their eyes and ears. Cast not down - They were cautious not to give me any occasion to change my countenance towards them.

25. I chose - They sought to me for advice in all difficult cases, and I directed them what methods they should take. Sat - As a prince or judge, while they stood waiting for my counsel. A king - Whose presence puts life, and courage, into the whole army. As one - As I was ready to comfort any afflicted persons, so my consolations were always welcome to them.

XXX

Job's honour is turned into contempt, ver. 1-14. His prosperity, into fears, pains, and a sense of the wrath of God, ver. 15-22. He looks for nothing but death, ver. 23. And rest therein, ver. 24. Reflects on his former sympathy with the afflicted, ver. 25. And describes his own present calamities, ver. 26-31.

1. Younger - Whom both universal custom, and the light of nature, taught to reverence their elders and betters. Whose fathers - Whose condition was so mean, that in the opinion, of the world, they were unworthy to be my shepherds the companions of my dogs which watch my flocks.

3. Solitary - Although want commonly drives persons to places of resort for relief, yet they were so conscious of their own guilt, that they shunned company, and for fear or shame fled into, and lived in desolate places.

4. Who cut - Bitter herbs, which shews their extreme necessity. Juniper - Possibly the word may signify some other plant, for the Hebrew themselves are at a loss for the signification of the names of plants.

7. Brayed - Like the wild asses, for hunger or thirst. Thorns - Under which they hide themselves, that they might not be discovered when they are sought out for justice.

10. Spit - Not literally, for they kept far from him, but figuratively, they use all manner of reproachful expressions, even to my face. Herein, also we see a type of Christ, who was thus made a reproach of men, and despised of the people.

11. He - God. Cord - Hath slackened the string of my bow, and so rendered my bow and arrows useless; he hath deprived me of my strength or defense. Let loose - They cast off all former restraints of humanity, or modesty, and do those things before mine eyes, which formerly they trembled lest they should come to my ears.

12. Right hand - This was the place of adversaries or accusers in courts of justice. The youth - Hebrew. young striplings, who formerly hid themselves from my presence, chap. xxix, 8. Push - Metaphorically, they endeavour to overwhelm me. Ways - Cause- ways, or banks: so it is a metaphor from soldiers, who cast up banks, against the city which they besiege. Destruction - To destroy me.

13. Mar - As I am in great misery, so they endeavour to stop all my ways out of it. Set forward - Increasing it by their invectives, and censures. Even they - Who are themselves in a forlorn and miserable condition.

14. Waste place - In the waste place; in that part of the bank which was broken down. They rolled - As the waters, come rolling in at the breach.

15. Terrors - If he endeavoured to shake them off, they turned furiously upon him: if he endeavoured to out run them, they pursued his soul, as swiftly and violently as the wind.

20. I stand - I pray importunately and continually.

21. Turned - As if thou hadst changed thy very nature, which is kind, and merciful, and gracious.

22. Thou - Thou exposest me, to all sorts of storms and calamities; so that I am like chaff or stubble lifted up to the wind, and violently tossed hither and thither in the air. Substance - By which, my body is almost consumed, and my heart is melted within me.

23. House appointed - The grave is a narrow, dark, cold house, but there we shall rest and be safe. It is our home, for it is our mother's lap, and in it we are gathered to our fathers. It is an house appointed for us, by him that has appointed the bounds of all our habitations. And it is appointed for all living. It is the common receptacle for rich and poor: we must all be brought thither, and that shortly.

24. To the grave - The hand of God's wrath will not follow me beyond death; I shall then be safe and easy: Tho' men cry in his destruction: tho' most men cry and are affrighted, while they are dying, while the body is sinking into destruction; yet I desire it, I have nothing to fear therein, since I know that my redeemer liveth.

25. Did not I - Have I now judgment without mercy, because I afforded no mercy to others in misery? No; my conscience acquits me from this inhumanity: I did mourn over others in their miseries.

26. Upon me - Yet trouble came upon myself, when I expected it not.

27. Affliction - Came upon me suddenly, and unexpectedly, when I promised myself peace and prosperity.

28. Without the sun - Hebrew. black, not by the sun. My very countenance became black, tho' not by the sun, but by the force of my disease.

29. A brother - By imitation of their cries: persons of like qualities are often called brethren. Dragon - Which howl and wail mournfully in the deserts.

XXXI

Job's protestation of his innocence, with regard to wantonness, ver. 1-4. Fraud and injustice, ver. 5-8. Adultery, ver. 9-12. Haughtiness and severity toward his servants, ver. 13-15. Unmercifulness to the poor, ver. 16-23. Confidence in his wealth, ver. 24, 25. Idolatry, ver. 26-28. Revenge, ver. 29-31. Neglect of poor strangers, ver. 32 Hypocrisy, or not reproving others, ver. 33, 34. He wishes God would answer and that his words might be recorded, ver. 35-37. Protests his innocence, as to oppression, ver. 38-40.

1. I made - So far have I been from any gross wickedness, that I have abstained from the least occasions and appearances of evil.

2. For - What recompence may be expected from God for those who do otherwise. Above - How secretly soever unchaste persons carry the matter, so that men cannot reprove them, yet there is one who stands upon an higher place, whence he seeth in what manner they act.

5. Walked - Dealt with men. Vanity - With lying, or falsehood. Deceit - If when I had an opportunity of enriching myself, by wronging others, I have readily and greedily complied with It.

6. Let me - I desire nothing more than to have my heart and life weighed in just balances, and searched out by the all-seeing God. That God - Or, and he will know; (upon search he will find out: which is spoken of God after the manner of men:) Mine integrity - So this is an appeal to God to be witness of his sincerity.

7. Heart - If I have let my heart loose to covet forbidden things, which mine eyes have seen: commonly sin enters by the eye into the heart. A blot - Any unjust gain.

8. Increase - All my plants, and fruits, and improvements.

10. Then - Not as if Job desired this; but that if God should give up his wife to such wickedness, he should acknowledge his justice in it.

11. This - Adultery. It is - Hebrew. an iniquity of the Judges; which belongs to them to take cognizance of, and to punish, even with death; and that not only by the law of Moses, but even by the law of nature, as appears from the known laws and customs of the Heathen nations.

12. Destruction - Lust is a fire in the soul; it consumes all that is good there, the convictions, the comforts; and lays the conscience waste. It consumes the body, consumes the substance, roots out all the increase. It kindles the fire of God's wrath, which if not quenched by the blood of Christ, will burn to the lowest hell.

16. If I - Denied them what they desired of me. To fail - With tedious expectation of my justice or charity. Job is most large upon this head, because in this matter Eliphaz had most particularly accused him.

18. Youth - As soon as I was capable of managing mine own affairs. With me - Under my care. A father - With all the diligence and tenderness of a father. Her - The widow mentioned ver. 16. From -

From my tender years; ever since I was capable of discerning good and evil.

19. Perish - When it was in my power to help them.

21. When - When I saw I could influence the Judges to do what I pleased.

23. For - I stood in awe of God and of his judgments. I could not - I knew myself unable either to oppose his power, or to bear his wrath. Even good men have need to restrain themselves from sin, with the fear of Destruction from God. Even when salvation from God is a comfort to us, yet destruction from God should be a terror to us. Adam in innocency was awed by a threatning.

26. I - This place speaks of the worship of the host of heaven, and especially of the sun and moon, the most eminent and glorious of that number, which was the most ancient kind of idolatry, and most frequent in the eastern countries. Shined - In its full strength and glory.

27. Kissed - In token of worship, whereof this was a sign.

28. The judge - The civil magistrate; who being advanced and protected by God, is obliged to maintain and vindicate his honour, and consequently to punish idolatry. Denied God - Not directly but by consequence, because this was to rob God of his prerogative, by giving to the creature, that worship which is peculiar to God.

29. Lift up - Hebrew. stirred up myself to rejoice and insult over his misery.

31. If - My domesticks and familiar friends. His flesh - This is farther confirmation of Job's charitable disposition to his enemy. Although all who were daily conversant with him, and were witnesses of his and their carriage, were so zealous in Job's quarrel, that they protested they could eat their flesh, and could not be satisfied without. Yet he restrained both them and himself from executing vengeance upon them.

33. As Adam - As Adam did in Paradise.

34. Did I fear - No: all that knew Job knew him to be a man of resolution, that boldly appeared, spoke and acted, in defense of religion and justice. He durst not keep silence, or stay within, when called to speak or act for God. He was not deterred by the number, or quality, or insults of the injurious, from reproving them, and doing justice to the injured.

35. Had written - Had given me his charge written in a book or paper, as the manner was in judicial proceedings. This shews that Job did not live, before letters were in use. And undoubtedly the first letters were those wrote on the two tables, by the finger of God. He wishes, his friends, who charged him with hypocrisy, would draw up the charge in writing.

36. Take it - As a trophy or badge of honour.

37. Him - My judge, or adversary. My steps - The whole course of my life. A prince - With undaunted courage and confidence.

38. Cry - Because I have gotten it by fraud or violence.

39. Without money - Either without paying the price for the land, or by defrauding my workmen of their wages. Life - Killing them that I might have undisturbed possession of it, as Ahab did Naboth.

XXXII

Some account of Elihu, and his sentiments concerning the dispute between Job and his friends, ver. 1-5. He excuses his own youth, ver. 6-10. and pleads, that he had heard all they had to say, ver. 11-13. That he had something new to offer, ver. 14-17. Could not refrain from speaking, ver. 18-20. And would speak impartially, ver. 21, 22.

1. Because - So they said: but they could not answer him.

2. The Buzite - Of the posterity of Buz, Nahor's son, Gen. xxii, 21. Ram - Or, of Aram; for Ram and Aram are used promiscuously; compare 2 Kings viii, 28; 2 Chron. xxii, 5. His pedigree is thus particularly described, partly for his honour, as being both a wise and good man, and principally to evidence the truth of this history. He justified - Himself not without reflection upon God, as dealing severely with him, he took more care to maintain his own innocency, than God's glory. The word Elihu signifies, my God is he. They had all tried in vain to convince Job: but my God is he who both can and will do it.

3. No answer - To Job's arguments as to the main cause. Condemned - As a bad man.

4. 'Till Job - And his three friends.

6. Afraid - Of being thought forward and presumptuous.

8. Spirit - The spirit of God. Giveth - To whom he pleaseth.

9. Judgment - What is just and right.

12. Convinced - By solid and satisfactory answers.

13. Left - God thus left you to your own weakness, lest you should ascribe the conquering or silencing of Job to your own wisdom. God - This is alleged by Elihu, in the person of Job's three friends; the sense is, the judgments which are upon Job, have not been brought upon him by man originally, but by the hand of God, for his gross, though secret sins: but, saith Elihu, this argument doth

not satisfy me, and therefore bear with me if I seek for better.

19. Bottles - Bottles of new wine.

22. I know not - The more closely we eye the majesty of God as our maker, the more we dread his wrath and justice, the less danger shall we be in of a sinful fearing or flattering of men.

XXXIII

Elihu offers himself to Job as the person he had so often wished for, ver. 1-7. He charges him with reflecting upon God, ver. 8-11. He aggravates this by shewing him God's sovereign power over man, and the various means he uses to do him good, ver. 12-14. Particularly dreams, ver. 15-18. And sickness, ver. 19- 30. He requests Job to answer him, or let him go on, ver. 31-33

3. My words - I will not speak passionately or partially, but from a sincere desire to do thee good. Clearly - What I speak will be plain, not hard to be understood.

4. Life - I am thy fellow creature, and am ready to discourse with thee upon even terms, according to thy desire.

6. Behold - I will plead with thee in God's name and stead, which thou hast often wished, and I am God's creature like thyself.

9. Clean - Not absolutely, for he often confesses himself to be a sinner, but no such transgression, as might give God just occasion to punish him so severely, as is implied, where he blames God for finding occasions against him, implying that he had given him none by his sins. And thus far Elihu's charge was just, and herein it differs from the charge of Job's three friends, who often accuse him, for asserting his own innocency; although they did it, because they thought him an hypocrite, whereas Elihu does it upon other grounds, even because Job's justification of himself was accompanied with reflections upon God.

11. Marketh - He narrowly prys into all my actions, that he may find matter against me.

12. Not just - Thou art in the wrong. Greater - Not only in power and majesty, but also in justice, and wisdom, and goodness, and therefore thou dost foolishly, in censuring his judgments, thou castest off that awe and reverence which thou shouldest constantly maintain towards thy sovereign Lord.

13. He - Useth not to give an account to his creatures of the grounds and reasons of his judgments or dispensations as being the supreme governor of all persons and things, in whose will it becometh all men to acquiesce.

14. Yet - Although he doth not give men an account of his matters, yet he doth that which is sufficient for them. Twice - When once speaking doth not awaken men, God is graciously pleased to give them another admonition: though he will not gratify men's curiosity in enquiring into his hidden judgments, yet he will acquaint them with their duty. God speaks to us by conscience, by providence, and by ministers, of all which Elihu here treats at large, to shew Job, that God was now telling him his mind, and endeavouring to do him good. He shews first, how God admonishes men by their own consciences.

16. Sealeth - He imprints those instructions upon their minds.

17. Pride - And God by this means is said to hide pride from man, because by these glorious representations of his Divine majesty to man, he takes him off from the admiration of his own excellency, and brings him to a sight of his own weakness, and to an humble and ready submission to his will.

18. Keepeth - By his gracious admonitions whereby he leads him to repentance.

19. Pain - The second way whereby God instructs men and excites them to repentance.

22. The destroyers - The pangs of death, here called the destroyers, are just ready to seize him.

23. A messenger - A prophet or teacher. To expound the providence, and point out the design of God therein. One, &c. - A person rightly qualified for this great and hard work, such as there are but very few. To shew - To direct him to the right way how he may please God, and procure that mercy which he thirsts after; which is not by quarrelling with God, but by an humble confession. and supplication for mercy through Christ the redeemer.

24. He - God. A ransom - Although I might justly destroy him, yet I will spare him, for I have found out a way of ransoming sinners from death, which is the death of my son, the redeemer of the world, and with respect to which I will pardon them that repent and sue for mercy. Observe how God glories in the invention! I have found, I have found a ransom; a ransom for poor, undone sinners! I, even I am he that hath done it.

26. Render - He will deal with him as with one reconciled to him through the mediator, and turning from sin to righteousness.

28. Life - His life which was endangered, shall be restored and continued. Yea, farther, God shall Deliver his soul from going into the pit of hell: and his life shall see the light, all good, in the vision and fruition of God.

29. Lo - All these ways God uses to convince, and save sinners.

30. To bring - That he may save men from being forever miserable, and make them forever happy. "Lord, what is man, that thou shouldest thus visit him? This should engage us, to comply with God's designs, to work with him for our own good, and not to counter-work him. And this will render those that perish inexcusable, that, so much was done to save them, and they would not be healed." So Mr. Henry. Excellent words! But how much did God do to save them? Did he ever do any thing to save them? Did he ever design to save them? If not, how does that which was never done, no nor designed, "render them inexcusable?"

XXXIV

Elihu proceeding bespeaks the attention of the company, ver. 1-4. Charges Job with other indecent expressions, ver. 5-9. Shews God's justice, sovereignty, power, omniscience, ver. 10-25. His severity against sinners, ver. 26-28. His over-ruling providence, ver. 29, 30. Teaches Job what he ought to say, ver. 31, 32. Appeals to his own conscience, and concludes with reproving him for murmuring, ver. 33-37.

2. Ear - The ear, is put for the mind to which things are conveyed by it.

4. Let us - Not contend for victory, but for truth and equity. Know - Let us shew one another who hath the best cause.

5. Said - I am so far righteous, that I have not deserved, such hard usage from God. Had taken - So Job had said, chap. xxvii, 2, he denies me that which is just and equal, to give me a fair hearing.

6. Should I lie - So Job had said in effect, chap. xxvii, 4, 5, 6, should I falsely accuse myself of sins of which I am not guilty? Without transgression - Without any such crying, sin, as might reasonably bring down such terrible judgments upon my head.

7. Like water - Abundantly and greedily: who doth so break forth into scornful expressions, not only against his friends, but in some sort against God himself.

8. Who goeth - Although I dare not say, that he is a wicked man, yet in this matter he speaks and acts like one of them.

9. He said - Not in express terms, but by consequence; because he said that good men were no less, nay, sometimes more miserable here than the wicked.

12. Pervert - As Job hath affirmed.

13. Who - Who or where is his superior that made the world, and, then delivered the government of it to God? God himself is the sole creator, the absolute Lord of all, and therefore cannot do unjustly: because the creator and Lord of the world must needs have all possible perfections in himself, and amongst others, perfect justice. Disposed - Or, committed, to him, to be governed by him, in the name, of his Lord, to whom he must give an account.

15. All - The design of this and the foregoing verse is the same with that of ver. 13, namely, to declare God's absolute and uncontrollable sovereignty over all men.

17. Shall he - That is unrighteous. Govern - Elihu's argument is the same with that of Abraham, Gen. xviii, 25, and that of St. Paul, Rom. iii, 5, 6. If God be unrighteous, how shall he judge or govern the world? And the argument is undeniable: if God were unjust, there would be nothing but injustice and confusion in the world, whereas we see there is a great deal of justice administered in the world, and all this must proceed from him who is the fountain of all justice, and rule, and authority. And he that makes men just, shall he be unjust? Most just - God, who hath given so many clear and unquestionable evidences of his justice, in giving just and holy laws, in encouraging and rewarding righteous persons in this life, and inflicting dreadful judgments upon tyrants and oppressors.

18. Wicked - Though a king may be wicked, yet his subjects neither may nor dare call him so.

21. For - God doth not destroy either prince or people unjustly, no nor out of his mere pleasure, but for their sins, which he sees exactly, although they use all possible arts to hide them.

26. As - Because they are wicked men. In the open light - In publick view for their greater shame, and for the greater glory of his justice.

28. Cry of the poor - Their case is bad, who have the prayers and tears of the poor against them: for these will draw down vengeance sooner or later, on the heads of their oppressors.

29. Whether - God can carry on his work either of mercy or justice, as irresistible upon an whole nation as upon one particular person.

30. Reign not - May not continue his tyranny, lest the people be ensnared, lest the people should be longer kept in the snares of oppression; God doth this to free poor oppressed people from the snares which ungodly men lay for them.

32. That - The secret sins which I cannot discover, manifest thou to me.

33. Should it be - Doth God need thy advice how to govern the world, and whom, and when to reward or punish? Refuse - To submit as is expressed, ver. 32. Therefore - If thou canst say any thing

for thyself, I am ready to hear thy defense.

34. Let - I am content that any wise man should judge of my words, and let such consider what I say.

36. End - Throughly and exactly, 'till the cause be brought to an issue. Wicked men - On their behalf; he hath put arguments into their mouths against God and his providence.

37. Addeth - He sinned before, by impatience under his afflictions, now he is grown obstinate, and instead of humbling himself for his sins, justifies himself, and accuses the blessed God. Clapped - Insulting and triumphing. Against God - In effect, though not directly.

XXXV

Our righteousness profits ourselves, not God, ver. 1-7. Our wickedness hurts not him, but other men, whom God would help, if they cried to him sincerely, ver. 8-13. Why he delayed to help Job, ver. 14-16.

2. Thou saidst - Not that Job said this in express terms, but he said those things from which this might seem to follow, as that God had punished him more than he deserved.

3. Thou saidst - Another imputation upon God. Unto thee - Unto me; such changes of persons being frequent in the Hebrew language. What profit, &c. - God does not reward so much as I deserve. But it was not fair to charge this upon Job, which he had neither directly nor indirectly affirmed.

5. Clouds, &c. - They are far above us, and God is far above them. How much then is he out of the reach either of our sins or our services?

9. Cry - Thus one man's wickedness may hurt another.

10. None - Few or none of the great numbers of oppressed persons. God - They cry out to men, but they seek not God, and therefore if God do not hear their cries it is not unjust. Maker - Who alone made me, and who only can deliver me. Who when our condition is ever so dark and sad, can turn our darkness into light, can quickly put a new song in our mouth, a thanksgiving unto our God.

11. Who - This is an aggravation of mens neglect of God in their misery. God hath given men, what he hath denied to beasts, wisdom to know God and themselves. Therefore they are inexcusable, for not using that wisdom, by calling on God in the time of trouble.

12. Because - God doth not answer their cries, because they are both evil, wicked and impenitent, and proud, unhumbled for those sins for which God brought these miseries upon them.

13. Vanity - Vain persons, that have no wisdom or piety in them.

14. See him - Thou canst not understand his dealings with thee. Here Elihu answers another objection of Job's: and tells him that though God may for a season delay to answer, yet he will certainly do him right. Judgment - Justice is at his tribunal, and in all his ways and administrations. Trust - Instead of murmuring, repent of what is past, humble thyself under God's hand, wait patiently in his way, 'till deliverance come; for it will certainly come if thou dost not hinder it.

15. Because - Because Job doth not acknowledge God's justice and his own sins. He - God. Anger - Hath laid grievous afflictions upon him. He - Job is not sensible of it, so as to be humbled under God's hand.

XXXVI

Elihu desires a farther hearing, ver. 1-4. Describes the methods of providence, ver. 5-15. Warns and counsels Job, ver. 16-21. Shews God's sovereignty and omnipotence, ver. 22-33.

3. Afar - From remote times, and places, and things. I will not confine my discourse to thy particular case, but wilt justify God by declaring his great and glorious works of creation and providence both in the heaven and in the earth, and the manner of his dealing with men in other parts and ages of the world. Ascribe - I will clear and maintain this truth, that God is righteous in all his ways.

4. He, &c. - Thou hast to do with a God of perfect knowledge, by whom all thy words and actions are weighed.

5. Despiseth - His greatness doth not make him (as it doth men) despise, or oppress the meanest. Wisdom - His strength is guided by wisdom, and therefore cannot do any thing unbecoming God, or unjust to his creatures.

6. But - He will certainly in his time deliver his oppressed ones.

7. He - Never ceases to care for and watch over them. Exalted - They continue to be exalted; they are not cast down from their dignity, as the wicked commonly are.

8. If - Through the vicissitude of worldly affairs, they are brought from their throne into a prison, as sometimes hath been done.

9. Work - Their evil works, by these afflictions he brings them to a sight of their sins. Exceeded -

John Wesley

That they have greatly sinned by abusing their power and prosperity; which even good men are too prone to do.

10. *Openeth* - He inclines them to hearken to what God speaks by the rod.

13. *Cry not* - Unto God for help. *Bindeth* - With the cords of affliction.

14. *Die* - They provoke God to cut them off before their time. *Unclean* - Or, Sodomites; to whose destruction, he may allude. They shall die by some exemplary stroke of Divine vengeance. Yea, and after death, their life is among the unclean, the unclean spirits, the devil and his angels, forver excluded from the new Jerusalem, into which no unclean thing shall enter.

15. *Openeth* - Causeth them to hear, and understand, and do, the will of God.

16. *He would* - If thou hadst opened thine ear to God's counsels. *Into* - A state of ease and freedom.

17. *The judgment* - Or, the sentence, thou hast justified the hard speeches which wicked men utter against God. *Therefore* - Therefore the just judgment of God takes hold on thee. Thou hast maintained their cause against God, and God passes against thee the sentence of condemnation due to wicked men.

18. *Wrath* - Conceived by God against thee. *Then* - If once God's wrath take hold of thee, no ransom will be accepted for thee.

19. *Thy riches* - If thou hadst as much of them as ever. *Forces* - The strongest forces.

20. *The night* - The night of death, which Job had often desired, for then, thou art irrecoverably gone: take heed of thy foolish and often repeated desire of death, lest God inflict it upon thee in anger.

21. *Chosen* - Thou hast chosen rather to quarrel with God, and censure his judgments, than quietly to submit to them.

22. *Behold* - God is omnipotent; and therefore can, either punish thee far worse, or deliver thee, if thou dost repent. He is also infinitely wise; and as none can work like him, so none can teach like him. Therefore do not presume to teach him how to govern the world. None teacheth with such authority and convincing evidence, with such condescension and compassion, with such power and efficacy as God doth, he teaches by the bible, and that is the best book; by his son, and he is the best master.

24. *Remember* - Call to mind this thy duty. *Magnify* - Every work which he doth; do not condemn any of his providential works, but adore them as done with admirable wisdom, and justice. *Behold* - With admiration and astonishment.

25. *It* - The power, and wisdom, and greatness of God are so manifest in all his works, that all who are not stupid, must see and acknowledge it. *Afar off* - The works of God are so great and conspicuous, that they may be seen at a great distance. Hence Elihu proceeds to give some instances, in the works of nature and common providence. His general aim is to shew,

1. That God is the first cause and supreme director of all the creatures; whom therefore we ought with all humility and reverence to adore,

2. That it is presumption in us to prescribe to him in his special providence toward men, when the operations even of common providence about the meteors, are so mysterious and unaccountable.

26. *Neither* - He is eternal, as in his being, so in all his counsels; which therefore must be infinitely above the comprehension of short-lived men.

27. *For* - Having affirmed that God's works are incomprehensibly great and glorious, he now proves it from the most common works of nature and providence. And hence he leaves it to Job to consider how much more deep and inconceivable the secret counsels of God must be. *Water* - He orders matters so wisely, that the waters which are in the clouds, do not fall down at once in spouts, which would be pernicious to the earth and to mankind; but by degrees, and in drops. *According* - According to the proportion of vapors which the heat of the sun hath drawn up by the earth or sea. So it notes that great work of God by which the rain is first made of vapors, and afterwards resolved into vapors, or into the matter of succeeding vapors, by a constant rotation.

29. *Understand* - Whence it comes to pass, that a small cloud, no bigger than a man's hand, suddenly spreads over the whole heavens: how the clouds come to be suddenly gathered, and so condensed as to bring forth thunder and lightning. *Noise* - The thunder produced in the clouds, which are often called God's tent or tabernacle.

30. *Light* - The lightning; fitly God's light, because God only can light it. *It* - Upon the cloud, which is in a manner the candlestick in which God sets up this light. *The sea* - The lightning spreads far and wide over all the parts of the sea, and pierceth deep, reaching even to the bottom of it.

31. *Judgeth* - By thunder and lightning, and rain from the clouds, he executes his judgments against ungodly people. *Meat* - Giveth meat. By the same clouds, he provides plentiful showers dropping fatness on the earth.

32. *Clouds* - With thick and black clouds spread over the whole heavens. *Light* - The sun. *The cloud* - Which God interposes as a veil between the sun and earth.

33. *The noise* - The thunder gives notice of the approaching rain. *Also* - And as the thunder, so also the cattle sheweth, concerning the vapor, concerning the coming of the rain, by a strange instinct, seeking for shelter, when a change of weather is near.

XXXVII

Elihu observes the hand of God, in thunder and lighting, ver. 1-5. In frost and snow, rain and wind, ver. 6-13. Challenges Job to account for these, ver. 14-22. Concludes, that God is great and greatly to be feared, ver. 23,

2. Hear - It is probable that while Elihu was speaking it thundered, and that tempest was begun, wherewith God ushered in his speech. And this might occasion his return to that subject of which he had discoursed before. Voice - The thunder is called God's voice. Because by it God speaks to the children of men, to fear before him. Mouth - That is produced by God's word or command, which is often signified by his mouth.

3. Directeth - His voice: which he guideth like an arrow to the mark, that it may do that work for which he sends it.

4. After - After the lightning, which is seen before the thunder is hard. Them - The lightnings spoken of in the beginning of the verse.

6. Strength - Those storms of rain which come with great force and irresistible violence.

7. Sealeth - By these snows and rains he drives men out of the fields, and seals or binds up their hands from their work. That - They may seriously contemplate on these, and other great and glorious works of God.

9. Cold - Freezing winds.

10. The waters - The waters which had freely spread themselves before, are congealed and bound up in crystal fetters.

11. Watering - The earth. They spend themselves and are exhausted watering the earth, until they are weary. Wearieth - Them with much water, and making them to go long journeys to water remote parts, and at last to empty themselves there: all which things make men weary; and therefore are here said to make the clouds weary by a common figure. Scattereth - As for the white and lightsome clouds, he scatters and dissolves them by the wind or sun.

12. Turned - The clouds are carried about to this or that place. Not by chance (though nothing seems to be more casual than the motions of the clouds) but by his order and governance.

13. Correction - To scourge or correct men by immoderate showers. Earth - The whole earth, which is said to be the Lord's, Psalm xxiv, 1; l, 12, and so this may denote a general judgment by excessive rains inflicted upon the earth, and all its inhabitants, even the universal deluge, which came in great measure out of the clouds. Mercy - For the benefit of mankind and for the cooling of the air and improving the fruits of the earth.

14. Consider - If there be so much matter of wonder in the most obvious works of God, how wonderful must his secret counsels be?

15. Them - The things before mentioned, the clouds, rain, snow, and other meteors. Did God acquaint thee with his counsels in the producing and ordering of them? His cloud - Probably the rainbow, seated in a cloud, which may well be called God's cloud, because therein God puts his bow, Gen. ix, 13.

16. Balancings - How God doth as it were weigh the clouds in balances, so that although they are full of water, yet they are kept up by the thin air.

17. Quieteth - The air about the earth. From the south - By the sun's coming into the southern parts, which makes the air quiet and warm.

18. With him - Wast thou his assistant in spreading out the sky like a canopy over the earth? Strong - Which though it be very thin and transparent, yet is also firm and compact and steadfast. Looking glass - Made of brass and steel, as the manner then was. Smooth and polished, without the least flaw. In this, as in a glass, we may behold the glory of God and the wisdom of his handy-work.

19. Teach us - If thou canst. Say unto him - Of these things. Order - To maintain discourse with him, both because of the darkness of the matter, God's counsels being a great depth; and because of the darkness of our minds.

20. Shall - I send a challenge to God, or a message that I am ready to debate with him concerning his proceedings? Speak - If a man should be so bold to enter the lists with God. Swallowed up - With the sense of his infinite majesty.

21. Light - The sun; which is emphatically called light, and here the bright light: which men cannot behold or gaze on, when the sky is very clear: and therefore it is not strange if we cannot see God, or discern his counsels and ways. Them - The sky by driving away those clouds which darkened it.

22. North - From the northern winds which scatter the clouds, and clear the sky. Elihu concludes with some short, but great sayings, concerning the glory of God. He speaks abruptly and in haste, because it should seem, he perceived God was approaching, and presumed he was about to take the work into his own hands.

23. Find - We cannot comprehend him: his power, wisdom, justice, and his counsels proceeding

from them are past our finding out. Power - Therefore as he doth not need any unrighteous action to advance himself, so he cannot do it, because all such things are acts of weakness. Judgment - In the just administration of judgment, he never did, nor can exercise that power unjustly, as Job seemed to insinuate. Afflict - Without just cause.

24. Fear - Fear or reverence him, and humbly submit to him, and not presume to quarrel or dispute with him. Wise of heart - Wise in their own eyes.

XXXVIII

God begins with an awakening challenge, ver. 1-3. Proceeds to several proofs of Job's inability to contend with him, because of his ignorance and weakness: for he knew nothing of the founding of the earth, ver. 4-7. The limiting of the sea, ver. 8- 11. Of the morning light, ver. 12-15. The recesses of the sea and earth, ver. 16-21. Of the treasures in the clouds, ver. 22-27. He could do nothing toward the making of his own soul, the producing of rain, frost, lightning, or the directing of the stars and their influences, ver. 28-38. He could not provide for the lions or the ravens, ver. 39-41. How then should he direct God's secret counsels? Here God takes up the argument, begun by Elihu, and prosecutes it in inimitable words, exceeding his, and all other mens in the loftiness of the style, as much as thunder does a whisper.

1. Lord - The eternal word, Jehovah, the same who spake from Mount Sinai. Answered - Out of a dark and thick cloud, from which he sent a tempestuous wind, as the harbinger of his presence. In this manner God appears and speaks to awaken Job and his friends, to the more serious attention to his words; and to testify his displeasure both against Job, and them, that all of them might be more deeply humbled and prepared to receive, and retain the instructions which God was about to give them.

2. Counsel - God's counsel. For the great matter of the dispute between Job and his friends, was concerning God's counsel and providence in afflicting Job; which Job had endeavoured to obscure and misrepresent. This first word which God spoke, struck Job to the heart. This he repeats and echoes to, chap. xlii, 3, as the arrow that stuck fast in him.

3. Gird up - As warriors then did for the battle.

4. Where - Thou art but of yesterday; and dost thou presume to judge of my eternal counsels! When - When I settled it as firm upon its own center as if it had been built upon the surest foundations.

5. Measures - Who hath prescribed how long and broad and deep it should be. Line - the measuring line to regulate all its dimensions.

6. Foundations - This strong and durable building hath no foundations but God's power, which hath marvelously established it upon itself. Cornerstone - By which the several walls are joined and fastened together, and in which, next to the foundations, the stability of a building consists. The sense is, who was it that built this goodly fabrick, and established it so firmly that it cannot be moved.

7. Stars - The angels, who may well be called morning-stars, because of their excellent lustre and glory. Sons of God - The angels called the sons of God, because they had their whole being from him, and because they were made partakers of his Divine and glorious image. Shouted - Rejoiced in and blessed God for his works, whereby he intimates, that they neither did advise or any way assist him, nor dislike or censure any of his works, as Job had presumed to do.

8. Doors - Who was it, that set bounds to the vast and raging ocean, and shut it up, as it were with doors within its proper place, that it might not overflow the earth? Break forth - From the womb or bowels of the earth, within which the waters were for the most part contained, and out of which they were by God's command brought forth into the channel which God had appointed for them.

9. The cloud - When I covered it with vapors and clouds which rise out of the sea, and hover above it, and cover it like a garment. Darkness - Black and dark clouds. Swaddling band - Having compared the sea to a new-born infant, he continues the metaphor, and makes the clouds as swaddling-bands, to keep it within its bounds: though indeed neither clouds, nor air, nor sands, nor shores, can bound the sea, but God alone.

10. Break up - Made those hollow places in the earth, which might serve for a cradle to receive and hold this great and goodly infant when it came out of the womb. And set - Fixed its bounds as strongly as if they were fortified with bars and doors.

12. Morning - Didst thou create the sun, and appoint the order and succession of day and night. Since - Since thou wast born: this work was done long before thou wast born. To know - To observe the punctual time when, and the point of the heavens where it should arise; which varies every day.

13. That - That this morning light should in a moment spread itself, from one end of the hemisphere to the other. Shaken - From the face of the earth. And this effect the morning-light hath upon the wicked, because it discovers them, whereas darkness hides them; and because it brings them to condign punishment, the morning being the usual time for executing judgment.

14. It - The earth. Turned - Is changed in its appearance. By the seal - The seal makes a beautiful

impression upon the clay, which in itself hath no form, or comeliness. So the earth, which in the darkness of night lies like a confused heap without either form or beauty, when the light arises and shines upon it, appears in excellent order and glory. They - The men and things of the earth, whether natural, as living creatures, herbs and trees; or artificial, as houses or other buildings. Stand - Present themselves to our view. Garment - Wherewith the earth is in a manner clothed and adorned.

15. Withheld - That light which enjoyed by others is withholden from them, either by their own choice, because they chuse darkness rather than light; or by the judgment of God, or the magistrate, by whom they are cut off from the light of the living. Arms - Their great strength which they used to the oppression of others.

16. Springs - Hebrew. the tears; the several springs out of which the waters of the sea flow as tears do from the eyes. Walked - Hast thou found out the utmost depth of the sea, which in divers places could never be reached by the wisest mariner? And how then canst thou fathom the depths of my counsels?

17. Death - Hast thou seen, or dost thou know the place and state of the dead; the depths and bowels of that earth in which the generality of dead men are buried. Death is a grand secret? We know not when or by what means we shall be brought to death: by what road we must go the way, whence we shall not return. We cannot describe what death is; how the knot is untied between soul and body, or how the spirit goes "To be we know not what, and live we know not how." With what dreadful curiosity does the soul launch out into an untried abyss? We have no correspondence with separate souls, nor any acquaintance with their state. It is an unknown, undiscovered region, to which they are removed. While we are here in a world of sense, we speak of the world of spirits, as blind men do of colours, and when we remove thither, shall be amazed to find how much we were mistaken.

18. Breadth - The whole compass and all the parts of it?

19. Dwelleth - Hath its constant and settled abode. Whether goes the sun when it departs from this hemisphere? Where is the tabernacle and the chamber in which he is supposed to rest? And seeing there was a time when there was nothing but gross darkness upon the face of the earth, what way came light into the world? Which was the place where light dwelt at that time, and whence was it fetched? And whence came that orderly constitution and constant succession of light and darkness? Was this thy work? Or wast thou privy to it, or a counsellor, or assistant in it?

20. Take it - Bring or lead it: and this it refers principally to the light, and to darkness, as the consequent of the other. Bound - Its whole course from the place of its abode whence it is supposed to come, to the end of its journey. Know - Where thou mayst find it, and whence thou mayst fetch it.

22. Treasures - Dost thou know where I have laid up those vast quantities of snow and hail which I draw forth when I see fit?

23. Trouble - When I intend to bring trouble upon any people for their sins.

24. Distributed - In the air, and upon the face of the earth. This is variously distributed in the world, shining in one place and time, when it doth not shine in another, or for a longer time, or with greater brightness and power than it doth in another. All which are the effects of God's infinite wisdom and power, and such as were out of Job's reach to understand. Which - Which light scattereth, raises the east-wind, and causes it to blow hither and thither upon the earth? For as the sun is called by the poets, the father of the winds, because he draws up those exhalations which give matter to the winds, so in particular the east-wind is often observed to rise together with the sun.

25. Overflowing - For the showers of rain which come down orderly, and gradually, as if they were conveyed in pipes or channels; which, without the care of God's providence, would fall confusedly, and overwhelm the earth. Lightning - For lightning and thunder? Who opened a passage for them out of the cloud in which they were imprisoned? And these are joined with the rain, because they are commonly accompanied with great showers of rain.

26. To cause - That the clouds being broken by lightning and thunder might pour down rain. No man - To water those parts by art and industry, as is usual in cultivated places.

27. To bring forth - Hitherto God has put such questions to Job, as were proper to convince him of his ignorance. Now he comes to convince him of his impotence. As it is but little that he can know, and therefore he ought not to arraign the Divine counsels, so it is but little he can do; and therefore he ought not to oppose Divine providence.

28. Father - Is there any man that can beget or produce rain at his pleasure?

31. Bind - Restrain or hinder them. Pleiades - The seven stars, which bring in the spring. Bands - By which it binds up the air and earth, by bringing storms of rain and hail or frost and snow. Orion - This constellation rises in November, and brings in winter. Both summer and winter will have their course? God indeed can change them when he pleases, can make the spring cold, and so bind the influences of Pleiades, and the winter warm, and so loose the bands of Orion; but we cannot.

32. Bring forth - Canst thou make the stars in the southern signs arise and appear? Arcturus - Those in the northern. His sons - The lesser stars, which are placed round about them; and attend upon them, as children upon their parents.

33. Ordinances - The laws which are firmly established concerning their order, motion, or rest, and their powerful influences upon this lower world. Didst thou give these laws? Or dost thou perfectly know them? Canst thou - Manage and over rule their influences.

34. Cover thee - Thy land when it needs rain.

38. Mire - By reason of much rain.

39. Hunt - Is it by thy care that the lions who live in desert places are furnished with necessary provisions? This is another wonderful work of God.

41. Raven - Having mentioned the noblest of brute creatures, he now mentions one of the most contemptible; to shew the care of God's providence over all creatures, both great and small. Their young ones are so soon forsaken by their dams, that if God did not provide for them in a more than ordinary manner, they would be starved to death. And will he that provides for the young ravens, fail to provide for his own children.

XXXIX

The more fully to convince Job of his ignorance, God here discourses, Of the wild goats and hinds, ver. 1-4. Of the wild ass, ver. 5-8. Of the unicorn, ver. 9-12. Of the peacock and ostrich, ver. 13-18. Of the horse, ver. 19-25. Of the hawk and eagle, ver, 26-30.

4. Young ones - Notwithstanding their great weakness caused by their hard entrance into the world. Grow up - As with corn, that is, as if they were fed with corn. Go forth - Finding sufficient provisions abroad by the care of God's providence.

5. Sent - Who hath given him this disposition that he loves freedom, and hates that subjection which other creatures quietly endure? Loosed - Who keeps him from receiving the bands, and submitting to the service of man.

7. Scorneth - He feareth them not when they pursue him, because he is swift, and can easily escape them. Driver - He will not be brought to receive his yoke, nor to do his drudgery.

8. Mountains - He prefers that mean provision with his freedom, before the fattest pastures with servitude.

9. Unicorn - It is disputed whether this be the Rhinoceros; or a kind of wild bull.

16. Her labour - In laying her eggs is in vain, because she hath not the fear and tender concern for them, which she should have.

17. Deprived - Because God hath not implanted in her that instinct, and affection, which he hath put into other birds and beasts toward their young.

18. Lifteth - To flee from her pursuer: to which end she lifts up her head and body, and spreads her wings. Scorneth - She despises them thro' her swiftness; for though she cannot fly, yet by the aid of her wings she runs so fast, that horse-men cannot reach her.

19. Thunder - A strong metaphor, to denote force and terror.

21. Valley - Battles used to be pitched in valleys, or low grounds, especially horse battles.

23. Quiver - The quiver is here put for the arrows contained in it, which being shot against the horse and rider, make a rattling noise.

24. Swalloweth - He is so full of rage and fury, that he not only champs his bridle, but is ready to tear and devour the very ground on which he goes. Believeth - He is so pleased with the approach of the battle, and the sound of the trumpet calling to it, that he can scarce believe his ears for gladness.

25. Ha, ha - An expression of joy and alacrity declared by his proud neighings. Thunder - The loud and joyful clamour begun by the commanders, and followed by the soldiers when they are ready to join battle.

26. Fly - So strongly, constantly, unweariedly, and swiftly. South - At the approach of winter, when wild hawks fly into warmer countries, as being impatient of cold. The birds of the air are proofs of the wonderful providence of God, as well as the beasts of the earth. God instances in two stately ones.

27. Mount - Flies directly upward 'till she be out of thy sight; which no other bird can do.

29. Her eyes - Her sight is exceeding sharp and strong, so that she is able to look upon the sun with open eyes, and to behold the smallest prey upon the earth or sea, when she is mounted out of our sight.

33. Blood - There are divers eagles who do not feed upon carcases, but many eagles do feed on them. She - In an instant, flying thither with admirable celerity.

XL

Job humbles himself before God, ver. 1-5. God challenges him to vie with him, in justice, power, majesty, and dominion over the proud, ver. 6-14. And gives an instance of his power in the Behemoth, ver. 15-24.

1. Answered - Having made a little pause to try what Job could answer. This is not said to be spoken out of the whirlwind, and therefore some think God said it in a still, small voice, which wrought more upon Job, (as upon Elijah) than the whirlwind did. Tho' Job had not spoken any thing, yet God is said to answer him. For he knows mens thoughts, and can return a fit answer to their silence.

2. Reproveth - That boldly censureth his ways or works; it is at his peril.

5. Answer - Speak again; I will contend no more with thee. Twice - Often, the definite number being used indefinitely.

6. Whirlwind - Which was renewed when God renewed his charge upon Job, whom he intended to humble more throughly.

8. Wilt thou - Every word is emphatical, wilt (art thou resolved upon it) thou (thou Job, whom I took to be one of a better mind) also (not only vindicate thyself, but also accuse me) disannul (not only question, but even repeal and make void, as if it were unjust) my judgment? My sentence against thee, and my government and administration of human affairs? Wilt thou make me unrighteous that thou mayst seem to be righteous?

10. Deck - Seeing thou makest thyself equal, yea, superior to me, take to thyself thy great power, come and sit in my throne, and display thy Divine perfections in the sight of the world.

13. Hide - Kill every one of them at one blow. Bind - Condemn or destroy them. He alludes to the manner of covering the faces of condemned persons, and of dead men. In secret - In a secret place, bury them in their graves.

15. Behemoth - Very learned men take the leviathan to be the crocodile, and the behemoth to be the river-horse, which may fitly be joined with the crocodile, both being well known to Job and his friends, as being frequent in the adjacent parts, both amphibious, living and preying both in the water and upon the land. And both creatures of great bulk and strength. Made - As I made thee. Grass - The river-horse comes out of the river upon the land to feed upon corn, and hay, or grass, as an ox doth, to whom also he is not unlike in the form of his head and feet, and in the bigness of his body, whence the Italians call him, the sea-ox.

16. Strength - He hath strength answerable to his bulk, but this strength by God's wise and merciful providence is not an offensive strength, consisting in, or put forth by horns or claws, as it is in ravenous creatures, but only defensive and seated in his loins, as it is in other creatures.

17. Tail - Which though it be but short, yet when it is erected, is exceeding stiff and strong. Thighs - The sinews of his thighs. His thighs and feet are so sinewy and strong, that one of them is able to break or over-turn a large boat.

19. The chief - He is one of the chief of God's works, in regard of its great bulk and strength.

20. Mountains - Though he lives most in the water, yet he often fetches his food from the land, and from the mountains or hills, which are nigh the river Nile. Play - They not only feed securely, but sport themselves by him, being taught by experience that he is gentle and harmless.

22. Brook - Or, of the Nile, of which this word is often used in scripture. His constant residence is in or near this river, or the willows that grow by it.

23. River - A great quantity of water, hyperbolically called a river. Hasteth not - He drinks not with fear and caution; but such is his courage, that he fears no enemy either by water or by land. He drinks as if he designed, to drink up the whole river. He mentions Jordan, as a river well known, in and nigh unto Job's land.

24. Sight - Can any man take him in his eyes? Openly and by force? Surely not. His strength is too great for man to overcome: and therefore men are forced to use wiles and engines to catch him.

XLI

To convince Job of his wickedness, he is here challenged to subdue and tame the leviathan, ver. 1-10. A particular description of him. ver. 11-34.

1. Leviathan - Several particulars in the following description, agree far better with the crocodile, than the whale. It is highly probable, that this is the creature here spoken of. Cord - Canst thou take him with a hook and a line, as anglers take ordinary fishes.

2. Thorn - Or, with an iron hook, or instrument as sharp as a thorn; wherewith thou usest to carry little fishes.

3. Supplications - Doth he dread thine anger or power? Or will he earnestly beg thy favour? It is a

metaphor from men in distress, who use these means to them to whose power they are subject.

7. Fill - A whale's you may: but the skin of a crocodile is so hard that an iron or spear will not pierce it.

8. Lay - Seize upon him, if thou darest. Battle - But ere thou attempt it consider what thou art doing, and with whom, thou art going to fight. Do no more - Proceed no farther, draw back thy hand.

9. Hope - The hope of taking or conquering him.

10. Stand - To the battle. Me - To contend with me who created him?

11. Prevented - Hath laid the first obligation upon me, for which I am indebted to him. Who can be before-hand with me in kindnesses, since all things under heaven are mine.

13. Discover - Or, uncover, or take off from him. Face - The upper or outward part of his garment, or, the garment itself: the word face being often redundant. And by the garment is meant the skin which covers the whole body; who dare attempt to touch his very skin? Much less to give him a wound. His double bridle - His fast jaws, which have some resemblance to a double bridle: whence the Greeks call those parts of the face which reach to the jaws on both sides, the bridles.

14. Doors - His mouth. If it be open, none dare enter within, and if it be shut, none dare open it.

15. Shut - Closely compacted together, as things that are fastened together by a seal. This likewise is true of the crocodile, but the skin of the whale is smooth and entire without any scales at all.

18. Sneesings - This the crocodile is said frequently to do. Eyes - To which they seem very fitly compared, because the eyes of the crocodile are dull and dark under the water, but as soon as they appear above water, cast a bright and clear light; like the morning light, suddenly breaking forth after the dark night.

19. Lamps - This also better agrees with the crocodile, which breathes like the river-horse, of which ancient authors affirm, that his nostrils are very large, and he breathes forth a fiery smoke like that of a furnace.

21. Kindleth coals - An hyperbolical expression, denoting extraordinary heat.

22. And sorrow - Sorrow is his companion and harbinger, which attends upon him wheresoever he goes. So anger and fear are said by the poets to accompany the God of war.

24. Nether mill-stone - Which being to bear the weight of the upper, ought to be the harder and stronger of the two.

25. Raiseth - Upon the top of the waters. Mighty - Even the stout-hearted. Breakings - By reason of their great danger and distress; which is expressed by this very word, Psalm lx, 2 Jonah ii, 4. Purify - Those who ordinarily live in the neglect of God, they cry unto God in their trouble, and endeavour to purge their consciences from the guilt of their sins.

26. Hold - Hebrew. cannot stand, cannot endure the stroke, but will be broken by it. The crocodile's skin, no sword, nor dart, nor musquet bullet can pierce.

28. Turned - Hurt him no more than a blow with a little stubble.

30. Stones - His skin is so impenetrable, that the sharpest stones or shells are as easy unto him as the mire.

31. Boil - To swell, and foam, and froth by his strong and vehement motion, as any liquor does when it is boiled in a pot, especially boiling ointment. The sea - The great river Nile, is called a sea, both in scripture, as Isaiah xi, 15, and in other authors, as Euphrates is called the sea of Babylon, Isaiah xxi, 1 Jer. li, 36. Lakes also are most frequently called seas both in the Old and New Testament: and in such lakes the crocodiles are as well as in the Nile.

32. Shine - By the white froth or foam upon the waters. The same may be observed in the wake of a ship by night.

34. King, &c. - He can tame both the behemoth and leviathan, as strong and stout-hearted as they are. This discourse concerning them was brought in, to prove that it is God only, who can look upon proud men and abase them, bring them low, and hide them in the dust, he it is that beholdeth all high things, and wherein men dealt proudly, he is above them. He is king over all the children of pride, brutal or rational, and makes them either bend or break before him.

XLII

Job throughly humbles himself before God, ver. 1-6. God reproves his friends, for whom Job intercedes, and God accepts them, ver. 7-9. God blesses and restores Job to his prosperity, ver. 10-15. His age and death, ver. 16, 17

2. Thou canst, &c. - Job here subscribes to God's unlimited power, knowledge and dominion, to prove which was the scope of God's discourse out of the whirlwind. And his judgment being convinced of these, his conscience also was convinced, of his own folly in speaking so irreverently concerning him. No thought can be withholden from thee - No thought of ours can be withholden from thy knowledge. And there is no thought of thine, which thou canst be hindered from bringing into

execution.

3. Who - What am I that I should be guilty of such madness! Therefore - Because my mind was without knowledge. Knew not - I have spoken foolishly and unadvisedly of all things far above my reach.

4. Hear - Hear and accept my humble confession. Inquire - I will no more dispute the matter with thee, but beg information from thee. The words which God had uttered to Job by way of challenge, Job returns to him in way of submission.

5. Seeth thee - The knowledge which I had of thy nature, perfections and counsels, was hitherto grounded chiefly, upon the instructions of men; but now it is clear and certain, as being immediately inspired into my mind by this thy glorious apparition and Revelation, and by the operation of thy Holy Spirit; which makes these things as evident to me, as if I saw them with my bodily eyes. When the mind is enlightened by the spirit of God, our knowledge of Divine things as far exceeds what we had before, as knowledge by ocular demonstration, exceeds, that by common fame.

7. Eliphaz - As the eldest of the three, and because he spoke first, and by his example led the rest into the same miscarriages. Two friends - Elihu is not here reproved, because he dealt more mercifully with Job, and did not condemn his person, but only rebuked his sinful expressions. Ye have not, &c. - This is not to be understood absolutely, but comparatively. Job was not so much to be blamed as they, because his opinion concerning the methods of God's providence, and the indifferency of its dispensations towards good and bad men was truer than theirs, which was, that God did always reward good men and punish sinners in this life.

8. My servant - Whom though you condemned as an hypocrite, I own for my faithful servant. Offer - By the hand of Job, whom I hereby constitute your priest to pray and sacrifice for you. Lest I deal - Lest my just judgment take hold of you for your false and foolish speeches.

9. Accepted Job - And as Job prayed and offered sacrifice for those who had grieved and wounded his spirit, so Christ prayed and died for his persecutors, and ever lives, making intercession for transgressors.

10. Captivity - All his bodily distempers were thoroughly healed, and probably in a moment. His mind was calmed, his peace returned, and the consolations of God were not small with him. Prayed - Whereby he manifests his obedience to God and his true love to them.

11. Then - When Job had humbled himself, and God was reconciled to him. Sisters - His kindred. Eat - Feasted with him, to congratulate with him God's great and glorious favour. Bemoaned - They declared the sense which they had of his calamities while they were upon him, although they had hitherto wanted opportunity to express it.

12. Blessed - Not only with spiritual, but also with temporal blessings. Just double to what they were, chap. i, 3. This is a remarkable instance of the extent of the Divine providence, to things that seem minute as this, the exact number of a man's cattle; as also of the harmony of providence, and the reference of one event to another: for known unto God are all his works, from the beginning to the end.

14. Jemima - The day, either because of her eminent beauty, or because she was born in the day of his prosperity, after a dark night of affliction. Kezia is the name of a spice of a very fragrant smell, commonly called Cassia. Keren-happuch signifies plenty restored.

15. So fair - In the Old Testament we often find women praised for their beauty, but never in the New, because the beauty of holiness is brought to a much clearer light by the gospel.

16. After this, &c. - Some conjecture, that he was seventy when his trouble came. If so his age was doubled, as his other possessions.

17. Full of days - So coming to his grave, as Eliphaz had spoken, like a ripe shock of corn in its season.

John Wesley

NOTES ON THE BOOK OF PSALMS

WE have now before us one of the choicest parts of the Old Testament, wherein there is so much of Christ and his gospel, as well as of God and his law, that it has been called the summary of both Testaments. The history of Israel; which we were long upon, instructed us in the knowledge of God. The book of Job gave us profitable disputations, concerning God and his providence. But this book brings us into the sanctuary, draws us off from converse with men, with the philosophers or disputers of this world, and directs us into communion with God. It is called, the Psalms, in Hebrew Tehillim, which properly signifies Psalms of praise, because many of them are such; but Psalms is a more general word, meaning all poetical compositions, fitted to be sung. St. Peter styles it, The book of Psalms. It is a collection of Psalms, of all the Psalms that were divinely inspired, composed at several times, on several occasions, and here put together, without any dependence on each other. Thus they were preserved from being scattered and lost, and kept in readiness for the service of the church. One of these is expressly said to be the prayer of Moses. That some of them were penned by Asaph, is intimated, 2 Chron. xxix. 30, where they are said to praise the Lord, in the words of David and Asaph, who is there called a seer or prophet. And some of the Psalms seem to have been penned long after, at the time of the captivity in Babylon. But the far greater part were wrote by David, who was raised up for establishing the ordinance of singing Psalms in the church of God, as Moses and Aaron were for settling the ordinance of sacrifice. Theirs indeed is superseded, but this will remain, 'till it be swallowed up in the songs of eternity. There is little in the book of Psalms of the ceremonial law. But the moral law is all along magnified, and made honourable. And Christ the foundation, corner and top-stone of all religion, is here clearly spoken of; both his sufferings, with the glory that should follow, and the, kingdom he would set up in the world.

1

This psalm was put first as a preface to all the rest, as a powerful persuasive to the serious study of the whole book, and of the rest of the holy scripture, taken from that blessedness which attends upon the study and practice of it. It shews us, the holiness and happiness of a good man, ver. 1-3 The sinfulness and misery of a wicked man, ver. 4, 5. The ground and reason of both, ver. 6.

1. Blessed - The Hebrew words are very emphatical: O the blessedness of that man! Counsel - That doth not lead his life according to their counsel, or manner of living. Standeth - Which notes a more settled abode in it. Way - In their manner of conversation. Seat - Which notes a constant and resolved perseverance in their wicked courses. Scornful - Of those who make a mock of sin, and scoff at goodness and goodmen. Divers observe a gradation in this verse; the following clause still exceeding the former, for standing is more than walking, and sitting more than standing; and sinners in scripture use, are worse than the ungodly, and the scornful are the worst of sinners.

2. Day and night - Not seldom and slightly, but diligently, and constantly.

3. Whither - His happiness is not short and transitory, but, like those trees which are continually green and flourishing.

4. Ungodly - Their condition is far different. Chaff - They are restless and unquiet: their seeming felicity, hath no firm foundation, but quickly vanishes and flees away as chaff before the wind.

5. Not stand - Not endure the trial. Judgment - In the great and general judgment of the world.

6. Knoweth - He approves, loves, and delights in them, and therefore will recompence them. Perish - All their designs and courses shall come to nothing, and they shall perish with them.

2

There is nothing in this psalm which is not applicable to Christ, but some things which are not all applicable to David. Threatenings denounced against the adversaries of Christ's kingdom, ver. 1-6. Promises made to Christ, ver. 7-9. Counsel given to all, to submit to him, ver. 10-12.

1. Heathen - Who did so against David, 2 Sam. v, 6, 17; 1 Chron. xiv, 8, and against Christ, Luke xviii, 32 Acts iv, 25, &c.

2. **The kings** - Herod, and Pilate and others with or after them. **Earth** - So called in way of contempt and to shew their madness in opposing the God of heaven. **Set** - The word denotes the combination of their counsels and forces. **Anointed** - Against the king whom God hath chosen and exalted.

3. **And cast** - The same thing expressed with more emphasis. Let us not only break off their yoke and the cords by which it is fastened upon us, but let us cast them far away.

4. **Sitteth** - As the king of the whole world. **Heavens** - As an evidence both of God's clear and certain knowledge of all things that are done below, and of his sovereign and irresistible power. **Laugh** - Shall despise them and all their crafty devices.

6. **Yet** - Notwithstanding all their artifices and combinations. **My king** - Who ruleth in my stead, and according to my will, and for my glory. **Zion** - Over my church and people. Zion strictly taken, was an hill on the north part of Jerusalem, where there was a strong fort, called the city of David, but in a more large sense it is put for the city of Jerusalem, for the temple of Jerusalem, built upon the hill of Moriah, which was either a part of mount Sion, or adjoining to it; for the church of the Jews, and for the Christian church.

7. **The decree** - The will and appointment of God concerning this. **My son** - Which tho' it may in some sort be said to, or of David, yet much more properly belongs to Christ, who is commonly known by this title both in the Old and New Testament, and to whom this title is expressly appropriated by the holy ghost, who is the best interpreter of his own words, Acts xiii, 33 Heb. i, 5. **This day** - This may be understood either,

1. Of his eternal generation. This day, from all eternity, which is well described by this day, because in eternity there is no succession, no [yesterday,] no [tomorrow,] but it is all as one continued day or moment without change or flux; or,

2. Of the manifestation of Christ's eternal son-ship in time; which was done both in his birth and life, when his being the son of God was demonstrated by the testimony of the angel, Luke i, 32, and of God the Father, Matt. iii, 17; xvii, 5, and by his own words and works; and in his resurrection, which seems to be here mainly intended, of which day this very place is expounded, Acts xiii, 33. When Christ was in a most solemn manner declared to be the son of God with power, Rom. i, 4.

8. **Earth** - Not only the Jewish nation, but the whole world.

9. **Them** - Those that will not quietly submit to thee, shall be crushed and destroyed by thee. This was in part fulfilled, when the Jews who persisted in unbelief, were destroyed by the Roman power: And in the destruction of the Pagan power, when the Christian religion came to be established. But it will not be compleatly fulfilled, 'till all opposing power and principality be put down.

10. **Now** - While you have time for repentance and submission.

11. **Fear** - With an awful sense of his great and glorious majesty. **Rejoice** - Do not esteem his yoke your dishonour and grievance; but rejoice in this inestimable grace and benefit. **Trembling** - This is added to warn them of taking heed that they do not turn this grace of God into wantonness.

12. **Kiss** - In token of your subjection and adoration; whereof this was a sign among the eastern nations. **The son** - The son of God. **Ye perish** - Be taken out of the way by death or destruction. **Wrath** - The least degree of his anger is terrible.

3

David complains to God of his enemies, ver. 1, 2. Comforts himself in God, and the experience of his goodness, ver. 3-6. Triumphs in the salvation of God, ver. 7, 8 A psalm of David, when he fled from Absalom his son.

2. **My soul** - Of me: the soul being commonly put for the person. **In God** - God hath utterly forsaken him. **Selah** - This word is no where used but in this poetical book, and in the song of Habakkuk. Probably it was a musical note, directing the singer either to lift up his voice, to make a pause, or to lengthen the tune. But withal, it is generally placed at some remarkable passage; which gives occasion to think that it served also to quicken the attention of the singer and hearer.

3. **A shield** - My defense. **My glory** - Thou hast formerly given, and wilt farther give occasion of glorying in thy power and favour. **Lifter up** - Thou wilt restore me to my former power and dignity.

4. **His hill** - Out of heaven, so called, chap. xv, 1.

5. **Slept** - Securely, casting all my cares upon God. **Awaked** - After a sweet and undisturbed sleep.

7. **Cheek bone** - Which implies contempt and reproach. **Teeth** - Their strength and the instruments of their cruelty. He compares them to wild beasts.

4

David prays, reproves the wicked, and testifies the happiness of the righteous, ver. 1-3. Exhorts them to consider and serve God, ver. 4-5. Declares his own experience of the grace of God, ver. 6-8. To the chief musician on Neginoth, A psalm of David. Title of the psalm. Chief musician - The director of the musick of the temple. Neginoth - Or, on stringed instruments, as this word is translated, Hab. iii, 19.

1. O God - The witness and defender of my righteous cause.

2. My glory - By his glory probably he means that honour which God had conferred upon him. Vanity - Wickedness. Lying - Those calumnies which they raised against him, to make him odious to all the people.

3. Godly - Me, whom, though you traduce as an hypocrite, God hath pronounced to be a man after his own heart, 1 Sam. xiii, 14. For himself - In his stead, or to be his vicegerent, as all kings are, and especially the kings of God's own people.

4. In awe - Be afraid, if not of me, yet of God, who hath engaged in my cause. Sin not - By prosecuting your rebellion against God's authority. On your bed - Calmly consider these things in the silent night, when you are at leisure from distracting business. Be still - Compose your tumultuous minds.

5. Offer - Unto God, that he may be reconciled to you. Righteousness - Righteous sacrifices; which requires that the persons offering them be righteous and do righteous things, and offer them with an honest mind, with faith and true repentance. Without which, he intimates, that all their sacrifices were of no esteem with God, and would be wholly unprofitable to them.

6. Many - Of my followers, who are weary of waiting upon God. Who - Who will put an end to our troubles, and give us tranquility. Lift up - Upon me and my friends. Give us an assurance of thy love, and evidence it by thy powerful assistance.

7. Thou hast - Whatsoever thou shalt do with me for the future, I have at present unspeakable satisfaction in the testimonies of thy love to my soul; more than worldly persons have in the time of a plentiful harvest.

8. In peace - In tranquility of mind, resting securely upon God's promises.

5

David beseeches God to hear his prayer, ver. 1-3. Assures himself of God's justice against his enemies, ver. 4-6. Declares his resolution: to serve God, ver. 7. Prays for himself and the people of God, and against his enemies, ver. 8-12. To the chief musician upon Nehiloth, A psalm of David. Title of the psalm. Nehiloth - This is no where else used in scripture. It is thought to signify a wind-instrument, as Neginoth signified stringed instruments.

1. Meditation - My prayer accompanied with deep thoughts and fervent affections of soul.

3. Morning - Every morning. As soon as I wake, I am still with thee, as he saith, chap. lxxxix, 18. The first thing that I do is to pray to thee.

4. Surely - Thou dost not approve of, nor delight in them, or in their prayers. Dwelt - Have any fellowship with thee.

7. Come - With holy boldness and confidence. Mercy - Trusting only in thy great mercy. Fear - With an holy dread and reverence of thy majesty. Towards - Looking towards it, when I cannot come to it.

8. Righteousness - In thy righteous laws. Because - That I may give them no occasion of slandering me, or religion for my sake. The way - The way wherein thou wouldst have to one walk. Plain - That I may clearly discern it, and readily walk in it.

9. Throat - Wide opened ready to devour all that come within their reach. A metaphor from wild beasts gaping for the prey.

10. Destroy - Condemn and punish them. Cast - Out of thy land, and from among thy people.

6

David being sick both in body and mind, because he had offended God, presents his misery before him, ver. 1-3. Begs the return of his favour, ver. 4-7. Assures himself of an answer of peace, ver. 8-10. To the chief musician on Neginoth, upon Sheminith, A psalm of David Title of the psalm. Upon Sheminith - Or, upon the eighth. It is thought to be the loftiest note, as Alamoth is the lowest; but this is only conjecture; the Jews themselves have no certain knowledge of their own ancient musick.

2. Bones - My inmost parts.

5. *In death* - Among the dead. *Remembrance* - He speaks of the remembrance or celebration of God's grace in the land of the living, to the edification of God's church, and the propagation of true religion among men; which is not done in the other life.

6. *With my tears* - It well becomes the greatest spirits to be tender, and to relent under the tokens of God's displeasure. David who could face Goliath himself, melts into tears at the remembrance of sin, and under the apprehension of Divine wrath, and it is no diminution to his character.

8. *Hath heard* - By the workings of God's grace upon his heart, he knew his prayer was accepted. His tears had a voice, in the ears of the God of mercy. Silent tears are no speechless ones. Our tears are cries to God.

10. *Ashamed* - Of their vain confidence. *Return* - Repent of their sins and return to their obedience.

7

David prays for deliverance from his enemies, ver. 1, 2. Appeals to God for his innocence, ver. 3-5. Prays to him to judge his cause, ver. 6-9. Expresses his confidence in God, ver. 10-17. Shiggaion of David, which he sang unto the Lord, concerning the words of Cush the Benjamite Title of the psalm. *Shiggaion* - This seems to be the name of a kind of song, or instrument, which then was well known, but now is only matter of conjecture. *Words* - The false report raised by him. *Cush* - Probably some eminent commander or courtier under Saul.

2. *Lest* - Mine enemy. *Tear* - Out of my body.
3. *Hands* - Which Cush and others falsely lay to my charge. *Iniquity* - In my actions.
4. *Deliver* - When it was in my power to destroy him, as 1 Sam. xxiv, 2-6.
6. *Lift up* - Glorify thyself, and shew thyself to be above them. *Commanded* - To execute that righteous sentence, which thou hast commanded, appointed, and declared by thy prophet Samuel.
7. *Compass* - They will come from all parts to worship thee, and offer to thee praises and sacrifices. *High* - To thy tribunal, to sit there and judge my cause. An allusion to earthly tribunals, which generally are set up on high above the people.
9. *O* - Put a stop to their wicked practices.
11. *Every day* - Even then, when his providence seems to favour them, and they are most secure and confident.
12. *He will* - God will hasten, and speedily execute his judgments upon him.
13. *Him* - For the wicked. *Ordaineth* - Designs or fits for this very use. Of all sinners, persecutors are set up as the fairest marks of Divine wrath. They set God at defiance but cannot set themselves out of the reach of his judgments.
14. *Travelleth* - This metaphor denotes his deep design, and vigourous endeavours for doing mischief, and his restlessness and pain 'till he have accomplished it.

8

David extols the majesty, power, and providence of God, ver. 1, 2. And his loving-kindness to mankind, ver. 3-5. In giving him dominion over this lower world, ver. 6-9. To the chief musician upon Gittith, A psalm of David. Title of the psalm. *Gittith* - This also is supposed to be the name of a tune, or instrument.

1. *In* - Not only in Israel, but among all nations. Which shews that this psalm speaks of the Messiah, and the times of the New Testament. *Heavens* - Where thy throne of glory is established, where the blessed angels celebrate thy praises, where Christ sitteth at thy right hand in glorious majesty, from whence he poureth down excellent gifts upon babes.
2. *Babes* - Weak and foolish, and contemptible persons, who are frequently called babes or children. Such are very unfit to grapple with an enemy: and therefore when such persons conquer the most powerful and malicious enemies, it must needs confound them, and advance the glory of God: as indeed it did, when such mean persons as the apostles, and disciples of Christ, maintained and propagated the gospel, in spite of all the wit, power, and rage of their enemies. *Ordained* - Perfectly or firmly settled strength; that is, the praise of his strength or power, Matt. xxi, 16, it is rendered praise. *Still* - Silence and confound them. *Avenger* - The devil, and all who are his vassals and espouse his quarrel.
3. *The moon* - Either the sun is included under this general title: or he omitted it, because he made this psalm by night. *Ordained* - Placed in that excellent and unalterable order, and directed to their several motions.
4. *What is man* - How mean and inconsiderable a thing is man, if compared with thy glorious

majesty. Man - Hebrew. infirm, or miserable man. By which it is apparent that he speaks of man, not according to the state of his creation, but as fallen into a state of sin and misery, and mortality. Mindful - Carest for him, and conferest such high favours upon him. The son - Hebrew. the son of Adam, that great apostate from God, the sinful son of a sinful father, his son by likeness of disposition and manners, no less than by procreation. All which tends to magnify the following mercy. Visitest - Not in anger, as that word is sometimes used, but with thy grace and mercy.

5. For - Thou hast in Christ mercifully restored man to his primitive estate, wherein he was but one remove below the angels; from which he was fallen by sin. Crowned - Man, fallen and lost man: who is actually restored to glory and dominion in Christ his head and representative, who received this crown and dominion for man's good, and in his stead; which he will in due time communicate to his members. And so the two expositions of this place concerning mankind and concerning Christ, may be reconciled. For he speaks of that honourable estate conferred first upon Christ, and then by his hands upon mankind. But the words more literally rendered are, Thou madest him a little less than God. And hence some have inferred, that man in his original state was the highest of all creatures.

9

David praises God for giving him victory over his enemies, ver. 1-6. Triumphs in confidence that God would judge the world and protect his people, ver. 7-10. Calls others to praise him, ver. 11, 12. Prays for help, and praises God, ver. 13-20. To the chief musician upon Muth-labben, A psalm of David Title of the psalm. Muth-labben - This also seems to be a title of some tune, or instrument: of which we may be content to be ignorant, as the Jewish doctors are.

3. Turned back - Put to flight.
7. But - Though cities and people may perish, yet the Lord abides forever. Which is sufficient for the terror of his enemies, and the comfort of his church.
10. Thy name - Thy infinite power and wisdom, and faithfulness and goodness. The name of God is frequently put for God. Put their trust - The experience of thy faithfulness to thy people in all ages, is a just ground for their confidence.
11. Zion - Whose special and gracious presence is there. People - To the heathen nations.
12. Blood - The bloodshed of his innocent and holy ones: which though he may not seem to regard for a season, yet he will certainly call the authors of it to a severe account. Them - The humble, as it follows, or the oppressed, ver. 9, that trust in him, and seek to him, ver. 10, whom he seemed to have forgotten.
14. Gates - In the great assemblies. These gates he elegantly opposes to the former. Of - Of the people who live or meet together in Zion. For cities are as it were mothers to their people, and the people are commonly called their daughters. So the names of the daughters of Egypt, Jer. xlvi, 11, and of Edom, Lam. iv, 21, 22, and of Tyre, chap. xlv, 12, are put for the people of those places.
16. Higgaion - This is either a musical term, or a note of attention, intimating that the matter deserves deep meditation, or consideration, as the word signifies.
17. Forget - That do not regard God, nor his precepts, nor his threatenings and judgments.

10

David complains of and describes the wicked, ver. 1-15. Prays to God to appear against them, and rejoices in the prospect of it, ver. 12-18.

3. Boasteth - He glorieth in his very sins which are his shame, and especially in the satisfaction of his desires.
4. Countenance - So called, because though pride be properly seated in the heart, yet it is manifest in the countenance.
5. Judgments - Thy threatenings denounced against, and punishments inflicted upon sinners. Are far - He doth not regard or fear them: yea he despises them, being confident that he can blow them away with a breath. This is a gesture of contempt or disdain, both in scripture, and other authors.
7. Tongue - Under his fair and plausible speeches, mischief is hid and covered. Vanity - Or, injury, the vexation or oppression of other men.
8. Sitteth - Not within the villages, but in the ways bordering upon them, or leading to them, as robbers use to do. Are set - Hebrew. Are hid. He watches and looks out of his lurking-place. He alludes still to the practices of robbers.
10. Croucheth - Like a lion (for he continues the same metaphor) which lies close upon the ground, partly that he may not be discovered, and partly that he may more suddenly and surely lay hold on his prey.

13. Contemn - Why dost thou by giving them impunity, suffer and occasion them to despise thee?

14. Requite - Hebrew. to give (to restore or pay the mischief which they have done to others) with thy hand, by thy own extraordinary providence, because the oppressed were destitute of all other succors. Fatherless - Of such as have no friend or helper, one kind of them being put for all.

15. Seek - Search for it, and punish these wicked atheists. 'Till - No such wickedness be left in the world, or at least in the church.

16. Is king - To whom it belongs to protect his subjects. Therefore his peoples case is never desperate, seeing he ever lives to help them. The heathen - The Canaanites; whom God, as king of the world, expelled, and gave their land to his people. By which great example he confirms his faith and hope for the future. His land - Out of Canaan, which God calls his land, because he gave it to them, and fixed his presence and dwelling in it.

17. Prepare - By thy grace and good spirit, that they may so pray as thou wilt hear.

18. To judge - To give sentence for them, and against their enemies. The man - Earthly and mortal men, who yet presume to contend with thee their maker.

11

David encourages himself in God, against the attempts of his enemies, ver. 1-3. Asserts the dominion and providence of God, ver. 4-7 To the chief musician, A psalm of David.

1. Ye - Mine enemies.
2. For lo - David having directed his speech to his enemies, now turns it to God, and pours out before him his complaints. Ready - They lay designs for my destruction and make all things ready to execute them.
3. Foundations - Piety, justice, fidelity, and mercy, which are the pillars or foundations of a state or kingdom. What - The condition of all righteous men will be desperate.
4. Temple - In heaven; which is mentioned as an evidence of his glorious majesty, of his sovereign power and dominion over all men and things, and of his accurate inspection into all men and their actions. Throne - Where he sits to examine all causes, and to give righteous sentence according to every man's works. Try - He throughly discerns all men, their most inward and secret actions: and therefore he sees and will reward my innocency, notwithstanding all the calumnies of mine enemies; and withal he sees all their secret designs, and will discover and defeat them.
5. Trieth - He chastens even righteous persons, yet still he loves them, and therefore will in due time deliver them. But as for the wicked, God hates them, and will severely punish them.
6. Rain - Send them plentifully, swiftly, and suddenly, as rain commonly falls from heaven. Snares - Grievous plagues or judgments, which are called snares, because wicked men are often surprized with them when they least expect them. And because they cannot escape them, or get out of them; but are held fast and destroyed by them. Horrible tempests - Dreadful judgments so called, in allusion to the destruction of Sodom by these means. But this he seems to speak not so much of present calamities, as of eternal punishments. This - Is their portion, and as it were the meat and drink appointed them by God.

12

David begs help of God, having no man whom he could trust, ver. 1, 2. Describes the wicked and assures himself, that God would punish them, and preserve the just, ver. 3-8. To the chief musician upon Sheminith, A psalm of David. Title of the psalm. Sheminith - The same title is prefixed to chap. vi, 1.

4. Prevail - By raising and spreading evil reports concerning him. Our own - At our own disposal to speak what we please, who can control or restrain us?
5. Puffeth - From him that despises him, and hopes to destroy him with a puff of breath.
6. Pure - Without the least mixture of falsehood; and therefore shall infallibly be fulfilled.
7. Thou shalt keep them - Thy words or promises: these thou wilt observe and keep, both now, and from this generation forever. 8. Walk - They fill all places, and go about boldly and securely.

13

David complains to God, ver. 1, 2. Prays for help, ver. 3, 4. Rejoices in hope, ver. 5, 6. To the chief musician, A psalm of David.

2. How long - Shall I be in such perplexities, not knowing what course to take?
3. Lighten - Revive and comfort, and deliver me from the darkness of death, which is ready to come upon me.

6. I will sing - It is a common thing for David and other prophets to speak of future deliverances as if they were already come, that so they may signify both the infallible certainty of the thing, and their firm assurance thereof.

14

The atheism and corruption of mankind, ver. 1-3. An expostulation with sinners, ver. 4-6. A prayer for the salvation of God, ver. 7. To the chief musician, A psalm of David.

1. The fool - The wicked man. Good - That is, actions really good or pleasing to God.
2. Looked - God knoweth all things without any enquiry: but he speaks after the manner of men. Upon - Upon the whole Israelitish nation, and upon all mankind for he speaks of all except his people, and the righteous ones, who are opposed to these, ver. 4, 5.
3. Gone - From God, and from the rule which he hath given them. Filthy - Loathsome and abominable to God.
4. Bread - With as little remorse, and with as much greediness. Call not - They are guilty not only of gross injustice towards men, but also of horrid impiety and contempt of God.
5. There - Upon the spot, where they practiced these insolences, God struck them with a panick fear. For - God is on their side, and therefore their enemies have cause to tremble.
6. Because - This was the ground of their contempt, that he lived by faith in God's promise and providence.
7. O that - These words immediately concern the deliverance of Israel out of that sinful state, in which they now were; which having described, he concludes, with a prayer to God to help them out of Zion, where the ark then was, but principally they design the spiritual redemption and salvation of all God's Israel by the Messiah. The captivity - His captive people. The children of Jacob, as Aaron is named for his sons, 1 Chron. xii, 27.

15

The scope of this short, but excellent psalm, is to shew us the way to heaven. Here is a question proposed, ver. 1. The answer to it, ver. 2-5. A psalm of David.

1. Who - Who shall so dwell in thy church here, as to dwell with thee forever in heaven?
2. Uprightly - Loving, and serving God, and loving his neighbour not in word only, but in truth; and this constantly. Worketh - Makes it his business to do justly, to give to every one his due, first to God, and then to men. Speaketh - His words and professions to God and men, agree with the thoughts and purposes of his heart.
3. He - He that doth not speak evil of his neighbour. neighbour - That is, any man. Nor taketh - Into his mouth, doth not raise it, neither spread or propagate it; or believe it without sufficient reason.
4. Vile - An ungodly man. honoureth - He highly esteems and loves them, though they be mean as to their worldly condition, and though they may differ from him in some opinions or practices of lesser moment. Sweareth - A promissory oath. Hurt - To his own damage. As if a man solemnly swear, that he will sell him such an estate at a price below the full worth; or that, he will give a poor man such a sum of money, which afterwards he finds inconvenient to him. Changeth not - His purpose, but continues firm and resolved to perform his promise.
5. To usury - In such a manner as is contrary to God's law: of which see otherwise, Exod. xxii, 25 Levit xxv, 36, 37, &c. Reward - Or, a bribe for him who hath a bad cause. Moved - He shall abide with God here, and when he dies be forever with the Lord.

16

David professes his trust in God, his adherence to him and love of his people, ver. 1-3. His satisfaction in God, ver. 4-7. He speaks in the person of Christ, of Gods presence with him, of his resurrection and the glory that should follow, ver. 8-11. Michtam of David. Title of the psalm. Michtam - This seems to be a title belonging to the musick or the song, which, with the rest, is now lost and unknown. As David was both a member, and an eminent type, of Christ, he speaks of himself sometimes in the one and sometimes in the other capacity: and therefore having spoken of himself as a member of Christ, in the former part of the psalm, he proceeds to consider himself as a type of Christ, and being inspired by the holy Ghost: towards the close he speaks such things, as though they might be accommodated to himself in a very imperfect sense, yet could not properly, belong to any but to Christ, to whom therefore they are justly appropriated in the New Testament.

2. To thee - Thou dost not need me or my service, nor art capable of any advantage from it.

3. But - I bear a singular respect and love to all saints, for thy sake, whose friends and servants they are, and whose image they bear. This more properly agrees to David, than to Christ, whose goodness was principally designed for, and imparted to sinners.

4. Sorrows - Having shewed his affection to the servants of the true God, he now declares what an abhorrency he has for those that worship idols. Offerings - In which the Gentiles used sometimes to drink part of the blood of their sacrifices. Names - Of those other gods mentioned before.

5. The Lord - I rejoice in God as my portion, and desire no better, no other felicity. Cup - The portion which is put into my cup, as the ancient manner was in feasts, where each had his portion of meat, and of wine allotted to him. Lot - My inheritance divided to me by lot, as the custom then was.

6. Lines - My portion, which was measured with lines. Are fallen - In a land flowing with milk and honey, and above all, blessed with the presence and knowledge of God.

7. The Lord - Hath inspired that wisdom into me, by which I have chosen the Lord for my portion, and am so fully satisfied with him. Reins - My inward thoughts and affections, being inspired and moved by the Holy Spirit. Instruct - Direct me how to please God, and put my whole trust in him. Night - Even when others are asleep, my mind is working upon God, and improving the silence and solitude of holy meditations.

8. I have set - I have always presented him to my mind, as my witness and judge, as my patron and protector. Hitherto David seems to have spoken with respect to himself, but now he is transported by the spirit of prophecy, and carried above himself, to speak as a type of Christ, in whom this and the following verses were truly accomplished. Christ as man did always set his father's will and glory before him. Right-hand - To strengthen, protect, assist, and comfort me: as this assistance of God was necessary to Christ as man. Moved - Though the archers shoot grievously at me, and both men and devils seek my destruction, and God sets himself against me as an enemy, yet I am assured he will deliver me out of all my distresses.

9. My glory - My tongue, which is a man's glory and privilege, above all other living creatures. Rejoiceth - Declares my inward joy. For this word signifies not so much eternal joy, as the outward demonstrations of it. My flesh - My body shall quietly rest in the grave. Shall rest - in confident assurance of its incorruption there, and of its resurrection to an immortal life: the flesh or body is in itself, but a dead lump of clay; yet hope is here ascribed to it figuratively, as it is to the brute creatures, Rom. viii, 19.

10. Hell - In the state of the dead. Holy one - Me thy holy son, whom thou hast sanctified and sent into the world. It is peculiar to Christ, to be called the holy one of God. To see - To be corrupted or putrefied in the grave, as the bodies of others are.

11. Life - Thou wilt raise me from the grave, and conduct me to the place and state of everlasting felicity. Presence - In that heavenly paradise, where thou art gloriously present, where thou dost clearly and fully discover the light of thy countenance; whereas in this life thou hidest thy face and shewest us only thy back-parts. Right-hand - Which he mentions as a place of the greatest honour, the place where the saints are placed at the last day, and where Christ himself is said to sit, chap. cx, 1. Pleasures - All our joys are empty and defective: But in heaven there is fulness of joy. Our pleasures here are transient and momentary; but those at God's right hand are pleasures forevermore. For they are the pleasures of immortal souls, in the enjoyment of an eternal God.

17

David appealing to God for his integrity, begs for defense against his enemies, ver. 1-9. Describes their wickedness, ver. 10-12. Prays for deliverance from them, and rests in hope, ver. 13-15. A prayer of David.

1. The right - Regard my righteous cause.

2. Sentence - Judgment on my behalf. Come - From thy tribunal.

3. Proved - Or, searched or tried it, by many temptations and afflictions. Night - When mens minds being freed from the distraction of business, and from the society of men, they act more vigorously and freely, according to their several inclinations. Tried - As gold-smiths do metals. Nothing - Nothing of unrighteousness. Purposed - I have resolved, upon deliberation, as the word implies. Mouth - I am so far from practicing against Saul's life, as they charge me, that I will not wrong him so much as in a word.

4. Concerning - Observing the works of the men of this age, how wicked they are, I was resolved to take more care in ordering my own actions. By - By the help of thy blessed word. Paths - The customs and practices. Destroyer - Or, of the violent man: such as Saul, and his courtiers and soldiers.

7. By - By thy great power.

10. They - They live in splendour and prosperity.

11. Steps - In all our ways. We go from place to place, to rocks, and caves, and woods; but wheresoever we go they are at hand, and ready to surround us. Eyes - They keep their eyes fixed upon us. Bowing - Couching down upon the earth, that they may watch the fittest opportunity to surprize us.

13. Sword - Thy instrument to execute vengeance upon thine enemies. Do not punish me with this rod: let me fall into thy hands, and not into the hands of men.

14. Thy hand - Wherewith thou dost correct me. World - Who set their hearts upon this world, and neither have, nor desire any other portion. Belly - Mind or appetite, as that word is used, Job xx, 20. Prov. xx, 30. Treasure - With extraordinary wealth and glory. Children - When many of thy faithful servants are barren, these are blessed with a numerous posterity.

15. I will - I do not place my portion in earthly treasures, but in beholding God's face, in the enjoyment of God's presence and favour; which is enjoyed in part in this life, but not fully. Satisfied - The time is coming, wherein I shall be abundantly satisfied with beholding thy face. Awake - When I arise from he dead. Likeness - With the image of God stamped upon my glorified soul.

18

David triumphs in God, ver. 1-3. Praises God for his past deliverances, ver. 4-19. Takes the comfort of his integrity, which God had thereby cleared up, ver. 20-28. Gives God the glory of all his victories, ver. 29-42. Express his hope of what God would do farther, ver. 43-50. This psalm with some few and small variations, is written, 2 Sam. xxii, 1-51. It was composed by David towards the end of his life, upon the occasion here mentioned. To the chief musician, A psalm of David, the servant of the LORD, who spake unto the LORD the words of this song, in the day that the LORD delivered him from the hand of all his enemies, and from the hand of Saul, and he said: Title of the psalm. Servant - Who esteems it a greater honour to be thy servant, than to be king of Israel. Saul - After the death of Saul, and the conquest of all his succeeding enemies, and his own firm establishment in his kingdom.

1. Love - Most affectionately, and with my whole soul; as the Hebrew word signifies.

2. Rock - To which I flee for refuge, as the Israelites did to their rocks. Horn - It is a metaphor from those beasts whose strength lies in their horns.

4. Death - Dangerous and deadly troubles. Floods - Their multitude, and strength, and violent assaults, breaking in upon me like a flood.

5. Sorrows - Which brought me to the brink of the grave. Death - Had almost taken hold of me, before I was aware.

6. Temple - Out of his heavenly habitation.

7. Then - Then God appeared on my behalf in a glorious manner, to the terror and confusion of all mine enemies, which is here compared to an earthquake.

8. There went, &c. - All these seem to be figurative expressions, denoting the greatness of his anger.

9. Bowed - By producing thick and dark clouds, whereby the heavens seem to come down to the earth. Came - Not by change of place, but by the manifestation of his presence and power on my behalf.

10. Cherub - Or, upon the cherubim, upon the angels, who are also called God's chariots, chap. lxviii, 17, upon which he is said to sit and ride. All which is not to be understood grossly, but only to denote God's using the ministry of angels, in raising such storms and tempests. Fly - As swiftly as the wind.

11. Darkness - He covered himself with dark clouds. Waters - Watery vapors.

12. At - His glorious and powerful appearance. Passed - Or, passed away, vanished, being dissolved into showers.

14. Arrows - Lightnings. Them - Mine enemies.

15. Discovered - By mighty earthquakes, which overturned the earth, and made its lower parts visible.

18. Prevented - They had almost surprized me.

19. Brought - Out of my straits and difficulties, into a state of freedom and comfort. So he ascribes all his mercies to God's good pleasure, as the first spring of them.

20. Righteousness - Just cause. The innocency of my actions towards Saul, from whose blood I kept my hands pure.

22. Judgments - I diligently studied and considered them.

24. Iniquity - From that sin which I was most inclined or tempted to.

25. Upright - Thou metest to every one the same measure, which he meteth out to others; and therefore thou wilt perform mercy and truth, to those who are merciful and true to others.

26. Pure - Free from the least mixture or appearance of unrighteousness, or unfaithfulness. Froward - Thou wilt cross him and walk contrary to him.

28. Lightest - Given me safety, and comfort, and glory, and posterity also.

29. Troop - Broken through the armed troops of mine enemies. Wall - I have scaled the walls of their strongest cites.

30. Perfect - His providence, though it may sometimes be dark, yet is always wise and just, and unblameable. Tried - The truth of God's promises is approved by innumerable experiences.

31. Who - Our Lord is the only God, and therefore there is none, that can hinder him from accomplishing his own work.

32. Perfect - Perfectly plain and smooth, and clear from impediments.

33. High-places - Confirms me in that high estate into which he hath advanced me.

35. Salvation - Thy protection, which hath been to me like a shield. Held - Kept me from, falling into those mischiefs, which mine enemies designed. Gentleness - Thy clemency, whereby thou hast pardoned my sins; thy grace and benignity.

36. Slipt - As they are apt to do in narrow and uneven ways.

43. People - From contentions, and seditions, under Saul, and Ishbosheth, and Absalom. Heathens - Of the Ammonites, Moabites, Edomites, Syrians, and others. Not known - Even barbarous and remote nations.

44. Hear - As soon as they understand my will and pleasure, they shall instantly comply with it.

45. Close places - Out of their strong holds, where they shall lurk for fear of me.

46. The Lord - He and he only is the true living God.

48. Violent man - From Saul: whom for honour's sake he forbears to mention.

49. Heathen - David is here transported beyond himself, and speaks this in special relation to Christ who was to be his seed, and of whom he was an eminent type, and by whom alone this was done. And therefore this is justly applied to him, and to his calling of the Gentiles, Rom. xv, 9.

50. His king - To the king whom God himself chose and anointed, and to all his posterity; and especially to the Messiah, who is called David's seed, Acts xiii, 23 Rom. i, 3.

19

The book of the creatures shews us the power and Godhead of the Creator, ver. 1-6. The book of the scriptures shews us his will; the excellency thereof, ver. 7-11. A prayer against sin, ver. 12, 14. To the chief musician, A psalm of David.

1. The heavens - They are as a legible book, wherein he that runs may read it. The glory - His eternal power and Godhead, his infinite wisdom and goodness. Firmament - Or, the expansion, all the vast space extended from the earth to the highest heavens, with all its goodly furniture.

2. Day - Every day and night repeats these demonstrations of God's glory. Uttereth - Or, poureth forth, constantly and abundantly, as a fountain doth water; So this Hebrew word signifies. Knowledge - Gives us a clear knowledge or discovery of God their author.

3. Heard - Or, understood; there are divers nations in the world, which have several languages, so that one cannot discourse with, or be understood by another, but the heavens are such an universal teacher, that they can speak to all people, and be clearly understood by all.

4. Line - Their lines, the singular number being put for the plural. And this expression is very proper, because the heavens do not teach men audibly, or by speaking to their ears, but visibly by propounding things to their eyes, which is done in lines or writings. Gone - Is spread abroad. Earth - So as to be seen and read, by all the inhabitants of the earth. Words - Their magnificent structure, their exquisite order, and most regular course, by which they declare their author, no less than men discover their minds by their words. Sun - Which being the most illustrious and useful of all the heavenly bodies, is here particularly mentioned.

5. Bridegroom - Gloriously adorned with light as with a beautiful garment, and smiling upon the world with a pleasant countenance. Chamber - In which he is poetically supposed to have rested all night, and thence to break forth as it were on a sudden. Strong man - Conscious and confident of his own strength.

6. The ends - His course is constant from east to west, and thence to the east again. So that there is no part of the earth which doth not one time or other feel the benefit of his light and heat.

7. The law - The doctrine delivered to his church, whether by Moses, or by other prophets. Having discoursed hitherto of the glory of God shining forth in, the visible heavens, he now proceeds to another demonstration of God's glory, which he compares with and prefers before the former. Perfect - Completely discovering both the nature and will of God, and the whole duty of man, what he is to believe and practice, and whatsoever is necessary to his present and eternal happiness. Whereas the creation, although it did declare so much of God, as left all men without excuse, yet did not fully manifest the will of God, nor bring man to eternal salvation. Converting - From sin to God, from whom all men are naturally revolted. Testimony - His law, so called because it is a witness between God and man, what God requires of man, and what upon the performance of that condition, he will do for man.

John Wesley

Sure - Hebrew. faithful or true, which is most necessary in a witness: it will not mislead any man, but will infallibly bring him to happiness. Simple - Even persons of the lowest capacities.

8. Right - Both in themselves, and in their effect, as guiding men in the ready way to eternal happiness. Rejoicing - By the discoveries of God's love to sinful men, in offers and promises of mercy. Commandment - All his commands. Pure - Without the least mixture of error. The eyes - Of the mind, with a compleat manifestation of God's will and man's duty: both which, the works of nature, and all the writings of men discover but darkly and imperfectly.

9. The fear - The law and word of God, because it is both the object and the rule, and the cause of holy fear. Clean - Sincere, not adulterated with any mixture. Constant and unchangeable, the same for substance in all ages. Judgments - God's laws are frequently called his judgments, because they are the declarations of his righteous will, and as it were his judicial sentence by which he expects that men should govern themselves, and by which he will judge them at the last day.

12. Who - Thy law, O Lord, is holy and just and good. But I fall infinitely short of it. Cleanse - Both by justification, through the blood of thy son; and by sanctification thro' thy Holy Spirit. Though the first may seem to be principally intended, because he speaks of his past sins. Secret - From the guilt of such sins as were secret either, from others; such as none knows but God and my own conscience: or, from myself; such as I never observed, or did not discern the evil of. Pardon my unknown sins, of which I never repented particularly, as I should have done.

13. Presumptuous - From known and evident sins, such as are committed against knowledge, against the checks of conscience, and the motions of God's spirit. Dominion - If I be at any time tempted to such sins, Lord let them not prevail over me, and if I do fall into them, let me speedily rise again.

14. Let - Having prayed that God would keep him from sinful actions, he now prays that God would govern, and sanctify his words and thoughts: and this was necessary to preserve him from presumptuous sins, which have their first rise in the thoughts. Redeemer - This expression seems to be added emphatically, and with special respect to Christ, to whom alone this word Goel can properly belong.

20

A prayer for the king, ver. 1-4. The king and the people rejoice in God, and pray for his help, ver. 5-9. To the chief musician, A psalm of David.

1. God of Jacob - God had made a covenant with Jacob and his posterity.
2. Sanctuary - From the tabernacle in Zion, where the ark then was; toward which the Israelites directed their prayers.
5. Rejoice - Hereby they shew their confidence in God, and their assurance of the victory. Name - To the honour of God. Set up - In way of triumph.
6. Now - We are already sure of victory by the consideration of God's power and faithfulness and love to David, and to his people. They speak as one person, because they were unanimous in this prayer. Saveth - Will certainly save. Strength - This shews how God will hear him, even by saving him with a strong hand.
7. Remember - Trust in it.
8. Brought down - From their horses and chariots, to which they trusted. Stand - Stand firmly, and keep the field.
9. Let the king - God, the supreme monarch, the king of kings, and in a peculiar manner the king of Israel.

21

A thanksgiving for blessings received, ver. 1-6. An expression of confidence in God, ver. 7-13. To the chief musician, A psalm of David. Title of the psalm. Of David - The subject of this psalm is the same with the former, both being made for the peoples use, concerning the king. Only the prayers there used, are here turned into praises, for the blessings received in answer to their prayers. And as David was an illustrious type of Christ, so in many of these expressions he looks beyond himself to Christ, in whom they are properly, and fully accomplished.

3. Prevent - Crowning him with manifold blessings, both more and sooner than he expected. With - With excellent blessings.
4. For ever - Thou gavest him a long life and reign here, and after that didst translate him to live with thee forever. But this was more eminently fulfilled in Christ, who asked of his father, life, or to be saved from death, Heb. v, 7, though with submission to his will: but his father, though he saw it necessary to take away his temporal life, yet instantly gave him another, far more noble, even the

perfect possession of an everlasting life both in his soul and body, at his right hand.

5. Glory - His fame or renown. Salvation - By reason of those great and glorious deliverances which thou hast wrought both for him, and by him.

6. Countenance - Smiling upon him, by thy grace and favour.

9. Oven - Like wood, which when it is cast in there, is quickly consumed.

10. Fruit - Their children. God will take away both root and branch, the parents and all that wicked race.

11. Thee - Against God, not directly, but by consequence, because it was against David, whom God had anointed, and against the Lord's people, whose injuries God takes as done to himself.

13. Exalted - By thy own power, or by the manifestation thereof.

22

It is confessed that David was a type of Christ, and that many passages of the Psalms, though literally understood of David, yet had a further and mystical reference to Christ. But there are some other passages, which were directly, and immediately intended for, and are properly to be understood of the Messiah; though withal there may be some respect and allusion to the state of the penman himself. And this seems to be the state of this psalm, which is understood of the Messiah, by the Hebrew doctors themselves, and by Christ himself and by his apostles. And there are many passages in it, which were literally accomplished in him, and cannot be understood of any other. In this psalm David speaks of the humiliation of Christ, ver. 1-21. Of the exaltation of Christ, ver. 22-31. To the chief musician upon Aijeleth Shahar, A psalm of David. Title of the psalm. Shahar - This was the title of some musical instrument, name, or song, which was usually sung in the morning.

1. My God - Who art my friend and father, though now thou frownest upon me. The repetition denotes, the depth of his distress, which made him cry so earnestly. Forsaken - Withdrawn the light of thy countenance, the supports and comforts of thy spirit, and filled me with the terrors of thy wrath: this was in part verified in David, but much more fully in Christ. Roaring - My out-cries forced from me, by my miseries.

3. But thou art - Just and true in all thy ways, this he adds to strengthen his faith, and to enforce his prayers, and prevail with God for the honour of his holy name, to hear and help him. Inhabitest - Whom thy people are perpetually praising.

6. A worm - Neglected and despised. People - Not only of the great men, but also of the common people. Which doth not so truly agree to David as to Christ.

7. Shoot out - They gape with their mouths, in mockery. This and the next verse are applied to Christ, Matt. xxvii, 39, 43.

12. Bulls - Wicked and violent, and potent enemies; for such are so called, Ezek xxxix, 18 Amos iv, 1. Of Bashan - As the cattle there bred were, and therefore fierce and furious.

14. Water - My spirits are spent and gone like water which once spilt can never be recovered; my very flesh is melted within me, and I am become as weak as water. Bones - I am as unable to help myself, and as full of torment, as if all my bones were disjointed. Wax - Melted, through fear and overwhelming grief.

15. Dried - I have in a manner no more moisture left in me, than is in a dry potsherd. Cleaveth - Through excessive thirst and drought. Death - Thy providence, delivering me into the power of mine enemies, and by thy terrors in my soul.

16. Dogs - So he calls his enemies for their insatiable greediness, and implacable fierceness against him. Pierced - These words cannot with any probability be applied to David, but were properly and literally verified in Christ.

17. May tell - By my being stretched out upon the cross.

18. They part - This also cannot be applied to David, but was literally fulfilled in Christ, Matt. xxvii, 35 John xix, 24.

20. Darling - Hebrew. my only one; his soul, which he so calls, because it was left alone and destitute of friends and helpers.

21. Heard - Answered and delivered me.

22. Declare - When thou hast delivered me. Thy name - that power and faithfulness and goodness, which thou hast manifested on my behalf. Congregations - The same whom he calls the congregation, and the seed of Jacob and Israel: which also does not so fitly agree to David, who never gives this title to any, but such as were near a-kin to him, as it does to Christ, who extends this name to all his disciples, Matt. xii, 48, 49, and to whom this very text is applied, Heb. ii, 11, 12.

24. Abhorred - He did not turn away his face from it, as men do from things which they abhor. From him - For ever: tho' he did so for a time.

25. Great congregation - In the universal church, of Jews and Gentiles.

26. Satisfied - This is doubtless to be understood, of those spiritual blessings, that grace and peace, and comfort, which all believing souls have in the sense of God's love, the pardon of their sins, and the influences of God's spirit. Seek him - That seek his favour. Your heart - He speaks of the same persons still, though there be a change from the third to the second person, as is usual in these poetical books. For ever - Your comfort shall not be short and transitory, as worldly comforts are, but everlasting.

27. The world - All nations from one end of the world to the other. So this is an evident prophecy of the calling of the Gentiles, and a clear proof, that this psalm immediately speaks of Christ; to whom alone, this and divers other passages of it, belong. Remember - They shall remember their former wickedness with grief and shame, and fear; particularly in worshiping dead and impotent idols. They shall remember their great and manifold obligation to God, which they had quite forgotten, his patience in sparing them so long, in the midst of all their impieties, and in giving his son for them: they shall remember the gracious words and glorious works of Christ, what he did, and suffered for them; which possibly divers of them had been eye and ear-witnesses of. The Lord - Into the only true God, and unto Jesus Christ, to whom this name of Jehovah is often ascribed in scripture.

28. For - This is added as a reason, why the Gentiles should be converted, because God is not only God and the Lord of the Jews, but also of the Gentiles, and of all nations.

29. Fat - Kings and princes, and the great men of the world. Shall eat - Shall feed upon the bread of life, Christ and all his benefits. Worship - This is added to shew what kind of eating he spoke of. Go down - That is, all mankind, for none can escape death.

30. A seed - Christ shall not want a seed or posterity, for though the Jewish nation will generally reject him, the Gentiles shall come in their stead. A generation - That believing seed shall be reputed both by God and men, The generation, or people of the Lord, as the Jews formerly were.

31. They - The seed last mentioned. Come - From Judea and Jerusalem (from whence the gospel was first to go forth) to the Gentile world, to the several parts whereof the apostles went upon this errand. His - God's righteousness: his wonderful grace and mercy unto mankind, in giving them Christ and the gospel; for righteousness is often put for mercy or kindness. Unto - Unto succeeding generations. Whereby David gives us a key to understand this psalm, and teaches us that he speaks not here of himself, but of things which were to be done in after-ages, even of the spreading of the gospel among the Gentiles, in the time of the New Testament. That he - They shall declare that this is the work of God, and not of man.

23

David extolls the goodness of God as his shepherd, and expresses his confidence in him, ver. 1-6. A psalm of David.

2. Lie down - To repose myself at noon, as the manner was in those hot countries. Green - Where there is both delight and plenty of provisions.

3. Restoreth - Hebrew. He bringeth it back; from its errors and wandering. For - Not for any worth in me, but for the glory of his justice, and faithfulness, and goodness.

4. Thy rod and thy staff - Two words denoting the same thing, and both designing God's pastoral care over him.

5. A table - Thou furnishest me with plenty of provisions and comforts. Oil - With aromatic ointments, which were then used at great feasts; thy comforts delight my soul. Runneth over - Thou hast given me a plentiful portions, signified by the cup, given to the guests by the master of the feast.

24

This psalm is generally thought to have been composed by David, upon bringing the ark of God from the house of Obed-edom, into the tabernacle which David had built for it, 2 Sam. vi, 12, 17. Wherein he hath a farther prospect to the temple, which he earnestly desired and intended to build. Moreover because the tabernacle, and temple, and ark, were types of Christ, and of his church and of heaven. David extended his thoughts to them also, or at least the Holy Ghost designed to comprehend them under these typical expressions. He shews God's sovereignty over the world, ver. 1, 2. Who shall receive his blessing, ver. 3-6. An exhortation to receive Christ, ver. 7-10. A psalm of David.

2. Seas - The whole collection of waters, as well as the sea and the rivers running into it, as that great abyss of waters which is contained in the bowels of the earth.

3. The hill - Zion or Moriah, the place of God's sanctuary and special presence. Having asserted God's dominion over all mankind, he now proposes an important question, by whom God will be served, and his blessing enjoyed? Stand - To minister before him. Standing is the posture of ministers or servants. Who shall serve God, with God's acceptation. Holy place - In the place which he hath

sanctified for his service.

4. He - Whose actions and conversation are holy and unblameable. Pure heart - Careful to approve itself to God, as well as to men; ordering a man's very thoughts and affections according to God's word. Vanity - Who doth not value or desire the vain things of this life, such as honours, riches, pleasures; but makes God his portion.

5. The blessing - Grace and glory, and all other good things.

6. The generation - The true progeny which God regards. Face - His grace and favour, which is often called God's face.

7. Lift up - He speaks here of the gates and doors of the temple, which by faith and the spirit of prophecy, he beheld as already built, whose doors he calls Everlasting, not so much because they were made of strong and durable materials, as in opposition to those of the tabernacle, which were removed from place to place. These gates he bids lift up their heads, or tops, by allusion to those gates which have a portcullis, which may be let down or taken up. And as the temple was a type of Christ, and of his church, and of heaven itself; so this place may also contain a representation, either of Christ's entrance into his church, or into the hearts of his faithful people, who are here commanded to set open their hearts and souls for his reception: or of his ascension into heaven, where the saints or angels are poetically introduced as preparing the way, and opening the heavenly gates to receive their Lord and king, returning to his royal habitation with triumph and glory. The king - The Messiah, the king of Israel, and of his church, called the King, or Lord of glory, 1 Cor. ii, 8 James ii, 1, both for that glory which is inherent in him, and that which is purchased by him for his members.

8. The Lord - He is no ordinary person, no other than Jehovah, who hath given so many proofs of his almightiness, who hath subdued all his enemies, and is now returned in triumph.

9. Lift up - The same verse is repeated again, to awaken the dulness of mankind, who are so hardly brought to a serious preparation for such solemnities; and to signify the great importance of the matter, contained under these expressions.

10. Of hosts - Under whose command are all the hosts of heaven and earth, angels and men, and all other creatures.

25

David distrest, takes refuge in God, ver. 1-7. Shews the goodness of God to them that fear him, ver. 8-15. Prays for help against his enemies, and for the church, ver. 16-22. A psalm of David.

2. Ashamed - Disappointed of my hope.

3. Cause - Without any provocation of mine.

4. Teach - Teach me my duty, and cause me to keep close to it, notwithstanding all temptations.

8. Upright - Holy and true, in all his declarations and offers of mercy to sinners. Therefore - He will not be wanting to such poor sinners as I am, but will guide them into the way of life and peace.

9. The meek - Such as meekly submit themselves to God, and are desirous to be directed and governed by him. Judgment - In the paths of judgment, in the right way.

10. Paths - All the dealings of God with them, yea even those that are afflictive, are done in kindness and faithfulness to them.

11. For - Or, though (as this particle is often rendered) it be great. Possibly he speaks of his sin against Uriah and Bathsheba. Great - Or, much or manifold. For the Hebrew word signifies both great and much.

12. Chuse - Which God appointeth.

13. At ease - Hebrew. in Good; in the possession and enjoyment of the true good. The land - Canaan; which was given as an earnest of the whole Covenant of Grace, and all its promises.

14. The secret - His love and favour, which is called his secret, Job xxix, 4 Prov. iii, 32, because it is known to none but him that enjoyeth it. Will shew - He will make them clearly to understand it, both its duties and its blessings; neither of which ungodly men rightly understand.

15. Pluck - He will deliver me out of all my troubles.

20. Soul - My life.

22. Israel - If thou wilt not help me, yet spare thy people who suffer for my sake, and in my sufferings.

26

David professes his integrity, ver. 1-8. Deprecates the doom of the wicked, ver. 9, 10. Casts himself upon the mercy of God, ver. 11, 12. A psalm of David.

1. Trusted - I have committed my cause and affairs to thee.

3. For - I dare appeal to thee, because thou knowest I have a deep sense of thy loving-kindness, by which I have been led to love and obey thee.

4. Sat - Continued with them. I have been so far from an imitation of their wicked courses, that I have avoided their company. Vain - With false and deceitful persons. Go in - Into their company.

6. Compass - Approach to thine altar with my sacrifices: which I could not do with any comfort, if I were conscious of those crimes, whereof mine enemies accuse me.

8. House - Thy sanctuary and worship. honour - Thy glorious and gracious presence.

9. Gather not - Do not bind me up in the same bundle, or put me into the same accursed condition with them.

12. Standeth - I stand upon a sure and solid foundation, being under the protection of God's promise, and his almighty and watchful providence. Congregations - I will not only privately, but in the assemblies of thy people celebrate thy praise.

27

David declares his confidence in God, ver. 1-3. His desire to be in the house of God, ver. 4-6. He prays for light and salvation, ver. 7-12. And exhorts others to wait upon God, ver. 13, 14. A psalm of David.

2. Light - My counsellor in all my difficulties, and my comforter and deliverer in all my distresses. Strength - The supporter and preserver of my life.

3. In this - That God is my light.

4. Dwell. &c. - Have opportunity of constant attendance upon God. To behold - That there I may delight myself, in the contemplation of thy amiable and glorious majesty, and of thy infinite wisdom, holiness, justice, truth, and mercy.

5. The secret - In his tabernacle, into which mine enemies cannot come. He alludes to the ancient custom of offenders, who used to flee to the tabernacle or altar. Rock - A place high and inaccessible.

9. Away - From thy face or presence, or from the place of thy worship.

11. Because of - That I may neither fall into their hands by my folly, nor give them any occasion of triumphing over me.

13. The living - David was thus earnestly desirous of this mercy in this life, not because he placed his portion in these things; but because the truth and glory of God, were highly concerned in making good the promise of the kingdom to him.

28

A prayer for help, ver. 1-3. The doom of the wicked, ver. 4, 5. A thanksgiving, closed with prayer, ver. 6-9. A psalm of David.

2. Towards - Towards the holy of holies, because there the ark was; from whence God gave oracular answers to his people.

3. Draw not - Do not drag me; as thou dost these, to execution and destruction.

5. Regard not - The providential works of God towards his people.

7. I am helped - He speaks of it as past, because God assured him by his spirit, that he had heard and accepted his prayers.

29

It is probable David wrote this psalm, during a storm of thunder, lightning, and rain; as that he wrote the eighth in a moon-shining night, and the nineteenth in a sun-shining morning. He calls on the great to give glory to God, ver. 1, 2. Observes his power in thunder and lightning, Ver. 3-9. His dominion over the world and care over the church, ver. 10, 11. A psalm of David.

1. Ye - Ye potentates and rulers of the earth. Glory - By an humble and thankful acknowledgment of it.

2. Give, &c. - The honour which he deserves: own him as the Almighty, and the only true God. Holiness - Or, in his holy and beautiful house.

3. The waters - Above in the clouds, which are called waters, Gen. i, 7 chap. xviii, 11. The Divine power displays itself in those high places, which are far above the reach of all earthly potentates. Many - Upon the clouds, in which there are vast treasures of water, and upon which God is said to sit or ride, chap. xviii, 10, 11; civ, 3.

5. Lebanon - A place famous for strong and lofty cedars.

6. Them - The cedars; which being broken by the thunder, the parts of them are suddenly and violently hurled hither and thither. Sirion - An high mountain beyond Jordan joining to Lebanon. Lebanon and Sirion are said to skip or leap, both here, and chap. cxiv, 4, by a poetical hyperbole.

7. The flames - The lightnings.

8. Kadesh - An eminent wilderness, vast and terrible, and well known to the Israelites, and wherein possibly they had seen, and observed some such effects of thunder.

9. To calve - Through the terror it causes, which hastens the birth. He names the hinds, because they bring forth their young with difficulty, Job xxxix, 1, 2. Discovereth - Hebrew. maketh bare, of its trees, which it breaks or strips of their leaves. Glory - Having shewed the terrible effects of God's power in other places, he now shews the blessed privilege of God's people, that are praising God in his temple, when the rest of the world are trembling under the tokens of his displeasure.

10. The flood - The most violent waters, which sometimes fall from the clouds upon the earth. These are fitly mentioned, as being many times the companions of great thunders. And this may be alleged as another reason, why God's people praised him in his temple, because as he sends terrible tempests and thunders, so he also restrains and over-rules them. Sitteth - He doth sit, and will sit as king forever, sending such tempests when it pleaseth him.

30

He praises God for delivering him, and exhorts others to praise him, ver. 1-5. Recollects his former security, and his prayer when in trouble, ver. 6-10. And stirs himself up to thankfulness, ver. 11, 12. A Psalm and song, at the dedication of the house of David. Title of the psalm. Song - A psalm to be sung with the voice to an instrument. David - At the dedication of David's house, which was built, 2 Sam. v, 11, and doubtless was dedicated, as God had commanded.

5. Cometh - Speedily and in due season.

7. Mountain - My kingdom: kingdoms are usually called mountains in prophetical writings.

9. Profit - What wilt thou gain by it? The dust - Shall they that are dead celebrate thy goodness in the land of the living? Or, shall my dust praise thee?

11. Sackcloth - Given me occasion to put off that sackcloth, which they used to wear in times of mourning, Esth iv, 1 chap. xxxv, 13 Isaiah xxxii, 11 Joel i, 13. Girded - With joy, as with a garment, surrounding me on every side.

12. My glory - My tongue.

31

David professes his confidence in God, intermixing prayer to him, ver. 1-8. Complains to God and prays for deliverance, ver. 9-18. Concludes with giving glory to God, and encouraging others to trust him, ver. 19-24. To the chief musician, A psalm of David.

1. Ashamed - Of my confidence in thy promise. Deliver me - According to thy faithfulness and goodness.

5. My spirit - My soul or life; to preserve it from the malice of mine enemies. For - Thou hast delivered me formerly, and therefore I commit myself to thee for the future. O Lord, &c. - Who hast shewed thyself so, in making good thy promise.

6. Vanities - Idols, which are often called Vanities, as Deut. xxxii, 21. Or, curious arts, and all sorts of divinations.

7. Known - Loved me, and cared for me.

8. Room - Made way for me to escape, when I was encompassed by them.

9. Grief - With continual weeping.

10. Iniquity - For the punishment of mine iniquity. Consumed - The juice and marrow of them bring almost dried up with grief.

11. A fear - They were afraid to give me any countenance or assistance. Fled - To prevent their own danger and ruin.

12. A broken vessel - Which is irreparable, and useless, and therefore despised by all.

13. Fear - Just cause of fear.
15. My times - All the affairs and events of my life, are wholly in thy power.
19. Laid up - His favour is not always manifested, to them, but it is laid up for them in his treasure, whence it shall be drawn forth when they need it, and he sees it fit. Before - Publickly and in the view of the world.
20. The secret - Or, as in the secret of thy presence: either,
1. As if they were in thy presence chamber, where thine own eye and hand girdeth them, from all the assaults of their enemies; called his secret, partly, because the greatest part of the world are strangers to God and his presence: and partly, because it is a safe and secure place, such as secret and unknown places are. Or,
2. As if they were in the secret of God's tabernacle, as it is called, chap. xxvii, 5, the place of God's special presence, where none might enter save the high-priest. With thy secret favour and providence, which saves them by hidden and unknown methods. From - From their vain-glorious boasting and threats, and from their bad and insolent attempts. Pavilion - Or, tabernacle. Strife - From contentious and slandering tongues.
21. City - In Keilah: where God wonderfully preserved me.
22. Haste - When my passion took away my consideration, and weakened my faith. Cut off - Cast out of thy sight, and out of the care of thy gracious providence.

32

The happiness of them whose sins are forgiven, ver. 1, 2. The necessity of confessing our sins, and of prayer, ver. 3-6. God's promise to them that trust in him, ver. 7-10. An exhortation to rejoice in God, ver. 11. A psalm of David, Maschil. Title of the psalm. Maschil - Or, an instructor. This psalm is fitly so called, because it was composed for the information of the church, in that most important doctrine, the way to true blessedness.

2. Imputeth - Whom God doth not charge with the guilt of his sins, but graciously pardons and accepts him in Christ. No guile - Who freely confesses all his sins, and turns from sin to God with all his heart.
3. Silence - From a full and open confession of my sins. Old - My spirit failed, and the strength of my body decayed. Roaring - Because of the continual horrors of my conscience, and sense of God's wrath.
4. Hand - Thy afflicting hand. My moisture - Was dried up.
5. The iniquity - The guilt of my sin.
6. For this - Upon the encouragement of my example. Found - In an acceptable and seasonable time, while God continues to offer grace and mercy. Waters - In the time of great calamities. Not come - So as to overwhelm him.
8. I will - This and the next verse seems to be the words of God, whom David brings in as returning this answer to his prayers. Mine eye - So Christ did St. Peter, when he turned and looked upon him.
9. Will not - Unless they be forced to it by a bit or bridle. And so all the ancient translators understand it.
10. Sorrows - This is an argument to enforce the foregoing admonition.

33

The Psalmist exhorts the righteous to praise God, for his truth, justice and goodness, ver. 1-5, For creating the world, ver. 6-9. For his providence in governing it, ver. 10-17. For his peculiar favour to his people, encouraging them to trust in him, ver. 18-22.

2. Harp, &c. - These instruments were used in the publick worship of God in the tabernacle.
3. A new song - Renewed or continued from day to day.
4. The word - All God's counsels and commands are wise, and just, and good. His works - All his works of providence agree with his word, and are the accomplishment of his promises or threatenings.
5. Goodness - He not only doth no man wrong, but he is kind and merciful to all men.
6. The word - God made this admirable structure of the heavens, and all its glorious stars; not with great pains and time, but with one single word. Host - The angels: or the stars.
7. Store-houses - Either in the clouds, or in the bowels of the earth.
10. The Lord - Thus he passes from the work of creation, to the works of providence, and from the instances of his power, in senseless and irrational creatures, to his power in over-ruling the thoughts and wills, and actions of men, whether single or united.

11. The Counsel - All his purposes and designs are always successful.

13. All men - Although he hath a relation to Israel, yet he hath a general care over all mankind, all whose hearts and ways he observes.

15. Fashioneth - Having said that God sees and observes all men, he now adds, that he rules and governs them; yea, even the hearts which are most unmanageable, he disposes and inclines according to the counsel of his will. Alike - Or, equally, one as well as another: whether they be Jews or Gentiles, princes or peasants; all are alike subject to his jurisdiction. Their works - Both outward and inward, all the workings of their minds and actions, and all their endeavours and actions.

16. No king - He instances in these, as the most uncontrollable persons in the world, and most confident of themselves. By which he strongly proves his general proposition, of God's powerful providence over all men. By an host - But only by God's providence, who disposes of victory and success, as he pleases, and that frequently to the weakest side.

17. An horse - Though he be strong and fit for battle, or for flight, if need requires. And so this is put for all warlike provisions. Vain things - Hebrew. a lie; because it promises that help and safety which it cannot give.

18. The eye - Whosoever therefore would have safety, must expect it only from the watchful eye, and almighty hand of God. That fear - These are the chief objects of his care and favour. Hope - That place their hope and trust, and happiness, not in any creature, but only in God, and in his mercy and blessings.

34

David praises God for his goodness to himself and others, ver. 1-7. Encourages the righteous to trust in him, ver. 8-10. Exhorts them to fear God and depart from evil, ver. 11-14. God's favour to the righteous and displeasure at the wicked, ver. 15-22 A psalm of David, when he changed his behaviour before Abimelech: who drove him away, and he departed. Title of the psalm. When - A psalm made upon that occasion, though not at that time, when he counterfeited madness. Wherein whether he sinned or not, is matter of dispute; but this is undoubted, that his deliverance deserved this solemn acknowledgment. Abimelech - Called Achish, 1 Sam. xxi, 10. But Abimelech seems to have been the common name of the kings of the Philistines, Gen. xx, 2; xxvi, 1, as Pharaoh was of the Egyptians.

2. Shall boast - Shall glory in this, that I have so powerful and so gracious a master. The humble - The righteous.

3. Together - Not in place, for David was now banished from the place of God's publick worship, but in affection: let our souls meet, and let our praises meet in the ears of the all-hearing God.

5. Lightened - Comforted and encouraged. Ashamed - They were not disappointed of their hope.

6. This man - David.

7. The angel - The angels, the singular number being put for the plural.

8. O taste - Make trial, of it by your own experience of it. Good - Merciful and gracious.

9. Fear - Reverence, serve, and trust him: for fear is commonly put for all the parts of God's worship.

12. Life - A long and happy life, begun in this world and continued forever in the next. Good - In which he may enjoy good, prosperity or happiness.

13. Evil - From all manner of evil speaking, from all injurious, false and deceitful speeches.

14. Depart - From all sin. Do good - Be ready to perform all good offices to all men. Seek - Study by all means possible to live peaceable with all men. Pursue it - Do not only embrace it gladly when it is offered, but follow hard after it, when it seems to flee away from thee.

16. The face - His anger, which discovers itself in the face.

18. Nigh - Ready to hear and succor them. To - Those whose spirits are truly humbled under the hand of God, and the sense of their sins, whose hearts are subdued, and made obedient to God's will and submissive to his providence.

20. Bones - All the parts and members of their bodies.

35

David prays for deliverance from his enemies, and prophecies their destruction, ver. 1-10, Describes their wickedness, ver. 11-21. Foretells their confusion, the joy of the righteous, and his own thanksgiving, ver. 22-28. A psalm of David.

3. Say - By thy spirit assuring me of it: and by thy providence effecting it.

6. Their way - By which they flee, being chased.

7. For - Out of mere malice.

10. My bones - My whole body, as well as my soul.

13. Returned - Although my fastings and prayers did them no good.

15. Gathered - They were so full of joy, that they could not contain it in their own breasts, but sought to communicate it to others. Abjects - Or, vile persons, either for the meanness of their condition, or for their wickedness. Knew not - While I had no suspicion of them. Tear me - My good name with calumnies, and reproaches and curses.

16. Mockers - They made themselves buffoons and jesters, and accustomed themselves to mock and deride David, that thereby they might gain admittance to the tables of great men, which was all they sought for.

17. Look on - Without affording me pity or help. Darling - My soul, Hebrew. my only one; which is now left alone and forsaken by my friends, and hath none to trust in but God.

18. I will - When I shall be restored to the liberty of the publick assemblies.

20. For - They breathe out nothing but threatenings and war; they use not open violence but subtile artifices, against me and my followers, who desire nothing more than to live quietly and peaceably.

21. Wide - To pour forth whole floods of scoffs and slanders. \Aha - An expression of joy and triumph. Our eye - What we have long desired and hoped for.

22. This - Thou also hast seen, all their plots and threats, and all my distresses and calamities. Keep not - Be not deaf, to my prayers. The same word signifies, both to be silent, and to be deaf.

23. Awake - To plead my cause against mine adversaries.

36

The grievous state of the wicked, ver. 1-4. The goodness of God, ver. 5-9. David prays, in confidence of deliverance, ver. 10- 12. To the chief musician, a psalm of David, the servant of the Lord.

1. No fear - When I consider the manifold transgressions of ungodly men, I conclude within myself, that they have cast off all fear of the Divine majesty.

2. Flattereth - He deceiveth himself with vain persuasions, that God does not mind his sins, or will not punish them. Found - Punish, as the same phrase is used, Num. xxxii, 23.

3. Left off - Once he had some degrees of wisdom, but now he is become an open apostate.

4. Deviseth - Freely, from his own inclination, when none are present to provoke him to it.

5. Thy mercy - Mine enemies are cruel and perfidious, but thou art infinite in mercy, and faithfulness. Heavens - Is infinite and incomprehensible. Faithfulness - The truth both of thy threatenings against thine enemies, and of thy promises made to good men. The clouds - Is far above our reach, greater and higher than we can apprehend.

6. Mountains - Stedfast and unmoveable: eminent and conspicuous to all men. Judgments - The executions of thy counsels. Deep - Unsearchable, as the ocean. Man - The worst of men; yea, the brute-beasts have experience of thy care and kindness.

7. Loving-kindness - Though all thine attributes be excellent, yet, above all, thy mercy is most excellent, or precious and amiable.

8. Satisfied - Who trust in thee, as he now said. Fatness - With those delightful provisions, which thou hast prepared for them in heaven. The river - Which denotes both their plenty, and their perpetuity.

9. Life - It is in God as in a fountain, and from him is derived to us. But - Of that glorious and blessed, and endless life, which alone is worthy of the name. Light - In the light of thy glorious presence, which shall be fully manifested, when we see thee face to face. Light - Joy and comfort, and happiness: the word light is elegantly repeated in another signification; in the former clause it is light discovering, in this light, discovered or enjoyed.

11. The foot - Of my proud and insolent enemies. Come - So as to overthrow me.

12. There - He seems as it were to point at the place, as if it were already done.

37

David exhorts to patience and confidence in God, ver. 1-8. Shews the different state of the righteous and the wicked, ver. 9- 40. A psalm of David.

1. Fret not - Because they prosper in their wicked enterprizes.

5. Commit - All thy cares and business, and necessities, commend to God by fervent prayer.

6. Judgment - It shall be as visible to men, as the light of the sun, at noon-day.

7. Rest - Do not repine at his dealings, but quietly submit to his will, and wait for his help.

8. Fret not - Either against the sinner for his success; or against God. Do evil - If grief arise in thee, take care that it do not transport thee to sin.

9. The earth - This for the most part was literally fulfilled in that state of the church.

10. Not be - He shall be dead and gone. Diligently - Industriously seeking him. His place - His place and estate, and glory.

11. But - Those who patiently bear God's afflicting hand, and meekly pass by injuries. Peace - Partly of outward peace and prosperity, which God in his due time will give them: but principally of inward peace, in the sense of God's favour and the assurance of endless happiness.

13. His day - The day appointed by God for his punishment or destruction.

18. Knoweth - Observes with care and affection. The days - All things which befall them, their dangers and fears, and suffering. For ever - To them and their seed forever: and when they die their inheritance is not lost, but exchanged for one infinitely better.

20. Fat - Which in an instant melts before the fire.

23. Established - So that he shall not fall into mischief.

24. Fall - Into trouble.

25. Forsaken - These temporal promises, were more express to the Jews in the times of the Old Testament, than to Christians.

26. Blessed - Not only with spiritual, but with temporal blessings.

27. Dwell - Thou shalt dwell in the land, and afterwards in heaven.

30. The mouth - Having shewed, God's singular care over the righteous, he proceeds to give a character of them. Judgment - Of God's judgment, word or law.

31. Heart - His thoughts, meditations and affections are fixed upon it. Slide - Slide, or swerve, from the rule, from God's law.

35. Bay-tree - Which is continually green and flourishing even in winter.

36. Yet - He was gone in an instant. But - There was no monument or remainder of him left.

37. Peace - Though he may meet with troubles in his way, yet all shall end well.

38. Together - All without exception.

38

David complains of God's displeasure and his own sin, ver. 1-5. Of his bodily sickness, ver. 6-10. Of the unkindness of his friends and the injuries of his enemies, ver. 11-20. Prays to God for help, ver. 21, 22. A psalm of David to bring to remembrance. Title of the psalm. To bring, &c. - Either, to God, that by this humble and mournful prayer, he might prevail with God, to remember and pity him; or, to himself, that by reviewing this psalm afterwards, he might call to mind his former danger and misery, and God's wonderful mercy in delivering him; and that others also might remember what God had done to him.

2. Arrows - Thy judgments outward and inward.

3. Sin - Which hath provoked thee to deal thus severely with me.

4. Iniquities - Or, the punishment of mine iniquities, as this word is frequently used. Are gone - Like deep waters wherewith I am overwhelmed.

5. Foolishness - Sin.

7. Disease - The disease might be some burning fever, breaking forth outwardly in carbuncles, or boils. It is true, this and the other expressions may be taken figuratively, but we should not forsake the literal sense of the words without necessity.

12. Deceit - They design mischief, but cover it with fair pretenses.

13. Dumb - Was silent, to testify his humiliation for his sins, and his acceptation of the punishment which he had brought upon himself.

16. When - When I fall into any misery, they triumph in the accomplishment of their desires.

17. To halt - just falling into destruction. Before me - I am constantly sensible of thy just hand, and of my sins the cause of it.

18. Declare - To thee.

19. Strong - Are thriving and flourishing.

39

David relates the struggle which had been in his breast, ver. 1-3. He meditates on man's frailty and mortality, ver. 4-6. He prays for pardon, deliverance from trouble, and respite from death, ver. 7-13. To the chief musician, even to Jeduthun, A psalm of David. Title of the psalm. Jeduthun - One of the three chief masters of the sacred musick, 1 Chron. xvi, 41, 42.

1. I said - I fully resolved. Take heed - To order all my actions right, and particularly to govern my tongue.

2. Dumb - Two words put together, expressing the same thing, to aggravate or increase it. I held - I

forbear to speak, what I justly might, lest I should break forth into some indecent expressions. Stirred - My silence did not assuage my grief, but increase it.

4. My end - Make me sensible of the shortness and uncertainly of life, and the near approach of death.

5. Before thee - If compared with thee, and with thy everlasting duration.

6. Vain shew - Hebrew. in a shadow or image; in an imaginary rather than a real life: in the pursuit of vain imaginations, in which there is nothing solid or satisfactory: man in and his life, and all his happiness in this world, are rather appearances and dreams, than truths and realities. Disquieted - Hebrew. They make a noise, bustling, or tumult, with unwearied industry seeking for riches, and troubling and vexing both themselves and others in the pursuit of them.

7. Mow Lord - Seeing this life and all its enjoyments are so vain and short. My hope - I will seek for happiness no where but in God.

10. Remove - Take off the judgment which thou hast inflicted upon me. I am - Help me before I am utterly lost.

11. Beauty - His comeliness and all his excellencies or felicities. Moth - As a moth consumeth a garment, to which God compares himself and his judgments, secretly and insensibly consuming a people, Isaiah li, 8.

12. A stranger - I am only in my journey or passage to my real home, which is in the other world.

13. No more - Among the living, or in this world.

40

This psalm is a celebration of God's great goodness to him, and all his people. In it there are some passages which cannot belong to Christ, and some which do not properly belong to David, or to that time and state of the church, but only to Christ, and to the times of the New Testament. He praises God for delivering him out of deep distress, ver. 1-5. Thence takes occasion to speak of the work of our redemption by Christ, ver. 6- 10. Prays for mercy and grace both for himself and for his brethren, ver. 11-17. To the chief musician, A psalm of David.

2. Pit - Desperate dangers and calamities. Rock - A place of strength and safety. Established - Kept me from falling into mischief.

3. And fear - Shall stand in awe of that God, whom they see to have so great power, either to save or to destroy.

4. The proud - Or, the mighty, the great and proud potentates of the world, to whom most men are apt to look and trust. Turn - From God, in whom alone they ought to trust. To lies - To lying vanities, such as worldly power and wisdom, and riches, and all other earthly things, or persons, in which men are prone to trust: which are called lies, because they promise more than they perform.

5. Many - This verse seems to be interposed as a wall of partition, between that which David speaks in his own person, and that which he speaks in the person of the Messiah, in the following verses.

6. Sacrifice - These and the following words, may in an improper sense belong to the time of David; when God might be said, not to desire or require legal sacrifices comparatively. Thou didst desire obedience rather than sacrifices, but in a proper sense, they belong only to the person and times of the Messiah, and so the sense is, God did not desire or require them, for the satisfaction of his own justice, and the expiation of mens sins, which could not possibly be done by the blood of bulls or goats, but only by the blood of Christ, which was typified by them, and which Christ came into the world to shed, in pursuance of his father's will, as it here follows, ver. 7, 8. So here is a prediction concerning the cessation of the legal sacrifice, and the substitution of a better instead of them. Opened - Hebrew. bored. I have devoted myself to thy perpetual service, and thou hast accepted of me as such, and signified so much by the boring of mine ears, according to the law and custom in that case, Exod. xxi, 5, 6. The seventy Jewish interpreters, whom the apostle follows, Heb. x, 5, translate these words, a body hast thou prepared me.

7. Them - These words literally and truly belong to Christ, and the sense is this; seeing thou requirest a better sacrifice than those of the law, lo, I offer myself to come, and I will in due time come, into the world, as this phrase is explained in divers places of scripture, and particularly Heb. x, 5, where this place is expressly applied to Christ. Volume - These two words, volume and book are used of any writing, and both express the same thing. Now this volume of the book is the law of Moses, which is commonly and emphatically called the book, and was made up in the form of a roll or volume, as the Hebrew books generally were. And so this place manifestly points to Christ, concerning whom much is said in the books of Moses.

8. I delight - This is eminently true, of Christ, and is here observed as an act of heroic obedience, that he not only resolved to do, but delighted in doing the will of God, or what God had commanded

him, which was to die, and that a most shameful, and painful, and cursed death. My heart - I do not only understand it, but receive it with heartiest love, delighting both to meditate of it, and to yield obedience to it.

9. Righteousness - Thy faithfulness. Great congregation - In the most public and solemn assemblies: not only to the Jews, but also to all nations; to whom Christ preached by his apostles, as is observed Eph. ii, 17. Not refrained - From preaching it, even to the face of mine enemies.

11. With-hold not - David, having been transported by the spirit of God to the commemoration of the great mystery of the Messiah, he now seems to be led back by the same spirit, to the consideration of his own case.

12. Taken hold - Mens sins are figuratively said to take hold of them, as an officer takes hold of a man whom he arrests. To look - Unto God or men, with any comfort: I am ashamed and confounded.

15. Shame - Their sinful and shameful actions.

41

David on a sick bed lays hold on God's promise and prays for mercy, ver. 1-4. Complains of the pride and malice of his enemies, ver. 5-9. Flees to God for succor, and praises him, ver. 10, 13. To the chief musician, A psalm of David.

3. Make his bed - Give him ease and comfort, which sick men receive by the help of those who turn and stir up their bed, to make it soft and easy for them.

4. Heal - The soul is said to be healed, when it is pardoned and purged. For - For I acknowledge that I have sinned.

6. His heart - Even when he is with me, and pretends hearty affection, his heart is devising mischief against me.

9. Yea - These words were literally fulfilled in David, and yet the Holy Ghost looked farther in them, even to Christ and Judas, in whom they received a fuller accomplishment. Lift up - A phrase implying injury, joined with insolency and contempt; taken from an unruly horse, which kicks at him that owns and feeds him.

10. Requite - Punish them for their wicked practices; which being now a magistrate, he was obliged to do.

11. By this - Because hitherto thou hast supported me, and prolonged my days to the disappointment of their hopes.

12. Settest - Or, hast confirmed me in thy presence, under thine eye and special care: to minister unto thee, as a king over thy people. And in regard of his posterity, the kingdom was established forever. 13. Amen - Signifies an hearty assent and approbation, and withal an earnest desire of the thing, to which it is annexed. And as the Psalms are divided into five books, so each of them is closed with this word; the first here: the second, chap. lxxii, 19, the third, chap. lxxxix, 52, the fourth, chap. cvi, 48, the last in the end of chap. 1l, 6, the doubling of the word shews the fervency of his spirit, in this work of praising God.

42

The psalmist longs for the public service of God, ver. 1-4. Stirs himself up to trust in God, ver. 5-9. Reproached by his enemies, still hopes in him, ver. 10, 11. To the chief musician, Maschil, for the sons of Korah. Title of the psalm. Sons of Korah - Who were an eminent order of singers in the house of God, 1 Chron. vi, 33.

1. Panteth - After the enjoyment of thee in thy sanctuary.

2. Thirsteth - Not after vain useless idols, but after the only true and living God. Appear - In the place of his special presence and publick worship.

4. Remember - My banishment from God's presence, and mine enemies triumphs. In me - I breathe out my sorrows and complaints to God within my own breast. The multitudes - Israelites, who went thither in great numbers. Holy-day - Or that kept the feast, the three solemn festival solemnities, which they kept holy unto the Lord.

5. For - Hebrew. for the salvations of his face, for those supports, deliverances and comforts which I doubt not I shall enjoy both in his presence and sanctuary, and from his presence, and the light of his countenance.

6. Therefore - Therefore that I may revive my drooping spirits. Remember - I will consider thy infinite mercy and power, and faithfulness. Mizar - From all the parts of the land, to which I shall be driven; whether from the parts beyond Jordan on the east: or mount Hermon, which was in the northern parts.

7. Deep - One affliction comes immediately after another, as if it were called for by the former. A metaphor taken from violent and successive showers of rain; which frequently come down from heaven, as it were at the noise, or call of God's water spouts.

8. Command - Will effectually confer upon me. Loving-kindness - His blessings, the effects of his loving-kindness.

10. As - As a sword, which cutteth the very bones, so painful are their reproaches.

43

The psalmist appeals to God, ver. 1, 2. Prays to be restored to the public ordinances, and trusts in God, ver. 3-5.

1. Nation - So he calls the company of his enemies for their great numbers. Man - Probably Achitophel or Absalom.

3. Send out - That is, actually discover them. Truth - Thy favour, or the light of thy countenance, and the truth of thy promises made to me; or the true-light, the illumination of thy spirit, and the direction of thy gracious providence, whereby I may be led in the right way, to thy holy hill. Hill - Of Zion, the place of God's presence and worship.

44

The church commemorates past mercies, ver. 1-8. Complains of present troubles, ver. 9-16. Professes her integrity, ver. 17-22. Prays for succor, ver. 23-26. To the chief musician for the sons of Korah, Maschil.

4. My king - The whole people speak as one man, being united in one body.

11. Scattered - Those who were not slain are carried into captivity, and dispersed in several places.

16. Avenger - Who executeth both God's and his own vengeance upon me.

17. Yet - Although we cannot excuse ourselves from many other sins, yet through thy grace we have kept ourselves from apostacy and idolatry, notwithstanding all examples and provocations.

18. Turned - From thy worship to idols.

19. Broken us - By inflicting upon us one breach after another, thou hast at last brought us to this pass. The place - A place extremely desolate, such as dragons love, Isaiah xiii, 21, 22, and therefore full of horror, and danger. Covered us - With deadly horrors and miseries.

22. Yea - Because we are constant in thy worship, which they abhor.

25. Our soul - Our persons. Our belly - We are not only thrown down to the earth, but we lie there like dead carcases.

45

This psalm is an illustrious prophecy of the Messiah, and points at him only, as a bridegroom espousing the church to himself, and as a king ruling in it. And our saviour probably alludes to this, where he compares the kingdom of heaven to a royal marriage. We have no reason to think, it has any reference to Solomon's marriage with Pharaoh's daughter. It is meant purely of Christ, and no other, and to him it is applied in the New Testament. After the preface, it speaks of the person and victories of the royal bridegroom, ver. 1-5. The righteousness of his government, ver. 6, 7. The splendour of his court, ver. 8, 9. Of the royal bride, the church, her consent gained, ver. 10, 11. The nuptials solemnized, ver. 12-15. The issue of this marriage, ver. 16, 17. To the chief musician upon Shoshannim, for the sons of Korah, Maschil. A song of loves. Title of the psalm. Shoshannim - Is supposed to mean, an instrument of six strings. This is a song of loves, of the holy love which is between Christ and his church.

1. Enditing - Hebrew. boileth, or bubbleth up like water over the fire. This denotes that the workings of his heart, were fervent and vehement, kindled by God's grace, and the inspiration of the Holy Ghost. Made - Have composed. Pen - He was only the pen or instrument in uttering this song; it was the spirit of God, by whose hand this pen was guided.

2. Fairer - Than all other men: which is most true of Christ; but not of Solomon; whom many have excelled, in holiness and righteousness, which is the chief part of the beauty celebrated in this psalm. Grace - God hath plentifully poured into thy mind and tongue the gift of speaking wisely, eloquently, and acceptably. Therefore - And because God hath so eminently qualified thee for rule, therefore he hath blessed thee with an everlasting kingdom.

3. Thy sword - To smite thine enemies. And the sword is here put for all his arms, as it is in many other places.

4. And - Being thus magnificently girt and armed. Ride - March on speedily and successfully against thine enemies. The word - That is, the gospel: which is called the word of truth, Eph. i, 13, and may no less truly be called the word of meekness, because it is not delivered with terror, as the law was at Sinai, but meekly and sweetly; and the word of righteousness, because it brings in everlasting righteousness, and strongly excites all men to the practice of righteousness and holiness. And so the gospel is compared, to an horse or chariot, upon which Christ is said to ride, when the gospel is preached, and carried about from place to place. Teach thee - Thou shalt do exploits, which shall be terrible to thine enemies. But the phrase, thy right hand shall teach thee, is not to be taken properly; the meaning is, his hand should shew him, discover and work before him.

5. Arrows - The same with the sword, and this is no other than his word, which is sharp and powerful, and pierceth the hearts of men. The kings - Of thine enemies. Fall - Prostrate at thy feet, after the manner of conquered persons.

6. O God - It is evident, that the speech is still continued to the same person whom he calls king, ver. 1, 11, and here God, to assure us that he doth not speak of Solomon, but a far greater king, who is not only a man, but the mighty God, Isaiah ix, 6. A right scepter - Thou rulest with exact righteousness and equity.

7. Therefore - Therefore God hath exalted thee far above all men and angels, to a state of joy and endless glory at his right hand; which is fitly compared by the oil of gladness. Thy God - According to thy human nature, John xx, 17, though in respect of thy Divine nature, thou art his fellow, Zech xiii, 7, and his equal, Phil ii, 6, and one with him, John x, 30. Oil - So called, because it was a token of gladness, and used in feasts, and other solemn occasions of rejoicing. Fellows - Above all them who partake with thee in this unction: above all that ever were anointed for priests or prophets, or kings.

8. Myrrh - Wherewith they used to perfume their garments: this may denote those glorious and sweet smelling virtues, which, as they were treasured up in Christ's heart, so did they manifest themselves outwardly, and give forth a grateful smell, in the whole course of his life and actions. Palaces - The king is here supposed to reside in his ivory palaces, and his garments are so fragrant, that they not only perfume the whole palace in which he is; but the sweet favour is perceived by those that pass by them, all which is poetically said, and with allusion to Solomon's glorious garments and palaces. The heavenly mansions, may not unfitly be called ivory palaces, as elsewhere in the same figurative manner they are said to be adorned with gold and precious stones, from which mansions Christ came into the world, into which Christ went, and where he settled his abode after he went out of the world, and from whence he poured forth all the fragrant gifts and graces of his spirit, although there is no necessity to strain every particular circumstance in such poetical descriptions; for some expressions may be used, only as ornaments, as they are in parables; and it may suffice to know, that the excellencies of the king Christ are described by things which earthly potentates place their glory. Whereby - By the sweet smell of thy garments out of those ivory palaces, or the effusion of the gifts and graces of thy spirit from heaven; which as it is a great blessing to those who receive them, so doth it rejoice the heart of Christ, both as it is a demonstration of his own power and glory, and as it is the instrument of bringing souls to God. Made thee - Thou art made glad.

9. Among - Among them that attend upon thy spouse, as the manner was in nuptial solemnities. As the queen is the church in general, and so these honourable women are particular believers, who are daily added to the church, Acts ii, 47. And although the church is made up of particular believers, yet she is distinguished from them, for the decency of the parable. And these believers may be said to be Kings daughters, because among others, many persons of royal race embraced the faith, and because they are in a spiritual sense, Kings unto God, Rev. i, 6. Right hand - The most honourable place. Ophir - Clothed in garments made of the choicest gold. By which he designs the graces wherewith the church is accomplished.

10. Hearken - The prophet having hitherto spoken to the bridegroom, now addresseth his speech to the bride. O daughter - He speaks like an elder person, and as her spiritual father and counsellor. Incline - He uses several words, signifying the same thing, to shew his vehement desire of her good. Forget - Comparatively.

11. So - So thou shalt be acceptable to thy husband; which will abundantly recompence thee, for the loss of thy father's house. Thy Lord - As he is thy husband, and also as he is thy king, and God.

12. The daughter - The people of Tyre; as the daughter of Zion or Jerusalem, are put for their inhabitants: he mentions the Tyrians; because they among others, and before many others, were to be converted to Christ, but they are here put for all the Gentiles, whom that city fitly represents, as being the mart of the nations. A gift - To testify their homage. The rich - Of other nations.

13. Daughter - The spouse; so called, because she was the daughter of one king, and the wife of another. Within - In her soul. Her cloathing - She is outwardly adorned with virtuous and honourable actions.

14. Brought - He alludes to the custom of conducting the bride to the bride-groom's house. Companions - Her bride-maidens attending upon her.

16. Instead - Having directed his speech to the bride, he now returns to the bridegroom, as may be gathered both from the Hebrew words, which are of the masculine gender; and from the next verse, which unquestionably belongs unto him, and therefore this cannot be understood of Solomon, and his marriage with Pharaoh's daughter, because he had no children by her, and but very few by all his wives and concubines; and his children were so far from being made Princes in all the earth, that they enjoyed but a small part of their father's dominions, but this was fully accomplished in Christ: who instead of his fathers of the Jewish nation, had a numerous posterity of Christians of all the nations of the earth, which here and elsewhere are called princes and kings, because of their great power with God and with men.

17. Remembered - As he began the psalm with the celebration of the king's praises, so now he ends with it, and adds this important circumstance, that this nuptial song should not only serve for the present solemnity, but should be remembered and sung in all successive generations.

46

The safety of the church under God's care, ver. 1-7. An exhortation to behold his works, and to trust in him, ver. 8-11. To the chief musician for the sons of Korah, A song upon Alamoth.

2. Though - Though there should be nothing but confusion, and desolations round about us: which are often expressed by such metaphors.

4. A river - This may design the gracious presence, and blessing of the Lord, which is frequently described under the name of waters. Make glad - Shall not barely preserve it from danger, but give great occasion for rejoicing and thanksgiving. The city - Jerusalem, the place where God's holy tabernacle is settled.

7. Raged - Against God, and against his people. Uttered - He spake to them in his wrath. The earth - The inhabitants of the earth were consumed.

8. Desolations - Among those who were vexatious to God's people.

9. To cease - He hath settled as in a firm and well-grounded peace. The land - Of Israel: from one end of it to the other. The bow - The bows and spears, and chariots of their enemies.

11. Be still - Stir no more against my people. God - The only true and almighty God; your gods are but dumb and impotent idols. Exalted - I will make myself glorious by my great and wonderful works.

47

This psalm seems to have been composed upon the occasion of carrying the ark from the house of Obed-edom into the city of Zion, 2 Sam. vi, 12, 17. But as Zion was a type of the church, and the ark a type of Christ, so it has a farther reference, even to Christ's ascension into heaven, and to the spreading of his kingdom in all parts of the world. It contains an exhortation to rejoice in God, ver. 1-4. A prophecy of Christ's ascension, and of the calling of the Gentiles, ver. 5-9. To the chief musician, A psalm for the sons of Korah.

3. Subdue - He speaks this in the name of the whole church, to which all particular believers were to submit themselves in the Lord.

4. Chuse - He will appoint and bestow upon us. Inheritance - The presence and worship, and blessing of God. This God had chosen for the Israelites and resolved to chuse or set apart for the Gentiles. Of Jacob - Of the people of Jacob or Israel, who are frequently called Jacob, for these did actually enjoy the presence of God in his sanctuary. Loved - Not for any peculiar worth in them, but for his free love to them, as he declareth, Deut. vii, 7, 8.

5. God - This is meant literally of the ark: but mystically of Christ's ascension into heaven, as may be gathered by comparing this with Eph. iv, 8, where the like words uttered concerning the ark upon the same occasion, chap. lxviii, 18, are directly applied to Christ's ascension.

7. The king - Not only ours, but of all the nations of the world. Sing - Not formally and carelessly, but seriously, considering the greatness of this king whom you praise, and what abundant cause you have to praise him.

8. The throne - Heaven is often called God's throne, whence God is said to behold and to rule all nations; of which general dominion of God, he here speaks. And Christ sits at his father's right-hand, for that purpose.

9. The princes - The Gentiles, who were divided in their principles, and interests, and religions, are now united and gathered together to Christ, laying their scepters at his feet, and jointly owning his worship and service. And altho' he mentions their conversion only, yet the conversion of their people might reasonably be supposed. Of the God - He doth not say the people of Abraham, lest this should be appropriated to the Israelites; but the people of the God of Abraham who worship the God of Abraham,

whether they be Jews or Gentiles. The Shields - The princes or rulers, who are called shields, Hosea iv, 18, because by their office they are the common prosecutors of all their people. These are the Lord's, at his disposal, or subject to his dominion, both as to their hearts and kingdoms. Exalted - By this means God shall be greatly glorified.

48

The glory and excellency of the church, ver. 1-3. Which God preserves from her enemies, ver. 4-8. God is praised for this, ver. 9, 10. Who effectually provides for its safety, ver. 11-14 A song and psalm for the sons of Korah.

1. The city - In Jerusalem. Mountain - In his holy mountain.

2. The joy - This is spoken prophetically, because the joyful doctrine of the gospel was to go from thence to all nations. The city - Of God, who justly calls himself a great king.

3. Known - By long experience. Palaces - Possibly he may point at the king's palace and the temple, which was the palace of the king of heaven; which two palaces God did in a singular manner protect, and by protecting them, protected the whole city and people.

4. The kings - Either those kings confederate against Jehoshaphat, 2 Chron. xx, 1, or the Assyrian princes; whom they vain- gloriously called kings, Isaiah x, 8. Passed - In their march towards Jerusalem.

5. Saw it - They did only look upon it, but not come into it, nor shoot an arrow there - nor cast a bank against it, 2 Kings xix, 32. Marvelled - At the wonderful works wrought by God.

6. Fear - At the tidings of Tirhakah's coming against them, 2 Kings xix, 9, and at that terrible slaughter of their army, ver. 35.

7. Breakest - Thou didst no less violently and suddenly destroy these raging enemies of Jerusalem, than sometimes thou destroyest the ships at sea with a fierce and vehement wind, such as the eastern winds were in those parts.

8. Heard - The predictions of the prophets have been verified by the events. Establish - God will defend her in all succeeding ages. And so God would have done, if Jerusalem had not forsaken him, and forfeited his protection.

9. Thought - It hath been the matter of our serious and deep meditation, when we have been worshipping in thy temple.

10. So - Thou art acknowledged to be such an one as thou hast affirmed thyself to be in thy Word, God Almighty, or All- sufficient, the Lord of hosts, and a strong tower to all that trust in thee. Righteousness - Of righteous actions; by which thou discoverest thy holiness.

11. Judgments - Upon thine and their enemies.

12. Tell - He bids them mark well her towers, bulwarks, and palaces, with thankfulness to God, when they should find upon enquiry, that not one of them were demolished.

13. Tell it - That they may continue their praises to God for this mercy, by which they hold and enjoy all their blessings.

49

The preface, ver. 1-4. We need not fear the wicked, ver. 5. They cannot by their riches save either their friends or themselves from death, ver. 6-10. They cannot secure happiness to themselves, either in this world or the world to come, ver. 11-14. He comforts good men against the fear of death, or of the prosperity of the wicked, ver. 15-20. To the chief musician, A psalm for the sons of Korah.

4. I will - I will hearken what God by his Spirit speaks to me, and that will I now speak to you. A parable - Which properly is an allegorical speech, but is often taken for an important, and withal, dark doctrine or sentence. Open - I will not smother it in my own breast, but publish it to the world. Dark - So he calls the following discourse, because the thing in question ever hath been thought hard to be understood.

5. In the days - In times of great distress and calamity, when wicked men flourish, and good men are oppressed. Supplanters - This character fitly agrees to David's enemies, who were not only malicious, but deceitful and treacherous.

6. Trust - As that which will secure them from calamities. Having said that good men had no cause of fear, from their present sufferings from ungodly men, now he proceeds to shew, that the ungodly had no reason to be secure because of their riches.

7. Redeem - Neither from the first death, nor from the second. Brother - Whom he would do his utmost to preserve.

8. Soul - Of their life. Precious - Hard to be obtained. Ceaseth - It is never to be accomplished, by any mere man, for himself or for his brother.

10. He seeth - Every man sees that all men die, the wise and the foolish; the evil and the good. To others - He saith not to sons or kindred; but to others, because he is wholly uncertain to whom he shall leave them, to friends, or strangers, or enemies; which he mentions as a great vanity in riches. They neither can save them from death, nor will accompany him in and after death; and after his death will be disposed, he knows not how, nor to whom.

11. Thought - Tho' they are ashamed to express, yet it is their secret hope. Houses - Either their posterity, often called mens houses: or their mansion-houses, as it is explained in the next clause. For ever - To them and theirs in succeeding generations. Call - Fondly dreaming by this means to immortalize their memories.

12. Man - Living in all splendour and glory. Abideth not - All his dreams of perpetuating his name and estate, shall be confuted by experience.

13. Way - Their contrivance to immortalize themselves.

14. Sheep - Which for a season are in sweet pastures, but at the owner's pleasure are led away to the slaughter. Death - The first death shall consume their bodies, and the second death shall devour their souls. The upright - Good men whom they abused at their pleasure. Morning - In the day of the general judgment, and the resurrection of the dead. Beauty - All their glory and felicity. Dwelling - They shall be hurried from their large and stately mansions, into a close and dark grave.

15. God - Tho' no man can find out a ransom to redeem himself, yet God can and will redeem me. The grave - The grave shall not have power to retain me, but shall be forced to give me up into my father's hands. Receive - Into heaven.

16. Afraid - Discouraged.

18. Blessed - He applauded himself as an happy man. Men - And as he flatters himself, so parasites flatter him for their own advantage. When - When thou dost indulge thyself, and advance thy worldly interest.

19. He - Now he returns to the third person: such changes are frequent in this book. Go - To the grave and hell, where he shall meet with his wicked parents, who by their counsel and example, led him into his evil courses. See - Neither the light of this life, to which they shall never return: nor of the next life, to which they shall never be admitted.

20. Understandeth not - Hath not true wisdom. The beasts - Though he hath the outward shape of a man, yet in truth he is a beast, a stupid, and unreasonable creature.

50

The design of this psalm is to reprove the common miscarriages of many professors of religion, who satisfied their own consciences, and fancied that they pleased God with their external and ceremonial performances, notwithstanding their neglect of piety, justice, and charity: and to instruct men concerning the nature of the true and acceptable worship of God. The glorious appearance of the great judge, ver. 1-6. Instructions given how to worship him, ver. 7-15. A reproof of those who pretend to worship him, while they disobey his commands, ver. 16-20. Their doom read, and warning given to all, to order their conversation aright, ver. 21-23. A psalm of Asaph. Title of the psalm. Asaph - Who was not only the chief of the sacred singers, but also a prophet, 2 Chron. xxix, 30, and a composer of several psalms, 2 Chron. xxix, 30.

1. Called - All the inhabitants of the earth, from one end to the other: whom he here summons to be witnesses of his proceedings in this solemn judgment, between him and his people, which is here poetically represented. For here is a tribunal erected, the judge coming to it, the witnesses and delinquents summoned, and at last the sentence given.

2. Zion - The place where he was supposed to reside, and where he would now sit in judgment. The perfection - The most amiable place of the whole world, because, of the presence and worship, and blessing of God. Shined - Hath manifested himself in a glorious manner.

3. Our God - The prophet speaks this in the persons of the worshippers of God. Though he be our God, yet he will come to execute judgment upon us. Cease - Or delay to sit in judgment. Tempestuous - This is a farther description of that terrible majesty, wherewith God would clothe himself when he came to his tribunal.

4. Call - To the inhabitants of them, all angels and men, whom he calls in for witnesses of the equity of his proceedings.

5. Gather - O ye angels, summon and fetch them to my tribunal. Which is poetically spoken, to continue the metaphor, and representation of the judgment. My saints - The Israelites, whom God had chosen and separated them from all the nations of the earth, to be an holy and peculiar people to himself, and they also had solemnly devoted themselves to God; all which aggravated their apostacy. Those - Who have entered into covenant with me, and have ratified that covenant by sacrifice. This seems to be added, to acquaint them with the proper nature, use and end of sacrifices, which were

principally appointed to be signs and seals of the covenant made between God and his people; and consequently to convince them of their great mistake in trusting to their outward sacrifices, when they neglected the very life and soul of them, which was the keeping of their covenant with God.

6. Declare - God will convince the people of his righteousness, and of their own wickedness, by thunders and lightnings, and storms, or other dreadful signs wrought by him in the heavens. Himself - In his own person. God will not now reprove them, by his priests or prophets, but in an extraordinary manner from heaven.

7. Hear - Having brought in God, as coming to judgment, he now gives an account of the process and sentence of the judge. Testify - I will declare my charge against thee. Thy God - Not only in general, but in a special manner, by that solemn covenant made at Sinai; whereby I avouched thee to be my peculiar people, and thou didst avouch me to be thy God.

8. I will not - This is not the principal matter of my charge, that thou hast neglected sacrifices which thou shouldst have offered.

9. Bullock - Be not so foolish, as to imagine that thou dost lay any obligations upon me by thy sacrifices.

11. The fowls - Such as are wild and fly up and down upon mountains.

14. Offer - If thou wouldest know what sacrifices I prize, and indispensably require, in the first place, it is that of thankfulness, proportionable to my great and numberless favours; which doth not consist barely in verbal acknowledgments, but proceeds from an heart deeply affected with God's mercies, and is accompanied with such a course of life, as is well-pleasing to God. Vows - Those substantial vows and promises, which were the very soul of their sacrifices.

15. Call - And make conscience of that great duty of fervent prayer, which is an acknowledgment of thy subjection to me, and of thy trust and dependance upon me. Glorify - Thou shalt have occasion to glorify me for thy deliverance.

16. But - With what confidence darest thou make mention of my grace and favour, in giving thee such a covenant and statutes.

21. Kept silence - I did not express my displeasure against thee in such judgments as thou didst deserve. Thoughtest - Thou didst misconstrue my patience and long-suffering, as if it had proceeded from my approbation of thy evil courses. Set in order - I will bring to thy remembrance, and lay upon thy conscience all thy sins.

23. Glorifieth - He and he only gives me the honour that I require, and not he who loads my altar with sacrifices.

51

David prays for pardon, ver. 1, 2. Confesses his sins, ver. 3- 5. Prays for renewing grace, ver. 6-14. Promises unfeigned thankfulness, ver. 15-17. Prays for the whole church, ver, 18, 19. To the chief musician, A psalm of David, when Nathan the prophet came unto him, after he had gone in to Bathsheba.

4. Thee only - Which is not to be, understood absolutely, because he had sinned against Bathsheba and Uriah, and many others; but comparatively. So the sense is, though I have sinned against my own conscience, and against others; yet nothing is more grievous to me, than that I have sinned against thee. Thy sight - With gross contempt of thee, whom I knew to be a spectator of my most secret actions. Justified - This will be the fruit of my sin, that whatsoever severities thou shalt use towards me, it will be no blemish to thy righteousness, but thy justice will be glorified by all men. Speakest - Hebrew. in thy words, in all thy threatenings denounced against me. Judgest - When thou dost execute thy sentence upon me.

5. Behold - Nor is this the only sin which I have reason to bewail before thee; for this filthy stream leads me to a corrupt fountain: and upon a review of my heart, I find, that this heinous crime, was the proper fruit of my vile nature, which, ever was, and still is ready to commit ten thousand sins, as occasion offers.

6. Truth - Uprightness of heart; and this may be added; as an aggravation of the sinfulness of original corruption, because it is contrary to the holy nature and will of God, which requires rectitude of heart: and, as an aggravation of his actual sin, that it was committed against that knowledge, which God had wrote in his heart.

7. Hyssop - As lepers, are by thy appointment purified by the use of hyssop and other things, so do thou cleanse me a leprous and polluted creature, by thy grace, and by that blood of Christ, which is signified by those ceremonial usages.

8. Joy - By thy spirit, seal the pardon of my sins on my conscience, which will fill me with joy. Rejoice - That my heart which hath been sorely wounded may be comforted.

10. Create - Work in me an holy frame of heart, whereby my inward filth may be purged away.

Right - Hebrew. firm or constant, that my resolution may be fixed and unmoveable. Spirit - Temper or disposition of soul.

12. The joy - The comfortable sense of thy saving grace, promised and vouchsafed to me, both for my present and everlasting salvation. Free - Or, ingenuous, or liberal, or princely. Which he seems to oppose to his own base and illiberal and disingenuous and servile spirit, which he had discovered in his wicked practices: a spirit, which may free me from the bondage of sin, and enable me cheerfully to run the way of God's precepts.

14. Thy righteousness - Thy clemency and goodness.

15. My lips - Which are shut with shame and grief.

16. Not sacrifice - This is not to be understood absolutely, with respect to David's crimes, which were not to be expiated by any sacrifice.

17. A broken spirit - This is of more value than many sacrifices.

18. Good pleasure - Thy free and rich mercy. Build - Perfect the walls and buildings of that city, and especially let the temple be built, notwithstanding my sins.

52

The wickedness of Doeg, and his doom, ver. 1-5. The righteous will see it and fear, ver. 6, 7. David comforts himself in God, ver. 8, 9. To the chief musician, Maschil, A psalm of David, when Doeg the Edomite came and told Saul, and said unto him, David is come to the house of Ahimelech.

1. Continually - God is continually doing good: thou art continually doing mischief. O mighty - He speaks ironically. O valiant captain! To kill a few weak and unarmed persons.

2. Deviseth - Expresses what thy wicked mind had devised. Deceitfully - Doeg pretended only to vindicate himself from disloyalty, 1 Sam. xxii, 8, but he really intended to expose the priests, to the king's fury.

5. Pluck thee - Violently and suddenly as the Hebrew word signifies, from thy house and lands, and all the wages of thy righteousness. Root - Though thou seemest to have taken deep root, yet God shall pluck thee up by the very roots, and destroy thee both root and branch.

6. Fear - Reverence God's just judgment.

8. The house - In God's church, or among his people.

9. Thou hast - Destroyed mine and thine implacable enemies, and established me in the throne, of which I am no less assured, than if it were already done. I will continue in thy way, placing my whole confidence in thy power and goodness, and faithfulness. Before - In the presence of thy saints.

53

David here describes the wickedness of mankind, nearly in the same words as in chap. xiv. To the chief musician upon Mahalath, Maschil, A psalm of David. Title of the psalm. Mahalath - This also seems to be the name of a musical instrument, or tune.

5. Scattered - Hath not only broken their bones, their strength, and force, but also dispersed them hither and thither, so as there is no hope of a restoration. Thee - Against my people. Thou - Thou oh Jerusalem, which they besiege.

54

David prays for help against his enemies, ver. 1-3. Comforts himself with the assurance of deliverance, ver. 4-7. To the chief musician on Neginoth, Maschil, A psalm of David, when the Ziphim came and said to Saul, Doth not David hide himself with us.

1. Name - By thy own strength. Judge - Plead my cause.

3. Strangers - The Zephites, whom, though Israelites, he calls strangers in regard of their barbarous and perfidious carriage.

5. Thy truth - Whereby thou art engaged to fulfil thy promises and threatenings.

55

David complains to God, ver. 1-8. Prays for help against his enemies, ver. 9-15. Assures himself of God's protection, ver. 16- 18. And their destruction, ver. 19-23. To the chief musician on Neginoth, Maschil, A psalm of David.

3. Voice - Their clamours and threats, and slanders. Cast - They lay many crimes to my charge.
4. The terrors - Deadly terrors; such as seize upon men in the agonies of death.
8. Tempest - From the force and fury of mine enemies.
9. Destroy - Destroy them by dividing. Tongues - Their speech, as thou didst at Babel, Gen. xi, 9, their votes, and opinions, and counsels. Which was eminently done among Absalom's followers, 2 Sam. xvii, 23. Strife - Injustice and fraud, oppression and contention rule here, instead of that public justice and peace which I established. City - In Jerusalem; which in Absalom's time was a sink of all sins.
10. They - Violence and strife. Go about - Do encompass it, as it were a garrison. Walls - In the outward parts, as also in the very midst of it. So that all parts were horribly corrupted.
11. Streets - The places of buying and selling, and of public commerce.
12. Hated - With a manifest or old hatred.
13. Equal - Not in power, but in reputation, for wisdom, and influence upon my people. Guide - Whose counsel I highly prized, and constantly followed. All which agrees to Achitophel.
15. Them - All such as pretend to religion, and have manifestly apostatized both from the profession and practice of it. The grave - Cut off by a sudden and violent death. Among them - Hebrew. in their inwards. Wickedness is deeply rooted in their hearts.
17. Evening, &c. - The three stated times of prayer among the Jews.
18. He hath - He speaks of a future deliverance, as a thing done, because of the certainty of it. He hath restored me to my former peace and tranquility. For - For there were more with me than against me; even the holy angels whom God employed to defend and deliver me.
19. Hear - My prayers. Eternity - Who is eternal, and therefore unchangeable, and almighty. Because - They meet with no crosses nor disappointments. Therefore - Their success makes them go on securely, without any regard to God, or dread of his judgments.
20. He - They, the persons last mentioned.
22. Burden - All thy crosses, and cares, and fears, lay them upon the Almighty, by faith and prayer. He directs this speech to his own soul, and to all good men in like circumstances. Suffer - As he doth wicked men. Tho' he may for a season suffer them to be shaken, yet not to be overwhelmed.
23. Them - The wicked. Not live - But shall be cut off by an untimely and violent death. Trust in thee - And in this confidence I will quietly wait for deliverance.

56

David complains of his enemies, and begs for mercy, and help against them, ver. 1-7. Expresses his confidence in God, ver. 8-13. To the chief musician upon Jonath-elem-rechokim, Michtam of David, when the Philistines took him in Gath. Title of the psalm. Jonath-elem-rechokim. Which is supposed to be the name of a song.

4. Will praise - I will praise the Lord for his word, for his promises of protection and deliverance, made to his people. Flesh - Infirm and mortal men, called flesh by way of contempt, as chap. lxxviii, 39 Isaiah xxxi, 3.
6. They gather - After they have severally employed their thoughts against me, they meet together to compare them, and to put them in execution. Hide - They lurk secretly, that they may pry into my most private actions. Steps - That they may find some occasion to reproach me. Soul - Or, life, to take it away.
7. Escape - Shall they secure themselves by injurious and malicious practices. The people - These who are mine enemies.
8. Wanderings - How I have been hunted from place to place. Put - Regard and pity them. Are they not - But why do I pray to God to do that which he hath already done?
12. Thy vows - I had made vows to express my gratitude, and resolve to perform them.
13. Walk - That I may serve and glorify thee. The light - In this life.

57

David here begins with prayer and complaint, tho' not as without hope, ver. 1-6. He concludes with joy and praise, ver. 7- 11. To the chief musician Al-taschith, Michtam of David, when he fled from Saul in the cave. Title of the psalm. Al-taschith - The word signifies, destroy not. Which some think to be a preface, containing the sum of the psalm. The cave - Either

1. That of Adullam, 1 Sam. xxii, 1, or
2. That of Engedi, 1 Sam. xxiv, 1.
3. Send forth - Will discover them, by affording his gracious help in pursuance of his promises.
4. Lions - Fierce and bloody men. I lie - I have my abode. On fire - From hell. Who are mere fire-brands, breathing out wrath and threatenings, and incensing Saul against me.
5. Excited - Glorify thy power, and goodness, and justice, and faithfulness, by my deliverance. Above, &c. - To the highest degree possible.
7. Fixed - In a stedfast belief of thy promises.
8. My glory - My tongue, the instrument of singing. Awake - I will employ all the powers of my soul and body.
9. The people - Among the Israelites, and among the Heathens, as I shall have occasion.

58

David describes his enemies, ver. 1-5. Foretells their ruin, ver. 6-9. Which would be to the comfort of good men, and to the glory of God, ver. 10, 11. To the chief musician, Al-taschith, Michtam of David.

1. O congregation - The word seems to point at Saul's Judges and counsellors; who met together to consult what they should do against David. Sons of men - So he calls them; to mind them that they were men, and must give an account to God for all their hard speeches.
2. Heart - With free choice and consent. Hands - He intimates that they did great wrong under the pretense of justice, and while they seemed exactly to weigh the true proportion between the actions and the recompenses allotted to them, they turned the scale; and pronounced an unjust sentence. Land - Or, in this land, where God is present, and where you have righteous laws to govern you.
3. Estranged - From God, and from all goodness. Their very natures are corrupt, even from their birth: they are the wicked offspring of sinful parents. Astray - By actual sins, from their childhood, as soon as ever they were capable of the exercise of reason.
4. Poison - Their malicious disposition.
5. Not hearken - As they commonly say of the adders, such really are these men: deaf to all my counsels, to their own consciences, and to God's law. Of the charming or enchanting of serpents, mention is made both in other places of scripture, and in all sorts of authors, ancient and modern, Hebrew and Arabick, and Greek and Latin. And particularly the Arabick writers (to whom these creatures were best known) name some sorts of serpents, among which the adder is one, which they call deaf, not because they are dull of hearing, but, as one of them expressly faith, because they will not be charmed.
6. Their teeth - Their powerful instruments of doing mischief.
7. Melt away - As waters arising from melted snow, which at first run with great force, but are suddenly gone.
8. Melteth - Which is quickly dissolved.
9. Before - Before your pots can be heated. Take them - Violently and irresistibly. Living - Alive, as he did Korah.
10. Rejoice - For the blessed effects of it; the vindication of God's honour, and the deliverance of himself and of all good men. Wash - There shall be so great a slaughter of his enemies that he might, if he pleased, wash his feet in their blood.

59

David prays for deliverance from his enemies, ver. 1-7. He foretells their destruction, ver. 8-17. To the chief musician, Al- taschith, Michtam of David: when Saul sent and they watched the house to kill him.

4. Run - To and fro, to receive Saul's commands, and to execute them with all speed.
5. The God - A God in covenant with all true Israelites, whom thou hast promised to protect and bless. The heathen - Or, these heathens, who though they are Israelites by birth; yet in their dispositions

they are mere Heathens. Be not - For indeed thou canst not according to thy word, be merciful to such incorrigible offenders.

6. Return - Watching for me: which they did at this time all the night long, 1 Sam. xix, 11. A dog - When he is pursuing his prey. Go round - When they did not find him in his own house, they sought for him in other parts of the city.

7. Pour out - Sharp and bitter word's, abundantly and vehemently, as a fountain doth waters, as this word signifies. Swords - Words as keen and mischievous as swords. For who - David doth not hear us, and God either doth not hear, or not regard what we say.

10. Prevent - Thou wilt help me sooner than I expect.

11. My people - Over whom thou hast appointed me to be governor in due time. Forget - Their former danger, and thy glorious mercy in delivering them. Scatter - Let them wander from place to place, that they may carry the tokens of thy justice, and their own shame to all places.

12. Pride - For their proud and insolent speeches against thee. Lying - For their execrations and lying reports, which they have spread concerning me.

13. Not be - In the land of the living any more.

60

David remembering God's judgments on the land, prays for help, ver. 1-5. Triumphs in confidence of receiving it, ver. 6-12. To the chief musician upon Shushan-eduth, Michtam of David, to teach; when he strove with Aram-naharaim, and with Aram-zobah, when Joab returned, and smote of Edom in the valley of salt, twelve thousand. Title of the psalm. Shushan-eduth - This seems to be the name of an instrument, or tune, then well known, but now unknown and forgotten. To teach - For the special instruction of God's people. Aram-naharaim - The Syrians (so called from Aram, the son of Shem, Gen. x, 22,) of the two rivers, or of Mesopotamia, the country between Tygris and Euphrates. Aram-zobah - The Syrians of Zobah, part of Syria so called.

2. Tremble - A poetical expression, signifying great changes among the people.

3. To drink - Thou hast filled us with no less honour, than men intoxicated with strong drink.

4. A banner - Which is a sign and instrument,

1. Of union. This people who were lately divided, thou hast united under one banner, under my government:

2. Of battle. Thou hast given us an army, and power to oppose our enemies; which blessing God gave to Israel, for the sake of those few sincere Israelites who were among them. The truth - Not for any merit of ours, but to shew thy faithfulness in making good thy promises.

5. Beloved - Thy beloved people.

6. Rejoice - Therefore I will turn my prayers into praises, for what God has already done. Divide - Which supposeth possession and dominion. Shechem - A place within Jordan, in mount Ephraim. Succoth - A place without Jordan. He mentions Shechem, and Succoth; for all the land of Canaan, within and without Jordan.

7. Gilead - All the land beyond Jordan, which was possessed by Reuben and Gad, and half of the tribe of Manasseh. Manasseh - The other half of that tribe within Jordan. The strength - A chief part of my strength, either to offend mine enemies, or to defend myself. For this tribe was very numerous, and valiant and rich. Law-giver - The chief seat of my throne and kingdom, and of the inferior throne of judgment, chap. lxxii, 5.

8. Wash-pot - In which I shall wash my feet. I shall bring them into the lowest degree of servitude. Shoe - I will use them like slaves; a proverbial expression. Triumph - It is an ironical expression, signifying that her triumphs were come to an end.

9. Who - None can do it but God. City - The cities; the singular number for the plural. Having beaten his enemies out of the field, he desires God's assistance to take their strong-holds, and so secure himself from farther attempts. Edom - Which was an high and rocky country, Obad 1-3, fortified by nature, as well as by art, and therefore not to be subdued without a Divine hand.

10. Hadst cut off - But now hast graciously returned to us.

61

David flees to God, and resolves to trust him, ver. 1-4. Praises God from an assurance of future blessings, ver. 5-8. To the chief musician upon Neginah, A psalm of David.

2. The end - To which David was driven. Lead me - Convey me into some high and secure fortress.
4. I will - I shall, I doubt not, be restored to the tabernacle, and worship thee there all my days.
5. Heritage - Thou hast granted me this singular mercy, to live in God's land, to enjoy his presence, and to worship in his tabernacle; which is the heritage that all that fear thee, prize and desire above all things.
6. Prolong - The years of my life and reign. Thus he speaks because his kingdom was not like Saul's, but established to him and his heirs; and because Christ, his son and heir, should actually, and in his own person possess the kingdom forever. 7. Abide - In the throne. Before God - Living and ruling as in God's presence, serving God and worshipping him in his tabernacle. Truth - Thy truth in giving me those mercies which thou hast promised, and thy mercy in giving me such further blessings as I needs.

62

David expresses his confidence in God, ver. 1-7. Excites others to trust in him, ver. 8-12. To the chief musician, to Jeduthun. A psalm of David. Title of the psalm. Jeduthun - A famous musician, 1 Chron. ix, 16.

3. Ye - Mine enemies; to whom now he turns his speech. Against - Against me, a man like yourselves, whom common humanity obliges you to pity.
9. Vanity - Vain, and helpless creatures. A lie - They promise much, but generally deceive those who trust in them.
10. Vain - Feeding yourselves with vain hopes of felicity, from those riches which you take from others by violence.
11. Spoken - Frequently, both immediately as at Sinai, and by his holy prophets, from time to time. That - That power is God's prerogative; and consequently all creatures, either against or without him, are poor impotent things.
12. Therefore - God is almighty, therefore he can easily destroy all his enemies: he is also merciful, and therefore will pardon good mens failings. Renderest - And this as he is obliged to do by his holy nature, so is he able to do it, being omnipotent, and willing to do it to the godly (which was the only thing that might be doubted, because of their manifold miscarriages) because he is merciful and gracious.

63

David's desire and esteem of God, ver. 1-4. His satisfaction, and communion with God, ver. 5, 6. His joyful dependence upon God, ver. 7, 8. His holy triumph in him, ver. 9-12. A psalm of David, when he was in the wilderness of Judah.

1. Early - Hebrew. in the morning, Which implies the doing it with diligence and speed. Thirsteth - For the enjoyment of thee in thy house and ordinances. Flesh - The desire of my soul, is so vehement, that my very body feels the effects of it. No water - In a land where I want the refreshing waters of the sanctuary.
2. To see - To enjoy. Power - The powerful and glorious effects of thy gracious presence.
5. Satisfied - When thou shalt fulfil my earnest desire of enjoying thee in the sanctuary.
9. Shall go - Into the grave.
10. Foxes - Their carcases shall become a prey to wild and ravenous creatures.
11. The king.- I who am already anointed king. Everyone - That sweareth by the name of God, in truth, and judgment, and righteousness. Every sincere servant and worshipper of God. Shall glory - Shall rejoice in my deliverance.

64

David describes his enemies and prays for deliverance from them, ver. 1-6. Foretells their destruction, ver. 7-10. To the chief musician, A psalm of David.

6. Iniquities - They study diligently, to find new ways of doing mischief. Deep - Cunning, both to contrive and conceal, and to execute their plots.
8. Flee - Through fear of being involved in their destruction.
10. Glad - For the honour of God, which by this means is vindicated.

65

David praises God for hearing prayer, pardoning sin, satisfying and protecting his people, ver. 1-5. For fixing the mountains, calming the sea, preserving the succession of day and night, and making the earth fruitful, ver. 6-13. To the chief musician, A psalm and song of David.

4. Approach - To draw near to God in his house and ordinance, by prayer and praise, and other acts of communion with him. Satisfied - With the blessings there conferred upon thy people, the favour and fellowship of God, remission of sins, renovation of heart and life, joy and peace, and well-grounded assurance of eternal life.
5. Righteousness - By virtue of thy faithfulness, and goodness. Wilt thou - Thou wilt graciously answer our prayers. The confidence - Thou art the stay and support of all mankind, by thy powerful and gracious providence.
7. Tumult - No less wild and impetuous.
8. Thy tokens - Terrible thunders and lightnings, and earthquakes, and comets or other strange meteors, or works of God in the air. Morning - The successive courses of the morning and evening; or of the sun and moon which go forth at those times. Thus the whole verse speaks of the natural works of God, the former clause, of such as are extraordinary and terrible, the latter of such as are ordinary and delightful.
9. River - With rain, which he very significantly calls a river for its plenty, and the river of God, of God's immediate providing. Them - The inhabitants of the earth. Provided - Or, disposed, the earth, which without this would be hard and barren.
10. Bringest down - For the rain dissolves the high and hard clods of earth.
12. Wilderness - Which though neglected by men, are furnished with food for beasts.
13. Sing - They are abundantly satisfied with thy goodness, and in their manner sing forth the praise of their benefactor.

66

The psalmist calls on all people to praise God, for his sovereign power over the whole creation, ver. 1-7. For his special favour to his people, ver. 8-12. Praises him for his goodness to himself in particular, ver. 13-20. To the chief musician, A song or psalm.

1. All lands - Ye people of all nations. He invites the Gentile world, to the contemplation and celebration of God's works.
6. We - Our nation, or our ancestors, in whose loins we then were.
10. Proved us - As it were in a burning furnace; and with a design to purge out our dross.
11. Net - Which our enemies laid for us.
12. To ride - To use us like slaves.
15. I will go - One speaks in the name of all the rest. Incense - With the fat of rams, which is no less pleasing to God than incense.
18. Iniquity - Any sin. In heart - If my heart had been false to God, although I might have forborne outward acts. If I had been guilty of that, by heart was set upon sin, or I desired only that which I resolved in my heart to spend upon my lusts.

67

A prayer for Israel, ver. 1. For the conversion of the Gentiles, ver. 2-5. A prospect of glorious times, ver. 6, 7. To the chief musician on Neginoth, A psalm or song.

2. *Thy way* - The way of truth, or the true religion; the same which in the next clause is called his saving health, and both together signify the way of salvation; deal so graciously with thy people, that thereby the Gentile-world may at last be allured to join with them.

4. *Judge* - Rule them. Govern - Hebrew. lead; gently, as a shepherd doth his sheep; and not rule them with rigor, as other lords had done.

6. *Them* - When the people of the earth shall be converted to God, God will cause it to yield them abundance of all sorts of fruits. Under which one blessing, all other blessings both temporal and spiritual are comprehended. *Our own* - He who is Israel's God in a peculiar manner.

68

The occasion of this psalm, seems to have been David's translation of the ark to Zion, which was managed with great solemnity and devotion. For the first words are the very same which Moses appointed for such occasions, Num. x, 35, and the following verses pursue the same matter. Thence he falls into a description of some of the glorious works of the God to whom this ark belonged. But because David knew that both himself and the ark were types of Christ, and that the church of Israel were a type of the catholick church, consisting of Jews and Gentiles, and that the legal administrations were types of those of the gospel, he therefore by the spirit of prophecy, looked through the types, to the great mysteries of Christ's resurrection and ascension, and of the special privileges of the Christian church, and of the conversion of the Gentiles, and intermixes passages, which immediately belong to these things, although the words be so ordered, that they carry a manifest allusion to the present actions, and may be applied to them, in a secondary sense. He first prays against God's enemies, and for his people, ver. 1-3. Then praises God, for his greatness and goodness, ver. 4-6. For his wonderful works, ver. 7-14. For his special presence in his church, ver. 15- 17. The ascension of Christ, and the salvation of his people, ver. 18-20. His victories over his enemies, and favours to his church, ver. 21-28. The accession of the Gentiles to the church, ver. 29- 31. An awful acknowledgment of the glory and grace of God, ver. 32-35. To the chief musician, A psalm or song of David.

4. *Jah* - Is an abbreviation of the name Jehovah, which the Heathens pronounced Jao. *Before him* - Before the ark where he is present, as David is said to dance before the Lord, upon this occasion, 2 Sam. vi, 14.

5. *Habitation* - In heaven.

6. *Rebellious* - Those who rebel against God.

7. *Wentest* - In the cloudy pillar, as their captain leading them up out of Egypt.

8. *Dropped* - Poured down great showers, which accompanied those mighty thunders.

9. *Weary* - Dry and thirsty, and parched with excessive heat, and ready to faint for want of rain, chap. lxiii, 1.

10. *Thy congregation* - The people of Israel. *It* - This land for the use of thy people: which God did by designing it for them, and expelling the old inhabitants; by furnishing it with all sorts of provisions, and making it fruitful by his special blessing. *Poor* - Such thy really were, when God undertook the conduct of them into Canaan.

11. *Gave* - He put this triumphant song into their mouths.

12. *Kings* - The kings of Canaan, and other nations who came forth against the Israelites, accompanied with great and numerous armies. *The spoil* - There was enough, not only for those who took it, but also to be divided to their wives and children, when they came home.

13. *Ye* - Ye Israelites. *Ye are* - Tho' you have formerly been exposed to great reproach and misery, yet God hath changed your condition. *Gold* - Beautiful and glorious, like the feathers of a dove, which according to the variety of its postures, and of the light shining upon it, look like silver and gold.

14. *Therein* - In Canaan, at the coming of the Israelites. The land was as white as mount Salmon is with the snow.

15. *The hill* - Zion, the seat of God's ark. *High hill* - Which is not to be understood of external height, but of its spiritual height, or exaltation, in regard of the glorious privileges of God's presence, and worship.

16. *Leap* - Why do you triumph and look upon Zion with contempt? He speaks to the hills by an usual figure. *Will dwell* - This hill, though despicable in your eyes, is precious in God's, and chosen by him for his perpetual residence.

17. *Chariots* - The armies (whereof chariots were an eminent part in those times) which attend

upon God to do his pleasure. Twenty thousand - An innumerable company, a certain number being put for an uncertain. Among them - Here the psalmist seems to be transported by the prophetic spirit, from the narration of those external successes, to the prediction of the Messiah; and of the transcendent privileges and blessings accruing to mankind thereby. As in Sinai - God is no less gloriously, though less terribly present here, than he was in Sinai, when the great God attended with thousands of his angels, solemnly appeared to deliver the law. Yea, here is a greater privilege than Sinai had, The Lord Jehovah descending from heaven into an human body, as appears by his ascending thither again, which the next verse describes.

18. Ascended - This has a manifest reference to Christ, and his ascension into heaven, in whom alone it is literally accomplished, and to whom therefore it is ascribed, Eph. iv, 8. Although the expressions are borrowed from the ancient custom of princes, who, after some glorious achievements, used to go up into their royal cities in triumphant chariots, being attended by their captive enemies, and afterward to distribute gifts to their soldiers and subjects, and sometimes to do some acts of clemency even to their rebels and enemies. Captivity - Those whom thou hast taken captive; death and sin, and the devil, and all the enemies of Christ, and of his people, whom Christ led in triumph, having spoiled them, and making a shew of them openly, Colossiansii, 15. Received - According to thy manhood thou hast received from God all the treasures of wisdom and knowledge, and all those gifts and graces of the Holy Spirit, which are necessary either to the perfection of thy nature, or to the good of thy church and people. Rebellious - Thy most stubborn and rebellious enemies, whether Jews or Gentiles. Might dwell - That he who as man is ascended into the highest heavens, might, as God, come down to them, and dwell with them, not only in and by his ordinances in which he is present, but also by his spirit dwelling in their hearts.

20. Issues - Escapes or deliverances.

21. Hairy - In ancient times many people used to wear long and shaggy hair, that their looks might be more terrible to their enemies.

22. Bring again - I will give my people as great deliverances as I formerly did, when I saved them from Og, king of Bashan. The sea - From the Egyptians at the Red Sea.

23. That, &c. - And as it was at the Red Sea, and at Bashan before, so yet again thine enemies shall be slain in such numbers, that thou mayst wade in their blood, and thy dogs lick it up in the field.

24. They - Men saw and observed it. Goings - The procession of the ark to Zion, the solemnity whereof is particularly described in the following verses. The sanctuary - The tabernacle prepared for it.

26. Fountain - All ye people of Israel.

27. There is - Present in this solemn pomp of carrying the ark to Zion. Little - Called little, because it was exceedingly diminished, and almost extinguished under the Judges, Judg. xx, 35; xxi, 3 &c. Ruler - The tribe which had lately swayed the scepter, but now submitted to David. Company - The people of that tribe who waited upon them. Zebulun, &c. - He mentions these tribes, because they lived in the remotest parts of the land of Canaan. And so by naming two of the nearest tribes, and two of the farthest, he intimates that the other tribes also came upon this occasion, as is manifest from 2 Sam. vi, 15-19.

28. Thy God - Having spoken of Israel, he now directs his speech to them. Commanded - Hath ordained or effectually procured. Thy strength - all that strength and power which thou hast put forth at any time

29. thy temple - The temple which Solomon shall build. Kings - Kings of the Gentiles: which was done in part, in the times of Solomon and Hezekiah, but more fully when the Lord was come into his temple.

30. Rebuke - Chastise those that will not bring presents to thee. The bulls - The fierce and furious adversaries of God, and of his church; the calves, are people or soldiers depending upon them. Delight - That merely out of a love to mischief and spoil, make war upon others, and upon us particularly.

31. Ethiopia - He names these, as the ancient enemies of God, and of his people; but by them he understands all other nations of the like character. Unto God - Begging mercy of him. This prophecy, as also the next verse, evidently belongs to the times of the Messiah.

33. Heavens - The highest heavens; dwelling there in infinite glory, and from thence looking down upon all the inhabitants of the earth, and ruling them by his almighty power. Of old - From the beginning of the world; whereas the ark was only some hundred years old. A voice - His gospel, published by Christ and his apostles, assisted by the Holy Spirit sent from heaven; which might well be called God's voice, and that a mighty voice, because it produced such great and wonderful effects.

34. Ascribe - Acknowledge that he is able to do whatsoever he pleaseth. Excellency - His excellent power and goodness. Is over - Dwells among them. He is indeed the universal Lord, but in a special manner, he is the God of Israel.

35. Terrible - Deservedly to be feared.

69

David complains of his troubles, and begs help from God, ver. 1-21. Foretells the judgments of God upon his persecutors, ver. 22-29. Concludes with praise and thanksgiving, ver. 30-36. In all this David was a type of Christ, and several passages of this psalm are applied to him in the New Testament. So that, like the 22nd psalm, it begins with the humiliation, and ends with the exaltation of Christ. To the chief musician upon Shofhannim, a psalm of David.

1. Waters - Tribulations.
4. I restored - For peace sake.
5. My sins - But O Lord, although I have been innocent to mine enemies, I am guilty of many sins and follies against thee.
6. For my sake - Because of my sad disappointments. For if they see me forsaken, they will be discouraged by this example.
7. For thy sake - For my obedience to thy commands, and zeal for thy glory.
9. Zeal - That fervent love which I have for thy house and service, and glory, and people. Eaten - Exhausted my spirits. Upon me - I have been as deeply affected with thy reproaches, as with mine own. This tho' truly belonging to David, yet was also directed by the spirit of God in him, to represent the disposition and condition of Christ, in whom it was more fully accomplished, to whom therefore it is applied in the New Testament, the first part of it, John ii, 17, and the latter, Rom. xv, 3.
10. Wept - For their impiety. Reproach - They derided me for it.
11. Proverb - A proverb of reproach.
12. That sit - Vain and idle persons, that spend their time in the gates and markets.
13. In the truth - Or, According to thy saving truth, or faithfulness; grant me that salvation, which thou hast graciously promised.
21. Gall - Instead of giving me that comfort which my condition required, they added to my afflictions. Vinegar - These things were metaphorically fulfilled in David, but properly in Christ, the description of whose sufferings was principally intended here by the Holy Ghost.
22. Their table - And this punishment in their table, exactly answers their sin, in giving Christ gall for his meat, ver. 21. A snare - Their table or meat, which is set before them, shall become a snare: the occasion of their destruction.
23. Eyes - Not the eyes of their bodies, but of their minds: as they that shut their eyes and will not see, so they shall be judicially blinded. To shake - To take away their strength.
26. For - Which is an act of barbarous cruelty. Talk - Reproaching them, and triumphing in their calamities.
27. Wilt add - Give them up to their own lusts. Not let them - Partake of thy righteousness, or of thy mercy and goodness.
28. Living - Of eternal life.
29. On high - Out of the reach of mine enemies.
31. This - This hearty sacrifice of praise, is more grateful to God, than the most glorious legal sacrifices. Hath horns - That is both tender and mature, as it is when the horns bud forth, and the hoofs grow hard.
32. The humble - Those pious persons who are grieved for their calamities, will heartily rejoice in my deliverance. Live - Or, be revived, which were dejected, and in a manner dead with sorrow.
33. Prisoners - Those who are in prison or affliction for his sake.
35. Sion - His church and people. They - His servants, as is explained in the following verse. There - In the literal Canaan for a long time, in the heavenly Canaan forever.

70

This psalm is copied almost word for word from the eleventh psalm, and perhaps is for that reason entitled, A psalm to bring remembrance. For it may sometimes be of use to pray over again the prayers we have formerly made to God on like occasions. David here prays, that God would send help to him, shame to his enemies, and joy to his friends. To the chief musician, a psalm of David, to bring to remembrance.

71

David wrote this psalm in his old age, of which the former part is prayer, ver. 1-13. The latter part, joyful praise and thanksgiving, ver. 14-24.

7. A wonder - For my many and sore calamities.
15. The numbers - Of thy salvations and mercies vouchsafed to me.
16. Make mention - To support and comfort myself with the remembrance of it. Righteousness - Of thy faithfulness in making good all thy promises.
19. Very high - Most eminent.
20. Bring me - From the grave.

72

Divers passages of this psalm, do not agree to Solomon, nor to any other king but the Messiah. It must therefore be acknowledged, that, this is a mixt psalm, belonging to Solomon imperfectly, but to Christ, clearly and fully: diverse expressions being so ordered, that the reader might be led by them to the contemplation of Christ, and of his kingdom. Which was the more necessary for the support of God's true Israel, because the spirit of God foresaw Solomon's dreadful apostacy, and the great miscarriages and calamities of his successors, and of the kingdom under their hands, and therefore was pleased to fortify their hearts with that glorious condition, which they should certainly enjoy under the Messiah. It is probable, David dictated this psalm, a little before he died, when he gave orders to proclaim Solomon king. After a short prayer for his successor, he foretells the glories of his reign, ver. 1-17. And concludes with praise to the God of Israel, ver. 18-20. A psalm for Solomon.

1. Judgments - He saith judgments in the plural number, because though the office of judging and ruling was but one, yet there were divers parts and branches, of it; in all which he begs that Solomon may be directed to do as God would have him to do.
2. Thy afflicted ones - For such are thine in a special manner, thou art their judge and patron.
3. The mountains - Which are so dangerous to passengers, in regard of robbers and wild beasts. Hereby it is implied, that other places should do so too, and that it should be common and universal.
4. Judge - Vindicate them from their oppressors.
5. Thee - Thee, O God, this shall be another blessed fruit of this righteous government, that together with peace, true religion shall be established, and that throughout all generations, which was begun in Solomon's days, but not fully accomplished 'till Christ came.
6. He shall come - Christ did come down from heaven, and brought or sent down from heaven his doctrine, (which is often compared to rain) and the sweet and powerful influences of his spirit.
8. Dominion - From one sea to another, or in all the parts of the habitable world. This was accomplished in Christ, and in him only. The river - Euphrates: which was the eastern border of the kingdom of Canaan, allotted by God, but enjoyed only by David, Solomon, and Christ. Of whose kingdom this may be mentioned, as one of the borders; because the kingdom of Christ is described under the shadow of Solomon's kingdom.
10. The sea - Of remote countries, to which they used to go from Canaan by sea; which are frequently called isles in scripture; the kings that rule by sea or by land.
11. All nations - Which cannot be said of Solomon with any truth or colour, but was unquestionably verified in Christ,
14. Deceit and violence - The two ways whereby the lives of men are usually destroyed. Precious - He will not be prodigal of the lives of his subjects, but like a true father of his people, will tenderly preserve them, and severely avenge their blood upon those who shall shed it.
15. Live - Long and prosperous, as Solomon: yea, eternally as Christ. Gold - This was done to Solomon, 1 Kings x, 15, and to Christ, Matt. ii, 11. But such expressions as these being used of Christ and his kingdom, are commonly understood in a spiritual sense.
16. A handful - This intimates the small beginnings of his kingdom; and therefore does not agree to Solomon, whose kingdom was in a manner as large at the beginning of his reign, as at the end, but it exactly agrees to Christ. The earth - Sown in the earth. Mountains - In the most barren grounds. Shake - It shall yield such abundance of corn, that the ears being thick and high, shall, when they are shaken with the wind, make a noise not unlike that which the tops of the trees of Lebanon, sometimes make. Of the city - The citizens of Jerusalem, which are here put for the subjects of this kingdom.
20. The prayer - This psalm is the last which David composed: for this was wrote but a little before his death.

73

It is probable, Asaph was the author of this psalm; for we read of the words of David and the words of Asaph the seer, which were used in praising God in Hezekiah's time, 2 Chron. xxix, 30. He begins with laying down a general principle, ver. 1. Confesses his temptation to envy the wicked, ver. 2-14. Tells how he gained the victory over it, and advantage by it, ver. 15-28. A psalm of Asaph.

1. A clean heart - To all true Israelites, who love God, and serve him in spirit and truth.
2. My feet - My faith in God's providence, was almost overthrown.
4. No bands - They are not dragged to death, by the sentence of the magistrate, which they deserve.
5. As other men - As good men frequently are.
8. And speak - Boasting of their oppressions.
9. Against - Against God, blaspheming his name, and deriding his providence. Walketh - Using all manner of liberty, reproaching all sorts of persons.
10. Turn - To this wicked company. Waters - And partake of the same prosperity with their leaders. God seems to give them a full cup of consolation, as if he would wring out all his blessings upon them.
12. Behold - These seem to be the words of the psalmist, summing up the matter.
13. In vain - Hence I was sometimes tempted, to think that religion was a vain, unprofitable thing. True religion is here described by its two principal parts, the cleansing of the heart, and the hands.
15. Offend - By grieving, discouraging and tempting them to revolt from God.
16. To know - To find out the reason of this providence.
17. Until - 'Till I consulted the word of God. He alludes to the practice of those times, which was, in difficult cases to resort to God's sanctuary, and the oracle therein. Their end - There I learned that their prosperity was short.
19. Terrors - With God's dreadful judgements unexpectedly seizing upon them.
20. They awake - Out of the pleasant dream of this vain life. Despise - Thou shalt make them despicable both to themselves and to all others; raise them to shame, and everlasting contempt. Image - All their felicity and glory, which shall be evidently discerned to be, no real or substantial thing, but a mere image or shadow.
21. Pricked - I was deeply wounded with disquieting thoughts.
22. Nevertheless - Although I gave thee just cause to cast me off, yet thou didst continue thy care and kindness to me. Hast held - That my faith might not fail.
27. Go a whoring - Those who revolt from thee, to work wickedness; which is called whoredom in scripture.

74

This psalm, which so particularly describes the destruction of Jerusalem, was probably written by another Asaph, who lived at the time of the captivity. He, in the name of the Jews, complains of the miseries they suffered, ver. 1-11. Encourages himself by recollecting the mighty works of God, ver. 12-17. Prays for deliverance, ver. 18-23. Maschil of Asaph Title of the psalm. Maschil of Asaph - Not composed by that famous Asaph, who flourished in David's time, but by some of his posterity, who is called by their father's name, as this psalm speaks of the destruction of the temple and of Jerusalem, and of God's people by the Chaldeans.

2. Thy congregation - Thy people. Thine inheritance - The tribe of Judah, which thou hast in a special manner chosen for thine inheritance, and for the birth of the Messiah. Nor is it strange that he mentions this tribe particularly, because the calamity here remembered, did principally befall this tribe, and Benjamin, which was united with it.
3. Lift up - Come speedily to our rescue. Because - Because otherwise our destruction is irrecoverable.
4. Roar - In a way of triumph. Midst, &c. - In the places where thy people used to assemble for thy worship. Set up - Monuments of their victory.
5. Famous - The temple was so noble a structure, that it was a great honour to any man to be employed in the meanest part of the work, though it were but in cutting down the trees of Lebanon.
6. Axes and hammers - These words are not Hebrew, but Chaldee or Syriack, to point out the time when this was done, even when the Chaldeans brought in their language, together with their arms, among the Israelites.
8. Destroy them - All at once. So they intended, although afterwards they changed their council, and carried some away captive. Burnt up - All the public places wherein the Jews used to meet together

to worship God every sabbath-day.

9. Signs - Those tokens of God's gracious presence, which we used to enjoy. The temple and ark, and sacrifices, and solemn feasts, were signs between God and his people. Prophet - Who can foretell things to come. Probably Ezekiel and Jeremiah were dead when this psalm was composed; and David was involved in civil affairs, and did not teach the people as a prophet. Knoweth - How long their captivity should continue.

11. Why - Why dost thou forebear the exercise of thy power? Bosom - In which thou now seemest to hide it.

12. King - It belongs therefore to thy office to protect and save me. Midst - In the view of the world.

13. Dragons - He means Pharaoh and his mighty men.

14. Leviathan - Pharaoh. The people - To the ravenous birds and beasts of the desert. These creatures are significantly called the people of the wilderness, because they are the only people that inhabit it.

15. The flood - Thou didst by cleaving the rock, make a fountain and a stream to flow from it, for the refreshment of thy people in those dry deserts. Driedst - Jordan and the Red Sea; for the sea itself; yea, a greater sea than that, is called a river, Jonah ii, 3, where the Hebrew word is the same which is here used. And the same title is expressly given to the sea, by Homer, and other ancient writers.

16. The light - The moon, the lesser light.

17. Set - Thou hast fixed the bounds of the habitable world in general, and of all the countries and people upon the earth. And as this clause shews God's power over all places, so the next displays his dominion over all times and seasons.

18. Remember - Though we deserve to be forgotten, yet do not suffer our enemies to reproach the name of the great and glorious God.

19. Soul - The life. Turtle-dove - Of thy church, which is fitly compared to a turtle-dove, because simple and harmless, and meek, and faithful.

20. The covenant - Made with Abraham, whereby thou didst give the land of Canaan to him, and to his seed forever. Dark places - This dark and dismal land in which we live.

21. Return - From the throne of thy grace, to which they make their resort.

75

Probably David wrote this psalm, at his coming to the crown, after the death of Saul, and delivered it to that Asaph, who was chief of the musicians. Herein he thanks God for bringing him to the throne, checks the insolence of his enemies, owns the sovereignty of God in all affairs, and promised to lay himself out for the public good. To the chief musician, Al-taschith, A psalm or song of Asaph. Title of the psalm. Asaph - This psalm seems to relate to the time when David had entered upon, but not got full possession of the kingdom.

1. Thy name - Thy self; art present with us, and ready to help.

2. Receive - The whole congregation, all the tribes.

3. Dissolved - Or, destroyed; by intestine divisions and wars. I hear - I support it, by maintaining religion and justice, by setting up good magistrates, and encouraging good ministers, and good men, who are indeed the pillars of a nation.

4. I said - I charged them. Deal not - Desist from your practices. Lift not up - Do not carry yourselves scornfully and maliciously.

5. Lift not - A metaphor from untamed oxen, which will not bow their heads to receive the yoke. Stiff neck - With pride and contempt.

8. For - God is here compared to the master of a feast, who then used to distribute portions of meat and drink to the several guests. A cup - Of vengeance. Red - Such as the best wine of Judea was. Mixture - The wine is mingled not with water, but with strengthening and intoxicating ingredients. Dregs - The worst and most dreadful part of those tribulations. Shall wring - This dreadful draught was brought upon them by their own choice and wickedness.

9. Declare - The praises of God.

10. Horns - Their honour and power, which they made an instrument of mischief. Will - When I shall be advanced to the throne. But - Good men shall be encouraged and promoted.

76

Asaph congratulates the church, in having God so nigh, ver. 1-3. He celebrates the power of God, shewn in some late victory over their enemies, ver. 4-6. He shews that all ought to fear him on this account, ver. 7-9 And that his people ought to trust him, and to pay their vows, ver. 10-12. To the chief musician on Neginoth, A psalm or song of Asaph.

2. Salem - In Jerusalem, which was anciently called Salem. Zion - Largely so called, as it includes Moriah, an adjoining hill.

3. There - At Jerusalem. Sword - Both offensive and defensive weapons. Battle - All the power of the army, which was put in battle-array.

4. Thou - O God. Than - The greatest kings and empires of the earth, which in prophetic writings are often compared to mountains. And they are called mountains of prey, because they generally were established by tyranny, and maintained by preying upon their own subjects, or other kingdoms.

5. Sleep - Even a perpetual sleep.

6. Chariot - The men who rode upon, and fought from chariots and horses.

8. Thou - Didst execute judgment upon thine enemies, by an angel from heaven: which is said to be heard, either because it was accompanied with thunders and earthquakes, or because the fame of it was quickly spread abroad. Feared - The rest of the world were afraid to disturb Israel.

10 Surely - The furious attempts of thine enemies, shall cause thy people and others to praise thee for thy admirable wisdom, power, and faithfulness.

11. Vow - A sacrifice of thanksgiving for this wonderful deliverance. Let all - All the neighbouring nations submit to the God of Israel.

12. Cut off - As men do their grapes in time of vintage; so the Hebrew verb implies. The spirit - Their breath and life, as he did in the Assyrian army.

77

The psalmist complains of deep distress, and temptations to despair, ver. 1-10. He encourages himself to hope, by the remembrance of what God had done formerly, ver. 11-20. To the chief musician, to Jeduthun, A psalm of Asaph.

2. Night - Which to others was a time of rest and quietness.

3. Troubled - Yea, the thoughts of God were now a matter of trouble, because he was angry with me. Overwhelmed - So far was I from finding relief.

4. Waking - By continual grief.

5. The days - The mighty works of God in former times.

6. My song - The mercies of God vouchsafed to me, and to his people, which have obliged me to sing his praises, not only in the day, but also by night.

7. Cut off - His peculiar people.

10. I said - These suspicions of God's faithfulness proceed from the weakness of my faith. The years - The years wherein God hath done great and glorious works, which are often ascribed to God's right-hand.

13. In holiness - God is holy and just, and true in all his works.

16. Afraid - And stood still, as men astonished, do.

17. Poured - When the Israelites passed over the sea. Arrows - Hail-stones or lightnings.

19. Not known - Because the water returned and covered them.

20. Leddest - First through the sea, and afterwards through the wilderness, with singular care and tenderness, as a shepherd doth his sheep.

78

This psalm is a narrative of the great mercies God had bestowed upon Israel, the great sins wherewith they had provoked him, and the many tokens of his displeasure at them. Here is, The preface, ver. 1-8. The general scope of this psalm, ver. 9-11. As to the particulars, we are told, what God had done for them; how ungrateful they were for his favours; how God had justly punished them; and how graciously he had spared them, notwithstanding all their provocations, ver. 12-72. Maschil of Asaph.

1. My law - The doctrine which I am about to deliver. 2. Parable - Weighty sentences. Dark sayings - Not that the words are hard to be understood, but the things, God's transcendent goodness, their unparallel'd ingratitude; and their stupid ignorance and insensibleness, under such excellent teachings of God's word and works, are prodigious and hard to be believed. Of old - Of things done in

ancient times.

5. Established - This is justly put in first place, as the chief of all his mercies. A testimony - His law, called a testimony, because it is a witness between God and men, declaring the duties which God expects from man, and the blessings which man may expect from God.

9. Ephraim - That Ephraim is here put for all Israel seems evident from the following verses, wherein the sins, upon which this overthrow is charged, are manifestly the sins of all the children of Israel, and they who are here called Ephraim are called Jacob and Israel, ver. 21, and this passage may refer to that dreadful overthrow related, 1 Sam. iv, 10, 11, which is particularly named, because as the ark, so the flight was in that tribe. And the psalmist having related this amazing providence, falls into a large discourse of the causes of it, namely, the manifold sins of that and the former generations, which having prosecuted from hence to ver. 60, he there returns to this history, and relates the sad consequence of that disaster, the captivity of the ark, and God's forsaking of Shiloh and Ephraim, and removing thence to the tribe of Judah and Mount Zion. Bows - These are put for all arms.

12. Field - In the territory. Zoan - An ancient and eminent city of Egypt.

15. Wilderness - In Rephidim, and again in Kadesh.

16. Streams - Which miraculously followed them in all their travels, even to the borders of Canaan.

17. Wilderness - Where they had such singular obligations to obedience. This was a great aggravation of their sins.

18. Tempted - Desired a proof of God's power. Lust - Not for their necessary subsistence, but out of an inordinate and luxurious appetite.

22. Trusted not - That he both could, and would save them from the famine which they feared.

23. Heaven - Which he compares to a store-house, whereof God shuts or opens the doors, as he sees fit.

25. Angels food - Manna, so called, because it was made by the ministry of angels.

26. South wind - First an eastern, and afterwards a southern wind.

27. Fowl - But God took away from them the use of their wings, and made them to fall into the hands of the Israelites.

31. Mightiest - The most healthy and strong, who probably were most desirous of this food, and fed most eagerly upon it.

33. Vanity - In tedious and fruitless marches hither and thither. Trouble - In manifold diseases, dangers, and perplexities.

34. Returned - From their idols. Inquired - Speedily sought to God for ease and safety.

35. Redeemer - That God alone had preserved them in all their former exigencies, and that he only could help them.

36. Lied - They made but false protestations of their sincere resolutions of future obedience.

42. Hand - The glorious works of his hand. Enemy - That remarkable day, in which God delivered them from their greatest enemy, Pharaoh.

45. Flies - These flies were doubtless extraordinary in their nature, and hurtful qualities. And the like is to be thought concerning the frogs.

46. labour - The herbs which were come up by their care and labour.

47. Sycamore-trees - Under these and the vines, all other trees are comprehended. This hail and frost destroyed the fruit of the trees, and sometimes the trees themselves.

49. Evil angels - Whom God employed in producing these plagues.

51. Ham - Of the Egyptians, the posterity of Ham, the cursed children of a cursed parent.

54. Holy place - The land of Canaan, separated by God from all other lands. Mountain - The mountainous country of Canaan; the word mountain is often used in scripture for a mountainous country.

57. Deceitful bow - Which either breaks when it is drawn, or shoots awry, and frustrates the archer's expectation.

59. Heard - Perceived or understood, it is spoken of God after the manner of men.

60. Shiloh - Which was placed in Shiloh. Among men - Whereby he insinuates both God's wonderful condescension, and their stupendous folly in despising so glorious a privilege.

61. His strength - The ark, called God's strength, 1 Chron. xvi, 11, because it was the sign and pledge of his strength put forth on his people's behalf. Glory - So the ark is called, as being the monument and seat of God's glorious presence. Enemies - The Philistines.

64. Priests - Hophni and Phinehas. No lamentation - No funeral solemnities; either because they were prevented by their own death, as the wife of Phinehas was, or disturbed by the invasion of the enemy.

66. Smote - Them with the piles. Reproach - He caused them to perpetuate their own reproach by sending back the ark of God with their golden emrods, the lasting monuments of their shame.

67. Refused - He would not have his ark to abide any longer in the tabernacle of Shiloh, which

was in the tribe of Joseph or Ephraim.

68. Chose - For the seat of the ark and of God's worship.

69. Sanctuary - The temple of Solomon. Palaces - Magnificent and gloriously. Established - Not now to be moved from place to place, as the tabernacle was, but as a fixed place for the ark's perpetual residence.

79

This psalm seems to have been written by the later Asaph, upon the destruction of Jerusalem by the Chaldeans. It contains, a representation of the deplorable condition of the Jews, ver. 1-5. And a petition for deliverance, ver. 6-13. A psalm of Asaph.

8. Prevent - Prevent our utter extirpation.

11. The prisoner - Of thy poor people now in captivity.

80

This psalm was composed upon occasion of some calamity, which befel the tribes of Israel after their division into two kingdoms, and before the captivity of either of them. In which time all the evils mentioned herein did befall them, sometimes in one part, and sometimes in another. The psalmist prays for the tokens of God's presence, ver. 1-3. Complains of heavy distress, ver. 4-7. Illustrates this, by the comparison of a vine, ver. 8-16. Concludes with a prayer for mercy, ver. 17-19. To the chief musician upon Shoshannim Eduth, A psalm of Asaph. Title of the psalm. Shoshannim Eduth - It seems to be the name of a musical instrument.

1. Joseph - The children of Joseph or Israel. The name of Joseph, the most eminent of the patriarchs, is elsewhere put for all the tribes. Cherubim - Which were by the mercy seat above the ark.

2. Before Ephraim - Here is an allusion to the ancient situation of the tabernacle in the wilderness, where these tribes were placed on the west-side of the tabernacle, in which the ark was, which consequently was before them.

3. Turn us - To thy self.

9. Preparedst - Thou didst root out the idolatrous nations. Deep root - Thou gavest them a firm settlement.

10. The hills - They filled not only the fruitful valleys, but even the barren mountains.

11. The river - They possessed the whole land, from the mid-land sea to the river Euphrates.

12. Hedges - Taken away thy protection.

16. They - Thy people, signified by the vine. So now he passes from the metaphor to the thing designed by it.

17. Be - To protect and strengthen him. Right-hand - Benjamin signifies the son of the right hand, a dearly beloved son, as Benjamin was to Jacob. Son of man - The people of Israel, who are often spoken of as one person, as God's son and first-born.

18. Go back - Revolt from thee to idolatry or wickedness. Quicken - Revive and restore us to our tranquility.

81

This psalm may assist us in our solemn feast-days, in praising God, for what he is, and what he has done, ver. 1-7. In admonishing one another, concerning our obligations to God, the danger of revolting from him, and the happiness of keeping close to him, ver. 8-16. To the chief musician upon Gittith, A psalm of Asaph.

5. Joseph - Among the people of Israel. Testimony - For a witness of that glorious deliverance. He - God. Went - As a captain at the head of his people. Egypt - To execute his judgments upon that land. I - My progenitors, for all the successive generations of Israel make one body, and are sometimes spoken of as one person. A language - The Egyptian language, which at first was unknown to the Israelites, Gen. xlii, 13, and probably continued so for some considerable time, because they were much separated both in place and conversation from the Egyptians.

6. Pots - This word denotes all those vessels wherein they carried water, straw, lime, or bricks.

7. Calledst - At the Red Sea. Secret place - From the dark and cloudy pillar, whence I thundered against the Egyptians.

8. Testify - This God did presently after he brought them from Meribah, even at Sinai.

10. Wide - Either to pray for mercies, or to receive the mercies which I am ready to give you.

15. Him - Unto Israel. Their time - Their happy time.
16. Honey - With all pleasant and precious fruits.

82

We have here the dignity and duty of magistrates, ver. 1-4. The wickedness of some magistrates, and their doom, ver. 5-7. A prayer to God, ver. 8. A psalm of Asaph.

1. Standeth - To observe all that is said or done there. Mighty - Kings or chief rulers. By their congregation he understands all persons whatsoever of this high and sacred order. Judgeth - Passes sentence upon them. The gods - Judges and magistrates are called gods, because they have their commission from God, and act as his deputies.
2. How long - The psalmist speaks to them in God's name. Accept - By giving sentence according to your respect or affection to the person.
5. They - The magistrates of whom this psalm treats. Know not - The duty of their place. Nor will - Their ignorance is wilful. Walk on - They persist: it is their constant course. In darkness - In their sinful courses. The foundations - This corruption of the supreme rulers, flows from them to their inferior officers and members.
6. Have said - I have given you my name and power to rule your people in my stead. All - Not only the rulers of Israel, but of all other nations. Children - Representing my person, and bearing both my name and authority.
7. Like men - Or, like ordinary men.
8. Arise - Take the sword of justice into thine own hand.

83

A remonstrance of the designs and endeavours of Israel's enemies, ver. 1-8. A prayer, that God would defeat them, preserve his church, and get himself glory, ver. 9-18. A song or psalm of Asaph.

3. Hidden ones - Thy people of Israel, who are called God's hidden or secret ones, to intimate the respect which God has to them, as to his peculiar treasure.
6. The tabernacles - The people dwelling in them. Ishmaelites - Some of the posterity of Ishmael, called by their father's name, as others of them are supposed to be called Hagarens from their grandmother Hagar.
7. Gebal - An Arabian people so called by ancient writers dwelling in the southern border of Canaan, where most of the people here mentioned had their abode.
8. Of Lot - Moab and Ammon.
13. A wheel - Whereas they promise to themselves a sure possession, let them be like a wheel, which is very unstable, and soon removed.
14. The mountains - The woods upon the mountains, which in those hot countries, when they have once taken fire, burn with irresistible violence.
16. May seek - May own and worship thee as the only true God.

84

The psalmist declares his love for the ordinances of God, and the happiness of those that enjoy them, ver. 1-7. A devout prayer, and expression of faith in him, ver. 8-12. It is generally supposed, David wrote this, when he was driven out of the land by Absalom. To the chief musician upon Gittith, A psalm for the sons of Korah.

4. They-That constantly abide in thy house; the priests and Levites, or other devout Jews who were there perpetually, as Anna, Luke ii, 36-37. They will - They are continually employed in that blessed work.
5. Whose strength - Who trusteth in thee as his only strength. Thy ways - Blessed are they whose hearts are set upon Zion and their journey is thither.
6. Baca - A dry valley in the way to Jerusalem, here put for all places of like nature. Make a well - They dig divers little pits or wells in it for their relief. The rain - God recompenses their diligence with his blessing, sending rain wherewith they may be filled.
7. They go - They grow stronger and stronger. Appeareth - This is added as the blessed fruit of their long and tedious journey.
9. Look - Cast a favourable eye towards him. Anointed - Of me, who though a vile sinner, am thine anointed king.

10. Than dwell - In the greatest glory and plenty.

11. A sun - To enlighten and quicken, and direct and comfort his people. Shield - To save his people from all their enemies. Grace - His favour, which is better than life. Glory - The honour which comes from God here, and eternal glory.

85

A recital of past, and prayer for present mercy, ver. 1-7. A prediction of a favourable answer, ver. 8-13. To the chief musician, A psalm for the sons of Korah.

1. Captivity - The captives.

4. Turn us - Restore us to our former tranquillity, and free us from the troubles which we yet groan under.

6. Revive us - Give us a second reviving in bringing home the rest of our brethren, and in restraining our enemies.

8. Will hear - Diligently observe. Will speak - What answer God will give to my prayers. Peace - He will give an answer of peace. Saints - Not to all that are called God's people, but only to those who are truly such.

9. His salvation - That compleat salvation for which all the Israel of God wait; even the redemption by the Messiah; of which not only Christian, but even Jewish writers understand this place; and to which the following passages properly belong. And the psalmist might well say this salvation was nigh, because the seventy weeks determined by Daniel were begun. Glory - The glorious presence of God, and the God of glory himself, even Christ, who is the brightness of his father's glory.

10. Kissed - That great work of redemption by Christ, shall clearly manifest God's mercy in redeeming his people Israel, and in the conversion of the Gentiles; his truth in fulfilling that great promise of sending his son, his righteousness in punishing sin, on his son, and in conferring righteousness upon guilty and lost creatures; and his peace or reconciliation to sinners, and that peace of conscience which attends upon it.

11. Truth - Truth among men. Righteousness - And God's justice shall be satisfied: he shall look down upon sinful men with a smiling countenance.

13. Before him - As his harbinger. He shall fulfil all righteousness, he shall satisfy the righteousness of God, and shall advance righteousness and holiness among men. Set us - Shall cause us to walk in those righteous ways wherein he walketh.

86

David prays for the favour and blessing of God, ver. 1-6. Expresses confidence in him, by praise mingled with prayer, ver. 7-17. A prayer of David.

2. Holy - Sincerely devoted to thy service.

11. Truth - In the way of thy precepts, which are true and right in all things. My heart - Knit my whole heart to thyself.

13. Hell - From extreme dangers and miseries.

87

This psalm contains a commendation of Zion, a type of the gospel-church, which is here preferred before the rest of the land of Canaan, ver. 1, 2, 3. And before any other place, as being filled with more eminent men, and more of divine blessings, ver. 4-7. A psalm or song for the sons of Korah.

1. Its foundation - The foundation of the temple of God.

2. Zion - That is, Zion itself, or Jerusalem, which was built upon and near Mount Zion. He saith Zion rather than Jerusalem, to intimate that he loved Jerusalem for Zion's sake, or for the temple, which he chose for his peculiar dwelling place.

4. Rahab - Egypt, so called, either from its pride or natural strength. Babylon - Under these two and Philistia, the constant enemies of Israel, he seems to understand all the enemies of the church of God, who shall now be not only reconciled but united to them. Arabia - The nations on every side of them, for Tyre was on the north, Arabia on the South; those nearest to them, and those more remote from them.

5. Zion - Of Jerusalem, or the church of God. Said - It shall be acknowledged. Man - Hebrew. Man and man, all sorts of men without difference of nations. Establish - And this shall not be a transient, but a lasting work; Zion shall continue in its strength and fertility because the Almighty God is her founder

and protector.

6. When - When God, the maker and governor of this city shall take a survey of all his citizens. It is an allusion to princes or governors of cities that use to write and keep a register of all their people.

7. Singers - There shall be great rejoicing and praising God, both with vocal and instrumental musick, for this glorious work of the conversion of the Gentiles. He describe's evangelical worship, by legal phrases and customs, as the prophets frequently do. In thee - In Zion or the church. These words may be here added as the burden of the song, which these singers are supposed to have sung, in the name of all the people of God. All our desires and delights are in thee, all the springs of mercy, grace, and glory, flow to us only in and thro' thee.

88

This is the most melancholy of all the Psalms: it is all lamentation, and mourning, and woe. Here we have the pressure of spirit which the psalmist was under, ver. 1-9. His humble pleadings with God, ver. 10-14. A farther declaration of his affliction, ver. 15-18. A song or psalm for the sons of Korah, to the chief musician upon Mahalath Leannoth, Maschil of Heman the Ezrahite. Title of the psalm. Leannoth - Which seems to be the name of the instrument. Heman - Probably the same person who was famous in David's time, both for his skill in musick, and for wisdom.

4. Counted - I am given up by my friends for a lost man.
5. Free - Well nigh discharged from the warfare of the present life, and entered as a member into the society of the dead. Whom - Thou seemest to neglect and bury in oblivion.
7. Waves - With they judgments, breaking in furiously upon me like the waves of the sea.
10. Wonders - In raising them to life. To praise thee - In this world?
12. Forgetfulness - In the grave, where men are forgotten by their nearest relations.
13. Prevent - Come to thee before the dawning of the day, or the rising of the sun.
17. Water - As the waters of the sea encompass him who is in the midst of it.

89

This psalm manifestly treats of the declining state of the house and kingdom of David, in or about the Babylonish captivity. The psalmist praises and rejoices in God, ver. 1-18. He builds all his hopes on God's covenant with David, ver. 19-37. He laments the present calamities of the king and royal family, ver. 38-45. Expostulates with, prays to God, and praises him, ver. 46- 52. Maschil of Ethan the Ezrahite. Title of the psalm. Ezrahite - Not him who is mentioned, 1 Kings iv, 31, but some person of the same name, and inspired by the same spirit, who lived long after.

1. Sing - He prefaces this, lest the following complainers of present miseries should argue ingratitude for former mercies. Faithfulness - Whatsoever hath befallen us, it proceeded not from thy unfaithfulness.
2. Establish - As firmly and durably as the heavens themselves.
3. Chosen - With David; whom I have chosen to the kingdom.
4. Build up - I will perpetuate the kingdom to thy posterity; which was promised upon condition, and was literally accomplished in Christ.
5. Heavens - The inhabitants of heaven. Faithfulness - Understand, shall be praised; which supplements are usual in scripture.
6. Among - The highest angels.
7. Feared - With a fear of reverence. Saints - The whole society of angels. All that - That encompass his throne.
8. Round thee - Like a girdle encompassing thee. It appears in all thy words and works.
10. Rhahab - Egypt.
12. Tabor - The several parts of the land of Canaan, both within Jordan, where mount Tabor is; and without it, where Hermon lies. Rejoice - Shall be fruitful and prosperous, and so give their inhabitants cause to rejoice. In - By thy favour.
14. Justice and judgment - Justice in judging.
15. Know - Who enjoy the presence of God and his ordinances, to which they are called by the sound of trumpets. Walk - Under the comfortable influences of thy favour.
16. Name - In the knowledge and remembrance of thy name, of thy infinite power and goodness.
17. The glory - To thee alone belongs the glory of all their valiant achievements.
19. Vision - Which then was the usual way by which God spake to the prophets. Holy one - To thy holy prophets; the singular number being put for the plural; especially to Samuel and Nathan. Laid help - I have provided help for my people. Upon - Upon a person of singular courage and wisdom.

22. Exact - Not conquer him or make him tributary.
25. Set - Establish his power and dominion. The sea - The mid-land sea. The rivers - Euphrates, called rivers, in regard of divers branches of it, and rivers which flow into it. So here is a description of the uttermost bounds of the promised land.
27. My first-born - As he calls me father, ver. 26, so I will make him my son, yea my first-born; who had divers privileges above other sons. This and the following passage in some sort agree to David, but are properly accomplished in Christ. Higher - This also was in some sort accomplished in David, but more fully in the Messiah.
29. For ever - To sit upon the throne forever, as the next words explain it. This was accomplished only in Christ.
37. A witness - The rainbow, which is God's faithful witness, a token of God's everlasting covenant between God and every living creature for perpetual generations, Gen. ix, 12, 16.
38. But - Having hitherto declared the certainty of God's promises, he now humbly expostulates with God about it.
45. Youth - The youthful and flourishing estate of David's kingdom was very short, and reached not beyond his next successor.
47. Short - Our time, the time of our king and kingdom, in whose name the psalmist puts up this petition. Wherefore - Wherefore hast thou made us and our king (and consequently all other men, whose condition is nothing better than ours) in vain, or to so little purpose? Didst thou raise us and him, settle the crown upon David's head by a solemn covenant, and vouchsafe so many and great promises and privileges, and all this but for a few years, that our crown and glory should be taken from us, within a little time after it was put upon our heads?
48. What man - All men at their best estate are mortal and miserable; kings and people must unavoidably die by the conditions of their natures; and therefore, Lord, do not increase our affliction.
50. How I - We thy servants; our king and his people; of whom he speaks as of one person.
51. Anointed - By whom he seems to understand either first the kings of Judah, the singular number being put for the plural; and by their footsteps may be meant either their ways or actions, or the memorials of their ancient splendour; or secondly the Messiah, whom the Jews continually expected for a long time, which being well known to many of the Heathens, they reproached the Jews, with the vanity of this expectation. And by the footsteps of the Messiah, he may understand his coming.
52. Blessed - Let thine enemies reproach thee and thy promises concerning the sending of the Messiah, I will heartily bless and praise thee for them, and encourage myself with them.

90

Probably Moses wrote this psalm, on occasion of the sentence passed on the Israelites, that their carcases should fall in the wilderness. Herein he considers the eternity of God, ver. 1-3. And the frailty of man, ver. 4-6. He submits to the righteous sentence of God, ver. 7-11. And prays for the return of his favour, ver. 12-17. A prayer of Moses the Man of God. Title of the psalm. A prayer of Moses - Who considering that terrible sentence of God, concerning the cutting off all that sinful generation in the wilderness, takes occasion to publish these meditations concerning man's mortality and misery. V.

1. Dwelling place - Although we and our fathers, for some generations, have had no fixed habitation, yet thou hast been instead of a dwelling-place to us, by thy watchful and gracious providence. And this intimates that all the following miseries were not to be imputed to God but themselves.
2. Thou - Thou hadst thy power, and all thy perfections, from all eternity.
3. Turnedst - But as for man, his case is far otherwise, though he was made by thee happy. and immortal, yet for his sin thou didst make him mortal and miserable. Saidst - Didst pronounce that sad sentence, return, O men, to the dust out of which ye were taken, Gen. iii, 19.
4. Past - Indeed time seems long when it is to come, but when it is past, very short and contemptible. A watch - Which lasted but three or four hours.
5. Them - Mankind. Away - Universally, without exception or distinction. A sleep - Short and vain, as sleep is, and not minded 'till it be past.
7. Are consumed - Thou dost not suffer us to live so long as we might by the course of nature.
8. Hast set - Thou dost observe them, as a righteous judge, and art calling us to an account for them. Secret sins - Which though hid from the eyes of men, thou hast brought to light by thy judgments.
10. Our years - Of the generality of mankind, in that and all following ages, some few persons excepted. Flee - We do not now go to death, as we do from our very birth, but flee swiftly away like a bird, as this word signifies.
11. Thy fear - According to the fear of thee; according to that fear which sinful men have of a just God. So - It bears full proportion to it, nay indeed doth far exceed it.

12. Teach us - To consider the shortness of life, and the certainty and speediness of death. That - That we may heartily devote ourselves to true wisdom.

13. Return - To us in mercy. How long - Will it be before thou return to us? Repent thee - Of thy severe proceedings against us.

14. Early - Speedily.

17. The beauty - His gracious influence, and glorious presence. In us - Do not only work for us, but in us,

91

This psalm is a dialogue, wherein one declares the safety of them, who take God for their keeper, ver. 1. David declares this to be his resolution, ver. 2. Various promises are made to him, ver. 3-13. Which God himself confirms, ver. 14-16.

1. He - He that makes God his habitation and refuge.

3. Pestilence - From the pestilence, which like a fowler's snare takes men suddenly and unexpectedly.

5. By night - When evil accidents are most terrible and least avoidable. Arrow - The pestilence, or any such destructive calamity; such are frequently called God's arrows. By day - Thou shalt be kept from secret and open mischiefs.

6. Darkness - Invisibly, so that we can neither foresee nor prevent it.

12. Bear thee - Sustain or uphold thee in thy goings, as we do a child.

13. The lion - Shall lie prostrate at thy feet, and thou shalt securely put thy feet upon his neck. Dragon - By which he understands all pernicious creatures, though never so strong, and all sorts of enemies.

14. Because - This and the two following verses are the words of God.

92

God is praised for his works, ver. 1-5. The doom of the wicked, from the eternal God, ver. 6-9. The prosperity of the righteous, ver. 10-15. A psalm or song for the sabbath-day.

5. Thoughts - Thy counsels in the government of the world and of thy church.

6. A brutish man - Who is led by sense, not by reason and faith. This - The depth of God's counsels and works.

10. Anointed - I shall have cause of testifying my joy by anointing myself, as the manner was at all joyful solemnities.

12. Palm-tree - Which is constantly green and flourishing.

13. Planted - Whom God by his gracious providence has fixed there. The house - In its courts; he means in the church of God, whereof all good men are living members.

14. Old age - Their last days shall be their best days, wherein they shall grow in grace, and increase in blessedness.

93

This and the six following psalms, according to the opinion of the Hebrew doctors, belong to the times of the Messiah. The glory of God's kingdom, both of providence and glory, ver. 1-6.

1. Clothed - That majesty and strength which he always had, he will shew in the eyes of all people. Moved - He will overrule all the confusions in the world, so that they shall end in the erection of that kingdom of the Messiah, which can never be moved.

3. Floods - The enemies of thy kingdom.

5. Testimonies - Thy promises, which no less than the precepts are God's testimonies, or the witnesses, or declarations of his will to mankind. He seems here to speak of those precious promises concerning the erection of his kingdom in the world by the Messiah. Holiness - It becometh thy people to be holy in all their approach to thee.

94

The danger and folly of persecuting the children of God, ver. 1-11. Assurance given to the persecuted, that God will deliver them, ver. 12-23.

4. Utter - Or pour forth freely, constantly, abundantly, as a fountain doth waters (so this Hebrew word signifies.) Hard things - Insolent, and intolerable words against thee and thy people.
7. Of Jacob - He who takes that name to himself, but has no regard to his people.
9. Planted - The word is emphatical, signifying the excellent structure of the ear, or the several organs belonging to the sense of hearing. Formed - By which word he intimates the accurate and curious workmanship of the eye.
10. Know - Mens thoughts and words and actions.
11. Thoughts - Yes, he knoweth all things, even the most secret things, as the thoughts of men; and in particular your thoughts; much more your practices.
12. Blessed - Those afflictions which are accompanied with Divine instructions are great and true blessings.
15. But - God will declare himself to be a righteous judge, and will again establish justice in the earth. Follow - They will all approve of it, and imitate this justice of God in all their actions.
16. Rise - To defend and help me. I looked hither and thither, but none appeared; God alone helped me.
17. Dwelt - In the place of silence, the grave.
19. Thoughts - While my heart was filled with various and perplexing thoughts, as this Hebrew word signifies. Comforts - Thy promises, and the remembrance of my former experience of thy care and kindness.
20. Shall - Wilt thou take part with the unrighteous powers of the world who oppress thy people. A law - By virtue of those unrighteous decrees which they have made.

95

The author of this psalm was David, as is affirmed, Heb. iv, 7. It has a special reference to the days of the Messiah; as it is understood by the apostle, Heb. iii, 7, &c. and Heb. iv, 3-9. Herein we are called upon, to praise God, as a great and gracious God, ver. 1-7. To hear God's voice, and not harden our hearts, lest we fall as the Israelites did, ver. 8-11.

3. God's - Above all that are called God's angels, earthly potentates, and especially the false gods of the Heathen.
4. Hand - Under his government. Strength - The strongest or highest mountains.
7. Pasture - Whom he feeds and keeps in his own pasture, or in the land which he hath appropriated to himself. The sheep - Which are under his special care. Today - Forthwith or presently.
8. Harden not - By obstinate unbelief. Provocation - In that bold and wicked contest with God in the wilderness. Temptation - In the day in which you tempted me.
9. Works - Both of mercy, and of justice.
10. Do err - Their hearts are insincere and bent to backsliding. Not known - After all my teaching and discoveries of myself to them; they did not know, nor consider, those great things which I had wrought for them.
11. My rest - Into the promised land, which is called the rest, Deut. xii, 9.

96

This psalm is a part of that which was delivered to Asaph and his brethren, 1 Chron. xvi, 7, on occasion of bringing up the ark to the city of David. Here is a call to praise God, as a great and glorious God, ver. 1-9. To rejoice in his judging all the world, ver. 10-13.

1. O sing - Upon this new and great occasion, not the removal of the ark, but the coming of the Messiah.
4. Gods - The gods of the nations, as the next verse expounds it.
6. Before him - In his presence.
9. Beauty - Cloathed with all the gifts and graces, which are necessary in God's worship.
10. Reigneth - God hath now set up his kingdom in the world. Established - The nations of the world shall by the means of it enjoy an established and lasting peace.
13. Before - At the presence and approach of their Lord and Maker. Cometh - To set up his throne among all the nations of the earth.

97

Christ is the Alpha and Omega in this psalm. His government speaks terror to his enemies, ver. 1-7. And comfort to his friends, whom he preserves and delivers, ver. 8-12.

1. Isles - The Gentile nations, as this word, used Isaiah xlii, 4, is expounded, Matt. xii, 21.
2. Darkness - A dark cloud doth encompass him.
6. Heavens - The angels, yea God himself from heaven.
7. Confounded - Let them be ashamed of their folly. Gods - All you whom the Gentiles have made the objects of their worship.
8. Zion - Thy people dwelling in Zion or Jerusalem, to whom Christ came. Heard - The fame of thy judgments, and the setting up the kingdom of the Messiah.
11. Light - Joy and happiness. Sown - Is laid up for them.

98

This psalm sets forth the glory of the Redeemer, ver. 1-3. And the joy of the redeemed, ver. 4-9. A psalm.

2. Salvation - The redemption of the world by the Messiah: which was hitherto reserved was a secret among the Jews, yea was not throughly known by the most of the Jews themselves. Righteousness - His faithfulness in accomplishing this great promise.

99

Israel is required to praise God, for their hasty constitution both in church and state, ver. 1-5. Some instances of the happy administration of it, ver. 6-9.

1. People - Such as are enemies to God and his people. Sitteth - Upon the ark. He is present with his people. Earth - The people of the earth. Moved - With fear and trembling.
3. Them - All people.
4. Judgment - Though his dominion be absolute, and his power irresistible, yet he manages it with righteousness. The king's strength is by a known Hebraism put for the strong, or powerful king. Equity - In all thy proceedings.
5. Foot-stool - Before the ark, which is so called, 1 Chron. xxviii, 2. Holy - It is consecrated to be a pledge of God's presence.
6. Moses - Moses before the institution of the priesthood executed that office, Exod. xxiv, 6. That call - Who used frequently and solemnly to intercede with God on the behalf of the people.
7. Spake - To some of them: to Moses and Aaron, Exod. xix, 24; xxxiii, 9-11; 1 Sam. vii, 9, &c.
8. Them - The intercessors before mentioned. Forgavest - The people for whom they prayed, so far as not to inflict that total destruction upon them which they deserved;

100

An exhortation to praise God and to rejoice in him, ver. 1- 5 A psalm of praise

101

This psalm was composed by David between the time of God's promising the kingdom to him and his actual possession of it. The general scope of David's vow, at his entrance on his government, ver. 1, 2. The particulars of it, ver. 3-8. A psalm of David.

1. I will sing - I will praise thee, O Lord, for thy mercy and justice, which thou hast so eminently discovered in the government of the world, and of thy people; and I will make it my care to imitate thee herein.
2. I will - I will manage all my affairs with wisdom and integrity. When - God is often said in scripture to come to men, when he fulfills a promise to them. House - In my court and family, as well as in my public administrations.
4. Depart - Shall be turned out of my court. Know - Not own nor countenance.
8. Early - Speedily; as soon as I am seated in the throne.

102

A complaint of pressing afflictions, ver. 1-11. Motives of comfort, ver. 12-28. A prayer of the afflicted when he is overwhelmed, and poureth out his complaint before the LORD. Title of the psalm. Complaint - This psalm contains a prayer for the use of all true Israelites, in the name and behalf of the church of Israel. It seems to have been composed in the time of their captivity, and near the end of it, ver. 13, 14.

3. An hearth - An hearth is heated or burnt by the coals which are laid upon it.
5. Skin - My flesh being quite consumed.
6. A pelican - Is a solitary and mournful bird.
9. Bread - The sense is, dust and ashes are as familiar to me as the eating of my bread; I cover my head with them; I sit, yea, lie down in them, as mourners often did.
10. Lifted me - As a man lifts up a thing as high as he can, that he may cast it to the ground with greater force.
12. Remembrance - Thy name, Jehovah, which is called by this very word, God's remembrance, or memorial, and that unto all generations, Exod. iii, 15.
13. The set time - The end of those seventy years which thou hast fixed.
18. This - This wonderful deliverance shall be carefully recorded by thy people.
19. Looked - From heaven.
20. To loose - To release his poor captives out of Babylon, and from the chains of sin and eternal destruction.
21. To declare - That they might publish the name and praises of God in his church.
22. When - When the Gentiles shall gather themselves to the Jews, and join with them in the worship of the true God.
23. He - God. The way - In the midst of the course of our lives. Some think the psalmist here speaks of the whole commonwealth as of one man, and of its continuance, as of the life of one man.
24. I said - Do not wholly destroy thy people Israel. In the midst - Before they come to a full possession of thy promises and especially of that fundamental promise of the Messiah. Thy years - Though we die, yet thou art the everlasting God.
26. Perish - As to their present nature and use.
28. Continue - Though the heavens and earth perish, yet we rest assured that our children, and their children after them, shall enjoy an happy restitution to, and settlement in their own land.

103

The psalmist stirs up himself to praise God for all his benefits, ver. 1-19. Calls upon all his works to assist him therein, ver. 20-22. A psalm of David.

5. The eagles - Which lives long in great strength and vigour.
11. So great - So much above their deserts and expectations.
14. Knoweth - The weakness and mortality of our natures, and the frailty of our condition, so that if he should let loose his hand upon us, we should be irrecoverably destroyed.
21. His hosts - A title often given to the angels, in regard of their vast numbers, mighty power, unanimous concurrence, and exquisite order. Ministers - This Hebrew word is commonly used of the highest and most honourable sort of servants,

104

David in the foregoing psalm praises God for his love to his people; in this, for his works of creation and providence. He gives God the glory of his majesty in the upper world, ver. 1-4. The creation of the sea and dry land, ver. 5-9. The provision he makes for all the creatures, ver. 10-18. The regular course of the sun and moon, ver. 19-24. The furniture of the sea, ver. 25, 26. God's care and sovereign power over all the creatures, ver. 27-32. Concludes with a resolution to continue praising God, ver. 33-35.

2. Light - With that first created light, which the psalmist fitly puts in the first place, as being the first of God's visible works.
3. Waters - In the waters above the heavens, as they are called, Gen. i, 7.
4. Spirits - Of a spiritual or incorporeal nature, that they might be fitter for their employments. Fire - So called for their irresistible force and agility, and fervency in the execution of God's commands.
5. Who laid - Hebrew. he hath established the earth upon its own basis, whereby it stands as fast

and unmoveable, as if it were built upon the strongest foundations. Forever - As long as the world continues. God has fixt so strange a place for the earth, that being an heavy body, one would think it should fall every moment. And yet which way so ever we would imagine it to stir, it must, contrary to the nature of such a body, fall upwards, and so can have no possible ruin, but by tumbling into heaven.

6. The deep - In the first creation, Gen. i, 2, 9.

7. Rebuke - Upon thy command, Gen. i, 9. Fled - They immediately went to the place which God had allotted them.

8. Go up - In that first division of the waters from the earth, part went upwards, and became springs in the mountains, the greatest part went downwards to the channels made for them.

9. A bound - Even the sand of the sea-shore.

11. Wild asses - Stupid creatures, and yet plentifully provided for by the Divine providence.

13. The hills - Which most need moisture. From - From the clouds. Satisfied - By this means all the parts of the earth, are made fruitful. The fruit - With the effects of those sweet showers.

15. Oil - He alludes to the custom of those times and places, which was upon festival occasions to anoint their faces with oil. Bread - Which preserves or renews our strength and vigour.

16. Trees - Which come up, and thrive not by man's industry, but merely by the care of God's providence.

19. For seasons - To distinguish the times, the seasons of divers natural events, as of the ebbing and flowing of waters, and other seasons for sacred and civil affairs, which were commonly regulated by the moon.

21. Roar - They roar when they come within sight of their prey. Seek - Their roaring is a kind of natural prayer to God, for relief.

25. Creeping - This word is common to all creatures that move without feet.

26. Leviathan - The whale. Therein - Who being of such a vast strength and absolute dominion in the sea, tumbles in it with great security, and sports himself with other creatures.

20. Darkness - Which succeeds the light by virtue of thy decree.

29. Hidest - Withdrawest the care of thy providence.

30. Spirit - That quickening power of God, by which he produces life in the creatures from time to time. For he speaks not here of the first creation, but of the continued production of living creatures. Created - Other living creatures are produced; the word created being taken in its largest sense for the production of things by second causes. Renewest - And thus by thy wise and wonderful providence thou preservest the succession of living creatures.

31. Rejoice - Thus God advances the glory of his wisdom and power and goodness, in upholding the works of his hands from generation to generation, and he takes pleasure in the preservation of his works, as also in his reflection upon these works of his providence.

32. He looketh - This is a farther illustration of God's powerful providence: as when he affords his favour to creatures, they live and thrive, so on the contrary, one angry look or touch of his upon the hills or earth, makes them tremble and smoke, as Sinai did when God appeared in it.

35. Praise ye the Lord - Hebrew. Hallelujah. This is the first time that this word occurs. And it comes in here on occasion of the destruction of the wicked. And the last time it occurs, Rev. xix, 1, 3, 4, 6, it is on a like occasion, the destruction of Babylon.

105

In the former psalm we praise God for his common providence; in this, for his special favours to his church. The first eleven verses of it David delivered to Asaph, (1 Chron. xvi, 7, &c.) to be used in the daily service of the sanctuary. Here is the preface, ver. 1-7. The history itself in several articles: God's covenant with the patriarchs, ver. 8-11. His care of them in a strange land, ver. 12-15. His raising up Joseph, ver. 16-22. The increase of Israel in Egypt, and their deliverance out of it, ver. 23- 38. His care of them in the wilderness, and their settlement in Canaan, ver. 39-45.

3. Glory - Glory in the God whom you serve, as the only true God.

4. Seek - The Lord in his strength, in his sanctuary, or before the ark, which is called God's strength. Face - His gracious presence.

5. Judgments - The punishments which he brought upon Egypt by his mere word.

6. Of Jacob - The only branch of Abraham's seed to whom the following blessings belong.

7. Judgments - God executes his judgments upon all nations and people.

8. Remembered - So as to perform it. The word - The promise. Commanded - Established. Thousand generations - To all generations.

9. Oath - Wherewith he ratified the covenant with Isaac, Gen. xxvi, 3.

10. A law - That it might be as firm and irrevocable as a law.

11. Lot - The portion assigned to you by lot.

13. They went - Both in Canaan, where there were seven nations, and in Egypt.

15. Anointed - My prophets, Abraham, Isaac, and Jacob; who are called God's anointed, because they were consecrated to be his peculiar people, and to be kings and princes in their families. And they are called prophets, because God familiarly conversed with them and revealed his will to them, and by them to others.

16. Staff of bread - Bread, which is the staff or support of our lives.

19. His word - That word or Revelation which came first to Pharaoh in a dream, and then to Joseph concerning the interpretation of it. Purged - From those calamities which were cast upon him, and so prepared the way for his release.

23. Ham - Ham was the father of Mizraim, or the Egyptians, Gen. x, 6.

25. Turned - That is, suffered them, to be turned.

28. They - Moses and Aaron, who inflicted that plague after Pharaoh had threatened them.

30. Land - Their country. In chambers - Which entered into the chambers. Kings - Of Pharaoh and his sons, and his chief nobles and governors.

31. Coasts - In all their land, even to the utmost borders of it.

37. Feeble - Diseased or unable for his journey: which in so vast a body, and in a people who had been so dreadfully oppressed, was wonderful.

39. Covering - To protect them from the heat of the sun.

40. Quails - He speaks of the first giving of quails, Exod. xvi, 13, which God gave them as a refreshment, notwithstanding their sin in desiring them, which he graciously pardoned. Bread - With manna which came out of the air, commonly called heaven.

41. River - They flowed in channels which God provided for them, and followed the Israelites in their march.

44. labour - The fruits of their labour; their cities, vineyards, olive-yards.

106

The foregoing psalm was an history of God's goodness to Israel; this is an history of their rebellion: against him; probably both were wrote by David at the same time, as we find the first verse and the two last in that psalm, which he delivered to Asaph, 1 Chron. xvi, 35, &c. Herein we have the preface, ver. 1-5. The narrative of all of the sins of Israel, aggravated by the great things God did for them; their provocations at the Red-sea, ver. 6-12. Lusting, ver. 13-15. Mutinying, ver. 16-18. Worshiping the golden calf, ver. 19-23. Murmuring, ver. 24-27. Worshiping Baal- peor, ver. 28-31. Quarreling with Moses, ver, 32, 33. Mixing with the nations of Canaan, ver. 34-39. God rebuked them, yet saved them from ruin, ver. 40-46. The conclusion, ver. 47, 48. It begins and ends with Hallelujah.

4. Me - He speaks here in the name, and on the behalf of the whole nation. With-With those favours which thou dost usually and peculiarly give to thy people.

5. See - Enjoy. Chosen - Of thy chosen people; such as are Israelites indeed. Gladness - Such joy as thou hast formerly afforded unto thy beloved nation. Glory - That we may have occasion to glory in God's goodness towards us. Inheritance - In the congregation of thy people.

6. Glory - As our fathers did.

7. At the sea - When those wonders were but newly done, and fresh in memory.

8. Saved them - That he may vindicate his name from the blasphemous reproaches, which would have been cast upon it, if they had been destroyed.

9. Led them - As securely as if they had walked upon the dry land.

13. Soon - Even within three days, Exod. xv, 22, 23. Waited not - They did not wait patiently upon God for supplies, in such manner and time as he thought fit.

14. Lusted - For flesh.

15. Souls - Into their bodies. So their inordinate desire of pampering their bodies, was the occasion of destroying them.

16. The saint - So called, because he was consecrated by God for that sacred office of the priesthood, in which respect all the priests are said to be holy, Lev. xxi, 6-8. Hereby he intimates, that their envy and rebellion was not only against Aaron, but against God himself.

19. A calf - When they were but just brought out of Egypt by such wonders, and had seen the plagues of God upon the Egyptian idolaters, and when the law of God was but newly delivered to them in such a tremendous manner.

20. Their glory - God, who was indeed their glory. Into - Into the golden image of an ox or calf, which is so far from feeding his people, as the true God did the Israelites, that he must be fed by them.

23. Breach - God had made a wall about them; but they had made a breach in it by their sins, at which the Lord, who was now justly become their enemy, might enter to destroy them; which he had certainly done, if Moses by his prevailing intercession had not hindered him.

24. Despised - Preferring Egypt, and their former bondage, before it, Num. xiv, 3, 4.
25. The voice - To God's command, that they should boldly enter into it.
26. Lifted up - He swear. Of this dreadful and irrevocable oath of God, see Num. xiv, 11, 12.
27. Overthrow - He swear also (tho' not at the same time) that he would punish their sins, not only in their persons, but in their posterity.
28. Joined - They had communion with him, as God's people have with God in acts of his worship.
31. And - It was accepted and rewarded of God as an act of justice and piety.
37. Devils - They did not worship God as they pretended, but devils in their idols; for those spirits, which were supposed by the Heathen idolaters to inhabit in their images, were not good spirits, but evil spirits, or devils.
43. Counsel - By forsaking God's way, and following their own inventions.
45. Repented - Changed his course and dealing with them.

107

The psalmist here observes God's providential care of the children of men in general, and shews how he helps those that are in any distress, in answer to their prayers. He instances in banishment and dispersion, ver. 1-9. Captivity and imprisonment, ver. 10-16. Sickness, ver. 17-22. Distress at sea, ver. 23-32. The disposal of families and nations, ver. 33-13

3. Gathered - Into their own land.
4. No city - Or rather, no town inhabited, where they might refresh themselves.
6. The Lord - Hebrew. Unto Jehovah, to the true God. For the Heathens had, many of them, some knowledge of the true God.
7. Forth - Out of the wilderness.
10. Darkness - In dark prisons or dungeons.
12. Heart - The pride and obstinacy of their hearts. Fell - They fell into hopeless miseries.
17. Afflicted - With sickness.
20. Word - His command, or blessing.
32. Exalt him - In public assemblies, and before all persons, as they have opportunity. Elders - The magistrates or rulers; let them not be ashamed nor afraid to speak of God's wonderful works, before the greatest of men.
33. Rivers - Those grounds which are well watered, and therefore fruitful. And so the water-springs, here, and the standing water, ver. 35 are taken. Into - Into a dry ground, which is like a parched and barren wilderness.
34. For - He doth not inflict these judgments without cause, but for the punishment of sin in some, and the prevention of it in others.
35. Water - Into a well-watered and fruitful land.
36. Hungry - Poor people who could not provide for themselves.
39. They - These men, who when they are exalted by God, grow insolent and secure. Low - By God's just judgment.
40. Contempt - Renders them despicable. Wander - Banishes them from their own courts and kingdoms, and forces them to flee into desolate wildernesses for shelter.

108

The five first verses of this psalm are taken out of psalm 57, the rest out of psalm 60. David thanks God for personal mercies, ver. 1-5. Prays for national mercies, ver. 6-13. A song or psalm of David.

1. Glory - With my tongue.

109

David complains of his enemies and appeals to God, ver. 1-5. Foretells their destruction, ver. 6-20. Prays that God would succor him in his low condition, ver. 21-29. Concludes with a joyful hope of deliverance, ver. 30, 31 To the chief musician, A psalm of David.

1. God - The author and matter of all my praises.
4. Adversaries - They requite my love with enmity, as it is explained ver. 5.
6. A wicked man - Who will rule him with rigor and cruelty. Satan - To accuse him; for this was the place and posture of accusers in the Jewish courts.
7. Sin - Because it is not from his heart.

10. Desolate places - Into which they are fled for fear and shame.

11. Catch - Hebrew. ensnare, take away not only by oppression but also by cunning artificers. Stranger - Who hath no right to his goods.

17. Delighted not - In desiring and promoting the welfare of others.

18. Garment - Which a man wears constantly. Like water - Water in the cavity of the belly, between the bowels, is almost certain death. And oil soaking into any of the bones, will soon utterly destroy it.

20. That speak evil against my soul - With design to take away my life.

21. Is good - Above the mercy of all the creatures.

23. When - Towards the evening, when the sun is setting. The locust - Which is easily driven away with every wind.

110

That this psalm belongs to the Messiah, is abundantly evident both from the express testimony of the New Testament, Acts ii, 34; 1 Cor. xv, 25 Heb. i, 13; x, 13. and from the consent of the ancient Hebrew doctors. Of him, it is directly and immediately to be understood; the spirit of God wisely so ordering this matter, that it might be a convincing testimony against the unbelieving Jews, concerning the true Messiah, and concerning the nature and quality of his kingdom. His prophetic office, ver. 2. His priestly office, ver. 4, His kingly office, ver. 1, 3, 5, 6. His states of humiliation and exaltation, ver. 7. A psalm of David.

1. The Lord - God the father. Said - Decreed it from eternity, and in due time published this decree, and actually executed it; which he did when he raised up Christ from the dead, and brought him into his heavenly mansion. Unto - Unto his son the Messiah, whom David designedly calls his Lord, to admonish the whole church, that although he was his son according to his human nature, yet he had an higher nature, and was also his Lord, as being God blessed forever, and consequently Lord of all things. The Hebrew word Adon is one of God's titles, signifying his power and authority over all things, and therefore is most fitly given to the Messiah, to whom God hath delegated all his power Matt. xxviii, 18. Sit - Now take thy rest and the possession of that sovereign kingdom and glory, which by right belongeth to thee; do thou rule with me with equal power and majesty, as thou art God; and with an authority and honour far above all creatures, as thou art man. Make - By my almighty power communicated to thee as God by eternal generation, and vouchsafed to thee as mediator. Enemies - All ungodly men, sin and death, and the devil. Footstool - Thy slaves and vassals.

2. The rod - Thy strong or powerful rod, and the rod is put for his scepter, or kingly power: but as the kingdom of Christ is not carnal, but spiritual, so this scepter is nothing else but his word. Zion - From Jerusalem.

3. People - Thy subjects, shall offer thee as their king and Lord, not oxen or sheep, but themselves, their souls and bodies, as living sacrifices, and as freewill-offerings, giving up themselves to the Lord, 2Cor viii, 5, to live to him, and to die for him. The day - When thou shalt take into thy hands the rod of thy strength, and set up thy kingdom in the world. In the beauties - Adorned with the beautiful and glorious robes of righteousness and true holiness. The dew - That is, thy offspring (the members of the Christian church) shall be more numerous than the drops of the morning dew.

4. Sworn - That this priesthood might be made sure and irrevocable.

5. The Lord - God the son; the Lord, who is at thy right-hand. Strike - Shall destroy all those kings who are obstinate enemies to him.

6. Judge - Condemn and punish them. The places - Or, the place of battle. Dead bodies - Of his enemies. Heads - All those princes who oppose him. But this and the like passages are not to be understood grossly, but spiritually, according to the nature of Christ's kingdom.

7. Drink - He shall have a large portion of afflictions, while he is in the way or course of his life, before he comes to that honour of sitting at his father's right-hand. Waters in scripture frequently signify sufferings. To drink of them, signifies to feel or bear them. Therefore - He shall be exalted to great glory and felicity.

111

This and several of the following psalms seem to have been wrote for the service of the church in their solemn feasts. It is composed alphabetically, each sentence beginning with a several letter of the Hebrew alphabet. The psalmist here praises God for his works, ver. 1-9. Recommends the fear of God, ver. 10.

2. Sought - Diligently meditated upon.

3. Work - Either all his works, or that eminent branch of those works, his providence towards his people. Righteousness - His justice or faithfulness in performing his word.

4. Remembered - By their own nature, and the lasting benefits flowing from them, which are such as cannot easily be forgotten.

5. Meat - All necessary provisions for their being and well-being.

7. The works - All that he doth on the behalf of his people, or against their enemies. Truth - Are exactly agreeable to his promises, and to justice. Commandments - His laws given to the Israelites, especially the moral law. Sure - Constant and unchangeable.

8. Done - Constituted or ordered.

9. Redemption - The deliverance out of Egypt, which was a type of that higher redemption by Christ. Commanded - Appointed, or established firmly by his power and authority. For ever - Through all successive generations of his people to the end of the world. Reverend - Terrible to his enemies, venerable in his peoples eyes, and holy in all his dealings with all men.

10. The fear - True religion. Beginning - Is the only foundation of, and introduction to, true wisdom.

112

This also is an alphabetical psalm. We have here the character and blessedness of the righteous, ver. 1-9. The iniquity of the wicked, ver. 10.

2. Generation - The posterity.

3. Righteousness - The fruit or reward of his righteousness, which is God's blessing upon his estate.

4. Darkness - In the troubles and calamities of life. He - The upright man.

5. Lendeth - Gives freely to some, and lends to others according to the variety of their conditions. Affairs - His domestick affairs. Discretion - Not getting his estate unjustly, nor casting it away prodigally, nor yet withholding it from such as need it.

6. Moved - Though he may for a season be afflicted, yet he shall not be eternally destroyed.

7. Evil tidings - At the report of approaching calamities.

9. Dispersed - His goods, freely and liberally. Righteousness - His liberality, or the reward of it. Ever - What he gives is not lost, but indeed is the only part of his estate, which will abide with him to all eternity.

10. The desire - Either of the misery of good men; or of his own constant prosperity.

113

We are here exhorted to praise God, ver. 1-3. Particularly for his glory and greatness, ver. 4, 5 And for his grace and goodness, ver. 6-9.

6. Humbleth - Who is so high, that it is a wonderful condescention in him to take any notice of his heavenly host, and much more of sinful and miserable men upon earth.

8. Princes - As he did Joseph, David, and others. His people - Who in God's account are far more honourable than the princes of Heathen nations.

114

This and the four following psalms, the Jews were wont to sing at the close of the paschal supper. It is a solemn commemoration of God's delivering Israel, giving them the law, and water out of the rock, ver. 1-8.

2. Judah - Or Israel, one tribe being put for all. Judah he mentions as the chief of all the tribes.
4. The mountains - Horeb and Sinai, two tops of one mountain, and other neighbouring mountains.
7. Tremble - The mountains did more than what was fit at the appearance of the great God.

115

We are to give glory to God, not to ourselves or idols, ver. 1-8. By trusting in his promise and blessing, ver. 9-15. And by praising him, ver. 16-18.

8. Are like them - As void of all sense or reason as their images.
9. Their - Who trust in him.
10. Aaron - You priests and Levites.
11. Ye that fear - All of you who worship the true God, not only Israelites, but even Gentile proselytes.
12. Mindful - In our former straits, and therefore we trust he will still bless us.
13. Both small - Of whatsoever quality, high and low, rich and poor.
16. The Lord's - In a peculiar manner, where he dwelleth in that light and glory, to which no man can approach. Given - As the foregoing verse declares, that God was the creator of heaven and earth, so this asserts that he is also their Lord and governor to dispose of all men and things as he pleases.
17. Silence - Into the place of silence, the grave.

116

This psalm is a solemn thanksgiving to God. Wherein the psalmist professes his love to God, for delivering him out of great straits and dangers, ver. 1-8. Prays for his future protection, and promises to praise him, and to walk holy before him, 9-19.

3. The sorrows - Dangerous and deadly calamities. Pains - Such agonies and horrors, as dying persons use to feel.
7. Rest - Unto a chearful confidence in God.

117

An exhortation to all nations to praise God for his mercy and truth, ver. 1, 2.

118

The form of this psalm seems to be dramatical, and several parts of it are spoken in the name of several persons; as it is in the book of the Song of Solomon, and in one part of Ecclesiastes. David speaks in his own name from the beginning to ver. 22, from thence to ver. 25, in the name of the people; and thence to ver. 28, in the name of the priests; and then concludes in his own name. He calls upon all about him to praise God, ver. 1-4. Encourages himself and others to trust in God, from the experience he had had of his power and mercy, ver. 5-18. He gives thanks for his advancement to the throne, as it was a figure of the exaltation of Christ, ver. 19-23. The people, the priests, and the psalmist himself triumph in the prospect of the Redeemer's kingdom, ver. 24-29.

10. Nations - The neighbouring nations, Philistines, Syrians, Ammonites, Moabites, who were stirred up, by the overthrows which David had given some of them, by their jealousy at his growing greatness, and by their hatred against the true religion.
11. Yea - The repetition implies their frequency and fervency in this action.
12. Bees - In great numbers. Thorns - Which burns fiercely, but quickly spends itself.
13. Thou - O mine enemy. The singular word is here put collectively for all his enemies.
14. Salvation - My saviour.
15. Doth valiantly - These are the words of that song of praise now mentioned.
16. Exalted - Hath appeared evidently, and wrought powerfully and gloriously.

19. **Open** - O ye porters, appointed by God for this work. **The gates** - Of the Lord's tabernacle: where the rule of righteousness was kept and taught, and the sacrifices of righteousness were offered.

20. **The righteous** - As David was a type of Christ and the temple of heaven, so this place hath a farther prospect than David, and relates to Christ's ascending into heaven, and opening the gates of that blessed temple, both for himself and for all believers.

22. **The builders** - The commonwealth of Israel and the church of God are here and elsewhere compared to a building, wherein, as the people are the stones, so the princes and rulers are the builders. And as these master-builders rejected David, so their successors rejected Christ. **Head stone** - The chief stone in the whole building, by which the several parts of the building are upheld and firmly united together. Thus David united all the tribes and families of Israel: and thus Christ united Jews and Gentiles together. And therefore this place is justly expounded of Christ, Mark xii, 10 Acts iv, 11 Rom. ix, 32 Eph. ii, 20. And to him the words agree more properly than to David.

24. **Made** - Or sanctified as a season never to be forgotten.

25. **We** - These seem to be the words of the Levites, to whom he spake ver. 19.

26. **Blessed** - We pray that God would bless his person and government. **Cometh** - To the throne; or from his Father into the world: who is known by the name of him that cometh or was to come, and of whom this very word is used, Gen. xlix, 10 Isaiah xxxv, 4. **Name** - By commission from him. **We** - We who are the Lord's ministers attending upon him in his house, and appointed to bless in his name, Num. vi, 23 Deut. x, 8. So these are the words of the priests.

27. **The Lord** - Or, The mighty God, as this name of God signifies, and as he shewed himself to be by this, his wonderful work. **Who** - Who hath scattered our dark clouds, and put us into a state of peace, and safety, and happiness. **The horns** - These are supposed to be made for this very use, that the beasts should be bound and killed there. These three last verses are David's words.

119

Because this psalm was very large, and the matter of it of the greatest importance, the psalmist thought fit to divide it into two and twenty several parts, according to the number of the Hebrew letters, that he might both prevent tediousness, and fix it in the memory. Each part consists of eight verses. All the verses of the first part beginning with Aleph, all the verses of the second with Beth, and so on. It is observable, that the word of God is here called by the names of law, statutes, precepts or commandments, judgments, ordinances, righteousness, testimonies, way and word. By which variety, he designed to express the nature and perfection of God's word. It is called his word, as revealed by him to us; his way, as prescribed by him for us to walk in; his law, as binding us to obedience; his statutes, as declaring his authority of giving us laws; his precepts as directing our duty; his ordinances, as ordained by him; his righteousness, as exactly agreeable to God's righteous nature and will; his judgments, as proceeding from the great judge of the world, and being his judicial sentence to which all men must submit; and his testimonies, as it contains the witness of God's will, and of man's duty. And there is but one of these one hundred and seventy six verses, in which one or other of these titles is not found. The general scope and design of this psalm is, to magnify the law and make it honourable: to shew the excellency and usefulness of divine Revelation, and recommend it to us, by the psalmist's own example, who speaks by experience of the benefits of it, for which he praises God, and earnestly prays for the continuance of God's grace, to direct and quicken him in his way.

6. **Respect** - A due respect, which implies hearty affection, diligent study, and constant practice. **To all** - So as not to allow myself in any known sin, or in the neglect of any known duty.

7. **When** - When by thy good spirit I shall he more fitly instructed in the meaning of thy word.

8. **Forsake me not** - For then I shall fall into the foulest sins.

9. **A young man** - Or, any man. But he names the young man, because such are commonly void of wisdom and experience, and exposed to many and great temptations. **Cleanse** - Purge himself from all filthiness of flesh and spirit.

11. **Hid** - I have laid it up in my mind like a choice treasure, to be ready upon all occasions to counsel, quicken or caution me.

17. **Live** - Safely and comfortably.

18. **Open** - Enlighten my mind by the light of thy Holy Spirit, and dispel all ignorance and error. **Behold** - Those great and marvelous depths of Divine wisdom and goodness, and those profound mysteries of Christ, and God's grace to mankind, and of that everlasting state, which are not to be known but by Divine illumination.

19. **A stranger** - I am not here as in my home, but as a pilgrim travelling homeward in a strange land. **Commandments** - Which are my chief support and guide in my pilgrimage.

20. **Breaketh** - Faints, as it frequently does, when a thing vehemently desired is delayed. **Judgments** - To a more sound knowledge and serious practice of them.

21. The proud - Obstinate and presumptuous sinners, who sin with an high hand. Err - Or, wander, knowingly or wilfully.

25. The dust - I am in danger of present death: I am like one laid in the grave. Quicken - Preserve my life, or raise me out of the dust. Word - According to thy promise.

26. My ways - My sins; and all my cares, and fears, and troubles.

27. Understand - More throughly.

28. Melteth - Like wax before the fire.

29. Grant me - Vouchsafe me an accurate knowledge of thy word, and let me govern myself by it in all things.

30. Laid - Or, set before me as a mark to aim at; as a rule to direct me.

32. Run - I will obey thy precepts with all readiness, fervency, and diligence. Enlarge - When thou shalt replenish my heart with wisdom, and love to thee and thy law.

36. Covetousness - He mentions this in particular, because it is most opposite to God's testimonies, and does most commonly hinder men from receiving his word, and from profiting by it: and because it is most pernicious, as being the root of all evil.

37. Vanity - The vain things of this present world, such as riches, honours, pleasures: from beholding them, with desire or affection. Quicken - Make me lively, vigourous and fervent in thy service.

38. Stablish - Confirm and perform thy promises.

39. I fear - For my instability in thy ways; which in respect to my own weakness, I have great cause to fear.

40. Longed - After a more solid knowledge and constant performance of them. In - According to thy faithfulness.

43. Take not - Do not deal so with me, that I shall be ashamed to mention thy word. Judgments - In thy word.

45. At liberty - Enjoy great freedom and comfort in thy ways.

48. Lift up - To receive and embrace thy precepts and promises.

49. Thy word - Thy promises.

52. Judgments - Thy ancient dispensations to the children of men in punishing the ungodly.

53. Horror - A mixed passion, made up of abhorrence of their sins, and dread and sorrow at the consideration of the judgments of God coming upon them.

54. The house - In this world, wherein I am a stranger and pilgrim, as all my fathers were.

55. Thy name - Thy holy nature and attributes, thy blessed word, and thy wonderful works. In the night - When darkness causes fear in others, I took pleasure in remembering thee; and when others gave themselves up to sleep, my thoughts and affections were working towards thee.

56. This - This comfortable remembrance.

57. Said - I have professed and owned it.

59. Thought - I seriously considered both my former courses, and my duty in all my future actions.

61. Robbed - Done me many injuries, for my respect to thy law.

66. Judgment - Whereby I may rightly discern between truth and falsehood. Knowledge - A spiritual experimental knowledge.

70. Fat - They are stupid and insensible.

74. Glad - For the encouragement they have by my example to trust in God. See me - Alive and in safety. Word - In thy promise, and have not been disappointed of my hope.

75. Judgments - Thy corrections. Of faithfulness - In pursuance of thy promises, and in order to my good.

79. Known - Loved and practiced them.

80. Sound - That I may love and obey them sincerely, constantly, and universally.

81. Fainteth - With long desire and earnest expectation.

83. Bottle - A leathern bottle. My natural moisture is dryed and burnt up.

84. The days - The days of my life. I have but a little while to live; give me some respite before I die.

85. Who - Who have no respect to thy law.

86. Faithful - Just and true.

89. In heaven - With thee in thy heavenly habitation.

91. They - The heaven and the earth. Ordinances - As thou hast appointed. For - All things are subject to thy power and pleasure.

96. Perfection - Of the greatest and most perfect enjoyments in this world. Commandment - Thy word; one part of it being put for the whole. Broad - Or, large, both for extent, and for continuance: it is useful to all persons: it is of everlasting truth and efficacy; it will never deceive those who trust to it, as all worldly things will, but will make men happy both here and forever.

100. Because - The practice of religion is the best way to understand it.

102. Taught me - By thy blessed spirit, illuminating my mind, and working upon my heart.

108. Offerings - The sacrifices of prayer and praise.

109. Is - Exposed to perpetual danger.

118. Deceit - Their deceitful devices, shall bring that destruction upon themselves which they design for others.

121. Judgment, &c. - Just judgment.

122. Surety - Do thou undertake and plead my cause.

123. The word - For the performance of thy faithful or merciful promise.

126. To work - To put forth thy power for the restraint of evil-doers. They - The wicked. Made void - Or, abrogated thy law, have openly cast off its authority.

127. Therefore - Because the general apostacy of others makes this duty more necessary.

129. Wonderful - In regard of the deep mysteries, the most excellent directions, and the exceeding great and precious promises of God contained in them.

131. Panted - I thirst after thy precepts, and pursue them eagerly.

133. Steps - My motions and actions.

136. Rivers - Plentiful tears, witness of my deep sorrow for God's dishonour, and for the miseries which sinners bring upon themselves.

140. Pure - Without the least mixture of falsehood.

142. Everlasting - The same in all ages and places.

143. Trouble - Outward troubles and anguish of spirit.

148. Watches - The middle watch, which was set in the middle of the night; and the morning watch, which was set some hours before the dawning of the day.

149. Judgment - According to thy word.

150. Nigh - To me, they are at hand and ready to seize upon me. Are far - They cast away from them all thoughts of thy law.

152. Of old - By long experience. Founded - Thou hast established them upon everlasting foundations.

160. The beginning - From the beginning of the world.

161. But - But I feared thine offense and displeasure more than their wrath.

164. Seven times - Many times; a certain number being put for an uncertain.

165. Offend - Hebrew. they shall have no stumbling-block, at which they shall stumble and fall into mischief.

175. Judgments - Thy word or testimonies, which are the only ground of my hope in thy help.

120

David prays against lying tongues, and denounces judgment against them, ver. 1-4. Complains of his wicked and unpeaceable neighbours, ver. 5-7. A song of degrees. Title of the psalm. Of degrees - Or, of accents, as the word properly signifies. This title is given to this and the fourteen following psalms, probably because they were sung upon the fifteen degrees, steps, or stairs of the temple, which the Jewish writers mention.

4. Arrows - The wrath and vengeance of the mighty God, which in scripture is often compared to arrows, and here to coals of juniper, which burn very fiercely and retain their heat for a long time.

5. Mesech - Mesech and Kedar are two sorts of people often mentioned in scripture, and reckoned amongst the barbarous nations. But their names are here to be understood metaphorically. And so he explains himself in the next verse.

121

David assures himself of help from God, ver. 1, 2. He assures others of it, ver. 3-8. A song of degrees.

1. Hills - To Sion and Moriah, which are called the holy mountains.

5. Shade - To keep thee from the burning heat of the sun.

6. Smite - With excessive heat. Moon - With that cold and moisture which come into the air by it. Intemperate heats and colds are the springs of many diseases.

122

This psalm seems to have been wrote for the use of the people, when they came to Jerusalem at the three solemn feasts. David here shews the joy with which they were to go up to Jerusalem, ver. 1, 2. The esteem they were to have of it, ver. 3-5. The prayers they were to make for its welfare, ver. 6-9. A song of degrees of David.

4. The tribes - Whom God has chosen to be his people. Unto - Unto the ark, called the testimony, because of the tables of the covenant laid up in it, which are called God's testimony, and the tables of the testimony. And this is called the testimony of, or to Israel, because it was given by God to them. Give thanks - To worship God; this one eminent part thereof being put for all the rest.
5. Judgment - The supreme courts of justice for ecclesiastical and civil affairs. Thrones - The royal throne allotted by God to David and to his posterity, and the inferior seats of justice under his authority.

123

The psalmist expresses and prays for deliverance from trouble, ver. 1-4. A song of degrees.

2. Look - For supply of their wants, and for help and defense against their oppressors. Until - Until he help and save us.

124

David describes the danger he and his people had been in, ver. 1-5. Blesses God for delivering them, ver. 6-8. A song of degrees of David.

5. The proud - Our enemies, compared to proud waters, for their great multitude and swelling rage.

125

The safety of them that trust in God, and the fate of the wicked, ver. 1-5. A song of degrees.

3. The rod - Their power and authority. Not rest - Not continue long. The lot - Upon the habitations and persons of good men. Lest - Lest they should be driven to indirect courses to relieve themselves.
5. Lead them - Unto sinful courses. Israel - Upon the true Israel of God.

126

This psalm was probably composed by Ezra, at the return of Israel from Babylon. Those who are returned, are called upon to be thankful; those who still remain there, are prayed for and encouraged, ver. 1-6. A song of degrees.

1. Turned - Brought the captive Israelites out of Babylon into their own land. Dream - We were so surprized and astonished.
4. Turn - As thou hast brought us home, bring also the rest of our brethren. As - As thou art pleased sometimes to send floods of water into dry and barren grounds, such as the southern parts of Canaan were.

127

We must trust in God for success in all enterprizes, ver. 1, 2. And for children, ver. 3-5. A song of degrees of Solomon.

1. Build - Assist and bless those that build it.
2. You - Builders, or watchmen. To sit - To use constant and unwearied diligence. So - By his blessing. Giveth - Freely, without that immoderate toiling, wherewith others pursue it.
3. Children - The chief of these blessings. Heritage - Only from God's blessing, even as an inheritance is not the fruit of a man's own labour, but the gift of God.
4. Youth - These he prefers before other children, because they live longest with their parents, and to their comfort and support, whereas children born in old age seldom come to maturity before their

parents death.

5. Full - Who hath a numerous issue. Shall speak - They shall courageously plead their cause in courts of judicature, not fearing to be crushed by the might of their adversaries.

128

The happiness of them that fear God, ver. 1-6. A song of degrees.

3. Olive-plants - Numerous, growing and flourishing.

129

The people of God commemorate their deliverance out of sore afflictions, ver. 1-4. The destruction of their enemies, ver. 5- 8. A song of degrees.

1. From my youth - From the time that I was a people.
4. Righteous - Faithful or merciful. The cords - Wherewith the plow was drawn. By these cords he understands all their plots and endeavours.
6. House-tops - Which there were flat. Which - Having no deep root, never comes to maturity. And so all their designs shall be abortive.
8. The blessing - Which was an usual salutation given by passengers to reapers: so the meaning is, it never continues 'till the harvest comes.

130

The psalmist confessing his sins, expresses his hope in God, ver. 1-6. And exhorts Israel to hope in him, ver.7, 8. A song of degrees.

3. Mark - Observe them accurately and punish them as they deserve. Stand - At thy tribunal.
4. Forgiveness - Thou art able and ready to forgive repenting sinners. Feared - Not with a slavish, but with a childlike fear. This mercy of thine is the foundation of all religion, without which men would desperately proceed in their impious courses.
5. I wait - That he would pardon my sins.
6. They - Whether soldiers that keep the night-watches in an army, or the priests or Levites who did so in the temple.
7. Israel - Every true Israelite. Plenteous - Abundantly sufficient for all persons who accept it upon God's terms.

131

David testifies his humility, and exhorts Israel to trust in God, ver. 1-3. A song of degrees of David.

2. Surely - When my mind was provoked. Weaned - Wholly depending upon God's providence, as the poor helpless infant, relies upon its mother for support.

132

Probably this psalm was wrote by Solomon to be sung at the dedication of the temple, of which he desires God would come and take possession, ver. 8, 9, 10. With these words he concluded his prayer, 2 Chron. vi, 41, 42. He pleads David's piety towards God, ver. 1-7. And God's promise to David, ver. 11-18. A song of degrees.

1. Afflictions - All his sufferings for thy sake.
5. Until - Until I have raised an house in which the ark may be put.
6. It - Of the ark. Ephratah - In the tribe of Ephraim, which was called also Ephratah. Found it - Afterwards we found it in Kirjath- jearim, which signifies a city of woods, in the territory whereof the ark was seated for twenty years.
7. Tabernacles - Into his temple. Footstool - The ark, is often said to sit between the cherubim, which were above the ark.
8. Rest - Into thy resting place, the temple so called, Isaiah lxvi, 1, where thou hast now a fixed

habitation. The ark - The seat of thy powerful and glorious presence.

10. David's sake - In regard of thy promises vouchsafed to David. Turn not - Cast me not out of thy presence. Of - Of me whom thou hast anointed to be king over thy people.

16. Salvation - With thy saving graces and blessings.

17. There - In Jerusalem. To bud - His power and glory to flourish. A lamp - A successor to continue forever in his family, as this phrase is expounded 1 Kings xi, 36; xv, 4, and particularly one eminent and glorious light, namely, the Messiah.

133

The happiness of brotherly love, ver. 1-3. A song of degrees of David.

2. Ointment - It is no less grateful and refreshing than that oil which was poured forth upon Aaron's head at the time of his consecration to the priestly office. Skirts - Not to the lower skirt or bottom of his sacerdotal garment, but to the upper skirt of it, or the mouth of it, as the Hebrew word properly signifies.

3. Zion - It is as desirable as the dew which falls upon mount Hermon, nay, as desirable as that heavenly dew of God's ordinances and graces which he hath commanded to fall upon the mountains of Zion and Moriah, and others which are round about Jerusalem. There - Where brethren live in peace and unity.

134

In this Psalm the priests or Levites who watched all night in the temple, exhort one another, and pray for one another, ver. 1-3. A song of degrees.

1. Servant - Peculiarly so called, priests and Levites. Night - Not only by day, but also by night, when their watch was more necessary. Stand - Serve or minister.

3. Thee - Thee whosoever thou art who dost faithfully perform the duty here commanded.

135

An exhortation to praise God for his greatness and mighty works, ver. 1-7. For destroying his enemies, ver. 8-11. For his mercy toward Israel, ver. 12-14. The vanity of idols, ver. 15-18. Another exhortation to praise God, ver. 19-20.

2. Ye - Ye priest and Levites.

6. Seas - In the visible seas, and in the invisible depths both of the earth and of the waters.

7. From - From all parts of the earth, from one end to another. Rain - An eminent instance of his good providence.

14. Judge - Will in due time plead the cause of his people. Repent - He will recall that severe sentence which for their sins he had passed upon them.

136

We must praise God as great and good in himself, ver. 1- 3. As the Creator of the world, ver. 4-9. As Israel's God, ver. 10- 22. As our Redeemer, ver. 23, 24. As God over all, ver. 25, 26.

2. The God of gods - Who is infinitely superior to all that are called gods, whether angels, or princes, or idols.

22. Israel - He speaks of all that people as of one man, because they were united together in one body in the worship of God.

25. Food - To all living creatures. For which God deserves great praises, which the psalmist teaches us to render to God for them, because those who are most concerned, either cannot, or do not perform this duty.

137

Probably this psalm was wrote toward the end of the Babylonish captivity. Herein the captives complain of the scoffs of their enemies, yet remember Jerusalem, and foresee the downfall of Babylon, ver. 1-9.

1. Sat - The usual posture of mourners.
2. Harps - Harps are here put for all instruments of musick.
3. A song - Such songs as you used to sing in the temple of Zion.
4. The Lord's - Those songs which were appointed by God to be sung only in his service.
6. If - If I do not value Jerusalem's prosperity more than all other delights.
7. The day - In the time of its destruction.
8. Happy - As being God's instrument to vindicate his honour, and execute his just judgments.

138

David praises God for his goodness, and foretells that other kings will praise him, ver. 1-5. He rejoices in hope of still greater blessings, ver. 6-8. A psalm of David.

1. The gods - Before kings and princes.
2. Temple - Where the ark was. He was not permitted to enter into it. Magnified - For thou hast glorified thy word or promise unto me more than any other of thy glorious perfections.
4. The kings - A prophecy of the calling of the Gentiles. Hear - The gospel preached among then.
5. The ways - His wonderful counsel and gracious providences.
8. Perfect - Will finish the great work of my deliverance. Forsake not - Or, do not give over, the work of my salvation, which is thus far advanced, not by any human help, but by thy power and providence.

139

This psalm is, by many of the Jewish doctors, esteemed the most excellent in the whole book. The omniscience of God is here asserted, ver. 1-6. Proved by two arguments; That he is everywhere present, ver. 7-12. And that he made us, ver. 13-16. This may fill us with pleasing admiration of God, ver. 17, 18. With an holy hatred of sin, ver. 19-22. And with an holy satisfaction in our own integrity, ver. 23, 24. To the chief musician, A psalm of David.

2. Afar off - Thou knowest what my thoughts will be in such and such circumstances, long before I know it, yea from all eternity.
3. Compassest - Thou discernest every step I take. It is a metaphor from soldiers besieging their enemies, and setting watches round about them.
5. Beset me - With thy all-seeing providence. And laid - Thou keepest me, as it were with a strong hand, in thy sight and under thy power.
6. I cannot - Apprehend in what manner thou dost so presently know all things.
8. Hell - If I could hide myself in the lowest parts of the earth.
9. The wings - If I should flee from east to west: for the sea being the western border of Canaan, is often put for the west in scripture. And wings are poetically ascribed to the morning here, as they are elsewhere to the sun, and to the winds.
16. Imperfect - When I was first conceived. Book - In thy counsel and providence, by which thou didst contrive and effect this great work, according to that model which thou hadst appointed.
17. Thoughts - Thy counsels on my behalf. Thou didst not only form me at first, but ever since my conception and birth, thy thoughts have been employed for me.
18. Them - Thy wonderful counsels and works on my behalf come constantly into my mind.
22. Perfect hatred - See the difference between the Jewish and the Christian spirit!

140

David prays and hopes for deliverance from his enemies, ver. 1-7. Foretells their destruction, ver. 8-13. To the chief musician, A psalm of David.

3. Tongues - Using words as sharp and piercing as the sting of a serpent.
9. Mischief - The mischief which they design against me, shall fall upon themselves.
10. Coals - Divine vengeance, which is compared to coals of fire.
13. Dwell - Shall constantly enjoy thy gracious and powerful presence.

141

David prays for acceptance and assistance, ver. 1-6. For the deliverance of himself and friends, ver. 7-10. A psalm of David.

4. Incline not - Suffer it not to be inclined. Heart - Keep me not only from wicked speeches, but from all evil motions of my heart. Dainties - The pleasures or advantages which they gain by their wickedness.
5. Smite - By reproofs. Break - Not hurt, but heal and greatly refresh me. Calamities - In the calamities of those righteous persons who reproved him. When they came into such calamities as those wherein he was involved he would pity them and pray for them.
6. Judges - The chief of mine enemies. Overthrown - Or, cast down headlong by thine exemplary vengeance. Hear - Hearken unto my counsels and offers which now they despise.
7. Our bones - Our case is almost as hopeless as of those who are dead, and whose bones are scattered in several places.

142

David complains to God and trusts in him, ver. 1-7 Maschil of David; A prayer when he was in the cave.

3. Knowest - So as to direct me to it. My path - What paths I should chuse whereby I might escape.
4. Right-hand - The place where the patron or assistant used to stand.
5. Portion - Even in this life.
7. Prison - Set me at liberty. Compass - Shall flock to me from all parts, to rejoice and bless God with me and for me.

143

David complains and prays for pardon and help, ver. 1-12. A psalm of David.

2. Justified - Upon terms of strict justice.
3. For - This is not a reason of what he last said, but an argument to enforce his petition delivered, ver. 1. Soul - My life; nothing less will satisfy him. Dead - I am in as hopeless a condition in the eye of man, as those that have lain long in the grave.
5. The days - What thou hast done for thy servants in former times.
6. As land - Thirsteth for rain.
8. Morning - Seasonably and speedily.

144

David blesses God for his mercies, ver. 1-4. Prays against his enemies, ver. 5-8. Promises to praise him, ver.9-11. The happiness of those who serve God, ver. 12-15. A psalm of David.

2. Subdued - Who hath disposed my peoples hearts to receive and obey me as their king.
5. Come - To help me. Smoke - As Sinai did at thy glorious appearance, Exod. xix, 18. This is a figurative and poetical description of God's coming to take vengeance upon his enemies.
7. Strange children - Either of the Heathen nations: or of the rebellious Israelites.
8. Vanity - Vain brags and threatenings which shall come to nothing. Falsehood - Deceiving themselves, by being unable to do what they designed; and others, by not giving them that help which

they promised.

12. That - This mercy I beg not only for my own sake, but for the sake of thy people, that they may enjoy those blessings which thou hast promised them; and particularly, that our sons, who are the strength and hopes of a nation, may be like plants, flourishing and growing in height and strength, as plants do in their youth; for when they grow old, they wither and decay. Cornerstone - Strong and beautiful.

14. Breaking in - Of enemies invading the land, or assaulting our cities, and making breaches in their walls. Going out - Of our people, either out of the cities to fight with an invading enemy: or out of the land into captivity.

145

This also is an alphabetical psalm. In it David praises God for his greatness, ver. 1-7. For his goodness and everlasting kingdom, ver. 8-13. For his providence, ver. 14-16. For his mercy to his servants, ver. 17-21. David's psalm of praise.

14. All - All that look up to him for help.
15. All - Of all living creatures. Wait - Expect their supplies wholly from thy bounty. Expectation is here figuratively ascribed to brute creatures.
18. Nigh - To answer their prayers. In truth - With an upright heart.

146

The psalmist praises God, and exhorts all to trust in him alone, ver. 1-5. Because of his power, faithfulness and everlasting kingdom, ver. 6-10.

4. That day - As soon as ever he is dead. Thoughts - All his designs and endeavours either for himself or for others.
6. For ever - Both because he liveth forever to fulfil his promises, and because he is eternally faithful.

147

The psalmist praises God for his care over the church, ver. 1-14. His government over all, ver. 15-18. His giving his word to Israel, ver. 19, 20.

4. Calleth them - He exactly knows them as we do those whom we can call by name.
9. Ravens - Which he mentions because they were most contemptible, especially to the Jews, to whom they were unclean: and because they are not only neglected by men, but also forsaken by their dams as soon as ever they can fly, and so are wholly left to the care of Divine providence.
10. Delighteth not - As if he needed either the one or the other for the accomplishment of his designs.
13. Thy gates - Thy strength consists not in thy walls, and gates, and bars, but in his protection.
14. Borders - In all thy land, even to its utmost borders.
15. Commandment - Which is sufficient without any instruments to execute whatsoever pleaseth him. Swiftly - The thing is done without delay.
16. Like wool - Not only in colour and shape, and softness, but also in use, keeping the fruits of the earth warm. Ashes - In colour and smallness of parts, as also in its burning quality.
17. Ice - Great hail-stones, which are of an icy nature, and are cast forth out of the clouds, like morsels or fragments.

148

An exhortation to all creatures in heaven and earth, man especially, to praise God, ver. 1-14.

4. Heavens of heavens - Ye highest heavens, the place of God's throne. Waters - Ye clouds which are above a part of the heavens.
6. Established - He hath made them constant and incorruptible, not changeable, as the things of the lower world. A decree - Concerning their continuance.
7. Dragons - Either serpents, which hide in the deep caverns of the earth; or whales, and other sea-monsters, which dwell in the depths of the sea.

John Wesley

8. Fire - Lightnings and other fireworks of the air. Vapor - Or, fumes: hot exhalations. Fulfilling his word - Executing his commands, either for the comfort or punishment of the inhabitants of the earth.
13. Above - Above all the glories which are in earth and in heaven.
14. The horn - In scripture commonly denotes strength, victory, glory, and felicity.

149

An exhortation to praise God for his love to his people, ver. 1-5. And for enabling them to overcome their enemies, ver. 6- 9.

4. The Lord - He rejoiceth over them to do them good. Beautify - Hebrew. adorn, make them amiable and honourable in the eyes of the world, who now hate and despise them. The meek - All true Israelites are such.
5. In glory - For the honour which God putteth upon them. Beds - By night as well as by day.
7. Vengeance - For all their cruelties and injuries towards God's people. This was literally accomplished by David upon the Philistines, Ammonites, Syrians and other neighbouring nations.
9. Written - Appointed and declared in the holy scripture.

150

An exhortation to praise God with all sorts of musical instruments, ver. 1-6.

1. Sanctuary - In his temple. The firmament - In heaven: there let the blessed angels praise him.
6. Also - Every living creature in heaven and in earth.

www.ingramcontent.com/pod-product-compliance
Lightning Source LLC
Chambersburg PA
CBHW020642230426
43665CB00008B/281